Sexual Offenses and Offenders

Sexual Offenses and Offenders

Theory, Practice and Policy

SECOND EDITION

KAREN J. TERRY

John Jay College of Criminal Justice

WADSWORTH
CENGAGE Learning·

Australia • Brazil • Japan • Korea • Mexico • Singapore • Spain • United Kingdom • United States

WADSWORTH
CENGAGE Learning·

Sexual Offenses and Offenders:
Theory, Practice and Policy,
Second Edition
Karen J. Terry

Editor-in-Chief: Linda Ganster

Acquisitions Editor:
Carolyn Henderson Meier

Development Editor:
Virginette Acacio

Editorial Assistant: Casey Lozier

Media Editor: Andy Yap

Marketing Manager:
Michelle Williams

Senior Marketing
Communications Manager:
Heather Baxley

Manufacturing Planner:
Judy Inouye

Rights Acquisitions Specialist:
Thomas McDonough

Design Direction,
Production Management,
and Composition:
PreMediaGlobal

Cover Designer: Riezebos
Holzbaur/Brieanna Hattey

Cover Image: © Nick Daly

For product information and
technology assistance, contact us at **Cengage Learning
Customer & Sales Support, 1-800-354-9706**

For permission to use material from this text or product,
submit all requests online at **www.cengage.com/permissions**
Further permissions questions can be emailed to
permissionrequest@cengage.com

Library of Congress Control Number: 2012939583

ISBN-13: 978-1-133-04982-1

ISBN-10: 1-133-04982-6

Wadsworth
20 Davis Drive
Belmont, CA 94002
USA

Cengage Learning is a leading provider of customized learning solutions with office locations around the globe, including Singapore, the United Kingdom, Australia, Mexico, Brazil, and Japan. Locate your local office at **www.cengage.com/global**

Cengage Learning products are represented in Canada by Nelson Education, Ltd.

To learn more about Wadsworth, visit
www.cengage.com/wadsworth

Purchase any of our products at your local college store or at our preferred online store **www.cengagebrain.com**

Printed in the United States of America
2 3 4 5 6   19 18 17 16 15

About the Author

KAREN J. TERRY is a Professor in the Department of Criminal Justice at John Jay College of Criminal Justice, City University of New York. She holds a doctorate in criminology from Cambridge University. Dr. Terry's research focuses on sexual abuse and victimization, and she has published widely on the management and supervision of sex offenders. Most recently, she was the principle investigator for two national studies on the sexual abuse of minors by Catholic priests.

Brief Contents

PART I   Understanding Sexual Offending: Incidence, Prevalence, and Causes   1

1 Sexual Offenses and Offenders   3

2 Historical Perspectives on Sexual Behavior   24

3 Etiology of Sexually Deviant Behavior   44

4 Cycle of Sexual Offending   71

PART II   Offender Typologies, Special Groups of Offenders, and Victims   91

5 Types and Typologies of Sexual Offenders   93

6 Juvenile Offenders   118

7 Commercial Sexual Exploitation of Children   139

8 Sexual Offending in Institutional Settings   161

9 Victims   186

PART III   Responses to Sexual Offenders: Treatment, Punishment and Community Regulations   213

10 Management and Supervision of Sex Offenders in the Community   215

11 Assessment and Treatment of Sexual Offenders   247

12 Incapacitating Sex Offenders   276

Contents

PREFACE   xiii

PART I   Understanding Sexual Offending: Incidence, Prevalence, and Causes   1

1   Sexual Offenses and Offenders   3
What Is a Sexual Offense?   4
Prevalence of Sexual Offending and Victimization   7
Official Data on Sexual Victimization   10
Research Estimates   16
Reporting Sexual Abuse   18
Telescoping   21
Chapter Summary   22
Discussion Questions   23

2   Historical Perspectives on Sexual Behavior   24
Historical, Religious, and Cultural Perspectives of Sexual Behavior   24
Changing Perceptions of Deviant Sexual Behavior: The 20th Century   27
1885–1935: The First Wave of Panic   28
1936–1976: The Rise of the Sexual Psychopath   32
1976–Present: The Emergence of a Sexually Violent Predator   39

Chapter Summary   42

Discussion Questions   42

3   Etiology of Sexually Deviant Behavior   44

Paraphilias and Other Sexual Disorders   45

Noncontact and Minimal Contact Paraphilias   46

High-Contact Paraphilias   48

Psychodynamic Theories   54

Biological Theories   55

Feminist Theories   57

Attachment Theories   58

Behavioral and Cognitive-Behavioral Theories   60

Psychosocial Theories   61

Routine Activities Theory   63

Integrated Theories and Empirical Research   64

Chapter Summary   69

Discussion Questions   69

4   Cycle of Sexual Offending   71

The Offense Cycle   71

Grooming and Planning   73

Persistence of Offending Behavior   77

Cognitive Distortions   77

Victim Empathy   83

The Role of Fantasies   85

Behavioral Triggers   87

Chapter Summary   89

Discussion Questions   89

PART II   Offender Typologies, Special Groups of Offenders, and Victims   91

5   Types and Typologies of Sexual Offenders   93

Specialization and Generalization of Offending Behavior   94

Typologies of Rapists   96

Sexually Motivated Offenses   98

Nonsexually Motivated Offenses   99

Typologies of Child Sexual Abusers   101
 Intrafamilial and Extrafamilial Abusers   102
 The Fixated-Regressed Typologies   105
 The FBI Typologies   108
 The MTC:CM3 Typologies   109
 Other Typologies   111
Typologies of Female Sex Offenders   111
Chapter Summary   116
Discussion Questions   117

6 Juvenile Offenders   118
Who Are Juvenile Sexual Offenders?   119
 Prevalence, Recidivism, and Characteristics   119
 History of Abuse   122
 Female Juvenile Sex Offenders   123
 Juvenile Sex Offenders and Non-Sex Offenders:
 A Comparison   124
Why Juveniles Sexually Offend   126
 Experimental or Criminal Behavior?   126
 Theories and Antecedents of Offending Behavior   127
 Typologies of Juvenile Sex Offenders   129
Assessment and Treatment of Juvenile Offenders   131
 The Assessment Process   132
 The Treatment Process   134
Management of Juvenile Offenders   134
Chapter Summary   136
Discussion Questions   137

7 Commercial Sexual Exploitation of Children   139
Sexual Offenders and the Internet   140
 Accessing Child Pornography   140
 Scope of the Problem   143
 Characteristics and Typologies of Cyber Sex Offenders   144
 Victims of Child Pornography   145
 Crossover between Child Pornography and Child Sexual
 Abuse   147
 Regulating and Policing Child Pornography   148
Sexting and Self-Produced Pornography   152

Juvenile Prostitution   154

Human Trafficking   157

Chapter Summary   159

Discussion Questions   160

8   **Sexual Offending in Institutional Settings   161**

Sexual Abuse within Child and Adolescent-Oriented Institutions   162

    Schools   162

    Child Care Settings   162

    Boy Scouts of America   163

    Big Brothers Big Sisters   164

    Athletic Organizations   165

    Professional and Legal Remedies   167

Sexual Abuse in Religious Institutions   167

    Child Sexual Abuse within Non-Catholic Religious Organizations   168

    Sexual Abuse within the Catholic Church   172

Sexual Abuse within Prisons   177

    Prevalence and Reporting   178

    Effects of Victimization   179

    Characteristics of Sexual Assaulters and Victims in Prison   180

    Prison Rape Elimination Act   181

    Preventing Sexual Assault in Prison   182

Sexual Abuse within the Military   183

Chapter Summary   184

Discussion Questions   184

9   **Victims   186**

Overview of Research on Sexual Victimization   187

Effects of Victimization   190

    Physical Harm   191

    Psychological Reactions   192

    Rape Trauma Syndrome and the Stages of Victimization   195

    Secondary Victims   196

Responding to Reports of Sexual Abuse: The Medical and Criminal Justice Processes   197

    The Hospital   198

The Police 200

The Adversarial Process 202

Victim Treatment and Counseling 209

Chapter Summary 212

Discussion Questions 212

PART III **Responses to Sexual Offenders: Treatment, Punishment and Community Regulations 213**

10 Management and Supervision of Sex Offenders in the Community 215

Overview of Sex Offender Laws 216

Jacob Wetterling Crimes against Children and Sexually Violent Offender Registration Act (1994) 216

Megan's Law (1996) 217

Pam Lychner Sex Offender Tracking and Identification Act (1996) 218

Protection of Children from Sexual Predators Act (1998) 218

Campus Sex Crimes Prevention Act (2000) 218

Prosecutorial Remedies and Other Tools to End the Exploitation of Children Today (PROTECT) Act (2003) 219

Adam Walsh Child Protection and Safety Act (2006) 219

Registration and Community Notification Laws 220

RCNL Regulations and Guidelines 220

Legal Challenges to RCNL 223

Risk Assessment 227

The Adam Walsh Act: Uniformity and Controversy 230

Efficacy of RCNL 232

Residence Restrictions 235

GPS Monitoring 237

The Containment Approach: Collaborating for Effective Management 239

Reentry and Reintegration 242

Housing 242

Employment and School 243

Recreation and Social Relationships 244

Chapter Summary 245

Discussion Questions 246

11 Assessment and Treatment of Sexual Offenders 247

History of Treatment 248

"Nothing Works" 250

Professionalization of Treatment 251

Assessment for Treatment 252

Background Information 252

Physiological Testing 253

Psychometric and Actuarial Testing 253

Types of Treatments 254

Cognitive-Behavioral Treatment 254

Medical Treatment 260

Community versus Prison Treatment 262

Variables and Controversies with Treatment 265

Ethics of Sex Offender Treatment 265

Treatment Staff 267

Assessment for Treatment Participation: Exclusion Criteria 268

Measuring Treatment Effectiveness 269

Methodological Considerations 270

Study Findings 272

Chapter Summary 274

Discussion Questions 274

12 Incapacitating Sex Offenders 276

SVP Legislation 277

Definition of an SVP 277

The Commitment Process 278

State Variation in SVP Statutes 279

The Role of Mental Health in SVP Legislation 281

Assessing "Dangerousness" 281

Treatment 283

Release 284

Legal Arguments about SVP Legislation 284

Understanding the Goals and Efficacy of SVP Legislation 289

Chapter Summary 291

Discussion Questions 291

BIBLIOGRAPHY 293

INDEX 351

Preface

Most books on sexual offending cover a specific topic area related to offenses, offenders, or victims. This book is unique in that it provides a comprehensive overview of psychological, sociological, and legal issues related to sexual offending. It explores why people commit sexual offenses, discusses the different types of sexual offenders, and explains the legal and treatment responses to sexual offending.

This book is divided into three parts. Part I is an analysis of the incidence, prevalence, and causes of sexual offending. It provides an overview of what is known about the nature and scope of sexual offending in society, historically and today. Part II is an overview of offender typologies, special groups of offenders, and victims. Though much of the recent research on sexual offending disputes the utility of categorizing offenders into discrete typologies, it is important to understand the characteristics of sexual offenders who target particular victims (such as those exclusively attracted to children). It is also important to understand how discreet groups of offenders, including juveniles, Internet predators and child pornographers, and those who abuse within an organizational setting, may exhibit unique characteristics in their offending patterns. Part III of this text addresses the public response to sex offenders, including the monitoring, supervision, punishment, and treatment of offenders. With the proliferation of sex-offender policies that emerged from the 1990s onward, it is necessary to understand the efficacy of these policies, how they have developed, and the trajectory of the legislation.

This is the second edition of *Sexual Offenses and Offenders: Theory, Practice, and Policy*, and it follows a similar outline to the first but with several important additions. First, it provides updated material from the first edition, including incidence and prevalence statistics, recent empirical studies, and developing legislation. Second, it contains new chapters on sexual offending within organizations, including the Catholic Church, prisons, and the military, as well as new information about child pornography, trafficking, prostitution, and sexual solicitation.

Like the first edition, this text contains data from interviews with sex offenders in prisons in England, but it also contains additional empirical data on sexual offenders from more recent studies.

The goal of this book is to provide an extensive overview of sexual offending and victimization, with the most accurate and updated material available. However, a secondary goal of this book is to challenge readers into thinking progressively about sexual offending and what the responses should be to this type of behavior. Knowledge of sexual offending has developed substantially over the last few decades, and even since the first edition of this text. Examples of new developments include:

- *Theoretical frameworks for explaining sexual abuse* New frameworks have been developed to explain sexually deviant behavior, from integrated pathways models to situational perspectives. How can these help us to develop prevention strategies?

- *Specialization in offending* Research over the last decade has consistently shown that most sex offenders are not "specialists" but instead "generalists," committing more nonsexual offenses than sexual ones. Research also indicates that most sexual offenders do not target a particular type of victim, such as a child versus adult, a boy versus a girl, a child in the family or outside the family. What are the implications for this in abuse prevention? What does this mean for policies such as registration and notification?

- *Risk assessments* Risk assessment strategies and instruments continue to develop. What do we know about the dangerousness of sex offenders as a unique group, and how is that changing?

- *Legislation* Policies regarding the supervision and monitoring of sex offenders continue to expand, regulating where sex offenders can live, conditions for living in the community, and length of time under which they must abide by these regulations. Federal legislation also now requires states to conform to uniform standards for registration and notification. What will be the likely effects of such legislation?

Society will inevitably continue to think of sex offenders as a unique group, more dangerous than other types of offenders and requiring more severe sanctions. Despite the lack of evidence as to the efficacy of regulatory policies, they raise a critical issue that must be addressed: What is the balance between appropriate sanctions that help to protect the community and the rights of the sex offenders who are living in this community?

ACKNOWLEDGMENTS

I would like to thank all the reviewers of this text who helped to shape its development. I would also like to recognize those who assisted in the research for this edition of the text. In particular, I would like to thank Michelle Cubellis, whose assistance was invaluable with these revisions. Additionally, I would like to recognize Margaret Leland Smith, Christina Massey, Brenda Vollman, and Delene Bromirski for their work on the *Causes and Context* report, which I cited in several places in this text. Finally, I would like to thank Carolyn Henderson Meier at Cengage, who has assisted me throughout the publication process.

PART I

Understanding Sexual Offending: Incidence, Prevalence, and Causes

1 Sexual Offenses and Offenders

2 Historical Perspectives on Sexual Behavior

3 Etiology of Sexually Deviant Behavior

4 Cycle of Sexual Offending

1

Sexual Offenses and Offenders

There are few groups of individuals who are more reviled than sexual offenders. Though this has been true for more than a century, the past two decades have brought forth intense scrutiny from the public, politicians, and policy-makers. Several emotionally-charged cases of child sexual abuse were highly publicized in the 1980s and 1990s, reigniting public intolerance for sexual offenders. And although the incidence of sexual offenses has been decreasing, sanctions for sex offenders have been constantly increasing over the last two decades. Unfortunately, empirical research does not show that such sanctions significantly deter offenders or reduce recidivism, and yet this legislation creates significant financial strain for local jurisdictions and states that must implement the policies (Zgoba et al., 2008). Despite the questionable efficacy of these laws, there is no sign of reducing the sanctions for this group.

This is not the first time historically that society has exhibited a "moral panic" about the dangers of sexual abuse. This panic has waned and ebbed throughout the last century. Jenkins (1998, p. 4) explains that the perception of sex offenders is the effect of "socially constructed realities" influenced by existing social and political ideologies. The public desire to incapacitate sex offenders today is similar to social attitudes in the 1930s, when sexual psychopathy laws emerged to incapacitate those considered to be "unfortunate but dangerous wretches" (Robson, 1999, p. 2). So although empirical research has consistently shown that sex offenders constitute a heterogeneous population of individuals for whom a one-size-fits-all policy will not be effective, such policies regarding the supervision, monitoring, and incapacitation of sexual offenders have gone full circle since the beginning of the century.

The purpose of this text is to provide the reader with a general understanding of sex offenders and the societal responses to them. Historically, sex offender research has focused on why sex offenders commit such offenses, and the characteristics of different types of offenders. Sex offender research today is centered around three general topic areas: (1) the factors associated with sexual offending, including personal characteristics as well as situational variables; (2) sex offenders' risk of recidivism; and (3) the efficacy of policies and programs for sex offenders. Before addressing the issue of why people commit sexual offenses and how best to prevent them, however, it is necessary to understand the nature and scope of sex crimes in the United States today.

WHAT IS A SEXUAL OFFENSE?

More than 100 years ago, Richard von Krafft-Ebing (1886/1965, p. 241) made the following observation about sexual behavior:

> Nothing is so prone to contaminate—under certain circumstances, even to exhaust—the source of all noble and ideal sentiments, which arise from a normally developed sexual instinct, as the practice of masturbation in one's early years. It despoils the unfolding bud of perfume and beauty, and leaves behind only the coarse, animal desire for sexual satisfaction. If an individual, thus depraved, reaches the age of maturity, there is lacking in him that aesthetic, ideal, pure and free impulse that draws the opposite sexes together. The glow of sensual sensibility wanes, and attraction toward the opposite sex is weakened. This defect in the morals, character, fantasy and instinct of the youthful masturbator, male or female, in an unfavorable manner, even causing, under certain circumstances, desire for the opposite sex to become entirely absent; thus masturbation becomes preferable to the natural mode of sexual satisfaction.

At that time, masturbation, homosexuality, and other sexual practices regarded as common today were not only condemned, but were also considered pathological and loathsome. Attitudes toward sexual behavior are structured through social and political ideologies, and they have changed drastically throughout the centuries. Some harmful sexual acts are—and should continue to be—illegal in nearly every community. One such example is rape, which constitutes a violation of the person and can cause irreparable harm both physically and psychologically. In describing rape, the Policy Advisory Committee on Sexual Offences in England stated that

> rape involves a severe degree of emotional and psychological trauma; it may be described as a violation which in effect obliterates the personality of the victim.... Rape is also unpleasant because it involves such intimate proximity between the offender and the victim. (Criminal Law Revision Committee, 1984)

The legally and socially accepted boundaries of other sexual behaviors, however, are not as clear, and sexual violence is not unique to any one culture or historical period (Stermac, Segal, & Gillis, 1990). Sexual behaviors other than those for the purposes of procreation (for example, homosexuality, incest, adultery, masturbation, bestiality, and sexual activity with children) have vacillated among social acceptance, stigmatization, and illegality.

Sexual offenses vary across time and cultures, and even across various jurisdictions in the United States. The types of sexual acts that may be criminalized can be broadly categorized in four ways, though these are not necessarily mutually exclusive:

1. *Sexual acts with contact.* Most sexual offenses are within this category, where there is touching of the intimate part(s) of the body or penetration either without the consent of the victim or when one person is incapable of consenting under the law (for example, a person who has not yet reached the age of consent, a person who is not conscious, or a person who is dead). This category involves all contact acts, from touching over the clothes to forced sexual intercourse.

2. *Noncontact sexual behavior.* This involves acts that are for the purpose of sexual gratification, but no contact is made between the perpetrator and the victim (for example, exposure of the genitals, voyeurism (peeping), and telling children to perform sexual acts).

3. *Viewing, possessing, or producing child pornography.* This third category includes any act involving the viewing or producing of any visual material of a child that is for the purpose of sexually gratifying an adult. This may include sexual contact with children or the sexual exploitation of children in photos and films. Recent examples include "sexting," or texting sexual pictures of oneself to another person (discussed further in Chapter 7).

4. *Sexual solicitation or trafficking.* Acts included in this category are based upon sexual services exchanged for financial or other types of compensation. Sexual solicitation may involve prostitution in a traditional sense (solicitation of sexual services through face-to-face meetings). Alternatively, adults may seek sexual relationships with adolescents, usually online, which may or may not result in a face-to-face meeting. Trafficked victims may be adults or minors, domestic or international, and are generally lured into performing sexual services for promises of money and/or a better life.

There are some offenses common across all jurisdictions in the United States, though the terminology differs depending on the jurisdiction. For example, although most states use the term *rape* to define offenses involving nonconsensual oral, anal, and/or vaginal penetration, this is called *sexual imposition* or *gross sexual imposition* in North Dakota and is called *sexual assault* in Colorado. Additionally, the specific definitions of this crime differ in terms of who can be a victim or an offender (male and/or female), the class of felony or misdemeanor, and the age of the victim (some define the different degrees by age ranges, with acts committed against younger victims being more serious offenses).

Many states also label some consensual sexual acts as offenses. Thirteen states listed consensual sodomy as a criminal act as recently as 2003, when sodomy laws were invalidated and declared unconstitutional by the Supreme Court (*Lawrence v. Texas*, 2003). Other consensual acts that continue to be illegal in some states include incest (intergenerational and between siblings), adultery, bigamy, female genital mutilation, fornication, masturbation for hire, indecent dancing, prostitution, and public indecency (Leiter, 1999). In addition to these offenses, other crimes that are not necessarily sexual in nature are registerable offenses, such as kidnapping.

For most sexual offenses, there must be a lack of consent on the part of the victim and some level of intent on the part of the offender. The laws in most states stipulate that consent is lacking from a sexual act when:

- The act is the result of force, threat, or duress;
- A reasonable person would understand that the victim did not consent due to a clear or implied statement that he or she would not want to engage in the sexual act; or
- The victim is incapable of consenting because he or she is below the age of consent (this ranges from age 16 to age 18 in various states), is mentally disabled, is mentally incapacitated, is physically helpless, is under the custody of correctional services, or is placed within the care of children and family services (or any other organization in charge of monitoring and caring for those in care of the state).

Offenses vary by type, degree of severity, class of offense, and length of sanction. In some states, these are defined simply by class of felony or misdemeanor. In other states, they are divided into first, second, and third degree offenses, with first degree offenses being the most severe. For example, Table 1.1 shows how

T A B L E 1.1   New York Penal Code Definition of Rape

Code Section	Offense	Degree	Definition
§130.25	Rape	Third	He or she engages in sexual intercourse with another person, to whom the actor is not married, who is incapable of consent and is not less than 17 years old; actor is over 21 years old and engages in sexual intercourse with someone less than 17 years old. Class E Felony.
§130.30		Second	Actor is over 18 years of age and he or she engages in sexual intercourse with someone less than 14 years of age; victim is otherwise mentally disabled or mentally incapacitated. Class D Felony.
§130.35		First	He or she engages in sexual intercourse with a person by forcible compulsion; who is incapable of consent because he or she is physically helpless; who is less than 11 years of age; who is less than 13 years old and the actor is over 18. Class B Felony.

SOURCE: New York Penal Law (2000)

VIGNETTE

SEXTING : The Emergence of New Sexual "Offenses" in the 21st Century

Accepted sexual behaviors change over time and by place, and are regulated by social and cultural norms. Over the last few decades, there has been an emergence of new behaviors, often related to developing technology, that are being considered sexual offenses. One such phenomenon is "sexting," in which people text nude or semi-nude photos of themselves to others. Though this has become a widespread practice generally, it is particularly common among adolescents. A survey of 1300 teens conducted by the National Campaign to Prevent Teen & Unplanned Pregnancy and CosmoGirl.com found that one in five teens had sexted, even though the majority knew it was a crime.

Several sexting cases have made media headlines, since sexting can have serious legal consequences for those who partake in this activity. One such example was of Phillip Albert, a teenager in Orlando, Florida. After an argument with his 16-year-old girlfriend, Phillip, then 18, sent a picture of his naked girlfriend that she had texted him to her family and friends. Phillip was charged with sending child pornography, convicted, and sentenced to five years of probation. Additionally, he is required to register as a sex offender until age 43. Phillip's attorney is appealing the conviction, noting that "sexting is treated as child pornography in almost every state and it catches teens completely off-guard because this is a fairly natural and normal thing for them to do. It is surprising to us as parents, but for teens it's part of their culture" (Feyerick & Steffen, 2009).

Another high-profile sexting case occurred in Pennsylvania. Marissa Miller was 12 years old when she and a friend took pictures of themselves wearing training bras while at a slumber party. The picture soon surfaced on another classmate's cell phone. The district attorney for the county told Miller and her friend that they could take probation and re-education classes or be charged with sexual abuse of a minor. Miller's mother, along with another family, refused to take the deal; instead, they contacted the ACLU (American Civil Liberties Union) and with its help is suing the district attorney to stop him from filing charges.

Phillip Albert's attorney noted that "Some judges have the good sense and reasonableness to treat this as a social problem and others are more zealous in their efforts to put everybody away and I think it's time as a society that we step back a little bit and avoid this temptation to lock up our children" (Feyerick & Steffen, 2009).

Questions
1. What should be the consequences for teens who "sext"?
2. What are the potential harms that can result from "sexting"?
3. Explain the similarities and differences between sexting and transmitting or possessing child pornography.

© Cengage Learning

New York classifies rape into three degrees. The sanctions associated with the degree of the offense increase as the severity of the offense increases.

PREVALENCE OF SEXUAL OFFENDING

AND VICTIMIZATION

It is impossible to accurately assess the extent of sexual offending and the characteristics of offenders. Most data on sex offenders relate to those who are either arrested or convicted, a group that represents a small portion of all sexual offenders. From 1992 to 2000, only 31 percent of rapes and sexual assaults were reported to the police (Hart & Rennison, 2003). Of those that are reported, not all end in arrest, and not all of those go on to indictment or conviction. This "funnel" system means that the further researchers are from the point at which the crime was committed, the further they are from knowing the true nature and scope of the problem of sexual offending. Furthermore, nearly all data on sex offenders relate to the male population of offenders. As such, the female sex offender population constitutes an even higher rate of the underreported and underresearched proportion of the total sex offender population (Righthand & Welch, 2001; Travin, Cullen, & Protter, 1990).

What is certain about sexual abuse, particularly child sexual victimization, is that it is widespread, and it remains so despite the precipitous decline in abuse cases in the 1990s (see Child Maltreatment Report, 2001; Hanson & Morton-Bourgon, 2004; Jones & Finkelhor, 2004). One meta-analysis summarizing prevalence studies found that overall rates of sexual victimization were approximately 30 percent for girls and 13 percent for boys in one's lifetime (Bolen & M. Scannapieco, 1999). According to Finkelhor (2008), children who experience sexual abuse often experience multiple types of abuse. Finkelhor, Ormrod, Turner, and Hamby (2005) found that in 2002– 2003, nearly half (49 percent) of the youth sampled in their study had experienced more than one form of direct (assault, maltreatment, sexual victimization) or indirect (witnessed) victimization. The concept of "multiple victimization" is consistent with findings from longitudinal studies by Cathy Widom and her colleagues (see Horwitz, Widom, McLaughlin & White (2001); Widom, Czaja, & Dutton, 2008).

The high rate of sexual victimization is not simply a criminal justice problem, but is also a public health problem (Abel et al., 1994). Those who are victimized as youths show higher levels of mental health problems as adults (Horwitz et al., 2001). Confounding this issue is the low rate of reporting of victimization, or when it is reported, the delay in disclosure. The literature shows that several factors are commonly associated with the delay in disclosure (see Terry & Tallon, 2004), including the relationship between the victim and the perpetrator (Arata, 1998; Hanson et al., 1999; Smith et al., 2000; Wyatt & Newcomb, 1990); the severity of abuse (Gries et al., 1996; Kogan, 2005; DiPietro et al., 1997); the likely consequences of the disclosure (Berliner & Conte, 1995; Hershkowitz et al., 2007; Lamb & Edgar-Smith, 1994; Roesler & Weissmann-Wind, 1994; Sorenson & Snow, 1991); age, developmental, and cognitive variables (Campis et al., 1993; Keary & Fitzpatrick, 1994; Lamb & Edgar-Smith, 1994); and "grooming" behavior that offenders use to entice children to participate in the sexually abusive behavior (Pryor, 1996).

Most studies indicate that when compared with their male counterparts, females are more likely to have been sexually abused during childhood. Furthermore, females are more likely than males to disclose information regarding sexual abuse, and male victimization seems to be acutely underreported (Brochman, 1991; Devoe & Coulborn-Faller, 1999; Finkelhor, 2008; Gries et al., 1996; Lamb & Edgar-Smith, 1994; McMullen, 1992; Tewksbury, 2007; Walrath, Ybarra, & Holden, 2003). That being said, reports are beginning to emerge about high rates of sexual abuse of boys in particular institutions and organizations. The lack of knowledge about male sexual victimization is striking; because so few males report, most information about their victimization is anecdotal or derived from studies with small sample sizes. As such, little statistical knowledge is available about males' long-term physical, psychological, and emotional effects, or about abuse events themselves.

Knowledge of sex offenders and rates of victimization are based upon two primary sources: official data (including criminal justice reports, victimization surveys, and social service data) and empirical studies. Table 1.2 shows the strengths and weaknesses of the different data sources.

T A B L E 1.2   Comparison of Data Sources
© Cengage Learning

Source of Data	Strengths	Weaknesses
Uniform Crime Reports (UCR)	■ Most common source of official criminal justice data in the United States ■ Reliable because it measures the same offenses each year ■ Makes it possible to compare the crime rate in jurisdictions of varying sizes	■ Hierarchy rule ■ Relies on official statistics, voluntary reporting by police ■ Definitions of some offenses incomplete
National Incident-Based Reporting System (NIBRS)	■ Gathers incident-based data ■ Detailed information available on offenders, victims, properties, and locations of offenses	■ Not yet widely implemented ■ Complicated, time consuming reporting system
National Crime Victimization Survey (NCVS)	■ Provides information on the dark figure of crime ■ Gives information on why crimes are underreported ■ Most extensive bounded study	■ Self-reports not totally reliable
National Incidence Study (NIS)	■ Extensive data collection in four reports ■ Reports data on children reported to CPS, screened out, and reported by "sentinels" ■ Data from a nationally representative sample from 126 CPS agencies in 122 different counties	■ Abuse underreported and not always recognized

Continues

TABLE 1.2   Comparison of Data Sources (*continued*)

Source of Data	Strengths	Weaknesses
National Child Abuse and Neglect Data System (NCANDS)	■ Provides annual reports of child abuse ■ State-by-state information distinguished by types of child abuse	■ Information is not always reported to social services and thus may be incomplete
Empirical Studies	■ Can provide deeper analysis of issues by observing samples of the population	■ Studies use varying methodologies and definitions, and thus may not be comparable

Official Data on Sexual Victimization

Official statistics on sexual offending are derived from several sources. The primary criminal justice data sources include arrest and conviction rates. Since it is difficult to gather this on a local level, the most common sources used to understand prevalence rates are federal reports, including the Uniform Crime Reports (UCR), and National Incident-Based Reporting System (NIBRS). Victimization surveys, namely the National Crime Victimization Survey (NCVS), provide data about the amount of victimization that is underreported in official statistics. Social service data sources provide more detailed information about the extent and nature of child sexual abuse allegations, and the key sources for this information include the National Incidence Study (NIS) and the National Child Abuse and Neglect Data System (NCANDS). Though not evaluated in this text, key resources for crime data internationally include the *European Sourcebook of Crime and Criminal Justice Statistics* (2006) and the *International Crime Victimization Survey* (Van Dijk, Van Kesteren, & Smit, 2008).

Criminal Justice Data Sources   In the 1920s, the government began to measure and track crime trends on a federal level for the first time through the UCR. The UCR is compiled annually by the Federal Bureau of Investigation (FBI) and contains information provided by nearly 17,000 local police departments (Grant & Terry, 2011). The local police agencies or state agencies give their arrest data to the FBI on a voluntary basis, and the FBI then tabulates the data on a national level. Despite its voluntary nature, there is a 97 percent compliance rate among police agencies.

The UCR consists of two sections: Part I and Part II offenses. Part I offenses, which are also called *index offenses*, are divided into categories of violent and property offenses, of which there are four each. The four violent offenses are murder (and nonnegligent manslaughter), forcible rape, robbery, and aggravated assault, and the four property offenses are burglary, larceny-theft, motor vehicle theft, and arson. Part II offenses consist of all other offenses, including simple assaults, other sexual offenses, forgery, fraud, vandalism, embezzlement, vice crimes such as gambling and prostitution, weapons violations, alcohol and drug violations, and curfew violations.

The UCR is used to determine the crime rate in the United States and in local jurisdictions. In order to compute the crime rate, you take the number of total reported crimes, divide by the total population of the reporting area, and multiply by 100,000. The most significant strength of the UCR is its reliability; it measures crimes using the same definitions every year and across all jurisdictions. Therefore, it allows jurisdictions to understand how their crime rates change each year and how they compare to crime rates in other jurisdictions, even those with different populations (for example, rural and urban areas).

Unfortunately, the UCR has several weaknesses. Most significantly, crime is underreported, and this measures only the number of crimes that are reported and cleared by arrest or exceptional means. Since sexual offenses are the least-reported crimes, the UCR is not necessarily a valid measure of sexual offense statistics. A second weakness with the UCR is that it follows the "hierarchy rule," meaning that it compiles data only on the most serious offenses if multiple offenses are committed at one time. In other words, if a person breaks into a house, rapes the occupant, murders her, and steals her car, only the murder will be counted in the UCR. A third weakness of the UCR is that it uses one definition for each crime, yet the definitions of crimes vary by jurisdiction. This is particularly troublesome for sexual offenses, as the UCR defines forcible rape as "the carnal knowledge of a female forcibly and against her will. Attempts or assaults to commit rape by force or threat of force are also included; however, statutory rape (without force) and other sex offenses are excluded" (Uniform Crime Report, 2009). Thus, the UCR is beneficial in giving us a comparison of statistics on the forcible rape of women by men, but not other sexual offenses. These are complied into the broad category of "sexual offenses" in Part II crimes, defined as "Statutory rape and offenses against chastity, common decency, morals, and the like. Attempts are included" (Uniform Crime Report, 2009).

Despite its weaknesses, the UCR remains the best source of official statistics for crimes. According to the Uniform Crime Report (2009), the rate of forcible rape was estimated at 56.6 rapes per 100,000 people, a 3.4 percent decrease from 2008. Rapes by force accounted for 93 percent of the reported rapes in 2009, whereas attempts or assaults to commit rape accounted for 7 percent. The forcible rape rate decreased 10.4 percent from 2000.

In an effort to improve the compilation and reporting of crime data, the FBI devised the NIBRS database in 1989. NIBRS is an incident-based reporting system, and as such allows for the calculation of multiple offenses, multiple victims, multiple offenders, and multiple arrests within a single incident. It still has flaws, however. Currently, police departments representing only 17 percent of the population submit data to NIBRS. Also, like the UCR, the NIBRS relies on reported offenses. However, it does eliminate the hierarchy rule by counting all offenses in each incident. It is also beneficial in that it collects detailed data on the offenders, victims, locations, properties, and arrests on each single crime incident, thus offering insight into offenses not currently available with the UCR.

Victimization Surveys Victimization surveys provide valuable information on the extent of sexual abuse. The NCVS, in particular, is the largest and most significant national survey in the United States and is central to our understanding of the "dark figure" of crime, or the extent to which crimes are underreported.

In order to better understand the magnitude of the underreporting of crime and the reasons why it is underreported, the Bureau of Justice Statistics began conducting an annual survey of approximately 49,000 households in 1972. The survey collects self-report data on all crimes against the household and individuals in the household who are over the age of 12. The NCVS finds that crime is severely underreported, with only about 37 percent of all crimes reported to the police. It has found that crime is underreported for numerous reasons, including that the offenses were personal (particularly domestic violence and sexual offenses), the victim believes that the police will not be able to do much about catching the offender, the victim does not trust the police, the victim fears that his or her own criminal behavior (for example, drug use) would be exposed, the victim fears that his or her reputation would be damaged, and the victim thinks the perpetrator will retaliate.

Like all sources of official statistical data, however, there are some drawbacks to victimization surveys. In particular, the reliability of self-reported data is questionable, and the NCVS does not provide a way to gather victimization information from young children who may be victims of abuse. Nonetheless, victimization surveys tell us the following in regard to race and ethnicity, age, and victim–offender relationship for victims aged 12 and older (Rennison, 2001; Rennison & Rand, 2003):

- *Race and Ethnicity* Though there are differences in victimization rates, there is no significant distinction between victims of sexual offenses on the basis of race and ethnicity. Whites are victims of sexual offenses at a rate of .8 per 1000 in the population, Blacks are victimized at a rate of 2.5, and those of other races are victimized at a rate of 1.2. Additionally, Hispanics were victimized at a rate of .7 per 1000. The rate of victimization for Blacks increased from 2000, when the rate was 1.2 per 1000. At the same time, the rate of victimization for Whites decreased, from 1.1 per 1000.

- *Age* The highest rate of victimization for a sexual offense is with victims aged 16–19, whose rate of victimization in 2000 was 4.3 per 1000 and rose to 5.5 in 2002. In 2002, those at the next highest level of risk were aged 20–24 (at a rate of 2.9) and aged 12–15 (at a rate of 2.1). The NCVS does not collect data on victims under the age of 12, which would likely be a large percentage of the victim population based on arrest and conviction statistics.

- *Victim–Offender Relationship* It was more common for both male and female victims to be abused or assaulted by a nonstranger than a stranger. With male victims, 52 percent were abused by nonstrangers, all of whom were friends or acquaintances (this was based on a small sample size, so the results may not be generalizable). Female victims know the perpetrator in 69 percent of the cases, with the highest percentage of abusers (57 percent of all cases) being friends or acquaintances.

Another victimization survey on sexual abuse is the Minnesota Student Survey. This self-report survey was administered to 6th, 9th, and 12th grade students in Minnesota in 1989, 1992, 1995, 1998, and 2001, and more than 90 percent of students in these grades in Minnesota participated in the surveys each year. The survey contains two questions about sexual abuse, the results of which show a slight rise in abuse between 1989 and 1992, followed by a 22 percent drop from 1992 to 2001.

Social Service Data   There are two primary sources of social service data through which the incidence of child sexual abuse is estimated: The NIS and the NCANDS. The NIS is a congressionally-mandated effort from the Department of Health and Human Services to assess the overall incidence of child maltreatment in the United States (U.S. Department of Health & Human Services, 2010). Data were collected in 1979 and 1980 for the NIS–1, followed by the NIS–2 in 1986 and 1987, and the NIS–3 in 1993 and 1995. The Fourth NIS (NIS–4) provides estimates of the incidence of child abuse and neglect in the United States 2005–2009 based on substantiated and unsubstantiated cases. These studies provide child, perpetrator, and family characteristics, and demographical information about the nature and severity of the maltreatment, as well as the extent of changes in the incidence over time.

In order to measure the scope of child abuse and neglect, the NIS includes not only children who were investigated by Child Protective Services (CPS) agencies, but also children who were not reported or who were screened out by CPS agencies. The study expanded its data by utilizing a sentinel methodology, which required community professionals to look for victims or possible victims of child abuse and neglect. The "sentinels," as they are called, are staff members who have contact with children and families in various social service contexts (such as law enforcement agencies, medical services, educational institutions, and other social services). This methodology is designed to look beyond official abuse reports and include children who come to the attention of community professionals.

The NIS–4 includes a nationally representative sample of data collected from 126 CPS agencies in 122 different counties. The 126 CPS agencies provided demographic data on all children who were reported and accepted for investigation between September 4 and December 3, 2005 and between February 4 and May 3, 2006. Data for the NIS–4 were also collected from 10,791 community professionals in 1094 sentinel agencies. A total of 6208 forms were collected from the sentinels and 10,667 forms were completed on cases at participating CPS agencies.

Children were evaluated according to standard definitions of abuse and neglect as previously used in the NIS–2 (1986) and NIS–3 (1993). In order to be classified as abuse or neglect, the *Harm Standard* requires that an act or omission result in demonstrable harm. The *Endangerment Standard* includes all children who meet the Harm Standard, but also includes children deemed by the sentinels and their professional opinion as endangered or if the child's maltreatment was substantiated in a CPS investigation. Only children who fit these standards of abuse (physical, sexual, and emotional) and neglect (physical, emotional, and educational) were used to generate national estimates.

According to the Harm Standard from the NIS–4, one child in every 58 in the United States experienced maltreatment. The number of children who experienced physical, sexual, and/or emotional abuse under the Harm Standard decreased 26 percent from the NIS–3 to the NIS–4. The estimated number of sexually abused children decreased 38 percent from the NIS–3 along with a 44 percent decrease in the rate of sexual abuse. The estimated number of physically abused children decreased 15 percent from the NIS–3 along with a 23 percent decrease in the rate of physical abuse. The estimated number of emotionally abused children decreased 27 percent from the NIS–3 along with a 33 percent decrease in the rate of emotional abuse. There were no significant changes in neglect since the NIS–3. Results showed a 57 percent decrease in the number of children for whom injury could be inferred due to the nature of the maltreatment. Overall, the NIS–4 shows a 19 percent decrease in the total number of maltreated children in the United States since the NIS–3 in 1993. This decline in incidence is significant compared to the 56 percent increase between the NIS–2 in the mid-1980s and the NIS–3 in the mid-1990s.

According to the Endangerment Standard, one child out of every 25 in the United States has been maltreated. Results, however, did not show any reliable change since the NIS–3. Of those who were maltreated, 29 percent of children were abused and 77 percent were neglected. Of the 29 percent who were abused, 22 percent were sexually abused. In all of the NIS reports, girls were more likely to be sexually abused than boys.

The other well-known source of information for child abuse statistics is NCANDS, a national data collection and analysis system created for the purpose of documenting the scope and nature of child maltreatment reporting (Family Life Development Center, n.d.). The NCANDS Child File consists of case-specific data of all investigated reports of maltreatment to state child protective service agencies. NCANDS defines maltreatment as an "act or failure to act by a parent, caretaker, or other person as defined under State law which results in physical abuse, neglect, medical neglect, sexual abuse, emotional abuse, or an act or failure to act which presents an imminent risk of serious harm to a child" (Family Life Development Center, n.d.). Child File data are collected annually through the voluntary participation of states and include the demographics of children and their perpetrators, types of maltreatment, investigation dispositions, risk factors, and services provided.

Reports of child maltreatment are collected by social services across the United States; however, states are not required to submit data to NCANDS. The reporting agency investigates and decides whether the case of abuse is substantiated by evidence or not. Reports may contain information about multiple children, abuse types, and perpetrators. Information is not collected about the perpetrator(s) for unsubstantiated cases. Data on substantiated cases, however, include the perpetrator's gender, race, and relationship to the child. Additionally, the Child File also contains information about the support services provided to the family and any problems identified for the child, caretaker, or family.

Annual datasets for calendar years from 1990 through 2002 are available from NCANDS. In 2003, the data collection period changed to fiscal years. The 2004 dataset included a total of 3,134,026 records from 44 states and Washington, DC, whereas the 2003 dataset included 1,216,626 total records from 22 states and Washington, DC. The most recent available data are for federal fiscal year 2004.

The state-level rates of child sexual abuse in 1992 range from a minimum of 87 per 100,000 children in New Jersey to a maximum of 688 per 100,000 children in Alaska. The average for 48 states and the District of Columbia is 246 children per 100,000. Table 1.3 shows the state-by-state comparison of child sexual abuse statistics in 1992 and 2000, and how there was a significant decrease in nearly every state during that decade.

T A B L E   1.3   Child Sexual Abuse Statistics (1992 and 2001)

© Cengage Learning

State	Percentage Children Abused (1992)	Percentage Children Abused (2001)	Rate of Children Abused per 100,000 (1992)	Rate of Children Abused per 100,000 (2001)	Percentage Change Between 1992 and 2001
AL	0.43%	0.17%	427	174	−59.33%
AK	0.69%	0.78%	688	778	+13.19%
AZ	0.31%	0.02%	307	23	−92.40%
AR	0.31%	0.31%	307	310	+1.12%
CA	0.34%	0.11%	338	113	−66.58%
CO	0.22%	0.05%	220	48	−78.21%
CT	0.14%	0.06%	138	56	−59.16%
DE	0.12%	0.08%	116	82	−29.72%
DC	0.03%	0.10%	27	96	−252.80%
FL	0.28%	0.17%	283	171	−39.38%
GA	0.30%	0.10%	299	100	−66.61%
HI	0.10%	0.09%	101	92	−8.96%
ID	0.34%	0.08%	343	79	−77.04%
IL	0.18%	0.09%	178	85	−52.15%
IN	0.50%	0.27%	496	274	−44.76%
IA	0.19%	0.14%	193	141	−27.10%
KS	0.13%	0.14%	127	142	+11.61%
KY	0.27%	0.12%	271	116	−57.21%
LA	0.11%	0.07%	108	71	−34.28%
ME	0.21%	0.29%	209	292	+40.03%
MA	0.18%	0.07%	177	74	−58.04%
MI	0.10%	0.06%	102	64	−37.77%
MN	0.11%	0.07%	114	70	−38.51%
MS	0.25%	0.10%	246	97	−60.49%
MO	0.21%	0.16%	211	158	−25.18%
MT	0.36%	0.13%	364	126	−65.50%
NE	0.17%	0.08%	166	85	−49.01%
NV	0.12%	0.04%	120	42	−65.25%
NH	0.10%	0.08%	104	75	−27.93%
NJ	0.09%	0.04%	87	36	−58.78%
NM	0.17%	0.09%	171	90	−47.41%
NY	0.16%	0.06%	157	64	−59.37%
NC	0.09%	0.06%	89	62	−30.26%

Continues

T A B L E   1.3   Child Sexual Abuse Statistics (1992 and 2001) (*continued*)

State	Percentage Children Abused (1992)	Percentage Children Abused (2001)	Rate of Children Abused per 100,000 (1992)	Rate of Children Abused per 100,000 (2001)	Percentage Change Between 1992 and 2001
ND	0.13%	0.07%	127	70	−44.42%
OH	0.40%	0.27%	403	272	−32.56%
OK	0.14%	0.12%	138	117	−15.50%
OR	0.40%	0.11%	404	111	−72.53%
PA	0.15%	0.08%	153	80	−47.78%
RI	0.26%	0.08%	258	79	−69.48%
SC	0.20%	0.09%	197	89	−54.88%
SD	0.27%	0.08%	266	83	−68.67%
TN	0.23%	0.17%	229	166	−27.46%
TX	0.21%	0.11%	212	110	−48.12%
UT	0.38%	0.32%	382	317	−17.18%
VT	0.56%	0.29%	563	291	−48.41%
VA	0.15%	0.07%	152	68	−55.13%
WA	0.46%	0.03%	463	26	−94.30%
WI	0.54%	0.34%	542	335	−38.14%
WY	0.28%	0.08%	283	82	−70.92%

Research Estimates

In the 1980s, there was a rise in the number of reports involving sexual offenses by acquaintances, whether in regard to child sexual abuse or rape. These allegations shattered the stereotyped images of sex offenders at the time, leading to further research of this population. Studies found that there was an increase in cases of date rape, rape in marriage, and intrafamilial abuse—cases that would have largely gone unreported prior to that time for reasons of stigma, self-blame, fear of not being believed, or a desire to protect the friend or family member who committed the offense (Scully, 1990). Even today, those who are most likely to serve prison sentences for sexual offenses are those who have raped strangers, used weapons, had multiple minor victims, physically injured their victims, and/or committed other crimes in addition to the sexual offense (Grant & Terry, 2001). As of 2008, an estimated 235,000 individuals convicted of sex offenses were under the supervision of the criminal justice system. Approximately 60 percent of these were supervised within the community (Demichele, Payne, & Button, 2008).

Studies have found that sexual offending does not discriminate on the basis of age, race, ethnicity, socioeconomic status, educational level, or any other stable characteristics for either offenders or victims. Sex offenders, particularly those who abuse children, do not necessarily "age out" of their deviant behavior, as do many property offenders, and sex crimes are generally considered to be psychologically motivated offenses. Sexual offenders are often diagnosed with personality or mental disorders, particularly paraphilias (discussed in Chapter 5) (Abel, Becker, & Cunningham-Rathner, 1984), and this makes them a unique population. Despite the heterogeneity in offenders and the etiology of their offending behavior, there are many similarities in the population as a whole. They tend to have poor social and relationship skills, most have had poor relationships with their parents, many abuse alcohol or drugs, and many were either physically and/or sexually abused as children.

It is difficult for researchers to ascertain a true assessment of the prevalence and incidence of sexual abuse, which refer, respectively, to the total number of cases in a given population at a specific time and the rate of occurrence over a period of time. Individuals who are sexually abused by family members or acquaintances are least likely to report the sexual abuse to the criminal justice system. Thus, most individuals who were sexually abused as children or were sexually abused as an adult by someone known to them do not report the abuse to criminal justice authorities.

Studies on the incidence of sexual abuse, which concentrate on estimating the number of new cases occurring over a particular period of time, gained greater urgency in the 1980s, indicating that the scope of sexual victimization is extensive.

Studies often show varying levels of prevalence of sexual abuse. As an example, study statistics show that:

- One in six women has been raped (Tjaden & Thoennes, 2006), and one in three girls is likely to be abused by an adult (Russell, 1984).

- Seventeen to twenty-two percent of women and 2 to 8 percent of men have been victims of sexual assault (Levenson & D'Amora, 2007).

- 12.8 percent of females and 4.3 percent of males reported a history of sexual abuse during childhood (MacMillan et al., 1997).

- Nearly a quarter of all children will be sexually assaulted before their 18th birthday; 74 percent of those assaulted as children are girls (Spinazzola, Ford, & Zucker, 2005).

- Twenty-seven percent of females and 16 percent of males disclosed a history of childhood sexual abuse; 42 percent of the males were likely to never have disclosed the experience to anyone, whereas 33 percent of the females never disclosed (Finkelhor, Hotaling, Lewis, & Smith, 1990).

- The lifetime prevalence of sexual assault among 12–17-year-olds is 1 in 12 (Finkelhor, Ormrod, Turner, & Hamby, 2005), and 74 percent of child victims know the abuser well (Snyder, 2000).

- The overall prevalence of sexual abuse of male children is 13 percent and female children is between 30 and 40 percent (Bolen & Scannapieco, 1999).

Official statistics indicate that rates of sexual abuse have declined in the past decade. Research findings corroborate this, and indicate that there has been a simultaneous reduction in related factors such as domestic violence incidents among intimate adults, and pregnancies and births among teenagers. It is not clear what has caused this reduction in sexual abuse or related factors, though it coincides with a reduction in various types of violent and property crime. It also coincides with increased sanctions for sexual offenders, including an increased likelihood of incarceration and civil sanctions such as registration, notification, civil commitment, and residency restrictions (to be discussed in Part III).

REPORTING SEXUAL ABUSE

Crime is underreported. Sexual crimes are the most underreported offenses, though more individuals reported their victimization to the police in 2000 than in any year of the previous decade (Hart & Rennison, 2003). In order to understand how accurate statistics are on sexual offending, it is important to understand who reports, why, after how long, and with what accuracy.

The NCVS shows the following about individuals over the age of 12 who reported their sexual assaults to the police from 1992 to 2000 (Hart & Rennison, 2003, p. 5):

- *Gender* Victims were more likely to report sexual offenses to the police if the offender was male (32 percent) than female (13 percent).
- *Race* Victims were more likely to report sexual offenses if the offender was Black (39 percent) than White (29 percent).
- *Age* Victims reported sexual offenses to the police 40 percent of the time when the perpetrator was 12–14 years of age, the highest percentage of reporting in any age category.
- *Number of Perpetrators* Victims were more likely to report the sexual abuse to police if there were two perpetrators (44 percent) rather than one perpetrator (33 percent).
- *Victim-Offender Relationship* Victims were more likely to report sexual offenses committed by strangers (41 percent) than nonstrangers (27 percent).
- *Use of Weapons* Victims were more likely to report a sexual offense if the perpetrator had a weapon present during the offense (49 percent), particularly a firearm (62 percent), than if no weapon was present (28 percent).
- *Reasons for Reporting* The most common reason for victims to report sexual offenses to the police was to prevent future violence. The most common reason for victims *not* to report sexual offenses to the police was because of privacy issues.

Empirical research supports the findings in the NCVS, though the benefit of such studies is that they can also include victims under the age of 12. Child sexual abuse is the least reported of sexual offenses. Studies that analyze reporting trends of child sexual abuse all indicate that a high percentage of victims who report their abuse to authorities do so many years after the abuse occurred, and many do not ever disclose. The most common studies conducted to analyze reporting trends on child sexual abuse are adult retrospective studies. Like the NCVS, these studies found that the process of disclosing childhood sexual abuse depends on numerous variables. Of note:

- Only one-third of the victims reported the abuse to authorities before age 18, and the average age of disclosure was 25.9 (Roesler & Weissmann-Wind, 1994, in a study of 228 adult female victims of child sexual abuse by adult—primarily male—family members).

- The average age of child sexual abuse victims was just over 8, and approximately 41 percent of victims disclosed the abuse at the time it occurred (Arata, 1998, in a study of 204 female victims of child sexual abuse).

- The average age at the time of the child sexual abuse was 10, and 64 percent of the victims disclosed the abuse as adults (Lamb & Edgar-Smith, 1994, in a study of 45 adult female and 12 adult male child sexual abuse victims).

- The majority of victims waited more than eight years to report their childhood sexual abuse (Smith, Letourneau, & Saunders, 2000, in a study assessing disclosure rates of females raped when they were children).

- Disclosure of child sexual abuse by minors may be spontaneous or prompted, and many children and adolescents need assistance with disclosure (DeVoe & Coulborn-Faller, 1999).

- Disclosure of childhood sexual abuse may be purposeful or accidental, with accidental disclosure more common in preschool-aged children and purposeful disclosure more common in adolescents (Sorenson & Snow, 1991).

A significant factor in whether a child reports sexual abuse and the manner in which the abuse is reported is the potential for the person to whom the child is disclosing to believe his or her report on the abuse, especially law enforcement (Campbell, 2005). Approximately half of the children who recant their reports of childhood sexual abuse do so under pressure from their guardians (Bradley & Wood, 1996). The Child Sexual Abuse Accommodation Syndrome, a model of reporting outlined by Summit (1983) that consists of five components, suggests reasons why child sexual abuse victims delay disclosure. First, the abuse is usually carried out in privacy, and the abuser encourages secrecy. Second, because children are obedient to adults, they are helpless and maintain the secrecy that the adult encourages. Third, the child becomes entrenched in the abusive situation, begins to feel guilt and responsibility for the abuse, and continues to accommodate the perpetrator. Fourth, the victim delays disclosure because of the promise of secrecy and feelings of guilt and shame. Finally, after delayed disclosure, the victim often retracts the report due to disbelief about the abuse by those trusted by the victim.

In addition to a general delay in disclosure of child sexual abuse, many victims report the abuse in stages. Sorenson and Snow (1991) identified four stages of disclosure in their study of 630 victims of child sexual abuse: denial (experienced by 72 percent of the victims in their sample), disclosure (78 percent of the victims progressed from tentative to active disclosure), recantation (experienced by 22 percent of the victims), and reaffirmation (93 percent of those who recanted later confirmed their original reports).

Adult retroactive studies not only help us to understand the process of disclosure, but also explain the reasons that victims disclose. The most significant variables that seem to hinder disclosure of abuse are the age of the victim at the time the abuse occurred, the victim-perpetrator relationship, the gender and cognitive or developmental abilities of the victim, the type of sexual abuse that occurred, and the chance of negative consequences related to disclosure.

The gender of the victim has an impact on the disclosure of sexual abuse, as females are more likely both as children and as adults to report sexual abuse than are males (DeVoe & Coulborn-Faller, 1999; Gries, Goh, & Cavanaugh, 1996; Lamb & Edgar-Smith, 1994; Walrath, Ybarra, & Holden, 2003). Paine and Hansen (2002) do show, however, that although gender is an important factor in the decision to report abuse, victim-perpetrator relationship is the most important factor in determining whether a victim of child sexual abuse will eventually disclose.

Several studies indicate that a victim is less likely to report or delay the report of child sexual abuse if the perpetrator is well known to the child (Arata, 1998; Hanson, Saunders, Saunders, Kilpatrick, & Best, 1999; Smith et al., 2000; Wyatt & Newcomb, 1990). This relationship is most significant if the perpetrator is a relative or stepparent. Arata (1998) showed that 73 percent of victims did not disclose the abuse in such a situation; when the perpetrator was an acquaintance 70 percent of the victims did not report. The desire not to report familial sexual abuse is compounded if the victim feels responsible for the abuse, and in such cases the victim often waits longer to disclose the abuse (Goodman-Brown, Edelstein et al., 2003; Roesler & Weissmann-Wind, 1994).

The gender of the perpetrator also seems to be an important factor in reporting, as offenses by female offenders are reported less often than those by male offenders (Righthand & Welch, 2001). There are several reasons why victims may not report sexual abuse by females. Many female-perpetrated offenses are within the family and, as indicated earlier, intrafamilial acts of abuse are the least-reported sexual offenses. Also, women are traditionally seen as caregivers, nonviolent nurturers who are either not willing or not capable of harming children. Many adult and adolescent males are also reluctant to report abuse because of the shame of being a victim. Alternatively, they may not view the actions against them as abuse (Elliot & Briere, 1994). Kasl (1990) states that underreporting is the result of a social taboo, and that the stigma caused by female sexual abuse must be abolished.

In order to report the abuse in a timely manner, it appears that children need to feel as though they will be supported by the person to whom they disclose the abuse. Children who believe that they will not be supported when they disclose abuse will wait longer to report, often until adulthood when they can choose a person they trust to support them (Lamb & Edgar-Smith, 1994). Shame and guilt also appear to play a role in the decision about disclosure. Older children who are able to understand and anticipate social consequences of sexual abuse are less likely to report the abuse than are younger children (Campis, Hebden-Curtis, & DeMaso, 1993; Keary & Fitzpatrick, 1994).

Some researchers have found that children are less likely to report sexual abuse if the abuse is severe (Arata, 1998; DiPietro et al., 1997; Gries, Goh, & Cavanaugh, 1996) or they fear further harm as a result of their disclosure (Berliner & Conte, 1995; Roesler & Weissmann-Wind, 1994; Sorenson & Snow, 1991). Sorenson and Snow (1991) found that victims who fear further reprisals will not report the abuse if the perpetrator is present or the disclosure could lead to further abuse, and Roesler and Weissmann-Wind (1994) found that one-third of the victims they spoke to delayed reporting until adulthood because they feared for their safety. Hanson et al. (1999), on the other hand, found the inverse relationship true of severity of abuse and disclosure. They discovered that in a sample of women who were raped when they were children, the more severe the sexual abuse the more likely the victims were to report the abuse sooner.

Telescoping

When victims report their crimes or complete victimization surveys long after the crime occurred, they often remember the crime as occurring earlier or later than it actually happened (Sudman & Bradburn, 1973, as cited in Schneider & Sumi, 1981). This phenomenon is called *telescoping*, and it occurs in two forms: *forward telescoping*, or recalling an event that occurred prior to the reporting period in question, and *backward telescoping*, which is recalling an event that occurred after the reporting period. Telescoping is not unique to crime victims. All individuals "telescope" events that they recall long after the events happened. However, telescoping events of victimization creates challenges for researchers trying to understand criminal statistics (Schneider & Sumi, 1981). Accurate crime statistics are deemed essential by government agencies, and as such controlling for temporal telescoping is imperative to attain analyzable, accurate data.

In the 1970s, many researchers began conducting studies on telescoping to better understand its effect on crime statistics. Not surprisingly, researchers found that memory disorientations, including telescoping, occur more often in older respondents, particularly those over age 55 (Sudman & Bradburn, 1974, as cited in Gottfredson & Hindelang, 1977). Researchers also found that forward telescoping is more common than backward telescoping (Schneider & Sumi, 1981) and that the more prominent the event, the more likely the person is to forward telescope (Neter & Waksberg, 1964, as cited in Gottfredson & Hindelang, 1977). The problem with this, in terms of crime statistics, is that individuals are going to report crime as occurring more recently than it did. Another issue is that victims of nonreported events tend to telescope more than victims who report events of victimization to the police (Schneider & Sumi, 1981), thus creating a potential flaw with chronological information included in victimization surveys.

Researchers are also interested in the prevalence of telescoping, and have conducted many surveys to determine the scope of the problem. Skogan (1975, as cited in Levine, 1976) found in a Washington, DC, pilot survey that 17 percent of victimizations reported by respondents actually occurred prior to the six-month period specified. Another study revealed that 22 percent of larcenies reported by respondents occurred prior to the reference period mandated by the survey (Schneider & Sumi, 1981). Murphy and Cowan (1976, as cited in Schneider & Sumi, 1981) claim that crime victimization interviews have shown that victimization can be overstated by 40 to 60 percent in some surveys.

One factor that influences the accuracy of interviews is whether the survey is bounded or unbounded. Studies have demonstrated that *bounded interviews*, or interviews conducted after a previous visit with the respondent has occurred, show a much higher accuracy level in data gathered. Those in *unbounded interviews*, or those where there was no previous visit with the respondent, tend to report nearly twice as much crime as respondents of bounded interviews in the same time period (Turner, 1972, as cited in Skogan, 1975, p. 25).

CHAPTER SUMMARY

- Sexual offenses vary by type, degree of severity, class of offense, and length of sanction. They can be broadly categorized as contact offenses (where touching occurs), noncontact offenses (where only viewing or talking occurs), sexual solicitation (where sexual acts are traded for compensation) and pornographic offenses (where movies or pictures are involved).

- Statistics on the prevalence of sexual offending are derived from three types of data: arrest and conviction rates, victimization surveys, and empirical studies. It is difficult, if not impossible, to ascertain the true prevalence of offending in the population. Many researchers and research organizations have calculated rates of victimization.

- Rates of victimization have decreased in the past decade. The best estimates of victimization rates are that one in four women and one in seven men are sexually abused in their lifetimes.

- Victims of child sexual abuse often wait many years to report the abusive behavior. The length of delay depends on many factors, including victim-offender relationship, severity of the abuse, cognitive and developmental variables, fear of negative consequences, and gender of the victim.

- After a delay in reporting, many victims suffer from "telescoping," and do not report the time of the abuse correctly.

DISCUSSION QUESTIONS

1. What are the best sources of statistical information on sexual offenses and offenders? How do these sources of information differ?

2. What are the most significant problems in determining the true prevalence of sexual abuse?

3. How accurate are reports of sexual offending many years after the abuse occurred? What factors influence the accuracy?

4. What should be done to increase reporting of sexual abuse?

DID YOU KNOW...?

- **Did you know** that most sexual offenses are committed by family members or acquaintances? Many reports about sexual offenders in the media relate to sexual assaults by strangers, but in fact most perpetrators know their victims.

- **Did you know** that recidivism rates for sex offenders are low—substantially lower than recidivism rates for most other crimes? Sexual offenses are greatly underreported, so the true rate of sexual offending is not clear. However, official statistics show that most sexual offenders are not convicted of multiple sexual offenses.

- **Did you know** that not all victims of sexual abuse go on to abuse others? Many sex offenders were sexually abused themselves; however, most people who were sexually abused do not go on to become abusers.

© Cengage Learning

2

Historical Perspectives
on Sexual Behavior

As explained in Chapter 1, the concept of "normal" sexual behavior is a socially constructed reality that is continually adapting (Jenkins, 1998). Actions that are defined as sexual offenses vary across religions, cultures, nations, and even states. Additionally, these definitions change over time, adapting to the prevailing social norms and cultures. There are few objective standards for acceptable sexual behavior, and tolerance of various sexual acts depends largely upon the political and social ideologies of the day. An evaluation of sexual behavior over centuries and in various cultures shows the evolution of attitudes toward sexual acts that have intermittently been considered taboo, including homosexuality, bestiality, sadomasochism, adultery, masturbation, and pederasty.

HISTORICAL, RELIGIOUS, AND CULTURAL
PERSPECTIVES OF SEXUAL BEHAVIOR

The sexual activity of Greek and Mediterranean cultures has been extensively detailed in art, literature, poetry, mythology, and theater (Dover, 1978). Though there was no word equivalent to *homosexuality* until 1869, same-sex conduct was displayed in visual arts as early as the sixth century B.C. One of the most prominent philosophical depictions of homosexual relationships occurs in Plato's *Symposium*, which contemplates the nature of a relationship between Socrates and a young, attractive male. Artistic depictions of transgenerational homosexuality were not uncommon, and many vases and murals show scenes of older males touching the genitals of nude young males (Dover, 1978). Men also wrote love poems about younger boys, particularly those in late adolescence, and sexual activity between older men and younger boys was acceptable and considered beautiful (Breiner, 1990).

Though same-sex relationships occurred regularly in Greece, the men were not considered homosexual in the sense of the word today. It was acceptable for men to have relationships with both men and women, and same-sex relationships were common to supplement the sexual relationship with a wife. Women were not highly respected and were typically viewed as "mad, hysterical, and possibly dangerous and destructive to men" (Breiner, 1990, p. 41). Marriage was considered a necessity for procreation, though sexuality was not linked to marriage and sexual pleasure could thus be received outside the marriage (Mondimore, 1996). The ideal relationship was that of an active older male and a passive younger male (Breiner, 1990; Mondimore, 1996), evident even in Greek mythology, which depicts Zeus as attracted to a young boy of legendary beauty (Dover, 1978).

Homosexuality was institutionalized into the Greek culture, and this was apparent by the arts and practices of the people. Plays, particularly comedies, were very sexual in nature and often included overt sexual acts on stage. There were also orgies to the gods that included repeated sexual acts and often the sacrifice of a child (Breiner, 1990). It was common for young boys to be sold into slavery, and socially prominent men would have slaves for their own sexual use. Though the majority of sexual behavior revolved around males, there were also women who were involved in homosexual practices. The most famous of these is Sappho, resident of Lesbos (from which the word *lesbian* is derived), who wrote love poems to women.

The Greek culture was not the only one to promote homosexuality, pederasty, and the importance of the male figure in society. Boy brothels were also found in Rome, and the Romans believed that sexual relationships with young boys would aid their mental development (Breiner, 1990). Although the Greeks viewed man-boy relationships as beautiful, Romans often subjected boys (particularly slave boys) to violence and abuse. Sadistic activities were enjoyed for entertainment, and this included watching women and children being raped and having sex with animals.

The Egyptians were similar to the Greeks and Romans in their admiration of the male figure and their acceptance of homosexuality. Other sexual behaviors common to the Egyptians included polygamy, incest, sexual play among children, and sexual touching of children by adults (Breiner, 1990). Children participated in sexual play at an early age, and it was expected that this would teach them about sexual behavior. By A.D. 200, brother-sister marriages were common, especially among those in the middle class. Though intercourse between adults and children was considered taboo, adults commonly sucked the penises of boys in order to prepare them for sexual activity later. Sexual activity among adults was very open in Egypt, and the pharaoh in particular was expected to partake in extensive sexual activity with his wives and other women while traveling (Breiner, 1990).

Open sexual activity continued in such a fashion until the early Middle Ages, at which time homosexuality became a crime in Europe. This shift in moral thinking about sexuality was influenced by the church, and all sexual acts that were for enjoyment rather than procreation were considered to be sinful (Holmes, 1991; Mondimore, 1996). Sodomy was the catchall category of all "unnatural" sexual acts, including masturbation, bestiality, anal intercourse, fellatio, and heterosexual intercourse in anything other than the missionary position. By the 14th century, sodomy was illegal throughout Europe, and perpetrators could potentially be sentenced to death. Homosexual acts were particularly discouraged, and in 1326 King Edward II of England was brutally killed because of his relationship with another male (Mondimore, 1996, p. 25). Though the church continued to have an influence on sexual mores for several hundred years, transgenerational sexual acts became socially acceptable in 16th- and 17th-century Europe. It was common for adults to touch and fondle the genitals of their prepubescent children, though the touching stopped when the children developed into adolescence (Breiner, 1990; Jenkins, 1998).

In the 18th century, many children were sent to workhouses and brothels and were victims of murder, assault, or rape. With this exception, there was little danger from adult offenders outside the home. The main focus on sexual behavior continued to be within the home, and separate courts were developed for criminal and moral offenses. Although acts such as incest had been accepted in ancient cultures, the church declared incest an ecclesiastical offense, and incestuous marriages were invalidated (Thomas, 2000). Moral offenses, such as masturbation, were brought before the church courts throughout the beginning of the 20th century. Other types of behavior that were considered more serious offenses—including homosexuality, bestiality, and sexual intercourse with prepubescent children—were brought before the criminal courts and were punishable by sentences as severe as death.

Though the Catholic Church dominated regulation of sexual behavior in Europe, other religions and cultures differed in their sexual mores. Polygamy was (and in some cultures, still is) regularly practiced by Muslims, Mormons, and Hebrews. Hebrew families had strict puritan regulations on sexual behavior, and, like the Catholic Church, considered homosexuality an abhorrence (Breiner, 1990). Masturbation was prohibited; for young men this was equivalent to premarital sex, and a married man who masturbated was guilty of adultery. Men were even discouraged from touching their genitals while urinating, as this was thought to encourage masturbation (Breiner, 1990).

In opposition to the puritan sexual mores of various religious sects, Native American and African cultures often practiced sexual activities similar to those of the ancient Greeks. There was evidence of homosexuality in both North and South American tribes, where sexual play among children was also tolerated. Many tribes believed that sexual activity between children and adults was a necessary aspect of sexual development, and that a boy would have to be sexually intimate with an older man in order to develop masculine qualities (Mondimore, 1996). African tribes had similar rituals, and female circumcision was (and is still) common to many African cultures. That such acts are regularly practiced in other cultures but are condemned in Western societies shows the influence of social ideologies on accepted sexual behavior. There is no objective standard for the types of sexual behavior that should be prohibited, and sexual mores have changed drastically even throughout the previous century.

CHANGING PERCEPTIONS OF DEVIANT SEXUAL BEHAVIOR: THE 20TH CENTURY

The beginning of the 20th century witnessed a new philosophy of sexual morality. It was at that time, during the Progressive Era, that concerns began to emerge about a number of issues, including the sexual behavior of women and the abuse of children. With the Industrial Revolution causing vast urban growth, adolescent women began entering the workplace in large numbers for the first time. Subsequently, they began participating in social activities outside of their local neighborhoods, experiencing unprecedented freedom from their families (Odem, 1995). It was this change in social structure that instigated the modification of "age of consent" laws for sexual behavior, and it was at this time that the courts began to regularly monitor sexual behavior.

Researchers during the Progressive Era began focusing on serious sexual offenders, classifying their behavior as a medical problem. Many sexual deviants were labeled pathological or insane and were sent to mental hospitals, where they were treated until they regained their sanity. Shortly thereafter, researchers began to study the possible correlation between hormones and sexually deviant behavior, hypothesizing that organic treatments were necessary in order to control such behavior. Research in the 1950s began to show that sexually deviant behavior might not be simply the result of hormones or psychopathology; the underlying problems might be behavioral in nature. There continued to be a lack of understanding about the complexities of sexually deviant behavior, however, and it was only in the 1970s that researchers began to link sexually deviant behavior to social problems. Researchers at this time began to take into consideration the effects of cognitive processes on the behavior of sexual deviants, and research continues in this area today.

Whether researchers looked at those who committed deviant sexual acts as having medical, psychological, or moral problems, most looked at the population of sexual deviants as unique. Because the motivation of their behavior was not—and is still not—clearly understood, reactions to their behavior have been erratic. Despite the various therapies and legislative acts that have been imposed upon those who commit sexual offenses, the reactions to this population are distinctly cyclical. Figure 2.1 outlines the cycle of legislative proposals, showing how policies regarding sexual offenders are implemented after waves of emotionally-charged, notorious sex crimes occur.

Though new information about sexual offenders was continually attained throughout the century, societal reaction to sexually deviant behavior has shown a repetitive pattern. At three distinct points in the 20th century, there were public outcries to control sexual "fiends," "psychopaths," and "predators." It was the highly publicized cases of sexual abuse, or, more specifically, cases involving

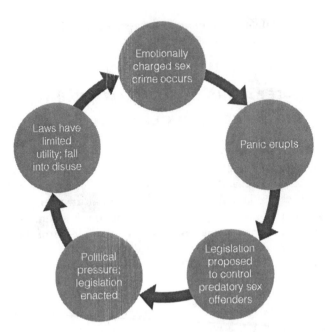

FIGURE 2.1   Cycle of moral panic and reactions to sex offenders
© Cengage Learning

the sexual murder of children by strangers, that largely influenced such public reactions (Jenkins, 1998). In between these peaks of interest in stranger attacks, little public attention was paid to sexual abuse. Most considered it to be a problem within the family that was not shared with the public or the courts. Figure 2.2 shows the public perception of sexual abuse and abusers throughout the century.

In order to understand legislative reactions to sex offenders today, it is essential to observe the influence of research, political ideologies, and societal reactions to deviant sexual behavior throughout the 20th century.

1885–1935: The First Wave of Panic

Prior to the 1880s, little was known about those who committed "deviant" sexual acts. It was Richard von Krafft-Ebing (1886/1965) who, in his groundbreaking book *Psychopathia Sexualis*, first claimed that deviant sexual acts were the result of psychopathological problems in the individual. He attributed various sexual disorders to psychological abnormalities, stating that the sexual disorders were a permanent part of a person's character and could not be changed. His book contains case studies of individuals—both male and female—who experienced various sexual disorders and paraphilias, though a significant portion of the book focuses on homosexual activity. Krafft-Ebing said that homosexuality could be blamed on hereditary factors, or it could be acquired from the practice of masturbation. He concluded that sexual deviants, particularly homosexuals, were mentally ill, pathological, loathsome, and a threat to social hygiene.

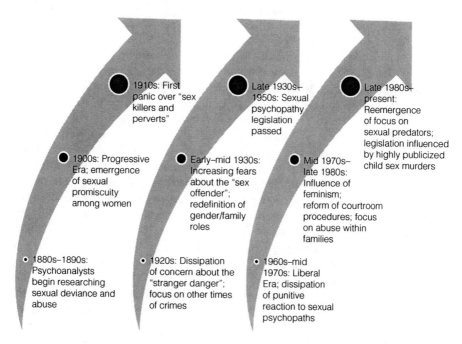

FIGURE 2.2 Changing concepts of deviant sexual behavior in the 20th century, showing periodic increases in concern about the "stranger danger."
SOURCE OF INFORMATION: Jenkins (1998)

He published 12 editions of *Psychopathia Sexualis,* and his work opened flood-gates of research on sexual behavior.

Two other influential researchers at the time were Havelock Ellis and Sigmund Freud. Ellis (1899/1942) wrote a two-volume, multipart book on the psychology of sex, in which he discussed issues ranging from menstruation to marriage to sexual morality. He recognized that a changing social environment defines sexual morality, and that standards of morality are continually changing. His opinion differed from Krafft-Ebing's on the issues of homosexuality and masturbation, as he did not consider sexual deviates to be mentally ill or patho-logical. Though Ellis did not consider homosexuals to be "normal," he did not think there was reason to try to cure them. He did not believe that homosexuals who went through treatment for their deviation could be cured, and with this Freud agreed. Like Krafft-Ebing, Freud believed that deviant sexual behavior was rooted in psychopathology, and he attributed sexual deviation to character dis-orders in a 1905 essay on neuroses (Freud, 1953). He explained that "neurotic symptoms represent the patient's sexual activity," with more complex symptoms representing the patient's fantasies (Freud, 1959, p. 281). Much of Freud's research focused on the sexual activity among family members; he stated that incest was a common occurrence and was consequently the root of problems for many girls.

While researchers were focusing on the causes of sexually deviant behavior, in the 1880s the public began receiving information about sexual immorality from social groups. The Women's Christian Temperance Union (WCTU)—a group primarily consisting of white, middle-class women—began lobbying vigorously in 1889 for the modification of age of consent laws in the United States (Odem, 1995, p. 8). They wanted to raise the age of consent from 10 (in most states) to 18,[1] claiming that "male vice and exploitation were responsible for the moral ruin of young women and girls" (Odem, 1995, p. 16). Although it was true that many men were taking advantage of young working-class girls, some of the young women themselves were acting promiscuously. The number of women working in factories and other industrial centers nearly tripled from the 1880s to 1910, and working-class women began participating in new social activities outside the home and local neighborhoods. The purity reformers of the WCTU acknowledged the need to protect the sexual autonomy of these women, saving them from "male seducers" who would lead them into vices such as prostitution (Odem, 1995, p. 18). Their campaign literature highlighted the increasing frequency of sexual attacks upon women and young girls, and they called for legislative changes in the punishment for these crimes (Odem, 1995, p. 9).

The legislative changes they were seeking did materialize, and by 1920 the age of consent was 16 or 18 in nearly every state.[2] It was not just the religious moral reformers who were concerned about sexual activity during this era, however. While they were waging a campaign against "white slavery," a general panic was rising about sex "fiends" and "perverts" who were preying on children. It was becoming apparent in the larger cities, particularly New York, that child prostitution was rampant among both boys and girls. The number of brothels that would prostitute effeminate boys increased, and they were frequented by some of the more respectable men in the cities. The moral vicissitude was brought about in part by the spreading of venereal diseases, syphilis and gonorrhea in particular, by homosexuals and pedophiles, whose behavior was under scrutiny at this time (Jenkins, 1998, p. 27).

It was between 1910 and 1915 that the United States reached its first retributive climax against sexual offenders. This was largely the result of a rise during this time period in sex-related child homicides, many of which were attributed to serial killers. There were sexual murders in New York City, Colorado, North Dakota, Alabama, Washington, and Atlanta (Jenkins, 1998, p. 36). The media and the police managed to create a panic in the public by defining the "Jack the Rippers" as intelligent, manipulative criminals who were easily able to elude detection. In an effort to reduce serious sex crimes, police intervention increased for all sexual offenders who committed offenses in public—namely, homosexuals and other public "nuisances"—whereas there was a dearth of intervention for intrafamilial offenders.

---

1. The age of consent was 7 in Delaware and 12 in Arkansas, the District of Columbia, Kentucky, Louisiana, Missouri, Nevada, Virginia, Washington, and West Virginia.

2. In Georgia, the age of consent was 14.

During this five-year period, a number of factors influenced legislation and research on sexual offenders. Indeterminate sentences were introduced for serious offenders in most states, and these nearly always affected sex offenders. There was a move toward positivism—the belief that people are social beings who want to conform, but are compelled to commit offences for reasons beyond their control—that came simultaneously with increasing research from European academics and increasing media coverage on the problem of deviant behavior. Because the focus of criminological research at this time was primarily biological and physiological, such as with the newly translated research of Cesare Lombroso (the Italian "father of scientific criminology" who studied biological and physiological theories of crime in the 19th century), remedies for deviant sexual behavior were also physiological. The concept of eugenics, which supposed that some people were genetically unfit and should therefore not procreate, was a popular one. Among criminals fitting this description were sex offenders, and the practice of sterilization was common. In addition to sterilization, surgical castration was a method used to reduce the sexual drive of, and therefore the number of offenses committed by, sexual criminals. At the time, the concept of eugenics was unquestioned, and the sterilization of habitual criminals was allowed until 1942, when it was declared unconstitutional in the case of *Skinner v. Oklahoma* (1942). It was only at this time that the science of hereditary criminality was seriously questioned.

Most of the early research on child sexual abusers focused on serious offenders, often men with psychiatric problems. Even though the researchers studied serious offenders who had been convicted or otherwise incapacitated, the sex offenders in these early studies presented a unique typology in terms of characteristics and likelihood of recidivism. For example, Frosch and Bromber (1939) conducted a psychological study of 709 sex offenders passing through a psychiatric court clinic in New York City. Among their findings were that sex offenders had a low rate of recidivism (a finding that has consistently been replicated in contemporary studies); many were men over age 40 who reported having a strong religious affiliation; alcoholism and mental deficiency were only minor factors in their offending; many of the men in this sample had a maladjusted sex life; and, "pedophiles" had a higher rate of psychopathic personalities and neurotics. In their study of 250 male nonpsychotic pedophiles and exhibitionists at Bellevue Hospital, Apfelberg et al. (1944) found that more than a quarter of the offenders were married and living with their wives at the time of their offenses; 32 percent had been previously charged with sex offenses; and, 38 percent had been charged with other types of offenses.

The panic over sexual killers subsided in the 1920s. The reasons for this were numerous. First, the focus began to turn away from stranger assaults and toward child molestation and incest. The high amount of venereal disease among children was still questioned, though it was attributed largely to child abuse by relatives or to prostitution rather than to rape. Second, by 1917 the WCTU had essentially completed its campaign to save women and children for a life of social purity. They had, by this time, achieved their main goals: women's suffrage and an increased age of consent. Third, by the 1930s issues other than sexual offenses became more topical in the media; namely, organized crime and Prohibition. Fourth, the focus of criminologists and sociologists was shifting, and research focused largely on issues in policing (corruption, brutality), organized crime, and juvenile delinquency (Jenkins, 1998, p. 46). The trend of medicalizing criminal acts did not diminish in the 1920s, however. Research on incarcerated offenders to determine the levels of psychopathy in criminals increased. It was this trend that led to the hospitalization of sexual offenders in the 1930s.

1936–1976: The Rise of the Sexual Psychopath

As had happened at the beginning of the century, an awareness of stranger sex crimes during the 1930s led to new legislation for sexual offenders. Child murderers such as Albert Fish permeated the media coverage in the mid-1930s. He committed numerous offenses against children, including rape, murder, and cannibalism. Though his offenses were indeed horrific, recidivist offenders such as Fish were—and are—atypical. The number of arrests for sexual offenders increased dramatically in the late 1930s, but this was due not as much to an increase in sexual offenses as it was to a change in law enforcement policies (Karpman, 1954). The police in most large cities began to crack down on minor sexual offenses, such as homosexuality and frotteurism (the sexual urge to touch or rub another person) (Tappan, 1950). Though the media fueled the idea that the nation was overrun by sex crimes, this was based more on hysteria than fact. For instance, New York City was noted as having a particularly large population of sexual criminals, yet the majority of arrests were for either consensual acts or misdemeanors. Arrests for sodomy more than doubled there from 1932 to 1938, because officers were required to pick up all those known to commit sexually deviant acts, and the high level of homosexual activity in the subway became known as a "queer threat" (Jenkins, 1998). Despite the high number of minor offenses, the focus of political and media attention was on the relatively rare habitual sex offender. This, combined with the emerging physiological theories of criminology, created a new label for sex offenders in 1937: "sexual psychopaths."

Criminal sanctions alone were not considered sufficient to incapacitate recidivist offenders. Thus, in an effort to skirt the criminal justice system, sexual psychopathy legislation was initiated to civilly commit habitual sexual criminals, or Mentally Disordered Sex Offenders. Michigan was the first state to pass a psychopathy law in 1937, and 28 other states followed suit over the next 50 years (Schwartz, 1999, pp. 3–4). Michigan's law, like those that followed, allowed for the commitment of sexual "degenerates" or perverts if they had mental disorders and posed a threat to the public. Statutes were passed on the principle that sexual psychopathy was a disorder that could be diagnosed and treated, and violent sexual predators would remain civilly committed in mental institutions until they were "cured" (Alexander, 1993). The premise of the legislation was ostensibly therapeutic, yet the result was primarily retributive. The commitment process itself was grossly subjective, and those who were committed remained hospitalized for many years.

There was no consensus for the definition of sexual psychopathy, and it differed from state to state (Tappan, 1950). In California, the offender would have had an "utter lack of power to control his impulses," yet an offender in Iowa had only to have the "criminal propensities towards the commission of sex offences" (Grubin & Prentky, 1993, p. 383). The standard necessary to commit sexual psychopaths was twofold: there had to be proof that the individuals suffered from a mental illness and that they were a danger to themselves or others. Dangerousness was a subjective standard, and because it could not be predicted with any sense of accuracy, commitment standards were questionable (Sutherland, 1950). Civil commitment replaced criminal incarceration, and the critical factor in commitment was that it was not punishment but rather treatment. Therefore, individuals who remained dangerous but not mentally ill were no longer supposed to be civilly confined.

That all sex offenders were a public threat was a concept promoted at this time by various persons with public influence. The media promoted the image of the serious sex fiend through newspaper articles and magazines. The police and the Federal Bureau of Investigation (FBI) were concerned with the inability of the criminal justice system to retain these sex fiends in the prison system, focusing specifically on two factors: the escalation of offending behavior and the use of parole. Offenses such as exhibitionism did not warrant severe sentences, yet this was seen as a gateway action into more serious deviant acts. FBI Director J. Edgar Hoover publicized his opinions during the 1930s and 1940s by describing "degenerate sex offenders" as one of the most severe problems facing children, despite the relatively low crime rate at that time (Jenkins, 1998). The FBI warned families of a looming "stranger danger"; these warnings continued through the 1960s. Parole was considered one source of recidivism, as many of the child sexual killers were repeat offenders who had been released from prison early, on parole. Politicians, too, were using the public's fears about sex crimes to promote their own campaigns. In Minnesota, for example, a young girl went missing in 1938 and was allegedly kidnapped, molested, and killed by a "sexual pervert," though her body was never found. One gubernatorial candidate claimed that he would protect the community from such "unfortunate but dangerous wretches" should he be elected, and, upon his election, sexual psychopathy laws were passed unanimously in 1939 (Robson, 1999, p. 2).

The use of civil commitment under sexual psychopathy laws increased throughout the 1940s and early 1950s. It was not just sex offenders who were subject to adverse public reactions at this time, however. Mental hospitals had lax commitment standards for all those perceived as a social threat. The population of state hospitals increased drastically, largely with those civilly committed due to feeblemindedness or mental illnesses that deemed them a danger to society. States were vague about the types of sexual offenses that could result in the label of sexual psychopath, and some statutes included behaviors such as peeping, lewdness, and impairing morals. Both felonies and misdemeanors could result in commitment, as well as both forced and statutory offenses (for example, statutory rape, which is an offense only because of the age of the victim).

At the height of the panic over sexual psychopaths, some researchers were divided on the issue of civil commitment. For instance, Karpman (1954, p. 38) stated that sexual offenders were not a particularly vicious group of individuals and there was little truth to the supposition that minor offenses escalate to more serious deviant behavior. Yet he also supported indefinite commitment for sexual psychopaths to hospitals for study and treatment until such a time that they were no longer a risk to the community (Karpman, 1954, p. 225). Homosexual activity was still a socially unacceptable sexual alternative, and some researchers linked homosexuals and pedophiles in terms of their "perverse" sexual interests. There was said to be an inevitable connection between an attraction to one's own gender and children, both showing an "arrested psychosexual development" (Jenkins, 1998, p. 62). But by the late 1940s, many researchers began to resist the "stranger danger" belief, citing exaggerated claims of sexually related homicides (Sutherland, 1950). Most researchers opposed the idea of civil commitment for sexual psychopaths, believing—correctly—that such laws would result in the overcommitment of minor offenders.

One researcher published a report on the problems of sexual psychopathy statutes, challenging the validity of the statutes due to, at the most basic level, the erroneous views about sex offenders that led to the legislation (Tappan, 1950). He pointed out 10 primary fallacies concerning the sex offender (pp. 13–16), strikingly applicable to the myths prevalent today:

1. Sex offenders are not usually homicidal sex fiends, and most are minor offenders. Citing Sutherland (1950), he stated that there is more danger of murder by an acquaintance or relative than by an unknown sex fiend, and that a truly dangerous sex fiend is rare.

2. Sex offenders have a low rate of recidivism, and they repeat their offenses less frequently than any other property or violent offenders except those convicted of homicide.

3. There is rarely an escalation of behavior in sex offenders. Though escalation does occur in some serious offenders, most find a sexual act that gives them satisfaction (for example, exhibitionism) and persist in that behavior.

4. It is not possible to predict dangerousness in this population, a point supported by many prominent psychiatrists. He stressed the importance of this point, because sex offenders are indefinitely committed to institutions based on their perceived risks.

5. "Sex psychopathy" is not a clinical entity, and there is much disagreement on what this term means. The offenders who are committed exhibit a variety of psychological problems, and there is no clear definition as to what does or should constitute a sexual psychopath.

6. Sexual offenders are not oversexed individuals, but tend to be undersexed. Organic treatments such as castration are not effective remedies for deviant sexual behavior, because sexual urges are not the driving force of the offender.

7. There is no treatment that can "cure" sex offenders, and commitment to a mental hospital does not mean that a sexual offender will be treated.

Sex offenders are often confined indefinitely and offered no treatment (a problem with sexual predator legislation that is discussed in greater detail in Chapter 12).

8. Though sexual psychopathy legislation was passed in order to incapacitate the serious sexual fiend, the individuals who are most often committed are minor offenders.

9. Due process rights of the accused are disregarded because the commitment procedure is of a civil nature. Tappan asserts that there is a violation of human rights and due process in the commitment procedure, stating that "regardless of the type of court employed to attain this result, it is in effect a serious punishment in which liberty and due process are vitally involved. Reasoning to the contrary is founded in a technical legalism of the most vicious sort" (Tappan, 1950, p. 16).

10. The "sex problem" will not go away merely because a law was passed. The only purpose of the statute is to satisfy the public, and that experience with these laws "reveals the futility of ineffectual legislation" (Tappan, 1950, p. 16).

At the time the report was published, 14 states had passed sexual psychopathy legislation. The most important point of the report is the discord between psychiatrists and lawmakers. Tappan stated that "sixty-five out of sixty-six psychiatrists … expressed the belief that there was insufficient accord in the field to justify legislation specifically for the sexual psychopath" (1950, p. 37). Additionally, he outlined the dangerous precedents set by sexual psychopathy legislation, including civil adjudication of individuals without due process; indefinite commitment to hospitals for offenders who are neither insane nor seriously psychologically impaired; and that sex offenders can be indefinitely committed into hospital until "cured," though they are not necessarily being treated and the cost of commitment to taxpayers is extraordinary (p. 16). Despite Tappan's assertions, the number of states with sexual psychopathy legislation doubled over the next two decades.

At the height of the sexual psychopathy discussions in mid-century, publications about sex offenders continued to focus on the pathology of offending behavior. In his book *The Sexual Criminal*, based on case studies of extreme offenders, De River (1949) described anecdotal examples of sex "degenerates" and "perverts." He claimed that "pedophiles" were psychosexually immature, had a predilection for young children, had mental or physical handicaps, and were often shy or uneasy around adults. It was publications like this that helped develop the popular image of the sexual "pervert" at the time, even though the stereotypes were not based upon empirical analyses.

Empirical research was also ongoing at this time, though the samples of offenders generally consisted of the most serious, incarcerated offenders. In addition to studying skewed samples, most researchers in mid-century were also studying offenders from a psychodynamic perspective. As a result, though the studies provided information about sexual offenders and their histories, demographics, and attitudes, the study findings were often highly skewed since they only focused on the most serious offenders and from a single perspective.

For example, in a study of 102 sexual offenders at Sing Sing, Abrahamsen (1950) found that all of the men in his sample expressed the same characteristics, including hostility toward authority, mental disorders, the prominence of alcohol in many offenses, prior commission of sex crimes (one-third of the sample had previously committed sex crimes), and the developmental delay of conscience in most offenders. Hammer and Glueck (1957) studied approximately 200 sex offenders over a five-year period at Sing Sing prison, and they also found consistent psychological patterns. They noted that all offenders exhibited five key characteristics: a reaction to massive Oedipal entanglements; castration fear or feelings and fear of approaching mature females psychosexually; interpersonal inhibitions of schizoid to schizophrenic proportions; weak ego-strength and lack of adequate control of impulses; and, concrete orientation and minimal capacity for sublimation.

Scholarly articles focusing only on child sexual abusers also had the same limitations. Toobert, Bartelme, and Jones (1959) published an article arguing that pedophiles are not always aggressive, but rather their behavior stemmed from a sense of weakness, inadequacy, or low self-regard, and that such behavior correlated with some type of family disruption during childhood. Gigeroff, Mohr, and Turner (1968) analyzed three distinct groups of pedophiles: the adolescent pedophile, who is often still in puberty; the middle-aged pedophile (aged 35 to 39), who is usually married, shows severe marital and social maladjustment, and exhibits abusive behavior; and the senescent pedophile (aged mid-50s to 60s), who is characterized by loneliness and social isolation and whose abusive behavior evolves "out of a situation in which a particular child is the only one the man can emotionally relate to." They noted that recidivism rates are low for most sexual offenders—between 6 and 8 percent—however, those with a previous sexual offense conviction had recidivism rates of 30 percent and those with sexual and nonsexual offenses had recidivism rates of 50 percent.

As researchers were studying sex offenders in prison or committed to institutional treatment centers in mid-century, other sex researchers were studying "normal" sexual behavior. In two controversial reports, Alfred Kinsey (1948) and Kinsey, Pomeroy, Martin, and Gebhard (1953) analyzed the prevalence of sexual acts that were considered by most to be deviant at the time, such as masturbation and homosexual behavior. He discovered that a high percentage of individuals had, in fact, participated in these behaviors, therefore creating questions about the use of the term *deviant* to describe them. Other studies of normal sexual behavior were carried out in the next two decades, which focused on determining the prevalence of certain sexual practices, such as masturbation, and on understanding how various sexual acts could add pleasure to traditional relationships (see Hite, 1976, 1982; Laumann et al., 1994; Masters & Johnson, 1966). Despite the controversy associated with the methodological flaws of the Kinsey reports and with sex research in general, this body of work was highly influential at the time and demonstrated that normal sexual behavior could be documented using empirical analyses.

Sex researchers also began to study issues of gender identity in the 1950s and 1960s. Notable for his work was John Money, who studied sexual behavior for over 50 years. In 1955, he coined the term *gender role*, later expanded to "gender-identity/role," and in 1966 helped establish the Gender Identity Clinic at Johns Hopkins. The clinic performed sex-reassignment surgeries, and in 1972 Money published the controversial book, *Man and Woman, Boy and Girl* (Money & Ehrhardt, 1972). In this work, he expressed the view that gender is malleable and can be altered through external factors such as prescribed hormones and behavior therapy. Though some of this work was ethically questionable, his impact on study of gender identity was substantial.

The 1960s and early 1970s brought about a social and sexual revolution, and as the Liberal Era emerged there was a dissipation of punitive reaction to sexual psychopaths. Sexual psychopathy statutes fell into disuse in many states, and the main focus on sexual behavior was the changing societal attitudes toward acts that were previously considered to be socially stigmatizing. There was a sexual liberation in the 1960s, and sexual behavior among young people was becoming openly pronounced. Additionally, homosexuality became a more socially acceptable sexual alternative as a result of the gay liberation movement, initiated in 1969 after the Stonewall Riots in New York City. The 1970s brought forth an era of social change for women, with the legalization of abortion in *Roe v. Wade* (1973). While the social and political ideologies were changing, so, too, were theories on sexual offending.

Research on child sexual abuse began progressing in the 1960s. In a methodologically sophisticated research project, Gebhard and Gagnon (1964) studied sexual offenders who abused young children (and notably did not label all of the offenders pedophiles). The authors stated that the regression to sexually abusing children is a function of a breakdown in control over sexual behavior that results from a current environmental stressor and the disposition for this behavior was based on disordered childhood relationships. They did state, however, that they were not able to determine exactly what would constitute the childhood precursors of acts of sexual abuse of children.

Several mid-century studies compared groups of offenders who committed abuse against children of the same sex to those who abused children of the opposite sex. Fitch (1962) found no significant differences between the "homosexual" and "heterosexual" offenders with respect to age at time of offense, age at first conviction for sexual offense, and intelligence. However, the study found major differences in employment level, marital status, sentence decreed, and pattern of previous and subsequent convictions. This study showed that sexual recidivists were predominantly single, homosexual offenders who had a history of previous convictions for sexual offenses.

Notable research on rape in the late 1960s came from feminist researchers. It was becoming evident at this time that male and female constructions of social reality differed (Scully, 1990, p. 2), and the women's movement against sexual violence arose as an attempt to combat the prevailing negative views of female victims. Police practices, courtroom procedures, and even academic research condemned the victims of sexual abuse as partially or primarily responsible for their victimization. Amir (1971), for example, studied forcible rapes in Philadelphia and claimed that 19 percent were victim precipitated and that in many cases the victim initiated the interaction. It wasn't until the 1980s that the women's movement succeeded in changing the public perception of victims of sexual violence, and it was at this time that allegations of child sexual abuse within the family became more frequent. But by the end of the 1980s, a new panic emerged about the sexual homicide of children by strangers. This panic still exists today and is the source of the backlash against sexual offenders.

DID YOU KNOW...?

Sexual Behavior and Changing Social Norms: Homosexuality

Perceptions of "normal" sexual behavior change over time and differ by culture. One of the best examples of these changing views of sexuality and sexual behavior can be seen in the changing views of homosexuality.

The terms *homosexual* and *heterosexual* were first used in personal written communications in 1868 between a writer and a sex reformer (Katz, 1997). *Homosexual* appeared in public in 1869, and by 1900, was being used as a negative classification within the medical field. *Heterosexual* was also being used by the medical community in reference to those men and women who practiced nonprocreative intercourse. In the United States, the terms appeared in print in a medical journal in 1892 defining "two kinds of sexual perversion, judged according to a procreative standard ... 'to abnormal methods of gratification' " (Katz, 1997, p. 177). For the next 50 years, homosexuality continued to be considered a socially unacceptable behavior, and some researchers linked homosexuals and pedophiles through their "perverse" sexual interests (Jenkins, 1998).

By the end of the 1950s, views of homosexuality slowly began changing. For example, the Wolfendon Committee on Homosexual Offences and Prostitution in England, which convened and released a report in 1957, was charged with reviewing whether same-sex behavior and prostitution should be considered offenses and, if so, what the sanctions for those offenses should be. The Committee decided that the sanctions for prostitution should increase, while the homosexual behavior between consenting adults in private should not be a criminal offense. This recommendation for the decriminalization of homosexual behavior was well ahead of its time, as the *Diagnostic and Statistical Manual of Mental Disorders* (DSM) still considered homosexuality to be a mental disorder. Despite the fierce debates about the Wolfendon report, however (see Ronan, 1957), the report's recommendations ultimately led to the passage of the Sexual Offences Act of 1967, which did make legal sexual behavior between consenting adults (over the age of 21) of the same gender in private.

Homosexuality was starting to be viewed as a socially acceptable sexual alternative at about the same time in the United State largely as a result of the gay liberation movement, exemplified in 1969 by the Stonewall Riots in New York City. By 1973, homosexuality was removed from the DSM-II (though it was replaced with a category of disorder called sexual orientation disturbance). Laws continued to change throughout the next 30 years, but many states continued to have laws banning this behavior until the U.S. Supreme Court stated that sodomy laws were unconstitutional in *Lawrence v. Texas* (2003).

Questions
1. Are there any sexual behaviors that are now considered "deviant" that may become accepted sexual practices in the future?
2. Are there cultures where homosexual behaviors are still considered deviant?
3. How is the controversy over same-sex marriage linked to the controversy over homosexual behavior generally?

© Cengage Learning

1976–Present: The Emergence of a Sexually Violent Predator

Toward the end of the 1970s, a number of issues were emerging that were not previously in the public forum. Problems with mental health such as depression and eating disorders were being discussed for the first time as common problems of normal people, and individuals were seeking therapy at rapid rates for cures to their ills. Childhood sexual abuse was also being discussed in open forums, particularly the courts. This new discourse was beneficial in many respects: it allowed for more information about the issues to be publicized, and it modified the stereotype that the victims of abuse were to blame rather than the perpetrators. Before long, however, a new problem evolved.

In the 1980s, the courts witnessed an influx of lawsuits from adults claiming they had been sexually abused as children. These adults claimed that they had repressed the memories for years, and only after several therapy sessions was the abuse recalled. The courts were initially hesitant to accept such claims (for example, *Tyson v. Tyson*, Wash. 1986), though they gradually altered their views and began awarding damages to the plaintiffs (for example, *Hammer v. Hammer*, Wis. Ct. App. 1987). The statutes of limitation were extended in many American states, because the alleged abuse was often recalled decades after it occurred. Repressed memories were generally retrieved during therapeutic sessions when individuals—the majority of whom were women—sought psychological therapy for problems other than the alleged abuse. Therapists suggested that the patients read self-help books (Bass & Davis, 1988; Blume, 1990; Fredrickson, 1992), many of which indicated that individuals experiencing psychological problems were likely to have been sexually abused as children. Some of these books described lists of symptoms attributable to repressed abuse; these lists included characteristics as common as eating disorders, fear of being alone in the dark, and drug or alcohol abuse (Blume, 1990).

During therapeutic sessions, various retrieval processes were used to induce recall of repressed memories, the most common being hypnosis and Amytal (Green, 1994). Hypnosis, a sleeplike condition achieved through relaxation and concentration on a particular topic, lacks scientific elucidation because it is not well-understood what happens in the mind to reproduce memories. Accurate information has emerged under hypnosis by individuals who witnessed an event, as details can be recollected immediately after the event through sensory recall and mental exercise with some accuracy. Individuals attempting to recall entire events from the past, however, consistently recall information that is incorrect more often than information that is correct. This is particularly true with hypnotic age regression, where the recalled events occurred before the age of five, a time represented by "childhood amnesia" (Loftus, 1994). Amytal, the other common method used to retrieve memories, is a barbiturate that induces a hypnotic drowsiness in individuals. Although said to function as a truth serum, it has been asserted that "Amytal has no legitimate use in recovered memory cases.... It is worse than useless, as it [encourages] patients' beliefs in completely mythical events" (Piper, 1993, pp. 447, 465). Amytal is similar to hypnosis in that it increases confidence in a subject's recollections and the quantity of such recollections; however, there is no increase in the accuracy of such memories, and without independent corroboration there is no distinction between verifiable and fantasized memories (Watkins, 1993).

The validity of repressed memories eventually surfaced as a critical issue, because many of those who were accused denied the allegations, claiming that ideas of abuse were being inadvertently planted by therapists through various memory-retrieval techniques. There was a contention that during therapeutic sessions, therapists were unintentionally planting false memories through leading questions and through associations of sexual abuse to other psychological problems. As therapists probed for traumatic past experiences, they suggested on the basis of a particular symptom that sexual abuse had occurred to the patient during childhood. With the idea of such abuse planted, many of the vulnerable patients accepted the explanations as the basis of their current problems. For example, Laura Stratford consulted with a therapist to find the source of scars across her body. Though she "remembered" being abused, evidence eventually led to the conclusion that all of her physical scars were self-inflicted (Jenkins & Maier-Katkin, 1991). In another case, George Franklin was convicted of murder based solely on his daughter's retrieved memories. Eventually, it came out that not only had she revised her account of the offense to fit the facts of the case, but the facts she retrieved were originally reported in local newspapers (Loftus, 1993).

Many of the repressed memory cases included claims of childhood sexual abuse in conjunction with ritualistic satanic abuse. The first publicized account of this abuse was in *Michelle Remembers* (Smith & Pazder, 1980), and Michelle Smith's story is similar to many subsequent cases. After experiencing problems of sexual dysfunction, low self-esteem, eating disorders, and a miscarriage, she underwent therapy for a year and concluded that 22 years earlier she had been the subject of childhood satanic abuse. Extraordinary stories involving many reputable individuals surfaced about rituals of chanting, baby breeding, human and animal sacrifices, starvation, and torture. Smith's story is remarkable but not unique; almost every claim of satanic abuse concerns similar stories, implying an international satanic conspiracy if the accusations were to be confirmed (Green, 1994). However, despite the existence of a "satanic panic," evidence has yet to be found to corroborate any of these extraordinary satanic abuse claims.

Those who believe in the existence of satanic practices claim that within the past 30 years the remnants of physical evidence have deteriorated or been exhumed so as to avoid detection. While this claim cannot be discounted, it is highly unlikely that satanic rituals have been taking place for at least three decades and yet no evidence has been found regarding these rituals anywhere in the world. Therapeutic transcripts for these cases show how some psychologists ask leading questions about satanic rituals until the patients agree to the elaborate stories. In the McMartin preschool case, children were asked questions such as "Did you ever see people walking around in dark robes?" and "Did anyone touch you *here* (indicating private areas)?" (Hicks, 1991). The questions were asked repeatedly until the children answered affirmatively regarding the existence of satanic rituals in conjunction with sexual abuse. Despite children's statements, charges were dropped in all cases claiming satanic abuse due to lack of physical evidence to support the given claims.

As cases of repressed memories became more frequent, some defendants began to file countersuits against the therapists who were responsible for retrieving false memories (see, for example, *Ramona v. Isabella*, 1994). Few cases of repressed memories are brought up in the courts today, and none result in convictions without corroborating evidence. There are, however, thousands of cases brought before the courts on a daily basis involving child sexual abuse within the family. Despite the prevalence of this type of sexual abuse—which accounts for the majority of cases—another "stranger danger" panic erupted in the late 1980s. It was this panic, based upon a few highly publicized cases of child rape and murder, that initiated the current trend toward sex offenders: the emergence of the sexually violent predator.

In the late 1980s, two child molesters committed horrific acts in the state of Washington. Both offenders had a long history of sexual offending, and there was a common belief that the criminal justice system was ineffective at keeping recidivist sex offenders incapacitated. Wesley Alan Dodd sexually molested, tortured, and murdered three young boys, saying that if he were released he would do it again—and enjoy it. Earl Shriner had a long history of child molestation charges and a homicide charge from when he was a juvenile. In and out of institutions since the age of 15, he had just been released after a decade in prison when he kidnapped and tortured a seven-year-old boy. In prison, he confided in a journal and to other inmates that he fantasized about killing again, and explained in great detail about how, when released, he would buy a van in which he would kidnap boys and take them into the woods to torture them. There was nothing the state could do to keep him in prison. Dodd was executed, but it was the case of Earl Shriner that prompted the implementation of a legislative act for "sexually violent predators" (SVPs) who had the potential to be released from prison one day.

Washington was the first state to enact SVP legislation, though several states implemented legislation in the 1990s and 2000s. An SVP is defined as any person who has been convicted of or charged with a sexually violent offense and who suffers from a mental abnormality or personality disorder that makes the person likely to engage in predatory acts of sexual violence. A mental abnormality was defined as "a congenital or acquired condition affecting the emotional or volitional capacity which predisposes the person to commit sexually violent offenses in a degree constituting such person a menace to the health and safety of others" (Dorsett, 1998, p. 125). This legislation was essentially a modification of the sexual psychopathy laws, though there were a few significant variations. Most important, civil commitment was not intended to replace incarceration, but instead to supplement it. Upon completion of a criminal sentence, sexual offenders who have a mental disorder and are deemed dangerous can be committed to some type of secure mental hospital until they are "rehabilitated."

In Washington, The Community Protection Act also established a system of notification to the community when offenders are convicted or released from prison. It was only with the implementation of Megan's Law in 1996 that registration became a federal regulation. Megan's Law, the registration and notification scheme that originated in New Jersey, is named after seven-year-old Megan Kanka, who was sexually abused and killed by a convicted child molester living in her neighborhood. Her parents claimed that if a convicted sex offender is living in the area, the community has a right to know so that the parents can protect their children. Though registration has broader consequences (discussed in Chapter 10), this legislation focuses primarily on sexual attacks by strangers, not abuse within the home. The death of Megan Kanka was an emotionally charged sex crime against a child by a recidivist offender, and politicians had little choice but to implement laws protecting the community against the "stranger danger."

Though the cases of kidnapping and child murder are horrific, these are not the norm. SVP legislation, like that of sexual psychopathy laws from the 1930s, was passed to incapacitate a small portion of the population. However, the number of offenders referred for civil commitment is growing, and there are now similar problems with the SVP population that were prevalent with those convicted as sexual psychopaths. All of the problems with the psychopathy population presented by Tappan (1950) are relevant in regard to the SVP population, and it is likely that the statutes will eventually fall into disuse in a similar manner.

CHAPTER SUMMARY

- Accepted sexual behavior has changed significantly throughout history, and from the time of first writings of the ancient Greeks, "normal" sexual acts have depended on accepted social and political ideologies.

- Sexual assaults by strangers have had a significant influence on legislation throughout the 20th century. Yet, the majority of sexual offenses are committed by an acquaintance or relative of the victim, and the legislation also engulfs these individuals.

- There were three distinct cycles of moral panic regarding sex offenders in the 20th century. Each cycle is characterized by legislative policies based on emotionally charged, notorious sex crimes.

- Research on sexual offending has developed greatly over the last century. Studies in the early mid-twentieth century were often methodologically flawed and based on samples of serious sexual offenders who were in prison or incapacitated in mental institutions.

DISCUSSION QUESTIONS

1. Why is it important to understand the historical context of the social perception of sexual behavior?

2. What is the primary cause of the "moral panic" over child sexual abuse throughout the 20th century?

3. What are the key similarities between sexual psychopathy and sexually violent predator legislation?

4. What problems may result from implementing legislation that is primarily based on "stranger" sexual abuse of children?

5. What roles did researchers, the media, and politicians play concerning public attitudes toward sexual offenders throughout the 20th century?

VIGNETTE

SEXUAL FIENDS AND MONSTERS: The Fear of the Extreme

Sexual offenses cause a level of fear in the public that is unique from other crimes. Despite the fact that sexual assaults by strangers are rare—even more so for sexual assaults against children—the public fears the sexual fiends, monsters, and predators that they hear about in the media. The media tends to report on the most heinous, frightening cases of sexual assault, kidnapping, and murder. As a result, public opinion strongly favors severe legislative sanctions against sex offenders with the understanding that such policies will keep them safe. What follows are examples of cases that led, at least indirectly, to sex offender legislation.

Albert Fish Albert Fish raped and murdered children in the early 20th century. Though no one has definitely proven how many victims he had, Fish claimed to have offended against more than 100 children in every state and admitted to cannibalism in some of those cases. Additionally, he was a sexual deviant with a penchant for masochism (discussed in Chapter 3). He practiced infibulation, which involves fastening by ring, clasp, or stitches the foreskin in boys (or the labia majora in girls) in order to prevent sexual intercourse, and upon his execution it was realized that he had more than two dozen piercings in his genital area (Holmes, 1991, p. 61). At the time he was executed in 1936, the United States had just begun to experience the rising fear of the sexual psychopath.

Earl Shriner From the 1960s to 1980s, Earl Shriner had a history of serious sexual offenses against children and adolescents in the state of Washington. His final victim was seven-year-old Ryan Alan Hade, whom he kidnapped, raped, cut off his penis, stabbed, and left for dead. Ryan survived, and Shriner was convicted and sentenced to 131 years in prison. While incarcerated for a previous sexual offense, Shriner had disclosed his fantasies about the rape and torture of children, but the state had no way to keep him confined. As a result of the community outrage about him, the state of Washington passed the Community Protection Act of 1990, the first modern-day legislation that encompassed both registration and civil commitment clauses.

Questions
1. What role does the media have in informing public opinion about sexual offending?
2. What are the positive and negative effects of media attention on serious sexual offenders?
3. Should legislation be implemented based upon the small but serious cases of sexual offending, like those of Albert Fish and Earl Shriner?

3

Etiology of Sexually Deviant Behavior

There are many possible explanations as to why individuals commit sexual offenses. The literature on sexual offending provides biological, psychological, and sociological bases of the origins of deviant behavior. However, no one factor is responsible for causing someone to commit a sexual offense, and no single theory is capable of explaining the etiology of deviant sexual behavior for such a heterogeneous group of individuals (Robertiello & Terry, 2007).

Notwithstanding the complexity of the task, researchers since the beginning of the century have produced models and hypotheses to explain such behavior through biological or psychological abnormalities. By mid-century, the understanding of sexual disorders (paraphilias) was beginning to develop, and this development continues to the present day. By the end of the 1960s, the theoretical approach to understanding sexual offenders began transforming. Few explanations were based on abnormalities beyond the control of the individual; rather, the theoretical frameworks incorporated behavioral and cognitive-behavioral approaches. Concurrently, feminist and sociocultural theorists emerged with a competing school of thought, choosing to define sexually aggressive behavior through societal explanations. They voiced a global critique of men and society rather than focusing on individual causes of deviant behavior.

One deficiency that unites these traditional explanations of sexual offending is their lack of empirical support. By contrast, current theories are rooted in empirical research, emphasizing developmental, interpersonal, personality, epidemiological, sociological, and situational variables, all of which have helped to develop data-driven models of offending behavior (Lanyon, 1991, p. 36). Though still developing, these integrated theories provide a more thorough framework for understanding why men, women, and juveniles commit sexual offenses. This chapter outlines the various explanations of the etiology of sexual offending.

PARAPHILIAS AND OTHER SEXUAL DISORDERS

Some sexual offenders are diagnosed with paraphilias or other sexual disorders, as identified in the *Diagnostic and Statistical Manual of Mental Disorders (DSM).*[1] The features of all paraphilias are recurrent, intense sexually arousing fantasies or urges involving either nonhuman objects, suffering or humiliation of oneself or one's partner, children or other nonconsenting persons (American Psychiatric Association, 2000). For some paraphiliacs, these fantasies or stimuli are necessary in order to achieve erotic arousal, whereas for others they are episodic and the individual can be stimulated otherwise. The behavior, urges, and fantasies cause clinically significant distress or impairment in social, occupational, or other areas of functioning. Many paraphiliacs suffer from more than one paraphilia, or have at some point in their lives experienced multiple paraphilic interests (Abel, Becker, Mittelmen, Cunningham-Rathner, Rouleau, & Murphy, 1987).

There are eight primary paraphilias listed in the *DSM IV-TR*: exhibitionism, voyeurism, frotteurism, sadism, masochism, fetishism, transvestic fetishism, and pedophilia. Additionally, there are several other disorders labeled paraphilias not otherwise specified (NOS). It is important to note the distinction between the disorder (paraphilia) and the criminal act. Media reports about sexual offending often use interchangeable language that indicates a person can be convicted of a paraphilia, which is incorrect. For instance, a person cannot be *convicted* of pedophilia, but instead a person who has been *diagnosed* with pedophilia may sexually abuse a child and be convicted of rape, sexual abuse, aggravated sexual abuse, etc. (depending on the nature of the criminal act and the nomenclature for that act by jurisdiction).

Most paraphilic acts do not come to the attention of authorities for several reasons (American Psychiatric Association, 1999). These are often private acts that take place in the home, and they only come to the attention of authorities (or therapists) when they become habitual, involve a victim, or result in a criminal act. Many paraphilic acts (for example, exhibitionism, frotteurism, voyeurism), involve strangers and take place quickly. As such, the victims rarely get a sufficient view of the perpetrator that would enable them to provide a full description to the police. Additionally, some victims do not know they are subject to this abuse (for example, voyeurism) and are unable to notify authorities.

Paraphilias differ greatly; some involve no contact with a victim (for example, exhibitionism), some involve minor contact (for example, frotteurism), whereas others contain much contact and even violence (for example, sadism). Research

---

1. Information about paraphilias in this chapter is based upon the *DSM IV-TR*, the current version at the time of publication. The *DSM V* is scheduled for release in May 2013.

T A B L E 3.1   Eight Main Paraphilias of the *DSM IV*

Paraphilia	Description – Sexual Fantasies, Urges or Behaviors Involving:
Exhibitionism	Exposure of genitals to a stranger; may include exposure only or masturbation during the exposure
Frotteurism	Touching or rubbing up against a nonconsenting person in a crowded area; may rub genitals against or fondle the victim
Voyeurism	Watching a stranger who is naked, disrobing, or engaging in a sexual act; no sexual activity sought with the victim
Fetishism	Sexual attraction to nonliving objects, such as a shoe or undergarment; individual often masturbates while holding the object or has a partner wear the object during sexual encounters
Transvestic Fetishism	Cross-dressing; heterosexual man is sexually aroused by himself wearing the female clothing
Sexual Masochism	The act of being humiliated, bound, beaten, or made to suffer in some way; may occur with a partner or during masturbation
Sexual Sadism	The act of humiliating, binding, beating, or making another person suffer in some way; sexual excitement the result of control over the victim
Pedophilia	Sexual attraction to a prepubescent child; may involve own children or nonrelated children, males or females
Paraphilia Not Otherwise Specified (NOS)	Sexual fantasies, urges or behaviors about individuals, objects or other nonconsenting persons other than the above paraphilias, which cause distress or other serious problems for the person diagnosed

SOURCE OF INFORMATION: American Psychiatric Association (2000)

shows that paraphiliacs typically have more than one paraphilia, and that there is crossover between types of acts committed by paraphiliacs. For instance, one report states that "paraphilac persons tend to cross over between touching and non-touching of their victims, between family and nonfamily members, between female and male victims, and to victims of various ages" (American Psychiatric Association, 1999, p. 47). The primary paraphilias are summarized in Table 3.1.

Noncontact and Minimal Contact Paraphilias

The most common noncontact paraphilia that comes to the attention of therapists and authorities is *exhibitionism*, or the exposure of genitals to a stranger. Exhibitionism is almost exclusively male, though there are some females known to be exhibitionists. Sometimes, the offender masturbates when he exposes himself, and at other times the act is simply to shock the stranger. However, many exhibitionists fantasize that the stranger is aroused by their exposure, and they go home to masturbate about this fantasy after the act occurs. Those who expose themselves tend to do so frequently, and often expose themselves many times before being caught and arrested. Additionally, they have the highest known number of sexual offenses per offender (Abel et al., 1987). Researchers have found that exhibitionists, like rapists and child sexual abusers, often experience loneliness and have intimacy deficits (Marshall, 1989), and they show higher levels of arousal to consensual adult sexual relations than to exhibiting (Marshall, Anderson, & Fernandez, 1999). This indicates that sexual needs are not the only motivating factor for exhibitionists, and their primary motivation may be non-sexual in nature.

Another common paraphilia, though one that comes to the attention of authorities far less frequently than exhibitionism, is fetishism. *Fetishism* involves sexual fantasies and urges involving nonliving objects. The sexual attraction may also center on behaviors (for example, stepping on bugs) or body parts (also called partialism), though technically these are not fetishes but other types of paraphilias. For those diagnosed with fetishism, the object of the fetish is usually required for sexual excitement; without it there is some level of erectile dysfunction. The range of fetishes is vast; though the most common fetish objects are clothing, particularly women's lingerie and shoes, there are also fetishes about nearly every object and behavior imaginable. Such attractions can be quite harmless, or they may involve dangerous or criminal behavior. There are too many fetishes to name here, but examples include the sexual attraction to stuffed animals (*plushophilia,* or more commonly "plushies"); urine (*urophilia*); feces (*coprophilia*); eyes (*oculophilia*); statues, dolls or mannequins (*agalmatophilia*); small bugs or animals being squished ("crush" fetish); people with impaired mobility (*abasiophilia*); amputees (*acrotomophilia*); watching or staging accidents (*symphorophilia*); and being eaten (*vorarephilia*).

Though the most common fetish involves women's clothing, this is not the same as dressing up in women's clothing. *Transvestic fetishism* is another type of paraphilia; this involves men who keep a collection of women's clothing and intermittently use it to cross-dress. While dressed, the man will usually mastur-bate and imagine he is the object of his sexual fantasy. This occurs only in het-erosexual males, or males whose primary sexual preference is to be with women. As with all paraphilias, there are different degrees of transvestic fetishism. For some males cross-dressing creates a peace of mind, whereas others are severely distressed about their need to do so. One convicted rapist who cross-dresses describes his experience with transvestic fetishism in the following way[2]:

> I was leaving the house at night, going off, dressing up, and spending the night dressed up in the stuff, which made me feel totally different. But it also put a strain on my relationship, so I turned to the drugs. Because I would get so low, my self-esteem would go so far down, that I would take drugs to bring myself back up.... I want to be a normal human being, I don't want to be weird. I want to be a normal person, a father to my kids, a husband to my wife.

---

2. Quote taken from an interview with a rapist in prison in England, 1996.

A fourth minimal-contact paraphilia is *frotteurism*, which is touching and rubbing up against a nonconsenting person. This occurs in a crowded place, such as a subway car during rush hour, and is an almost exclusively male paraphilia. The frotteur may touch his genitals against the person or "accidentally" rub the other person's genitals or breasts. He usually fantasizes about having an exclusive relationship with this person, and he will generally masturbate about the contact at a later date.

Another noncontact paraphilia is *voyeurism*, which is the observation of unsuspecting individuals in the process of either disrobing or engaging in sexual activity. No sexual activity is sought with the "victims," though the voyeur may masturbate while watching the persons or later in response to the memory. Though this is a noncontact behavior, some offenders who commit serious sexual offenses such as rape often begin their deviant sexual behavior through "peeping" (Terry, 1999). For example, a rapist described the escalation of his behavior in the following way[3]:

> I went out and got drunk one night and walked by a clothesline and
> saw some women's underwear and [stole] them. Then I started peeping
> in women's windows. And then I started fantasizing about having sex.
> I started fantasizing about raping and, it wasn't only rape, it was about
> me hitting her on the head, and her unconscious and then having sex
> with her, because that is the only way I thought I would get sex.

This excerpt shows an individual with more than one paraphilia—voyeurism and fetishism—and it shows how there was an escalation of paraphilias into a serious, violent fantasy. Most paraphiliacs do not become violent, though some voyeurs do eventually desire sexual contact with an individual they are watching.

In addition to the noncontact or minor contact paraphlias discussed, the *DSM IV-TR* lists paraphilias NOS, many of which are also noncontact. For example, telephone scatologia is the urge to make obscene phone calls, and the paraphiliac repeatedly calls strangers and speaks to them sexually. These are not consensual phone calls, and the caller is sexually aroused sometimes by a conversation that ensues and sometimes by the shock that is caused (Holmes, 1991). The common element between the noncontact or minimal-contact paraphilias is that the offender typically is excited by his behavior and masturbates in response to the behavior later. With exhibitionism, frotteurism, and scatologia, the offender envisions excitement by the victims. He misperceives the victims' cues of shock, anger, or fear as sexual excitement at his exposure, touch, or sexually suggestive words. Though these paraphilias have minimal contact with potential victims, other paraphilias could be more dangerous if acted upon.

High-Contact Paraphilias

Serious paraphilias are those involving violence, children, or other nonconsenting persons. *Pedophilia* involves the sexual attraction to prepubescent children and, if these desires are acted upon, could cause significant harm. For an individual to be classified as a pedophile, he must have recurrent, intense sexually

---

3. Quote taken from an interview with a rapist in prison in England, 1996.

arousing fantasies, sexual urges or behavior involving a *prepubescent* child over a period of time (American Psychiatric Association, 2000). Additionally, the individual would be at least 16 years of age and at least five years older than the child (American Psychiatric Association, 2000).

Not all child sexual abusers are pedophiles because, like rapists, they are not all driven by sexual needs and therefore may not experience these intense sexual urges. Neither are all pedophiles child sexual abusers, because they might not act on these intense sexual urges. Additionally, many of the children who are sexually abused are not prepubescent. Although not considered a formal diagnosis in the *DSM IV-TR*, many clinicians and researchers consider those with recurrent sexual fantasies, urges, or behaviors regarding adolescents to be a unique group that displays the characteristics of paraphilias. The term applied to this disorder is *ephebophilia* or *hebophilia* (these terms are used interchangeably). The American Psychiatric Association (APA) considered including ephebophilia in the *DSM V*, though a determination was made not to include this as a specific disorder. However, there is a proposed revision for pedophilia to become pedohebophilia in the *DSM V*, with subtypes of pedophilic type (attraction to prepubescent children) and hebophilic type (with an attraction to pubescent children) (American Psychiatric Association, 2010).

Sexual attraction to children is not the only paraphilia with potential harm. Other dangerous paraphilias involve violence or prohibited sexual acts, the most common of which are sexual sadism and sexual masochism. *Sexual masochism* is the act of being humiliated, beaten, bound, or otherwise made to suffer. Some acts are conducted on the person's own, such as binding themselves, shocking themselves electrically, sticking themselves with pins, or similar actions. Other times acts are committed with partners, such as bondage, blindfolding, and whipping. *Sexual sadism* takes place when the individual derives sexual excitement from the psychological or physical suffering of another person. This involves the same actions as in masochism, but performing instead of receiving. The acts can be minor and cause little damage, such as humiliating one's partner, or the acts may potentially cause a lot of damage, such as *hypoxia* (the deprivation of oxygen). Sexually sadistic acts often increase in severity over time, and sadists who are diagnosed with antisocial personality disorders may cause serious injury or even death to their victims (American Psychiatric Association, 2000).

Many sadists and masochists experience both of these paraphilias, and as such they are often combined into one disorder: sadomasochism. Sadomasochists partake in giving and receiving pain, humiliation, and degradation. Though called a paraphilia, there are many "normal" couples who participate in sadomasochistic activities. This once again illustrates how our changing societal acceptance of acts once considered deviant is modified over time, resulting in acts no longer being taboo. The only time sadomasochistic acts are brought to the attention of authorities is when the violence involved creates a negative outcome. One controversial case involving such activity occurred in England in 1987. In the case of *Brown and others* (1992), the police arrested three men who were in possession of videotapes of them performing sadomasochistic activities with 44 other men over a 10-year period. The activities included maiming of the genitalia (for example, piercing with fish hooks and needles), branding, and beatings with hands and instruments such as cat-o'-nine-tails, some of which drew blood and caused scarring.

All of the activities that occurred were consensual,[4] they took place in the privacy of the home, and they occurred for no other reason than sexual gratification. The case eventually was heard by the European Court of Human Rights in order to determine if the state has a right to interfere in private sexual encounters. The court stated that the state does have a right to intervene, even though the behavior constitutes a "private morality" because of the harm (potential and actual) resulting from the acts. The decision was based on the extreme nature of the acts and was deemed necessary for the protection of public health. The court compared the nature of the acts to drug abuse, declaring that the state has the obligation to intervene in activities that potentially may result in harm to an individual, even if that individual chooses to participate in that activity and it harms no one other than him- or herself.

Sexual sadism is a paraphilia that typically develops in adolescence, with interests piqued through masochistic masturbatory practices. *Autoerotic asphyxia* is a dangerous activity that constricts the oxygen during masturbation, accomplished with the use of a strangulation device (typically, a ligature with padding in order to prevent rope burns), a plastic bag, a chemical (for example, nitrous oxide), water, chest compression, or choking (Geberth, 1996; Hazelwood, Dietz, & Burgess, 1983). Both males and females participate in autoeroticism, and the purpose of it is to create a higher level of sexual excitement through the restriction of oxygen to the brain. The sexual excitement does not just occur through the restriction of oxygen, but as a combination of ritualistic behavior, oxygen deprivation, danger, and fantasy (Geberth, 1996, p. 319). Unfortunately, accidental deaths occur from this activity—estimated at 500 to 1000 per year in the United States—many of which are mistaken for suicides or homicides (Hazelwood et al., 1983).

Though autoerotic asphyxiation is generally linked to sexual masochism, not all individuals who partake in autoerotic activities are diagnosed with this paraphilia, and many exhibit other paraphilias. Hazelwood et al. (1983) conducted a study on autoerotic fatalities, with a sample of 150 subjects. Cited as the most extensive study on this issue (Geberth, 1996), the authors noted that subjects evidenced the following paraphilias in addition to masochism and/or sadism: fetishism, transvestic fetishism, pedophilia, voyeurism, coprophilia, and mysophilia (sexual attraction to mud or dirt). These diagnoses were substantiated through previous actions (for example, repeated abuse of children substantiated pedophilia), material the subject possessed (for example, drawings of sadistic activity), or the state in which they were found (for example, the bodies are often found dressed in women's clothing, indicating transvestic fetishism).

Like other forms of deviant sexual behavior, autoerotic asphyxiation has been documented historically, with the earliest known evidences found in a

---

4. Though consensual, one of the 44 men videotaped was under the age of 21. The age of consent for homosexual behavior was, at that time in England, 21 years of age. As such, the defendants were also charged with committing a sexual act with a minor.

Mayan relic dating to A.D. 1000 (Hazelwood et al., 1983). It was also documented in European artifacts and books from the 18th through the 20th centuries, presumably sparked by publication of papers by the Marquis de Sade (Hazelwood et al., 1983).

Another deviant sexual act that occurs with relatively high frequency is *bestiality*, or sexual activity with animals. Any sexual activity with animals is prohibited by law in the United States, yet it is practiced in many rural areas where animals are easily accessible. This is not always, and in fact often not, a paraphilia. In order to be diagnosed with a paraphilia—*zoophilia*—the individual must have a sexual attraction to animals that fits the criteria of a paraphilia. Yet, it is clear from the popularity of Internet sites containing images of bestiality that the practice is intriguing, if not avidly practiced, among a subsection of the general population.

Bestiality was also of concern to practitioners at the beginning of the century, as Krafft-Ebing (1886/1965) recorded several cases of bestiality in *Psychopathia Sexualis* involving intercourse with rabbits, hens, goats, dogs, and other domestic animals. He describes some of these cases as pathological in nature, and others resulting from perceived sexual inadequacy. For instance,

> A man was caught having intercourse with a hen. He was thirty years old and of high social position. The chickens had been dying one after another, and the man causing it had been wanted for a long time. When asked by the judge for the reason for such [an] act, the accused said that his genitals were so small that coitus with women was impossible. Medical examination showed that his genitals were, in fact, extremely small. (pp. 470–471)

Another serious paraphilia is *necrophilia*, or the sexual attraction to dead bodies. Rosman and Resnick (1989) describe three types of necrophiles, with varying degrees of severity. The first is the *pseudo necrophile*, also called a *fantasy necrophile*; this is an individual who either fantasizes about sex with dead bodies or has sex with dead bodies only periodically. The pseudo necrophile prefers the sexual partner to be alive but pretend to be dead, and there are many reports from prostitutes that their clients make them partake in this behavior. A second classification of necrophile is the *regular necrophile;* this is an individual who regularly has sexual intercourse with dead bodies. He is attracted to corpses and frequently works in an occupation where there is access to dead bodies, such as a coroner, or in a place like a morgue or graveyard.

Though the pseudo and regular necrophiles are dangerous and partake in prohibited behavior, they do not kill the victims in order to have sexual intercourse with them. This describes the third degree of necrophilic behavior, where the person is labeled a *homicidal necrophile*. This person kills in order to have intercourse with dead bodies, which is an extreme form of the paraphilia. Some serial killers are homicidal necrophiles, the most infamous being Jeffery Dahmer. Dahmer lured young men to his apartment and then proceeded to drug, strangle, dismember, and cannibalize them. He kept them alive for several days, turning them into "love slaves" by torturing them prior to killing them. Once dead, he had sexual intercourse with some of the victims before dismembering them and keeping body parts (and photos of the dismembered body parts) as trophies.

The case of Jeffery Dahmer is extreme, and most offenders who commit sexual homicides do not commit necrophilic acts. Rather, most sexual murderers achieve sexual gratification by killing a person. It is common after a sexual murder (also called *lust murder*) for the individual to masturbate over the body or to insert a foreign object into the vagina or rectum as an act of sexual substitution (Ressler, Burgess, & Douglas, 1988). Ressler et al. (1988) conducted a study of sexual murderers and found several commonalities between the offenders; most important, they have an active fantasy life, and their fantasies are violent and sexual in nature. They found a link between sadistic acts and fantasies, as sadists' violent fantasies can lead to sexual murder. It therefore follows that some sexual sadists are in danger of escalating into becoming sexual murderers if they are not detected and stopped.

In sum, paraphilias are diagnosable sexual disorders that can cause an individual to have intense sexual urges and fantasies about certain individuals, objects, or behaviors. Some of these paraphilias can lead to sexual abuse of children (for example, pedophilia) or the sexual assault of adults (for example, sadism). However, the etiology of offending behavior may be explained through the interaction of these disorders and other social, cultural, psychological, and biological factors.

DID YOU KNOW...?

Development of Paraphilias in the *Diagnostic and Statistical Manual of Mental Disorders*

Various organizations and agencies attempted to classify mental disorders beginning in the 19th century, but it was not until 1952 that the APA created the first edition of the *DSM*. Prior to this time, the majority of psychologists understood mental illness simply in terms of different types of psychoses and neuroses. The need of the Army and Navy for a formal system of diagnoses to better understand the conditions of men returning from World War II appears to have been a large influence on the publication of the first *DSM*. Sexual deviance and sexual disorders were mentioned only briefly in this first edition and the term "paraphilia" was not used until 1954. Sexual deviance at this point was considered only one of a host of "reactions" to sociopathic personality disturbance along with alcoholism (McAnulty, 1995).

The second edition of the *DSM* (*DSM-II*, 1968) was virtually unchanged from the first edition (Schmidt, Kotov, & Joiner, 2004). However, specific "sexual deviations" (paraphilias) were, in the second edition, listed under the category "Personality Disorders and Certain Other Non-Psychotic Mental Disorders" (McAnulty, 1995). As the *DSM* continued to follow a psychoanalytic perspective in the 1960s, behaviorists at this time theorized that paraphilias developed as a result of learning. In other words, certain objects, people, or situations could easily become associated with sexual arousal and could later serve as objects of sexual fantasies (Abel & Osborn, 1995). Treating paraphilias would mean reconditioning sexual arousal to be associated with other innocuous objects, people, or situations.

A major turning point in the understanding of paraphilias came in 1970 when Masters and Johnson published *Human Sexual Inadequacy*, which prompted an interest in sex-specific therapy methods and also a change in attitude toward sex disorders (Masters & Johnson, 1970; Segraves, Balon, & Clayton, 2007). Instead of paraphilias being a result of deficient intrapsychic development, Masters and Johnson suggested that these disorders were the result of certain interactions between people. To treat the paraphilia, clinicians should focus on the interaction as well as the person's unique psychological development. Masters and Johnson not only influenced the general public with their new ideas and attitudes but they were also instrumental in the third revision of the *DSM* (Segraves et al., 2007).

The *DSM-III*, published in 1980, represented a significant change in diagnostic methodology, as it incorporated an atheoretical approach that emphasized observable behavior (Coolidge & Segal, 1998; Schmidt, Kotov, & Joiner, 2004). Also in the third edition, conditions were officially called *disorders* and the manual included the implementation of the multiaxial (Axis I, Axis II) diagnostic system. Furthermore, personality disorders were separated from major clinical disorders in this edition, and medical and social influences were taken into account when assessing a person's overall level of functioning (Coolidge & Segal, 1998; Oken, 2007). Under this system, paraphilias were first listed by the names that are still used today and the diagnostic criteria stated that paraphilic fantasies were necessary for sexual excitement. These changes were an attempt to establish the diagnostic criteria as more reliable and to distinguish between occasional paraphilic behavior and chronic paraphilia (McAnulty, 1995). However, because the *DSM-III* was written with an atheoretical approach, diagnoses of paraphilias did not hint at their causes or what kind of treatment may have been best. Quite simply, a diagnosis was made if an individual displayed enough of the essential observable behaviors that were considered symptoms of that specific paraphilia. The *DSM-III-TR*, published in 1987, incorporated two changes to the diagnoses of paraphilias. First, the criteria in this edition specified that the individual in question must have acted on his or her paraphilic fantasies in some way, and could no longer be diagnosed solely based on their private thoughts and fantasies. Secondly, the criterion was added in this edition that these paraphilic fantasies must cause the individual subjective distress (McAnulty, 1995; Segraves et al., 2007).

In 1994, the *DSM-IV* was published, and its revision followed in 2000 (*DSM-IV-TR*). One modification to the diagnosis of paraphilias in the *DSM-IV* was a further elaboration on the matter of subjective distress; in the *DSM-IV-TR*, not only did the individual have to be experiencing distress for an official diagnosis, but the individual must have experienced "clinically significant distress." This addition further complicated the diagnostic criteria by requiring a high level of stress and ongoing impairment related to the paraphilia or the paraphilic fantasy. In other words, a man who was sexually attracted to children and who molested prepubescent children could not have been officially diagnosed as a pedophile unless his behavior and his attractions were distressing him enough to cause disruptions in other areas of his life.

Questions
1. Should a person be diagnosed with a paraphilia if he spends hours every day looking at pornography on the Internet? Why or why not?
2. How can diagnoses or paraphilias influence treatment of sexual offenders?

PSYCHODYNAMIC THEORIES

Austrian psychoanalyst Sigmund Freud is generally credited with examining sexual deviancy through a psychoanalytic framework, though his theories are no longer widely supported. Freud called individuals' sexual desires "perversions"—in particular, paraphilias such as exhibitionism, voyeurism, and pedophilia—and argued that sexual deviations were the consequence of childhood deprivation, developmental fixation, or regression back to any one of the four stages of sexual development (Freud, 1953). Freud labeled the four stages of development as oral, anal, phallic, and genital; unresolved problems brought about fixations during these stages of development. These fixations were sexual in nature, and included oedipal conflicts, castration anxiety, and penis envy.

The oedipal conflict, which Freud claimed that boys could develop during the phallic stage of development, is characterized by competition between father and son for the mother's affection. Castration anxiety and penis envy result from boys and girls discovering the differences in their genitalia; boys conclude that girls are actually boys whose fathers have cut off their penises, and girls are jealous of boys. Children should eventually outgrow these stages. It is when the boys do not resolve their oedipal conflicts that they develop a permanent aversion to adult females, whose appearance brings back their anxiety about castration.

Psychodynamic theory also explains the interaction of the three elements of the human psyche: the id, the ego, and the superego. The *id*, considered to be the "pleasure principle," is the basis of desire and the division of the psyche from which instinctual human drives originate. The id seeks instant gratification of these instinctual urges. The *ego*, or the "reality principle," is the mediator between the id and superego. The *superego*, or the "conscience," is responsible for decisions based on past experiences of rewards and punishments. These parts of the psyche are internalized and work together to help the individual develop a system of morals.

For more than a half century, psychoanalysts (for example, Fenichel, 1945; Hammer, 1957) expanded on Freud's explanations of sexual deviations. A common characteristic of these theories was the belief that deviant behavior was unlikely to go away. Psychoanalysts believed that the psychopathology of the offender is a deep-rooted aspect of the person's personality, and, if treatment is to occur, it must be lengthy and based on the restructuring of the character. While psychoanalysis at this time focused primarily on sexual dysfunction, paraphilias, and traits such as homosexuality, psychoanalytic theories in the 1970s began to shift toward serious sexual offenses.

In the 1980s, psychodynamic theorists proposed family-based etiological explanations for deviant sexual behavior. For instance, MacLeod and Sarago (1987) suggested a "family dysfunction model" whereby sexual problems are characterized by an ill, absent, or sexually frigid mother who provides an unsatisfying marriage for her husband. Loneliness and the need for intimacy develop, and the husband turns to his children for the undemanding love that he seeks. All types of sex offenders show intimacy deficits and expressions of loneliness (Marshall, 1989), yet these traits are not sufficient in themselves to explain deviant sexual behavior. Nonetheless, they may be significant factors in a multicausal explanation of the etiology of sexually deviant behavior.

BIOLOGICAL THEORIES

Many researchers have attempted to explain sexually deviant behavior through biological and physiological abnormalities. Most of these explanations are based on the assumption that abnormal hormonal levels adversely affect sexual behavior. Biological theorists (for example, Berlin and Rada) suggest that biological functions are likely to be only one component of multiple etiologies for sexual deviations—sexual behavior is multidetermined and is not likely based on hormone levels alone. Biological theories usually pertain to rape or sexual assault of adults rather than child sexual abuse, because rape is considered an act of violence and there has been a postulated correlation between aggression and high levels of testosterone (Money, 1970; Rada, Laws, & Kellner, 1976). Biological theories of child sexual abuse have been primarily concerned with abnormal hormonal and androgenic levels in the brain.

The primary focus of biological explanations of aggressive sexual behavior is the role of androgens and androgen-releasing hormones in males. Secretion of the androgens is controlled by the hypothalamus and the pituitary gland, and the anterior lobe of the pituitary carries the androgens to the testes. The testes control the level of hormones, particularly testosterone, that are released into the bloodstream. When testosterone circulates in the bloodstream, it may or may not be bound to proteins. If it is bound, androgens may become active if they come into contact with receptors for testosterone. This happens during puberty, at which time males experience physical changes, such as increases in body hair and muscle mass and penis enlargement, as a result of the androgenic effects (Hucker & Bain, 1990).

Because of this androgenic process, the level of testosterone in the testes increases dramatically in males when they reach puberty. Sex drive also increases at this time. As such, there is an implicit belief that testosterone is the primary biological factor responsible for sexual drive in males. Empirically, researchers have shown that increased levels of erotic activity correspond to increased levels of plasma testosterone. Pirke, Kockott, and Dittmar (1974) showed that the level of plasma testosterone for subjects watching an erotic film increased by approximately 35 percent over subjects who were not watching an erotic film. This correlation has not been consistently validated, however, as some biological studies have not shown a clear link between these variables. Despite these inconsistent results, Bancroft (1978) states that there is a general implication that hormone levels are affected by erotic stimulus.

The underlying question posed by biological theorists about rape is whether or not there is a connection between aggression and increased levels of testosterone, and, if so, whether this hormonal imbalance leads to sexual aggression. Aggression and sex appear to be mediated by the same neural substrates involving predominantly midbrain structures (the hypothalamus, septum, hippocampus, amygdala, and preoptic area), while the same endocrines activate sex and aggression (Marshall & Barbaree, 1990a, p. 259). Some self-report studies have shown a correlation between aggression and high testosterone levels (Olweus, Matteson, Schalling, & Low, 1980; Scaramella & Brown, 1978), and studies of convicted prisoners have shown that those with violent histories do have higher testosterone levels than nonviolent offenders (Kreutz & Rose, 1972). Although there has been some research showing a correlation between "aggressive feelings" and high testosterone levels in young men (Persky, Smith, & Basu, 1971), most studies show a tenuous correlation, if any, between paper-and-pencil tests measuring aggression and the level of plasma testosterone in males (Ehrenkranz, Bliss, & Sheard, 1974; Kreutz & Rose, 1972). Testosterone is not the only hormone important in mediating behavior (Marshall & Barbaree, 1990a). Even if aggression is linked to testosterone levels, it is unclear whether testosterone actually produces aggressiveness or simply causes an increase in muscle mass and strength, allowing individuals to manifest their aggression more effectively (Hucker & Bain, 1990, p. 98).

As for studies that measure levels of testosterone and *sexual* aggression, results are largely conflicting, and the correlations that do exist are slight. One study showed that rapists scored higher than controls on a hostility inventory, yet plasma testosterone levels were not related to hostility scores (Rada et al., 1976). A further study by these researchers showed no differences between hormonal levels in rapists and controls (Rada, Laws, Kellner, Stiristava, & Peake, 1983), with the lack of correlation between testosterone levels and sexual violence supported by other researchers as well (Bradford & MacLean, 1984). In some studies, only the most violent and/or sadistic offenders were found to have elevated plasma testosterone levels (Rada et al., 1976), whereas other studies did not establish this correlation (Langevin et al., 1985).

Most of the hormonal studies that have been conducted contained small samples and produced conflicting results (Hucker & Bain, 1990). Although testosterone is presumed to be the source of sexual drive in males, few researchers claim to find a link between sexually deviant acts and abnormal hormonal or androgenic levels. Most biological theorists conclude that even when a hormonal imbalance is present in a male to act as a physiological potentiator for violence, these factors must still be triggered by environmental and social learning factors in order for sexual aggression to occur (Hays, 1981; Hucker & Bain, 1990; Kreutz & Rose, 1972; Meyer-Bahlberg, 1987).

One controversial biological theory of rape was suggested by Thornhill and Palmer (2000). They explain rape from an evolutionary biological perspective, contending that males are driven to rape in order to reproduce. They state that although rape is not a morally good or even acceptable act, it is an act of natural selection. They support this by making claims such as that most rape victims are in their prime reproductive years. They contradict most sociological research and actually promote rape myths, stating that women should not dress provocatively because those who do so are more likely to be raped. Though highly publicized because of its unique perspective, other biological and evolutionary theorists have strongly criticized their work for being unscientific and based upon anecdotal evidence (Coyne & Berry, 2000).

FEMINIST THEORIES

Feminist theories about sexually deviant behavior focus primarily on rape; specifically, they center around the motivation of men to commit acts of sexual violence against women. These theories emerged in the late 1960s, when it became evident that the female victims were persecuted as much as the male offenders in cases of sexual violence. Most researchers at this time were male, and their explanations of deviant behavior focused on the victims' actions as much as the offenders'. The feminist movement was also moderately successful at changing the perception of female victims in the criminal justice system. With the increased public support for the active prosecution of offenders, the rate of reporting and convicting these offenders rose considerably through the 1980s.

A pioneer on research regarding sexual violence in the 1970s was Susan Brownmiller, who analyzed rape in a cultural, political, and historical context and cited sexual crime as an example of men's oppression of women (Brownmiller, 1975). She and other feminists regarded sexual assault as systemic to a patriarchal society of conditioned male supremacy. Accordingly, theories surmised that the use of coercion to achieve sexual conquest represented an exaggeration of prevailing norms rather than a departure from them (Brownmiller, 1975; Herman, 1990; Matthews, 1994). Sexual gratification is not considered by most feminists to be the primary motive for rape (Allison & Wrightsman, 1993; Brownmiller, 1975; Burt, 1980; Darke, 1990; Ellis, 1989). Rather, rape is used as just one other tool to dominate and control women, who are considered relatively powerless compared to men and, therefore, subservient to them (Allison & Wrightsman, 1993). From a theoretical perspective, rape is seen to be the consequence of deep-rooted social traditions of male dominance and female exploitation (Ward, 1995, p. 10). Men who commit sexual offenses are considered normal, rationalized through the epidemiological explanation that almost all sexual offenders are male and a notable proportion of the male population has committed a sexual offense (Herman, 1990).

Feminist theorists view rape as a cultural rather than an individual problem. Sexual violence is said to represent an extension of attitudes and practices surrounding male-female relations in a male-dominated culture (Darke, 1990). Cultures that encourage gender stereotyping create "gender socialization," whereby sexually aggressive men have been socialized to feel little need for intimacy and a low capacity for empathy (Lisak & Ivan, 1995). Social violence is not unique to any one culture or historical period (Stermac, Segal, & Gillis, 1990); however, some characteristics such as interpersonal violence, male dominance, and sexual separation are common to rape-prone societies (Sanday, 1981). Long-term prevention necessitates changing the societal conditions that generate sexual violence, such as belief in rape myths and sex-role ideology favoring restricted roles toward women. These attitudes may lead to gender socialization and thereby encourage and sanction a generalized hostility and, subsequently, sexual abuse, toward women (Brownmiller, 1975; Darke, 1990; Medea & Thompson, 1974; Sternmac et al., 1990; West, 1987).

Though feminist theories focus primarily on rape, sex-role stereotyping can also explain child sexual abuse. Whereas feminist theory describes men as having sexual entitlement over women, child sexual abusers express sexual entitlement over children (Hanson, Gizzarelli, & Scott, 1994). Child sexual abusers tend to be narcissistic and selfish, considering their own desires and ignoring potential harm caused by their own actions. Through their own narcissism, they exhibit "sexually specific sexist attitudes" similar to those of convicted rapists (Hanson et al., 1994, p. 198).

ATTACHMENT THEORIES

Due to the widespread reporting of intimacy deficits among sex offenders, researchers have sought to develop overarching theories to explain a possible pathway between intimacy deficits and sex-offending behaviors. Attachment theory follows the premise that humans have a natural propensity to form emotional bonds to others, and that models of bonding in infancy provide a framework for understanding attachment patterns in adulthood. Many sexual offenders exhibit a lack of close adult relationships as well as a lack of intimacy in their relationships generally (Marshall, 1989; 1993).

Though attachment theorists study bonds between individuals from infancy to adulthood, it is the period during adolescence that is most critical in the development of sexuality and social competence (Marshall & Barbaree, 1990a). By this time, adolescents with adequate parenting should have acquired prosocial behavior, including proper inhibitions on aggression and sexual behavior. Parents should also help instill in the adolescents a sense of self-confidence and the ability to form emotional attachments to others. If this is the case, adolescents should be able to transition to adulthood with both social constraints against aggression and the skills necessary to develop effective relationships with age-appropriate partners.

Individuals who have poor emotional attachments are more likely to commit a sexual offense than those with strong emotional attachments to others. Research shows that many of the men who sexually abuse children have poor social skills and little self-confidence, and thus, they have difficulty in forming intimate relationships with agemates (Marshall, 1989). This failure creates frustration in these men that may cause them to continue to seek intimacy with underaged partners. Seidman, Marshall, Hudson, and Robertson (1994) conducted two studies that showed that sex offenders have deficiencies in social skills that restrict the possibility of developing intimate relationships. In particular, sex offenders appear to misperceive social cues and do not act appropriately as a result of these deficiencies. These deficiencies in intimacy are common across various types of sex offenders. In the study by Seidman et al., rapists and nonfamilial child sexual abusers in the sample had the most significant deficiencies in intimacy.

According to attachment theorists, insecurely attached individuals may try to overcome feelings of loneliness through sexual activity, which runs the risk of involving inappropriate and unwanted advances given the overall level of inexperience with such behavior. Ward, Hudson, Marshall, and Siegert (1995) furthered this idea by suggesting that a lack of experience with intimate relationships may result in empathy deficits, which may, in turn, lead to sexual offending in certain individuals. Attachment models also focus on the sexual offender's ability to attribute appropriate thoughts and feelings to others. Keenan and Ward (2000) stated that sexual offenders may have deficits in their theory of mind, which is the awareness and understanding of others' beliefs, needs, and particular perspectives. These broad deficits lead to more specific deficits in intimacy, empathy, and cognition, which together put these individuals at risk for inappropriate interpersonal relations and behavior.

Regardless of the framework that most accurately describes the root and pathways of the relationship, empirical studies have shown that there does appear to be a link between intimacy deficits and sexual offending. In terms of romantic and sexual intimacy, Garlick (1989) and Seidman, Marshall, Hudson, and Robertson (1994) found that both incarcerated and nonincarcerated rapists and child sexual abusers reported higher levels of loneliness and lower levels of intimacy in adult relationships as compared to both nonsexual offenders and nonoffender controls from the community. More recent work has focused on intimacy across different types of adult relationships, including friendship, family, romantic, and sexual relationships. In one such study, Bumby and Hanson (1997) found widespread intimacy deficits in both incarcerated rapists and child sexual abusers, suggesting that these individuals experience a lack of intimacy in many different types of relationships including friendships with males, friendships with females, and relationships with family members. Rapists and child sexual abusers reported significantly more loneliness than nonsexual offenders and community control subjects, and child molesting behaviors were the best single predictor of degree of fear of intimacy.

Bartholomew (1990) has identified four categories of attachment styles: secure, preoccupied, fearful, and dismissing. These models of attachment explain the individual's self-concept as positive or negative, depending on the degree to which they believe they deserve to be loved (Bartholomew, 1990). An individual with a *secure* attachment style has a positive concept of himself and others, and as a result is able to make friends and have age-appropriate relationships. An individual with a *preoccupied* attachment style has poor self-esteem and low self-confidence but does have a positive attitude toward others and often needs their assistance to deal with personal matters. An individual with a *fearful* attachment style has a poor self-concept and a poor concept of others, thus often blaming himself for his problems but being too frightened to talk to others about these problems. An individual with a *dismissing* attachment style has both a positive self-concept and a high level of self-confidence, yet he has a negative concept of others and thus does not seek out help or support. The individual who is most likely to abuse a child is the person with a preoccupied, insecure attachment style (Ward et al., 1995, as cited in Marshall & Marshall, 2002).

BEHAVIORAL AND COGNITIVE-BEHAVIORAL THEORIES

Behavioral theorists began offering explanations as to the etiology of sexually deviant behavior in the late 1970s, led by researcher Gene Abel. Behavioral theories mainly relate to the assessment and treatment of sexually deviant behavior and view the behavior is, not as a disorder that can be treated. Unlike psychodynamic theories, behavioral theories are based on the assumption that there is no single underlying problem of which the deviant sexual behavior is a symptom. Abel's approach (Abel, Blanchard, & Becker, 1978) is based upon an implied model of etiology that is seen as underlying other disorders that are amenable to treatment through behavior therapy.

Langevin (1983) expanded upon Abel's theory and classified deviant sexual preferences according to their stimulus and response characteristics. As such, the deviant behavior is conditioned in the individual to the effect that "sexually indulgent behavior displays a pattern that is entrenched and perpetuated by intermittent positive rewards" (Kear-Colwell & Pollock, 1997, p. 21). Elaborating on the conditioning premise, Wolf (1985) developed a three-part theory as to the etiology of deviant sexual behavior. He alleged first that sexual offenders have a *disturbed developmental history*, including potentiators for later deviant attitudes; second, he stated that there is a presence of *disinhibitors* that will allow deviant behavior to occur; third, he concluded that the offender has *deviant sexual fantasies*. All three factors work together to develop and maintain deviant sexual behavior. A fourth behavioral theorist, Lanyon, states that sexual disorders are "conceptualized as an inappropriate frequency of one or more events (behavior, thoughts, or feelings), and this inappropriate frequency is thought to be maintained by the pattern of antecedents and consequences for the events" (Lanyon, 1991, p. 38).

Cognitive-behavioral theories were developed in an effort to build on the foundation of behavioral theories by taking into account the thoughts of offenders as well as their behaviors. Abel et al. (1984) explored the content of cognitions in sex offenders and analyzed the effect of cognitions on behavior. They found that sex offenders, like most individuals, are able to legitimize their behavior and the behavior of others through cognitive distortions (CDs). There are a number of CDs common to sex offenders, discussed in Chapter 4; these allow offenders to continue committing deviant sexual acts by averting blame from themselves and projecting it onto their victims or their environment. Some researchers (Ward & Keenan, 1999) claim that CDs derive from implicit theories that sex offenders have about themselves, their victims, and the world around them. Implicit theories, which are structured from the offenders' beliefs and desires, generate CDs that in turn permit inappropriate sexual behavior. They allow offenders to exist within a socially constructed reality and behave according to their beliefs about the world and their role in it. Ward and Keenan (1999) claim that implicit theories consider the following factors in relation to child sexual abuse:

- **Offenders View Children as Sexual Objects** They assume that children, like adults, are motivated by a desire for pleasure and thus desire and enjoy sexual behavior.

- **Offenders Are Entitled to the Sexual Behavior** The desires and beliefs of the offender are more important than those of the victim, which are either ignored or viewed as only of secondary importance.

- **The World Is Dangerous** The offender views other adults as being abusive and perceives that they will reject him in promotion of their own needs.

- **The Offender Has a Lack of Control** The offender perceives his environment as uncontrollable wherein people are not able to exert any major influence over their personal behavior and/or the world around them.

- **Sexual Behavior Is Not Harmful** The offender believes not only that there is no harm done to the victim, but that sexual activity is beneficial.

Offenders rarely modify these implicit theories, even when faced with evidence (behavior) to the contrary. Instead, the offender may simply reinterpret or reject a theory. For example, a child's friendly behavior might be evidence to the offender that the child wants to have sex with him. Though it is not clear how these implicit theories develop, it is likely from a combination of developmental, social, and psychological influences.

As for the etiology of deviant sexual behavior, cognitive-behavioral theory proposes that deviant sexual arousal is learned through classical conditioning (Hunter & Becker, 1994). As such, the effect of outcome on the offender's first deviant sexual act is important: if the act meets with no adverse consequences, an addictive pattern may be powerfully reinforced (Becker, 1990).

PSYCHOSOCIAL THEORIES

Psychosocial theories work from the viewpoint that deviant sexual behavior is a response to external factors, and that there is an interconnection between psychological and sociological variables that influence sexual behavior. Sexual behavior is a learned response to particular conditions, and deviant sexual behavior is the outcome of inappropriate socialization. This may result from personal experiences, such as childhood sexual abuse, or be influenced by general factors, such as pornography.

One trait common to rapists, child sexual abusers, and exhibitionists is poor social skills. These individuals tend to have difficulty formulating normal adult relationships and are described as suffering from "courtship disorder," in which "the terminal phase of courtship is exaggerated and distorted, and precoital courtship is virtually absent" (Freund, 1990). Rapists see violence as the only way to secure their goals of sexual gratification (Marshall & Barbaree, 1990a), and they use as much violence as necessary to achieve a sexual relationship.

Many child sexual abusers, on the other hand, have an inability to form age-appropriate relationships. In many cases of sexual abuse, regardless of victim type and motivation for the offense, sex offenders display characteristics of low self-esteem, poor self-image, and, subsequently, poor ability to socialize and form appropriate relationships with agemates.

Many sex offenders who lack proper relationship skills tend to misread social cues, and they do so in two ways. First, they misread cues from their victims, interpreting the victims' actions as sexual in nature. For instance, child sexual abusers often have a sexualized view of children (Hanson et al., 1994; Hartley, 1998; Ward & Keenan, 1999). They interpret children's actions as sexual in nature, and any overt symbol of affection is considered to be a sexual cue. Rapists, too, may misinterpret the actions of their victims as indicative of a sexual desire. For instance, if a woman dresses provocatively, it may be interpreted that she wants to have sex. Or if, when she is assaulted, she does not retaliate due to fear, this may be interpreted as a desire to comply with the sexual act.

Sex offenders not only misperceive cues of their individual victims, but also societal intimations. These cues can be in the form of patriarchal prerogatives of fathers for children (Hartley, 1998) or sex-role stereotyping of women (Burt, 1980). One societal condition that in Western cultures has been presumed to encourage sex-role stereotyping is pornography (Burt, 1980; Marshall, Anderson, & Fernandez, 1999). Feminist theorists recognize this as a definitive expression of male supremacy that also plays a role in masturbatory fantasy and sexual response (Herman, 1990). Some feminist researchers claim that a link exists between violent pornography and sexual violence (Allison & Wrightsman, 1993), although there has been no systematic empirical evidence to validate this statement. One study showed that some men are more likely to rape if given instructions that it is acceptable behavior (Quinsey, Chaplin, & Varney, 1981). However, another study showed that exposure to hard-core pornography enhances sexual aggression only in already angered males (Gray, 1982). In other words, pornography is not the origin of the deviant sexual behavior, but it can promote a relapse in offenders. This later study also showed that approximately one in three convicted sex offenders said that violent pornography stimulated their desire to offend after viewing it. Gray, as well as other researchers, however, concluded that violent pornographic depictions may act as potentiators for a few sadistic individuals to commit aggressive acts against women, yet most men will not be induced by this material to commit sexual assaults (Gray, 1982; Quinsey et al., 1981).

Though negative gender socialization may be one factor that influences rape, explanations of child sexual abuse often revert to the offenders' upbringing. In addition to the familial influences mentioned previously, researchers focus on the effect of childhood sexual abuse and whether this leads to a cycle of abuse (Freund & Kuban, 1994, p. 560). The "cycle of abuse" theory alleges that there are statistically significant links between childhood victimization and current sexual interest in children (Bagley, Wood, & Young, 1994). Though this hypothesis has several supporters (Garland & Dougher, 1990; Groth & Burgess, 1977), there are some inconsistencies with the abused-abuser theory. To begin with, it does not account for the fact that more female than male children are sexually abused, and yet there are more male than female sexual offenders. Additionally, it does not account for the fact that many offenders were not sexually abused as children. Similarly, the majority of children who were sexually abused do not go on to abuse others. Most researchers therefore conclude that childhood victimization is but one of many factors that may act as a prelude to later offending behavior.

ROUTINE ACTIVITIES THEORY

Most theories about sexual offending attempt to explain crime based on individual aspects of the offender. However, scholars have begun to assess the role that the environment plays in the commission of sexual offenses. The environment, and particularly the situations in which abuse occurs and the opportunities that offenders have to commit sexual offenses, play a critical role in whether or not abuse occurs. Based on this premise, offenders can be prevented from abusing if they feel that the opportunity to commit the crime presents too much risk, if the reward isn't big enough, or if too much effort is required (Terry & Ackerman, 2008 p. 645).

The theoretical approach that focuses on the crime element rather than the offender is routine activities theory (RAT). RAT holds that in order for a predatory crime to occur, three elements (the "crime triangle") must be present at the same time and in the same space: a motivated offender, a suitable target, and the lack of a capable guardian to prevent the crime from happening. Situational crime prevention (SCP) strategies are opportunity-reducing measures directed at highly specific forms of crime, and involve the management, design, or manipulation of the immediate environment in as systematic and permanent way as possible in order to make crime more difficult, risky, less rewarding or excusable for a wide range of offenders. SCP is based on the assumption that offenders are rational beings who weigh the costs and benefits of criminal behavior (Terry & Ackerman, 2008 p. 645). Potential offenders use the environment to their advantage and, thus, effectively implemented SCP can reduce criminal activity.

Based on the SCP approach, Felson and Clarke (1998) state that four opportunity reducing techniques must occur: increasing effort, increasing risk, controlling prompts, and reducing permissibility. Increasing effort entails making it more difficult or inconvenient to commit a crime through controlling access to facilities, target hardening, and controlling tools. Increasing risk is amplifying the threat of detection, mostly by providing guardianship. Controlling prompts refers to reducing situational triggers. Reducing permissibility refers to making potential offenders understand that their behavior is harmful to their victims. These techniques have generally been applied to property crimes, though researchers have recently begun to apply this paradigm to child sexual abuse (Marshall, Serran, & Marshall, 2006; Terry & Ackerman, 2008; Wortley & Smallbone, 2006a).

The most comprehensive analysis of situational factors related to sexual abuse has been conducted by Richard Wortley and Stephen Smallbone. In their study of sexual offenders in Australia, Wortley and Smallbone (2006a) observed seven factors that are consistent with a situational explanation of child sexual abuse. Specifically, they stated that child sexual abusers have: (1) a late onset of deviant behavior; (2) a low incidence of chronic sexual offending; (3) a high incidence of previous nonsexual offenses; (4) a low incidence of stranger abuse; (5) a low incidence of networking among offenders; (6) a low incidence of child pornography use; and (7) a low incidence of paraphilic behavior. The authors also note that location is an important factor in the commission of sexual offenses, for sexual abuse almost always occurs in private and often in the home of the offender.

Child sexual abuse is pervasive in situations in which adults have unguarded access to children, including in youth-serving organizations. Wortley and Smallbone (2006a) found that 20 percent of extrafamilial offenders reported having accessed children via an organized activity, with some 8 percent having joined a child or youth organization for the primary purpose of perpetrating a sexual offense. Colton, Roberts, and Vanstone (2010) found that adult male abusers were attracted to particular positions within educational institutions or voluntary organizations that would afford them easy access to potential victims and allow them to maintain the abuse without being detected. In a study of 41 "professional" perpetrators, Sullivan and Beech (2004) found that 15 percent reported having specifically picked their profession to access children while 41.5 percent reported that access to children was at least part of their motivation for having selected their profession. Indeed, over 90 percent of the abusers they studied were reported to have been aware of their sexual attraction to children prior to having begun their professional careers.

INTEGRATED THEORIES
AND EMPIRICAL RESEARCH

Although the individual theories discussed lend possible explanations as to the etiology of offending behavior, they are rarely sufficient explanations of all deviant behavior. The majority of offenders do not initiate sexually deviant behavior because of one variable, such as childhood sexual abuse or exposure to pornography. Rather, there are numerous interrelated factors that, when comprehensively studied, may better explain the etiology of offending behavior through multifactor models. Various researchers (for example, Finkelhor, 1984; Marshall, 1993; Marshall et al., 1999) claim that sexually deviant behavior results from a combination of psychological, developmental, and sometimes biological factors, including (among others) deviant sexual arousal and conditioning; few or poor intimate attachments to family, friends, or partners; loneliness; CDs and lack of empathy; and poor social and relationship skills.

Marshall, Anderson, and Fernandez (1999) claim that the most important factor that predisposes an individual to future deviant behavior is the strength of the bond between the child and his or her parents, for insecure children frequently lack social skills and have low self-esteem. This poor self-perception persists into adolescence and adulthood, leading to intimacy deficits and loneliness in relationships with family, friends, and partners (Bumby & Hanson, 1997). Children who have strong bonds to their parents develop a resistance to deviant behavior because of their beliefs, cognitions, skills, and emotional dispositions (Marshall et al., 1999, p. 28). Children from unhappy homes with poor attachments are most likely to offend, as they are most likely to accept and welcome attention and rewards from abusers. They are also the most likely to be vulnerable, be lonely, and develop a fear of intimacy, particularly in adult relationships.

The integrated theories, which envelop various developmental explanations for deviant behavior, indicate that childhood experiences predict a modeling effect because experiences in childhood relationships provide a basis for the formation of adult relationships. These theories also take into consideration possible biological explanations of deviancy. For example, boys who have weak bonds with their parents may have an inability to deal with stress and bodily changes once they reach puberty. At this time, the increase in testosterone in addition to social changes related to adolescence make the transition to adulthood difficult. Those with weak familial bonds tend to be vulnerable, and these vulnerable boys seek methods of power and control. With few outlets of sexual power available, the vulnerable boys may turn toward violent relationships or relationships with children. The availability of pornography, which encourages sex-role stereotyping, and even the popular media (for example, video games, movies) may encourage deviant attitudes in those adolescents who are already vulnerable.

In regard to child sexual abuse, David Finkelhor (1984) proposed a four-factor model of the preconditions of abuse, which integrate the various theories about why individuals begin to participate in sexually deviant behavior. This organizational framework addresses the full complexity of child sexual abusers, from the etiology of the abuse through the rationalization for it. Finkelhor's model focuses on the internal communications of child sexual abusers regarding their observations and opinions about the world around them. This internal communication creates an opportunity that allows the offenders to break through barriers that, until this time, had prevented them from acting out their feelings. They are able to rationalize their actions to themselves, reducing the barriers of guilt and shame. Once these barriers are absent, they can act on the opportunities they have created, thereby reducing their negative feelings of loneliness, isolation, and other such stressors.

In order to better explain this process, Finkelhor constructed an organizational framework consisting of four underlying factors that act as preconditions to sexual abuse. He states that in order to sexually abuse, an individual must (1) have motivation to sexually abuse, (2) overcome internal inhibitions, (3) overcome external factors that may act as inhibitors to the abuse, and (4) overcome the child's resistance to the abuse.

The first precondition, *motivation*, simply means that an individual must want to abuse the child. The abuser's motivation may result from many factors, such as the idea that he or she relates better to children than adults, that there is a sexual attraction to children, or that the abuse is addictive, like a drug. Next, the offender must *overcome internal inhibitions* to abuse a child, or must be able to justify the abuse to him- or herself in order to abuse. The offender may justify the abuse by saying, for example, that he or she was abused and enjoyed the abuse as a child, that the abuse is not harmful, or that it is educational. After overcoming internal inhibitions, the individual must *overcome external factors* that may inhibit the abuse. At this stage, the abuser begins creating opportunities for the abuse to occur. Opportunities may include any situation in which trust is built up between the abuser and the family of the child (if abuser and victim are not related), such as babysitting, coaching the child in a sporting event, or helping the child with homework. Finally, the abuser must *overcome the child's resistance* to the abuse. This often involves emotional manipulation of the child, such as telling the child how special he or she is, or that if the child tells someone, the abuser will go to prison.

In addition to these four preconditions to abuse, Finkelhor explains that adults who sexually abuse children experience "emotional congruence" to children, sexual arousal to children, blockage to adult relationships, emotional loneliness, a belief that there is no other way of obtaining this pleasure, a failure to understand damage caused, and poor impulse control. *Emotional congruence* describes the relationship between the adult abuser's emotional needs and the child's characteristics. For example, if an abuser's emotional needs are not fully mature, he or she may relate better to children than adults. These childish emotional needs may be exacerbated if the abuser has low self-esteem and inadequate social skills, thus making the abuser more comfortable in relationships with children in which he or she is able to exert more power and control.

Finkelhor also explains that adults who abuse children must have some level of sexual arousal to the children, whether it is innate or learned. Whether explained through social learning theory (through conditioning and imprinting, the abuser begins to find children arousing later in adulthood) or poor psychosexual development, sexual arousal to children is a necessary component of the motivation to abuse. Child sexual abusers also usually experience some type of *blockage*, or lack of ability to have their sexual and/or emotional needs met in adult relationships. The abuser's blockage may be developmental or situational; with *developmental blockage*, the abuser is prevented from moving into the adult sexual stage of development (an internal blockage), while *situational blockage* is when the abuser is unable to attain or maintain an adult relationship due to external factors, such as frustration from a relationship with an adult.

Overall, this organizational framework describes who is at risk to offend. It is likely that individuals who offend have been able to cope with many of the problems mentioned (for example, developmental blockage) and opportunities (for example, access to children) at different times. However, it is the combination of these problems, in addition to some type of demand on their coping system that contributes to an attitude supportive of sexual offending, thereby establishing a risk to offend. That risk increases the likelihood that a person may act out in a sexual fashion, because his or her belief system has filtered out the normal inhibitions toward sexual offending. Unfortunately, the relief that is associated with sexual offending is reinforcing, because it provides an emotional and physical response to coping in a way in which the offenders feel they have control, unlike many of the other parts of their lives.

Traits that appear to be most strongly connected to sexually deviant behavior are *dynamic variables*, or features that are changeable, such as cognitions, feelings, and attitudes. Unfortunately, it is these variables that are least understood, though empirical research in the past two decades has focused largely on them rather than *static variables* such as age and ethnicity. Empirical research generates data-driven models that are derived from a combination of theoretical perspectives rather than a specific theoretical approach. Empirical research tends to be developmental, cognitive, and social in nature, and it has led to the development of comprehensive theories of sexual offending.

Empirical studies on rape expanded at the time of the feminist movement, following the idea that rapists were not deviant characters, but rather like "the man next door" (Medea & Thompson, 1974; Russell, 1984). Empirical research has shown correlations between offending behavior and offender psychopathology, arousal patterns, attitudes, and social skills. A variety of factors have been measured, such as rape-supportive attitudes (Scully & Marolla, 1984) and prevalence of childhood sexual abuse in offenders (Seghorn, Prentky, & Boucher, 1987), as well as cognitive factors such as emotional disturbances and loneliness (Marshall, 1989). Some researchers have constructed equations that aim to predict factors of offending behavior (Malamuth, 1986), and others have utilized traditional theories such as Cohen's psychodynamic theories of rape to build empirical typologies of offenders to aid in the assessment for their management and treatment (Prentky & Burgess, 1990).

Other researchers who have proposed integrated theories to explain child sexual abuse focus on the offender's desire for sexual pleasure. For instance, O'Connell, Leberg, and Donaldson (1990) claim that child sexual abusers begin offending because of the attraction to the pleasure derived from the acts; they have a perception that this is the only way to obtain such pleasure; there is a lack of understanding about the damage resulting to the child from this pleasure; and there is a lack of inhibitors to prevent the offender from seeking this pleasure. Hall and Hirschman's (1992) quadripartite model identifies motivational precursors that increase the probability of offending. The four components of Hall and Hirschman's (1992) theory are physiological sexual arousal, inaccurate cognitions that justify sexual aggression, affective dyscontrol, and personality problems.

Ward and Seigert (2002) have critiqued many of the individual theoretical perspectives for explaining sexual abuse and present the most comprehensive integrated model of offending known as a pathways model. They explain that each distinct pathway has its own etiology. However, all sex offenders suffer from certain core deficits and "dysfunctional mechanisms." According to the pathways model, the four distinct and interlocking psychological mechanisms that are exhibited by sex offenders are (1) intimacy deficits; (2) deviant sexual scripts; (3) emotional dysregulation; and (4) antisocial cognitions. Sex offenders may also exhibit multiple dysfunctional mechanisms. Ward, Polaschek, and Beech (2006) provide an overview and critique of theories on sexual offending, including what they call Level I Theories (Multifactorial Theories), Level II Theories (Single-Factor Theories), and Level III Theories (Descriptive Models) of sexual offending.

T A B L E   3.2   Theories of Sexual Abuse
© Cengage Learning

Theory	Description of Theory
Paraphilias	Sexual disorders characterized by recurrent, intense, sexually arousing fantasies involving either nonhuman objects, suffering or humiliation of oneself or one's partner, children or other nonconsenting persons
Psychodynamic Theory	Sexual deviance is an expression of the unresolved problems experienced during the stages of development; the human psyche is composed of three primary elements: the id, the ego, and the superego; sexual deviancy occurs when the id is overactive
Biological Theory	Concerned with organic explanations of human behavior; physiological factors (e.g., hormone levels, chromosomal makeup) have an effect of sexual behavior; androgens promote sexual arousal, orgasm, and ejaculation, as well as regulate sexuality, aggression, cognition, emotion, and personality; abnormal levels of androgens lead to aggressive sexual behavior
Feminist Theory	Analyzes rape from a cultural, political, and historical context, and feminists cite sexual crime as an example of men's oppression of women; sexual gratification is not the primary motive for rape, but rape is a tool to dominate and control women
Attachment Theory	Humans have a propensity to establish strong emotional bonds with others, and when individuals have some loss or emotional distress, they act out as a result of their loneliness and isolation; intimacy deficits
Behavioral Theory	Deviant sexual behavior is a learned condition, acquired through the same mechanisms by which conventional sexuality is learned; it is acquired and maintained through basic conditioning principles
Cognitive-Behavioral Theory	Addresses the way in which offenders' thoughts affect their behavior; focus on the way in which sex offenders diminish their feelings of guilt and shame by rationalizing them through excuses and justifications
Psychosocial Theory	Deviant sexual behavior is a response to external factors, and there is an interconnection between psychological and sociological variables (e.g., social skills) that influence sexual behavior
Routine Activities Theory	Three factors must exist in time and place for an offense to occur: a motivated offender, a potential victim, and lack of a capable guardian; focus is on the criminal event rather than individual risk; crime reduction should focus on reducing opportunity
Integrated Theory	No single theory explains sexual offending behavior; multifactor models explain the preconditions to sexual abuse (motivation, overcoming internal and external factors, and overcoming child's resistance) and the pathways to abuse (distinct and interlocking dysfunctional mechanisms)

Despite years of research, theories on sexual offending are still inconclusive. There has been a shift in theoretical focus over the past three decades, and it is now clear that no single explanation accurately encompasses the myriad factors associated with the onset of deviant behavior. While comprehensive theories are able to explain general conditions associated with sexual offending, it is not possible to predict, on an individual level, who will offend based on these general characteristics. Table 3.2 summarizes theories of sexual abuse.

CHAPTER SUMMARY

- Theories developed throughout the century, focusing at various times on physiology, psychology, psycho-social factors, cognitive-behavioral factors, and ultimately integrated models of offending.

- The most thorough explanation of deviant sexual behavior lies in integrated theories. Integrated theories consider the preconditions to sexual abuse and take into consideration other factors such as attachments, emotions, and CDs.

- A common thread through most theories is that sex offenders tend to have poor social skills, low self-esteem, misperceive social cues, and are able to rationalize their behavior.

- Some sex offenders are diagnosed with paraphilias, which are sexual disorders that can explain the etiology of offending behavior. Some paraphilias are serious and can lead to significant distress for both the offender and the potential victim. Others are relatively minor, do not involve contact with the victim, and are practiced as consensual acts among "normal" adults.

DISCUSSION QUESTIONS

1. Why is it important to understand the theoretical underpinnings of sexual abuse?

2. Is there any crossover between different theoretical frameworks for explaining deviant sexual behavior?

3. What are some of the critical factors that play a role in explaining why people commit sexual offenses?

4. How do familial or other close relationships impact those who go on to become sexual abusers?

5. Why is it important to diagnose paraphilias?

6. What role do social skills play in sexual offending? How is this similar or different in offenders who abuse children and adults?

CASE STUDY

Aileen Wuornos, Serial Killer

Most sexual offenders are male, and nearly all known serial killers are also male. It is unusual to hear about violent female offenders, and particularly rare to hear about extreme cases, such as that of Aileen Wuornos. Wuornos was perhaps the highest-profile female serial killer in the United States. Between 1989 and 1990, she killed six truck drivers along Florida's highways. She claimed that these men had raped or attempted to rape her. Prior to the killings, Wuornos had worked these same highways as a prostitute. In 1989, she began picking up traveling truck drivers and taking them into nearby woods where she killed them (Shipley & Arrigo, 2004).

Aileen Wuornos had a difficult upbringing, and researchers have attempted to explain her behaviors through this difficult childhood. Wuornos was raised by alcoholic and abusive grandparents, and by the age of 11 she had begun trading sex for candy and cigarettes (Pearson, 2007). Her grandfather used to make her strip before beating her. At the age of 14, Wuornos became pregnant after being raped by one of her grandfather's friends. She gave birth to the child and then gave it up for adoption. When Wuornos turned 15, her grandfather threw her out and she turned to prostitution as a means of survival (McCloskey & Ramos-Grenier, 2006). Throughout her adult life she had run-ins with the police for various types of criminal behavior, including robbery, assault, fraud, and motor vehicle theft.

Those who have studied Wuornos's case argue that her childhood disrupted the development of safety and security that is important in early development, and as a result she had no ability to regulate her emotions. Additionally, her history of sexual abuse and, likely, physical and emotional abuse, may have led Wuornos to target individuals looking for prostitutes (Shipley & Arrigo, 2004). Assessments of Wuornos using the *DSM* have suggested that Wuornos suffered from Antisocial Personality Disorder, which is characterized by deceitfulness, impulsivity, and a reckless disregard for the safety of one's self and others (Pearson, 2007).

Wuornos was convicted for the murder of six men. She was executed by lethal injection in October 2002. She was the 10th woman to be executed in the United States since the reinstatement of the death penalty in 1976.

Questions
1.   Are theories of offending equally applicable to male and female offenders?
2.   What theories best explain Aileen Wuornos's behavior?

© Cengage Learning

4

Cycle of Sexual Offending

Whereas Chapter 3 outlined theories of why individuals begin to sexually offend and described the preconditions to sexual abuse, this chapter discusses the offense cycle. This includes the planning that goes into the offense as well as the cognitive processes that the offender uses to be able to continue offending. When individuals commit sexual offenses, they rarely do so spontaneously. Usually, there is a level of planning that leads up to the offense and, in the case of child sexual abuse, "grooming" behavior. Additionally, many offenders commit multiple offenses. In order to do so, they excuse or justify their behavior so that they feel little or no remorse, guilt, or shame. This rationalization allows the offender to continue the abusive behavior and, thus, the cycle of offending.

The *offense cycle* describes the interaction of the offender's thoughts, feelings, and behaviors. The cycle shows how sexual abuse is not a random set of acts, but rather is the result of a series of multideterminant decisions. Once begun, this offense cycle is able to continue because sex offenders neutralize their feelings of guilt, shame, and responsibility through cognitive distortions (CDs). These altered thought processes vary in both type and intensity, and they are crucial to the maintenance of the offenders' deviant fantasies, thoughts, and behaviors. Understanding the determinants of sexual offending is important in order to establish practical policies for treatment and supervision of sex offenders.

THE OFFENSE CYCLE

When committing sexual offenses, offenders make a series of decisions prior to the commission of these acts. Some of the decisions in this cycle transpire after a long period of time. Other decisions may occur quickly if the offender is in a situation where an abusive opportunity presents itself. Understanding this decision process helps explain the onset and persistence of offending behavior, because it is necessary to understand the conditions that create a pro-offending environment and how certain antecedents to sexual abuse vary among offenders.

Sexual offenders rarely make a straightforward decision to abuse a person. Instead, they tend to make a series of decisions that, when taken together, lead to sexual abuse. This series of seemingly irrelevant decisions (SIDs) (also known as *seemingly unimportant decisions* or *apparently irrelevant decisions*) creates a pro-offending environment for the offenders. For example, a rapist may decide to go to his neighborhood bar, even though his prior offense occurred against a woman he met at a bar while he was intoxicated. Another example is of a convicted child sexual abuser who goes to the corner deli at 3 P.M.—the exact time that kids in his neighborhood get out of school and stop to get snacks. Although the decisions in each example do not constitute deviant sexual behavior or even necessarily overt sexual thoughts, these SIDs place the offenders in environments in which they have access to potential victims through their routine activities. If the process is not stopped, the potential offender may continue to make SIDs until an offense takes place.

The offense cycle is more than just decisions, however. The offense cycle involves multiple determinants, including the interaction of thoughts, feelings, and behaviors. These determinants may be situational in nature (that is, the offender is in a situation in which offending is possible), they may involve negative affective states (in particular, depression, anger, or loneliness), they may be based on past learning (that is, the offender was abused in a similar way as a child), and the offender's actions may be reinforced (that is, from the pleasure derived from the abusive act). In other words, the offending cycle ties together the theoretical underpinnings of sexual abuse, as discussed in Chapter 3, including the preconditions of sexual abuse, the opportunity structure for abuse to occur, and the CDs of the offenders.

There are several steps involved in the offense cycle. At the outset, the offender has negative thoughts, often leading to self-pity and the idea that "nobody likes me" or "I'm no good." These self-pitying, negative thoughts lead to negative feelings, in particular anger, frustration, loneliness, and inadequacy. These negative thoughts and feelings interact and lead to negative (abusive) behavior. The thoughts and feelings lead the offender to make SIDs that, among other things, lead him or her to withdraw from others. The result is further loneliness and isolation, which results in a lack of communication that causes the original negative thoughts and feelings to go unresolved and further heightens the intimacy deficits of the offender.

Once the offender is ensconced in the negative thought-feeling-behavior cycle, he or she begins to experience inappropriate sexual thoughts or fantasies. These may be abstract fantasies about particular groups of individuals (for example, teenage boys, blond women, college students) or focused on a particular individual (for example, the neighbor). Though the offender may not act upon the fantasies immediately, the fantasies eventually lead to masturbation, where pleasure is derived as a result of the abusive fantasy. With this positive reinforcement, the offender's negative thoughts and feelings begin to wane, further reinforcing the negative behavior. It is at this point that the offender begins to take steps toward overtly deviant behavior if he has not done so already, targeting a victim and engaging in a fantasy rehearsal of the future abuse of that victim.

Once the offender has engaged in the fantasy rehearsal, he or she begins to plan the abusive act and "groom" the victim. Once adequate grooming has taken place, the offender will abuse the victim. Similarly to the masturbatory act, the abusive act itself is a tangibly positive reinforcement of the original fantasy. However, the abuse may also lead to negative feelings, particularly that of anxiety (What have I done?) and fear (Will I get caught?), despite the release of tension achieved through the sexual abuse. It is these negative feelings that lead to the desistance of the abuse cycle. Yet, the offender rarely addresses the original negative thoughts and feelings that led to the abusive behavior, and as a result the offense cycle often begins again if the offender has not been caught. Thus, the abusive behavior is cyclical.

GROOMING AND PLANNING

Throughout the offense cycle, offenders make a series of decisions that lead up to and allow the offender to commit the deviant act. Yet, many offenders do not recognize the amount of planning that occurs before a sexual offense is committed. Child sexual abusers tend to have a greater awareness of the planning than do those who sexually assault adults, because they generally "groom" children before engaging them in a sexual act. Grooming is a premeditated behavior intended to manipulate the potential victim into complying with the sexual abuse (John Jay College, 2004). Some child sexual abusers do not recognize their grooming patterns, or they may deny that such patterns exist, whereas others carefully develop elaborate schemes that encourage children to participate in sexual activity.

Pryor (1996, pp. 123–154) describes several methods by which child sexual abusers approach and engage their victims in sexual behavior, including verbal and/or physical coercion, seduction, games, and enticements. He explains how child sexual abusers are able to manipulate their victims into sexual compliance and how the offenders either continue the manipulation or adjust it in order to continue with the abuse. The first grooming tactic noted by Pryor is the seduction and testing of the child, whereby sexual activity is initiated after a common interaction such as tickling or bathing. Here, the child is seduced and sexual behavior is "tested," increasing incrementally unless the child overtly tells the offender to stop the action. The following two quotes are examples of this tactic. Both offenders were convicted of raping their daughters, though intercourse occurred only after years of touching and fondling.*

---

*From personal interviews with sex offenders in the English prison system.

[The abuse] actually started when Christine[1] was three and it went on until she was eleven. I started bathing her, and I touched her while I was bathing her.

Q: How did you groom her?

A: I would ask for a kiss and a cuddle, and that is how it all started. Then I got bolder and bolder, and eventually I had intercourse with her.

A second grooming tactic involves catching the victim by surprise (Pryor, 1996). This happens when the offender has planned for some length of time to abuse the victim, yet there was no opportunity for the abuse to occur. The offender either manipulates the situation so that he is alone with the victim or takes advantage of an opportunity that presents itself. The following offender utilized this tactic.

Q: How did the abuse start?

A: Handstands. She asked me if I would hold her legs while she did handstands, and so I said yes. So she did handstands, and I asked her if she wanted to do them again. When she did them a second time I put my hand down her pants.

A third tactic for engaging children in sexual behavior is verbal or physical coercion. Most child sexual abusers use manipulation, but few use physical force, weapons, or threats of physical force with their victims. Yet, some serious, repeat offenders do use physical and/or verbal force to make their victims comply. For example, an offender who was convicted of abusing six victims over a period of several years made the following statement. His victims were his nieces, his grandchildren, and their friends.

I was cunning, devious, you name it. I would use every trick in the book to get them to sit on my knee. I bribed them. I threatened them as well. I threatened, but I wouldn't really do it.... I threatened them with violence.... I threatened to hit them, even though it was not my jurisdiction to hit them.

Pryor (1996) describes another tactic used by child sexual abusers as masking sex in a game context. The offenders who use this tactic tend to be the more manipulative offenders and often have several victims. These schemes are well planned and premeditated, meant to trick the victims into participating in sexual acts. The first of the two excerpts is by an offender describing his first victim, his stepdaughter, when the abuse began at age 10. The second statement is by an offender who went to elaborate lengths to groom children and make them comfortable with the sexual nature of their games.

Q: How did you get her to comply *[with the abuse]*?

A: I acted like it was all a game, and she went along with it. I appreciate that now, she was looking at me as an authority figure and I let her down badly....

---

1. The names of all victims have been changed.

My grooming tactics were so good that the boys never said no. I started by play-fighting and wrestling and I took them swimming. I took them to a club ... that had a common changing room, that way I could see them undressing and they could get used to seeing me naked.

Perhaps the most common tactic used by child sexual abusers in order to groom the victims is emotional and verbal coercion. There are many ways in which this may occur, such as bribes or lack of disciplinary action in exchange for sexual favors, or emotional blackmail if the victim does not comply. The victims are almost always given incentives in order to comply with the abuse, such as money and gifts. This is often the tactic used with incest offenders or offenders who have regular contact with their victims. Following are two examples of this tactic. The first offender had sexual intercourse with his biological daughter, and the second had a sexual relationship with his stepson. In both the cases, the abuse went on for several years.

Q: What led up to the intercourse? Did she ever say "no" to the sexual acts?

A: I groomed her for several weeks. The first time I tried to touch her she ran away from me.

Q: Why did she eventually let you touch her?

A: Because I am her dad, and she probably just thought it was natural. I used to bathe her, and when I would touch her I would tell her it wouldn't hurt. She used to say "no, don't do it" sometimes, but I would buy her extra sweets.... I told her that if she told anyone, daddy will go away for a long time.

I don't see, I don't think I groomed them.... There were no treats or anything. Except with Danny. Danny was different. His treat was that he was allowed to stay up late for the simple reason so that we could masturbate each other.

Some child sexual abusers do not admit to initiating contact with the victim, but claim instead that the victim initiated the contact and instigated the sexual behavior. Pryor describes this as "taking over from the victim," in that the offenders carry on with the behavior once the victims initiate it. Though it is possible that such a scenario may occur, it is unlikely. A more plausible explanation is that the offenders have a distorted perception of the abuse and believe the victim to be culpable. The following excerpts are examples of this tactic:

From the time I first met him he was all over me. I tried to stop little Johnny from hanging around, but it didn't work.

She used to like to go to [soccer] matches.... And you see, she used to come to me and say to me, "I want to go to the [soccer] match Dad, so we can do you-know-what." I didn't used to buy her presents or anything like that, just take her out to [soccer] matches.

I know this sounds like I am minimizing, but this is the truth: it all started when I was sleeping, and I woke up and my nephew was giving me oral sex.

Rapists, particularly those who are opportunistic, often do not recognize the level of planning that goes into their offenses. Most claim that the decision to rape was made instantaneously and believe that only child sexual abusers plan offenses. Yet some rapists do eventually recognize that some planning went into the offenses. For instance, the following excerpt was taken from an offender who was convicted of sexual assaults against 10 prostitutes. The statement was taken after he completed a treatment program; prior to the treatment, he did not admit to planning any part of the offenses, saying they happened spontaneously.

Q: What else about the treatment stood out to you?

A: Just how you plan your offense. At the time you don't think about it, you know. But it is planned, it is all sectioned. When you look at it, you think

CASE STUDY

TED BUNDY: Planning His Offenses

In 1978, Ted Bundy was convicted of killing two female students at Florida State University. These were two of his estimated 30 murders, and he was ultimately executed in 1989 for the murder of a 12-year-old girl. His killing spree spanned five years and occurred across seven states. The question was, how was he able to become such a prolific killer without being caught?

During interviews about the homicides, Bundy admitted that he studied his victims' behavior prior to attacking them. Bundy noted that he was most organized while operating in his "predator mode," during which he selected a dump site, conducted research on his victims, and completed planning which included having an alibi and flight option. Bundy relied on his charm and social skills to ensure that his victims would feel comfortable enough to leave a populated area with him. Bundy would often rely on the same pattern, as he would feign an injury or pretend to be an authority figure. Using these guises, he would convince his victims to accompany him to his car where he would knock them unconscious with a crowbar. Bundy would then drive around with the victim, reaching his preselected dump site. It was here that he would again knock the victim unconscious and strangle her while raping her.

Bundy clearly illustrates the grooming and planning techniques utilized by sex offenders. Bundy used his likeable personality to his advantage, putting his victims at ease enough to lure them to areas where they would be alone. He also relied on his previously planned strategies, such as impersonating a police officer or pretending to be injured, to convince his victims that they had nothing to fear or could be of help to him. Bundy lured his victims to a desolate area where he was then able to catch them by surprise and act out his attacks. Bundy planned his attacks down to every detail and this planning contributed in part to his success in committing numerous murders and evading detection by law enforcement.

Questions
1. Are there similarities between the grooming/planning techniques of Ted Bundy and child sexual abusers?
2. How does the offense cycle apply to Ted Bundy? How could the cycle have been stopped?

yeah, I did do that.... *[My offense]* was all planned, all planned from start to finish. I used to, I took them to a park to attack them, and I used to go out to the park beforehand to make sure no one was there. And I knew exactly what I was gonna do before it happened. It wasn't spur of the moment, it was all planned. I knew where I was gonna take them, what I was gonna do, how much time I had, and when I had to pick the wife up from Bingo.

PERSISTENCE OF OFFENDING BEHAVIOR

Once there are motivational factors in place that create a predisposition to sexual offending, and once the offense cycle has begun, offenders must then overcome any internal or external inhibitions in order to commit an offense (Finkelhor, 1984). After the individual commits a sexual offense, additional factors must be present in order for the offender to maintain the deviant behavior. As with the etiology of offending behavior, there is no single variable that explains why sexual offenders continue perpetrating offenses. There are several variables, however, that have been associated with the maintenance of deviant sexual behavior. In particular, offenders almost universally exhibit distorted thought processes, or CDs, that allow for continuation of abuse without feelings of guilt or remorse for their actions (Murphy, 1990). Moreover, many sex offenders have fantasies about a victim, a particular type of victim (for example, young boys), or certain sexual practices, and the continuation of such fantasies is correlated to the maintenance of deviant behavior. The fantasies are not always sexual in nature; rather, many rapists and child sexual abusers fantasize about issues such as power and control. Additionally, child sexual abusers often fantasize about loving their victims, which, though not violent, is a CD and allows the offender to continue participating in the inappropriate relationship.

In addition to CDs and fantasies, sex offenders often blame their behavior on external factors, such as stress, alcohol, or strained marital relations. Though these disinhibitors are not causal, they do act as "triggers" for the sexual offense. The triggers can be either psychological (for example, use of alcohol) or socio-cultural (for example, weak criminal sanctions against sexual offenders) in nature (Hartley, 1998, p. 26). Researchers have identified CDs, fantasies, and triggering factors as pertinent to the persistence of offending behavior, and as such these variables are addressed at length in cognitive-behavioral treatment programs (discussed in Chapter 11).

Cognitive Distortions

When individuals commit wrongdoings, they often try to diminish their feelings of guilt and shame through "neutralizations" (Sykes & Matza, 1957). Individuals primarily neutralize feelings of wrongdoing through excuses and justifications for their behavior (Scott & Lyman, 1968; Scully, 1990). These neutralizations take the form of CDs that allow the offenders to remove from themselves any responsibility, shame, and guilt for their actions (Abel, Becker, & Cunningham-Rathner, 1984). These rationalizations of deviant behavior protect the individual from self-blame and allow the individual to validate the behavior through cognitive defenses.

CDs are not unique to sex offenders. Rather, all individuals distort thoughts regularly. For most individuals these distorted thoughts are not necessarily harmful (for example, a student who receives a bad grade on an exam assumes the teacher doesn't like him or her), but the distorted thoughts of sex offenders generally are harmful (for example, "She didn't fight with me so she must have wanted sex"). It is not the distortions themselves that are unique to sex offenders, but rather the content of the distortions (Marshall, Anderson, & Fernandez, 1999, p. 60). Though sex offenders do not form a homogeneous group of individuals, they show strikingly similar CDs about their victims, their offenses, and their responsibility for the offenses.

It is unclear as to whether CDs are conscious distortions or whether offenders genuinely believe these altered perceptions of reality. Some researchers suggest that CDs are self-serving and, thus, the offender consciously distorts thoughts initially (Abel et al., 1984). However, it is also suggested that the offenders eventually believe the distortions as they become more entrenched in their behavior (Marshall et al., 1999). Regardless, CDs are considered crucial to the maintenance of offending behavior for both rapists and child sexual abusers, because they serve the needs of the offenders to continue their behavior without feeling guilt for their actions.

There are many ways in which distortions manifest themselves in sex offenders. Sykes and Matza (1957) list five primary neutralization techniques, including the denial of responsibility, the denial of injury, the denial of the victim, the condemnation of the condemners, and the appeal to higher loyalties. Cognitive-behavioral theorists have explained these techniques in terms of CDs, the most common of which are minimization and/or denial of the offense and justification of the offense. Additionally, sex offenders often lack victim empathy and show an inability to recognize the level of planning that went into their offenses (including grooming of the victims). Some researchers also label sexual entitlement as a specific CD, resulting from the narcissistic attitudes of offenders who seek only to fulfill their own desires (Hanson, Gizzarelli, & Scott, 1994, p. 197). However broadly or specifically the CDs are defined, these distorted thoughts are conducive to the maintenance of deviant sexual practices.

Minimization and Denial   Most sex offenders minimize or deny their offenses, including the damage caused to the victim, the violence used, their responsibility for the offense, the planning of the offense, and the lasting effects as a result of the offense. Several researchers have categorized types of minimization and denial (Haywood et al., 1994; Marshall et al., 1999); these include complete or partial denial of the offense, minimization of the offense, minimization of their own responsibility, denial or minimization of harm to the victim, denial or minimization of planning, denial or minimization of deviant fantasies, and denial of the personal problems that led to the deviant behavior.

Some sex offenders deny all or part of their offenses. They may completely deny that they committed the offense—claiming, for instance, that the victim made up the story or they cannot remember what happened—or they may not admit to aggravating factors of the offense. Partial denial, as described by Marshall et al. (1999), includes refutation of a problem (for example, "I am not a sex offender") or the refusal to accept that an act was sexual abuse (for example, "The victim consented"). Though some researchers claim that denial is not an accurate predictor variable for recidivism (Hanson & Bussiere, 1998), there is a substantial body of literature that claims the opposite (Marques, Day, Nelson, & West, 1994; Simkins, Ward, Bowman, & Rinck, 1989). Few therapists allow deniers to participate in treatment until they at least admit that they committed the offense (Marques, Day et al., 1994).

Offenders with either adult or child victims may deny the offense by claiming that they were falsely accused or that they do not remember the offense. Some blame their memory loss on the extended period of time between the commission of the offense and the arrest, whereas others blame substances such as drugs or alcohol. The following excerpts from two child sexual abusers typify such denials.

Q: What about the USI *[unlawful sexual intercourse with a girl under the age of 16]?*

A: The USI, the reason I am guilty is because of medication, opium-based painkillers.... I don't remember what happened. If anything happened I will agree to it. But I can't remember because I was on medication.

This was a long time ago, 25 years ago. I have a very, very, poor memory.... This rape business, I have practically put it out of my mind, I never forget it but I have more or less put it out of my mind. *[He was convicted of raping his 10-year-old niece.]*

If offenders do not deny that they committed the offense, it is common for them to minimize the damage resulting from their acts. They rarely acknowledge the harm they caused the victim, and this is particularly true for child sexual abusers. Because most child sexual abusers are not violent toward their victims, they do not recognize the damage caused by what they view as a "consensual" relationship. They tend to see the assault on the child as the product of a mutual sexual interest, and they minimize any damage that might result from a child partaking in such a relationship. The first excerpt below is a statement made by a sex offender who was convicted of raping one daughter and indecently assaulting[2] another. The second is by an offender who was convicted of raping a 13-year-old girl.

In court she wouldn't say she consented, that is why it came back as rape.... The *affair* started in 1978, and the first time she said no at the last minute. *But after that it was consenting.*

A: I went out on a Sunday morning and the youngest daughter of Kathy asked me if she could go for a ride. We got along, we were laughing and joking,

---

2. Indecent assault is a charge in England equivalent to sexual assault in the United States. It involves inappropriate sexual touching in any way, and can include manual penetration, penetration with a foreign object, or oral sex.

and one thing led to another and, well, let's put it this way, I went a little farther than I should have done.

Q: What was going through your mind when she started screaming and crying?

A: I thought she was a virgin.

Although child sexual abusers rarely acknowledge that their "consensual" relationships are harmful, offenders with adult victims tend to minimize the damage they cause in other ways. They rarely recognize the level of coercion or violence used in order to make the victim comply with the assault. This is compounded if the victim is either a partner or spouse, or if the victim is involved in an occupation such as prostitution. In such cases, the offenders express a distorted thought of sexual entitlement, believing that they have the right to sexual intercourse with this person and that the act should not be considered rape. The following excerpts are from interviews with rapists. The first was convicted of raping his girlfriend, and his CD of entitlement to sex is clear from his description of his relationship with the victim. The second offender shows severe minimization of his actions and the harm caused by them. The victim was his girlfriend, whom he severely beat, throttled, and left unconscious when she said she did not want to have intercourse with him.

Q: Did you rape her?

A: We had a relationship, and there were times when we had sex and it was forceful. But she didn't leave me.... She ended up living with me. She didn't have to. She could have gone home.

My offense was not against the general public, it was against my girlfriend. ... I was brought up with ethics and so I tend to respect women. I have never committed an offense against anybody nor have I been rude to anybody in my life. This is the first time it happened. I didn't—I mean, there was no violence involved. It was just that the lady said no on this particular occasion, and I think she was more surprised than anything.

Justifications   In addition to minimizing or denying their offenses, sex offenders make excuses as to why they committed the deviant acts. By justifying their actions, offenders acknowledge their guilt in the acts but they do not take responsibility for them. Commonly, they blame the victims for their offenses or justify their offenses through the victims' actions.

Justification is common in the vast majority of sex offenders, as it assists in allaying remorse and guilt for the acts committed. Scully and Marolla (1984), who interviewed 114 incarcerated rapists, explain five ways in which rapists commonly justify their behavior. Rapists claim that (1) the victim is a seductress, and she provoked the rape; (2) women mean yes when they say no, or the victim did not resist enough to really mean no; (3) most women relax and enjoy it, and the rapists are actually fulfilling the woman's desires; (4) nice girls do not get raped, and prostitutes, hitchhikers, and promiscuous women get what they deserve; and (5) the rape was only a minor wrongdoing, so the perpetrator is not really an "offender."

Child sexual abusers also justify their actions by neutralizing their guilt. Common justifications include claims that they are helping the child to learn about sex; sexual education is good for the child; the child enjoys it; there is no harm being done to the child; the child initiated the sexual contact; and the child acts older than he or she is. Like offenders with adult victims, child sexual abusers often assert that the child did not resist and therefore must have wanted the sexual interaction. They fail to recognize any other explanations as to why the child might not have resisted, such as fear, uncertainty about what was happening, or the idea that the perpetrator is someone they knew and trusted. The following excerpt shows an offender justifying his contact with the young daughter of his friend because she did not resist his advances:

Q: What made you abuse her?

A: I don't know. The opportunity just was given to me. She came and sat in my lap and asked me how to draw something. So while she was drawing, I put my hand up her skirt. She didn't say no.

Many children, when abused, respond to the abusers by copying their actions or by doing what they are told to do. For instance, if a man shows a young girl how to masturbate him, she may comply without fully understanding the purpose or consequence of her actions. The offenders tend to assume that this type of compliance with a sexual act is indicative of the child's enjoyment of the act, and they are able to justify their actions accordingly. Other offenders sexually touch a child but do not have the child touch them. They are aroused by the touching and usually fantasize about the act at a later time. The offenders often believe that they are pleasuring the child, and they do not view this type of act as intrusive and harmful. Still others believe that they are teaching the child about sex, and that sexual intercourse is pleasurable and the child is enjoying the interaction. The following excerpts illustrate these points:

I was putting my thing on her private parts, mind you through her [underpants]. At no time did I force her to do anything, nor did I ever physically force her to touch me.

Q: Did you know what you were doing was wrong?

A: At the time I was giving myself the excuse, I was doing nothing wrong.... I would say to myself, she likes it. She has to learn that sometime, she has to learn sooner or later. I would make myself think I wasn't doing anything wrong.

Many children do not exert physical resistance to sexual advances. As discussed previously, this is largely due to the grooming techniques employed by the offender leading up to the abuse. Nonetheless, this lack of resistance to sexual advances signifies to most offenders that the child is enjoying the sexual interaction. Added to this are the natural biological reactions of the child to the sexual contact, such as when one offender told a researcher in an interview, "I remember touching her breasts at that point. And ... immediately her nipples got hard" (Pryor, 1996, p. 127). This is particularly applicable to offenders whose victims are girls who are just reaching puberty. The following excerpt is from an offender who abused his 12-year-old niece and justified his actions through all of the listed methods of neutralization:

Q: How did the abuse begin?

A: We used to kiss and cuddle, and then it progressed from there. She never really objected to any of it, only sometimes did she say she didn't like it. And only once did she say no, we can get in trouble for this. She was such a pretty little girl, so well developed for her age.... I suppose this must have mentally scarred her, but I know deep down that she really just loved it.

Many child sexual abusers seek out children who are vulnerable for abuse. This includes children who have been abused physically, emotionally, or sexually, and who often desire the attention paid to them by the offender. The offender is able to neutralize guilt in such a situation by believing that he is showing the child love as no one else does. Or, the guilt is neutralized because others have already abused the child and the offender is therefore not to blame. The following excerpt illustrates this point:

I abused my nephew and two of his friends. My brother was also abusing my nephew, and I guess I thought "He's already been abused, so I can abuse him too."

All types of sex offenders have a tendency to misread social cues by others and are poor at identifying emotions such as anger or fear in the victims. Both rapists and child sexual abusers often perceive their victims as initiating sexual contact and see their victims' actions as sexually provocative. Rapists view flirtatious actions by their victims as indicative of desiring a sexual relationship. Many do not understand prosocial boundaries to sexual contact and believe that if a sexual interaction has begun, then it should continue through intercourse. Thus, if the victims later make an attempt to terminate contact (victim says "No"), the rapists do not take the desire to stop the contact seriously (offender assumes she means "Yes"). Blaming the victim for initiating sexual contact alleviates the guilt of the act from them and transposes it to the victims.

Child sexual abusers misread cues from children in several ways, and the better they know the victim the more likely this is to happen. Children are naturally affectionate toward adults, particularly those whom they know well. Child sexual abusers view these naturally affectionate actions—such as sitting on an adult's lap—as sexual in nature and perceive the children as initiating sexual contact. They also perceive any sexual curiosity displayed by the child as a desire to know about sex, and they want to "teach" the child through sexual experiences. These misperceptions reinforce the offenders' narcissistic beliefs and detract from the ability of an offender to feel any empathy for his victims.

Victim Empathy

Research in cognitive psychology suggests that all individuals interpret situations differently, and they construct implicit theories about their worlds in order to explain the reality as it relates to them. The socially constructed reality of sex offenders revolves around two concepts: desires and beliefs (Ward & Keenan, 1999, p. 825). They form mental constructs about what they believe the victim wants, and because offenders exhibit narcissistic traits, they generally believe that the victim desires sexual activity with them (Hanson, Gizzarelli, & Scott, 1994). As such, they are often unaware of the damage that they cause to their victims. Without understanding the impact of their actions, or feeling empathy toward the victim, offenders are not likely to cease their offending behavior.

Empathy refers to the understanding of another's feelings and emotions. There are several components of empathy, including both cognitive and emotional factors (Davis, 1983; Moore, 1990). It is believed that prosocial empathic response patterns develop primarily during childhood, with parents having a significant impact on the development of behavior and emotional responses (Zahn-Waxler & Radke-Yarrow, 1990). Simply put, if parents show low empathic response patterns, it is likely that their children will model their conduct and also be deficient in empathic behavior. This deficiency in empathy is apparent in almost all sex offenders, and this is what allows them to continue offending despite the damage they cause to the victims.

Studies measuring general empathy in sex offenders show mixed results. Williams and Finkelhor (1990) claim that incestuous fathers lack empathy; Pithers (1994) claims that rapists lack empathy more than child sexual abusers; Hayashino, Wurtele, and Klebe (1995) claim that there is no difference in empathy between child sexual abusers and non-sex offenders. Additionally, sadistic rapists do not lack empathy, which is the failure to understand the feelings and emotional state of others. Rather, they do understand the pain, degradation, and humiliation of the victim and seek this out for sexual arousal.

Marshall, Hudson, Jones, and Fernandez (1995) propose that sex offenders do not necessarily lack empathy as a general trait, but they lack victim-specific empathy. Sex offenders do express empathic responses toward victims of sexual offenses. There are particularly pronounced group differences for empathic responses to victim harm: child sexual abusers are distressed about violence toward women, and rapists are sympathetic toward child victims. The following excerpt shows such a situation:

> I was very disturbed after hearing about [a rapist] who stabbed his victim's eyes out and then mutilated her genital area, and then I had to go back to my cell to think about it. Me, I never hurt my victims so this is disturbing.

The offender who made this statement was convicted of nearly 200 counts of child molestation. The victims were 11- to 14-year-old boys, and the abuse occurred over a 10-year period. Even after treatment, he failed to recognize the harm that he brought upon his victims, which is common to child sexual abusers when the victims display no overt resistance to the abuse (Stermac & Segal, 1989). Many offenders believe that there are degrees of offending behavior and, thus, degrees of harm (Ward & Keenan, 1999), and that the "consensual" nature of their offenses makes them less culpable than those with intrusive, violent offenses. The same offender went on to describe his relationship with his victims in the following way:

> I treat my boys, I mean my victims, better than I was ever treated.
> I have never forced them to do anything. I loved some of the boys.
> Some of them will not be affected; some will be homosexual anyway.
> This was just an earlier experience for them.

Many child sexual abusers feel similarly to this offender, and many believe that the victim enjoys the sexual behavior. Offenders who abuse adolescent boys most commonly feel this way, seeing the relationship as consensual rather than harmful. Two more examples of such relationships are as follows:

Q: Did you ever think about the consequences [of the abuse] for the victims?

A: Not with Danny. With him it was a mutual thing, it was something that we both wanted, even though he was only fourteen.

> I met my boyfriend [14-year-old victim] through another man and the boy told a friend of his. That is how I got caught. All the boys consented to the intercourse, but they were underage.

Child sexual abusers have a narcissistic view of their power, which is derived from the offenders' implicit theories about the importance of their desires taking precedence over those of the victims. Child sexual abusers made the following statements upon completion of a treatment program, exemplifying this type of narcissistic behavior:

> I thought I was not doing any harm, and yet it was so blatantly obvious that I was. I didn't pick up, or I didn't care, or I was so high in my ego that I didn't think about the other person.

Q: Why did you continue to abuse her [15-year-old victim]?

A: Because it was easier to keep abusing her than to get a regular partner. I was being totally selfish.

Q: Did you think she was enjoying herself?

A: Yes, because she did not complain.

Rapists, like child sexual abusers, lack victim empathy and express feelings of sexual entitlement, assuming the victim is less important and should exist to satisfy their sexual needs (Ward & Keenan, 1999, p. 828). They, too, have a narcissistic view of their power and importance. Feelings of sexual entitlement often develop at a younger age, as a child observes the interaction between his or her parents or other adults. The following excerpts are examples of such scenarios:

Q: You didn't think your first offense was rape?

A: No.... I honestly thought that men just coax women. I looked at it like, if a man buys a woman a drink in a bar, all you are doing is coaxing her at the end of the date to have a sexual relationship of some sort.

I think I had a lot of wrong messages given to me growing up as well. My father, the way he treated my *[mom]*, well, he sent a lot of the wrong messages. ... It was that you could take what you want when you want it. It was the same kind of scenario here. ... I was like, you look all right and I wouldn't mind having you. You've got no say in the matter.

This feeling of sexual entitlement is even more pronounced when the victim is a partner or someone viewed as promiscuous by the offender. Offenders feel they are allowed to treat such individuals either as property or as someone who should comply with their sexual requests. The following two excerpts are examples of this attitude:

Right up until I was sentenced I was saying this is ridiculous, I didn't rape my wife. But ... most of us *[sex offenders]* ... are very selfish. We think only about ourselves. You don't see it at the time; you just think of yourself. It's not until you start thinking about the other side, the victim, that you start realizing there are two sides.

I run a club ... and the girls who were around the club were promiscuous. So I started judging everybody else by the world I lived in. It was attitude. ... I just thought that all women were the same.

The Role of Fantasies

Historically, researchers assumed that sex offenders had deviant sexual fantasies, which in turn motivated them to commit deviant sexual acts. Additionally, it was believed that these deviant fantasies were conditioned through masturbation (McGuire, Carlisle, & Young, 1965) and that the fantasies could be modified through deconditioning or aversion therapy (Abel & Blanchard, 1974; Evans, 1968). Even the *Diagnostic and Statistical Manual of Mental Disorders* (American Psychiatric Association, 2000) lists sexually arousing fantasies as a condition of paraphilias, indicating that this belief continues to be prevalent (Langevin, Lang, & Curnoe, 1998).

Unfortunately, there is little empirical evidence to support the notion that sex offenders have more fantasies than non-sex offenders or that these fantasies are more deviant (Langevin et al., 1985). The prevalence and type of fantasies that the sex offenders have seem to vary by type of offender and extent of offending behavior. Pithers et al. (1989) claimed that only 17 percent of the rapists and 51 percent of the child sexual abusers in their study had deviant sexual fantasies. Marshall, Barbaree, and Eccles (1991) reported that 53 percent of child sexual abusers in their study had deviant sexual fantasies, and of those only 29 percent had fantasies prior to adulthood. Prentky et al. (1989) looked at a group of offenders convicted of sexual homicide and found that 86 percent of the serial sexual offenders had deviant fantasies, but only 23 percent of those convicted of only one offense had such fantasies. Additionally, it is impossible to know how many men who have never been convicted of a sexual offense have deviant sexual fantasies.

It is difficult to accurately measure fantasies in sex offenders, and it is equally difficult to know how to interpret the role of these fantasies in deviant behavior. Commonly, sex and non-sex offenders give self-reports about the types of fantasies they have, though many offenders either deny that they have fantasies or do not recognize that their fantasies are deviant. A second method of measuring arousal, and one that is more reliable than self-reports, is through the penile plethysmograph (PPG), which gauges the circumference of the penis through an elastic mechanism attached to it. Though the accuracy of PPG results is disputed because of methodological variance, the majority of results show that deviant sexual interest is a significant problem for extrafamilial child sexual abusers (Laws, Hanson, Osborn, & Greenbaum, 2000). Results are not as consistent for other groups of sex offenders, and many rapists and incestuous offenders show the same level of deviant arousal as non-sex offenders. For these offenders, there is often arousal to depictions of consensual adult erotica as well as deviant stimuli (Marshall et al., 1999). Even when arousal exists to the deviant stimuli, it is not clear whether the sex offenders fantasized about such issues prior to the commission of their offenses or whether the act itself caused the fantasies.

For those who do have deviant sexual fantasies, the types of fantasies vary widely depending on the type of offender and the motivation of the offense. Some offenders are motivated by sexual needs, while issues such as power and control motivate others. The fantasies may center on a particular sexual behavior, violence, power, control, or a specific victim or type of victim. As Marshall et al. (1999) point out, many offenders do not admit to fantasizing about deviant sexual behavior prior to their first deviant act. However, offenders who participate in a treatment program may admit to their deviant fantasies upon completion of the program. For example, the following excerpts are from a child sexual abuser prior and subsequent to treatment, when asked about his sexual attraction to children:

DID YOU KNOW...?

- **Did you know** that both male and female offenders may experience the offense cycle? Most of the literature on sexual offending relates to male offenders, but female offenders experience a similar cycle of offending. They are also likely to have CDs and participate in the grooming and planning of offenses.

- **Did you know** that many "normal" men experience sexual arousal to "deviant" sexual images? Measures of physiological arousal (from the plethysmograph) show little difference in the sexual attraction to deviant images, such as sexualized images of children, between men who have no history of sexual offending and those who do. This is one of many indications that sexual offending is not caused by sexual attraction alone. There are differences in some groups of serious sexual offenders and those who have diagnosed sexual disorders such as pedophilia.

© Cengage Learning

Q: Are you attracted to children?
Pretreatment:
I am not attracted to them, no, no.

Posttreatment:
You see, next door to me there was a woman with daughters, 13 and 15 years old, and they used to go out in the backyard in skimpy bathing suits in the summer. I used to fantasize about them. About the time my wife started rejecting me, I started fantasizing about these girls … and I used to go down to the beach, I used to go down there to watch the kids, sort of swimming and playing and all that. I wouldn't say I used to fantasize about them, but I liked watching them.

Some offenders compare their desire to commit deviant sexual acts to a drug addiction. They say that they have to have a "fix," and though they feel guilt while committing the acts, they desire the act again soon afterward. Whether or not the fantasies are related to the etiology of offending behavior is unclear, the fantasies do play a role in the maintenance of their behavior. The following excerpt illustrates this point:

All I had on my mind was sexual gratification. Sex is like a drug—you know that when you haven't got it the desire is always stronger than when you have some. So you need someone to give you that little kick.

Behavioral Triggers

Many sex offenders blame their sexual offending on situational and transitory factors such as drugs, alcohol, stress, and loneliness. Though these factors alone do not necessarily cause deviant behavior, they are often triggers to the commission of deviant sexual acts. These triggering factors can act either as *disinhibitors*, the most common of which is alcohol, or as *potentiators*, including negative affective states such as depression. Both disinhibitors and potentiators contribute to offending behavior, though they do so in different ways.

Disinhibitors such as alcohol allow the offender to justify the deviant behavior as being caused by an altered mental state. Many offenders are intoxicated before or at the time of their offenses, and intoxication acts as a link in the causative chain of events leading to the deviant act (Marshall et al., 1999). The offenders sometimes cite alcohol as the reason they committed their offenses, without recognizing other risk factors beyond the alcohol. For example, the following excerpt shows how one rapist used alcohol and drug use as an excuse in his offense:

Q: Were you drinking or on drugs the night of your offense?
A: Oh, yes.
Q: If you had not been drinking or on drugs, would this have happened?
A: If I had not been drinking or on drugs, no, it probably wouldn't have happened.

Q: What happened the night of your offense?

A: I went over to my *[friend's]* house and got ahold of some grass and started getting wasted. At 8:00 in the evening, I decided to go down to the shop and get some special lager, extra strength. I drank these five bottles within the space of a half-hour. Going into town, I bumped into the girl I had been going out with. I got the sense that she was not amused with me turning up at this pub. So I thought, fair enough, I'll just carry on drinking for the rest of the evening. And at each pub I went into I had a couple of bottles of Newcastle Brown Ale. In one of the pubs, I saw a dealer in there and bought some speed and some acid and I dropped them all in one go. So by this time I was quite intoxicated. By 11:00 I was a … mess. There were a lot of people who witnessed me sitting there smoking drugs.

It is likely that the drug-induced state of this offender was one causative link in the decision to commit the rape. However, the offender also explained during the interview that he had received divorce papers from his wife earlier that day and had argued with his girlfriend before going out that night. The negative affective states of anger, loneliness, and inadequacy were present, and these likely acted as potentiators for the offense he committed. His level of intoxication during the evening, however, acted as a disinhibitor and allowed him to justify his offense through a removal of responsibility.

Several researchers have shown a link between negative affective states and deviant sexual behavior. McKibben, Proulx, and Lusignan (1994) claim that rapists exhibit characteristics of loneliness, anger, humiliation, and inadequacy; Pithers, Kashima, Cumming, Beal, and Buell (1988) show a link between deviant sexual behavior and anxiety, depression, boredom, and resentment. When asked about their emotional state at the time of the offense, rapists and child sexual abusers made the following comments:

I was getting really depressed. At times I couldn't talk to anybody. People would come over to the house and I would just go upstairs.… It got so bad that I wanted to kill myself.

Before, I would be depressed an awful lot. I tried to get through that by artificial means at different times with the drugs, but they only work for a period of time.

I felt trapped.… I'd get pissed off, and anxious.… I felt claustrophobic when I got close to people. When I get close to people, I feel like they know me and they're trying to take me over. Not that they're trying to take control of me, but like they know me and I can't get away from them. I wind myself up over it. Maybe I won't do that now, but I used to let it affect me.

I was feeling frustrated.… I was feeling inadequate. During *[the offense]*, I was becoming more and more frustrated, and I was taking my frustrations out on her. I was angry but I felt like I was losing control, like

I was out of control on the inside but on the outside I was controlled.

Negative affective states such as the ones above may act as catalysts for deviant sexual behavior. However, they also may play a significant role in the maintenance of deviant behavior. Several offenders explained a link between their fantasies and their feelings of anger, frustration, and inadequacy. The following excerpt is from a rapist who said he would set himself up for rejection with women, which would in turn create feelings of anger and a desire for power over women:

My fantasies were about rape, taking off her clothes, trapping her. I think they started through lack of self-confidence, my own inadequacies, rejection. ... I was always setting myself up for rejection so that I would have an excuse to be angry. In my fantasy, I could do anything I wanted, I had complete control. But *[during the rape]* Lisa kept saying to me "I don't want to do that, why are you doing this to me?" This type of thing was not in my fantasy.

CHAPTER SUMMARY

- Sexual offenses do not just happen spontaneously. The offense takes place over a cycle, including a series of decisions regarding the potential victims and potential actions against the victims. This cycle includes planning the offense, fantasizing about the victim, grooming the victim (if the victim is a child), making decisions to commit the offense, and rationalizing the offending behavior.

- "Grooming" occurs when the offender participates in a premeditated behavior intended to manipulate the potential victim into complying with the sexual abuse. Not only does the offender groom the victim, but often grooms the family of the victim.

- Sex offenders have CDs that allow them to excuse and justify their behavior. The purpose of this rationalization is to alleviate feelings of guilt, shame, and remorse, and often the offender blames the victim for the offense.

- Sex offenders often lack victim empathy. Though they may empathize with victims generally, they lack victim-specific empathy or empathy for their own victim.

DISCUSSION QUESTIONS

1. What is grooming? What is the most common type of grooming behavior?
2. What are the key components of the offense cycle?

3. How are sex offenders able to maintain their abusive behavior without feeling guilt or shame? What types of sexual offenders are most likely to rationalize their behaviors?

4. Describe the role of fantasies in sexual offending. Is it possible to eliminate sexual fantasies? Change sexual fantasies?

5. Give examples of behavioral triggers and how they may lead to sexual abuse. What is the difference between potentiators and disinhibitors?

PART II

Offender Typologies, Special Groups of Offenders, and Victims

5   Types and Typologies of Sexual Offenders

6   Juvenile Offenders

7   Commercial Sexual Exploitation of Children

8   Sexual Offending in Institutional Settings

9   Victims

5

Types and Typologies
of Sexual Offenders

Reducing recidivism of sexual offenders is best accomplished by understanding and identifying the characteristics of offenders and the situations in which they offend. To better understand distinctions between types of offenders, researchers have created typologies, or classification schemes, that utilize offenders' characteristics and/or victim-choice information to outline a framework for analysis. Understanding the interpersonal and situational characteristics that are the basis of offending behavior will lead to a greater likelihood of controlling such behavior in the future.

Sex offenders, however, constitute a heterogeneous group of individuals and many offenders do not fit into discrete categories. Research in the last few decades has shown that sexual offenders do not fit into "stereotyped caricatures" (Hollin & Howells, 1991, p. 1). Sex offenders have unique personal and criminal histories, and the attitudes and beliefs that support their deviant behavior may vary (Gordon & Porporino, 1990). Additionally, the environment in which the sexual offense takes place should be taken into consideration when explaining who is offending, who is victimized, and in what situations (Wortley & Smallbone, 2006b).

Much of the research on sexual offenders has focused on the offenders' motivations for committing sexual offenses. Researchers have classified offenders into discrete typologies based on characteristics of the offenders and their offenses, considering both stable (historical) and dynamic (changeable) characteristics. Although some offenders might have similar characteristics, there is no single typology that can account for all offenders. Some background and cognitive traits are common to most sex offenders, yet the heterogeneity of offenders rarely allows for single typologies to be an adequate characterization. As such, some of the more sophisticated classification models (for example, Knight & Prentky, 1990) classify offenders among multidimensional axes. The usefulness of such classification systems, however, may be questionable based on recent research that shows few offenders are "specialists." Instead, most sex offenders are "generalists" who commit more nonsexual offenses than sexual ones.

This chapter provides an overview of the literature on specialization of offending and a summary of the existing typologies of male and female sex offenders (typologies of juvenile offenders are presented in Chapter 6 and child pornography offenders in Chapter 7).

SPECIALIZATION AND GENERALIZATION
OF OFFENDING BEHAVIOR

There is a significant amount of criminological literature devoted to the study of persistent offenders, or those who commit criminal behaviors over a long period of time (see Blumstein et al., 1986; Wolfgang et al., 1972). Longitudinal analyses have shown that a small number of individuals are responsible for committing a large percentage of all criminal acts. These "career criminals," or "persistent offenders," are also more likely to be "generalists" than to specialize in a particular type of criminal behavior throughout their careers (Farrington, 2003; Piquero et al., 2003). Research on sexual offenders has shown similar patterns (Hanson & Morton-Bourgon, 2004; Lussier, LeBlanc, & Proulx, 2005; Miethe et al., 2006; Simon, 2000; Smallbone & Wortley, 2004; Soothill et al., 2000; Zimring et al., 2007); sex offenders are more likely to be generalists than "specialists," and most do not persist in committing many sexual offenses over a long period of time.

The level of specialization within sexual offending is important in regard to both treatment and policy development (Lussier, LeBlanc, & Proulx, 2005). Many of the current treatment programs as well as supervision and management strategies (discussed at length in Section III of this book) are based on the assumption that sex offenders are a unique group of offenders who specialize in sex crimes (Simon, 2000). Sex offender-specific treatment may not be necessary or appropriate, for example, for an offender who has a career of property offenses and a single sexual offense. Additionally, registration and notification policies are based on the assumption that sex offenders are highly recidivistic. In fact, meta-analyses show that sex offender recidivism rates are relatively low; less than 14 percent of sex offenders are convicted of a new sexual offense and approximately 36 percent are convicted of any new offense within five years (Hanson & Morton-Bourgon, 2004).

Though sex offenders constitute a heterogeneous group of individuals, some researchers have distinguished between types of sex offenders to determine if some are more likely to recidivate or specialize than others. Studies show that child sexual abusers are more likely to specialize than rapists, but they still are more likely to commit a greater number of nonsexual offenses than sexual offenses. Simon (2000) found that incarcerated child sexual abusers are two times more likely to have another conviction of child molestation than other offenders. In a study of 10,000 sex offenders released from prison, Miethe et al. (2006) found that sex offenders as a whole specialized in offense type substantially less than other types of offenders. They did find that child sexual abusers specialized more than rapists, and that the most specialized child sexual abusers are comparable in their levels of specialization to nonsexual offenders. They also found few persistent sex offenders—only 8 percent of child sexual abusers in their sample had three or more convictions—and that the greater number of offenses, the greater the level of generalization. Lussier, LeBlanc, and Proulx (2005) found that both rapists and child sexual abusers were more likely to have previously committed property offenses than sexual offenses, and rapists were also more likely to have committed previous violent offenses than sexual offenses. They did note, however, that child sexual abusers have a later onset of offending behavior than rapists, commit less deviant behavior over their lifetime, and have a higher level of specialization in sexual offenses.

These findings about the versatility of offending have been consistent with populations of sex offenders internationally as well as populations of juvenile sex offenders. Soothill et al. (2000) examined a sample of convicted sex offenders in England and found that there was a high level of versatility among the offenders in their sample. They did find, however, that when sex offenders recidivated with another sexual offense, it tended to be the same one for which they were originally convicted. Zimring, Piquero, and Jennings (2007) analyzed juveniles with sex crime convictions in Racine, Wisconsin, and found that juvenile sexual offending had little predictive value on likelihood of committing sexual offenses in adulthood. The greatest predictor of adult sexual offending was a large number of nonsexual offenses. These findings were replicated in a longitudinal study of the Philadelphia birth cohort (Zimring, Jennings, Piquero, & Hays, 2009).

Some researchers have further explored the level of specialization among different types of child sexual abusers. Smallbone and Wortley (2004) studied 362 child sexual offenders in Queensland, Australia, and identified four types of offenders: intrafamilial, extrafamilial, mixed-type (consisting of both intra- and extrafamilial offenders), and deniers. They found that 64.4 percent of the offenders had previous convictions, but that 86.3 percent of those convictions were for nonsexual offenses. The mixed offenders—or those least likely to specialize in victim type—had the most sexual offenses of all groups, with 41.7 percent having previous sexual offense convictions. Sixty-two percent of the mixed offender group, however, had nonsexual convictions, indicating versatility even among those with more sexual offense convictions. Smallbone and Wortley (2004) also found that few offenders were driven by sexual disorders, or paraphilias. Less than 12 percent of the child sexual abusers in their sample had any given paraphilia other than pedophilia. In fact, they found that paraphilic activity was more likely to be significantly linked to nonsexual offending than sexual offending (Smallbone & Wortley, 2006). The Smallbone and Wortley (2006) findings were replicated on other populations of child sexual abusers, including child sexual abusers in the Catholic Church (Terry & Ackerman, 2008).

Because of the heterogeneous nature of sexual offenders, no system of classification based on the type and motivation of the offender has universal validity. However, it is important to understand characteristics common to the different types of offenders, as only then can they be treated and managed effectively.

TYPOLOGIES OF RAPISTS

Rapists,[1] like the general population of sex offenders, do not form a homogeneous group. In order to understand why individuals begin offending, researchers have tried to identify common characteristics among sexual assaulters. Although all rapists display differing characteristics, studies have found some cognitive factors to be present in many aggressive offenders, including negative views of women, endorsement of rape myths, condoning violence, and displaying a hyperidentification with the masculine role (Marshall, Laws, & Barbaree, 1990b; Scully, 1990). Many rapists also display personality deficits such as a sense of worthlessness and low self-esteem, a sense of vulnerability, impaired social relations, a dysphoric mood state (with an underlying mood state of anger, fear, and/or depression), and a mismanagement of aggression (Groth, 1983, p. 163). They also exhibit traits of social inadequacy, thus leading to negative emotional states and ultimately resulting in low self-esteem, stress, anxiety, anger, hostility, and aggressive behavior (Marshall, 1989; Marshall & Barbaree, 1990a; McKibben, Proulx, & Lusignan, 1994). Additionally, many rapists have difficulty processing information from women and misconstrue negative cues and messages (Lipton, McDonel, & McFall, 1987; Stermac, Segal, & Gillis, 1990).

Rapists often begin committing deviant sexual acts at a young age; half of the known population of sexual assaulters have attempted or committed their first deviant sexual acts before the age of 18 (Abel & Rouleau, 1990; Benoit & Kennedy, 1992; Epps, 1993; Groth, 1983). Rape-supportive attitudes are seen to be strongest in adolescence, and as such adolescence is critical in the development of sexually aggressive behavior (Groth, Longo, & McFadin, 1982; Herman, 1990; Marshall & Barbaree, 1990a). Because sex drives surge dramatically in young boys at puberty, it is important at this time to establish proper sociosexual interactions. Animal research has shown that the development of controls over sexual behavior arises from a socialization process, and it is necessary for human males to acquire inhibitory controls over this "biologically endowed propensity for self-interest associated with the tendency to fuse sex and aggression" (Marshall & Barbaree, 1990a, p. 257).

Researchers studying rape typologies have commonly classified rapists by the primary motivation of their offenses. Rape typologies can be most broadly categorized as sexual or nonsexual in nature (Barbaree et al., 1994). Though rape is a sexual offense, scholars have shown that nonsexual needs, in particular power and control, most commonly motivate rape (Brownmiller, 1975; Stermac & Segal, 1989). Feminist scholars have discussed how rape is a tool that men use to dominate

---

1. In this section of the text, the term *rapist* refers to a category of offenders who have sexually assaulted an adult. It is not referencing specifically convicted offenders, and does not include offenders who committed an act of assault against a child, even if that offense included penetration.

and control women (Allison & Wrightsman, 1993). Additionally, there is physiological evidence that rape is not driven by sexual needs alone. Some assessment studies of arousal indicate that most rapists are aroused more by consensual than nonconsensual sex (Marshall & Barbaree, 1990b). Rapists also tend to score almost equally to control groups consisting of non-rapists when exposed to violent erotic material (Barbaree et al., 1994). There is also a high incidence of sexual dysfunction during rapes (the offender is either unable to get an erection or ejaculate) (West, 1987). Although this could be attributed to the increased level of anxiety in such circumstances, it is unlikely that sexual dysfunction would occur if rape were based purely on the sexual needs of the offender.

Researchers have categorized rapists into typologies based on the earlier characteristics and motivations for committing offenses (see Burgess, Hartman, Ressler, Douglas, & MacCormack, 1986; Cohen, Garofolo, Boucher, & Seghorn, 1971; Groth, 1979; Knight & Prentky, 1990; Perkins, 1991; Rada, 1978; Scully & Marolla, 1985; Seghorn & Cohen, 1980). Though there are multiple classification systems for rapists, for the purpose of this book the typologies of rapists in the literature can be summarized and classified into four categories: *exclusively sexual*, *sadistic*, *power/control*, and *opportunistic*. Those classified as exclusively sexual and sadistic are motivated by sexual needs, whereas those classified as power/control and opportunistic rapists are motivated by nonsexual needs. Table 5.1 shows these typologies.

TABLE 5.1   Rape Typologies

Typology	Primary Motivation	Characteristics
Compensatory	Sexual	■ Offender uses only as much force as necessary to achieve sexual gratification; ■ May have "courtship disorder"; ■ Feelings of inadequacy; ■ "Gentleman" rapist.
Sadistic	Sexual	■ Offender achieves sexual gratification through pain and/or fear from the victims; ■ Often psychopathic; ■ Offense may lead to sexual murder.
Power/control	Non-sexual	■ An aggressive, pseudo-sexual act; ■ Offender desires power and dominance over the victim; ■ Motivation may be humiliation, degradation; ■ Offender is often angry.
Opportunistic	Non-sexual	■ Recreational/situational offender who leads impulsive, adventure-seeking lifestyle; ■ Assault often committed during another offense; ■ Poor impulse control.

SOURCE: Robertiello & Terry, 2007

The typologies are neither mutually exclusive nor exhaustive and should be regarded as an outline of the most common categorical classifications of rapists. Although some rapists will fit into one of the typologies, most will be cross-classified into one or more categories.

Sexually Motivated Offenses

Exclusively Sexual   Rarely is rape motivated purely by sexual needs; however, this type of rape is labeled here as *exclusively sexual*. These are sometimes labeled *sexual, nonsadistic* rapes (Knight & Prentky, 1990). Like the majority of rapists, offenders who commit a rape because of sexual needs have difficulty achieving normal relationships; they see violence as the only way to secure their goals of sexual gratification (Marshall & Barbaree, 1990a). Freund (1990) describes this as "courtship disorder," or the inability to form a normal relationship with a partner of the same age. Rapists often have problems with intimate relations and feel they lack the ability to establish a satisfying love relationship with a woman (Rada, 1978). These feelings of sexual inferiority are common to rapists and can lead to exaggerated masculine behavior and eventually rape.

Sadistic   Sexually motivated rapes can also be classified as *sadistic*, where offenders achieve sexual gratification from the victims' pain and/or fear (Perkins, 1991). These are the most dangerous sexual offenders, whose crimes may lead to sexual murder. Sadistic rapists tend to be predatory, exhibit a high rate of recidivism (which often occurs shortly after release from institutions), be strangers to their victims, use violence in their offenses, and show little empathy for their victims (Ganzar & Sarason, 1973; Hare & Jutai, 1983; Hare & MacPherson, 1984; Pithers, 1994; Quinsey, Rice, & Harris, 1990; Quinsey, Warneford, Pruesse, & Link, 1975; Serin, 1991; Serin, Malcolm, Khanna, & Barbaree, 1994).

Sadistic rapists share many of the same characteristics as individuals with antisocial personality disorder, though not all sadistic rapists are diagnosed with the disorder (Abel, Becker, & Skinner, 1980). Similar characteristics include impulsivity and aggressiveness, and both sadistic rapists and individuals with antisocial personality disorder tend to live unstable lives with no long-term plans (Hare & MacPherson, 1984; Serin, 1991). Sadistic rapists are often deceitful, irresponsible, and have a reckless disregard for the safety of others. Not only do they lack remorse and show little empathy for their victims, but the pain they cause sexually excites them. They seek out this pain and humiliation in order to become sexually excited, and the level of violence they use often escalates with each offense committed.

Dietz, Hazelwood, and Warren (1990) analyzed 30 sadistic offenders and described how they are different from nonsadistic offenders. Though there were only 30 offenders in their sample, their study provides insight into the sadistic criminal. They claim that the offenders showed a high degree of planning for their offenses, with most taking the victims to a preselected location, binding them, and intentionally torturing them. The types of torture varied, but included acts such as use of torture instruments, inserting foreign objects, beating, biting, whipping, and electric shock. The researchers admit that their study is not generalizable to all sexual sadists; however, it does give insight into this very serious type of offender.

Nonsexually Motivated Offenses

Power/Control   All rapes are inherently motivated by an element of power and control, and many are also motivated by elements of anger, hatred, and aggression. Groth defines rape as a pseudo-sexual act, emphasizing the desire of offenders to achieve power and dominance rather than sexual gratification. He states that rape is "the sexual abuse of power and the sexual expression of needs, motives, and issues that are predominantly nonsexual. It is the sexual expression of aggression rather than the aggressive expression of sexuality" (Groth, 1983, p. 165).

The explanation of rape as motivated by nonsexual needs is supported by feminist theories of rape, which view rape as the consequence of deep-rooted social traditions of male dominance and female exploitation (Ward, 1995). Some theorists expand upon this idea further by saying that sexual assaults are attempts to control and humiliate women (Darke, 1990; West, 1987). Darke proposes that the humiliation of women causes sexual arousal in the offenders, allowing the men to dominate and control vulnerable female victims. Although it may be argued that humiliation is a subjective term and the definition of "humiliating acts" lacks consensus, some researchers have noted an increase in "nastiness" of sexual assaults since the 1980s (Lloyd, 1991). Many victims claim that rapists use insulting and humiliating language during attacks, and force the victims to perform unusual sexual acts that they consider particularly degrading (West, 1987). Lloyd (1991) says that one interpretation of this could be that men who rape have an increasingly misogynistic attitude toward women and these acts are performed to humiliate them; however, these "humiliating" sexual acts could also be representative of consensual sexual acts that are now accepted sexual practices. It is nearly impossible to define "normal" sexual attitudes and behavior today, with society forming a "tolerantly critical acceptance of sexual acts" that would have previously been regarded with moral outrage (Saunders-Wilson, 1992).

The issue of power and control is also evident in rape cases where date-rape drugs, or Rohypnol (a.k.a. "roofies"), are used. This drug can cause the person ingesting it to black out, have memory loss, and lower his or her resistance to sexual abuse. These effects are increased if ingested with alcohol, and this is the likely form of ingestion when used as a date-rape drug. Victims generally report that they are drugged involuntarily when an acquaintance or date slips a dose of Rohypnol, which is odorless, tasteless, and colorless, into their drink. Though Sturman (2000) points out that drug rapes can be either planned or opportunistic, he states that in either situation the offender produces a situation in which he is in control of the victim.

The role of power and control as a motivation for rape is perhaps most apparent through the extensive accounts of rape during wartime. Soldiers in nearly every war have committed mass rapes of the enemy. Rarely, if ever, is rape during war motivated by sexual needs. Because rape is often associated with "the ideology of masculine aggressiveness" (West, 1987, p. 155), the motivation behind rape during wartime is the need for power and domination over other people. Usually occurring when victorious armies march through conquered territories, rape is used as a weapon to demoralize and destroy community honor (Lees, 1996, p. 59). Rape is often viewed as the ultimate humiliation of an enemy because it symbolizes a defiling of its people. War situations encourage an extreme type of machismo associated with a hegemonic form of masculinity (Connell, 1990). There is evidence that some soldiers have been given direct orders from superiors to rape victims both as a part of a military strategy and as a way to motivate hatred of the enemy (Lees, 1996). Although this helps to explain why some "ordinary Joes" (Brownmiller, 1975) are capable of performing sadistic acts that deviate from normal behavior, it does not explain the many victims' accounts that soldiers appeared to enjoy raping and demoralizing them (Seifert, 1993).

Rape in war has occurred throughout history, continuing in many cultures through present-day conflicts. It has been documented in wars of revolution, such as in George Washington's papers in 1780, and in wars of religion as far back as the First Crusade (Brownmiller, 1975). Nonetheless, few detailed accounts had been written about rape until World War I, and it was only with the mass rapes in Bosnia that the issue finally came into the public consciousness (Lees, 1996). Brownmiller has called the gang rape by soldiers a normal rather than abnormal aspect of war, although the extent of rape is dependent on the status of women in society. For example, the Vietcong consider women to have status equal to that of men, and as such they considered rape to be a serious crime (Brownmiller, 1975). In other societies, the women may be viewed either as objects that can be used and discarded (such as with the Jewish women in concentration and rape camps in World War II) or as objects that can be used to eradicate the enemy (such as with the "ethnic cleansing" of Bosnia). Even though international laws have been passed that make rape in wartime a serious offense, rape has continued to proliferate in wars that are both civil in nature (for example, Rwanda, Democratic Republic of Congo) and international (for example, Afghanistan, Iraq).

Opportunistic   Opportunistic offenders, the other category of rapists who are motivated by nonsexual needs, are adventure-seeking individuals who lead impulsive, delinquent lifestyles. Also called "recreational" (Scully & Marolla, 1985) or "situational" (West, 1987) offenders, they usually commit sexual assaults during the course of another crime such as burglary. They are "generalists" who commit more nonsexual crimes than sexual ones. They do not specialize in a particular type of sexual offense, but instead commit a rape in the context of their "routine activities" (as discussed in Chapter 3). In other words, they use the environment to their advantage and may commit an offense if an opportunity presents itself.

Opportunistic offenders tend to be compulsive, and they may have a history of antisocial behavior, characterized by poor social and relationship skills. Many offenders have experienced poor socialization in childhood, which does not allow them access to appropriate sociosexual interactions. This is often facilitated by a violent parenting style, resulting in feelings of resentment, hostility, and the use of aggression (Marshall & Barbaree, 1990a). Langevin et al. (1985) found that many rapists had parents who would administer punishment frequently but inconsistently. He described the fathers as often drunken, aggressive, and in trouble with the law, and said the sons are likely to reproduce this behavior. Knight et al. (1983) further claim that if a boy is taught antisocial behavior and grows up in a hostile home, then there is a greater likelihood that he will become a rapist. A perceived social inadequacy may increase the level of stress and anxiety, which will in turn disinhibit sexual aggression and facilitate offending behavior.

Although these rape typologies look at varying motivations to commit sexual assault, they do not take into consideration the relationship between the offenders and the victims. Some researchers have attempted to form typologies based on multiple axes that take into consideration all of these factors, believing that sexual assault is very different between strangers and acquaintances no matter the motivation (Knight & Prentky, 1990).

TYPOLOGIES OF CHILD SEXUAL ABUSERS

Prior to the 1980s, perpetrators of child sexual abuse were viewed as "a small group of individuals with psychological abnormalities whose emotional disturbances resulted in inappropriate sexual interest in children" (La Fontaine, 1990, p. 99), but this group proved to be neither small nor distinct. It was the emergence of the feminist movement (Brownmiller, 1975), an extensive national survey in Canada that looked at sexual offenses against children (Canada, 1984), and empirical research with large groups of child sexual abusers (for example, Abel & Rouleau, 1990; Finkelhor, 1986) that helped expose the true extent of child sexual abuse.

Many child sexual abusers display characteristics similar to rapists: they tend to be socially inept in adult relations, have low self-esteem, feelings of inadequacy, and a sense of worthlessness and vulnerability. However, they usually exhibit characteristics opposite to those rapists who are overly aggressive, act on impulse, and are insensitive to victims' feelings (West, 1987). Some child sexual abusers are violent; however, these are rare and tend to be extrafamilial offenders who abuse both girls and boys (Porter, 1984). Nonetheless, they usually seek a mutually comforting relationship with a child, and because of their poor social skills they find comfort in relationships with children that they consider to be passive, dependent, psychologically less threatening than adults, and easy to manipulate (Groth, 1983; West, 1987). Offenders who prefer relationships with agemates might regress to adult-child relationships because of a hindrance to normal adult relationships (Finkelhor, 1984; West, 1987). They frequently see themselves as physically unattractive, have problems with potency, have moral inhibitions, or have previously had frustrating experiences with adult relations. There is often a connection between negative affective states and deviant sexual behavior for child sexual abusers; however, unlike rapists, these tend to be states of inadequacy, humiliation, and loneliness rather than anger and hostility (McKibben et al., 1994).

Although several researchers have attempted to develop typologies of child sexual abusers (Groth, Hobson, & Gary, 1982; Howells, 1981; Knight & Prentky, 1990), the existing literature fails to render consistent psychological profiles and characteristics that can distinguish these offenders (Conte, 1991). Some researchers study child sexual abusers based on whether they abuse a child within their family (intrafamilial) or outside the family (extrafamilial). Other researchers explain child sexual abuse along three dimensions: age difference, specific sexual behavior, and sexual intent. Still others have classified offenders into subtypes based on an empirically derived classification system.

Intrafamilial and Extrafamilial Abusers

Most typologies of child sexual abusers distinguish between groups of offenders based on the motivation of their behavior. However, it is also important to understand whether there are differences between offenders based upon the type of victim they target. In this vein, much of the research on child sexual abusers has compared offenders based upon their victim choice and specifically whether the offender and victim are related. Overall, studies have generally found that intrafamilial offenders have a lower risk of reoffending than extrafamilial child sexual abusers. They tend to be older and more educated, and they are as, or more, receptive to treatment than other offenders (Gould, 1994). Many studies have found that alcohol and/or substance abuse is common among intrafamilial offenders, and intrafamilial offenders are more likely to be alcoholics than offenders diagnosed with pedophilia (Lang, Flor-Henry, & Frenzel, 1990). Family tensions and negative affective states are also common in the intrafamilial groups. According to Hanson, Stefly, and Gauthier (1993), intrafamilial offenders are less likely than other types of sex offenders to reoffend.

Langevin and Watson (1991) studied 122 cases of intrafamilial sexual abuse of daughters by fathers and stepfathers. They found that while most offenders had only one victim, the offenders showed high rates of anxiety, had problematic family backgrounds, and showed confused thinking. In a small, qualitative study of intrafamilial offenders, Hartley (2001) found that participants grew up feeling distant from their parents and were commonly rejected by at least one parent. Most offenders in Hartley's study were abused either physically or emotionally and experienced unstable childhoods. They also reported feeling stress in their lives due to jobs, relationships, alcohol, or self-esteem before they began sexually abusing their children. Moreover, these offenders did not have sexual relations with their partners as often as they wanted and had become dissatisfied with the relationship. Some stated that sex was important to them and started to have sexual contact with their daughters to fulfill the desire. Similarly, Miner and Dwyer (1997) found that incestuous fathers who engaged in sexual behaviors with their daughters perceived them as being second wives and expected them to respond as such. Further, Hanson, Gizzarelli, and Scott (1994) found that some intrafamilial offenders, mostly those with a stepdaughter victim, considered their abuse to be an affair.

The link between intrafamilial offenders and alcohol abuse has been consistent amongst several studies. Lang et al. (1988) examined aggressive behaviors and erotic attraction to females at various ages among a group of intrafamilial offenders, heterosexual pedophiles, violent offenders, and a group of volunteers from the community. The authors found that intrafamilial offenders were more likely to engage in alcohol abuse. They also found that intrafamilial offenders were older and often got angry or yelled at the victims to assume control, yet rarely resorted to violent physical behavior. Erickson, Walbek, and Seely (1987) noted differences between fathers and stepfathers who committed acts of sexual abuse; the biological fathers who abused their children were more likely to have anger and marital problems, be hostile, and have passive-aggressive personalities, whereas stepfathers were more likely to be alcoholics, not care about others' feelings, and have a tendency to act out.

Some researchers have studied the link between psychopathy and type of child sexual abuser, with consistent findings that intrafamilial offenders were the least likely group of child sexual abusers to show signs of psychopathy. Firestone, Bardford, Greenberg, and Serran (2000) found a negative relationship between psychopathy and deviant sexual arousal among intrafamilial offenders. This study showed that intrafamilial offenders were the oldest group of offenders and were the least likely to be violent. Similarly, Oliver (2004) examined the psychopathy of 638 extrafamilial child sexual abusers, 460 intrafamilial offenders, and 110 "mixed-type" offenders and found that intrafamilial offenders displayed the lowest amount of psychopathy and did not exhibit behavioral problems or have a lengthy criminal record.

Like other types of child sexual abusers, intrafamilial abusers have been shown to exhibit cognitive distortions that minimize the harm they cause to the victim. Hanson et al. (1994) compared the attitudes of 50 male intrafamilial offenders to those of 25 male batterers and a control group of 25 males who were not receiving any type of treatment. Analysis showed that intrafamilial offenders have more deviant attitudes than the control group and batterers and that they view children as "sexually attractive and sexually motivated." In the study by Hanson et al. (1994), about 58 percent of the intrafamilial offenders had more than one victim, with a majority being female victims. Most offenses in this study involved exposure or touching, with only 28 percent engaging in intercourse. Results indicate that intrafamilial offenders did not report feeling frustrated nor did they view affairs as being unacceptable.

Danni and Hampe (2000) analyzed 168 pedophiles, ephebophiles, and intra-familial offenders in order to differentiate between characteristics of these types of child sexual abusers. They gathered data from the presentence investigation reports and found that eight independent variables—sexually victimized as a child, prepubertal victim, seduction motive, age-appropriate relationships, stress, own child as victim, social façade, and anger—significantly discriminated between these types of sex offenders in approximately 90 percent of the cases. They found that pedophiles were the most likely group to have experienced sexual victimization when they were children, were the most likely to prefer and have prepubertal sex partners, and were the most motivated to seduce their victims. Alternatively, the ephebophiles were the most likely to have experienced external stress, and intrafamilial offenders were the most likely to feel a sense of entitlement to their victims.

Intrafamilial sexual abusers exhibit some types of psychological and emotional difficulties. In a study of the personality of biological intrafamilial abusers, nonbiological intrafamilial abusers (stepfathers), extrafamilial abusers, and non-sex offenders, Dennison et al. (2001) found that extrafamilial and nonbiological intrafamilial abusers have higher levels of anxiety. The study found no difference between levels of impulsiveness and hostility, but all sex offenders had high levels of depression and self-consciousness. Participants who committed intrafamilial abuse against immediate family members and extrafamilial members had low levels of extraversion while all intrafamilial offenders had low levels of both assertiveness and openness. These findings suggest the possibility that intrafamilial abusers are more conventional and closed minded. Nonoffenders had slightly higher levels of openness to experience; however, both nonoffenders and intra-familial abuser step-parents had higher levels of fantasies. Intrafamilial immediate family and extrafamilial offenders both showed low levels of deliberation showing that they were more likely to suffer from self-esteem and self-control problems.

Some researchers have evaluated the relationship between brain pathology and sexual behavior among child sexual abusers. Langevin et al. (1989) analyzed the probability of the presence of brain damage and dysfunction in 160 extrafa-milial child sexual abusers, 123 intrafamilial offenders, and 108 sexual aggressors as compared to a control group of 36 nonviolent and non-sex offenders. They found no differences between the different types of offenders in regard to alcohol and drug use, use of violence, educational levels, and whether the offenders admitted the abuse. However, intrafamilial offenders were significantly older than offenders in other groups.

Some research on intrafamilial offenders has shown that many offenders do not "specialize" in abusing a particular type of victim. Studer et al. (2002) analyzed past convictions and self-reports of 150 intrafamilial offenders and 178 extrafamilal offenders. This study found that 22 percent of the intrafamilial sexual offenders had other extrafamilial sexual offenses, and about 58 percent of the intrafamilial offenders had additional nonsexual crimes. About 53 percent of offenders who targeted biological children had additional extrafamilial victims while about 62 percent of the intrafamilial offenders who targeted nonbiological victims (stepchildren) had extrafamilial victims. Gould (1994) studied a sample of 86 extra-familial and intrafamilial abusers receiving outpatient treatment and 53 who were incarcerated. Though only 20 percent were previously arrested for other sex offenses and 15 percent were arrested for nonsexual crimes, 67 percent had been sexually involved with children before the arrest. Further, this study showed that 43 percent of intrafamilial offenders had extrafamilial victims while only 18 percent of extrafamilial offenders had incestuous victims.

Thus, while many "intrafamilial" sexual offenders do not necessarily specialize in abusing children within their families, they do tend to differ from child sexual abusers who primarily target victims outside the family. The intrafamilial offenders are generally characterized as regressed or situational offenders, discussed following, and exhibit the characteristics of those offenders. This has important implications for treatment, supervision, and management of these offenders.

The Fixated-Regressed Typologies

Classification of child sexual abusers began in earnest in the 1970s, when researchers began to distinguish the types of child sexual abusers based on their motivation for committing sexually deviant behavior. In the early 1980s, Groth, Hobson, and Gary (1982) proposed a fundamental classification scheme rooted around two basic concepts: the degree to which the deviant sexual behavior is entrenched in the abuser and the basis for psychological needs. Based on this distinction, Groth created the fixated-regressed dichotomy of sex offending, where the fixated offender is characterized as having a persistent, continual, and compulsive attraction to children and the regressed offender tends to be situational and precipitated by external stressors (Terry & Tallon, 2004). This classification system for child sexual abusers is the basis for most typologies of child sexual abusers, even those that add factors relating to social competence and level of interaction with children.

Fixated Offenders   *Fixated offenders* are individuals who exhibit persistent, continual, and compulsive attraction to children. They tend to be exclusively involved with children, and are usually attracted to children from adolescence (Finkelhor, 1984). Fixated offenders are most likely to choose extrafamilial victims who are either male adolescents or prepubescent girls (Abel & Rouleau, 1990; Simon, Sales, Kaskniak, & Kahn, 1992; West, 1987). Fixated offenders show psychological and emotional characteristics of children (Holmes & Holmes, 2002), and they do not develop sexually to the point of finding agemates attractive and desirable. They are often unable to attain any degree of psychosexual maturity and, during adulthood, have virtually no age-appropriate sexual relationships. The fixated offenders' desires are embedded in their psyche, and as such their actions usually do not result from the negative thoughts and feelings of the offense cycle discussed in Chapter 4.

Because of fixated offenders' sexual attraction to children or adolescents, researchers claim that they constitute both "a public health problem" (Abel,

Lawry, Kalstrom, Osborn, & Gillespie, 1994) and a "criminal problem" (Freeman-Longo, 1996). They recruit, groom, and develop relationships with vulnerable children (in an emotional and/or a situational sense), and these "relationships" often continue for several years (Conte, 1991). Because of their own inappropriate desires, many fixated offenders believe that their sexual relationships with children are caring and mutual, and that the child is able to derive pleasure and educational experience from the interaction (Abel & Rouleau, 1995; Marshall & Barbaree, 1990b).

Most fixated child sexual abusers have committed more offenses than those for which they have been convicted, and for that reason they constitute a high risk to the community. The extensive grooming process often creates a close personal relationship between the offender and the victim, and as a result the victims are less likely to report the abuse, or when they do report the abuse, there is a significant delay in reporting (Abel & Rouleau, 1990; Abel et al., 1994; Elliot, Browne, & Kilcoyne, 1995). Fixated offenders who abuse boys are likely to commit more offenses than other types of offenders, and of all child sexual abusers they seem to be at the highest risk of reoffending (Marques, Day et al., 1994; Marques, Nelson et al., 1994).

Regressed Offenders   Unlike the fixated offenders, child sexual abusers classified as *regressed* have a primary attraction to agemates. Their abusive behavior is not fixed, but rather is a temporary departure from their attraction to adults (Simon et al., 1992). The regressed offenders' behavior, which usually emerges in adulthood, tends to be precipitated by external stressors. These stressors, which are an important part of the offense cycle, can be situational in nature (for example, unemployment, marital problems, substance abuse), or they can be related to negative affective states (for example, loneliness, isolation). These stressors often lead to poor self-confidence, low self-esteem, and a self-pitying attitude (Schwartz, 1995), which subsequently lead to the abusive behavior.

Most regressed offenders develop normal relationships with agemates, and in fact many are married or cohabiting. They begin committing deviant sexual acts at times when they are having negative thoughts and feelings, like those represented in the offense cycle; commonly these negative thoughts and feelings develop at times of unrest with marital relations or as a result of stress, loneliness, and depression. Regressed offenders are rarely attracted to a particular type of child or adolescent in terms of age and gender. Instead, they victimize children to whom they have easy access—often their own children. Intrafamilial offenders tend to spend most of their time with their family and isolate the family from society in general (Miner & Dwyer, 1997). Intrafamilial relations are often more common and more severe in stepparent families, with the most frequent sexual relation occurring between stepfathers and stepdaughters (Redding Police Department, 1996).

Sexual abuse by a relative can be very traumatic, often more so than a stranger assault, because it is difficult for the victim to avoid contact with the perpetrator and cease such relations (West, 1987). Sexual acts among family members are also likely to be more intimate than abuse by strangers. Stranger assaults often consist of mild abuses such as exhibitionism or fondling, which are not physically intrusive in nature (La Fontaine, 1990). Though most intrafamilial offenders prefer heterosexual relationships, they form sexual relations with the children they have access to, regardless of the gender. Studies do not show child sexual abuse (either intrafamilial or extrafamilial) to be more prevalent in particular ethnic groups, and, contrary to popular perception, there is no significant difference between abuse in urban and rural areas and among various economic and social classes (La Fontaine, 1990).

Intrafamilial offenders almost always fit the regressed typology, since they tend to be attracted to agemates and develop relations with children for nonsexual reasons. Studies have found that incestuous offenders, like most regressed offenders, have similar arousal patterns to "normal" men (Freund, McKnight, Langevin, & Cibiri, 1972; Marshall & Eccles, 1991; Quinsey, Steinman, Bergerson, & Holmes, 1975). Sexual arousal is most commonly measured through a penile plethysmograph (PPG) as the male is shown erotic material. The control group ("normal" men) generally shows some level of arousal to photos of young children in erotic poses, and it is therefore difficult to differentiate between the groups of normal and regressed offenders. Fixated offenders, on the other hand, tend to show a strong level of attraction to the erotic material involving children. This indicates that, as with rapists, not all child sexual abusers are motivated by sexual needs to commit their offenses.

The fixated-regressed classification system is not only based upon the degree of sexual attraction to children, but also the degree of violence or force used in the sexually abusive act. Groth, Longo, and McFadin (1982) make a distinction between a sex-pressure offense and a sex-force offense. A *sex-pressure offense* is one where the offender either entices or entraps the victim into cooperating. Here the offender would prefer the victim to cooperate, and if the victim resists, it is unlikely that the offender will follow through with the abuse. Alternatively, in a *sex-force offense* the offender uses either intimidation or physical aggression. These offenders attempt to intimidate victims who can easily be overpowered and present little resistance toward the sexual advance. If the victim does resist, the sex-force offender is more likely to use physical aggression to commit the act of abuse, despite the resistance.

Since it was originally proposed, researchers have tested and expanded upon the fixated-regressed typology, though the concept of a motivation-based classification system has remained constant. The level of attraction to children is a common variable on which to base any classification system for child sexual abusers, though this is not a dichotomous typology. Rather, the fixated-regressed typology is a continuum. Offenders are not simply attracted to children or agemates, but they have varying levels of attraction toward children.

Simon et al. (1992), who attempted to empirically validate the fixated-regressed typology, found support in their study for such a continuum. They reviewed the cases of 136 child sexual abusers, looking at case history, Minnesota Multiphasic Personality Inventory (MMPI) results, presentence reports, and police report data. They found a continuous distribution of offenders rather than the bimodal, dichotomous classification, and said that in order for the

TABLE 5.2   Fixated-Regressed Typologies of Child Molesters

Typology	Motivation	Victim preference	Risk of reoffending
Fixated	■ Having never developed an attraction to age-appropriate partners, the fixated offender has a persistent, continual, and compulsive attraction to children; ■ Behavior emerges in adolescence; ■ Offenses are premeditated in nature and do not stem from stressors; ■ Most likely to be diagnosed with pedophilia/ephebohilia.	■ Extrafamilial; ■ Female (prepubescent), male (pubescent/adolescent); ■ Typically recruits vulnerable children and engages in extensive grooming in order to ensure the continuation of the abuse.	■ Higher risk of recidivism; ■ The risk of recidivism increases according to the number of victims.
Regressed	■ Offending stems from stressors in the individuals environment which undermine self esteem and confidence; ■ Behavior emerges in adulthood; ■ Offending is a departure from the offender's attraction to adults; ■ Similar to rapists, the offender is not necessarily motivated by sexual needs alone.	■ Intrafamilial, acquaintance; ■ Gender varies, depending on who is accessible; ■ Tend to victimize children to whom they have easy access.	■ Since they are not sexually fixated on children, they are at a lower risk of reoffending if treated; ■ Capable of feeling remorse for their actions.

SOURCE: John Jay College (2004)

fixated–regressed typology to be correct, it must be considered on a continuum. Table 5.2 outlines the fixated–regressed typologies of child sexual abusers discussed in this chapter.

The FBI Typologies

In constructing their classification system, the Federal Bureau of Investigation (FBI) used Groth's fixated-regressed typologies as a basis and expanded upon them, classifying child sexual abusers into seven distinct subgroups. These seven

TABLE 5.3   FBI Typologies of Child Molesters

Type of offender	Characteristics of offenders
	Situational offenders
Regressed	Offenders have poor coping skills, target victims who are easily accessible, abuse children as a substitute for adult relationships.
Morally indiscriminate	Offenders do not prefer children over adults and tend to use children (or anyone accessible) for their own interests (sexual and otherwise).
Sexually indiscriminate	Offenders are mainly interested in sexual experimentation, and abuse children out of boredom.
Inadequate	Offenders are social misfits who are insecure, have low self-esteem, and see relationships with children as their only sexual outlet.
	Preferential offenders
Seductive	Offenders "court" children and give them much affection, love, gifts, and enticements in order to carry on a "relationship."
Fixated	Offenders have poor psychosexual development, desire affection from children, and are compulsively attracted to children.
Sadistic	Offenders are aggressive, sexually excited by violence, target stranger victims, and are extremely dangerous.

SOURCE: Terry and Tallon (2004, p. 28)

subgroups correspond directly to the original regressed (regressed, morally indiscriminate, sexually indiscriminate, and inadequate) and fixated (seduction, introverted, and sadistic) typologies. Though these typologies are an expansion of the basic fixated-regressed classification system, little research has been done to empirically validate this classification system. As such, few scholars cite the FBI typologies today. Table 5.3 summarizes the characteristics of each of these types of offenders.

The MTC:CM3 Typologies

Like the FBI, Knight and Prentky (1990) also took into consideration issues of social competence and decision-making skills when they revised their original typologies of child sexual abusers and arranged a model based on their degree of fixation and degree of contact. They developed multidimensional typologies of child sexual abusers through a system known as the Massachusetts Treatment Center: Child Molester Typology, version 3 (MTC:CM3). This classification system is based on two axes: Axis I evaluates the level of fixation with children and the offender's level of social competence; Axis II evaluates the amount of contact, both interpersonal and sexual, that an offender has with children, including the amount and type of physical injury resulting from the contact. Each offender is assigned a separate Axis I and Axis II typology. Studies show that this classification system has a reasonable level of reliability and consistent ties to developmental antecedents of child sexual abuse (Knight & Prentky, 1990). This classification system also has distinctive prognostic implications, as shown in the preliminary results of a 25-year recidivism study conducted by the same researchers.

Other researchers have conducted studies to replicate the findings by Knight and Prentky. Looman et al. (2001) conducted a study in Canada, whereby they classified 109 child sexual abusers in accordance with the MTC:CM3 typology. They were able to classify all of the offenders except for the sadistic types into all subgroups with an acceptable level of reliability, thus replicating the original results. They found differences between the subgroups in phallometric assessments, with the high fixation–low social competence group showing the highest levels of sexual deviance on the Axis I assessment. The only group to show a clear fixation, or sexual preference for children, was the high fixation–low social competence group, the majority of whom preferred male victims and were more likely to have been victimized as children. The deviance indices for their sample for all four levels of Axis I indicated that child sexual abusers fail to differentiate between appropriate and inappropriate stimuli. The preferential (high fixation) child sexual abusers had the highest level of deviant sexual arousal and the greatest numbers of victims, but they caused the least amount of physical harm.

When analyzing the Axis II indices, Looman and colleagues found that low contact–high injury offenders were the most intrusive in their offenses and were the most likely to use physical force. This group also had a greater number of victims, were more likely to target strangers, and were the most likely to have deviant sexual arousal. Most offenders classified into Axis II groupings were equally likely to choose male and female victims except for the exploitative group, who were significantly more likely to choose female than male victims. Table 5.4 outlines the axes of the MTC:CM3 classification scheme.

T A B L E 5.4   **Knight and Prentky's MTC:CM3 Classification System**

Axis	Description of Axis Measurement
Axis I	▪ Assesses the extent to which the offender is fixated with children (on a continuum)
	▪ Measures the level of social competence of the offender
Axis II	▪ Assesses the amount of contact the offender has with children (e.g., exclusively involved with extrafamilial children, abuses own children)
	▪ Meaning of the contact (sexual and interpersonal)
	▪ Amount and type of physical injury involved in the contact (including threats and use of force)

SOURCE: Terry and Tallon (2004, p. 30)

Other Typologies

The level of fixation is not the only factor on which typologies of child sexual abusers are based. Some researchers have examined the static information related to sex offenders to see if their background history is linked to their current abusive behavior, creating typologies based on this information. For example, Baxter, Marshall, Barbaree, Davidson, and Malcolm (1984) conducted a study whereby they analyzed the criminal records, personal history, social-sexual competence, and phallometric responses of incarcerated pedophiles, ephebophiles, and rapists. Their results showed that each of these groups had significantly different criminal and personal backgrounds, though all showed traits of social and social-sexual inadequacy, lack of assertiveness, low self-esteem, and negative attitudes. Otherwise, pedophiles were older, more poorly educated, less likely to be married, were rarely involved in nonsexual crime, and had a higher level of recidivism for sexual offenses. They also showed a higher degree of deviant sexual arousal, or, more specifically, they failed to show a sexual response or erotic preference for adults.

In another study, Simkins (1993) conducted an exploratory investigation to determine how sexually repressed and nonrepressed child sexual abusers in therapy progress, measuring this change on a battery of personality and research instruments. He categorized 68 child sexual abusers as repressed, nonrepressed, or exploitive based on their psychosexual histories. He found that the sexually repressed child sexual abusers were significantly less likely to complete therapy. He also found the differences between these classifications of offenders on the MMPI, the Burt Rape Myth Scales, some of the Multiphasic Sexual Inventory Scales, and the Mosher's Sex Guilt Scale.

Laws, Hanson, Osborn, and Greenbaum (2000) conducted a study with 124 child sexual abusers who voluntarily participated in treatment, where the aim was to determine the extent to which multiple measures of pedophilic interest improved the diagnostic accuracy of any single measure. All participants admitted that they had a sexual attraction to children or had committed a sexual act with a child. Only 72 of the child sexual abusers completed the treatment program, and those completed a self-report card-sort measure of sexual interest and had their levels of sexual arousal measured with a PPG (with both audio and visual stimuli). All three measures used to assess pedophilic interest (that is, card sort, PPG slides, PPG audio) significantly differentiated boy-object and girl-object child sexual abusers. Though the card-sort measure showed the greatest classification accuracy, all three measures together showed a classification accuracy of 91.7 percent.

TYPOLOGIES OF FEMALE SEX OFFENDERS

Little is known about female sexual offenders. The research that exists on this population is comprised mainly of studies with small samples, many of which produce conflicting results. What we do know is that female sexual abuse is reported less than male sexual abuse (Travin et al., 1990), the age of onset is generally young (Ray & English, 1995), female sexual offenders usually have young victims (Fehrenbach & Monastersky, 1988), and their offending behavior is often linked to abusive backgrounds and/or psychological disorders (Bumby & Bumby, 1997).

Most studies on female sexual offenders have small sample sizes because there are so few females convicted of sexual offenses. While females make up about 2 percent of the adult sex offender population, they make up approximately 10 percent of adolescent offenders (13–18 years of age) and nearly 20 percent of child offenders (12 years of age and under) (Ray & English, 1995). Because of the small sample sizes, many studies of female sex offenders are case studies. As such, they produce valuable qualitative information about the female offenders, but this information is not necessarily generalizable to the larger female sex offender population.

Some of the larger studies of female sex offenders show that the average age of adult female sex offenders is mid-20s to mid-30s (Vandiver, Cheeseman Dial, & Worley, 2008; Vandiver & Walker, 2002). Their victims are usually children rather than adults, and the majority of their victims are under the age of 12 (Freeman & Sandler, 2008). They are just as likely to have male and female victims (Vandiver & Kercher, 2004), and they are often exposed to their victims in caretaking roles (Vandiver & Walker, 2002). Adolescent female offenders most often meet their victims through a babysitting role (Fehrenbach & Monastersky, 1988). Many adult female sex offenders have male co-offenders (Vandiver, 2006; Vandiver et al., 2008), and the victims in co-offending cases are more often female (Freeman & Sandler, 2008).

Most female sex offenders have been victims of abuse (Fehrenbach & Monastersky, 1988; Jennings, 2000; Lewis & Stanley, 2000; Vandiver et al., 2008), and many have a history of maltreatment and severe sexual victimization (Travin et al., 1990; Vandiver & Walker, 2002). The sexual abuse against them was most often perpetrated when they were prepubescent, generally by the age of 6 (Gannon, Rose, & Ward, 2008; Vandiver et al., 2008). Many female sex offenders are in abusive relationships at the time of their offending (Gannon, Rose, & Ward, 2008), and this is particularly true for those who are co-offenders (Vandiver, 2006). Female sex offenders are more likely than their male counterparts to use alcohol and illegal drugs (Freeman & Sandler, 2008), a characteristic consistent with "regressed" offending described earlier. Some qualitative studies have also indicated that female offenders have low IQs (bordering on mental retardation) (Lewis & Stanley, 2000).

Researchers have attempted to classify female sex offenders into typologies, though these typologies differ significantly from typologies of male offenders. The most established typologies for females offenders were proposed by Matthews, Matthews, and Speltz, (1989) and Vandiver and Kercher (2004). Matthews et al. (1989) constructed three typologies of adult female sex offenders: teacher/lover, male coerced/male accompanied, and predisposed (see Table 5.5). The *teacher/lover* typology is composed of women who initiate sexual abuse of

TABLE 5.5   Matthews et al (1989) Typologiesof Female Offenders

Typology	Description
Teacher/lover	■ Initiate sexual abuse of adolescent males and seek loving relationships with them; ■ Have significant cognitive distortions of justification and minimization of harm; ■ Do not regard their actions as abuse.
Male coerced/male accompanied	■ Influenced by male abusers to sexually offend; ■ Have a low self-esteem; ■ Often abuse drugs and/or alcohol; ■ Are often in an abusive relationship with the male who coerces them to offend.
Predisposed	■ Initiate the sexual abuse; ■ Most common victims are their own children; ■ History of sexual and physical abuse; ■ Deviant and/or violent sexual fantasies; ■ Seeking power and control; ■ May have serious psychological disorders.

SOURCE: Matthews et al. (1989)

adolescent males. These females tend to have severe cognitive distortions, particularly in denial of the harm they cause to the victims. They are often seeking a loving relationship and, like fixated male child sexual abusers, see their actions as loving and caring. They often do not regard their abuse of the victim as harmful, but rather see themselves in relationship with the children they are abusing.

The *male-coerced/male-accompanied* typology of female sexual offenders consists of females who are influenced by male abusers to sexually offend. These women tend to have low self-esteem, are often unassertive, have poor social and relationship skills, are dependent upon others, and often abuse substances. Their male partners who coerce them to offend are often abusive and violent, and there is likely a history of domestic violence among the partners. Many (approximately half of the adult female sexual offenders in most samples) are coerced into abusing by male partners. Nathan and Ward (2002) found that many of the females in the male-coerced typology were motivated by anger, rejection, and revenge. Though the male-coerced/male-accompanied typology is common among adult females, female adolescent offenders are rarely coerced into offending by male partners (Fehrenbach & Monastersky, 1988).

The *predisposed* female offender is the most dangerous and abusive classification of offenders. These females initiate the sexual abuse, often against their own children or other family members. Nearly all of these offenders were abused as children, both physically and sexually. They are often angry and may have deviant sexual fantasies in terms of both sexual attraction and violence (for example, sadism). They are often seeking power and control and are the most likely of the female offenders to have serious psychological disorders.

Syed and Williams (1996) enhanced the Matthews et al. (1989) typology system by adding two categories of offenders. The first is the angry-impulsive offender, who expresses anger and the need for power and control similarly to the predisposed offender, but has fewer psychosocial disorders. The second is the male-accompanied familial and nonfamilial offenders, to differentiate between incestuous and nonincestuous abusers, because nonincestuous abusers tend to be more serious in terms of number of victims and types of offenses.

Further expanding on these typologies, Vandiver and Kercher (2004) created typology system for female sex offenders consisting of six categories (see Table 5.6). These typologies are based upon the characteristics of the offenders and victims, and not on motivational factors.

According to Vandiver and Kercher (2004), the *heterosexual nurturers* are frequently in a caretaking role to the victim at the time of the offense. They usually view the relationship as nonabusive, and they are more likely to victimize males. *Noncriminal homosexual offenders* often work in conjunction with co-offenders and are more likely to have female victims. *Female sexual predators* are the most likely to be rearrested for a sexual offense. They were also more likely to have previous or future arrests for a crime other than a sexual offense. *Young*

TABLE 5.6   Vandiver and Kercher (2004) Typologies of Female Offenders

Typology	Description
Heterosexual nurturers	■ Frequently in a caretaking role to the victim; ■ View the relationship as non-abusive; ■ Most likely to victimize males.
Noncriminal homosexual offenders	■ Often have co-offenders; ■ More likely to have female victims.
Female sexual predators	■ Likely to have previous or future arrests for non-sexual offenses; ■ Highest level of recidivism.
Young adult child exploiters	■ Offenders are younger at the time of offense; ■ Often abuse their own children.
Homosexual criminals	■ Motivated by economic rather than sexual desires; ■ May force their victims into prostitution; ■ High likelihood of contact with law enforcement.
Aggressive homosexual offenders	■ Victims are adult women; ■ Offenders and victims are often in relationships prior to offense.

SOURCE: Vandiver & Kercher (2004)

adult child exploiters are the mothers who sexually abuse their own children. They are usually younger at the time of the offense. *Homosexual criminals* tend to be motivated by economic rather than sexual desires. They frequently force their victims into prostitution. These are the offenders most likely to come into contact with law enforcement. *Aggressive homosexual offenders* are most likely to victimize older women. This group accounts for sexual assault among homosexual couples.

All of the information about female sex offenders should be considered with caution, as most studies are not conducted on large samples. Little is known about the female sex offender population, especially when compared to the male sex offender population.

CASE STUDY

DEBRA LAFAVE: Understanding the Female Offender

Debra LaFave was a teacher at Grecco Middle School in Temple Terrace, Florida (LaFave & Simon, 2006). In 2004, at the age of 23, she met a 14-year-old student at one of the school's football games. She chaperoned a field trip that he attended, and later began spending more time with him (Crossing the Line, 2006). She began attending his football games, driving him home from games, inviting him to her classroom before school started, and frequently spoke to him on the telephone (LaFave & Simon, 2006).

When the boy left middle school, LaFave applied for a job at King High School to remain close to the boy. It was during this time that LaFave committed her first criminal act by performing oral sex on the boy while he was at her house one evening (Crossing the Line, 2006). A couple of days after this incident, LaFave and the young boy had sexual intercourse in her classroom. LaFave and the boy had sexual intercourse numerous times throughout the following weeks, all after LaFave picked him up from his home (Lafave & Simon, 2006).

The young boy's parents eventually found out about the meetings between LaFave and their son. After authorities placed wiretapping equipment on the boy's phone and overheard a conversation between the boy and LaFave in which the extent of their relationship was discussed, police arrested LaFave. LaFave was charged with two counts of lewd and lascivious battery on a person under the age of 16 in Hillsborough County as well as two counts of lewd and lascivious battery and one count of lewd and lascivious exhibition in Marion County, as she had engaged in sexual activity with the boy in a neighboring county (LaFave & Simon, 2006).

On November 22, 2005, LaFave plead guilty to two counts of lewd and lascivious battery. The sentence of three years house arrest and followed by seven years of probation; a 10 P.M. to 6 A.M. curfew; no living within 1000 feet of a school, church, or playground; no working with or around children; four years of psychological therapy; annual polygraph tests; no contact with the victim until he was 18 and the court approves; no profiting from her celebrity status; no possession of pornography; and no driving alone without the approval of a probation officer were approved by both county prosecutors (Rondeaux, 2005).

Questions
1. What is the typology that best fits Debra LaFave?
2. Is the punishment of three years of house arrest and seven years of probation appropriate? Why or why not?
3. Should she be allowed to have children? Explain the ethical arguments for and against this.

© Cengage Learning

DID YOU KNOW...?

- **Did you know** that female offenders have a lower rate of recidivism than male offenders?

- **Did you know** that most research on sex offender typologies has been conducted since the 1970s? Prior to that time, little was known about sex offenders as a unique group. Instead, the scholars who studied them primarily focused on individuals and case studies. How much do you think our knowledge will develop in the next half-century?

© Cengage Learning

CHAPTER SUMMARY

- Individuals who commit sexual offenses share a number of common characteristics, and as such it is possible to create typologies of offenders based on these commonalities. Although researchers have devised a variety of sophisticated typologies, very few offenders fit precisely into any one category.

- Most typologies are based on the offenders' motivation for committing the deviant acts (for example, sexual versus nonsexual needs). Other typologies consider the type of victim and/or the level of social competence of the offender.

- Rapists commonly commit offenses for nonsexual reasons, in particular out of a desire for power and control. This is also true of rapes that occur during wartime, as the rape leads to further humiliation of the enemy.

- The most common basic typology for child sexual abusers is the fixated-regressed model. Fixated offenders are primarily attracted to children, whereas regressed offenders are primarily attracted to agemates; they regress to abusing children at times of upheaval in their lives (for example, ending of a marriage, loss of a job, stress at work).

- Typologies for female offenders differ from those for male offenders. Some of the female typologies take into consideration the role of co-offenders as well the relationship between the offender and victim (for example, as caretaker). However, most studies of female offenders have small samples, and it is not clear whether these typologies are generalizable.

DISCUSSION QUESTIONS

1. What is the benefit of creating typologies of offenders?

2. What is the most common motivation of rapists? Explain through supporting evidence how we know this.

3. Typologies of child sexual abusers are based primarily on what factor? How have typologies of child sexual abusers evolved over the past 20 years?

4. Why do you think typologies cannot be applied to both male and female offenders? Should the typologies described in this chapter be applicable to offenders in other special groups (such as offenders in the church, military, or prison)?

5. If most sex offenders do not "specialize" in sexual offending or selecting particular types of victims, is it even necessary to create typologies?

6

Juvenile Offenders

Much of the literature on sexual offending relates to adult male offenders. Juvenile sexual offenders do, however, constitute a relatively significant percentage of the population of known sexual offenders. The juvenile population is unique from the adult sex offender population in their characteristics, in their motivations, and in the way that they are treated and supervised. Knowledge of this population is limited, largely because of the lack of reporting or delays in reporting. Much of the information that does exist on juvenile sex offenders comes from self-report studies of adults who retroactively discuss their deviant adolescent behavior (Weinrott, 1996). Despite the low level of empirical knowledge about juvenile sex offenders, they are being subject to increasingly harsh penalties in the criminal justice system. Recent longitudinal recidivism studies indicate, however, that extensive, harsh penalties are not warranted for the large majority of juvenile sex offenders (Zimring, Jennings, Piquero, & Hays, 2009; Zimring, Piquero, & Jennings, 2007).

Juveniles who sexually offend vary significantly in age, understanding of sexual issues, development, maturity, and availability of coping mechanisms (Knight & Prentky, 1993). Like adult offenders, they form a heterogeneous group and commit a variety of offenses (Harris, 2000). Clinicians and researchers note two distinct groups of juvenile offenders: adolescent and preadolescent offenders. Both groups offend for a variety of reasons, and there are no universally accepted theoretical models that can explain why either group begins and continues to offend (American Psychiatric Association [APA], 1999). There are, however, characteristics, pathologies, and histories common to many juvenile sex offenders. The aim of this chapter is to present an overview of juvenile sexual offenders, their characteristics, how they are treated and managed, and concerns about the increasing sanctions for them in the adult criminal justice system. For a much more in-depth understanding of issues related to juvenile sex offenders, see Ryan, Leversee, and Lane (2010).

WHO ARE JUVENILE SEXUAL OFFENDERS?

Because the majority of literature regarding sex offenders focuses on the adult male population, it is surprising to find that juveniles commit a large number of the known sexual crimes. There are some similarities between adult and juvenile sex offenders, particularly in terms of the etiology of offending behavior, their patterns of behavior, their social characteristics, and the cognitive distortions that help them to maintain the behavior (Ryan, 1999). However, Ryan states that when compared to adults, juveniles tend to be either less aware of the harm they cause as a result of their behavior or more aware and thus more uncomfortable. Shaw, Lewis, Loeb, Rosado, and Rodriguez (2000) found that there is no significant difference between the victims of juvenile and adult sex offenders in terms of the type of offense committed, whether there was penetration during the offense, and the amount of force used by the perpetrator. Alternatively, Allard-Dansereau, Haley, Hamane, and Bernard-Bonnin (1997) found that young sexual aggressors were more likely to engage in penetrative acts than were adult aggressors.

Epps (1999) found many traits in juvenile sex offenders that are similar to those in adult sex offenders, including low self-esteem, poor social skills, peer relationship difficulties, social isolation and loneliness, emotional problems, shyness and timidity, educational and academic problems, intellectual and neurological impairments, psychiatric problems, gender identity confusion, feelings of confused masculinity, problems arising from sexual and physical victimization, sexual deviancy and dysfunction, substance abuse, and family problems (p. 11). Though all studies on juvenile sex offenders do not support Epps's assertion that these characteristics are significantly increased in juvenile sex offenders compared to nonsexual offenders, nonoffenders, or adults, many find similar trends.

Prevalence, Recidivism, and Characteristics

It is pertinent to understand not only the prevalence of sexual offending by juveniles but also the likelihood that juveniles will continue to offend into adulthood. Several studies have shown that serious sexual predators who have a long history of sexual offending began those careers as juveniles. Additionally, paraphilias often develop prior to adulthood (Abel, Mittleman, & Becker, 1985). For this serious group of adult sexual offenders with a history of recidivism, those who had sexual convictions as adolescents generally commit more offenses as adults (Abel, Rouleau, & Cunningham-Rather, 1986). However, studies show that most juveniles who commit sexual offenses do not fit into this category of serious, recidivist offenders (Caldwell, 2007; Zimring et al., 2007, 2009).

Using longitudinal data, Zimring et al. (2007) analyzed the offending patterns of individuals in Racine, Wisconsin, who had sexual offense convictions as juveniles. They found that juvenile sexual offending had little predictive value on likelihood of committing sexual offenses in adulthood. The greatest predictor of adult sexual offending was a large number of nonsexual offenses. Zimring et al. (2009) replicated the findings of the Racine study using a separate longitudinal database in Philadelphia. They again found that juvenile sexual offenders tend to be generalists and commit more nonsexual than sexual offenses, and that a large number of nonsexual offenses is the best predictor of future offending. This is consistent with findings in other studies on juvenile sexual offenders (Burton & Meezan, 2004; Carpentier, Leclerc, & Proulx, 2011; Ryan et al., 2010). Burton and Meezan (2004) found that juveniles who sexually offend are about four times more likely to commit more nonsexual offenses than sexual ones. This is also fitting with research on juvenile offenders generally, the majority of whom are adolescent-limited rather than life-course persistent offenders (Moffitt, 1993).

Despite the low levels of recidivism for juvenile sexual offenders, it is important to understand the characteristics of the juveniles who have offended. The most prominent study on juvenile sexual offenders was published by the National Adolescent Perpetrator Network (NAPN) (1993), an organization that collected data on 1,600 juvenile sex offenders in 30 states. Though this report was published two decades ago, it is still cited today as one of the most comprehensive reports on juvenile sexual offending. That said, it is not without its critics, and some of the findings of the report have come under scrutiny (Zimring, 2004). The NAPN Task Force consisted of experts in the field of adolescent sexual abuse, who together produced a report that suggested treatment and institutional and legal reforms for juvenile sexual offenders. The report culminated in a list 387 "assumptions," or recommendations. Despite the comprehensiveness of the report, Zimring (2004) criticized the Task Force's lack of a distinction between sexual abuse and sexual deviancy, their insistence upon the necessity of punishment and treatment, the confusion between legal and medical issues, and the questions not asked by the Task Force.

With those limitations in mind, the NAPN (1993) report provided insight into the characteristics of juvenile sex offenders and their victims. It showed that 90 percent of juvenile sex offenders are male, and 60 percent penetrate the victim in some way. This study also showed that the majority of juvenile sex offenders have committed nonsexual offenses, and only about 7 percent committed only sexual offenses. In other words, most juvenile sexual offenders are not "specialists," as shown by Zimring et al. (2007, 2009). The age range for juvenile sex offenders in the NAPN data sample was 5 to 19, with an average age of just over 14 years. Broken down, the average age for male offenders was nearly 15 years, whereas females were younger, at just over 13 years. This estimate has been supported by other studies which have found that modal age for juvenile sex offenders is between 14 and 15 years old (Hanser & Mire, 2008). A literature review by Davis and Leitenberg (1987) showed the average age to be slightly higher, at 15.

The exact amount of sexually deviant behavior perpetrated by adolescents is not clear, though official statistics, studies, and self-report surveys give an idea as to the prevalence rate. Weinrott (1996) summarized official statistics from the Uniform Crime Reports (UCR) 1984–1993, which indicate that juveniles are responsible for 15.4 percent of forcible rape and 17 percent of other sexual offenses. Weinrott also summarized the self-reported data from the National Youth Survey, which show that approximately 3 percent of the adolescent population has committed a sexual offense—much higher than estimates given by the National Crime Victimization Survey (NCVS), which are lower than 1 percent. According to Becker et al. (1986), juveniles are responsible for approximately 20 percent of rapes and between 30 and 50 percent of cases of child sexual abuse. Letourneau, Bandyopadhyay, Armstrong, and Sinha (2010) estimated that juvenile sex offenders account for between 17 and 20 percent of all sex crimes, excluding prostitution. Ryan (1999) states that more than half of the male child victims and 20 to 30 percent of female child victims are abused by an older juvenile.

Most juvenile perpetrators are fewer than five years older than the victim, and in the NAPN sample, only 4 percent of juvenile sex offenders' victims were adults. A large amount of sexual offending by juveniles takes place in the home, and 90 percent of the perpetrators know their victims. Of those victims, the NAPN study showed that 39 percent are blood relatives, 10 percent peers, 6 percent total strangers, and many others are known in an acquaintance or authoritative capacity, such as a neighbor. These statistics are similar to the results of a study by Fehrenbach, Smith, Monastersky, and Deisher (1986). They show that of the 305 11- to 17-year-olds in their study, 60 percent had victims under the age of 12. One-third of the juveniles' victims in this study were family members, 12 percent were acquaintances, and fewer than 10 percent committed a rape against a peer. The researchers found the most common abuse situation occurred when the juveniles misused a position of authority (for example, a female in a baby-sitting situation). Graves, Openshaw, Ascione, and Ericksen (1996) conducted a meta-analysis of the literature and found that nearly all juveniles adjudicated delinquent for sexual offenses came from lower and middle socioeconomic status.

Repeat juvenile sex offenders tend to begin offending at a young age. Burton (2000) showed that 46 percent of the juveniles in his sample of 243 juvenile sex offenders began offending before the age of 12. Also, the offenders who began abusing prior to the age of 12 and continued abusing committed more serious offenses. The NAPN found that juvenile offenders often have multiple victims, with an average of 7.7 victims per offender.

Researchers have found numerous factors associated with an increased risk of recidivism. Miner (2002) states that juvenile sex offenders are at a higher risk of reoffense if they are young, have victims who are significantly younger than them, and show symptoms of impulsivity. Smith and Monastersky (1986) found that juveniles are more likely to recidivate if they have peer-aged, adult, or male victims, or if they commit noncontact offenses. Kahn and Chambers (1991) found that recidivism is linked to young offenders, young victims, cognitive distortions such as denial and minimization, and poor social skills. Langstrom and Grann (2000) found four factors associated with an increased risk of recidivism: commission of a previous sexual offense, poor social skills, male victim choice, and multiple victims. Deviant sexual interest also appears to be a strong predictor of sexual recidivism, especially in juvenile child sexual abusers (Kenny, Keogh, & Sidler, 2001; Worling & Curwean, 2000).

Despite the low levels of recidivism overall for juvenile sexual offenders, some juveniles are serious offenders with a significant history of criminal behavior. Some researchers have reconstructed the sexual histories of juvenile sex offenders to better understand the recidivism data. These studies indicate that a small group of serious juvenile sex offenders have extensive criminal backgrounds, often for both sexual and nonsexual offenses (Awad & Sanders, 1991; Fehrenbach et al., 1986). Other studies, however, have shown that sexually deviant behavior in juveniles is not strongly linked to other types of aggressive delinquent behavior (Smith, 1988). Broken down by offender type, Awad and Sanders (1991) showed that juveniles who sexually abused peers or adults were more likely to have committed previous delinquent acts than were child sexual abusers. Similarly, Ford and Linney (1995) found that juveniles convicted of rape were three times more likely than child sexual abusers to have prior offenses, and that more than 60 percent of juveniles who abuse children have no prior offenses. In a 10-year longitudinal study, Hagan, Gust-Brey, Cho, and Dow (2001) found that child sexual abusers (20 percent) have a higher likelihood of recidivism than either rapists (16 percent) or other delinquent juveniles (10 percent). Though their findings did not result in a significant difference between adolescent rapists and child sexual abusers, the authors noted that it is an important trend. Kemper and Kistner (2010) noted that juvenile sex offenders most commonly offend as either child sexual abusers or peer juvenile sex offenders and identified distinct differences between these groups. Juvenile child sexual abusers are more likely to victimize both genders, have higher rates of sexual abuse, and have fewer behavioral issues. Peer juvenile sex offenders almost exclusively victimize females, usually target acquaintances, and are more likely to have more extensive criminal backgrounds (Kemper & Kistner, 2010).

History of Abuse

Many reports indicate that a large number of perpetrators were physically and/or sexually abused at a young age (for example, Becker & Hunter, 1997; Fagan & Wexler, 1988; Fehrenbach et al., 1986; Hanser & Mire, 2008; Knight & Prentky, 1993; NAPN, 1993; Ryan, Miyoshi, Metzner, Krugman, & Fryer, 1996). NAPN (1993) shows that 42 percent of juvenile offenders have a history of physical abuse, 39 percent of known sexual abuse, and 26 percent of child neglect. Awad and Sanders (1991) found that juveniles who molested children were more likely to have been abused than those who offended against their peers. Nonetheless, many studies indicate that the prevalence of physical abuse is higher than the prevalence of sexual abuse in juvenile sexual offenders (Awad & Sanders, 1991).

Research shows that children are more likely to sexually abuse if they were abused (Becker, Cunningham-Rathner, & Kaplan, 1986). Not only are they more likely to abuse, but juvenile sex offenders who were abused generally begin offending at an earlier age, have more victims, are more likely to abuse both males and females, commit more intrusive offenses, and tend to show more psychopathology than those who were not abused (Cooper, Murphy, & Haynes, 1996; Hilliker, 1997). They are also more likely to recidivate with sexual offenses than juveniles who were not sexually abused (Mallie, Viljoen, Mordell, Spice, & Roesch, 2011).

Phan and Kingree (2001) showed that in a sample of 272 juvenile sex offenders, the females were more likely than the males to have experienced prior sexual abuse. Burton, Miller, and Shill (2002) found that juveniles who were sexually abused were more likely to abuse others if they had a male perpetrator (or both male and female perpetrators). Additionally, they found that they were more likely to abuse if they were abused over a long period of time and if the abuse included forceful acts or acts of penetration. Kobayashi et al. (1995) showed that juveniles who were physically abused were more likely to increase sexual aggression, but those who showed close bonding to their mother were less sexually aggressive. Prendergast (2004) identified three patterns of adaptation exhibited by youths who were sexually abused. Some deny that the abuse happened and simply repress it; others who "adjust" do not show any adverse symptoms after the abuse; and the final group "accepts" the abuse and believes they are in some way responsible for their victimization. Prendergast (2004) believes this can be used to determine the likelihood of sexual offending based on prior sexual abuse.

Female Juvenile Sex Offenders

Although females constitute a small proportion of the sex offender population, the percentage of sex offenders that is female increases as age decreases (Brown, Hull, & Panesis, 1984; Fehrenbach & Monstersky, 1988; Miccio-Fonesca, 1998; Ray & English, 1995). Whereas females make up approximately 1 to 2 percent of the adult sex offender population, they make up approximately 10 percent of adolescent offenders (13–18 years of age) and nearly 20 percent of child offenders (12 years of age and under) (Ray & English, 1995). Overall, the age of onset for sexual offending in females is younger than the age of onset for males.

As with male offenders, juvenile female sex offenders often know their victims. Most commonly, they are related to the victim or meet the victim in a babysitting situation (Hickey, McCrory, Farmer, & Vizard, 2008; Vandiver & Teske, 2006). Unlike adult female sexual offenders, juvenile female sex offenders rarely have a co-offender (Hickey et al., 2008). Instead, much of the victimization by adolescent females is the result of them exploring their sexuality in an unacceptable way (Vandiver & Teske, 2006).

Adolescent females who abuse were often abused when they were young and by more than one offender (McCartan et al., 2011; Righthand & Welch, 2001; Vandiver & Teske, 2006). Female adolescent sexual offenders are more likely than nonoffenders to have learning difficulties (McCartan et al., 2011). They also tend to experience abuse by more individuals than juvenile male sex offenders (Phan & Kingree, 2001), and the abuse is likely to have begun at a young age—often before age 6 (Hickey et al., 2008). Adolescent female sex offenders tend to enact the same type of abuse on their victims that they experienced (Vandvier & Teske, 2006). While both male and female juvenile sex offenders have low levels of recidivism for sexual offenses in adulthood, the rate of recidivism for females is substantially lower than that of males. The portrait of a "typical" juvenile female offender, then, is one of an adolescent who was repeatedly abused, often by more than one offender, who abuses younger children she knows and to whom she has access.

Juvenile Sex Offenders and Non-Sex Offenders: A Comparison

Many studies have compared juveniles who committed sexual offenses either to juveniles who have committed nonsexual offenses or to nonoffending juveniles in order to determine similarities and differences between the groups. Though these studies have provided important information, many have produced conflicting results as a result of methodological variation. For example, Jacobs, Kennedy, and Mayer (1997) found that there are no significant differences between sexual and nonsexual offenders in terms of IQ and academic testing. Similarly, the NAPN (1993) study states that the majority of juvenile sex offenders are either average or above average in their academic work, thereby not differentiating themselves from nonsexual offenders.

However, these results differ from most studies, which indicate that juvenile sex offenders perform poorly in academic settings (for example, Veneziano & Veneziano, 2002). Awad and Sanders (1991) claim that nearly half of juvenile sex offenders have diagnosable learning disabilities, and 83 percent have some difficulty in an academic setting. Ford and Linney (1995) found that the majority of juveniles in their sample had lower than average intelligence and many school suspensions. Ferrara and McDonald (1996) found that nearly one-third of juvenile sex offenders have a neurological impairment of some sort. Kahn and Chambers (1991) found that school behavioral problems are linked to an increased risk of recidivism in juvenile sex offenders.

Another difference is in terms of psychopathology and mental disorders. Many juvenile sexual offenders have diagnosable disorders, such as conduct disorder, depression, and attention deficit hyperactivity disorder (ADHD), but studies differ on whether the rate of these disorders is higher for sex offenders than other juveniles. Kraemer, Salisbury, and Spielman (1998) found that in their sample of juveniles in a residential treatment program, only 32.1 percent had no diagnostic disorders. Veneziano and Veneziano (2002) say that psychopathology is common to adolescent sex offenders, but Cooper et al. (1996) claim that it is only more common to adolescent sex offenders who were sexually abused. Frick (1998) says adolescent sex offenders are more likely than other types of adolescent offenders to show signs of psychopathy, as well as callousness and apathy. Smith, Monastersky, and Deischer (1987) found that juvenile sex offenders show a high level of impulsivity. Kavoussi, Kaplan, and Becker (1988) found that nearly half of their sample of child sexual abusers had conduct disorder, a finding similar to that of Graves et al. (1996). Becker et al. (1991) showed that sexual offenders scored twice as high on depression scales as nonoffending junior and senior high school students, and Veneziano and Veneziano (2002) found the link between social isolation and deviant sexual behavior to be very common. Alternatively, Fagan and Wexler (1988) found that most juveniles who abuse peers or adults are very similar in terms of psychopathology to nonoffenders. They claimed that the juvenile sex offenders showed high levels of prosocial behavior and did not differ significantly from a nonoffending population.

Another factor with contradictory results in the literature relates to substance abuse by the offenders and their families. Whereas several studies indicate that juvenile sex offenders are likely to abuse substances, all studies do not confirm these results. Lightfoot and Barbaree (1993) summarized the literature on this topic and found that substance abuse rates range from 3 to 72 percent. Overall, it seems that there may be a link between substance abuse and sexual abuse of peers or adults (Lightfoot & Barbaree, 1993), but not abuse of children (Becker & Stein, 1991). In terms of alcohol and substance abuse by the parents of juvenile offenders, a study by Graves et al. (1996) shows that alcohol abuse ranges from 17 to 43 percent, and substance abuse ranged from 43 (of mothers in their sample) to 62 percent (fathers) (Graves et al., 1996).

Both juvenile sexual and nonsexual offenders show more personal distress than nonoffenders (Lindsey, Carlozzi, & Eells, 2001). This means that they tend to be emotionally reactive, self-oriented, and are unable to focus on the distress of their victims. Though not significant, Lindsey et al. (2001) found that sex offenders tend to score slightly lower on an empathic scale than both nonsexual offenders and nonoffenders.

Juvenile sex offenders and nonsexual offenders do not differ on all factors, though. Hastings, Anderson, and Hemphill (1997) found that both groups experienced similar levels of stress and there are no significant differences between the groups on most static factors. Ford and Linney (1995) found that there are no differences between juvenile sexual and nonsexual offenders in terms of assertiveness, self-concept, and family history variables.

There are also differences between types of juvenile sexual offenders. Those who abuse younger children are more likely to show traits of schizoid personality disorders as well as dependent and avoidant traits. Alternatively, juveniles who sexually abuse adults or their peers are more likely to show narcissistic traits (Carpenter, Peed, & Eastman, 1995). Some studies have shown that juvenile sex offenders were likely to witness domestic violence within the home, even when they were not abused themselves (Caputo, Frick, & Brodsky, 1999). However, even though various types of juvenile sexual offenders were likely to observe or be victims of domestic violence within the home, child sexual abusers were more likely to experience this than rapists (Ford & Linney, 1995).

It is important to note that the methodology of all the studies on juvenile sex offenders discussed here vary greatly. This variability leads to differential findings, and it is difficult to know which studies provide the most accurate data.

Weinrott (1996) provides an overview of common difficulties and problems with studies of juvenile sex offenders.

WHY JUVENILES SEXUALLY OFFEND

As with adult offenders, many researchers have attempted to theorize about why juveniles commit sexually deviant behavior. Researchers do not all agree as to specific theoretical models that can explain juvenile sexual offending (APA, 1999), and some claim that there is a distinct difference in the etiology of offending for adolescent and preadolescent offenders. Until the 1980s, this behavior was almost universally dismissed, and sexually aggressive behavior was considered to be normal for adolescent males, or at the very least was a behavioral rather than sexual problem (Barbaree, Hudson, & Seto, 1993; Ryan, 1999).

Experimental or Criminal Behavior?

It is easy to identify acts as sexual "offenses" when an adult participates in sexual behavior with a child. However, when sexual acts are committed by juveniles it is often less clear. The behavior may be consensual, it may be sexual experimentation, or it may be abuse. After all, a juvenile who commits a sexual act with another child may be held responsible for a sexual offense, when that juvenile is not even old enough to consent to sexual behavior. This paradox makes for a complex understanding of culpability in juvenile sexual offense cases. Sexual acts by juveniles take place on a continuum of behavior, and the point at which they become abuse is often unclear. Some acts are quite serious, however, and as such juvenile sexual behavior should not always be dismissed as a "normal" sexual development process (Groth, Longo, & McFadin, 1982).

Most juveniles who are convicted of sexual offenses commit their offenses against children, and the children tend to be much younger than the child victims of adults (Russell, 1986; Shaw et al., 2000). With juvenile sex offenders, the age and social relationships between the perpetrator and the victim must be examined (Groth & Loredo, 1981). The greater the age discrepancy, the more inappropriate the sexual behavior is and the more likely that the act is not consensual.

In order to determine whether a juvenile's behavior is abusive, a number of factors in addition to the act must be taken into consideration. Specifically, what is the sexual knowledge of the juvenile, and is there any intent to commit a sexual offense? Many adolescent sex offenders have had some consensual sexual experience prior to the commission of their offense (Becker et al., 1986). Alternatively, some offenders were abused and act reactively, whereas others have minimal sexual knowledge. Because of the vast spectrum of knowledge among juvenile offenders about sexual behavior, some researchers classify juveniles into two groups of perpetrators—adolescents and children—in order to discern differences between the two groups (Calder et al., 2001).

The amount of sexual knowledge a child has is of particular importance in determining whether he or she has committed an offense. Sexual behavior is learned, and children can learn about sex and sexuality in many ways, such as through peers, television, their parents, self-exploration, and so forth. Some children learn about sex at a very young age, and this can occur through overt or covert sexual abuse, exposure to pornography, or witnessing adult sexual behavior. Some children react to this behavior by acting out and mimicking a learned response, but many do not go on to become adult sex offenders.

What is normal sexual behavior for children? It is normal for children to explore their own bodies and touch themselves. It is also normal for children to be curious about children of the opposite sex, and for a child to touch a sibling or another peer-aged relative. The question is then: At what point does this experimentation become an offense? The difficulty in this determination is particularly evident in the case of sibling incest. Finkelhor (1980) stated that sibling incest occurs in approximately 13 percent of the population (15 percent of females, 10 percent of males). Sibling incest generally occurs in households where the parents are either absent or inaccessible, or where there is a situation of excessive or open sexual behavior within the home and witnessed by children (Smith & Israel, 1987). The absence of the parents, either physically or emotionally, can lead to increased dependency on siblings (Smith & Israel, 1987).

Despite the apparent prevalence of sibling incest, many children and families ignore or do not report it (Araji, 1997). As with other sexual offenses, the victims of sibling incest may experience feelings of guilt, shame, and worthlessness. The taboo of incest may also lead to confusion and create a difficulty in establishing future sexual relationships (DiGiorgio-Miller, 1998). These feelings are often exacerbated if the family does not take the abuse seriously, press charges against the abusive sibling, and support the victim in the treatment process (DiGiorgio-Miller, 1998).

Theories and Antecedents of Offending Behavior

According to the literature, the most common antecedents of juvenile sexual offending are family dysfunction, particularly a family environment that fosters violence; lack of attachments and bonds, especially to parents; excessive use of pornography; a history of sexual abuse, physical abuse, and/or neglect; substance abuse by both the offender and the offender's family; and lack of empathy. Additionally, factors such as deviant sexual arousal and cognitive distortions may serve to facilitate this offending behavior.

Several researchers have noted a significant correlation between family dysfunction and sexually abusive behavior in juveniles. Despite the findings supporting this notion (for example, Smith, 1988), there are few patterns of family dysfunction in particular subsets of juvenile sex offenders (Weinrott, 1996). Though an abusive family situation may increase the level of violence or sexual violence in a juvenile, Kobayashi et al. (1995) found that bonding to the mother reduces the amount of sexual aggression.

Linked to this is the development of empathy. Empathy is a socialized construct, and therefore it is affected by familial interaction and bonding. Juvenile sex offenders often come from households where familial interaction is minimal or nonexistent, and many of these offenders often experience neglect. Juveniles who experience familial neglect appear to have a poor understanding of empathy (Lindsey et al., 2001). Similarly, many juvenile sex offenders with low empathy scores have poor social skills with peers and experience a high level of social isolation (Veneziano & Veneziano, 2002). Empathy deficit has thus been identified as an important etiological factor in juvenile sex-offending (Calley & Gerber, 2008; Farr, Brown, & Beckett, 2004).

Though debatable, some researchers claim that exposure to pornography enhances the likelihood of deviant sexual behavior in juveniles. In particular, they link excessive exposure to explicit sexual material, especially when young (that is, prepubertal), to deviant behavior (Harris, 2000; Zgourides, Monto, & Harris, 1997). Many juvenile sex offenders report exposure to both hard- and soft-core pornography. Becker and Stein (1991) reported that nearly 90 percent of their sample of adolescent offenders had some exposure to pornography, including magazines, videotapes, television, and books. It is likely that the percentage of adolescents viewing pornography has increased since the time of the Becker and Stein (1991) study, with the increased accessibility of pornography on the Internet. As such, it will be interesting to see future results of studies with juveniles who are consistently exposed to pornography on the Internet.

Deviant sexual arousal is also correlated to deviant sexual behavior in juveniles. Hunter and Becker (1994) in their summary of the literature found that individuals who abuse children often have deviant sexual arousal. Becker et al. (1989) found that there was more deviant sexual arousal in juveniles who had been sexually abused. Though this was true of the offenders despite the gender of their victims, those who had male victims scored higher on the pedophile coercion and noncoercion indices. Hunter and Becker (1994) found that there is generally early onset of pedophilia in adult males who abuse children. Additionally, Kahn and Chambers (1991) found a link between deviant sexual arousal and recidivism. As such, it is important to determine whether adolescent sex offenders have deviant sexual arousal. If they do, these arousal patterns must be addressed in the treatment goals.

Though all these factors are important to understand, they do not explain the etiology of offending behavior. Epps (1999) points out that deviant sexual behavior in juveniles can and should be explained through biological, psychodynamic, behavioral, social-cognitive, social-emotional, developmental, cognitive, trauma, family, and sociological explanations, much like the etiology of sexual offending behavior for adults. One theory about the onset of deviant sexual behavior is the social learning theory (Burton, Miller, & Shill, 2002), which is derived from a developmental perspective. Ryan (1999) explains that this perspective supports the view that deviant sexual behavior is learned, and that juvenile offenders should be able to learn socially acceptable sexual behavior despite any developmental deficits. Some researchers do not agree with the idea that deviant sexual behavior is learned based on the concept of conditioning. Marshall and Eccles (1993) stated that deviant sexual behavior may be one factor in the etiology of deviant behavior, but it is likely a predispositional rather than a causal factor.

Ryan et al. (1987) created a model of a sexual abuse cycle that follows a theoretical framework for conceptualizing abusive patterns. The cycle begins when the juvenile has a negative self-image. There are a number of factors that may create a low self-image in the child, primarily relating to his or her upbringing. Many juveniles who abuse are sexually or physically abused, and many others come from chaotic or violent households. All of these factors can lead to low self-image, low self-esteem, and situations of social isolation for the child. This low self-image can lead to poor coping strategies when negative situations arise, or it can cause the juvenile to predict negative reactions from others. This anticipation of negative reactions may lead to further social isolation, withdrawal, and fantasies stemming from lack of power and control. If the juvenile experiences a triggering event, these thoughts, feelings, and behaviors can lead to the commission of an offense. This offense, in turn, facilitates the low self-image in the juvenile, thus creating a sexual abuse cycle.

Once the offending cycle begins, cognitive distortions often help to facilitate the offending behavior. Common cognitive distortions in juvenile sex offenders include the minimization of responsibility, blaming the victim, and minimizing the harm to the victim (Knight & Prentky, 1993; Lakey, 1992). Juveniles also may have distorted thoughts regarding social roles (that is, supporting rape myths) and sexuality. However, Weinrott (1996) states that few empirical studies have yet been conducted to determine the extent of cognitive distortions and their role in the etiology of offending behavior.

Typologies of Juvenile Sex Offenders

Juvenile sex offenders constitute a heterogeneous population similarly to adult sex offenders, and as such, different offenders have varying characteristics and needs and create varying risks. Several researchers have attempted to categorize juvenile sex offenders into typologies in order to better understand subsets of the juvenile sex offender population. One early example of such a classification system was derived by O'Brien and Bera (1986).

First, they identified the *naïve experimenters*. These offenders tend to be young, lack social skills and sexual knowledge, and participate in situational acts. Their second category of offenders is the *undersocialized child exploiters*. Like the naïve experimenters, these juveniles generally do not have a history of delinquent behavior, but they tend to show a more severe degree of social isolation. They often come from families with a high level of dysfunction, and they have a high level of insecurity and a poor self-image. The third typology consists of *sexual aggressives*. These juveniles are the most likely to use force and violence during the commission of their offense, and they will most likely abuse peers or adults. They may have a history of delinquent behavior, substance abuse, a high level of impulsivity, and come from a household rife with dysfunction and violence. *Sexual compulsives* make up the fourth typology; these offenders have deviant sexual fantasies that become compulsive. They may be quiet, anxious, and exhibit paraphilic behavior such as voyeurism. Unlike the sexual aggressives, they are likely to come from a rigidly strict and perhaps religious household.

The fifth typology is the *disturbed impulsives*, whose actions are impulsive and may result from psychiatric disorders. The sixth typology consists of *group-influenced offenders*, who commit offenses to impress their peers. The final category is the *pseudo-socialized*, who show characteristics similar to psychopaths. They tend to exhibit psychological disorders such as narcissism, lack intimacy, have many superficial relationships with peers, and show a high level of intelligence.

O'Brien and Bera's (1986) classification system is quite thorough because it addresses major psychological and sociological issues related to the etiology and maintenance of offending behavior. Similarly, Prentky, Harris, Frizzell, and Righthand (2000) created an empirical classification of juvenile sex offenders consisting of six typologies based on their clinical work with the population. Their classification scheme is based on a more basic offending structure than O'Brien and Bera's. First, they differentiated between *child sexual abusers* and *rapists*. The third typology is of *sexually reactive children*, or those who follow a method of socially learned behavior. Their fourth category includes less invasive offenders, labeled *fondlers*. They also distinguished *paraphiliac offenders*, or those who as juveniles committed offenses such as voyeurism and exhibitionism. Finally, recognizing that typologies cannot be mutually exclusive or exhaustive, they added a category for sex offenders who do not fit into the defined typologies.

Though O'Brien and Bera (1986) and Prentky et al. (2000) are the most cited early typology models for juveniles, others also created typology systems. Jacobs (1999) claims that there are three ways by which juveniles should be classified: by the *age differential* between offender and victim, by the *intrusiveness* of the offense committed, and by the *gender* of the victim(s). Graves (as defined by Weinrott, 1996) claims that juvenile sex offenders can fit into three typologies: *pedophilic*, or those who consistently abuse children at least three years younger than themselves; *sexual assault*, or those who abuse peers or adults; and *undifferentiated*, or those who abuse a variety of victims. Becker and colleagues have studied the pathways to offending for juveniles and the outcomes for different types of juvenile offenders. For instance, Becker and Kaplan (1998) identify three paths of behavior for juveniles once they began offending: *continued delinquency, continued sexual offending, and no further offending*.

O'Brien and Bera's (1986) and Prentky et al.'s (2000) typology systems served as foundational sources for understanding juvenile sex offenders. However, more recent juvenile typology research has differentiated between juvenile sex offenders with psychosocial deficits and those with more general conduct problems (Leversee, 2010). For example, Hunter, Figueredo, Malamuth, and Becker (2003) studied differences between juvenile sex offenders who abused children and those who abused adolescents. They found significant differences between these groups, most notably that adolescent males who abused prepubescent children had greater psychosocial deficits and were not as aggressive as those who abused adolescents. Using the Millon Adolescent Clinical Inventory (MACI), Richardson, Kelley, Graham, and Bhate (2004) classified juvenile sex offenders based upon personality patterns. They identified five types of personality patterns—*normal, antisocial, submissive, dysthymic/inhibited*, and *dysthymic negativistic*—but were unable to link personality characteristics and particular types of offending. Similarly, Oxnam and Vess (2006) used the MACI to identify three groups of offenders—*antisocial/externalizing, withdrawn/socially inadequate*, and those with no clinical elevation. Most importantly, they showed that juvenile sex offenders exhibited personality profiles similar to nonsexual offending juveniles. Worling (2001) also used a personality inventory to identify subgroups of juvenile sex offenders. He identified four groups of offenders—*antisocial/impulsive, unusual/isolated, overcontrolled/reserved*, and *confident/aggressive*—but adolescent offenders in these groups were not significantly differentiated based upon characteristics of their offending patterns such as their victims' ages or genders.

Clearly, there is still much to be learned about the different types of adolescent sex offenders and their motivations for offending. Though there are many ways to classify offenders, with little agreement on specific methods or categories, these typology schemes are helpful in understanding the pathways to offending and the most appropriate ways in which to assess, treat, and supervise the offenders (Worling, 2001). By breaking up heterogeneous groups into identifiable and relatively homogeneous categories, treatment providers can better assess the risks and needs of offenders.

ASSESSMENT AND TREATMENT
OF JUVENILE OFFENDERS

Several influential studies of juveniles, including the NAPN (1993) report, indicate that assessment and treatment of juvenile sexual offenders is critical in order to reduce the likelihood of recidivism and life-course persistent offending. However, this claim has been criticized in the last decade (see Zimring, 2004). Letourneau and Miner (2005) noted that substantial clinical interventions for juveniles has resulted from three false assumptions that are not supported by existing data: that there is an epidemic of juvenile sexual offending, juvenile sex offenders have much in common with adult sex offenders, and without treatment juvenile sex offenders will reoffend. That said, some juveniles do commit serious sexual offenses, have developmental and psychological problems appropriate for treatment, and would benefit from participation in a treatment program.

Studies that assess the recidivism rates for juvenile sex offenders show that adolescents who participate in treatment have low recidivism rates (Davis & Leitenberg, 1987; Sipe, Jensen, & Everett, 1998; Smith & Monastersky, 1986). Those who reoffended were most likely to commit property crimes (Brannon & Troyer, 1995). The rate of recidivism is higher for violent juvenile sex offenders, who are more likely to commit further sexual offenses than are nonviolent sexual offenders (Sipe et al., 1998). Early research showed that recidivism rates are lower for juveniles who are offered treatment early on in their offending careers (Freeman-Longo & McFaddin, 1981; Groth, 1979). One flaw in these studies, however, is that they rarely considered recidivism rates for juvenile offenders who were treated compared to those who were not. More recent research shows that most juvenile sex offenders, regardless of whether they participated in treatment, have low recidivism rates for sexual offending in adulthood.

The treatment schemes commonly used for juvenile sex offenders include family therapies, cognitive-behavioral therapies, relapse prevention, and psychoeducational interventions. In order for treatment to be effective, the juvenile must be accurately assessed so that the therapist fully understands his or her treatment needs (Lane, 1997). Brannon and Troyer (1995, p. 324) claim that "successful" treatment emphasizes high levels of community involvement, stress–challenge education, student interpersonal problem-solving activities, energetic administrative leadership, and extensive staff training.

Studies have shown that inappropriate matching of risks and needs can actually increase recidivism among offenders (Andrews, Bonta, & Hoge, 1990). This is especially true of adolescent offenders when their behavior is misdiagnosed or considered to be "normal" (Longo, 1983). Additionally, many juveniles who participate in treatment programs do not complete them. This is particularly true of residential treatment programs, as one group of researchers consistently found that just over half of the participants completed the program (Kraemer et al., 1998). Kraemer et al. found two factors significantly associated with failure to complete a residential treatment program: impulsivity and age. They found that older adolescent offenders and those who showed generally impulsive behavior were the least likely to complete the program successfully. This supports other research that indicates younger children are more amenable to treatment. They found that treatment completion did not depend on the juvenile's IQ, ethnicity, or grade level. Hagan, King, and Patros (1994) looked at the number of adolescent rapists in a residential treatment program who were able to successfully complete the program (that is, they were not convicted of a future sexual offense in the following two years). Though 58 percent of their sample committed another delinquent act in this time, only 10 percent were convicted of another sexual offense.

Treatment should focus on offense-specific interventions to address the realities of the developmental needs and deficits of the juveniles. Treatment should also address offense-related issues such as substance abuse, eating disorders, childhood abuse, domestic violence that the juvenile may have witnessed, other crimes such as property offenses and arson, self-abusive behavior such as eating disorders and suicidal tendencies, and any behavior that harms others (Ryan, 1999). Because their sample showed a high level of generally delinquent behavior, Hagan et al. (1994) stated that treatment should also focus on antisocial criminal behavior. They found that antisocial behavior is likely to continue post-treatment if it is not specifically addressed in the program.

The Assessment Process

The assessment process for adolescent sex offenders is very detailed and time consuming, because these assessments require multiple interviews with the adolescents and their parents (APA, 1999). Though the process varies from institution to institution, the National Task Force on Juvenile Sexual Offending promotes six stages of evaluations: the *pretrial investigative assessment;* the *presentence risk assessment* to determine placement and prognosis; the *post-adjudication clinical assessment* to address treatment issues and modes; a *needs assessment* for treatment planning and progress in treatment; an *assessment for release or the termination from treatment program*, which aims to determine community safety and successful application of treatment tools; and a *follow-up assessment* to monitor the juvenile in the community. Most clinicians recommend this thorough assessment process, based on multiple resources rather that a single clinical or actuarial risk assessment tool (Rich, 2011).

The primary goal of the assessment process is to accurately identify the risks and needs of the offenders, and to make sure that the juvenile understands the dynamics of his or her offense (DiGiorgio-Miller, 1994). This means that the treatment provider must find out detailed information about the deviant act, including the degree of damage inflicted on the victim and whether the goal of the act was to control, degrade, or embarrass the victim, as these are factors that alert experts to juveniles suffering from paraphilias. Additionally, it is important to establish the sophistication of the deviant sexual act and to assess whether the knowledge demonstrated is beyond the average knowledge of children in the particular age group (APA, 1999). If so, this likely means that the child was abused or has been exposed to deviant sexual behavior previously.

Treatment providers must also aim to find out the true rate of abuse caused by the juvenile. In their research of three treatment programs, Baker, Tabacoff, Tornusciolo, and Eisenstad (2001) found that more than half of the juveniles in the sample disclosed more offenses and/or victims than those for which they were convicted. Throughout the treatment, the juveniles also revealed more information about previous sexual and physical abuse, and information about the abusive household they live in (often with the father subjecting the mother to domestic violence incidents).

In order to accurately identify the risks and needs of the juveniles, the treatment provider should use various assessment tools including official documents (that is, police records, victim statements), interviews, phallometric testing, polygraphs, and psychometric testing (Righthand & Welch, 2001). The official documents are necessary to understand the specifics of the crime committed, including the amount of harm caused to the victim. The interviews allow the treatment provider to assess the offender's sexual knowledge, family history, abuse history, and cognitive distortions, including the amount of denial, minimization, justification, and whether the offender feels any empathy toward his or her victim. Phallometric testing should be used to determine the level of deviant sexual arousal in the offender. Though this is ethically questionable and should not be considered an entirely accurate method by which deviant sexual arousal can be measured, it can give the treatment provider some basic understanding of the offender's arousal patterns. Polygraphs should be used throughout both the assessment and treatment processes to ensure that the offender is being truthful about his or her offense and offense history. Finally, psychometric tests are pertinent in understanding factors such as the offender's IQ, whether he or she has any diagnosable disorders, whether he or she shows traits of psychopathy, and his or her opinions about sexual issues (that is, supporting rape myths).

The Treatment Process

Once the juvenile offender is fully assessed, the treatment provider should determine what type of program is appropriate for the juvenile. Many clinicians promote a cognitive-behavioral approach to treating juvenile offenders, similarly to those used for adults (for example, Charles & McDonald, 1996; O'Reilly, Morrison, Sheerin, & Carr, 2001), though there is no consensus that this approach is best for all juveniles. For instance, Brannon and Troyer (1995) suggest that specialized programs are equivalent to general treatment programs that work to improve social skills, self-esteem, and other general problems that the juvenile may be experiencing. Also, juveniles diagnosed as psychopathic should be considered high-risk offenders who need extensive treatment beyond the core cognitive-behavioral program (Reiss, Grubin, & Meux, 1996).

O'Reilly et al. (2001) claim group-based cognitive-behavioral approaches are the most beneficial for the majority of juvenile offenders. The group-based approach, specifically in terms of relapse prevention, helps to motivate juvenile sex offenders to change their behavior. The cognitive-behavioral group treatment process aims to help juvenile offenders address problems with their interpersonal relationship skills, which are often an antecedent to deviant sexual behavior. This process also helps the offender learn to take responsibility for his or her actions, reduce and restructure cognitive distortions, and learn about sex education (Grant & MacDonald, 1996).

There are several goals of a juvenile sex offender treatment program. According to Righthand and Welch (2001, p. 43), the target areas of treatment are impaired social skills; empathy deficits; cognitive distortions; deviant sexual arousal; problematic management of emotions; impulsive, antisocial behavior; and consequences of personal history of child maltreatment. Focus on antisocial behavior is especially pertinent as numerous studies have suggested that sexual offending is one antisocial behavior in a midst of general criminal behavior. Though all of these factors must be addressed in treatment, Ryan (1999) states that the key to treatment for juveniles is victim empathy and empathic accountability. She states that "the absence of empathic accountability is the most obvious deficit in abusers" (p. 428). This is particularly important for offenders who have experienced neglect, which may be linked to a lack of empathy. Early interventions (for example, treatment early on in the juvenile's offending career) may help to increase empathic accountability (Hagan et al., 1994).

MANAGEMENT OF JUVENILE OFFENDERS

Supervision and management strategies for sex offenders have increased in frequency and severity in the last two decades. Unfortunately, this has also trickled down to include juvenile as well as adult offenders. In particular, the Sex Offender

Registration and Notification Act (SORNA) of the Adam Walsh Child Protection and Safety Act (Adam Walsh Act), passed in 2006, requires that juveniles adjudicated delinquent of aggravated sexual abuse, who were at least 14 years of age at the time of the offense, register as a sex offender and submit to notification. Such requirements will lead to juveniles being registered sex offenders for decades or even life, restriction of residency location and types of jobs, and notification to the community about the acts committed. Considering the statistics that show how the large majority of juvenile sex offenders are not life-persistent offenders, these consequences for juveniles are quite extreme. This act, and the collateral consequences that may result from it, is discussed in more detail in Chapter 10.

When juvenile sex offenders are living in the community, there are numerous agencies involved in their supervision process including child protection services, child and family services, social services, treatment providers, the police, and probation. For serious juvenile sex offenders who are at high risk to reoffend, the key to effective treatment, supervision, and management is a multiagency approach in which the agencies work together to reduce the chance of recidivism (Erooga & Masson, 1999).

With the passing of SORNA, the agencies most responsible for supervising juvenile sex offenders in the community have moved from social service agencies to criminal justice agencies. This is a move away from the goal of a juvenile justice system, which was to help the juvenile offender, provide services, and avoid stigmatization. Researchers almost universally disagree with the recent move toward increased criminal and civil sanctions (Zimring, 2004) and decreased judicial discretion for juvenile sex offenders (Bowater, 2008).

As of 2010, juveniles accounted for up to 10 percent of all registered sex offenders (Letourneau et al., 2010). If juveniles do account for 20 to 30 percent of rapes or attempted rapes, the number of registered juvenile sex offenders will increase substantially. As Becker (1998) noted more than a decade ago, there should be caution in applying such supervision and management techniques to the juvenile population, because there need to be further longitudinal studies on juvenile sex offenders to determine what their true long-term risks are.

DID YOU KNOW...?

Moving Away From the Juvenile Justice System Philosophy

The juvenile justice system was created in the late 19th century. Prior to this time, juveniles accused of committing crimes were processed through the adult criminal justice system. The focus of the juvenile justice system was to rehabilitate juveniles, rather than to imprison and punish them. The juvenile justice system essentially acted as the parents of the child, a philosophy known as *parens patriae*. In doing so, the court would make decisions about what to do with the juvenile offender based on the juvenile's best interests.

Over the last three decades, juvenile courts have become the subject of debate, specifically as to whether to "get tough" or "treat." Advocates of the get tough philosophy have claimed that the juvenile justice system is lenient, does not deter crime, and does not protect the community. Advocates of the *parens patriae* philosophy claim that most juveniles only commit minor offenses, punishment can do more harm than good, most juveniles age-out of delinquent behavior, and that the adult system will label and stigmatize juveniles. The research on juvenile sexual offenders also shows that most do not go on to become adult sexual offenders. Despite all the potential setbacks of harsh sentences for juveniles, the justice system is increasingly creating harsher sanctions for juveniles for many offenses.

Questions
1. What should be the primary focus of the justice system when a juvenile commits a sexual offense—community protection or the best interests of the juvenile offender? What are the drawbacks of each of these?
2. What might be the long-term effects of having juvenile sex offenders register and be subject to community notification?

© Cengage Learning

CHAPTER SUMMARY

- Like adults, juveniles who commit sexual offenses make up a heterogeneous group of individuals. They have various family histories, offend for a number of different reasons, and require different methods of treatment and supervision.

- Most juveniles who commit sexual offenses are not persistent life–course offenders. Instead, the majority are adolescent–limited offenders. Additionally, most adolescent sexual offenders commit more nonsexual offenses than sexual ones.

- As with adults, researchers classify juvenile sex offenders into typologies. However, unlike with adults, the juvenile typologies tend to be based on levels of psychosocial development and/or attachment and bonds to family.

- Juveniles are often dismissed out of the criminal justice system prior to conviction. However, when their cases do go to court and the juveniles are found delinquent, they receive an extensive assessment process and treatment regime.

- Many juvenile sex offenders are now subject to registration and notification schemes like adults. Researchers have indicated that such sanctions can lead to more harm than good for juveniles, and there is no evidence yet as to the effectiveness of these management strategies for reducing recidivism in the juvenile population.

DISCUSSION QUESTIONS

1. What are some of the similarities and differences between adult and juvenile sexual offenders?

2. How can criminal justice officials or psychologists distinguish between juveniles who are "experimenting" with sexual behavior and those who are committing criminal acts?

3. Explain the benefits and the problems with juveniles having to register as sex offenders.

4. Should juvenile sex offenders be allowed to attend school? Should the offenders' classmates be notified about their offending behavior?

CASE STUDY

GENARLOW WILSON: Does the Punishment Fit the Crime?

On December 30, 2003, 17-year-old Genarlow Wilson attended a New Year's Eve party with a group of friends in Douglas County, Georgia. Wilson was a star athlete of the football and soccer teams, was an honor student, and Douglas County High School's first ever homecoming king (Dewan, 2006). The party was held at a local hotel and partygoers participated in drug use, alcohol consumption, and sexual activity. One of the attendees brought along a video camera to document the party. It was on this video camera that Genarlow Wilson was seen receiving oral sex from a 15-year-old girl also attending the party (Redmon & Joyner, 2007).

Under Georgia's 1995 Child Protection Act, oral sex with a 15 year old constituted aggravated child molestation. This crime was punishable by a mandatory minimum sentence of 10 years in prison and lifetime registration on Georgia's sex offender registry (Downey, 2008). The video showing Wilson and the 15-year-old girl engaging in oral sex was brought to prosecutors by a third party. Prosecutors then decided to charge Wilson with aggravated child molestation (Dewan, 2006).

Wilson claimed that the acts were consensual. So did the 15-year-old alleged victim and her mother, Veda Cannon (Redmon & Joyner, 2007). Despite these claims that the sexual activity was consensual, Douglas County District Attorney David McDade decided to pursue the charges against Genarlow Wilson and five other teenage boys seen engaging in sexual activity with another girl on the video tape. McDade argued that the six boys, including Genarlow Wilson, had gang raped a 17-year-old girl who attended the party and engaged in repeated sex acts with the 15-year-old girl (Dewan, 2007).

Despite arguments by Wilson's lawyer, B. J. Bernstein, that the acts were consensual for all parties involved, Georgia law stated that an individual under the age of 16 was unable to consent to any kind of sexual activity. As a result, prosecutor McDade charged Wilson with rape and aggravated child molestation. Upon reviewing the video tape, the jury disagreed with the prosecutor's charge of rape and acquitted Wilson of this charge. While the jury did not feel that Wilson was guilty of statutory rape due to the consensual nature of the act, according to law they were bound to find him guilty of aggravated child molestation (Dewan, 2007). On April 18 2005, Wilson was found guilty of aggravated child molestation and sentenced to 10 years in prison without the possibility of parole and lifetime registration as a sex offender (Redmon & Joyner, 2007).

The case just described illustrates how juvenile sex offenders can often be forced to register as sex offenders due to consensual and sometimes normal adolescent acts. The case of Genarlow Wilson brings to light the question of whether statutory rape laws should be applied to juveniles when the age difference is minimal. Wilson is not at a high risk of sexual offending in the future, but due to his conviction, he is forced to register as one for the rest of his life.

Questions
1. What are the benefits and problems of statutory rape laws?
2. Should there be a minimum age differential between victim and perpetrator for an act to be considered statutory "rape"?
3. Should sexual behavior between adolescents be policed?
4. What sanction, if any, should have been applied to Genarlow Wilson?

7

Commercial Sexual Exploitation of Children

The types and level of sexual exploitation of children and adolescents have increased substantially in the last few decades. Technological advances allow for the more discreet exploitation of children, with computers and digital cameras, and the Internet provides a forum for mass distribution as never before. Cameras on phones and computers provide the opportunity for children and adolescents to take photos of themselves, send them to friends or post them online. And while social media and other forums have provided access to a globalized world, it has also exposed children and adolescents to dangers in unprecedented levels.

The good news is that children are becoming more educated about the dangers of technology, particularly in regard to meeting and talking to strangers. Yet they underestimate the dangers of their own behaviors, such as texting naked photos of themselves to friends and posting personal information online. But the exploitation of juveniles is not just online; rather, some adolescent boys and girls have become involved in prostitution, either for money or survival (in exchange for a place to live, food, etc.). Recent studies about juvenile prostitution have just begun to show the reality of the population of juveniles who are sexually exploited by adults, how they became involved in prostitution, and why they cannot get out. Though pimps and human traffickers play a role, more juveniles are sexually exploited through peers or others close to them.

Research on the exploitation of children and responses to it are nascent, as the types of exploitation continue to evolve. This chapter provides an overview of the exploitation of children online and offline, the types of adults who exploit children and adolescents, and the laws that govern this behavior.

SEXUAL OFFENDERS AND THE INTERNET

The dangers of child pornography and the Internet are threefold: children are being exploited for pornographic images, children are accessing pornographic images, and children are being solicited online. Child pornography is the depiction of sexually explicit behavior involving a minor under the age of 18 years, though the exact definitions of "child" and "pornography" vary by state and country. In the United States, child pornography includes actual or simulated: vaginal intercourse, oral or anal intercourse, bestiality, masturbation, sexually sadistic or masochistic behavior, and exhibition of the genitals of minors under the age of 18 (U.S. Code, Title 18 § 2256). Some states have adapted this definition to also include offenses such as penetration of the vagina or rectum digitally or with foreign objects, and excretory functions performed in a lewd manner. Images are also considered pornographic if the child is the focal point of a sexually suggestive setting; the child is in an unnatural pose or in inappropriate attire; the depiction suggests coyness or willingness to engage in sexual activity; or the depiction is intended to elicit a sexual response in the viewer. As of 2003, when the PROTECT Act was enacted, virtual and computer-generated sexual images of children are also illegal.

The definition of, and response to, child pornography is a social construction, based upon the culture and time period (Jenkins, 2001). Though many international organizations, such as Interpol (International Criminal Police Organization) and ECPAT (End Child Prostitution, Child Pornography, & Trafficking of Children for Sexual Purposes), use vague definitions of child pornography, they agree on the general tenets of what constitutes this behavior. They describe child pornography as the visual, written and/or audio depiction of a child engaged in sexual activity or the depiction of the child's genitals (Carr, 2001). Thus, despite the jurisdictional differences based on cultural variation, there now exists a global consensus on the sexual behaviors that constitute child pornography and the harms these behaviors might cause.

One of the most thorough archives of child pornographic images is part of the COPINE (Combating Paedophile Information Networks in Europe) project at the University of Cork, Ireland. Founded in 1997, the COPINE researchers have archived child pornographic images and video clips that have been downloaded from websites, networks, and newsgroups. Based on the types of images they found, they created a COPINE scale of 10 types of exploitation based upon the method and severity of the depicted sexual acts (Taylor, Quayle, & Holland, 2001). The levels of abuse are described in Table 7.1.

Accessing Child Pornography

The growth of pornography on the Internet results largely from three factors: accessibility, affordability, and anonymity (Cooper et al., 2000). It also provides a unique social environment whereby individuals can access information that supports their sexual fantasies and can communicate with others who share similar fantasies (Taylor & Quayle, 2003). These social networks can provide

TABLE 7.1 **COPINE Scale of Sexual Images of Children**

Levels	Description
Indicative	Nonerotic and nonsexualized pictures showing children in their underwear, swimming costumes from either commercial sources or family albums. Pictures of children playing in normal settings, in which the context or organization of pictures by the collector indicates inappropriateness.
Nudist	Pictures of naked or semi-naked children in appropriate nudist settings, and from legitimate sources.
Erotica	Surreptitiously taken photographs of children in play areas or other safe environments showing either underwear or varying degrees of nakedness.
Posing	Deliberately posed pictures of children fully clothed, partially clothed, or naked (where the amount, context, and organization suggests sexual interest).
Erotic Posing	Deliberately posed pictures of fully, partially clothed, or naked children in sexualized or provocative poses.
Explicit Erotic Posing	Pictures emphasizing genital areas, where the child is either naked, partially clothed, or fully clothed
Explicit Sexual Activity	Pictures that depict touching, mutual and self-masturbation, oral sex and intercourse by a child, not involving an adult.
Assault	Pictures of children being subject to a sexual assault, involving digital touching, involving an adult.
Gross Assault	Grossly obscene pictures of sexual assault, involving penetrative sex, masturbation or oral sex, involving an adult.
Sadistic/Bestiality	a. Pictures showing a child being tied, bound, beaten, whipped, or otherwise subject to something that implies pain. b. Pictures where an animal is involved in some form of sexual behavior with a child.

SOURCE: Taylor, Quayle, & Holland (2001)

validation and justification for the beliefs of those attracted to children, thus lowering their inhibitions and lessening the social risk for them.

There are many methods of distributing and accessing child pornography on the Internet. Citing the work of Blundell et al. (2002), Calder (2004), Ferraro et al. (2004), Jenkins (2001), and the U.S. General Accounting Office (2003), Wortley and Smallbone (2006c, pp. 10–11) summarize eight key methods of accessing child pornography (see Table 7.2). These range from open websites to password-protected or encrypted sites specifically for individuals with high levels of involvement in trading pornographic images.

As policing the Internet for pornographic images of children has become more sophisticated, so too have the sites where pornography is distributed, exchanged, and viewed. Many of the methods for accessing child pornography listed previously are not accessible by the average Internet user; they may be hidden, not searchable, password-protected, or encrypted (Wortley & Smallbone,

TABLE 7.2 **Methods of Distributing and Accessing Child Pornography on the Internet**

Method	Description
Webpages and websites	Specific websites containing images of child pornography. They may be child-only sites, adult sites with child pornography embedded, or adult sites with models who look like minors. Nonrestricted child pornography websites are unusual because of the high level of oversight on the Internet for easily accessible illegal images.
Webcams	Provide images of abuse broadcast in real time, which may also allow for interaction between the broadcaster and the audience (e.g., to make requests).
Email	Distributors may send attachments of child pornography images in emails to individuals, groups, or subscribers to a particular site. Offenders may also send emails with pornographic images to minors as a method of grooming.
E-groups	Members can share pornographic images and exchange information about websites that contain child pornography.
Newsgroups	Forums to discuss sexual interest in children with others who have the same interests, and provide photos for exchange. Newsgroups are one of the most common methods of distributing child pornography.
Bulletin Board Systems (BBS)	Provide a forum for discussions about child pornography, websites, and advice to those seeking access to child pornography.
Chat rooms	Used to exchange pornography and locate potential victims. They may be open or password-protected.
Peer-to-peer (P2P)	Allow for closed groups to trade images of child pornography. These are often populated with the more serious cyber sex offenders.

SOURCE: Wortley & Smallbone (2006c)

2006c). The websites may require a link through a personal connection, or require that the user join a group. Some sites are for profit, requiring that users pay a monthly or annual fee, and others simply provide a forum for users to chat and exchange photos.

Because of the secrecy of child pornography, there are few comprehensive studies on child pornography users, how users access child pornography, and why. The most comprehensive empirical investigation into child pornography use and users is the National Juvenile Online Victimization Study (NJOV), conducted by researchers at the Crimes Against Children Research Center, University of New Hampshire. NJOV is a two-wave longitudinal study of 2,574 local, county, and state law enforcement agencies (see Wolak, Finkelhor, & Mitchell, 2005). In the first phase, the researchers mailed surveys to this nationally representative sample of agencies asking for details about arrests for Internet-related child pornography and sexual exploitation crimes (Wolak et al., 2005). In the second phase, the researchers conducted telephone interviews with agencies to collect further details about information in the surveys. The NJOV researchers found that approximately two-thirds of the offenders who were arrested for Internet-facilitated offenses against children accessed or purchased images on the Internet but did not produce them, while approximately one-third produced the images they exchanged or sold (Mitchell, Jones, Finkelhor, & Wolak, 2011). Most of the pornographic images depicted serious sexual abuse situations involving preteen children (Wolak, Fineklhor, & Mitchell, 2011); 83 percent of the offenders had images of children aged 6–12, 39 percent had images of children aged 3–5, and 19 percent had images of children under the age of 3 (Wolak et al., 2005). The offenders who used P2P networks had the most extensive collection of images and the most heinous images, including images of young children (under age 3) and images depicting sexual violence (Wolak et al., 2011).

Scope of the Problem

Pornography is a multibillion dollar industry and is one of the highest grossing industries in the United States. According to Ropelato (2012), every second: $3,075.64 is spent on pornography; 28,258 Internet users view pornography; and 372 users are using search engines to search for pornographic sites. Approximately 4.2 million websites (12 percent of all websites) with 420 million pages contain pornography. One quarter of all search engine requests are of pornographic terms, and 8 percent of all emails contain pornography. The most common system for downloading pornography is through P2P networks, which are responsible for 35 percent of all pornographic downloads (Ropelato, 2012).

Children and adolescents are exposed to pornography on the Internet early and at high levels. The average age in which children are first exposed to pornography on the Internet is 11, and 80 percent of 15–17-year-olds have been exposed to hard-core pornography (Ropelato, 2012). In 2003, one in four children who used the Internet regularly had been exposed in the previous year to pornographic images (Mitchell et al., 2003), and one in three youths had been sexually solicited online (Ropelato, 2012). By 2006, the number of sexual solicitations had decreased, with one in seven minors sexually solicited that year (Ropelato, 2012).

Though the majority of pornography online consists of adult images, this medium has also allowed for the escalating distribution of, and access to, child images. Most pornographic images of children are available through discreet networks or groups, making it difficult to quantify the true extent of child pornography on the Internet (Beech et al., 2008; Taylor & Quayle, 2003; Wortley & Smallbone, 2006c). Ropelato (2012) says there are approximately 100,000 websites containing child pornography images; however, Taylor and Quayle (2003) note that the number of active sites or images available is highly fluid. Information about the extent of child pornography comes from individual investigations (such as the Operation Avalanche and Operation Cathedral discussed in the vignette on page 150); international policing organizations, such as Interpol; and research projects such as COPINE. The Interpol Child Sexual Exploitation (ICSE) image database has images of more than 2,300 victims from 41 countries (Interpol, 2011), and the COPINE project contains an archive of more than 700,000 images and 400 videos of sexually exploited children (Holland, 2005). Another large database of child pornographic images is ChildBase, a database compiled by the Child Exploitation and Online Protection Centre in the United Kingdom. Initiated in 1998, this database contains more than 800,000 images seized by police during investigations. As Jenkins (2001) notes, however, the number of pornographic sites and images is not as important as the subculture that creates the demand for them.

Characteristics and Typologies of Cyber Sex Offenders

Like the general population of sex offenders, cyber sex offenders constitute a heterogeneous group of individuals (Tomak et al., 2009). They share some characteristics with the general population of sex offenders; for instance, both cyber offenders and offline sex offenders have higher levels of physical and sexual abuse than the general population (Babchishin et al., 2011). However, these two populations differ in some ways. A meta-analysis by Babchishin et al. (2011) found that cyber sex offenders are more likely to be White, single, and younger than the general population of sex offenders. Sex offenders tend to have a higher level of education than the general population of offenders, and cyber sex offenders tend to be even more educated (Wolak et al., 2005).

Despite the rapidly changing nature of pornography on the Internet, the characteristics of cyber offenders remain stable over time. In the two waves of NJOV data, there were no significant differences in the demographic make-up of cyber offenders. The 2000 and 2006 cohorts were both primarily White and socioeconomically diverse (Wolak et al., 2011). Both cohorts also possessed pornographic images depicting serious sexual abuse of preteen children. Cyber sex offenders who possess pornography do differ in characteristics from those distributing it. Mitchell et al. (2011) found that the cyber sex offenders who were profiting from their pornographic images were more dangerous in several ways than those who were purchasing images of children; they were significantly more likely to have prior arrests for both sexual and nonsexual offenses, have a history of violence, have committed offenses with other offenders (including females), and produced child pornography.

As with other types of sex offenders, some scholars have created typologies for the different types of cyber sex offenders, based upon factors such as level of severity or motivations for collecting and/or distributing the materials. These cyber sex offenders can be classified in several ways, including by their cyber actions (for example, viewing pornography, soliciting), by the frequency with which they view and/or send child pornography, and by the age of the victims they seek (Robertiello & Terry, 2007).

McLaughlin (1998) was one of the first scholars to identify specific typologies of cyber sex offenders, and he created a classification system consisting of four typologies: collectors, manufacturers, travelers, and chatters. "Collectors" are often single, socially isolated individuals who collect and trade pictures of children. They tend to seek out children with specific characteristics (in regard to age, gender, hair color), and they also often have jobs with a high level of access to children. "Travellers" may collect pornography but are most likely to chat online and solicit meetings with victims. They usually target adolescents, who they groom and may pay for travel for them. "Manufacturers" make child pornography. They take photos of children they know, or they take photos of children in public and post them online. Many of the manufacturers have sexually abused children and have had convictions for sexual offenses. "Chatters" tend to chat with victims, often adolescents, online and engage in "cybersex." They also groom the victims and try to escalate to phone contact or contact in person. They are less interested in child pornography and more interested in erotica.

Moran (2010), as cited in Aiken et al. (2011), created a simple typology of cyber sex offenders, based on a pyramid framework of most offenders/simplest technology up to the fewest offenders using the most sophisticated technology. The majority of users (bottom of the pyramid) are the "simple users"; above those are the "open traders"; next up the pyramid are "closed traders"; and the peak of the pyramid consists of "experts" (Aiken et al., 2011, p. 22). As the level of technological sophistication increases, the number of offenders at that level decreases, and the majority of users are "simple users" who simply download material from others.

Yet other researchers have created typologies of cyber sex offenders based on the psychometric scores of the offenders. Henry et al. (2010) identified three clusters of cyber sex offenders: "apparently normal" offenders, who were within the normal range on all the psychological measures; "inadequate" offenders, who exhibited socio-affective deficits but did not score high in pro-offending measures; and "deviant" offenders, who scored low in victim empathy measures. They found statistically significant differences between these three groups, with the inadequate and deviant groups showing higher levels of emotional inadequacy and deviancy.

Rather than creating complete classification systems, some scholars, such as Briggs et al. (2011), identified a single typology for cyber offenders. They differentiate between Internet chat room offenders and the general rapist/child sexual molester typologies that already exist. They state that the Internet chat room offender typology can be divided into two subgroups: those who solicit contact with adolescents offline and a fantasy-driven group who engage only in online behavior.

Summarizing the characteristics of cyber sex offenders suggested by Krone (2004), Wortley and Smallbone (2006c, p. 15–17) provide a more expansive typology system for cyber sex offenders that include nine different typologies. These are shown in Table 7.3. Unlike the Henry et al. (2010) and Briggs et al. (2011) models, these are not driven primarily by psychological motivation but rather by level of engagement in the behaviors.

Victims of Child Pornography

Despite the proliferation of pornographic images of children on the Internet, there is little information about who these children are or the level of their exploitation and victimization. Most children who are exploited in pornographic

TABLE 7.3   Wortley and Smallbone's Typologies of Cyber Sex Offenders

Typology	Description
Browsers	May accidentally see images of abuse, but knowingly save the images; no networking, no use of security strategies to avoid detection.
Private fantasizers	Create digital images for private use; no networking, no use of secure strategies to avoid detection.
Trawlers	Seek images on the web through open browsers; may network, but employ few strategies to maintain security
Nonsecure collectors	Seek images in nonsecure websites or chat rooms; high level of networking, few security strategies.
Secure collectors	Members of closed groups who engage in high levels of networking and employ sophisticated security strategies to avoid detection.
Groomers	Develop online relationships with children, may send them pornographic images as part of the grooming process.
Physical abusers	Sexually abuse children; pornographic images a part of the abuse process but not the primary focus.
Producers	Record abuse images in order to disseminate to networks.
Distributors	Disseminate images of abuse; often a financial rather than sexual interest in pornography.

SOURCE: Wortley & Smallbone (2006c)

images know the perpetrators, just as do those children who are sexually abused in contact offenses. The perpetrators who take the photos are often related to the victims, or otherwise acquainted in some way (Wortley & Smallbone, 2006c). However, once these photos are distributed on the Internet, it is not always possible to identify their location of origin. By the time these images are viewed by hundreds or thousands of other perpetrators, the children are anonymous images, selected because of their characteristics. The police often have difficulty identifying them, and most remain anonymous even after major sting operations that lead to the arrests of dozens or hundreds of people downloading, possessing, trading, and distributing such images.

Few empirical studies have been conducted on the sexual images of children that have been collected. Not only are there ethical issues associated with this type of research, but methodological limitations are vast. Agencies that keep databases of child pornographic images do analyze the images in an attempt to identify the children in the photos, and they periodically report the statistics on the victims. As of 2008, the National Center for Missing & Exploited Children had identified 1,660 children in photos in their database (Quayle & Jones, 2011).

Demographically, the majority of children in pornographic photos are young, White females. In the National Center for Missing & Exploited Children database, 73 percent of the children were female, more than 90 percent were

White, and 55 percent were prepubescent (6 percent of those were infants or toddlers) (Quayle & Jones, 2011). Similarly, the Canadian Centre for Child Protection identified more than 15,000 sites hosting child pornography and found that 83 percent of the images were of female children, 57 percent contained images of children under 8, and 25 percent contained images of children between 8 and 12 years of age (Bunzeluk, 2009). In their study of ChildBase, Quayle and Jones (2011) found that girls were four times more likely to be in images than boys, and odds of images portraying White children were 10 to 1.

The types of sexual behavior portrayed in child pornography ranges from sexually suggestive posing to serious sexual abuse. In the Canadian Centre for Child Protection database, children were being sexually assaulted in about 36 percent of the images, while 64 percent of the images consisted of children in sexual poses (Bunzeluk, 2009). The younger the children, the more likely they were to be in images depicting sexual abuse. Approximately two-thirds of the extreme images, including bestiality, bondage, torture, and defecation, were against children under the age of eight (Bunzeluk, 2009). Because of some of the serious sexual acts committed against young children in pornographic images, Mitchell et al. (2011) note that this group of victims is a high-risk subgroup of youth.

Crossover between Child Pornography and Child Sexual Abuse

A significant research question regarding offenders who view child pornography is whether they also abuse, or are at risk of abusing, children. Studies on this topic are in their infancy, and the research has produced conflicting results. The main reason for the difficulty in quantifying overlap is the low rate of official statistics for both child pornography and contact offending. Many Internet offenders who have admitted to viewing child pornography have not been convicted of any contact offenses, and contact offenders who view pornography often have not been convicted of cyber offenses. As such, most data are related to self-reported behaviors. Additionally, when both types of sexual-offending behaviors are present, it is difficult to identify the chronology of the behaviors and therefore the risk that cyber offenders will begin committing contact offenses.

Overall, studies indicate that there is some overlap between online offending and contact offenses with children. Seto et al. (2011) conducted two meta-analyses to understand the level of crossover; the first assessed whether cyber sex offenders had a history of contact offenses, and the second assessed recidivism rates of cyber sex offenders. They found that 12 percent of the cyber sex offenders had a previous conviction of at least one contact offense, but 55 percent admitted to having committed a contact offense. Their second meta-analysis showed that 2 percent of cyber sex offenders committed a contact sexual offense within two to six years after their conviction, and 3.4 percent committed a new cyber sex offense. Thus, Seto et al. (2011) concluded that there is a subgroup of cyber-only offenders who pose a low risk of recidivating or committing a contact offense.

The findings by Seto et al. (2011) are consistent with other findings of cyber sex offenders. Wolak et al. (2005) found that 40 percent of NJOV cyber offenders who were arrested for possessing child pornography were "dual offenders," both possessing pornography and abusing children. Similarly, Bourke and Hernandez (2009) found that cyber sex offenders are significantly more likely than not to have committed a contact offense, and the offenders who did commit a contact offense were likely to have offended against multiple victims. They also identified this crossover group as generalists, stating that they abused children of various ages and/or genders. In a study comparing two groups of cyber sex offenders, those with contact offenses and those without, McCarthy (2009) found that contact group could be distinguished by the ratio of adult to child pornography.

Though there appears to be a crossover in offending for at least some cyber offenders, psychologically, cyber sex offenders differ from the general population of sex offenders. They exhibit significantly higher levels of victim empathy than offline offenders, fewer cognitive distortions, lower levels of impulsivity, lower sexual offense convictions, and show higher levels of self-control (Babchishin et al., 2011; Elliott et al., 2009; McCarthy, 2009; Webb et al., 2007). However, cyber offenders also show higher levels of sexual deviancy, more psychological problems in adulthood, and less impression management than offline offenders (Babchishin et al., 2011; Webb et al., 2007). Additionally, cyber offenders score higher on fantasy scales and have a greater connection to fictional characters than offline offenders (Elliott et al., 2009). Though not significant, Bates and Metcalf (2007) found that cyber sex offenders experienced higher levels of emotional loneliness and underassertiveness. Bates and Metcalf (2007) also showed differences between groups on sexual attitudes; the cyber sex offenders scored lower on sexualized attitudes towards children, emotional congruence with children, and victim empathy distortions, thus indicating that they did not explicitly endorse the sexual abuse of children. Some psychological findings are contradictory; Seto, Cantor, and Blanchard (2006) found that there are no differences between cyber sex offenders and contact offenders in diagnoses of pedophilia, while McCarthy (2009) found that contact offenders are significantly more likely to be diagnosed with pedophilia.

Ultimately, more studies on this topic are necessary to understand the nuances of which cyber sex offenders are at risk to abuse, in what situations, and why. Rather than view this as a dichotomous issue, the risk that cyber sex offenders pose to commit contact offenses should be considered along a continuum (McCarthy, 2009). Research should be conducted to determine who is at a higher risk, and those who are at a low risk to commit contact offenses should be treated differently than those at a high risk.

Regulating and Policing Child Pornography

Several laws have been passed to help to safeguard children from sexual exploitation. As technology has developed and the collectors, producers, and distributors of child pornography have become more sophisticated, lawmakers have had to constantly adapt the laws. The key federal acts that have addressed child pornography are seen in Table 7.4. The first law to explicitly prohibit child pornography was passed in 1978, though it applied to minors under the age of 16. The laws passed subsequently expanded the definition of pornography,

TABLE 7.4 **Major Federal Legislation Prohibiting the Sexual Exploitation of Children**

Federal Legislation	Description
Sexual Exploitation of Children Act (1978)	First federal law that prohibited the distribution of obscene material of minors.
Child Protection Act (1984)	Specified that a minor is a child under 18, and any sexually explicit material of minors is child pornography.
Child Sexual Abuse and Pornography Act (1986)	Banned the advertisement of child pornography and increased penalties for recidivist child pornography offenders.
The Child Protection and Obscenity Enforcement Act (1988)	Explicitly prohibited the possession, sale, and distribution of child pornography via the Internet. In 1990, Congress clarified this stipulation, making it illegal to possess three or more pornographic images of children.
Child Pornography Prevention Act (1996)	Made it illegal to possess or distribute any images that appear to sexually exploit minors.
Child Online Protection Act (1998)	Requires commercial pornographers to have users verify they are over 18 before entering an adult pornographic website.
PROTECT Act (2003)	Clarified that material can be considered child pornography even when it does not involve real children.
Adam Walsh Act (2006)	Limits the defense's access to examination of child sexual exploitation material that is the subject of a criminal charge.

clarified the behaviors that were prohibited, raised the age of minors to 18, specified the types of images that were covered, and increased the sanctions for those who violate the laws.

Several legal cases have also had an impact in shaping legislation and sanctions related to child pornography. In particular, *New York v. Ferber* (1982) found that child pornography is not the same as obscenity and is not protected by the First Amendment. The second major case that shaped child pornography legislation was *United States v. Dost* (1986), which clarified what constitutes "lascivious exhibition of the genitals or pubic area." The court created six criteria of what could be considered lascivious conduct (the Dost test), though not all need to be met in order to constitute a pornographic image.

A more recent, and controversial, legal examination of child pornography involves the sexual images of children that are not real. In an effort to skirt the legal consequences of possessing and distributing child pornography, some individuals have created sexual images of "virtual" children. Virtual images appear to depict minors engaging in sexual activity, but the images are produced by some means other than the use of real children (such as computer-generated images of children or images of adults who look like children). Virtual, or fictitious, children are not protected by the Child Pornography Prevention Act of 1996, purportedly to protect the right of free speech. In the case of *Ashcroft v. Free*

V I G N E T T E

T O C A T C H A P R E D A T O R : Sting Operations and Child Pornography

Many Americans have seen the television show *To Catch a Predator*, where the host of the show pretends to be an adolescent girl who meets older men online. The host sets up a sting operation, going with the television crew to the older man's apartment. Though this makes for good, but disturbing, television, the reality is that sting operations often take years and a substantial amount of resources to achieve a successful outcome.

One example of a multiyear, multiagency global effort to remove child pornography from the Internet was Operation Cathedral. Led by the British National Crime Squad in cooperation with 13 additional agencies across the world, Operation Cathedral led to the seizure of more than 750,000 pornographic images of children that were part of the "Wonderland Club." Called the world's biggest pedophile ring, the Wonderland Club was based in the United Kingdom but had members worldwide. As a result of Operation Cathedral, 107 men were arrested globally.

Similar in scope was Operation Avalanche, a U.S.-led investigation into a child pornography ring in Fort Worth, Texas. The service, called Landslide, had more than 250,000 customers worldwide and brought in approximately $1.4 million per month. Unlike other child pornography services, Landslide was a "gateway" to pornographic sites worldwide that served to protect the identity of customers. Operation Avalanche was a complex investigation but eventually led to the arrest and conviction of the operators of Landslide, Thomas and Janice Reedy. By 2001, officers in the United States had made more than 100 arrests of suspects in 37 states. The investigation also led to the identification of thousands of individuals in other countries, initiating major investigations (such as Operation Ore in the United Kingdom).

As technology for downloading and distributing child pornography becomes more sophisticated, so do the law enforcement operations to catch the perpetrators. These early sting operations were complicated, and the agencies encountered several obstacles, such as realizing that several of the credit cards used for Landslide were used fraudulently. However, those who are convicted of distributing child pornographic images for profit are now serving prison sentences that range from decades long to life. After turning down a plea bargain, Thomas Reedy was found guilty and sentenced to 1,335 years in prison (later reduced to 180 years on appeal).

Discussion Questions
1. What is the appropriate sentence for a person convicted of possessing child pornography or distributing it for profit? Should these sentences be as long as a sentence for sexually abusing a child?
2. What type of legal sanction might deter a person from becoming involved with the multimillion dollar child pornography industry?

Speech Coalition (2002), the Court said that acts banning virtual child pornography are constitutionally vague and they violate the free speech clause of the First Amendment. The Court did recognize the dangers in allowing such material to be produced, but it also acknowledged that the virtual images are not fundamentally related to sexual abuse of children.

Shortly after the Court announced its decision to protect virtual child pornography, several legislators began revising the law so that images that are "virtually indistinguishable" from minors engaging in sexual activity will not be protected. As a result of these efforts, the PROTECT Act (2003) addressed the prohibition of virtual child pornography in a different way. Rather than criminalize virtual images, the Act prohibits the distribution of material that is intended to cause another to believe that the images are child pornography. This concept of "virtual" pornography was tested in *United States v. Williams* (2008), in which the Court stated that it is illegal to distribute or receive sexual images of virtual children if an individual involved in the transaction believes those images are real. The importance of the Williams case is that the Court restricted the ability to pander child pornography, thus making it possible to charge the businesspeople in the child pornography industry who are involved for profit (McGrain & Moore, 2010).

Cases involving virtual pornography continue to be dealt with on a case-by-case basis, as the courts try to balance First Amendment rights with the need to combat the growing child pornography industry. However, the courts have generally found that virtual images are not covered by the First Amendment (Perry, 2012). For instance, in *United States v. Hotaling* (2011), the defendant created virtual images by morphing photos of minors' heads onto the bodies of adults committing sexual acts. Because the faces of the minors were clearly recognizable and therefore created a risk of reputational harm, the courts stated that this was child pornography and not covered by the First Amendment. The definition of "victim" will continue to evolve through such decisions in the courts, as will the definition of what constitutes a pornographic image.

It is not just the definition of child pornography and victim that are difficult; investigating the possession, distribution, and circulation of child pornography is challenging because of the anonymity and globalization of the Internet. It is often unclear who should be investigating particular offenses, as "jurisdiction" generally refers to physical geography, and there is no geographical boundary for the Internet. Some local agencies have the duty to investigate cyber crime, though jurisdiction will usually fall on federal agencies. This is because much of the crime in cyberspace crosses state and even international boundaries, and therefore many of the crimes are cross-jurisdictional.

There is little physical evidence on the Internet like that available at a physical crime scene, so investigators must target offenders through their "conversations" and electronic "fingerprints." Any computer, computer system, computer network, or any software or data owned by the suspect that is used during the commission of any public offense involving pornography (or any other cyber crimes) or that is used as a repository for the storage of illegal software is subject to forfeiture. Unfortunately, there are few established boundaries as to how cyber searches can legally take place and what type of searches would be considered constitutional under the Fourth Amendment.

In order to conduct searches of computers, officers can use wiretaps that are similar to those used on telephones. In order to obtain a wiretap order, it must be either issued where the interception occurs or consensual. For consensual wiretaps, the party must consent, not the service provider. However, the Child Protector and Sexual Predator Punishment Act of 1998 mandates that Internet service providers (ISPs) report known incidents of child pornography to authorities.

The act does not require ISPs to actively monitor individual customers or sites, but they can do so in order to protect themselves. Additionally, the provider can disclose information that it inadvertently came across, if the information pertains to a crime. In terms of the Fourth Amendment, computers are equivalent to "containers"; the user does not have a special expectation of privacy, even though data can be erased (*Commonwealth of Pennsylvania v. Copenhefer*, 1991). As with a container, the officer must have probable cause to search the computer, which usually requires a warrant specifying exactly what is to be searched and what the officer is searching for. Once the officers look for material beyond the scope of their specified search, they violate the individual's Fourth Amendment rights. For instance, in the case of *United States v. Carey* (1999), the officers had a warrant to search the suspect's computer for drug-related information. Upon finding images of child pornography, the officers continued to search for further such images in the jpeg files. The Court invalidated the search, claiming that the officers should have stopped the search and obtained a warrant once they found the pornographic images.

In most cases, images of child pornography are discovered during investigations of child sexual abuse (Wolak et al., 2011). Investigations into child pornography usually begin with investigations of possession of sexual images, which then evolve into proactive investigations of child pornography production and distribution. Wolak et al. (2011) note that arrests for possession of child pornography have been increasing, though this is likely due to the enhanced law enforcement investigations rather than an actual increase in producers of child pornography. At this point, however, the understanding and enforcement of child pornography continues to rapidly evolve.

SEXTING AND SELF-PRODUCED PORNOGRAPHY

Much of the research on sexual images of children has focused on the commercial sexual exploitation of children by adults. However, in the last decade, adolescents have begun creating "self-produced pornography," taking photos of themselves and texting them to friends ("sexting") or posting them online. Sexting is not exclusive to adolescents, though this behavior is most prevalent among adolescents and young adults. Sexting refers to sending a friend or other trusted person a sexual image, but this may lead to a widespread distribution of the image against the will of the subject of the photo (Aiken et al., 2011).

Sexting has emerged as a common practice among adolescents and young adults along with the rise in the use of technology generally. Mitchell et al. (2008) describe children as "living on the Internet," and Stone (2011) states that adolescents constantly use digital technology as a method of peer networking. The number of teens and young adults who have sexted is unknown, and research estimates vary depending on the source and the way in which it is defined and measured. Wolak et al. (2011) note that sexting is widespread, based upon surveys of law enforcement agencies; yet the actual frequency with which sexting occurs is difficult to estimate. One reason for this, notes Forbes

(2011), is the social disapproval over sexting, which causes many teens to not report such incidents. A study by the National Campaign to Prevent Teen and Unplanned Pregnancy (NCPTUP) shows that one in five teens between the ages of 13 and 19 have either sexted explicit images or posted them online (NCPTUP, 2009). The Third Youth Internet Safety Survey showed that 1 in 10 youth between the ages of 10 and 17 had sent or received sexual images, though few of these images violated child pornography laws (Mitchell et al., 2011). The sexting trend is even more prominent with young adults; Forbes (2011) states that approximately 36 percent of women and 31 percent of men aged 20 to 26 have posted nude or seminude images of themselves online.

The consequences of sexting or posting sexually explicit photos online can be psychologically damaging. In particular, the distribution of a sexually explicit photo to unintended audiences can result in emotional trauma to the subject of the photo (Forbes, 2011). Additionally, the images may be distributed online widely and accessible to anyone, which can be detrimental to the futures of those in the images (Mitchell et al., 2011).

DID YOU KNOW...?

It is not just adolescents and young adults who sext; adults also send sexually explicit photos of themselves to others. There are several high-profile cases of politicians who have been caught sexting, sending explicit texts, soliciting under-age adolescents, or posting explicit photos online, acts that have led to the demise of their political careers. Examples include:

- Anthony Weiner, congressman from New York, sent many sexual texts and explicit photos to women while in office. After accidently posting a seminude photo of himself publicly on Twitter, he eventually resigned his congressional seat in humiliation.

- Chris Lee, congressman from New York, resigned after sending a shirtless photo of himself to a woman he met on Craigslist.

- Mark Foley, congressman from Florida, resigned after he was caught sending sexually explicit emails to underage congressional male aides.

- Brian Doyle, deputy press secretary in the Department of Homeland Security, solicited a 14-year-old girl, impersonated by a sheriff deputy, online. He was arrested and served time in prison.

© Cengage Learning

Legally, states' responses to sexting are still mixed, and there has been no clear response to this behavior from the criminal justice system (Stone, 2011). In some states, sexting is a registerable sexual offense, and both the sender of the photos and the recipients who later distribute the images may be charged with criminal offenses. In fact, the sexting "victims"—those whose image was distributed—may be charged with crimes that carry the same penalty as the person who distributes the photos. This is a unique type of offense in that the offender in the case may also be the victim. Additionally, those who are charged for sexting offenses may be subject to the same sanctions as sex offenders charged with possession or distribution of child pornography (Forbes, 2011). In some states, there is little discretion about the sentences for offenders convicted of child pornography charges; there are mandatory minimum sentences with no reduction possible. Yet Wolak et al. (2011) show that few youth are arrested for sexting, and the youth who must register as sex offenders have often committed other sexual offenses as well.

JUVENILE PROSTITUTION

Legislators and federal agencies have expressed concerns about the seemingly high levels of juvenile prostitution in the United States. There are many claims about the extent of juvenile prostitution, though only recently have there been any methodologically sound studies to determine the nature and scope of the problem nationally and in local jurisdictions. As such, there is no consensus on the magnitude or needs of the child prostitution population. There is little research on the characteristics of the youth who are prostituted, why, what services are available to them, and whether those are effective in assisting them. Even the term *prostitution* is controversial as applied to juveniles, since prostitution is illegal and the term implies culpability on the part of the juvenile who is being prostituted. Many scholars and service agencies instead apply terms such as *sexual exploitation of children* or refer to youth who are prostituted.

Juvenile prostitution is a complex issue, and one not easily defined. Some describe prostitution as any sexual acts exchanged for money, while others consider a wider definition that also includes sexual acts in exchange for drugs, food, or shelter (Curtis et al., 2008). The exchange of sexual favors as a means to survival, or "survival sex," is even more poorly understood than traditional forms of prostitution (for example, on a street), since much of survival sex goes unreported and unnoticed. Prostitution may also be categorized depending on whether the person involved in prostitution is on his or her own, or whether there is a third party overseeing the money he or she makes. Known colloquially as pimps, some scholars have broadened this term after noting that the third-party facilitators may be friends, family, or other partners that are more similar to business managers. Curtis et al. (2008) refer to these as "market facilitators." Mitchell, Wolak, and Finkelor (2010) refer to them as "third-party exploiters," differentiating them from cases of solo prostitution and conventional child sexual abuse with payment.

Several legislative acts have identified juvenile prostitution as a critical issue within the criminal justice system, affecting some of the more vulnerable adolescents who are in need of assistance. Some of these acts are spearheaded by agencies who cite the large number of juveniles that are being exploited, yet few of these numbers are derived from methodologically sound studies, and the estimates of juvenile prostitution vary widely. Nationwide, the U.S. Department of Justice has estimated that between 100,000 and three million youth were exploited in the last decade (ECPAT, 2005), though this estimate includes child pornography and trafficking in addition to prostitution. ECPAT estimates that there may be up to 400,000 youth exploited in prostitution in the United States (ECPAT, 2005), though it is not clear how this number was derived.

Some studies have tried to understand the scope of prostituted youth in particular jurisdictions within the United States. For example, several scholars and agencies have studied juvenile prostitution rates in New York City, where there are high levels of anonymity, mobility, and resources and therefore higher levels of prostitution generally. In a study commissioned by the New York State Legislature, Gragg, Petta, Bernstein, Eisen, and Quinn (2007) found that approximately 2,200 youth were being prostituted in New York City. These estimates are based upon quantitative and qualitative data collected from various city agencies in four boroughs. As thorough as this study was, it still did not reach the population of hidden youth who had no contact with agencies such as juvenile detention facilities, runaway and homeless service agencies, and rape crisis centers.

Another study conducted in New York City utilized a method of Respondent-Driven Sampling (RDS) to identify this hidden population of youth through their social networks (Curtis et al., 2008). Similar to snowball sampling, RDS is used to recruit statistically representative samples of hard-to-reach populations, but through a systematic recruiting scheme (Dank, 2008). Through an RDS sample of 329 youth, Curtis et al. (2008) estimated that the size of the juvenile prostitution population in New York City is 3,946. What is most surprising about the Curtis et al. (2008) study was the demographic characteristics of the youth: 54 percent of the sample was male, and the majority were involved in solo prostitution. Only 8 percent of the youth in their sample were recruited into the market by a pimp, and 10 percent were subsequently under the control of a pimp. This may have an effect on how the youths are treated in the criminal justice system, as juvenile prostitutes under the control of a third party are more likely to be treated as victims rather than delinquents. Mitchell, Finkelhor, and Wolak (2010) found that 66 percent of youth prostituted by third parties were treated as victims, whereas only 11 percent of youths in solo cases were treated as victims by law enforcement agencies (Curtis et al., 2008).

The Curtis et al. (2008) study provides insight into a less-researched population of juvenile prostitutes that adds to the existing body of literature. Previous studies have shown that female prostituted youth nearly always become involved in prostitution before the age of 16 (Busby et al., 2000), while males tend to get involved between ages 11 and 13 (Estes & Weiner, 2001). Though most services for assisting prostituted youth are geared towards girls, some studies have shown that male youth are also being exploited at high rates. Adolescent males, particularly those who are homosexual or bisexual, are more likely to engage in survival sex than adolescent girls (ECPAT 2005; Finkelhor & Ormrod, 2004). Most studies have found that the majority of prostituted youth are White (Estes & Weiner, 2001), but the Curtis et al. (2008) study in New York City showed a population of mixed races and ethnicities. Their sample was 29 percent Black, 23 percent White, 23 percent Hispanic, and 22 percent who identified as "multiracial." This is not surprising, however, considering the demographic population of New York City.

There are significant psychological, physical, and emotional problems associated with youth who have been involved in prostitution. Studies show that youth who are involved in prostitution are often runaways, victims or witnesses of domestic violence, and have been involved in the child welfare system (Brannigan & Gibbs Van Brunschot, 1997; Kidd & Krall, 2002). They also are at high risk of engaging in criminal behavior, developing substance abuse problems, and becoming victims of sexual abuse (Inciardi, Pottieger, Forney, Chitwood, & McBride, 1991; Loeber & Farrington, 1998; Schissel & Fedec, 1999). Psychologically, they are likely to suffer from problems such as depression, self-abusive behavior, and schizophrenia (Brannigan & Gibbs Van Brunschot, 1997; Schissel & Fedec, 1999). Physically, they are at a high risk of unplanned pregnancy and sexually transmitted diseases (Busby et al., 2000; Kidd & Krall, 2002), and their substance abuse problems—particularly intravenous drug use—puts them at a higher risk of diseases such as HIV and hepatitis.

According to Curtis et al. (2008), most (87 percent) of the youth involved in prostitution are interested in leaving "the life" and said they would do so if they had an alternative means of supporting themselves. However, there are few services available to help youth remove themselves from a life of prostitution. The most common services for prostituted children are enforced detention programs (Busby et al., 2000), shelters and safe housing (for example, Children of the Night; Office of the United Nations High Commissioner for Human Rights), and voluntary health, educational, and job training services (Office of the United Nations High Commissioner for Human Rights). Even in New York City, there is a discrepancy between the needs of the population of sexually exploited youth and the resources allocated to it. There is one agency specifically dedicated to assisting juvenile prostitutes, and that serves that population of girls who had been under the control of pimps (Curtis et al., 2008).

The federal government has taken some steps towards responding to needs of the juvenile prostitution population. In 2003, the Federal Bureau of Investigation launched an Innocence Lost initiative, which reconceptualizes prostituted children as victims and focuses on providing them with services, while increasing legal responses to the adults who exploit them (Dank, 2008). Additionally, some local jurisdictions have taken action to ensure that juveniles involved in prostitution are treated as victims rather than delinquents. In New York State, the governor signed into law the Safe Harbor for Exploited Youth Act in 2008. This decriminalizes first acts of prostitution for youth age 16 and under and classifies them as "persons in need of supervision" (PINS), and provides services to juvenile prostitutes under the age of 18.

Dank (2008, p. 89) makes the following policy recommendations based upon the findings of the Curtis et al. (2008) study.

- More services need to be available to boys and transgender youth, who make up a significant portion of the CSEC population. These services should include emergency shelter, long-term housing, intensive counseling, medical services, educational opportunities, life-skills, and job training and employment opportunities.

- Use social networks to deliver services. Mandating youth, either through the court system or by law enforcement, to partake in services is not likely to be effective at helping youth exit the life. As Curtis et al. (2008) demonstrated, prostituted youth are often times influenced by their peers, whether it is through recruitment into the market or reasons to remain in the life, and infiltration of these social networks can be instrumental in effectively delivering services. One possible way to do this is to find, with the help of existing youth agencies, individuals with the largest and most diverse CSEC network and have them conduct outreach to their peers.

- Properly train staff who work with the CSEC youth. Training youth agency staff and law enforcement is necessary in order to gain the trust of prostituted youth. Without the proper training, agency staff and law enforcement officials could discourage a youth from seeking help ever again. Almost, if not, all sexually exploited youth have severe, deep-seated issues with adults and authority, and if they are not approached with a nonjudgmental and empathetic ear, they will see no reason to leave the life.

HUMAN TRAFFICKING

In addition to pornography and prostitution, another form of commercial sexual exploitation is human trafficking. Victims of human trafficking can be children or adults, domestic or international. They can be trafficked for the purposes of the sex trade or as forced labor, debt bondage, and involuntary servitude (Uy, 2011). Human trafficking for the sex trade involves the transportation of individuals against their will for the purposes of prostitution, pornography, stripping, escort services, and other sexual services.

Human trafficking is often seen as being connected to a larger picture of economic globalization and transnational crime (Fry, 2008) and is worth an estimated $32 billion and $91 billion (Kotrla, 2010). Excessive debt is used as a tool to manipulate victims into human trafficking (Lagon, 2008), or a promise of money and a better life. Because the definitions of human trafficking are not always clear, it is difficult to collect accurate data about this phenomenon. There is often a mixture of data concerning trafficking, smuggling, and illegal migration, while the term trafficking is reserved for victims of sexual slavery only (Gozdziak & Collett, 2005). It has also been difficult to create a definition of human trafficking due to differences regarding the notion of "consent" and the age of the victim (Gozdziak & Collett, 2005). There is a clear distinction between adult and children victims of sex trafficking, as adults are considered victims if they are subjected to commercial sex acts by force, fraud, or coercion, while a child under the age of 18 is considered a victim simply based upon his or her age (Kotrla, 2010).

There is a lack of reliable information regarding the scope of human trafficking (Fry, 2008). One reason for this is the lack of systematic, empirical, and methodologically rigorous research on trafficking in human beings. The U.S. Department of State has been publishing global estimates of human trafficking since 2002; they estimate that between 600,000 and 800,000 people are trafficked globally annually (Fry, 2008), with 14,500–17,500 trafficked into the United States alone (Gozdziak & Collett, 2005). The majority of trafficking cases were characterized as part of the sex trade (82 percent), split between instances of adult sex trafficking and allegations of prostitution or sexual exploitation of a child (Banks & Kyckelhahn, 2011). Some experts suggest that there are as many as 100,000 domestic minor sex trafficking victims in the United States, while 350,000 more children are at risk of becoming victims (Gozdziak & Collett, 2005).

The media portrayal of sex trafficking is that of third world women and children being brought across borders and forced into commercial sex acts (Uy, 2011). However, that is not necessarily an accurate portrayal. The Human Trafficking Reporting System was designed to measure the performance of the federally funded task forces and is currently the only system that captures information on human trafficking investigations conducted by the state and local law enforcement agencies (Banks & Kyckelhahn, 2011). Among the 389 incidents confirmed to be human trafficking in their report, there were 488 suspects and 527 victims; 13 percent of the confirmed sex trafficking victims were age 25 or older; sex trafficking victims were more likely to be White (26 percent) or Black (40 percent); and 83 percent were identified as U.S. citizens (Banks & Kyckelhahn, 2011). Studies show that those children most at risk are those who are homeless, have a history of abuse, and those in foster care or child protective services (Kotrla, 2010). Children can also become victims to sex trafficking through the Internet, as traffickers search for victims online and advertise the children online to potential consumers (Kotrla, 2010).

For the cases of sex trafficking that are international, Kotrla (2010) suggests that countries have a "culture of tolerance" that supports sex trade markets. These cultures often glamorize pimping and prostitution, which are embodied in clothing, songs, television, video games, and other forms of entertainment. Bales (2007) found six factors that predict trafficking from a country. The most powerful predictor was government corruption, followed by percent of the population under 14 years old, infant mortality and food production, population pressure, and conflict, and social unrest. These factors explained 75 percent of the variance in trafficking from a country. Fry (2008), however, found only four significant factors: percent of male population aged 60 or older, government corruption, infant mortality, and food production.

The Trafficking Victims Protection Act of 2000 is the first comprehensive federal law in the United States to combat human trafficking and help victims. Under this act, human trafficking is defined as "the recruitment, harboring, transportation, provision, or obtaining of a person for one of three purposes: labor or services, through the use of force, fraud, or coercion for the purposes of subjugation to involuntary servitude, peonage, debt bondage or slavery; a commercial sex act through the use of force, fraud, or coercion; and any commercial sex act, if the person is under 18 years of age, regardless of whether any form of coercion is involved" (Banks & Kyckelhahn, 2011).

The UN General Assembly adopted an international treaty regarding trafficking, which requires that countries criminalize trafficking and related conduct, as well as impose appropriate penalties; facilitate and accept the return of their trafficked nationals; when returning trafficked persons, ensure that this happens safely; exchange information aimed at identifying perpetrators or victims; provide or strengthen training for law enforcement, immigration, and other relevant personnel; strengthen border controls to detect and prevent trafficking; take legislative measures to prevent commercial transport being used in the trafficking process; and take steps to ensure the integrity of travel documents issued on their behalf and to prevent fraudulent use (Fry, 2008).

Victim protection measures are also contained within the protocol, such as protecting the privacy of trafficking victims, providing for the physical and psychological recovery of victims, providing for physical safety of trafficking victims, ensuring that domestic laws provide victims with the opportunity of obtaining compensation, permitting victims to remain in territories temporarily or permanently, and establishing polices aimed at preventing trafficking and protecting victims from being revictimized (Fry, 2008).

For victims of trafficking in the United States who are not citizens, the Trafficking Victims Protection Act of 2000 created the "T" visa, which allows trafficking victims to remain in the United States to assist federal authorities in the investigation and prosecution of human trafficking cases (Lagon, 2008). From 2001 to 2008, the U.S. Department of Homeland Security granted approximately 2,000 "T" visas. These victims have come from 77 countries (Lagon, 2008).

CHAPTER SUMMARY

- Though the scope of child sexual exploitation is unknown, studies show that this is a vast problem in the United States and worldwide. Children and adolescents can be sexually exploited through pornography, prostitution, and trafficking.

- The anonymity of the Internet and the advances in technology have led to an increase in the creation, viewing, and distribution of child pornography. As with other types of sex offenders, cyber sex offenders can be categorized into typologies depending on the nature and scope of their interests and activities.

- Technology has led to new offenses, such as sexting, where (usually) adolescents text sexual images of themselves to others. Though many teens think this is harmless, it can lead to long-term psychological and legal consequences for those who participate.

- Juvenile prostitution and human trafficking are other forms of sexual exploitation of children. Only recently have researchers begun to understand the scope of the problem, the characteristics of the children and adolescents who are exploited, and the services necessary to assist them.

DISCUSSION QUESTIONS

1. Compare and contrast "online" and "offline" child sexual abusers. What are the similarities and differences between the two types of offenders?

2. Who is in danger of becoming sexually exploited by an adult? What can be done to protect potential victims?

3. Is it possible to measure the true extent of juvenile prostitution? Human trafficking? Why or why not?

4. Is it possible to control the incidence of "self-produced pornography", or the sexualized images that people text or post online of themselves? If so, how? What are the potential dangers of this behavior?

8

Sexual Offending in Institutional Settings

Sexual victimization is a highly prevalent societal problem, and one that can lead to substantial and long-term harm to victims. Sexual victimization is almost always perpetrated by an individual known to the victim and is most prevalent in situations where the victim and the perpetrator are able to spend time together alone. Thus, abuse of minors is most common in families and institutions where adults form mentoring and nurturing relationships with adolescents, including schools, religious organizations, sports, and social organizations. Sexual assaults of adults are most common among acquaintances, within relationships, in situations where there is an unequal power relationship (for example, abuse by a psychologist or a professor), or in closed institutions such as the military or prisons.

Scholars are increasingly assessing the role the environment plays in the commission of sexual offenses. The environment, and particularly the situations in which abuse occurs and the opportunities that offenders have to commit sexual offenses, plays a critical role in whether or not victimization occurs. Child sexual abuse in particular is pervasive in situations in which adults have unguarded access to children, including in youth-serving organizations. Colton et al. (2010), Sullivan and Beech (2004), and Wortley and Smallbone (2006b) found that many perpetrators accessed the children they abused through youth-oriented organizations, and some joined the organization specifically for that purpose. Institutions with power differentials, which are often male-dominated, perpetuate inappropriate sexual behavior, and the sexual assaults often go unreported. This chapter assesses what is known about abuse of minors and adults within specific institutions.

SEXUAL ABUSE WITHIN CHILD AND ADOLESCENT-ORIENTED INSTITUTIONS

Many reports have emerged in the last decade about the sexual abuse of children within youth-oriented organizations, including churches, schools, social organizations, and sports. Reports indicate that this is a serious and underreported problem, although there is little reliable data indicating the true prevalence of such behavior. Gallagher (2000) reports that 3 percent of social service referrals are for claims of sexual abuse by an authority figure within an institution, with the most prevalent institutional abusers being teachers, clergy, scout leaders, tutors, and social workers. Abusers in these settings are generally employees or volunteers having some authority over children (Wortley & Smallbone, 2006b). Empirical data on abusers in institutional settings are limited, coming from a combination of places including social services, law enforcement agencies, and journalists rather than from the institutions themselves. Moreover, many of the reports contain anecdotal information with limited generalizability. What follows is an overview of what is known about abuse within nonreligious youth-oriented organizations (Terry et al., 2011).

Schools

There have been no methodologically rigorous empirical studies of sexual abuse within schools. The most substantial report summarizing knowledge of sexual abuse by educators stated that "educator sexual misconduct is woefully understudied" (Shakeshaft, 2004, p. 51). In her report, Shakeshaft summarized the statistics and results of the existing literature on sexual misconduct in schools. Drawing upon the limited available research (Shakeshaft, 2004, p. 1), she found that physical, verbal, and visual forms of sexual misconduct are widespread in schools. The most thorough of studies that she drew upon was that by American Association of University Women (2001), which showed that nearly 7 percent of students in grades 8 to 11 experienced an unwanted sexual contact, with 21 percent of these unwanted contacts reportedly perpetrated by teachers. Importantly, specific job characteristics were associated with a higher rate of abuse; teachers whose job involved individual time with students, such as coaches or music tutors, were more likely to abuse.

Though the Shakeshaft report is an excellent first step toward understanding the prevalence of sexual misconduct within schools, it has substantial limitations. Most importantly, the studies she summarizes contain small samples of clinical or interview data, or surveys conducted in ways that limit their generalizability. Additionally, the studies do not rely on consistent definitions of sexual behavior, misconduct, or abuse. This problem is not unique to studies of abuse within schools, but rather is common amongst studies of sexual abuse generally.

Child Care Settings

Several studies published in the last two decades have focused on sexual abuse of children within day care or other child care settings (Colton, Roberts, & Vanstone,

2010; Finkelhor & Williams, 1988; Margolin, 1991; Moulden, Firestone, & Wexler, 2007; Sullivan & Beech, 2004). In their study of 270 center-based and family-based day care institutions between 1983 and 1985, Finkelhor and Williams (1988) found substantiated claims of sexual abuse regarding 1,639 victims and 382 abusers. They estimated that 5.5 out of every 10,000 children enrolled in day-care centers and 8.9 children out of every 10,000 children in families are reported to be sexually abused. Certain situational factors seemed to play a key role in the abuse, such as low staff presence. Moulden et al. (2007) found that age (younger than age 25) and being single were risk factors for child sexual victimization among nonfamilial child care providers. They also found that abuse was more likely to take place in informal care settings than in formal care settings, consistent with the findings of Margolin (1991).

Boy Scouts of America

The Boy Scouts of America (BSA) is one of the largest youth-serving organizations in the United States, having served over 100 million youths since its inception in 1910. For most of the years it has existed, scout leaders were able to spend time alone with individual boys or scout groups, creating opportunities for abuse to occur. In 1991, journalist Patrick Boyle investigated the confidential files of BSA and published his findings in a five-part series in *Washington Times* as well as in a book (Boyle, 1994). According to BSA records, 416 male Scout employees were banned between 1971 and 1989 as a result of sexual misconduct, and 1151 cases of sexual abuse were reported within this time period. The Boy Scouts had one million adult volunteers and four million Scouts (including Cub Scouts, Boy Scouts, etc.) during this time period. The majority of the victims were Boy Scouts, who typically range in age from 11 to 17. Boyle found that most of the abuse occurred during camping trips. The Scouts claimed that sexual abuse in this organization was not a major crisis, but Boyle argued that sexual abuse is more common in Scouting than accidental deaths and serious injuries combined.

The BSA now has an extensive youth protection training program. However, more than 50 lawsuits have been filed against the Scouts by families of boys who were abused prior to the introduction of this program. At the time his book was published, Boyle said BSA had paid more than 15 million dollars to settle cases out of court, with payments ranging from $12,000 to $1.5 million. One such case is that of *Doe v. Goff* 306 Ill. App. 3d 1131 (1999), in which a victim filed a lawsuit against the Scout leader who abused him, the BSA, and the Rainbow Council of Boy Scouts, the latter two of which he claimed were negligent in their investigation of Goff's moral fitness and in implementing appropriate child protection programs. However, the Court decided that the organization was not negligent and should not be held liable for the abuse. The majority opinion stated that the organizations could not reasonably have foreseen the abuse, that the overwhelming majority of Boy Scout leaders are not sexual predators, and that the organizations' subsequent implementation of child protection programs did not render them liable for the abuse.

Conversely, in a civil trial in April 2010 an Oregon jury awarded the largest known verdict in the history of the BSA, $18.5 million, to a former Scout (Zaitz & Dungca, 2010). The Court found the BSA to be liable for allowing a former assistant scoutmaster to continue to work with children after the abuser admitted to molesting 17 boys. During the trial, it came to light that the BSA began keeping records detailing sexual abuse within the organization soon after its inception in 1910. Between 1965 and 1985, the BSA had classified 1,600 individuals as "unfit" to work with children (Raw Story, 2010). The jury at the trial was shown 1200 files of abusers, though it is believed that there are more than 6,000 such files at the organization's headquarters (McGreal, 2010). As a practice, the BSA does not release detailed statistics on child sexual abuse (Bono, 2004) and most cases are settled out of court (Associated Press, 2010), so it is not known how many cases actually have been reported. Whatever the number of cases, it is likely to be much higher than that uncovered by Boyle more than two decades ago.

The BSA now has a requirement that all employees and volunteers must pass a background check in order to be employed by or work with the organization, and they have developed an extensive training program on the awareness of sexual abuse. They have also developed internal policies requiring a minimum of two adults at every event and prohibiting adults from being left alone with individual Scouts. The BSA has been criticized, however, for not making their youth training program mandatory (McCall, 2010; Zaitz & Dungca, 2010), and their recently implemented policies prohibiting homosexual Scout leaders have come under scrutiny by various civil rights organizations.

Big Brothers Big Sisters

Big Brothers Big Sisters is an organization that provides mentorship to economically disadvantaged youths. Like other organizations where mentoring relationships develop between adults and adolescents, it has experienced incidents of sexual abuse. There have been no published studies about the incidence of abuse in the organization; however, in 2002 the organization's president stated that Big Brothers Big Sisters receives fewer than 10 allegations of sexual abuse per year in an organization that matches 220,000 children with mentors (Bennett, 2002), and approximately half of the allegations end in conviction or an admission of guilt (Bono, 2004).

Though the numbers of reported incidents have been declining in the last decade, some notable cases have been reported upon in the media. In the case of *Doe v. Big Brothers Big Sisters of America*, the plaintiff sued the organization for negligent hiring practices and supervision, saying he had been repeatedly sexual abused by his mentor while enrolled in a Big Brothers program in Chicago ("Negligent Hiring," 2006). The Court ruled in favor of the organization, stating that the national organization was not liable because their hiring and supervision policies and procedures were not mandatory, but merely recommendations. A similar decision was reached regarding the organization's liability in a child sexual abuse case in New York, *Lamarche v. Big Brothers Big Sisters of America*.

Donald Wolff reviewed 100 allegations of sexual abuse in the Big Brother Big Sister organization and determined that, much like in the BSA, the majority of offenders were single and came from various professions (Boyle, 1994). The sexual abuse ranged from inappropriate touching to other sexual acts, and the abuse commonly occurred during camping trips and visits to the abuser's house. Offenders also appeared to target emotionally vulnerable children, as is common in most cases of child sexual abuse. In most cases where charges were filed, the perpetrators confessed or the case ended with a conviction. Many of the abusers were involved in multiple organizations involving children, such as the Boy Scouts, child care services, or educational institutions. Based on these findings, Big Brothers Big Sisters instituted a strict screening process that involves a criminal background check for all employees and volunteers.

Athletic Organizations

Several studies have been published since the mid-1980s about sexual abuse in sporting organizations (Bringer, Brackenridge, & Johnston, 2001), and media reports in the last decade have highlighted the problem of sexual abuse in sports. The abusers are most commonly coaches, though abusers may also include other authority figures such as sports medicine professionals, sports psychologists, and officials of the organization (Brackenridge, 1997; Bringer et al., 2001). In the first major study of the issue, Kirby and Greaves (as cited in Bringer et al., 2001) examined sexual harassment and abuse among 1200 Canadian Olympians. They found that 8.6 percent of respondents had experienced forced sexual intercourse with an authority figure in their sport, and 1.9 percent of victims were younger than 16 years of age at the time of abuse.

Sexual abuse incidents can occur in a variety of sport settings. Some of the sports are individual sports, such as tennis, swimming, and gymnastics, where coaches spend time alone with a single athlete. More recently, cases have come to light about abuse by coaches of team sports such as basketball, baseball, and football (Anderson, 2011). Most of the abusers identified in media reports had abused between 10 and 12 alleged victims. The abusers tend to target vulnerable children or groom them through socialization with the family or emotional manipulation about the sport (Stirling & Kerr, 2009). Brackenridge (1994) found that athletes often did not identify or define abusive behavior as such until years later. Furthermore, she found that victims were reluctant to report abuse out of fear of their coach or the possibility of being blacklisted from their sport. Brackenridge (1997) likened the power of a coach to that of a priest whose absolute knowledge is not questioned or challenged.

USA Swimming, the governing body for competitive swimming in the United States, has recently been criticized as a result of several cases of sexual abuse that have surfaced. However, the executive director of USA Swimming in 2010 denied widespread child sexual abuse within the organization (Chuchmach & Patel, 2010). He did acknowledge that 36 swim coaches were banned over the last 10 years due to sexual misconduct, but noted that this number represented 0.3 percent of the 12,000 coaches active during that time period. USA Swimming has been criticized for failing to act on reports of abuse and conspiring to cover up allegations for fear that its public image would be tarnished (Chuchmach & Patel,

2010). In the midst of lawsuits and media attention, USA Swimming developed a plan to protect swimmers, partnering with the Child Welfare League to develop new safeguards to prevent abuse (USA Swimming, 2010).

The criticism against USA Swimming is similar to the concerns expressed about high-profile college sports teams. Essentially, abuse often goes unreported or, when reported, is not acted upon swiftly, aggressively, or effectively. In 2011, reports of abuse emerged against Jerry Sandusky, a former assistant football coach at Penn State (see Box, this chapter). In addition to the outrage against him as an abuser, scathing reports emerged about how various university officials knew about the abuse allegations and did not report the abuse to authorities.

CASE STUDY

JERRY SANDUSKY: The Fall of Penn State's Football Legacy

In November 2011, a Pennsylvania grand jury released a report of their investigation into allegations of sexual abuse by Jerry Sandusky, the former defensive coordinator for the Penn State University football team. Sandusky was also the founder of an organization called The Second Mile, created in 1977 to help disadvantaged children. The grand jury report provided graphic details about abuse committed by Sandusky against eight young boys who he met through The Second Mile. The behaviors ranged from hugging to rape, and all cases included evidence of grooming behaviors such as tickets to football games and other material gifts.

The allegations of abuse against Sandusky created outrage. However, even more outrageous to the public was the lack of response by those who knew about the abuse years earlier. At least two witnesses saw him committing serious sexual offenses against victims, and both told others about the incidents. In one case, a graduate assistant witnessed Sandusky raping a boy in the shower andtold the head coach, Joe Paterno, about the incident the next day. He also discussed this the following week with the Athletic Director and another senior university official. No one called the police, and no one tried to find out what happened to the young victim, who was about 10 years of age.

After the grand jury report was released, Penn State fired several of those who knew about the abuse, including legendary football coach "Joe Pa." There were many discussions the following week about each person's culpability in this abuse scandal, and who should have reported, to whom, and when. Public opinion focused on the tolerance of sexual abuse of children to protect the reputation of one of the top football teams, and football coaches, in the history of college football. The case also illustrated how unsupervised access to minors, all of whom were vulnerable, created an opportunity for abuse that went undetected, or unreported, for years.

Questions
1. Compare the Penn State scandal to that of the Catholic Church. What are the similarities and differences?
2. Paterno reported the abuse to his superiors at Penn State, which fulfilled his legal obligation. In light of this, was it appropriate to fire him? Why or why not?

Professional and Legal Remedies

In a study of youth-based institutions and organizations, Gallagher (2000) noted that institutional abuse is a principal concern among policy makers, practitioners, and the public. He noted that many institutions respond to abuse, but that preventative actions are preferable. Hanson (2006b) and Moulden et al. (2007) recommend screening applicants for positions involving youths, noting that standard police checks may be insufficient given the low rate of reporting and conviction among professionals. Noting the importance of situational factors in facilitating abuse, Hanson (2006b) suggests that screening techniques should consider the match between individual characteristics and risks inherent in the position or context.

Several state legislatures and courts have implemented legal proceedings and statutes to protect minors from abuse within organizations (Weiss, 2002). These "position of authority" statutes take many forms. Some states consider sexual contact an offense despite the victim being of legal age to consent whereas others consider it an aggravating factor. A number of states categorize such actions as both an aggravating factor and a separate offense. States also vary in their definitions of what constitutes abuse of authority. Some require evidence of coercion but some individuals automatically qualify just by virtue of the position they hold. The variety in statutes is indicative of the complexities of abuse by individuals in positions of authority.

SEXUAL ABUSE IN RELIGIOUS INSTITUTIONS

Most media reports about child sexual abuse within religious organizations have focused primarily on abuse by Catholic priests. The first widespread reporting of sexual abuse in the Catholic Church occurred in 1983, when Reverend Gilbert Gauthe from the diocese of Lafayette was accused of sexually victimizing dozens of young boys. He was convicted in 1985 and served less than 10 years in prison. The next high-profile case of sexual abuse in the Catholic Church was in 1993, when reports emerged that Reverend James Porter had allegedly abused more than 100 young boys and girls in parishes across Massachusetts during the 1960s and 1970s. The *Boston Globe* dubbed him a "predator priest," and he was sentenced to 18 to 20 years in prison.

But it was the case of John Geoghan that brought a firestorm of media attention on the Catholic Church, and in Boston in particular. Geoghan was believed to have sexually molested over 130 young boys between 1962 and 1993, and the *Boston Globe* began publishing articles daily on him and other abusive priests (see *The Boston Globe*, 2004). Geoghan was identified in the media as a "predator priest," a "moral monster," a "pure predator," and a man of "no remorse" (Estes, 1999; Mashberg & Convey, 2002; *The Globe Spotlight Team*, 2006). He was eventually convicted, incarcerated, and killed in prison by another inmate.

These high-profile cases were upsetting not only for their severity and duration but also because of the men who committed them—religious leaders who had been trusted to work with and care for minors for years, without supervision. In 2002 and the years thereafter, thousands of adults reported that they had been sexually abused by Catholic priests when they were minors. This explosion of reporting led to what is referred to today as the sexual abuse "scandal" or "crisis" in the Catholic Church. However, sexual abuse within religious organizations is not confined to the Catholic Church. The intensity of media reports from 2002 onward led to higher levels of reporting at a given point in time, and more news coverage of high profile "predatory priests." As a result, the Catholic Church commissioned in-depth studies of sexual abuse within the organization. These studies aimed to better understand the nature and scope of the problem of sexual abuse by priests and why it happened. The key findings from those studies are reported later in this chapter.

Sexual abuse of minors within religious institutions is not limited to the Catholic Church alone, however. Though no other religious institutions have yet commissioned full-scale studies of abuse within their institutions, journalists, victims, and some researchers have discussed the prevalence of abuse within various religious institutions.

Child Sexual Abuse within Non-Catholic Religious Organizations

Sexual abuse of minors in religious organizations is similar to the abuse of minors in nonreligious organizations. In both, the abuse is often perpetrated by an adult who has developed a nurturing and mentoring relationship with the child and has regular, often unsupervised, access to minors. This section provides an overview of what is known about abuse within religious organizations other than the Catholic Church (see Terry & Litvinoff, 2012, for more detailed information about non-Catholic organizations). There is no empirical information or investigative journalist reports about abuse within certain religions, such as Islam and Scientology. This does not mean abuse does not occur within these religions, but there are no reliable reports on it. Abuse by Catholic priests is addressed separately, since there is substantially more empirical information about that population.

Protestant   It is difficult to estimate the extent of child sexual abuse within Protestant denominations, since the various churches have autonomous organizational structures and varied reporting systems. However, Jenkins, as cited in Donohue (1996), estimated that approximately 10 percent of Protestant clergy have been involved in sexual misconduct and about 2 or 3 percent have sexually abused children (Donohue, 1996). According to Moyer (2007), three insurance companies that provide liability coverage to an estimated 165,000 U.S. Protestant churches estimate that Protestant churches receive more than 260 reports of abuse of minors by clergy, church staff, volunteers, or congregation members annually (French, 2007).

Two of the three insurance companies released information regarding legal claims (Moyer, 2007). GuideOne reported that annually over the past five years the companies paid approximately $4 million for child sex abuse and sexual misconduct settlements, excluding attorney fees. Brotherhood Mutual reported about $7.8 million claims have been paid in the last 15 years for sexual misconduct and child sexual abuse cases. While these estimates provide some indication of the monetary cost of abuse within the organization, these figures do not reflect the numbers of accused clergy or whether the accusations were substantiated. Reformation.com, a website that catalogues newspaper articles about Protestant ministers alleged to have sexually abused children, had 838 ministers listed on the website as of July 2010, though this website has since been discontinued.

Southern Baptist   Sexual abuse of minors within the Baptist Church first caught the media attention in 2008, when an article in *Time* magazine noted that the Church failed to implement a "pedophile" database (Fitzpatrick, 2008). *Time* magazine labeled this one of the top ten underreported new stories in 2008, noting that media headlines about child sexual abuse remained largely focused on the Catholic Church. However, Fitzpatrick (2008) noted that this Protestant church lacks a hierarchical structure, making it more difficult to track abuse cases. Advocates from the Survivors Network for those Abused by Priests (SNAP) have pushed for better oversight of sexual abuse within the religion and claim that autonomy is an excuse for allowing abuse to continue. The website StopBaptistPredators.org, a SNAP affiliate, currently tracks the names of ministers who have been alleged to have committed sexual misconduct against children and acts as an information and resource center for interested parties.

Episcopalian   As with most religious organizations, it is not clear how many priests within the Episcopalian Church have been accused of sexual misconduct with adults or children. The Church has, however, created detailed procedures about education and responses to abuse (Watanabe, 2002). These were developed after a bishop was found liable in 1991 for concealing a case of sexual misconduct against a woman in the diocese, and the diocese had to pay her $1.2 million in damages (Watanabe, 2002). Though this case involved sexual misconduct of an adult, it led to the establishment of formal policies on all types of sexual abuse, including training, guidelines, videos, and discussions about abuse. The Episcopalian Church requires that all priests, staff, and laity who work with children participate. Furthermore, the church reports the names of priests suspended or dismissed in their annual yearbook and informs congregations of priests' misconduct. The Episcopal Church's policies and enforcement surrounding child sexual abuse have served as a model for other mainline Protestant denominations, including Methodists, Presbyterian, and Lutherans (Watanabe, 2002).

Jehovah Witnesses   In 2003, Laurie Goodstein wrote an article in the *New York Times* that described sexual abuse policies within the Jehovah Witnesses (Goodstein, August 2003). She revealed that policies are largely based on biblical standards, as allegations of abuse go before a panel of male elders who review the case privately. Reports may be substantiated in one of two manners: the child has two witnesses to verify his/her account or the abuser admits his/her actions. In the latter case, if the abuser repents then the congregation is notified that the individual has been disciplined, although the reason remains confidential. Elders then will report the abuser to Headquarters in Brooklyn, New York, where the abuser's name will be placed in a database and banned from serving in positions of authority. Of note is that the Jehovah Witnesses' guidelines do not discuss the role of criminal justice authorities, only church policy. Current church policy dictates that after 20 years and no confirmed reports of abuse the abuser can be re-appointed to authority positions within the organization (http://www.silentlambs.org).

Though it is not based on empirical data, a victim-support website specifically for Jehovah Witnesses reports that the names of 23,720 people accused or found guilty of sexual abuse are listed in the church's database. Information reported to be recorded includes details of the abuse, age of victim and abuser, whether the abuse was reported to secular authorities, and the actions of the elders. These files have been primarily used to protect the legal interest of the organization. Based on these figures, conservative estimates worldwide indicate that one in four congregations house a child sexual abuser (http://www.silentlambs.org).

Critics and former members, many who have been expelled for speaking out against child sexual abuse policies, contend that current policies protect abusers (Goodstein, 2003). The silent lambs website has collected more than 5000 witness statements, primarily from girls and young women, asserting that the church had mishandled child sexual abuse cases against both congregation members and elders. In 2007, MSNBC reported Jehovah Witnesses settled nine lawsuits that alleged their policies shielded men who sexually abused children over the course of many years (Meyers & Greenberg, 2007). The church settled without admitting wrongdoing. Though the amount was officially undisclosed, new reports stated that one victim received nearly $800,000 in compensation (Meyers & Greenberg, 2007).

Mormons   The scope of child sexual abuse within the Mormon faith is unknown, and no estimates on the prevalence of abuse have been released to the public (Fletcher-Stack, 1999). A news report in the *Salt Lake Tribune*, however, claimed rates of child sexual abuse within their ranks are comparable to rates of abuse in society generally (*Bringing Abuse to Light*, 1999). Critics claim that religious beliefs and practices within the Mormon Church have kept child sexual abuse outside the public eye (Hamilton, 2010).

One study has been conducted with Mormon women who were survivors of childhood sexual abuse (Gerdes et al., 1996). Of the 71 women in the sample, 61 talked to church leaders about the abuse. Forty nine described this as a negative experience, saying that the bishop was "judgmental," "unbelieving," or "protective of the abusers," and half felt guilt or frustration as a result of being admonished by their church leaders to forgive the abusers. Five of the women were either disfellowshipped—that is, denied privileges to pray and speak publicly at church—or excommunicated for behavior related to their abuse. Only three of the abusers were disciplined, and some abusers remained in good standing even after they were legally convicted.

More than 40 plaintiffs have alleged that church officials knew of molestation or ignored the warning signs and failure to notify the families or authorities (McCann, 1999). According to the attorney for the Mormons, Von Keetch, in the past 10 years there have been three or four lawsuits annually (*Transcript of interview*, 1999). Yet, this number does not account for cases that have not been reported or adjudicated. Confidential settlements shield the Church of Latter-Day Saints (LDS) from publicly disclosing more details of the claims. Since 1989, LDS has provided training for their clergy, who are all lay members, and distributed flyers on child sexual abuse (McCann, 1999). Additionally, in 1995 LDS established a 24-hour hotline for bishops to access information and advice on child sexual abuse allegations (*Transcript of interview*, 1999).

Jewish Community   Similarly to other religious organizations, there is no empirical evidence of the prevalence of sexual abuse in the Jewish Community, and what is known has come generally through media reports and survivor accounts. News stories have recently begun surfacing with regular frequency in Jewish newspapers such as *The Jewish Week* (http://www.thejewishweek.com) and two survivors organizations have emerged in the Jewish community: The Awareness Center (http://www.theawarenesscenter.org) and Survivors for Justice (http://www.survivorsforjustice.org). The Awareness Center lists names of 107 Rabbis accused of sexual misconduct, 279 other trusted officials (parents, counselors, etc.), and 85 unnamed abusers. Though not listing specific cases, the Survivors for Justice website notes that "The sexual abuse of children is at alarming proportions within our community (http://www.survivorsforjustice.org)."

Also similar to other religious organizations, the Jewish community has its own system of oversight for negative behavior (rabbinical courts), including sexual abuse. Compounding this issue, the Orthodox Jewish culture disapproves of involving secular agencies in family and business matters (Melloy, 2009), and a strict adherence to this policy has helped to keep child sexual abuse outside of the criminal justice system, instead being investigated by rabbinical courts (Melloy, 2009). As a result, abusers are rarely formally investigated, prosecuted, or punished for their crimes. As such, there are no reliable statistics on the prevalence of child sexual abuse within the Orthodox Jewish community.

Several studies have sought to examine child sexual abuse within the Orthodox Jewish community. A case study by Neustein and Lesher (2008) of alleged child sexual assault within the Orthodox Jewish community exemplifies the context in which alleged abuse takes place, including highlighting the roles of religious and secular authorities. A retrospective study conducted by Yehuda et al. (2007) found that 26 percent of respondents, self-identified as observant Jewish women, reported sexual abuse with 16 percent reporting the abuse occurred by the age of 13. Yet, the studies suffer from methodological limitations that prohibit extrapolation of their results to the larger community.

News articles and studies provide some insight into why families do not report child sexual abuse to secular authorities outside of religious beliefs, including strong community pressure; fear it would bring shame to their community and tarnish their family reputation; concern stemming from the stigma of abuse and likely social ostracism following reporting; denial; and repercussions to the entire family, such as being unable to marry daughters and obtain employment (Hamilton, 2010). The Brooklyn District Attorney's (DA's) Office has come under attack for not actively pursuing abusers within the Orthodox community (Kolker, 2006). As a result, the DA's Office implemented a program, Voice of Justice, which encourages victims to report abuse and conducts outreach to schools and community centers to discuss abuse (Vitello, 2009). Additionally, a hotline for Orthodox sex abuse victims was put in place (Michels, 2009). As a result, 26 men were tried in 2009 and 8 convicted (Vitello, 2009). This marks a departure from even a few years ago.

Sexual Abuse within the Catholic Church

More studies have been conducted to date on sexually abusive clergy in the Catholic Church than abusers in any other religious organization. However, prior to 2002, most studies that had been published were limited in scope because of small sample sizes or they were based upon clinical samples from a single treatment center. Though few of them were generalizable, these early studies provided insight into the psychological problems of abusers and the characteristics of their behaviors. For example (Terry, 2008, p. 550):

- Flynn (2000) collected self-reports from 25 women sexually abused by clergy;

- Mendola (1998) studied 277 Catholic priests and religious brothers referred for psychiatric evaluation;

- Goetz (1992) collected self-reports of 374 ordained pastors to find out how many had affairs;

- Irons and Laaser (1994) studied 25 sexually abusive priests who were in treatment to determine whether they had any particular sexual additions;

- Ukeritis (2005) studied 74 clergy who had abused children and found that approximately 38 percent primarily abused children under age 13 or younger, and while 62 percent abused adolescents between ages 14 and 18;

- Fones et al. (1999) studied 19 clergy (17 of whom were Roman Catholic) (in a nonrepresentative sample) and found that 39 percent of the sample had offended against adolescents and 52 percent characterized the nature of their sexual behavior as deliberate;

- Loftus and Camargo (1993) studied a clinical sample of 1322 priests and brothers and found that 27.8 percent engaged in a sexual relationship with an adult woman, and while 8.4 percent reported sexual misconduct with a minor; and

- Anthony Sipe (1990) found in a clinical sample that 2 percent of priests engaged in pedophiliac behavior, 4 percent of priests are sexually preoccupied with adolescent boys or girls, and 20 to 40 percent of priests engage in sexual misconduct with adults.

In addition to clinicians, various theological scholars within the Catholic Church have undertaken the task of assessing the extent of sexual abuse by clergy. Extrapolating from data presented by St. Luke's Institute, a treatment center for priests, Plante (2003) concluded that approximately 3000 clergy have abused about 24,000 victims in the last 50 years. However, Plante noted that this figure may be comprised of men from various religions, not just the Catholic Church. In a literature review conducted by the Catholic League for Religious and Civil Rights (2004), the figure for abusive clerics cited in the media ranged anywhere from 1 to 1.8 percent. Cafardi (2008) provided an historical analysis of the Catholic Church's response to the sexual abuse of children by priests, with a focus on the Church's reliance on canon law as well as therapeutic options for the abusers.

Journalists have also attempted to investigate the extent of abuse in the Catholic Church. Based on his coverage of abuse cases in Louisiana from 1984 to 1992, Jason Berry (1992) concluded that 400 priests and brothers had sexually abused children and the Catholic Church had spent nearly $400 million in legal, medical, and psychological expenses. An investigation conducted by *New York Times* reporter Laurie Goodstein (2003) found that by the end of 2002, there were more than 1,205 priests publicly known to have committed acts of abuse against 4,268 victims. These abuse cases occurred most frequently during the 1970s and 1980s, and approximately half of the priests with allegations had multiple victims.

The Vatican convened a panel of eight non-Catholic scientists to study the problem of abuse in the Church. In his critical review of the available literature, much of which was based on clinical samples, Kafka (2004) found that the typical child sexual abuser in the Catholic Church is a diocesan priest who is an ephebophile. He also found that clergy abusers exhibit fewer psychological problems than do nonclergy sex offenders. However, methodological limitations of the studies he analyzed preclude firm conclusions about groups of clergy who offend.

Though these studies helped to identify some aspects of the sexual abuse crisis in the Church, the lack of thorough information led to a surge of media interest in the topic. According to Jenkins (1995), the emphasis upon sexual abuse committed by the clergy is a result of a shift in media coverage beginning in the 1980s. At that time, reports began emerging about the "pedophile Priest" Gilbert Gauthe in Louisiana. In 1993 the media again focused on the "predator priest" James Porter. It was the case of John Geoghan in 2002, however, that led to the widespread and sustained media attention of sexual abuse by Catholic priests.

Questions about the sexual abuse crisis in the Catholic Church centered around two key issues: how could a priest commit such acts, and how could a religious organization knowingly allow the child sexual abuse to occur (Terry,

2008). Just as Catholic communities, survivors groups, and the general public were seeking answers to these questions, so was the Church. At the 2002 summer meeting of the United States Conference of Catholic Bishops (USCCB), the bishops created a Charter that aimed to understand the extent of the abuse crisis, why it happened, and how to respond to it. The Charter called for empirical studies of the sexual abuse of minors by Catholic priests. The Office of Child and Youth Protection and the National Review Board, two entities formed as a result of the Charter, commissioned two studies: *The Nature and Scope of Sexual Abuse of Minors by Catholic Priests and Deacons: 1950–2002* (the "Nature and Scope" study), and *The Causes and Context of Sexual Abuse of Minors by Catholic Priests in the United States, 1950–2010* (the "Causes and Context" study). The *Nature and Scope* study resulted in two reports (John Jay College, 2004, 2006) and provided information about the extent of the abuse crisis, the priests against who allegations were made, the victims of the abuse, and the financial impact of the crisis. The *Causes and Context* study report (Terry et al., 2011) focused on the causes of the crisis and the factors that permitted abusive behavior to persist, integrating research from socio-cultural, psychological, situational, and organizational perspectives.

Nature and Scope Study   The goal of the Nature and Scope study was to determine the extent of the sexual abuse of minors by Catholic priests nationally from 1950 to 2002. Specifically, the USCCB mandate was to compile information on the following;

- Data pertaining to the offenses, including the number of offenses per diocese, the nature and duration of the offenses, in what locations and during which activities they occurred, and the Church's response to the allegations of abuse;
- Data pertaining to the abusers, including demographic characteristics, information about their clerical roles and training, the personal and family history of the priest, and what happened to them as a result of the abuse allegations;
- Data pertaining to the victims, including age and gender, information about the abuse incidents, grooming behavior that occurred before/during the abusive relationship, length of time between the abuse and when the abuse was reported, and to whom the abuse was reported; and
- Financial impact of the abuse crisis.

The research team developed three surveys—a diocesan survey, a cleric survey, and a victim survey—and sent them to all dioceses and religious orders of men in the United States. Identities of all priests and victims were confidential, and the researchers employed a double-blind procedure to ensure the anonymity of the subjects. Overall, 97 percent of all dioceses and eparchies and 63 percent of all religious communities responded.[1]

---

1. For an in-depth review of the methodology of the Nature and Scope study, see Terry (2008).

The results of the Nature and Scope study showed that the total number of priests with allegations from 1950 to 2002 was 4,392, which was equivalent to 4 percent of priests in the ministry during that time. The number of individuals who made allegations of sexual abuse was 10,667. Abuse incidence peaked in the 1970s and early 1980s. This distribution was consistent across all regions of the Catholic Church in the United States,[2] as well as in all sizes of dioceses. Thus, despite the high-profile nature of offenders in Boston, the Nature and Scope study showed that this was a national problem. Even though incidents peaked in the 1970s and early 1980s, most abuse cases were reported years, and often decades, later.

The majority of priests with allegations of abuse were diocesan priests serving in the role of pastor (25 percent) or associate pastor (42 percent), and the abuse occurred during a range of activities (for example, on retreats, after mass) and in various places (for example, in the parish residence, in the home of the victims). Pastors and associate pastors have high levels of discretion, with low levels of supervision and oversight of their daily activities, thus giving them many opportunities to abuse. The priest abusers committed numerous and often multiple types of sexual offenses, ranging from touching outside the clothes to penetration. The majority of victims were male (81 percent), and victims were most commonly (51 percent) between the ages of 11 and 14. Though the majority of priest abusers (56 percent) had one known victim, 3.5 percent of priests with allegations were responsible for abusing 26 percent of the victims. These serial abusers who had 10 or more victims had a long duration of offending behavior, averaging nearly 20 years each.

Causes and Context Study   The goal of the Causes and Context study was to explain what factors were associated with the abuse crisis and why there was a surge in abuse incidents in the 1970s and early 1980s. The researchers analyzed data from psychological, sociocultural, organizational, and situational perspectives. Data were derived from the following sources:

- Existing longitudinal data sets of various types of social behavior (such as crime, divorce, premarital sex) over the time period to provide an historical framework;

- Seminary documents outlining the history and development of a curriculum on human formation;

- Surveys of various groups within the Catholic Church, including bishops and other diocesan leaders; vicars general; victim assistance coordinators; priests with allegations of abuse and a comparison sample of priests in active parish ministry who had not been accused (the identity and behavior survey); and a group of "priests with integrity" who served in some capacity to assist victims of abuse;

---

2. There are 14 regions of the Catholic Church in the United States, with a dozen or so dioceses per region.

- Primary data from a 1971 survey of 271 priests on the psychology of American Catholic priests; and

- Clinical data from files at three treatment centers on four groups of priests: those with allegations of abuse against minors, those with allegations of other sexual misconduct, those with behavioral or mental health problems, and a normative sample.

The findings of the Causes and Context study indicate that the abuse crisis was caused by a complex interaction of psychological, developmental, organizational, cultural, and situational factors. There was no single identifiable cause of the crisis, and no specific "high risk" characteristics to help identify potential abusers. As with nonclergy sex offenders, priests with allegations of abuse who sexually abused minors constitute a heterogeneous population and very few were "specialists" who sought out a particular type of victim (in regard to age and/or gender).

The clinical data collected for the Causes and Context study showed that priests who sexually abused minors were not significantly more likely than other priests to have personality or mood disorders, and there were no significant differences in IQ between abusers and others who were treated. Additionally, few abusers were driven by sexual pathologies such as pedophilia (in the two clinical samples with sexual disorder data, 5 percent of the priests with allegations of abusing children were diagnosed with pedophilia). Many of the abusers did exhibit poor psychosexual development or other problems, including emotional congruence with children or adolescents, intimacy deficits, and high levels of stressors from work. Sexual identity and sexual behavior prior to ordination did not predict sexual abuse of minors. Most priests (80 percent) who sexually abused children also had participated in sexual behavior with adults.

Access to victims played a critical role in victim choice. Few significant differences were found between the locations and situations in which boys and girls were abused, but priests had more access to boys until recently (primarily because parishes permitted girls as altar servers after 1983). Priests who abused minors exhibited behavior consistent with nonpriest abusers. In particular, the abusers "groomed" their victims (enticed them to participate in the abuse through gifts and other benefits or through emotional or spiritual manipulation), and they justified and excused their own behavior, often shifting responsibility to the victims or others.

The decade of ordination also had a significant impact on patterns of abusive behavior. The majority of abusive priests were ordained prior to the 1970s, and more abusers were educated in seminaries in the 1940s and 1950s than at any other time period. Seminary education has developed significantly since that time, particularly in regard to human formation (teaching priests to live a life of chaste celibacy). These developments were consistent with the drop in allegations of abuse from the 1980s onward.

The response to abusive priests was varied by decade as well as by diocese. In general, most diocesan leaders responded to allegations of abuse by helping the abusers, for example, through treatment, but paid little attention to the victims and the harm to them that resulted from the abuse. The type of diocesan response changed over time, however, and by the 1990s onward bishops were less likely to reinstate those priests with allegations of abuse.

In sum, priests who sexually abuse children are similar to sex offenders in the general population. However, they had unguarded access to children and a high level of trust with members of the community, giving them substantial opportunities to abuse. Though priests exhibited some characteristics such as intimacy deficits, they did not appear to be primarily driven by a strong sexual attraction to children. In other words, they fit the typology of regressed offenders.

SEXUAL ABUSE WITHIN PRISONS

Sexual behavior in prison, both consensual and abusive, is a complicated issue and can have serious physical, psychological, and behavioral consequences for those involved. Sexual assault occurs in male and female prisons of all security levels and is committed by inmates and correctional staff. Sexual behavior between inmates may be consensual, but it is prohibited in correctional institutions. Corrections officers have traditionally used their discretion as to whether to report instances of sexual behavior, and often do not report those they consider to be consensual sexual acts instead of coercive ones (Eigenberg, 2000). The prevalence of sexual assault in prison is not well known, and efforts to document the extent of the problem have generally relied on self-reports of victimization, inmate interviews, and written surveys (Mair et al., 2003). These indicate that sexual assault is highly prevalent, and victims may experience numerous attacks throughout their confinement by multiple assailants (Mair et al., 2003). The high rate of sexual assault in prisons has led some researchers to say that sexual violence in prison is an institutional as well as a social problem (Tewksbury & West, 2000).

According to Wyatt (2006), the primary causes of sexual assault in prison include: 1) prison overcrowding, which leads to an insufficient number of correctional officers and an inability to segregate dangerous prisoners; 2) the single-sex nature of prisons, with no outlets for the inmates' sexual impulses; and 3) inadequacies of legal solutions to combating prison rape. Wyatt (2006) points out that laws banning sexual behavior in prison have little effect without focusing on prevention and punishment of the acts. Other researchers have noted that sexual assault in prison is caused primarily by a need for power and control rather than sexual gratification (Jones & Pratt, 2008). Sexually assaulting another inmate thus allows a prisoner to reinforce a sense of self, personal worth, and control.

When sexual assault in prison was first studied, it was regarded as homosexual acts engaged in by homosexual inmates or by men with weak moral characters (Jones & Pratt, 2008). There was little distinction between sex between inmates that was consensual and that which was abusive (Jones & Pratt, 2008). Sykes (1958), as cited in Fowler, Blackburn, Marquart, and Mullings (2010), proposed that inmates suffer deprivations when entering prison, including liberty, goods and services, heterosexual relationships, autonomy, and security. In response to this deprivation, inmates form their own subculture that features its own argot, inmate code, roles, and values. There continues to be a subculture today, with various terms used to describe either the victim or aggressor of sexual violence in prison (for example, wolf, top men, fags, queens, fairies, girls) (O'Donnel, 2004).

Even when sexual behavior between inmates is consensual, it may be inherently coerced. There is often a power differential between inmates, and prisoners are vulnerable by virtue of their confinement and inability to remove themselves from potentially dangerous situations (Corlew, 2006). Many consensual relationships also evolve from formerly abusive relationships, with the victim providing sexual acts in exchange for protection from other inmates (Corlew, 2006). Banbury (2004) explains how inmates are often forced into a situation whereby they repay their debts with sexual favors. Though they do so consensually, it underlines the lack of true consent in such situations.

Prevalence and Reporting

The true prevalence of sexual assault in prison is not clear, and study findings indicate that between 10 and 25 percent of the inmate population are raped or sexually coerced while incarcerated. Most victimization studies indicate that approximately 20 percent of the incarcerated population in the United States has been sexually assaulted by other inmates or correctional staff (Corlew, 2006; Fowler et al., 2010). Some studies differentiate between the rates of rape and other types of sexual coercion, with sexual coercion being more common than completed rapes. In a study of seven mid-western prisons, 16 percent of inmates reported experiencing sexual coercion while rape was experienced by 7 percent of the sample (Mair et al., 2003). Prison inmates describe rape as a common event in prison and an accepted part of their punishment (Wyatt, 2006). Sexual assault rates are even higher for juveniles and mentally ill inmates (Wyatt, 2006), and many inmates who have experienced sexual assaults are repeat victims. Corlew (2006) found that approximately two-thirds of those prisoners who report victimization have been victimized more than once, with an average of nine assaults, and some prisoners report experiencing up to 100 incidents of sexual assault per year.

This variation in prevalence statistics for prison rape is the result of underreporting by offenders, the failure of authorities to identify a common definition of sexual assault, and the misinterpretation of coerced sexual activity as being consensual (Moster & Jeglic, 2009).

The studies that have been conducted are generally small in scale and often cannot be generalized to the national correctional population. Differing methodologies also provide varying results; interviews and surveys with institutional authorities provide much lower estimates of sexual assault in prison than interviews and questionnaires of prison inmates (Tewksbury, 1989). Given these limitations, the magnitude of sexual assault among inmates is still not well understood (Bureau of Justice Statistics, 2004).

Sexual abuse is significantly underreported in any population, and even more so in the prison population than the general population. Rape and sexual assault in prison is often not reported due to feelings of guilt, shame or embarrassment, lack of proof or fear of not being believed, ineffective officials who are biased and won't do anything, fear of reprisal, the desire to not be placed in protective custody, and the desire to not be labeled a snitch (Fowler et al., 2010; Wyatt, 2006). Cultural proscriptions in prison against cooperating with authorities and other traditional barriers to reporting sexual victimization also lead to low rates of reporting (Fowler et al., 2010). Those who report their abuse are often subject to increased victimization rather than protected from it. In order to protect inmates who are being victimized, officials often place them in isolation, which can also have negative effects on the inmates (Corlew, 2006). Reporting victimization to staff when the perpetrator is a corrections officer is also problematic (Fowler et al., 2010), and many inmates fear reprisal if they would do so.

Studies of inmate self-reports found that older inmates and those who viewed themselves as weaker were more likely to report their abuse or urge fellow inmates to report their abuse to authorities (Fowler et al., 2010). To encourage reporting of sexual assault without the fear of reprisal, the Department of Corrections in most states have implemented two strategies: a toll-free hotline to report their abuse and inmate educational programs to educate inmates on what sexual assault and violence is, while encouraging them to report this abuse (Fowler et al. 2010). The immediacy with which the assault is reported is important because the faster it is reported, the greater the chance it will be addressed (forensic evidence) (Fowler et al. 2010).

When sexual assaults are reported, correctional officials do not always respond appropriately. In 2002, the American Civil Liberties Union filed a civil suit against the Texas Department of Criminal Justice and various prison officials on behalf of a former prison inmate (Roderick Johnson) who was allegedly repeatedly raped during his incarceration and charging that prison officials failed to discipline the offenders or take measure to prevent the assaults (Wyatt, 2006). In *Farmer v. Brennan*, the Supreme Court ruled that prison officials violate the Eighth Amendment if they deliberately disregard the occurrence of male rape in prison. Some prison officials noted that they do not report instances of prison rape that they are aware of because they have not been trained in how to do so. Other guards feel that the prisoners deserve it and ridicule any inmates who come forward looking for help (Wyatt, 2006).

Effects of Victimization

In addition to the individual effects of sexual assault on inmates, prison rape constitutes a serious public health problem. Sexual assault in prisons brings with it a high risk of contracting sexually transmitted diseases and other communicable diseases such as HIV, AIDS, hepatitis B & C, and tuberculosis (Corlew, 2006; Hammett, Harmon, & Maruschak, 1999; Knowles, 1999; Wyatt, 2006). Muraschak (1999) stated that the rate of HIV transmission is approximately five times higher in prison than in the general population, while Corlew (2006) said the prevalence of HIV in prisons is 10 times that in the general population.

Sexual victimization in prison can alter the social climate of prisons; contribute to institutional violence; and result in physical, psychological, and emotional trauma for victims (Corlew, 2006; Jones & Pratt, 2008; Knowles, 1999; Mair et al., 2003; Wyatt, 2006). Some victims of rape in prison turn to suicide to escape further trauma or fear, and have a high risk of suicide and lifelong psychological and emotional trauma (Mair et al., 2003; Tewksbury, 1989; Wyatt, 2006). Prisoners who have been victimized are usually stigmatized as "queens," "punks," "bitches," and "turnouts," and they may feel perpetually vulnerable, because they are unable to escape from the abusive situation. Inadequate grievance and investigation procedures contribute to these feelings of fear and vulnerability (Corlew, 2006).

Prison rape also affects society in that many victims of sexual assault become violent aggressors while incarcerated and after their release (Mair et al., 2003). Rape in prison can take nonviolent offenders and turn them into people with a high potential for violence. The victims of prison rape often view society as responsible for their victimization and humiliation (Knowles, 1999), and brutalized inmates are often more likely to commit crime when they are released (Knowles, 1999; Wyatt, 2006).

Characteristics of Sexual Assaulters and Victims in Prison

In the prison population, those most likely to become victims of sexual assault include individuals who are physically weaker, younger, known to be homosexual, suffering from developmental or mental disorders, have substance abuse problems, are not affiliated with a gang, have "ratted" someone out, or who are known to have been previously sexually assaulted (Banbury, 2004; Corlew, 2006; Dumond, 2000). Additionally, many of those who are sexually assaulted in prison were sexually abused prior to entering prison (Harlow, 1999). Overall, the victimization literature shows that the most common thread among victims of sexual offenses is vulnerability, and these vulnerable victims are often assaulted multiple times (Farrell, 1995; Harlow, 1999). Victims of sexual assault in prison are at increased risk for victimization after being "marked" (Jones & Pratt, 2008), and male inmates who are raped must often serve their rapist for the remainder of their stay in prison.

Some researchers have argued that race plays a role in who is targeted for victimization, though studies have produced conflicting findings. Knowles (1999) stated that more than 90 percent of rapes are interracial, and traditionally most inmate victims have been White and most sexually assaultive inmates have been Black. Some researchers have suggested that male rape in prison is a form of racial retaliation (O'Donnell, 2004; Tewksbury, 1989). However, O'Donnell (2004) suggests that Blacks victimize Whites in prison using sexual violence more because of their disproportionate numbers in prison. Whites may also be targeted as victims since they are found to more isolated and less likely to belong to a network within the prison. Whatever the reason, Whites are more severely and frequently raped than any other ethnic group in prison (Knowles, 1999).

In Tewksbury's (1989) study of 150 prison inmates, he found that height and weight were the only variables significant in predicting an individual's fear of sexual assault (though not necessary whether they were victimized). An increase in weight led prisoners to be more fearful of sexual assault as they believed they were less able to defend themselves, and taller individuals were less likely to fear sexual assault. Tewksbury did not find race to be a significant factor in predicting fear of sexual assault.

Most of the studies on sexual assault in prison have focused on male inmates, and few empirical studies have been conducted about the incidence of assault against female inmates. Some researchers have argued that much sexual activity between female inmates is consensual (O'Donnell, 2004), and many of the studies on sexual activity among female inmates have focused on consensual sexual activity (Blackburn, Mullings, & Marquart, 2008). However, recent studies indicate that nearly 10 to 17 percent of the substantiated inmate-on-inmate sexual violence featured a female victim, (Blackburn et al., 2008). Blackburn et al. (2008) found that 17.2 percent of respondents reported being the victim of abuse in prison; 2.5 percent reported being the victim of an attempted sexual assault, while 3 percent reported being the victim of a completed sexual assault. The majority reported inappropriate touching or groping without their consent (Blackburn et al., 2008). Similarly to male victims, younger inmates were more likely to report sexual abuse in prison. Otherwise, there were no statistically significant differences between those women in prison who reported being victims of sexual abuse and those who did not.

The role of sexual identity among those participating in consensual or abusive sexual relationships is complex, with both male and female inmates. Sex roles in prison are complicated by the fact that prisons are single-sex institutions and inmates do not have access to sexual behavior with anyone of the opposite sex. As Ross and Richard (2002) note, any given prison population has heterosexuals, homosexuals, transsexuals, and other sexual variations. However, most inmates who participate in sexual behavior and those who rape other inmates in prison are heterosexual. Within prison, rape of another inmate is often a form of establishing status (Knowles, 1999) rather than indicative of sexual orientation or identity.

Prison Rape Elimination Act

In response to the growing crisis about sexual violence in correctional institutions, President George W. Bush signed into law the Prison Rape Elimination Act (PREA) of 2003. PREA was developed as a comprehensive piece of legislation that is intended to foster an understanding of prison rape and focus on prevention (Mair et al., 2003). Prison rape is defined broadly by PREA to include various coercive sexual acts (including penetration of any sort, oral sodomy, sexual assault with an object, and sexual fondling) that are achieved through physical force or intimidation and occurring in federal, state, or local confinement facilities (Corlew, 2006). In order for states to be eligible for federal funding for prisons, they must cooperate with prison rape studies and implement minimal national standards.

PREA has five main purposes (Mair et al., 2003): (1) to conduct annual studies of the incidence and impact of prison rape; (2) establish a review panel on prison rape, which every year reviews operation of the three prisons with the highest incidence of prison rape and the two with the lowest incidence of prison rape; (3) provide funding to states for personnel, training, technical assistance, data collection, and equipment to prevent and prosecute prison rape; (4) establish a national prison rape reduction commission consisting of nine members who have expertise in the issue of prison rape; and (5) publish a final rule within one year after receiving the Commission's report establishing national standards or detecting, preventing, reducing, and punishing prison rape.

According to the PREA, nearly 200,000 inmates who are currently incarcerated have been or will be the victims of prison rape and the total number of inmates who have been sexually assaulted in the past 20 years exceeds one million. PREA establishes a zero-tolerance standard for inmate sexual assault and rape, making prevention a top priority. It addresses both staff-on-inmate violence and inmate-on-inmate violence. It is not gender specific and includes events resulting from sheer physical force or exploitation of fear or the threat of violence, or when the victim is not able to give consent due to mental or physical handicaps.

Many of the policies implemented by the PREA require the support of prison administrators and wardens (Moster & Jeglic, 2009). Moster and Jeglic (2009) conducted a study after the implementation of PREA and found that the majority of U.S. wardens surveyed believed prison rape was not a significant issue in their facilities (below 1 percent) and sexual activity was not really occurring in the institution. The wardens viewed institutional policies and procedures and staff training as somewhat effective in preventing prison rape and sexual assault, and thought that increased inmate supervision was the most effective at preventing prison rape.

Preventing Sexual Assault in Prison

Because of the unspoken nature of sexual assault in prison, it is difficult to know what might be the best methods of preventing prison rape. Staff training, prisoner education, and increased supervision, as recommended in PREA, are certainly policies that should be implemented and evaluated. Some studies have also recommended conjugal visits, furlough programs, placing victims in separate housing, and providing vocational, educational, psychological, and athletic programs as prevention policies (Eigenberg, 2000).

Researchers have argued that conjugal visits can allow prisoners to keep their sense of masculine identity through normal, healthy relationships with women. The prisoners are able to maintain healthy bonds with their family and, thus, reaffirm their masculinity and reduce their need to establish a manly self-image by victimizing other inmates (Wyatt, 2006). However, Knowles (1999) and Wyatt (2006) note that conjugal visits will not eliminate the problem of prison rape, because it is based on power as well as a desire for sexual activity. Wyatt (2006) notes additional problems with conjugal visits as well, such as the unsupervised nature of the visits, the potential for visitors to bring in contraband, and the jealously that may be felt by inmates without partners.

According to Eigenberg (2000), studies have shown that better screening and classification procedures, improved staff supervision, faster and more certain punishment, increased utilization of single cells, and better training for inmates and staff could aid in limiting the occurrence of prison rape. However, any policies that are implemented must be evaluated for their effectiveness.

SEXUAL ABUSE WITHIN THE MILITARY

As explained in Chapter 5, rape is highly prevalent during wars and military conflicts. Soldiers have committed mass rapes of the enemy in nearly all conflicts, and scholars have argued that the motivation behind rape during wartime is the need for power and domination of another people. War situations encourage an extreme type of machismo associated with a hegemonic form of masculinity (Connell, 1990), and rape is often associated with "the ideology of masculine aggressiveness" (West, 1987, p. 155).

But despite the understanding of the prevalence of rape in wartime, until recently little attention has been devoted to the sexual violence that occurs within the military institution itself. As women have an increasing presence in military units, reports are emerging of the sexual violence against them. Many military women face sexual harassment and sexual abuse during their service, and this abuse is amplified during wartime (Kelty, Kleykamp, & Segal, 2010). The hyper-masculine culture of the military devalues feminine qualities and leads to both physical and symbolic violence against women.

Prevalence rates of sexual assault in the military are unclear. The study of sexual assault in the military is more difficult because of differences in reporting requirements for sexual abuse in the military. However, a study by Kelty et al. (2010) showed that 6.8 percent of women and 1.8 percent of men reported being sexually abused in the military. Valente and Wight (2007) stated that 4 to 9 percent of female military service members are sexually assaulted while in the military. This includes sexual assault and sexual harassment in military settings by intimate partners and active duty personnel. Some female military officers report being raped more than once, often being gang raped while on active duty (Valente & Wight, 2007). Many do not report, however, and Valente and Wight (2007) found that one-third of the sexual assault victims did not know how to report the abuse, and while one-fifth believed it was to be expected in the military. Additionally, many fail to report their abuse because they feel as though they will be ridiculed, their careers will be disrupted, they will face retribution, or they will be told to get over it (Valente & Wight, 2007).

The effects of sexual assault on those in the military can be traumatic, and victims can experience a form of Post-Traumatic Stress Disorder referred to as Military Sexual Trauma (MST) (Kelty et al., 2010). MST has lasting side effects;

women veterans who were sexually abused reported symptoms of PSTD, dissociative disorder, eating disorders, and personality disorders, while male veterans who experience MST reported symptoms of dissociative disorders and personality disorders. Veterans who experienced sexual assault while in uniform were also likely to attempt suicide or harm themselves at more than twice the rate of veterans who did not experience MST (Kelty et al., 2010).

CHAPTER SUMMARY

- Institutional settings provide opportunities for sexual victimization to proliferate, often going undetected or unreported to criminal justice authorities.

- Sexual abuse of minors is most common in families and institutions where adults form mentoring and nurturing relationships with adolescents, including schools, religious organizations, sports, and social organizations.

- Hypermasculine institutions, such as prisons and the military, often provide situational opportunities for sexual abuse to take place.

- There are few methodologically sound empirical studies examining the prevalence of abuse within institutions, which makes it difficult to understand the scope of the problem.

- High-profile, serious cases of sexual victimization are often the catalyst to exposing sexual abuse within particular institutions. The causes of sexual abuse within any institution and the responses to those who abuse are often complex and change over time. Most institutions that cater to children and adolescents now have educational programs for creating safe environments, as well as policies for preventing and responding to allegations of sexual abuse.

DISCUSSION QUESTIONS

1. What would be the best way to determine the prevalence of sexual abuse within institutions where adults form mentoring or nurturing relationships with children and adolescents?

2. What steps could have been taken to reduce the extent of the sexual abuse crisis in the Catholic Church?

3. What are the primary impediments to inmates reporting sexual assaults to authorities?

4. Should consensual sexual behavior be allowed within prisons? Why or why not?

5. What can be done to reduce the scope of sexual abuse within the military?

DID YOU KNOW...?

- **Did you know** that sexual misconduct is common in situations where professionals work with patients? It is unethical, and often grounds for dismissal from the job or a professional association, for a professional to engage in sexual relationships with those under their control. Examples of such professions include doctor-patient, professor-student, and pastor-congregant.

- **Did you know** that most institutions where adults work with children now require education and training about proper and improper behavior between adults and children. Many of these training programs discuss the potential for "boundary violations," or behavior that is inappropriate but not necessarily abusive, such as becoming friends on social networking sites or spending time together alone and unsupervised.

9

Victims

Sexual victimization is a serious and pervasive problem, and research shows that sexual abuse may cause extensive, irreparable harm to victims.[1] Many victims continue to be affected long after the abuse has ended. Studies show high rates of depression and anxiety among victims (Kendall-Tackett, Williams, & Finkelhor, 1993; MacMillan & Munn, 2001; Romano & DeLuca, 2001) as well as an increased risk of suicide and suicidal thoughts (Dube et al., 2005; Rossow & Lauritzen, 2001). Substance abuse is also a frequently reported response to child sexual abuse (Dube et al., 2005; Heffernan et al., 2000; MacMillan & Munn, 2001; Simpson & Miller, 2002). Many victims struggle with anger and resentment, low self-esteem, shame, and self-blame. Moreover, victims often have difficulty trusting others, exhibit anti-social behaviors, and have strained interpersonal relationships (Dube et al., 2005; MacMillan & Munn, 2001). The effects of child sexual abuse, in particular, may also manifest themselves in behavioral problems, including disordered eating and delinquency (Dube et al., 2005). Sexual problems, promiscuity, and confusion over sexual identity and orientation are also common effects amongst victims (Bensley, Van Eenwyk, & Simmons, 2000). These psychological, emotional, physical, and behavioral effects can be debilitating to some victims and permeate all aspects of their lives in both the short and long term.

Any person may become the victim of a sexual offense—an adult or a child, male or female. Sexual victimization is prevalent across various races and ethnicities, and across the spectrum of socioeconomic statuses. Victimization occurs

---

1. In much of the current literature, primarily that of victim support agencies, the term *victim* is substituted by the term *survivor*. This book utilizes the term *victim* to denote a person who has been sexually victimized at any age but recognizes that these individuals are, in fact, survivors.

within families; among friends, acquaintances, and neighbors; within organizations; and, less frequently, between strangers. When sexual offenses occur, the family, friends, coworkers, and acquaintances of the victims, referred to as secondary victims, are also affected. It is the people close to the person victimized who must help him or her deal with the trauma and recover, although the process may prove traumatic for the secondary victims as well. The fact that most victims know their attackers aggravates the recovery process. For instance, if a woman discovers that her husband is abusing her daughter, she must help her daughter to recover. Yet, she must also cope with the fact that her daughter was being abused in the home, and that she knew the perpetrator of the crime. Also, she must deal with the deterioration of the family unit as a result of the offense.

The prevalence and impact of victimization has been studied extensively since the 1970s. In a meta-analysis, Bolen and Scannapieco (1999) found that overall rates of sexual victimization were approximately 30 percent for girls and 13 percent for boys throughout the lifespan. Children who experience sexual abuse often experience multiple types of abuse (Finkelhor, 2008). Finkelhor, Ormrod, Turner, and Hamby (2005) found that nearly half (49 percent) of the youth sampled in their study had experienced more than one form of direct (assault, maltreatment, sexual victimization) or indirect (witnessed) victimization. The concept of "multiple victimization" is consistent with findings from methodologically rigorous longitudinal studies conducted by Cathy Spatz Widom and her colleagues (Horwitz et al., 2001; Widom, Czaja & Dutton, 2008).

This chapter examines the history of our understanding of victimization, the effects of victimization, the difficulties encountered by victims throughout the criminal justice process, and the support groups that assist them in the restorative process.

OVERVIEW OF RESEARCH ON SEXUAL VICTIMIZATION

Despite the myriad studies now published on the impact of sexual victimization, little was known about the harm of victimization prior to the 1970s. The victims' rights movement in the criminal justice system, which began in the late 1960s, consisted of three elements: guaranteeing victim participation in criminal proceedings, securing financial benefits and services for crime victims, and securing more certain and harsher punishment for perpetrators. Research in the field of "victimology"—a term that appeared for the first time in 1940—developed on the same time scale. The early focus of this research was on typologies of victims and victim precipitation of abuse, later shifting to understanding structural elements of victimization. The key concerns of victimology were to understand individual vulnerability to victimization, and the nature and impact of victimization. Prior to this time, little scholarly attention was focused on the prevalence and impact of victimization.

Researchers of crime and victimization in the 19th century dismissed the notion that victimization was common. For example, Freud claimed his patients' reports of abuse were a result of fantasy and unresolved Oedipal complexes (Freud, 1905). His view was supported by others at the time, such as John Henry Wigmore who stated in his *Treatise on Evidence*, "women and girls are predisposed to bring false accusations against men of good character ... any female complainant should be examined by a psychiatrist to determine her credibility" (Olafson, 2004).

The classification of victims into typologies began as early as 1907, when Karl Abraham classified victims into two categories: accidental (abuse is violent, perpetrator is a stranger, victim knows it is wrong) and participant victims (victim often knows perpetrator, victim does not fully understand and is often given a reward, often more than one experience) (Abraham, 1927). An attitude of victim-blaming continued through the 1930s; for instance, Lauretta Bender, one of the earliest to research adult–child sexual behavior, found that all victims she interviewed were "unusually attractive" children who acted in a seductive manner with the psychiatrists. She stated, "It is not remarkable that frequently we considered the possibility that the child might have been the actual seducer rather than the one being seduced" (Bender & Blaue, 1937).

Despite the dearth of knowledge about victimization and its impact at the time, some early studies provided information that is similar to contemporary studies regarding prevalence of abuse. For instance, Terman (1938) conducted a study of married women in the 1930s and found that 32 percent had experienced a "shocking" or "disgusting" sexual experience before age 15. Similarly, Landis (1956) spoke to children abused by "sex deviates" in a treatment clinic in San Francisco and found that 33 percent of girls and 26 percent of boys were frightened at the time of abuse.

Research on sexual victimization, particularly of children, began to increase in the 1960s.[2] Two federally funded studies showed that child sexual abuse was common, and one of those was the first to report two significant findings: that most perpetrators were adults who knew the children they abused, and the long-term damage to children who were abused could be devastating (De Francis, 1971). In the 1970s, family systems therapists focused on an "ecological model" for understanding child sexual abuse, asserting that children were not to blame for their victimization. Also in the 1970s, sexual abuse became a focus of child-protection professionals, and the activities of child welfare organizations increased in frequency. At the same time, rape and child sexual abuse were a major focus of the feminist movement. Feminists conceptualized any type of sexual assault as a violent crime similar to rape resulting from male political control subordinating

---

2. For a more thorough review of the development of research on rape at this time, see Chapter 3, Feminist Theories.

women through terror, humiliation, and degradation. They argued that abuse was the fault of the perpetrator and not the victim, and both rape and child sexual abuse were the result of women's inferior place in society as compared to men in a male-dominated society.

Empirical research on sexual victimization began in earnest in the 1970s, and research on the abuse of children became so prevalent that the journal *Child Abuse and Neglect* was launched in 1976. By the 1980s, federal agencies began to devote significant funds toward research on sexual victimization, with a particular focus on the impact of victimization. For example, the National Institute of Justice funded three key studies: *Crime Victims: Learning How to Help Them, Research in Action* (Davis, 1987); *Serving Crime Victims and Witnesses* (Finn & Lee, 1987); and *Victim Appearances at Sentencing Hearings Under California's Victims' Bill of Rights, Executive Summary* (Villmoare & Neto, 1987).

A critical issue that emerged in the 1970s was the extent of intrafamilial abuse and abuse by those in a position of authority over the victims. Weber (1977) stated that sexual abuse was far more common than once thought and, importantly, occurs across social, economic, and ethnic boundaries. She also found a correlation between child sexual abuse and adult psychological symptoms and disorders. Rush identified the same correlation, and blamed mental health professionals for suppressing information and evidence of child maltreatment by men (Rush, 1977). Hindelang, Gottfredson, and Garofalo (1978) explained abuse through a "lifestyle exposure model," focusing more on structural understanding of the process of becoming a victim, which in turn helped frame the development of the victimization survey.

Despite the increased research on victimization, some researchers continued to downplay the resultant harm. For instance, Kempe and Kempe (1978, p. 55) stated, "most sexual molestation appears to do little harm to normal children." Conversely, researchers in the 1980s began focusing on the trauma of sexual abuse. In the early 1980s, the mechanism of "psychological trauma" was identified. Subsequently, the International Society for Study of Posttraumatic Stress was formed, the *Journal of Traumatic Stress* was launched, the Traumatogenic Theory was proposed (stating that exposure to any event that caused psychological trauma could cause psychological damage), the DSM-III added PTSD as a diagnosis (in 1980), and by 1983 the harm of sexual abuse was considered a form of posttraumatic stress.

By the 1990s, the victimization and child protection movements were in full swing, as evidenced by various legislative initiatives such as implementation of the *Child Protection Act of 1990*. Additionally, court proceedings were becoming more victim-focused, such as with the introduction of victim impact statements in the sentencing phase of criminal trials. However, many questions about victimization still remained. In 1992, a two-volume publication on sexual abuse raised questions such as: How is sexual abuse to be defined? What are the effects of abuse? How can the victim be helped? How can abuse be prevented? Contributors to this publication included physicians, attorneys, psychologists, philosophers, social workers, and engineers, all of whom covered a wide spectrum of basic applied issues related to victimization (O'Donohue & Geer,

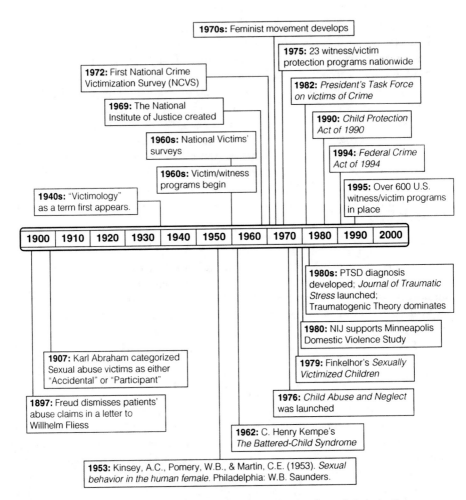

FIGURE 9.1 Development of the study and understanding of victimization
SOURCE: Terry et al., 2011

1992a, 1992b). The mid-1990s saw many additional contributions to the impact of child sexual abuse and prevention (for example, Burkhardt & Rotatori, 1995; Sebba, 1996; Vogeltanz et al., 1999), and scholarship on this topic continues to the present day. Figure 9.1 shows the development of the understanding of victimization as a concept over the last century.

EFFECTS OF VICTIMIZATION

Sexual assault victims are likely to experience a range of physical and psychological reactions to sexual abuse. The literature on effects of victimization is immense; the following sections provide an overview of the impact and phases of victimization.

Physical Harm

Types of sexual assault vary, and the more minor offenses (for example, touching above the clothing) are not likely to yield physical injuries. However, violent offenses that include penetration may well lead to serious injury (beyond the injury of the assault itself). When a victim is sexually assaulted, he or she may react in many different ways and thereby suffer varying degrees of physical harm. Some victims scream, some fight back, some are too shocked and afraid to react, and still others remain compliant so as to avoid possible additional violence (Rape Crisis Federation, 2002).

Victims of rape and sexual assault are not likely to face armed offenders. They are less likely to do so than victims of any other violent offense; approximately 6 percent of sex offenders threaten their victims with weapons (Rennison, 2001). The National Crime Victimization Survey (NCVS) shows that approximately one-quarter of all rape victims between 1992 and 1998 were physically injured during the attack in some way, however (other than the direct injuries resulting from the rape) (Simon, Mercy, & Perkins, 2001, p. 2). Although only a small percentage of those injuries involved wounds from weapons, broken bones, and severe bodily harm, they did include bruises, black eyes, cuts, or other such consequences. Some victims do not show any signs of physical violence, yet this does not mean that the experience is any less traumatic (Rape Crisis Federation, 2002).

It is also common for victims of sexual abuse, particularly those abused over a period of time when they were children, to experience medically unexplained symptoms. Called *somatization*, it is hypothesized that this allows the victim to express emotional pain through physical symptoms (Nelson, 2002). Common physical symptoms for which there is no obvious cause include back pain, pelvic pain, and headaches, and the victims tend to have negative perceptions of their health (Calhoun & Atkeson, 1991; Walker et al., 1992). Without an obvious organic cause to their pain, doctors may dismiss them as hypochondriacs. In fact, women who were sexually abused as children score higher on the hypochondriasis scale of the Minnesota Multiphasic Personality Inventory (MMPI) than women who have no history of abuse (Lundberg-Love, 1999). It is debatable whether the physical symptoms that victims experience are, in fact, somatic or whether they may be the result of physical trauma that occurred during childhood victimization (see Nelson, 2002).

In addition to the physical injuries, other medical problems, such as sexually transmitted diseases and pregnancy, may occur as the result of sexual assault. Though medical in nature, these are also likely to produce psychological harm. Sexually transmitted diseases occur in up to 30 percent of rape cases, with HIV being transmitted in approximately 0.2 percent of the cases (Resnick, Acierno, & Kilpatrick, 1997). Pregnancy also occurs in some cases, with an estimated 4.7 percent of raped women becoming impregnated (Homes, Resnick, Kilpatrick, & Best, 1992). Women who become pregnant must decide whether to carry the child through to term, and if so whether to raise it. This decision may have a significant impact on the victim, as even in a consensual relationship this choice is often stressful (see Strahan, 1991, for a review of psychological and socioeconomic effects of abortion on women). Whatever action is taken, the women are likely to experience some psychological symptoms as a result.

Psychological Reactions

The high rate of sexual victimization is not simply a criminal justice problem, but is also a public health problem (Abel et al., 1994). Those who are victimized as youths show higher levels of mental health problems as adults (Horwitz et al., 2001). Sexual abuse victims may experience a range of negative psychological reactions to the abuse. These include fear, anxiety, and depression (Calhoun & Atkeson, 1991; Lundberg-Love, 1999), emotional deprivation (Herman & Hirschman, 1977), and anxiety-related disorders, such as phobias, panic disorders, obsessive–compulsive disorders, eating disorders or other weight regulation practices, and sleep disturbances (Calhoun & Atkeson, 1991; Herman & Hirschman, 1977). Many victims experience low self-esteem and self-blame (Browning & Laumann, 1997), and they may withdraw from social interaction. Sexual abuse has a variety of effects on children depending on developmental factors such as their particular physical and cognitive growth, socialization, and other such factors (Finkelhor, 2008).

The most prevalent psychological reactions to sexual victimization are fear and anxiety, beginning with the fear created during the act itself. At this time, victims may fear for their lives, and this fear then leads to nervousness, specific anxiety about future sexual assaults, and ultimately a generalized anxiety (Calhoun & Atkeson, 1991, pp. 9–10). Depression is also a common consequence of abuse, particularly if the abuse was ongoing and the perpetrator was someone close to the victim (Lundberg-Love, 1999). Calhoun and Atkeson (1991, p. 11) describe how victims are likely to experience a number of depressive symptoms immediately following the sexual assault, including crying spells, fatigue, feelings of guilt and worthlessness, a sense of hopelessness, and suicidal thoughts. As a result of the depression, they are likely to withdraw from social interaction. This withdrawal can further perpetuate the cycle of depression, because when victims most need social support, they are instead avoiding those close to them. Victims generally show fewer of these symptoms after three or four months (Calhoun & Atkeson, 1991), though many victims do experience long-term depression or other disorders that help them cope with the trauma.

Several researchers have studied the traumatic impact of child sexual abuse, both at the time of the abuse and later in adulthood. While some researchers have concluded that sexual victimization can lead to the development of symptoms like those associated with Post-Traumatic Stress Disorder (PTSD) (Ullman, 2007), others argue that traumatic reactions often develop later in adulthood. For instance, Clancy (2009) notes that many of the adults in her sample who had been sexually abused as children experienced confusion at the time of the abuse, but later experienced negative psychological problems once the harmful nature of the behavior was understood. In an analysis of 45 studies of child sexual abuse, Kendall-Tackett, Williams, and Finkelhor (1993) did not find that trauma was a useful vehicle for understanding abuse. Likewise, Clancy (2009) and Nash and West (1995) found that the most common reaction at the time of abuse was "unpleasant confusion" and "embarrassment." Finkelhor (2008) notes that several developmental factors may impact the reaction to the abuse situation, including the child's support system, coping strategies, and environmental buffers. Despite the controversy over whether abuse is traumatic at the time it occurs, the literature consistently shows that abuse leads to negative long-term psychological and emotional consequences for many who experience it.

Some studies have shown a link between childhood victimization and future delinquency, including sexual offending (Brière & Runtz, 1989; Freund & Kuban, 1994; Lussier, Beauregard, Proulx, & Nicole, 2005). In their longitudinal analysis of 1,292 participants and 667 control subjects, Widom, Schuck, and White (2006) found a direct path from early victimization to later violence for males, though not for females. Weeks and Widom (1998) found that, among a sample of 301 convicted felons, perpetrators of sexual offenses reported higher rates (26.3 percent) of childhood sexual victimization than other offenders (12.5 percent). In a meta-analysis of 18 studies from 1965 to 1985, Hanson and Slater (1988) found that adult sex offenders who had perpetrated offenses against a male child were more likely to have a history of childhood sexual abuse (39 percent) than those who had perpetrated offenses against only female children (18 percent).

Sexual abuse also may affect victims' "sexual trajectories" (Hanson & Slater, 1988), leading to sexual dysfunction (Golding, 1996), an avoidance or loss of sexual satisfaction, and increased sexual activity (Ellis, Atkeson, & Calhoun, 1981). Smallbone and McCabe (2003) analyzed 48 written autobiographies of incarcerated offenders in Queensland, Australia, and found that offenders with a history of sexual abuse reported having begun masturbating at an earlier age than nonabused offenders. They hypothesized that these images of sexual abuse may be incorporated into early masturbation and tied to the development of deviant interests through classical conditioning. For men in particular, sexual abuse can lead to confusion and anxiety about sexual identity, and concern over gender identity (Watkins & Bentovim, 2000). As Coxe and Holmes (2001) note, factors such as victim age at the time of abuse, the relationship between the victim and the perpetrator, response to the report of sexual abuse as well as the frequency and duration of abuse may be important regarding the development of deviant beliefs and/or offense; yet there is not a strong link between early sexual victimization and becoming an adult sex offender.

Most studies indicate that when compared with their male counterparts, females are more likely to have been sexually abused during childhood. Furthermore, females are more likely than males to disclose information regarding sexual abuse, and male victimization seems to be acutely underreported (Brochman, 1991; Devoe & Coulborn-Faller, 1999; Finkelhor, Ormrod, Turner, & Hamby, 2005; Gries, Goh, & Cavanaugh, 1996; Lamb & Edgar-Smith, 1994; McMullen, 1992; Tewksbury, 2007; Watkins & Bentovim, 2000; Walrath, Ybarra, & Holden, 2003). That being said, reports are beginning to emerge about high rates of sexual abuse of boys in particular institutions and organizations including churches and sporting organizations. The lack of knowledge about male sexual victimization is striking; because so few males report, most information about their victimization is anecdotal or derived from studies with small sample sizes. As such, little statistical knowledge is available about males' long-term physical, psychological, and emotional effects, or about abuse events themselves.

Women and men experience many of the same physical, emotional, and psychological reactions to sexual abuse; however, there are some differences between the genders. Women are more likely to internalize their reactions, meaning they are more likely to suffer from psychological and emotional problems or physically harm themselves rather than others. Whereas some women need to talk about the experience of sexual assault in detail, many remain in the denial stage of abuse for a long time and do not talk about the abuse. Women are more likely than men to experience behavioral responses such as crying, pulling out hair, hitting or burning themselves, substance abuse, and adverse sexual behavior (Lundberg-Love, 1999, p. 7).

Some women do act out and abuse others or partake in other criminal acts. Harlow (1999, p. 2) examined the prior abuse of those serving correctional sentences and found that abuse was more common for women in the correctional than in the general population. She showed that 57.2 percent of females in state institutions, 39.9 percent in federal institutions, 47.6 percent in jail, and 40.4 percent of probationers had been abused prior to their sentences (with 39 percent, 22.8 percent, 37.2 percent, and 25.2 percent sexually abused while serving in each of the institutions, respectively). Although many men who were incarcerated were also abused (16.1 percent of men in state facilities, 7.2 percent in federal facilities, 12.9 percent in jail, and 9.3 percent of probationers were abused either physically and/or sexually [Harlow, 1999, p. 2]), women tended to be abused as both adults and juveniles, and by family members, acquaintances, and spouses. Additionally, three-quarters of the incarcerated women who were abused had parents who abused alcohol or drugs, and nearly two-thirds have at some point had a family member incarcerated. Women who were abused are more likely to act out and harm others if they do not have the support of a secure family unit.

Though they experience much of the same psychological trauma, men who are victims of sexual offenses are more likely to externalize their feelings than women. Male rape is most common in male-dominated institutions such as prison, military institutions, fraternities, and athletic organizations. As a reaction to the assault, some male victims attempt to reassert their masculinity through the stigmatization of others (Rogers & Terry, 1984; Watkins & Bentovin, 2000). This externalization comes from feelings of anger and a need to retain the socially constructed feelings of power and control that are associated with masculinity in today's society (McMullen, 1992). Because of the inclination to act out, some boys who were abused (though by no means all) go on to physically or sexually abuse others.

Socially, male rape can be stigmatizing, and for this reason male victims are hesitant to report the offense (Isley, 1991; Scarce, 1997). Men who rape and the male rape victims may be heterosexual or homosexual, yet male victims commonly experience confusion over their sexual identity as a reaction to the assault (National Center for Victims of Crime, 1997). Male rape, like female rape, is often wedded to feelings of power and dominance, and male victims are likely to experience feelings of self-blame and embarrassment that they could not prevent the victimization (Scarce, 1997). This is compounded if throughout the rape they experience an erection and then ejaculate. Though a common and reflexive reaction to the physical pain of the rape, many victims associate these actions with pleasure and consent (McMullen, 1992). Groth and Burgess (1980) explain how rapists try to get the victim to ejaculate, thereby reinforcing the feelings of power and control and the myth that the victim "wanted it."

Rape Trauma Syndrome and the Stages of Victimization

Some researchers have noted that rape may cause symptoms similar to PTSD in victims, in that it is based on a particular event in the victim's life that produces similar responses in nearly all who experience it. These symptoms have been identified as a result of rape trauma syndrome (RTS), which is clinically recognized as the "stress response pattern of the victim following forced, nonconsenting sexual activity" (Burgess, 1995, p. 239). Responses to sexual assault are often long term and include recurrent recollection of the event, reduced involvement in the environment, and hyperalertness, disturbed sleep patterns, guilt about the incident, or avoidance of activities that arouse recollection.

Much of the research on RTS details stages that victims experience as a result of a rape. Burgess and Holstrom (1974) identified two phases of RTS as the acute and the reorganization phases. The *acute phase* lasts a short period of time immediately after the assault and includes a variety of emotional responses from the victim (for example, crying, swearing, laughing). The *reorganization phase* involves learning how to accept and cope with life after the sexual assault. Some have since expanded on the two-phase model, such as the Rape and Rape Prevention researchers (1999), who listed six stages as *denial, anger, grief, depression, taking action,* and *acceptance.* Drawing on four sources of rape research, Koss and Harvey (1991, pp. 48–55) explain four stages of reactions, including the *anticipatory* phase (behavior before and during the assault, use of defense mechanisms to preserve a feeling of invulnerability); the *impact* phase (intense fear, anxiety, and guilt immediately after the assault); the *reconstitution* phase (an outward appearance of adjustment though a psychologically tumultuous phase); and the *resolution* phase (like the reorganization phase, learning to accept and cope with the abuse).

Holmes and Holmes (2002, p. 215) provided a basic yet thorough analysis of three stages of sexual victimization, which are shock, denial, and integration. When the victim is in *shock*, he or she experiences feelings of anxiety, guilt, and fear. Similar to the acute phase of RTS, this stage occurs for a short period after the victimization ends and is followed by a stage of denial. *Denial* occurs in most victims of sexual assault, and is when the victim tries to forget about the abuse. This could include complete or partial denial of the event, as well as suppression of any feelings of guilt and anxiety. Generally, the victim tries to forget about the event and return to a normal routine, which is also seen in Koss and Harvey's

(1991) reconstitution phase. Before victims move past this stage, they may begin to experience emotional problems such as grief and depression before they subsequently attempt to integrate the experience into their lives. As in the reorganization phase of RTS, they learn to cope with the trauma of what happened, and many of the initial psychological or physiological symptoms begin to subside (though not disappear). During this period of *integration*, the impact of the abuse is fully absorbed. The victim may have nightmares in which the experience is relived or there are resulting feelings of fear, stress, and anxiety. Personal and work relationships may also be affected, and there may be difficulties concentrating on work or professional duties. This stage is important, however, because it is the point at which victims begin to accept the abuse and try to adjust.

Though most sexual offense victims exhibit characteristics from these stages, the stages are by no means mutually exclusive or exhaustive. Victims clearly experience a distinct set of reactions to a traumatic event of this nature, but adjustment to sexual victimization is a long-term process and is affected by a complex interaction of variables that include level of social support, coping mechanisms, and demographic characteristics (Calhoun & Atkeson, 1991, p. 8). Other factors that influence the rate of recovery include the type and severity of the sexual assault, the environment in which the victim recovers, and the type and timing of interventions (Koss & Harvey, 1991; Ward & Inserto, 1990).

Secondary Victims

Secondary victims, or people close to the person who has been sexually abused, are also significantly affected by the sexual abuse. Additionally, these individuals must help the primary victim to cope with the abuse and work through any psychological reactions that emerge. Secondary victims include parents, siblings, partners, peers, colleagues, and employers (Ward & Inserto, 1990). Though all play different roles in the victim's life, many of these individuals may need counseling themselves in order to understand the offense and help the victim overcome the trauma.

When considering issues of child sexual assault, the most important role is that of the parents, particularly the mother. Parents of abused children have varying levels of knowledge of the abuse and, as a result, have varying feelings of guilt, negligence, and responsibility once the abuse is known. Johnson (1992, pp. 2–3) describes three models of mothers of incest survivors based on their knowledge of the abuse and reactions to it. The first model is the *collusive* mother, who knows the abuse is occurring and ignores it. Johnson explains that this mother not only is lacking guilt and anxiety about the abuse but also may herself be psychologically impaired and has pushed the daughter into the abusive situation. The second model is that of the *powerless* mother, who may want to help her child but cannot because she is weak and defenseless compared with the father. This mother is often a victim herself and is either physically or emotionally helpless in preventing the child abuse from occurring. The third model Johnson describes is that of the *protective* mother. She is able to assist the child once she becomes aware of the abuse because she has alternative resources available outside of the marriage. This mother is generally surprised to find out about the abuse and is likely to feel guilt that it happened and empathy toward her child.

Both parents and siblings of the victim are likely to experience emotional reactions to the abuse, including denial, disbelief, remorse, regret, and even trauma. When the abuse is interfamilial, the family is likely to go through significant changes, because in most cases either the victim or perpetrator will be removed from the home (Ward & Inserto, 1990). This uprooting will cause disruption for the entire family, and disruption may create emotional trauma for all involved— particularly the victim, who may feel responsible for the upheaval. The reaction toward the offender also varies: whereas some see the perpetrator as hateful and repugnant, others see him or her as sick and in need of help (Johnson, 1992).

The spouse or partner of a rape victim also plays a significant role in the recovery process. Whereas some partners are fully supportive, sympathetic, and helpful to the victim, others become withdrawn or blame the victim partially for the offense (Baker, Skolnik, Davis, & Brickman, 1991; Ward & Inserto, 1990). Rape elicits a stronger negative reaction from partners than other violent crimes (Baker et al., 1991), which in some cases leads to feelings of vengefulness or a lack of support for the victim. Though many of the partners are supportive, problems may emerge in the relationship due to feelings of uncleanliness or unfaithfulness (Ward & Inserto, 1990, p. 82). The study by Baker et al. (1991) showed that female peers of sexual assault victims show the most positive and supportive attitudes toward the victims, and as such this relationship is important for the victim who is recovering from the trauma.

If the victim does decide to report the sexual abuse to the authorities, he or she will become involved in a criminal justice process that may, ultimately, "revictimize" the victim. Victims often find this process to be as or more traumatic than the sexual assault itself.

RESPONDING TO REPORTS OF SEXUAL ABUSE: THE MEDICAL AND CRIMINAL JUSTICE PROCESSES

Once the victim reports a case of sexual abuse, a series of agencies become involved in the investigation of the case. The hospital must conduct a medical examination to collect evidence and test for any signs of sexual assault, while the police begin collecting evidence from the crime scene, victim, and offender (if known). Once a suspect is arrested, the prosecutor takes over the case and assesses whether charges should be made and, if so, what they should be. The prosecutor also has the option of offering the defendant a plea bargain. Unfortunately, victims of crime have little or no input into whether plea negotiations are offered or accepted. If the case goes to trial, the prosecution must show beyond a reasonable doubt that the sexual offense occurred, and the defense counsel will generally embark on severe questioning of the victim in order to break down the case. Whatever the outcome, the legal process is trying for the victim.

Victims' recovery from a sexual assault may be affected by the post-assault process (Campbell et al., 2001). There have been many institutional changes in the criminal justice system over the past two decades in response to victims of sexual assault. For instance, some police departments have implemented sex crime units, prosecutors' offices have implemented victim specialists and specialist prosecutors, there has been an increase in the numbers of rape crisis centers and victim advocates at those centers, and there are victim counselors at many hospitals (Burgess, 1995, p. 239). Nonetheless, the criminal justice process is a psychologically taxing experience for most victims of sexual offenses. In fact, many experience a condition of *critogenesis*, which is the exacerbation or genesis of a condition by legal processes (Gutheil, 2000). In other words, the criminal justice system causes more victimization when it should be addressing, helping, or reducing victimization. As long as the criminal justice system is offender rather than victim centered, critogenesis is likely to occur.

The Hospital

The hospital is a key institution in rape investigation because it is often the first place that victims go to be treated after an assault. It is the goal of the hospital to examine the victim and take evidence relating to the offense. Because the medical exam must be thorough, it is generally quite long and intrusive. A victim spends several hours at the hospital while the staff treats him or her both medically and psychologically (New York City Alliance Against Sexual Assault [NYCAASA], 2001). The procedures that the victim endures are lengthy, uncomfortable, and may cause the victim to feel further degraded and humiliated. As such, it is important to have specially trained hospital staff to work with the victims and victim advocates on call at the hospital.

The hospital has three duties in terms of helping victims of sexual abuse: the examination, the treatment, and postexamination (Ward & Inserto, 1990, p. 96). The examination includes a physical exam, a pelvic exam, and a collection of laboratory samples, as well as questions about the offense and perpetrators. The primary purpose of the examination is to determine if there are physical indications that a crime was committed and, if so, to preserve the evidence. However, there are many difficulties in doing this. In cases of both rape and child molestation, many victims do not go to the hospital immediately after the offense occurs. Even some who do go to the hospital shortly after the assault shower or bathe first, thereby eradicating any forensic evidence from their bodies. In cases where forensic evidence is available, the perpetrator may claim that sexual intercourse took place but was consensual. This is particularly prevalent in cases where an acquaintance, date, or spouse assaults the victim.

Another purpose of the hospital examination is to determine whether the victim has contracted any sexually transmitted diseases or has become pregnant. If the victim has been infected, the hospital must then offer treatment and/or counseling. Many hospitals now offer rape victims "morning after" pills in order to avoid pregnancy. If taken within 48 hours of intercourse, these work similarly to birth control pills and do not allow the egg to be fertilized. If the victim goes to the hospital more than 48 hours after the assault and is pregnant, she must make the decision as to whether she will continue or abort the pregnancy. The duty of the hospital in this situation is to counsel her about the options she has and arrange for a pregnancy termination, if so desired (Ward & Inserto, 1990).

Cases of child abuse present another set of difficulties in obtaining forensic evidence. To begin with, some doctors will not do vaginal examinations on children (Ward & Inserto, 1990), though guidelines exist for doctors to follow when performing exams on children suspected of being sexually abused (American Academy of Pediatrics Committee on Child Abuse and Neglect, 1991). When an examination is done, the purpose is to check for evidence of sexual abuse, usually penetration, and this is done through examination of the hymen. Unfortunately, this evidence is often inconclusive because the hymen can be stretched or broken in several ways, and the medical examination does not necessarily prove penetration (Prior, 2001). There is rarely any forensic evidence collected from children during the examination, because the abuse does not usually take the form of intercourse. Sexual intercourse is more prevalent in incestuous relations than extrafamilial relations (West, 1987), and because such abuse is likely to go on for a long time, it is unlikely that a child will go to the hospital directly after the intercourse takes place so that forensic evidence can be collected.

Studies show mixed results as to the effects of a hospital examination on children. Some researchers claim that hospital exams produce similar results to the sexual abuse—namely, fear, anxiety, pain, and anger, though rarely long-term anxiety or distress (Berson, Herman-Giddens, & Frothingham, 1993; Lazebnik et al., 1994). Other researchers, however, show that the hospital experience is not that traumatic for most children. In one study, more than two-thirds of the parents of sexually abused children said that the hospital did not have a negative impact on the child (Allard-Dansereau, Hebert, Tremblay, & Bernard-Bonnin, 2001). In fact, the hospital had a positive impact in that it reassured the children about the physical integrity of their bodies after the traumatic experience of abuse. Though it is unclear exactly what factors about the examination may have a negative impact on children, the study by Allard-Dansereau et al. indicates that one important factor is the demeanor of the doctor and the extent to which he or she explains the examination process.

In order to reduce the level of emotional trauma for adult and child victims, the hospital should offer support throughout the exam and the subsequent treatment. Additionally, all hospitals should have rape-designated facilities in order to ensure proper collection of evidence and medical and psychological treatment for the victims. Some states have such facilities available in designated hospitals, whereas others have gone further and established hospital-based sexual assault nurse examiners (SANEs). SANEs are forensically trained nurses who are specifically taught how to conduct evidentiary exams on sexual assault victims (Littel, 2001). They are involved in cases from the initial collection of evidence through the prosecution and can testify as experts in court as to the meaning of evidence.

This is true even in cases where the victim has no physical injuries or there is no sperm (and therefore no forensic evidence) available (Littel, 2001). In many communities, they create a link between the evidence collection in a hospital and the criminal justice process, thereby increasing the likelihood of conviction for the sexual offender (NYCAASA, 2001). The victim is never required to report the assault to the police, but when he or she does, the police face an arduous task of responding sensitively to the complainant while collecting evidence and finding the perpetrator of the crime.

The Police

Sexual assault differs from other criminal offenses in many ways, one being that it is a private offense that generally takes place in the home of the perpetrator and/or the victim. Sexual assault is a difficult crime to prevent, and the police response is almost always one of control after the crime has been committed. In this vein, the police have three primary duties in cases of sexual assault: to interview the victim, investigate the crime, and collect evidence (Office for Victims of Crime, 2001).

In most cases of sexual assault, whether the victims are children or adults, there are no witnesses to the offense. As such, it is pertinent for the police to interview the victim, who is likely the only witness to the crime. Adult victims are often reluctant to speak to the police, because sexual assault is such an intrusive and personal offense. The police should therefore be trained in interviewing victims of sexual assault so as not to appear patronizing or overprotective, and to be aware of the victims' desire for privacy about the situation (Office for Victims of Crime, 2001). In order to get the most accurate and thorough statement, the police may come across as interrogating the victim. The victim may interpret this as lacking in sensitivity or that the police do not believe his or her story. Additionally, when relaying the account of the offense, the victim might forget details of the crime. The police should not consider this, or any emotional outbursts, the result of a false allegation but rather the effect of a severe trauma (Office for Victims of Crime, 2001).

Child witnesses present a different set of difficulties. Though the majority of children's cases are handled through social services or family courts, the police may have to interview children who are victims of sexual abuse. The interviewer must be trained in interviewing children and have special skills in order to elicit truthful information from the child. Though the interviewer must establish rapport with any victim of sexual assault, it is particularly important with children. If the child is uncomfortable talking to the interviewer, he or she may not be willing to speak to the interviewer without the presence of a parent, if at all. Interviews are also more effective if the child is comfortable, which is more likely to occur if the child is in a familiar place like the home or a child advocacy center (Office for Victims of Crime, 2001; Ward & Inserto, 1990).

The National Institute of Justice (1992, pp. 33–42) describes three main techniques used in questioning. First, the interviewer may use anatomically correct dolls. Benefits to this approach include reducing stress for the child; reducing vocabulary differences between children and adults; and reducing embarrassment for the child. However, the dolls may have an adverse effect by provoking negative emotions related to the abuse or contaminating the child's memories at the sight of the genitalia. A second way in which children can be questioned is through normal interview techniques but with leading questions. This is risky though often necessary in order to elicit information. Children often do not report sexual behavior unless asked leading questions; however, presentation of inaccurate information may lead to a false memory being remembered (Loftus & Davies, 1984). A third method of questioning is to use videotapes, which are beneficial because they reduce the number of interviews, show the child's body language in response to questions, and can be used as evidence in court cases.

During the interview, the maturity and competency of the child must be established. The interview should begin with personal questions to establish rapport, with questions asking about the victim's name, address, pets, or siblings (Ward & Inserto, 1990). The interviewer can establish the level of development and maturity through personal questions such as religious affiliation, and establish the concept of time through asking about days of the week or month (Ward & Inserto, 1990, p. 69). Vocabulary must be age appropriate; it should not be too scientific or childish. Finally, the interviewer should provide reassurance and compassion to the child throughout the interview as well as praise, assuring the child that he or she is not in trouble.

Because children are considered the ultimate innocent victims, they are usually treated with sympathy and respect and their word is taken as truth despite the difficulties that arise from the interviews. Rape victims, however, are treated variably. If an offender attacks a stranger, the victim of the sexual assault is usually treated with respect and sympathy because this is seen as a "real rape." If the police see the victim as having any culpability in the assault, such as by drinking or hitchhiking, or because he or she is a prostitute, the police may treat the victim with less respect than they would a "real" rape victim. Many male rape victims also experience difficulties with the police (Pelka, 1995), though gender role stereotyping is less overt now than in previous years (Turner, 2000). To effectively elicit information and at the same time be supportive of all victims of sexual assault, the interviewer should show acceptance of the victim's statement, resourcefulness, empathy, sensitivity, persuasiveness, persistency, patience, and tolerance (Ward & Inserto, 1990, pp. 54–55).

The police response to victims is critical, and the ability of the victim to cope with the assault is largely dependent on the police reaction (Office for Victims of Crime, 2001). In order to reduce the disparity in the ways in which victims are treated, almost all police departments have employed training for interviewing victims of sexual assault or have established specialized sex crime units. Others have established specialized programs within the police department, such as Austin's Victim Assistance Program. The purpose of this program is to assist both the victim and the victim's family in the recovery process by providing them with emotional and psychological support (Parker, 2001). At the same time, the coordinator of this program ensures that the police are educated about the realities of sexual assault and the needs of the victims. Victim service agencies at the law enforcement level are particularly important, as very few crimes go on to prosecution, and those that do rarely end in conviction.

The Adversarial Process

Once the police have investigated the crime and arrested the perpetrator, the adjudication process begins. There are several stages to this process, and the case can be dropped or settled through plea negotiations at any stage. After the perpetrator is arrested, taken into custody, and booked, he or she goes before the court for an initial appearance. At this time, the judge or magistrate makes a decision about pretrial release. Unless the case contained a high degree of violence, such as rape using excessive force, it is likely that the defendant will be released either on his or her own recognizance or on bail. The pretrial release decision is based on several factors, including the nature of the crime, the safety of releasing the person into the community, and the best interest of the accused. Because many sex offenders are employed, have strong community ties, and show little likelihood of escape, they are usually released at this stage.

After the initial appearance, formal charges are filed against the defendant. At this time, the case is given to the prosecutor, who has the discretion to determine whether there is evidence to indicate that the defendant committed the offense and, if so, what the charges are going to be. If the prosecutor decides to proceed, the case will be brought before either the grand jury or the bench (in a preliminary hearing) to determine if there is probable cause to continue on to a trial. Once there is a formal charge, the defendant is arraigned and enters a plea. Most defendants plead guilty at this stage with the offer of a plea bargain, discussed in the next section. For those who plead not guilty, the case goes on to trial. Many cases do not make it to trial, however, and are dismissed at various stages throughout the adjudication process. One study found that 67 percent of cases are dismissed, and that 80 percent of the time this decision was made against the wishes of the victims (Campbell, 1998). When trials do take place, they generally take place many months or even years after the offense occurred due to factors such as legal maneuvering and overcrowding in the system. Because there are rarely witnesses to the offense, most victims have to testify against the offender and be cross-examined by the defense. Because of the high standard for conviction in criminal cases—proof beyond a reasonable doubt—sex offenders are rarely convicted if the case is based on the word of the victim, which contradicts the word of the only other witness: the defendant.

The adjudication process is often traumatic for victims, whether the case is dropped, the defendant pleads guilty, or the case goes to court. This begins with the decision made by the prosecutor about whether to charge the defendant at all. If the case goes to trial, the victim is usually revictimized in the courtroom. Though rape reform laws have emerged in the past decade to avert such abuses and victim advocates will assist the victims throughout the trial, many victims continue to feel a critogenic effect from the system.

Despite the offender-centered system, there are some fundamental changes that can be made in the way that victims are treated. An example of victim-centered legislation comes from the United Kingdom. In 1990, the Home Office created the Victims' Charter, a document outlining the rights of victims and what they can expect from the criminal justice agencies, which set out uniform standards of service for victim support. This nationally mandated code of practice ensures consistency throughout the country and is constantly developing in accordance with victim research. The general purpose of the charter is to set standards so that victims are treated with dignity, provided with information, protection, and support, and given information about their case. For victims of rape and sexual abuse, the charter also requires provision of specialized police officers to rape victims. Additionally, the charter establishes collaboration between agencies, primarily the police, probation, and Victim Support (the national charity for people affected by crime).

Role of the Prosecution: Dismissal, Plea Bargain, or Trial   Once a perpetrator is arrested and the case of sexual assault is passed on to the prosecutor, he or she must determine whether to prosecute and, if so, on what charges. There are many factors that go into the decision of whether to file charges; most important is the strength of the evidence. Beyond these factors, the prosecutor must also look at the credibility of the victim, who will inevitably take the stand as a witness. Though rape crisis counselors and rape advocates are available to support the victim throughout the criminal justice process, the duty of the prosecutor is simply to secure conviction. For this, the prosecutor may look for ways in which the victim displays rape-relevant behavior (for example, promiscuity) or has participated in criminal behavior in the past, behavior that the defense attorney will likely exploit at a trial. As one prosecutor states, "There is a difference between believing a woman was assaulted and being able to get a conviction in court" (Frohmann, 1995, p. 214). Some communities have established specialist lawyers to prosecute at rape trials in order to reduce the insensitivity of the approach and the amount of revictimization from the prosecution.

If the case goes to trial, it is the burden of the prosecutor to prove beyond a reasonable doubt that the defendant committed the crime in question. Unfortunately, there are low conviction rates with sexual offenses that do go to trial because of the lack of witnesses, the lack of forensic evidence, and clever defense tactics used to undermine the victim's testimony. Unless there are visible bruises, cuts, or other injuries, it is difficult to show physical coercion (a sexual act compelled by force). It is also difficult to prove emotional or mental coercion (a sexual act compelled by threats) when there is a prior relationship between the victim and offender, the victim is lacking in "moral turpitude" (for example, the rape of a prostitute), or there are "contributory factors" (for example, the victim was drinking). Those cases most likely to end in conviction are those committed by strangers where there is forensic evidence or cases of child abuse where there is clearly physical intrusion. As such, a prosecutor is only likely to take a sexual assault case to court if there is evidence corroborating the victim's story (Taslitz, 1999).

Because convictions are so difficult to obtain in court, the majority of cases do not ever go to trial. Approximately 90 percent of cases in the criminal justice system are settled through plea bargains, yet this number is even higher for sexual offense cases. Plea bargains, which are arranged among the prosecutor, the defense attorney, the defendant, and the judge, are negotiations of guilty pleas in exchange for reduced charges or lenient sentences. There are many benefits to plea bargaining for the prosecutor; most important, guilty pleas avoid the time, expense, and work of proving guilt at a trial, and they assure a conviction. It is beneficial to defendants as well, because they may receive a charge reduction, a dismissal of some charges, a softer label, or a lenient sentence. Plea bargains are beneficial to the correctional system, as lenient sentences result in shorter sentences or fewer prison sentences, thus reducing overcrowding. Plea bargains even benefit victims in the sense that the victim does not have to testify at a trial when the offender pleads guilty.

Another reason that prosecutors offer plea bargains is that there is a high rate of attrition at each stage of the criminal justice process. The primary reason for this is the increase in acquaintance and intimate rapes and child abuse within the family. These are the most difficult cases to support with evidence, and as a result they are often dismissed (Harris & Grace, 1999). The first point that cases can be dismissed is by the police after the investigation. If the case is lacking evidence, police will not pursue the allegation. The second place at which the case can be dismissed is at the initial appearance in court. At this time, approximately 24 hours after the perpetrator was arrested, it is not uncommon for the victim to recant his or her statement. Other reasons for dismissal are a voided arrest due to lack of probable cause, or lack of evidence even if probable cause does exist. A third point at which dismissal occurs is at the formal charge. If the grand jury or the judge during the preliminary hearing finds a lack of probable cause, there will be no true bill, or formal charge. The case can again be dismissed during the pretrial phase. When this happens, it is usually due to loss of evidence or confession or because the witness-victim is incompetent or mentally disabled and cannot testify.

Despite the benefits of plea bargaining, there are many problems with it as well. Though victims do not have to testify at trial when a plea bargain is offered, they are often dissatisfied with the lenient sentences given to offenders, and they rarely have a say in whether a plea is offered. The rationale behind this is that the adjudication process must look at facts rather than emotion, but the lack of inclusion of victims in the negotiation process may leave them feeling as though their plight is less important than that of the offenders'. Though the adjudication system in any state in the United States does not seem to be nearing change in this area, legislation in the United Kingdom was recently modified to become more victim centered. Under the Victims' Charter, the prosecutor is required to take into consideration the victim's views before a negotiation is offered.

It is difficult to obtain a conviction for rape or sexual assault against adults, though problems also arise in court trials when the children are victims. There are four main issues of concern in regard to child witnesses, which are competence, credibility, children's rights, and defendant's rights (Perry & Wrightsman, 1991). The National Institute of Justice (1992, p. 56) explains four competencies that the court has established for child witnesses. The first is *capacity for truthfulness*, or the basic understanding between truth and fantasy as well as an understanding of the necessity to speak the truth. The second competency is *mental capacity*, or the ability to accurately understand the act that took place. A third competency is *memory*, or the ability to recall correctly the specifics of the act. The fourth is *communication*, which is the ability for the child to explain in court what occurred and answer questions about the act. Though all states have different provisions relating to child competency, these four requirements must be present in order for a child to be a viable witness.

Once the child is declared competent, the prosecutor must determine the strength of the child's credibility, or how believable the child is (Mapes, 1995). Some children have difficulty in interpreting and explaining acts of sexual abuse, which detracts from their credibility (Loftus & Davies, 1984). Even when the child gives an accurate depiction of events, mock jury studies indicate that evidence in the case is of more concern than the testimony of the child (Ross, Miller, & Moran, 1987). Both children's and defendants' rights also present dilemmas. The child abuser may not be convicted if a child does not testify; yet, testifying may be a frightening experience for a child (Perry & Wrightsman, 1991). At the same time, the defendant has the Sixth Amendment right to face his or her accuser and confront the witness in court, though such a confrontation may be harmful to the child. The child should not have to relive the trauma of a frightening event unless it is absolutely necessary, and the prosecutor should consider whether this testimony is sufficiently likely to improve the chances of conviction.

Rape Reform Laws and Defense Tactics   If a sexual assault case does go to trial, the victim is likely to face an emotionally trying ordeal while testifying. The adjudication process, however, has changed considerably since the 1970s due to significant rape reform laws. At that time, the trial of a rape victim was likened to a "second rape," because the defense was allowed to bring up the victim's sexual history, her chastity (or lack of), and any motive she had to claim that a sexual encounter was rape (Estrich, 1987). The victim rather than the offender was blamed for the offense, as it was either suggested that she was lying about the offense, that she consented, or that she prompted the sexual encounter and it therefore was not rape (Cuklanz, 1996). It was not a crime for a man to rape his wife, following the traditional belief that she was his property. The laws were gender biased, so that a man could not be a rape victim and a woman could not be a rapist. A stranger who was raped was said to be "asking for it" if dressed provocatively, and if the victim lacked sexual experience it was suggested that she was repressed and "wanted it" (Taslitz, 1999). In order to convict, there had to be evidence corroborating the victim's account, and a woman had to show physical resistance to the offender in order for the act to be considered rape (Berger, Searles, & Neuman, 1995).

Rape law reforms were led by feminist researchers (for example, Brownmiller, 1975; Estrich, 1987; Griffin, 1979; Russell, 1975) who attempted to change not only the existing laws but also the public perception of both offenders and victims. The four legal areas of change represented by the reform agenda were definitions of sexual offenses, evidentiary rules, statutory offenses, and penalties for sexual offenses (Berger et al., 1995, p. 225). Socially, reformers felt that by reducing the prevalence of rape myths they could change public perception of victims and, ultimately, increase the number of sexual offense convictions. They believed that public perception and the law were interlinked, as the law promoted rape myths and represented male authority and female subversion in society (Berger et al., 1995). They were successful in many of their aims; legal definitions have changed and the gender bias has been all but eliminated. Physical resistance is no longer the only factor used to prove coercion, and lack of evidentiary corroboration of the victim's testimony does not imply that the victim is lying about the rape. Socially, the prevalence of rape myths has been reduced. The resultant increase in reporting of acquaintance and intimate rapes, as well as child abuse within the family, is testament to the success of their efforts. Unfortunately, sexual offenses are still difficult to prove, and defense tactics still create emotional stress for many of the victims.

Rape shield laws prohibit the defense from bringing up the promiscuity or character of the victim, and they limit the amount of information that can be introduced regarding the personal or sexual history of the victim. This includes information such as the victim's previous sexual partners, preferred type of clothing, occupation (for example, if the victim is a prostitute), or other such issues that may influence the victim's credibility. However, the defense can skirt the laws by asking questions that are indirectly correlated to the victim's character and may produce bias against the victim (Taslitz, 1999, p. 84). The defense lawyer may try to get the victim to offer statements about his or her personal or sexual life, after which the lawyer can ask any questions relating to the information offered. The language used by the lawyer might also introduce bias, such as asking about previous partners (plural), her "child's father" (as opposed to her husband), questions about regular use of drugs or alcohol (low moral turpitude), or comment on the victim's low social status (though completely unrelated to sexual behavior). Therefore, even though rape shield laws prohibit direct questions about the victim's character, the defense can either ask questions that are ultimately overruled (yet the jury hears the leading questions and may make assumptions about the victim's character) or ask questions irrelevant to the case whose only purpose is to paint a negative view of the victim.

Because the duty of defense attorneys is to get their clients acquitted, they use various strategies that aim to exculpate their clients. Some of these introduce bias against the victim, whereas others are simply intended to introduce reasonable doubt in the minds of the jurors; yet most put pressure and emotional stress on the victim. Ward and Inserto (1990, pp. 108–109) explain three defense ploys, the first of which is admitting that the victim was raped, but claiming that the defendant is not guilty and it is a case of mistaken identity. This is only possible if the rapist did not leave behind semen and therefore DNA, in which case the second ploy is to admit that sexual intercourse occurred but that it was consensual. This is a very common claim and is used often to introduce doubt in the mind of the jurors. If the victim did not go to the doctor immediately or the forensic evidence is ambiguous, the defense may employ a third tactic by admitting that a sexual encounter occurred but deny that intercourse took place.

CASE STUDY

JUSTIN BERRY: Victim or Offender?

Sometimes the line between victim and offender is blurred, particularly when it comes to juvenile offenders. The case of Justin Berry is a good example of such a situation.

In 2001, at the age of 13, Justin Berry began operating a pornographic website. Justin featured images and video of himself naked, masturbating, and engaging in sexual acts with female prostitutes, receiving money from more than a thousand men who paid to see his webcast. Today, he could be convicted of charges involving child pornography for such actions; but was he an offender or a victim?

Justin bought a webcam when he turned 13. He was a lonely teenager without many friends, and hoped the webcam would improve his social life. He posted innocent images of himself on an online photo website, and within minutes he received messages from child predators. These predators began sending him gifts, and he soon developed a friendship with many of them. After interacting with these men for a few weeks, one approached Justin online suggesting that if he took off his shirt the man would send him $50.00. The acts Justin committed online escalated as predators began to increase their demands and the money they were willing to pay. This business soon escalated into a monthly membership website featuring pornographic images of Justin. Justin eventually also began meeting some of these predators in person, where they performed sexual acts with him and gave him money for these meetings.

While Justin was clearly a victim of manipulation and sexual abuse by these men, he also became a developer and distributor of child pornography. He was eventually offered immunity for his testimony against the men who paid for memberships to his websites, even though he had committed crimes. The case of Justin Berry illustrates the reality that a large number of juvenile sex offenders were in fact victims of abuse themselves, and this abuse could have a long-term impact on his physical, emotional, and sexual development.

Questions
1. Do you think Justin is a victim or an offender? Can he be both?
2. What effects of victimization might Justin experience? What steps can or should be taken to best help reduce these effects?

Taslitz (1999, pp. 22–23) explains four other common defense strategies, most of which are meant to upset the victim while he or she is on the stand. First, the defense attorney may repeatedly ask questions about the rape. This serves two purposes: to unnerve the victim and to find any inconsistencies in the victim's version of events. A second tactic is to emphasize a delay in reporting the crime, if there was one. Here the defense is implying that if the victim really was raped, he or she would have been distressed enough to report it immediately. A third tactic is to reveal prior relationships, often indirectly, particularly if the relationship was with the defendant. Finally, the defense must try to undermine the general character of the victim and appeal to gender bias, if possible.

Though defense attorneys appear ethically void in their tactics of questioning sexual assault victims, it is their duty to defend their clients to the best of their ability. Some lawyers argue that to not introduce information that leads to

VIGNETTE

TRYING RAPE CASES IN THE MEDIA: The Problem of the Celebrity Offender

Victims of sexual assault are generally provided with a high level of anonymity. However, this is rarely the case when the alleged perpetrator of the abuse is a high-profile individual with a high level of public visibility. Cases of rape and child sexual abuse by athletes, politicians, actors, and businessmen have featured prominently in the media, and the credibility of the victims is nearly always mentioned. Many times these cases are dismissed, usually after the victim's credibility has been questioned. Other times, however, the alleged victims take advantage of the notoriety of the accused and try to use this notoriety to their advantage. Here are some examples of sexual assault cases that have high-profile alleged perpetrators:

- *Kobe Bryant.* Bryant, a basketball player for the Los Angeles Lakers, was accused of raping a 19-year old concierge at a resort in Vail, Colorado. Bryant's lawyers filed motions that his accuser had been prescribed an anti-psychotic drug, had made suicide attempts to get attention from an ex-boyfriend, and had semen from another man on her underpants that she wore to the hospital for her physical exam. After her name was leaked to the media and her sexual history was discussed publicly, Bryant's accuser refused to testify, and the case was dropped.

- *Ben Roethlisberger.* Two women accused Roethlisberger, quarterback for the Pittsburgh Steelers, of sexual assault against women in Utah and Georgia. Roethlisberger was not charged in either case, despite evidence in the latter case that included eyewitnesses, an immediate report of the incident, and a hospital exam. The alleged victim eventually stated that she did not want to go to trial because of the high level of media attention on the case.

- *Dominique Strauss-Kahn.* Then director of the International Monetary Foundation, Strauss-Kahn was accused of sexually assaulting a maid at a hotel in New York City. He was indicted, and there was evidence that sexual behavior had occurred. However, the case was dismissed after defense attorneys and the District Attorney noted that that the victim's credibility was questionable.

- *Roman Polanski.* Arrested in 1977 for having sex with a 13-year-old, this film director fled the country to avoid sentencing. He was arrested in Switzerland but not extradited, and the charges are still pending in the United States. His victim, who has been named in the media, claimed that the media and the courts have done more damage to her than Polanski, and accused the judge of using the case for his own personal gain.

Questions
1. Should public figures, including athletes, be treated differently in criminal cases? Why or why not?
2. How can victims in high-profile cases be better protected from media scrutiny?

© Cengage Learning

bias against the victim would "thereby undermine the lawyers' duty of zealous representation" (Taslitz, 1999, p. 106). Even the most conscientious of defense attorneys makes a distinction between victims of "real" rapes and rapes of women who may, in the eyes of some jurors, have some culpability in their victimization. By playing up the rape myths to juries, the defense attorney is able to "assault" the victim without even talking about her past or actions. He or she can talk about how men are brought up in a sexist society and when the woman went back to the defendant's apartment and was flirting with him, he took this to mean that she wanted something sexual. By directly talking about the defendant, the defense attorney indirectly talks about the victim and puts her in a negative view to the jury. In some areas, the rapist is even allowed to represent himself in court and cross-examine the victim (Beneke, 1995).

VICTIM TREATMENT AND COUNSELING

The researchers who focused on rape law reforms not only succeeded in changing legal and social perceptions of victims but also unveiled the need for victim support. Prior to the 1970s and consistent with social beliefs that rape was rare and victims played a role in their abuse, there were no government-sponsored agencies specifically devoted to assisting sexual assault victims (Koss & Harvey, 1991). At this time, rape crisis advocates began challenging the long-held perceptions of rape victims while informing the community about the realities of rape. They began forming individual rape crisis centers across North America, Europe, and Australia, and eventually gained the assistance of established groups such as the National Organization for Women (NOW) (Koss & Harvey, 1991). Today, there are rape crisis centers or victim advocate centers in nearly every major city in the United States.

Rape crisis centers have several purposes, the first of which is to supply the victim with information about medical issues such as pregnancy, abortion, and sexually transmitted diseases. Advocates from the centers can accompany victims to the police station, court, and hospital. Though they talk to the victims about their options in regard to medical and psychological treatment, they do not tell the victims what to do. They do not even persuade the victims to contact the police and report the assault; rather, they give them information about the criminal justice system and encourage them to do that with which they are comfortable. They provide the victim with assertiveness training through empowerment groups, as well as self-defense training for future protection. Most important, the centers provide counseling for victims by telephone or in person, on a short- or long-term basis, and on an individual or group basis.

Counseling is confidential and can assist victims in understanding the offense, their reactions to the offense, and how to protect themselves from future offenses (Largen, 1991). When counseling at a rape crisis clinic or hospital is sought, it is generally in the immediate postrape period (within two to three months after the assault) and is a short-term form of support. In fact, most victims attend a single intervention session, the reason for which is that shortly after this point they enter the denial stage of victimization (discussed earlier in the chapter). A primary purpose of this initial counseling session is to establish social support for the victim, accepting his or her story and building an empathic (though not dependent) relationship (Koss & Harvey, 1991). It is important for the victim to seek help during this immediate postrape period, because the counselors can help him or her cope through adaptive (rather than maladaptive) behavior (Minden, 1991).

Few rape victims seek extensive support immediately post-rape. Instead, they are more likely to seek group treatment or individual clinical treatment with a trained psychologist several months later, when they move out of the denial stage of victimization. The role of the clinician is similar to that of the counselor, though the clinician is more likely to focus on the long-term needs of the victim. Both counselor and clinician encourage the victim to express emotions resulting from the assault and provide the victim with factual information about medical and psychological symptoms they may experience (Calhoun & Atkeson, 1991; Koss & Harvey, 1991). The most important role for the clinician is to address any psychological problems that materialize as a result of the assault, such as depression, eating disorders, and suicidal thoughts. Victims who experience serious psychological disorders are encouraged to continue therapy for an extended period of time. Victims who experience fear, anxiety, stress, and other common feelings of vulnerability are encouraged to participate in a group treatment process.

Koss and Harvey (1991, pp. 208–210) explain nine benefits of the group treatment process for victims. First, it *reduces isolation* and helps the victim to see that others have shared a similar experience. Second, group treatment provides the victim with *positive support* that is adaptive and empowering. Third, it provides *validation* of the victim's feelings by helping him or her to understand that such reactions (for example, anger, rage, fear) are normal. Fourth, it provides *confirmation* of experience in that the victims can share their experiences and coping mechanisms with each other. This leads to the next benefit, which is that group treatment helps to *counteract self-blame* and *promote self-esteem* by removing blame from the victim and placing it on the offender. A sixth benefit to group treatment is the *egalitarian* rather than hierarchical mode of the session, where the victims not only seek support but also have a voice in the healing process of others. Group treatment also offers opportunities for *safe attachment*, with a safe context in which to meet, share similar feelings, and develop bonds with similar individuals. This links to the next benefit—groups provide a forum through which victims can *share grief* with others who understand their plight. Finally, the group experience allows victims to *contemplate and assign meaning to their experiences*, while committing themselves to recovering and moving on to the future.

Like their female counterparts, male victims of sexual assault also need counseling and treatment. Despite this, they are often presented with barriers when seeking support. Rape crisis centers were developed around a feminist philosophy, and several male victims have reported that the centers have negative attitudes toward men. The reason for this is that traditionally women have been the reported victims and males have been the aggressors (Mezey & King, 2000). As such, male victims are not necessarily comfortable in a setting that appears to be gender biased and at times hostile (Turner, 2000). Men are less likely to seek out treatment than women, and for those who do, there is a high attrition rate from the counseling. Male victims who receive a negative initial response when reporting the abuse (whether from the police, hospital, or acquaintances) are not likely to seek further support. Of those who do seek support, most have the same treatment needs as female victims (Mezey & King, 2000).

Perhaps most in need of treatment are children who have been abused. Because of the secretive nature of child sexual abuse and the grooming tactics used by perpetrators, the victims are highly likely to assign self-blame to the abuse. Child sexual abusers frequently use emotional coercion to get the child to comply with the abuse, and use emotional blackmail to keep the child from telling others (Pryor, 1996). The child sexual abuser will also frequently tell the child that the abuse occurred because he or she wanted it, thereby creating feelings of guilt, blame, fear, and anxiety in the child at a young age. Though children experience many of the same symptoms as adults, these symptoms may manifest themselves differently in the child. The child victim is far more likely than the adult victim to experience psychological disorders such as dissociation in order to cope with the trauma (Cairns, 1999). This helps the victim to separate the negative identity of abused child from the positive sense of being desired. Finkelhor (1986) explains four common responses to childhood sexual abuse as *traumatic sexualization* (confusion and distress resulting from inappropriate sexual behavior, which may lead to sexual dysfunction as an adult), *stigmatization* (applying self-blame once the child realizes the sexual contact is inappropriate), *betrayal* (due to the trusting relationship built up with the abuser, who is often a relative of the child), and *powerlessness* (they are unable to control the situation). If the abuse is revealed when the victim is a child, extensive therapy should begin immediately.

Unfortunately, most children do not report abuse immediately but only report it in adulthood. At this time there is a high prevalence rate of psychological disorders such as mood disturbances, sexual dysfunction, and interpersonal and relationship problems (Jehu, 1988). Because of the severity of the reactions, adult victims of childhood abuse are likely to receive individual rather than group therapy as a primary mode of treatment. Because childhood victimization often comes to attention in light of other problems (for example, marital or sexual problems), the victim may also participate in additional forms of treatment such as family or marital therapy. Whatever form the treatment takes, it is generally extensive and long term.

If the child reports the sexual abuse when it happens, he or she will go through a similar criminal justice process to that of adult victims of abuse. Unlike with adult victims, research on the effect of the criminal justice process on abused children is varied. Children who testify in juvenile court are seemingly helped by the process, as it purportedly restores a sense of power and control to the child. In most states, children are appointed a guardian *ad litem* (GAD) in juvenile court to act as a legal assistant and help them with the court process (National Institute of Justice, 1992). On the other hand, the criminal justice process is damaging to children who appear in criminal court, have to testify many times, are lacking maternal support through the process, are involved in the adjudication process for a long period of time, and whose cases are lacking corroborative evidence (National Institute of Justice, 1992). Whatever the effect of the system, children do need treatment to help them cope with the effects of sexual abuse, and the earlier this treatment takes place, the better the outcome.

CHAPTER SUMMARY

- Sexual abuse victims may experience physical, emotional, and psychological consequences of the abuse, some of which may be chronic and lifelong.

- The psychological trauma experienced by sexual abuse victims seems to be even greater if the abuse continues for a long period of time or is committed by someone close to the victim.

- Friends and relatives of the sexual abuse victim also experience trauma, particularly parents of abused children and partners of rape victims. These individuals are called secondary victims.

- The criminal justice process exacerbates the feelings of critogenesis for the victim, or revictimization as a result of legal processes. This revictimization is a result of the hospital exam (which is intrusive and long), the police interviews (the officer asks the same questions multiple times, appearing as though he or she does not believe the victim), and the adjudication process (during which the victim must explain the event and then be cross-examined by the defense attorney). If the defendant is famous, then the case may be tried in the media to the detriment of the victim.

- The level of revictimization has decreased in the past two decades because of rape shield laws. Prior to the enactment of these laws, blame for the sexual offense was placed primarily on the victim. Despite the rape shield laws, the victim still has little say in the criminal justice process. Despite the difficulties in alleviating victim anxiety resulting from the system, some communities have implemented schemes that reduce trauma and assist in the restorative justice process.

- Despite the assistance of laws that support victim rights, sexual offenses are still the most underreported of all offenses. This is particularly true for cases of childhood sexual abuse and the sexual abuse of males.

DISCUSSION QUESTIONS

1. How have victim rights evolved? What rights are victims afforded today? What improvements can be made with these laws while still upholding the rights of defendants?

2. What are the most common psychological or emotional consequences of sexual victimization of adults? Children? What effect does sexual victimization have on family and acquaintances of the victims?

3. How do the psychological consequences of sexual victimization differ between males and females?

4. What are the most important factors in reducing the long-term harm to children who were sexually abused?

PART III

Responses to Sexual Offenders: Treatment, Punishment and Community Regulations

10   Management and Supervision of Sex Offenders in the Community

11   Assessment and Treatment of Sexual Offenders

12   Incapacitating Sex Offenders

10

Management and Supervision of Sex Offenders in the Community

M any sex offender policies are enacted after an emotionally charged sex crime occurs, often the kidnapping, rape, and/or murder of a child by a stranger. The goal of these laws is to protect the community from recidivist sex offenders through enhanced sanctions and the regulation of their behavior. The courts have deemed these laws constitutional because they promote the state's interest in preserving public safety (Janicki, 2007). To date, however, few evaluation studies show that these laws are effective in that goal.

Since the 1990s, much of the sex offender legislation that has been enacted by the federal government regulates the supervision and monitoring of sex offenders living in the community. The primary focus of this legislation has been registration and community notification laws (RCNL), first through Jacob Wetterling Crimes Against Children and Sexually Violent Offender Registration Act, followed by "Megan's Law," and ultimately the Adam Walsh Child Protection and Safety Act of 2006. State and local jurisdictions have also enacted policies to enhance these core regulations, including residence restrictions, GPS tracking, and community supervision for life. This chapter provides an overview of current sex offender laws, with a particular focus on the guidelines, regulations, and legal issues related to registration and notification. It also discusses the evidence about efficacy of sex offender legislation and how any of the current policies fall short of reaching their intended goals.

OVERVIEW OF SEX OFFENDER LAWS

Legislation that regulates the behavior of sexual offenders is not new. As discussed in Chapter 2, there is a history of legislation throughout the last century in the United States that has focused on enhancing sanctions for sexual "fiends," "monsters," and "predators" (Jenkins, 1998). However, this legislative focus increased in the late 1980s, and by the 1990s public protection from sexual offenders became a high priority for the federal government. Most of the legislative acts that were passed were based on high-profile, emotionally charged cases of sexual abuse, kidnapping, and/or murder of a child by a stranger. Many, such as "Megan's Law," became memorial laws, named after a specific victim.

The first comprehensive, modern-day policy regulating the behavior of sex offenders was passed in Washington State. Called the Community Protection Act of 1990, it contained 14 provisions for increasing sanctions and regulatory monitoring of sex offenders in the state. Two cases in particular prompted this legislation. The first case involved Wesley Allan Dodd, a recidivist offender who sexually assaulted and murdered three young boys. When he was incarcerated prior to this offense, he had said if he were ever released he would offend again, and enjoy it. The second case involved Earl Shriner, who had a 24-year history of sexual violence. He kidnapped a seven-year-old boy, sexually assaulted him, cut off his penis, and left him for dead. In and out of institutions since the age of 15, Shriner had just been released after a decade in prison when he committed this offense. While incarcerated, he had bragged to inmates and confided in a journal that he fantasized about killing again. There was nothing the state could do to keep him or Dodd in prison, as both had finite sentences. The state was also prohibited from notifying the community about their release. The Community Protection Act was designed to give the state more discretion about what to do with sex offenders like Dodd and Shriner, who posed a high risk to the community.

Though the Community Protection Act is state legislation, the federal government has enacted similar laws. There are seven federal legislative acts that specifically allow for discretionary oversight of sex offenders living in the community. Though the federal legislation gives states discretionary power in how these policies are implemented, the federal statutes provide guidelines and, in some cases, require that states abide by certain conditions or risk losing federal funds. What follows is a brief description of these federal laws, which are also presented in Table 10.1.

Jacob Wetterling Crimes against Children and Sexually Violent Offender Registration Act (1994)

In 1989, 11-year-old Jacob Wetterling was riding his bike home from a convenience store in St. Joseph, Minnesota, with his 10-year-old brother and an 11-year-old friend. A masked gunman came out of a driveway and ordered the boys to throw their bikes into a ditch and lie face down on the ground. The gunman asked them some questions and then told Jacob's brother and friend to run into the woods. Despite the gunman's threat to shoot them if they turned around, both boys looked back in time to see the gunman take Jacob by the arm. By the time they reached the wooded area, both Jacob and the gunman were gone (see Jacob Wetterling Resource Center, 2008). Despite the efforts of friends, family members, the police, and the local community, Jacob has still never been found (Terry & Ackerman, 2009).

Although Jacob's abductor was never identified, many speculated that he was one of the sex offenders living in a halfway house in town. Jacob's mother, Patty Wetterling, became a policy maker, activist, and educator, leading the community effort to implement sex offender registration requirements in Minnesota and, subsequently, nationally (Wright, 2009). In 1994, Congress passed the Jacob Wetterling Crimes Against Children and Sexually Violent Offender Registration Act, part of the Federal Violent Crime Control and Law Enforcement Act of 1994, in Jacob's honor. The Jacob Wetterling Act required each state to create a registry for offenders convicted of sexual offenses. States that failed to comply with this act would forfeit 10 percent of federal funds from the Omnibus Crime Control and Safe Streets Act of 1968 (Terry & Ackerman, 2009). In 1997, the legislature passed the Jacob Wetterling Improvements Act, which added additional requirements to the original guidelines. Examples of such requirements include requiring offenders to register in the state where they work, if different from where they live; requiring states to set up procedures for registering out-of-state offenders; directing states to participate in the national sex offender registry; and giving states discretion to include additional offenses not specified in the original act.

Megan's Law (1996)

On July 19, 1994, seven-year-old Megan Kanka was killed by a recidivist pedophile living across the street from her in Hamilton Township, New Jersey. Jesse Timmendequas, who had been convicted of two previous sexual offenses against children, lured Megan into his house with the promise to see his puppy, and then raped and killed her. Megan's parents and community members wondered how recidivist sex offenders could be living in the community without the community's knowledge and awareness.

Megan's parents proposed that sex offender registration, as required by the Jacob Wetterling Act, was an insufficient form of community protection from sex offenders. They said that the community should also be notified of serious sexual offenders who are living in the neighborhood, claiming that the community has a right to know so that parents can better protect their children. The Kankas said that had they known a sex offender was living across the street from them, Megan would still be alive today. Eighty-nine days after her death, New Jersey enacted "Megan's Law." On May 17, 1996, then-president Bill Clinton enacted a federal version of Megan's Law that was a subsection of the Jacob Wetterling Act (Terry & Furlong, 2008). Together, the Jacob Wetterling Act and Megan's Law are referred to as RCNL. All states were required to implement RCNL by the end of 1997 or risk losing federal funding for state and local law enforcement. The last state to do so was Massachusetts, and by August 1996 all states were compliant.

Pam Lychner Sex Offender Tracking and Identification Act (1996)

Pam Lychner was a real estate agent in Houston, Texas. As she went to show a prospective client a home, an offender with a history of violence was waiting in the empty home and attacked her. Had her husband not arrived at the home in time, she likely would have been killed. After this attack, she formed a victim rights advocacy group called "Justice for All," which lobbied for tougher sentences for violent and sexual criminals (Terry & Ackerman, 2009). Tragically, Lychner and her two daughters were killed in the explosion of TWA Flight 800 in July 1996. Congress honored her memory by passing the Pam Lychner Sexual Offender Tracking and Identification Act later that year (Levenson & D'Amora, 2007).

The Pam Lychner Act established the National Sex Offender Registry (NSOR), the first national database which would be overseen by the FBI. It provided the FBI with various powers to supervise sex offenders, including verify the addresses of the offenders, disseminate information about them, and run background checks. This filled a gap in the existing legislation, since the Jacob Wetterling Act and Megan's Law provided states with discretion about RCNL guidelines, and there was little consistency across states in regard to registration and notification procedures. Despite its best efforts, the national database created as a result of the Pam Lychner Act faced several obstacles. Most importantly, the information in the national database was derived from the state databases. The problems with the state databases, discussed later, were therefore present in the national as well.

Protection of Children from Sexual Predators Act (1998)

In 1998, legislators passed the Protection of Children from Sexual Predators Act, which enabled the Bureau of Justice Assistance to assist states in complying with registration requirements. Additionally, it specified offenses and penalties for sexual offending behaviors, with a focus on trafficking and Internet crimes. Most human trafficking and child pornography offenses are regulated at the federal level, and as recognition of the extent of these offenses was becoming apparent the federal government recognized a need to enhance legislation for these offenses.

Campus Sex Crimes Prevention Act (2000)

In 2000, Congress again amended the Violent Crime Control and Law Enforcement Act of 1994 to include a new subsection with respect to sex offender registration requirements. As a result of this act, registered sex offenders would now be required to notify institutions of higher education that they attend for school or for employment about their status as a sex offender. This information would be provided to law enforcement agencies in the jurisdiction of the institution and would be entered into state registry records. Schools could request information at any time. The act also amended the Higher Education Act of 1965 to require institutions to provide notice of how information concerning registered sex offenders could be obtained.

Prosecutorial Remedies and Other Tools to End the Exploitation of Children Today (PROTECT) Act (2003)

In 2003 legislators enacted the PROTECT Act, the goal of which was to prevent abduction and eliminate sexual exploitation of children. The Act is extensive, providing enhanced methods for the investigation and adjudication of sex crimes. In regard to investigation, the act allows for the interception of all wire, oral, and electronic communications related to sexual abuse and sex trafficking and the interception of all related oral and electronic communications. Additionally, it created a national AMBER Alert Program that would allow better coordination between local and state programs. With respect to adjudication, it decreased pretrial release for offenders charged with certain crimes involving children and decreased the authority of judges to provide reduced prison sentences to certain sex offenders.

Most importantly, the PROTECT Act enhanced the sanctions for offenders and the supervision and monitoring of offenders in the community. It increased the penalty for child abduction to a minimum of 20 years in prison and increased the penalty for using a child for the production of pornography to 15–30 years. More generally, it strengthened the provisions on "virtual" child pornography and obscenity laws. The Act also lifted the 25-year statute of limitations for sexual and physical abuse and created "Two Strikes" laws that would provide lifetime imprisonment for offenders convicted of two serious sex offenses against children. In regard to release from prison, the Act authorized supervised release for offenders for life for those who committed sexual offenses against children.

Adam Walsh Child Protection and Safety Act (2006)

The Adam Walsh Child Protection and Safety Act of 2006 (Pub.L. 109-248) (AWA) is the most comprehensive act created to date that is related to the supervision and management of sex offenders in the community. It sets national standards for registration and notification, civil commitment, child pornography prevention, and Internet safety; makes failure to register a deportable offense for immigrants; and establishes grants to empirically assess the legislation. The AWA is named after Adam Walsh, who was abducted from a shopping mall in Florida in 1981 when he was six years old. He was killed, and his decapitated head was found 16 days after the abduction, though the perpetrator was not identified until 2008. The AWA was signed on the 25th anniversary of his abduction, and had been advocated by his father, John Walsh, host of *America's Most Wanted*.

The goal of the AWA is to provide uniform guidelines on the supervision, management, and punishment of sex offenders nationally. One of the most significant components of the act is the Sex Offender Registration and Notification Act (SORNA), which provides national standards for all sex offenders regardless of the state they live in. The Office of Sex Offender Sentencing, Monitoring, Apprehending, Registering, and Tracking (SMART Office) within the Department of Justice, Office of Justice Programs, oversees state compliance with SORNA. Additionally, the SMART office coordinates training and technical assistance for the states. The AWA also established a Sex Offender Management Assistance program within the Justice Department. The Applicability of the Sex Offender Registration and Notification Act (28 CFR Part 72), passed by the Department of Justice, is federal legislation specifying that SORNA's registration requirements are retroactive.

The AWA required that all states enact RCNL statutes in compliance with SORNA guidelines by July 2009 or risk losing 10 percent of their federal funding from the Byrne program law enforcement assistance funds. However, no states were compliant by that date. As a result, SMART extended the deadline for compliance each year through 2011. At the time of this publication in 2012, only eight states are compliant and several other states have guidelines being reviewed for compliance. Reasons for lack of compliance are discussed further.

REGISTRATION AND COMMUNITY NOTIFICATION LAWS

The goal of RCNL is to protect the community by providing them with knowledge about sex offenders who may be at risk to reoffend. It tracks sex offenders and provides information to the community about their risk level and where they live and work. However, RCNL consists of complicated guidelines and procedures that vary from state to state. The AWA set federal guidelines with which states must comply, but states do still have some discretion even within these narrow guidelines. Additionally, most states are still not compliant with the AWA guidelines and, thus, continue to manage sex offenders through the standards set out in their state-based Megan's Law statutes. This section provides information about RCNL regulations and guidelines, the factors that vary by state, an overview of the risk assessment process for sex offenders living in the community, challenges with RCNL, and efficacy of this legislation.

RCNL Regulations and Guidelines

After the enactment of Megan's Law, all states implemented some form of RCNL. Though each state was able to create its own regulations and guidelines, there were some consistent goals and processes by state. Offenders were responsible for registering with the police (or other designated agency) once convicted of a sexual offense or, in some states, an offense against a minor (for example,

TABLE 10.1   Federal policies related to the management and supervision of sex offenders

Name of Statute	Brief Description
Jacob Wetterling Crimes Against Children and Sexually Violent Predator Program (1994); Jacob Wetterling Improvements Act (1997)	Required each state to create a registry for offenders convicted of sexual offenses against and other certain other offenses against children.
Megan's Law (1996)	Subsection of the Jacob Wetterling Act that requires notification about high-risk sex offenders living in the community.
Pam Lychner Sexual Offender Tracking and Identification Act (1996)	Subsection of the Jacob Wetterling Act that established a national database at the Federal Bureau of Investigation (FBI) to track the whereabouts of all those who have been convicted of an offense against a minor or a sexually violent offense.
Protection of Children from Sexual Predators Act (1998)	Provides assistance to states to help them comply with registration requirements, and increases penalties for trafficking and cyber crimes.
Campus Sex Crimes Act (2000)	Requires sex offenders to provide information about institutions of higher education that they attended for school or for employment. This information is provided to law enforcement agencies in the jurisdiction of the institution and entered into state registry records.
PROTECT Act (2003)	Enacted to prevent the abduction of children and to eliminate sexual exploitation of children. Employs strategies such as the AMBER Alert, increases penalties for offenders, increases statute of limitation, and strengthens laws on child pornography.
Adam Walsh Child Protection and Safety Act (2006)	Act that sets national standards on the following measures: registration and notification, civil commitment, child pornography prevention, and Internet safety, and makes failure to register as a sex offender a deportable offense. It is one of the most comprehensive acts ever created to supervise and manage sex offenders. States that do not comply risk losing 10% of federal funding.

kidnapping, lewdness or lascivious behavior, assault on a child). The state would assess the risk level of the offenders to determine whether they were high (Tier 3), moderate (Tier 2), or low risk (Tier 1). Offenders would be required to register for a period of time, dependent upon the jurisdiction and the offense committed. Offenders had a certain period of time after conviction or release from a correctional institution to inform the registration agency of their whereabouts. They would provide the agency with a photograph, fingerprints, name, home address, place of employment or school, and in some states a

DNA sample. To verify the address that the offenders submitted, a letter would be mailed to the offenders' residence, and they would have to return the letter within a specified time period. If the letter was not returned or the offenders did not register within the given amount of time, they would have violated the registration statute and would be subject to a given sanction. If the offenders moved to a different address, they would be required to reregister with the local agency in the new community. The agency responsible for overseeing registration would notify the community about those offenders who were deemed to be a high risk to reoffend. Everyone in the community would be notified about Tier 3 offenders, and while certain groups in the community would be notified about Tier 2 offenders (for example, schools and day care centers would be notified about child sexual abusers).

Despite this generally similar process, state RCNL statutes varied in several ways. The most significant differences by state were as follows (Terry & Furlong, 2008).

- *Conviction/Type of Offense* Some states required registration only for individuals convicted of a sexual offense, whereas others allow registration when there was a finding of not guilty by reason of insanity, of a sexually motivated offense (for example, public exposure, murder with sexual intent, kidnapping of a minor), or of an attempted but not completed offense. Others, still, required registration only for offenders with child victims.

- *Retroactive Application of the Law* Some states applied registration retroactively, whereas in other states offenders only had to register if they were convicted after the implementation of RCNL. Though criminal statutes are not allowed to be applied retroactively, RCNL is considered a regulatory statute, not punishment, and the retroactive application of the law has therefore been deemed constitutional (discussed later in more detail).

- *Length of Registration* Offenders must register for different lengths of time depending on the state and the type of offense they committed. Currently, the registration period varies from 10 years to life.

- *Removal from the Registry* Some states that required lifetime registration allowed offenders to apply for expungement from the registry after a certain period of time, generally 10 or 15 years. In such a case, the offenders could petition the court to have their names removed from the registry, which would likely be granted if the offenders had committed no further offenses since the time of registration.

- *Time Period in Which to Register/Reregister* Each state gave the offenders a set amount of time to register with the given agency. The time period ranged from 48 hours to 10 days upon conviction or release into the community, and the offenders were required to reregister any time they moved or began a new job. Additionally, the offenders had to check in with the registration agency either annually or quarterly, depending upon level of risk.

- *Risk Assessment* All states assess the risk of sex offenders who must register, since notification procedures depend on the level of risk of the offenders.

However, states have varied in their risk assessment process. Some states assessed offender risk based upon the offense for which the offenders were convicted. Others used an actuarial risk assessment tool, along with a battery of psychological tests. The risk assessment process is complicated and a source of controversy, as discussed in more detail below.

- *Method of Notification* The method by which the registration agency notifies the community varied in each state, and also changed over time. At the outset, the agencies notified the community in a number of ways, such as by posting flyers or mailing them to members of the community; having an 800- or a 900-number for community members to call to find out information about a particular individual; and keeping a central registry at the agency that community members could check. However, by 2006 nearly all states used an Internet registry as their main source of providing information, and now all states are required to have this system of notification. Whether this passive system of notification (the community member is required to seek out the information) is more effective than an active system of notification (the information is sent to the community member) is debatable.

- *Sanction for Failing to Register* If offenders failed to register within the time period allotted, they would be subject to sanction. The type of sanction varied by state and by level of offender, ranging from a misdemeanor to a felony. Additionally, the sanction in most states would increase with each subsequent failure to register.

- *Registration of Juveniles* Some states required juvenile sex offenders to register, whereas others prohibited registration for anyone under age 18. Some states that required registration did not notify the community about the registered juvenile offenders. Whether juvenile sex offenders should register is a controversial issue, and one that has been subject of much debate. Specifically, some have argued that juveniles are likely to be harmed by being labeled as a sex offender. Others, however, have stated that the most important issue is the protection of the community, and for that reason the public should be notified about adult and juvenile sex offenders alike. This is one of the many issues addressed by the AWA, and one that has sparked substantial debate.

Legal Challenges to RCNL

When RCNL policies were enacted in the 1990s, many offenders who were subject to the requirements challenged the constitutionality of the legislation in the courts. Their primary argument was that RCNL is punishment. If the courts determined that RCNL constitutes punishment, then it could be deemed unconstitutional on four bases: double jeopardy, ex post facto application of the law, bill of attainder, and cruel and unusual punishment. *Double jeopardy*, which is prohibited by the Fifth Amendment, protects an individual from being tried twice for the same crime. Protection against *ex post facto application* of a law means that an individual is not subject to punishment for a law that was enacted after the crime was committed. In other words, a law cannot be applied retroactively if punishment can result from such an application. The *bill of attainder* clause prohibits infliction of punishment upon members of a group without judicial process. Finally, if registration and notification is punishment, then it must be proportionate to the offense committed; otherwise, it is unconstitutional under the Eighth Amendment's *cruel and unusual punishment* clause. In addition to the constitutional challenges that faced the statutes, some argued that registration creates problems for offenders, such as vigilantism, and for the community, such as a false sense of security for the public.

Because all four of these issues are related to punishment, the courts regarded them together in several key cases in the mid-1990s. No court determined registration to be unconstitutional on the basis that it is punishment, though the courts varied in their analysis of notification requirements early on. Hundreds of cases have been heard in the courts; however, it is the New Jersey case of *Doe v. Poritz* (1995) that set precedents for other registration and notification cases to follow.

In *Doe v. Poritz*, the court upheld RCNL, stating that it does not violate the constitutional rights of sex offenders subject to them. The court did state, however, that in order for the laws to be valid there must be some modification to the judicial review process for Tiers 2 and 3 offenders. The court said that the purpose of RCNL is to protect society from convicted sex offenders, and that the Constitution does not prevent society from employing such preventative measures. The court also stated that the community is allowed to employ these preventative measures for offenders who were convicted prior to enactment of the law, so long as the means of protection are reasonably designed only for the purpose of prevention and are not designed to punish. The court claimed, based on much case law, that this statute is not punitive but rather is remedial, despite the fact that it may have a deterrent effect. Because the court determined that RCNL is remedial and not punishment, it does not violate the bill of attainder clause, and does not constitute cruel and unusual punishment. Additionally, the court stated that retroactive application of the laws is acceptable in order to achieve the goal of the statute: community protection. If the laws were not applied ex post facto, it would take years to offer the protection they were designed to afford.

Though the courts determined that RCNL is not unconstitutional in theory, the application of it continued to present questions. One such issue was the retroactive application of the law to those who had been subject to plea bargaining agreements. Many offenders who were charged with a sexual offense prior to enactment of RCNL pled guilty either to the offense with which they were charged or to a lesser sexual offense. Once RCNL was enacted and applied retroactively, these offenders were subject to the requirements of the statute. Several offenders appealed their decision and requested the withdrawal of a guilty plea once they were told they had to register. However, the court upheld the duty to register even when a guilty plea was made prior to enactment of RCNL. For instance, in the *Opinion of the Justices to the Senate* (1996), the

Massachusetts court stated that there is no constitutional requirement to notify the defendant of the duty to register prior to when the defendant enters a plea, and the failure to notify the defendant of this duty does not negate a plea negotiation. The court in other states has supported this decision,[1] and it is unlikely that this will change.

Despite the declaration that notification does not violate substantive constitutional rights, the court stated that there is "sufficient impingement on protected liberty interests in privacy and reputation" so that there must be procedural safeguards in place where notification statutes are applied. The court in *Doe v. Poritz* determined that the state should establish specific guidelines by which the degree of risk of a further offense can be determined, focusing specifically on Tier 2 and 3 offenders because it is those offenders about whom the public is notified. It stated that notification is only allowed to members of the community who are "likely to encounter" the offender, and that this determination should be based on geographic location. Additionally, the court said it is necessary to construct a forum by which an offender designated into Tier 2 or 3 can object to such a classification. The court was careful to recognize that the individual rights of sex offenders must be protected; yet, the court also said "care should be exercised not to convert them into obstacles that prevent the enactment of honestly-motivated remedial legislation." The courts upheld notification statutes with similar justifications in several other cases immediately following *Doe v. Poritz*.[2]

There have also been arguments against RCNL in terms of due process rights of those to whom they are applied. The question in these cases has been twofold: Does RCNL trigger a due process analysis, and, if so, how much due process is necessary? The courts have been split on the issue, often on a case-by-case basis, and varying restrictions are put on the individual as a result of RCNL. Some cases, such as *Russell and Sterns v. Gregoire* (1997), claimed that there is no protected interest involved, and as a result the statute does not trigger a due process analysis. Other cases, such as *Artway v. Attorney General of New Jersey* (1996), stated that registration does not trigger a protected interest, yet notification does. Still others, such as *Doe v. Poritz* (1995), recognized differential due process rights for offenders classified into varying tiers. In these cases, offenders in Tier 1 have few, if any, due process rights, whereas Tier 3 offenders are entitled to due process because of the privacy restrictions that result from notification.

In terms of the constitutional right to privacy for sex offenders, the court has often quoted *Paul v. Davis* (1976). This case decided that the government could publicize records of official convictions as long as this does not impede a person's freedom. *Paul* is not related to registration, but it contains a thorough analysis of reputation as a result of publication of an arrest record. The defendant in this case was arrested for shoplifting, after which his name and photo were included in a

---

1. For example, *People v. McClellan* (1994); *State v. Skroch* (1994); *State v. Ward* (1987).

2. For example, *Artway v. Attorney General of New Jersey* (1996); *Doe v. Pataki* (1997); *E. B. and W. P. v. Verniero* (1997); *Opinion of the Justices to the Senate* (1996); *Russell and Sterns v. Gregoire* (1997); *Snyder v. State* (1996); *State v. Cameron* (1996).

police flyer distributed to store owners warning them of "active shoplifters" in the area. The Court in *Paul* stated, "Reputation alone ... was neither 'liberty' nor 'property' by itself sufficient to invoke the procedural protection of the due process clause." As such, the flyers were not unconstitutional under the Fourteenth Amendment because of the charge of defamation. Additionally, distribution of the flyers could not be based on an alleged violation of the constitutional right to privacy, since the plaintiff's claim of constitutional protection against the disclosure of the fact of his arrest for shoplifting was based not upon any challenge to the state's ability to restrict his freedom of action in a sphere contended to be "private," but instead was based on a claim that the state could not publicize a record of an official act such as an arrest.

Quoting *Paul*, the court has rendered similar decisions in cases involving community notification of sex offenders. In *Doe v. Pataki* (1996), the court said that RCNL does not deprive a convicted sex offender of the right to equal protection, specifically in regard to the constitutional right to privacy. The court in *Doe v. Poritz* (1995) did recognize that RCNL would have an inevitable impact on sex offenders in terms of loss of anonymity, yet this loss of anonymity "is no constitutional bar to society's attempt at self-defense." The court recognized the difficulty in balancing the rights of offenders versus those of the community, and said that so long as the extent of notification is based on the likelihood of reoffense, it is okay to protect potential victims from these offenders through notification. The court has claimed that the state has a strong interest in public disclosure, which substantially outweighs the sex offenders' interest in privacy. Therefore, the court concluded in *Doe v. Poritz* (1995) that because the registration and notification requirements of the statutes are rationally related to a legitimate state interest, the requirements of equal protection under the Fourteenth Amendment and the state constitution have been satisfied. Essentially, there is no reasonable expectation of privacy to any information contained in public records. Therefore, the state has a right to disclose the information (though the state's interest in disclosure outweighs the individual's interest in privacy, regardless).

In 2003, the U.S. Supreme Court decided on two cases related to the constitutionality of registration and notification statutes. In *Connecticut Department of Public Safety v. Doe* (2003), the Court addressed the issue of whether Connecticut was acting unconstitutionally by posting offender information on the Internet. Citing *Paul v. Davis* (1976), the Court said that this did not violate the offender's due process rights because injury to reputation alone is not a deprivation of liberty. Similarly, in the case *Smith v. Doe* (2003), the Court declared that registration and notification are constitutional even if applied ex post facto, because the law is nonpunitive. Thus, the U.S. Supreme Court upheld the decisions of lower courts: the enhanced supervision and management of sex offenders in the community is constitutional because these laws are regulatory and promote the state's interest in preserving public safety (Janicki, 2007).

The courts have also heard nonconstitutional challenges to RCNL. Particularly debatable issues include questions about what the appropriate sanctions (criminal) are for the failure to register (civil statute); the definition of "sex-based" offenses (for example, kidnapping, "sexting," public urination as indecent exposure); types and efficacy of risk assessment procedures and, relatedly, tier-level classifications; the application of laws as they apply to special groups of offenders (for example, homeless and juvenile offenders); and the broad scope of Internet notification (Terry, 2011). Risk assessment is particularly important, as it determines the level of supervision of offenders, potentially for the rest of their lives, while they live in the community.

Risk Assessment

The efficacy of sex offender legislation and treatment depends largely on the ability of designated professionals to be able to accurately assess the risks of the offenders. For treatment of sexual offenders, discussed in Chapter 11, it is critical that treatment providers match the risks and needs of the offenders. For supervision and management of offenders in the community, it is important to distinguish between offenders who pose a high risk to the public and those who do not. High-risk offenders are subject to enhanced registration and community notification policies, including a longer registration period, mandated treatment, and different methods of community notification (Blasko, Jeglic, & Mercado, 2011).

Prior to the enactment of the AWA, states had discretion in how to assess risk of offenders, as long as they had a systematic way in which to determine who was at a high risk of reoffending and notifying the community about those offenders. States used either an offender- or offense-based approach to risk assessment, though most used the offender-based approach. Offender-based approaches utilize actuarial assessment tools to determine risk, based upon the characteristics of the offenders. Offense-based risk assessment determines risk based on the offense for which the offender is convicted. The AWA requires the use of an offense-based risk assessment system, which is one of the most significant controversies about the law.

Actuarial and Sex Offender-Specific Tools   Actuarial assessments seek to evaluate an offender through interpretation of standardized scores on various risk assessment instruments. Risk is determined based upon a number of static and dynamic characteristics of the offenders. Static factors involve variables that are stable over time (for example, age, family history) whereas dynamic variables are subject to change (for example, cognitive distortions, levels of victim empathy).

A considerable amount of research has been conducted on actuarial risk assessment tools. Early studies of risk focused primarily on static factors, with little attention paid to dynamic variables (Hanson, 1998). Hanson and Harris (2000) addressed this issue by providing evidence that dynamic factors can be broken down further into stable dynamic risk factors (those expected to remain unchanged for a substantial period of time) and acute dynamic risk factors (factors that change rapidly). In their study of 208 sexual offense recidivists and 201 nonrecidivist sex offenders, the authors concluded that stable dynamic risk factors showed the greatest potential in differentiating the recidivists from the nonrecidivists. The assessment of both static and dynamic risk factors is important prior to treatment, as the treatment for sex offenders should focus on the individual characteristics associated with recidivism risk (Mann et al., 2010).[3]

Clinicians and researchers have developed a variety of actuarial assessment tools that can assess the risk of sex offenders based upon both static and dynamic characteristics. These instruments include the Sex Offender Risk Appraisal Guide (SORAG), Rapid Risk Assessment of Sexual Offense Recidivism (RRASOR), Static-99 (and the revised Static-99R and Static-2002), and the Minnesota Sex Offender Screening Tool-Revised (MnSOSTR). General recidivism tools such as the Violence Risk Appraisal Guide (VRAG) and the Psychopathy Checklist-Revised (PCL-R) have also shown promise in determining sex offender recidivism.

Several studies have evaluated the efficacy of these tools (Hanson, 2000). Barbaree et al. (2001) concluded that when these instruments were cross-validated on a sample of 215 sex offenders, the VRAG, SORAG, RRASOR, and Static-99 were capable of predicting general, violent, and sexual recidivism. MnSOSTR scores and guided clinical interviews were able to indicate general recidivism, but showed little sensitivity in discerning between serious or sexual reoffending. Out of all of these measures, the PCL-R, when used alone, was sensitive in predicting general and serious recidivism but was unable to predict sexual recidivism. Harris, Rice, and Quinsey (2003) also evaluated these four actuarial instruments in four samples of sex offenders (N = 396) for the prediction of violent and sexual reoffending. All four instruments predicted violent (including sexual) recidivism and recidivism known to be sexually motivated. However, predictive accuracy was higher for child sexual abusers than for rapists, especially for the Static-99 and the RRASOR. Kingston et al. (2008) compared the Static-99 and SORAG to yet another actuarial too, the Risk Matrix 2000, and found convergent validity between the instruments. Though they found that the Risk Matrix 2000 could predict risk above chance levels, they noted that the other instruments are better at predicting risk.

There are similarities between the actuarial assessment tools, and several studies have indicated convergent validity between them. However, the Static-99 (Hanson & Thornton, 2000) is the most common assessment tool used today for risk assessment. It is used not just for treatment purposes, but also for assessing risk of offenders living in the community and to determine whether offenders should be civilly committed (Boccaccini et al., 2012). The Static-99 is comprised of 10 items that focus on factors related to sexual deviance and nonsexual criminal history factors. The items focus on presence of any male victims, marital status, noncontact sex offenses, unrelated victims, stranger victims, prior sexual offenses, current nonsexual violence, prior nonsexual violence, four or more prior sentencing occasions, and whether the offender is 25 years or younger (Beauregard & Mieczkowski, 2009). These ten scores are summed producing a single score that is categorized into one of 4 risk groups: low (0–1), moderate–low (2–3), moderate–high (4–5), and high (6+).

---

3. For a through review of dynamic risk factors, see Hanson (2006c).

Out of 22 studies addressing the predictive validity of the Static-99 concerning sexual recidivism, 20 of the studies supported the risk assessment's predictive validity (Beauregard & Mieczkowski, 2009). However, Sreenivasan et al. (2007) found that the Static-99 scores may both under and overestimate risk due to the risk of false positives and negatives. They noted that the Static-99 was standardized on Canadian and U.K. samples that were predominantly white, which may limit its applicability to racially diverse prison samples in the United States. The Static-2002 was developed to increase coherence and conceptual clarity, and it has been found to have significantly greater accuracy in predicting sexual, violent, and any type of recidivism. The difference between the Static-99 and Static-2002 on predicting sexual recidivism was very small though (Helmus et al., 2011). For a thorough review of the research on the Static-99, 99R, and 2002, see http://www.static99.org/.

The various actuarial instruments have produced some consistent findings in regard to factors associated with high risk to reoffend. The strongest predictors of recidivism are criminal lifestyle variables (Hanson & Harris, 2000). Hanson and Harris (2000) also found that recidivists had poor social support, attitudes tolerant of sexual assault, antisocial lifestyles, poor self-management strategies, and difficulties complying with supervision. The recidivists showed similarities with the nonrecidivists concerning general mood, but the recidivists displayed more anger and subjective distress before reoffending. Other factors that are useful indicators of risk of recidivism include sexual preoccupations, conflict in intimate relationships, and emotional identification with children and hostility (Beauregard & Mieczkowski, 2009). Prentky et al. (1997) provided evidence illustrating that the strongest predictors of sexual offense recidivism include the degree of sexual preoccupation with children, presence of paraphilias, and the number of prior sexual offenses. The meta-analysis conducted by Hanson and Bussière (1998) illustrated that the best predictors of recidivism were sexual deviancy as measured by penile plethysmograph (PPG), history of sex crimes, psychological characteristics, negative relationship with mother, failure to complete treatment, and the presence of depression and anxiety. Harris et al. (2003) found that offenders who score high in both psychopathy and sexual deviance measures are an especially high-risk group (Harris et al., 2003).

It is important to note that the risk assessment tools described here are appropriate only for adult male offenders. These have not been standardized on adolescent or female offenders, or on specific groups of sex offenders (for example, clergy). Viljoen, Elkovitch, Scalora, and Ullman (2009) note that risk assessment tools used for juvenile sex offenders have not been adequately studied in regards to their prediction of sexual recidivism. In their study of adolescent offenders, Viljoen et al. (2009) also found that the Static-99 did not significantly predict sexual reoffending. Groups such as clergy offenders exhibit consistency in some of the risk variables in actuarial instruments, thus rendering them meaningless in terms of assessing recidivism. For example, there are no clergy under a particular age, Catholic clergy cannot marry, and all have high levels of education.

There are also concerns as to whether actuarial assessment tools will be as accurate for minority subsets of offenders, such as those offenders at an advanced age (Helmus et al., 2011). Age is an increasingly important variable, as the proportion of seniors in the general population and prison population has been increasing. As such, the age-risk variables should be reassessed. Hanson (2006a) found that older offenders had lower Static-99 scores than younger offenders and that Static-99 was moderately accurate in estimating relative recidivism risk in all age groups. Older offenders, however, had lower sexual recidivism rates than would be expected based on their Static-99 risk categories. Consequently, evaluators using Static-99 should consider advanced age in their overall estimate of risk (Hanson, 2006a). Helmus et al. (2011) found that the actuarial weights given to age at release in both the Static-99 and Static-2002 overestimate the risk of recidivism for older offenders. This is important as age is more strongly related to nonsexual violent recidivism than to sexual recidivism.

Conviction-Based Approach to Risk Assessment   While much research has been conducted about the efficacy of actuarial risk assessment tools, there are no empirical studies published to date on the efficacy of offense-based risk management. As a result of the offense-based approach, sex offenders are more likely to be considered moderate or high risk than under an offender-based risk assessment process. This is unnecessary at best, and harmful at worst. The conviction-based approach has been criticized because it removes the discretion of assessment provided by the actuarial instruments. It is no longer possible to take into consideration the aggravating and/or mitigating circumstances of the offenses (Levenson & D'Amora, 2007), or the important factors related to static and dynamic characteristics of offenders that have been significantly associated with risk. Yet, the AWA requires all states to comply with this type of assessment process.

The Adam Walsh Act: Uniformity and Controversy

Because of the inconsistencies in registration by state, the AWA was passed to provide uniformity to registration and notification statutes nationally. It created a baseline standard of registration and notification policies, but it also expanded the legislation to include additional offenses and offenders, enhanced supervision, and extended the time in which offenders would be subject to these requirements. As stated earlier, SORNA follows an offense-based risk assessment process. High-risk (Tier 3) offenses are those punishable by at least one year imprisonment and include offenses of sexual and aggravated sexual abuse, offenses against a minor under 13 years, kidnapping, and further offenses of a Tier 2 offender. Moderate-risk (Tier 2) offenses are those punishable by at least one year imprisonment that are not Tier 3 offenses and include sex trafficking, coercion and enticement, transportation with intent to engage in criminal sexual activity, abusive sexual contact, use of a minor in a sexual performance, solicitation of a minor for prostitution, and production of child pornography. Low-risk (Tier 1) offenses are all other offenses not categorized as Tier 2 or 3. According to the SORNA classification guidelines, high-risk offenders must be registered on a national database for life, moderate-risk sex offenders are required to register for 25 years and low-risk sex offenders for 15 years.

There are several criticisms of the new guidelines under SORNA. Prior to the enactment of the AWA, sanctions for failure to register varied by state. SORNA stipulates that failure to register or accurately and regularly update home, work, and school information will result in felony charges, punishable by up to 10 years in prison. This is a substantial criminal penalty for violation of a civil statute, and is one criticism about enhanced sanctions resulting from the AWA.

SORNA is also criticized for expanding the notification of offenders. It requires that all state registry websites include information for all sex offenders in their database—not just the information of high-risk and moderate-risk offenders. This is problematic because the community will no longer be able to discern which of the offenders are the most dangerous and most likely to recidivate, which was the original purpose of the notification legislation.

Importantly, and controversially, all juvenile sex offenders who are least 14-years-of-age at the time of the offense and who have been adjudicated for aggravated sexual abuse or some comparable offense will be subject to community notification provisions. This provision of SORNA has led to the reluctance on behalf of states to enact the AWA (Harris & Lobanov-Rostovsky, 2010). Unfortunately, these juveniles may be assessed as Tier 3 (high-risk) offenders, and they would therefore remain on the registry for life (Enniss, 2008). Not only is this policy inconsistent with the goal of the juvenile justice system (Letourneau, Bandyopadhyay, Armstrong, & Sinha, 2010), but it is also inconsistent with the empirical literature, which shows that the majority of juvenile sex offenders do not go on to commit offenses as adults (Caldwell, 2007; Zimring, Jennings, Piquero, & Hays, 2009; Zimring, Piquero, & Jennings, 2007). Further emphasizing this point, Caldwell, Ziemke, and Vitacco (2008) showed inconsistent risk designations for juveniles between SORNA guidelines and the validated risk assessment instruments for juveniles (Psychopathy Checklist: Youth Version and the Juvenile Sex Offender Assessment Protocol–II).

Finally, the AWA removes the discretion of states to use risk assessment guidelines that are considered to be best practices in assessing risk. Rather, it uses the offense-based system of assessment rather than an offender-based system, and there are no empirical studies that support this as an effective method of assessment. Some researchers have even argued that this system compromises public safety by reducing the discriminatory nature of the registry (Harris & Lobanov-Rostovsky, 2010). This provision is particularly troubling for juvenile offenders who must register, since it provides no ability to consider unique developmental factors related to juveniles (Letourneau & Miner, 2005).

Empirical researchers have long been critical about sex offender supervision and management policies, and are even more vocal about SORNA (Wright, 2009). It is not just the social scientists, however, that have been almost unanimously opposed to the AWA for its sweeping legislation and one-size-fits-all policies. Legal scholars have also been highly critical, variably called it misguided (Buntin, 2011), harmful (Baron-Evans, 2008), overbroad (Logan, 2008), constitutionality questionable (Frumkin, 2008; Visgaitis, 2011; Yung 2009), and potentially harmful to juvenile offenders (Bowater, 2008; Janus & Prentky, 2008). Even victim advocates have spoken out against legislation that goes too far.

The shortcomings of the AWA are evident beginning in the introduction to the Act. The AWA is dedicated to 17 victims, named in the legislation—Jacob Wetterling, Megan Kanka, Pam Lychner, Jetseta Gage, Dru Sjodin, Jessica Lunsford, Sarah Lunde, Amie Zyla, Christy Fornoff, Alexandra Zapp, Polly Klaas, Jimmy Ryce, Carlie Brucia, Amanda Brown, Elizabeth Smart, Molly Bish, and Samantha Runnion (42 USCS § 16901)—nearly all of whom were abducted, violently sexually assaulted, and/or killed by strangers. These cases highlight one of the flaws of the AWA and RCNL more generally; namely, registration is based upon the location of the offender's residence. Yet, empirical studies show that the location of the offenders' residences is not necessarily linked to the location of the abuse situation. The Minnesota Department of Corrections (2007a) conducted a study of sex offenders' proximity to their victims and found that of the 224 offenders in their sample, only 16 offenders lived within a one mile of the abuse location. This is true for the majority of the victims listed on the Adam Walsh Act, where in many cases the perpetrator traveled to a different neighborhood from where he was registered (for example, Jessica Lunsford), or even state (for example, Dru Sjodin), for the commission of the offense. In some of the cases (for example, Samantha Runion, Polly Klaas, Elizabeth Smart), notification would have been irrelevant because the victims were violently abducted and knowledge of the perpetrator's identity could not have prevented those offenses.

Most states have not yet implemented the AWA. This hesitation by states to implement in itself indicates the problematic nature of the legislation, which has become so far reaching that states either cannot afford to implement it or will not do so on principle. The cost of implementing SORNA has been prohibitive, because it requires system development, reclassification, expanded enforcement personnel, judicial and correctional costs, and legal costs related to prosecution, defense, and litigation (Harris & Lobanov-Rostovsky, 2010). Thus, while RCNL is not likely to be abolished, it is also likely that most states will not ultimately enact the AWA.

Efficacy of RCNL

Since their inception, researchers have been studying the efficacy of laws regulating the behavior of sex offenders. There is no single way in which to measure the effect of the laws, however, and studies have used varying definitions of efficacy and varying methods for studying it. Compounding this issue, the outcome of the studies can be interpreted differently. For example, does an increase in offending mean that the actual rate of offending is increasing, or that notification has led to a greater awareness of sexual offending and more people are reporting it? Additionally, would it be possible to discern the role of notification in the increase or decrease in reported cases of sexual abuse? The goal of RCNL is to reduce the amount of sexual abuse, but it is possible that the legislation actually causes a real increase in offending as a result of the collateral consequences of the laws. Such effects would be difficult to discern.

✦The goal of RCNL is public protection through education about offenders who are who are living in the community and are at a high risk to reoffend. As such, efficacy has most commonly been defined as a reduction in sexual offending, and specifically whether offenders modify their behavior as a result of the laws. As of 2010, 11 studies specifically evaluated the efficacy of RCNL on recidivism (Letourneau, Levenson, Bandyopadhyay, Armstrong, & Sinha, 2010), and most of these have shown that RCNL does not result in a significant decrease in sexual offending (Kernsmith et al., 2009). Five out of the six group-comparison studies failed to find support that RCNL reduced recidivism and, of the four studies that examined changes in crime rates over time, findings on efficacy were inconclusive. One of these studies found a positive effect on recidivism, one found a negative effect, and the last two found no clear effect on recidivism. Additionally, studies have found no significant differences between the recidivism rates of offenders who registered and those who failed to register. This includes both sexual recidivism and general recidivism rates (Levenson et al., 2010).

One of the most significant pre-post studies of RCNL was conducted in New Jersey, the first state to implement Megan's Law (Zgoba et al., 2008). The researchers studied 550 sex offenders released from prison or a treatment center between 1990 and 2000, comparing those released before and after the implementation of Megan's Law. Though there were differences by group in regard to levels of general recidivism, there were no significant differences between groups in regard to sexual recidivism (Zgoba, Veysey, & Dalessandro, 2010). The researchers also found that RCNL had no effect on the time to first rearrest, on the type of offense committed or on the number of offenses the offender committed. A study of RCNL in South Carolina produced similar results. In this study, Letourneau, Levenson, Bandyopadhyay, Armstrong, and Sinha (2010) found that the offender registration status at the time of the recidivating act was not associated with a reduced risk of sex crime recidivism or reduced time to detection of sex crime recidivism. The authors concluded that there was no evidence that South Carolina's broad RCNL decreased sex offender recidivism rates (Letourneau, Levenson, Bandyopadhyay, Armstrong, & Sinha, 2010, p. 452).

Most studies of RCNL efficacy have focused on adult offenders, and few have studied the impact of RCNL on juveniles (Letourneau, Bandyopadhyay, Sinha, & Armstrong, 2009). Prior to the enactment of SORNA, there were no reliable data on the deterrent effects of RCNL for juveniles, nor were data available on the collateral consequences on juveniles. Letourneau, Bandyopadhyay, Armstrong, and Sinha (2010) conducted a study of the effects of RCNL on juveniles in South Carolina and found that RCNL did not deter juvenile sex crimes. The authors argue that RCNL constitutes further retribution against sex offenders, both adults and juveniles.

Some recent studies have defined efficacy differently. Rather than focusing on the effect of RCNL on offenders, they studied the effect of RCNL on the public (Anderson & Sample, 2008; Bandy, 2011; Beck et al., 2004). Registration is intended to protect the public from sexual violence by increasing awareness of offenders in the community who had been convicted of sexual offenses (Kernsmith, Comartin, Craun, & Kernsmith, 2009). RCNL has been deemed constitutional in the courts based on the argument that the protection of the public takes precedence over the offenders' right to privacy (Bandy, 2011). The public's safety, then, would be dependent upon the protective behaviors they take once they find out about sex offenders living in the community. Yet little research exists on the degree to which registration policies have increased awareness of offenders in the community.

Studies that have evaluated the public response to sex offender registries have shown disappointing results. Few community members are aware of sex offender registries or take precautionary measures upon learning of the presence of a sex offender in their community (Kernsmith et al., 2009; Letourneau, Levenson, Bandyopadhyay, Armstrong, & Sinha, 2010). Kernsmith et al. (2009) found that the predictors of utilization of the registry included age, having children, and having been the victim of a sex crime, while the most frequently cited reason for not accessing the registry was a lack of interest or not having children. Additionally, community members take few precautionary measures when they are notified about sex offenders living in their community (Anderson & Sample, 2008; Bandy, 2011; Beck et al., 2004). This finding is consistent in communities of varying economic status, and undermines the assumptions on which RCNL is based (Bandy, 2011, p. 255).

Collateral Consequences   The purpose of RCNL is to reduce sexual offending and protect the community. However, laws that are overly punitive may have unintended consequences for both the offenders and the public that they intend to protect. In one of the first studies to examine the collateral consequences of RCNL, Tewksbury (2005) gathered data on 121 registered sex offenders in Kentucky. He found that RCNL resulted in high levels of social stigmatization; loss of relationships, employment, and housing; and assaults as a result of vigilantism. Studies have consistently shown that registered sex offenders are more likely to live in disadvantaged neighborhoods with high levels of social disorganization (Mustaine & Tewksbury, 2011; Mustaine et al., 2006). Kernsmith et al. (2009) noted that the social and financial constraints resulting from RCNL may actually increase sex offender recidivism and suggested that restricted notification only to public safety officials may mitigate the potential negative consequences.

Public registries may also have unintended consequences for the public, such as increasing fear and making victims less likely to report their victimization (Kernsmith et al., 2009). Registries may actually skew the sense of safety due to misperceptions that most sex offenders victimize children and are strangers to their victims (Kernsmith et al., 2009). In their study of the location of sex offender residences, Suresh et al. (2010) found that registered sex offenders living in disadvantaged neighborhoods were likely to live in clusters, and those clusters were likely to be near schools or other areas where children congregate. Thus, the legislation that has been enacted to protect the public may be unintentionally doing exactly the opposite.

In sum, laws regulating the monitoring and supervision of sex offenders in the community were not implemented based on sound theoretical models or an empirical bases, and studies conducted on their efficacy consistently show little, if any, effect on reducing recidivism (Levenson & D'Amora, 2007; Tewksbury & Lees, 2006; Welchans, 2005).

RESIDENCE RESTRICTIONS

In addition to the federal legislation related to the supervision and monitoring of sex offenders in the community, states and local jurisdictions have the discretion to enact additional regulatory laws to protect the public from sexual offenders. The most frequent types of legislation include residence restrictions and GPS monitoring (Vitiello, 2008). Residence restrictions limit the places where sex offenders can live, work, or loiter. The policies are based upon the premise that geographical proximity to offense opportunities increases the likelihood of offending (Terry & Ackerman, 2009). This is based on the criminological literature, which indicates that criminal offenses are dependent upon situational opportunities, and potential offenders will use the environment to their advantage in the commission of a crime (Cohen & Felson, 1979). According to this routine activities perspective, legislation that restricts sex offenders' movements in the community (including RCNL, residence restrictions, and GPS monitoring) reduces the opportunities for offenders to recidivate by limiting their access to potential victims and empowering potential victims to prevent attacks.

The goal of residence restriction statutes is to increase public safety protection by limiting sex offenders' access to the places "where children congregate." The places of congregation and the length of the restriction vary by jurisdiction. Residence restrictions typically bar offenders from living within a 1000- to 2500-foot distance from schools, day care centers, parks, playgrounds, or other places densely populated by children (Nieto & Jung, 2006). Though more than 30 states have implemented residence restrictions for sex offenders (Levenson, 2009), the specifics of the restrictions are usually determined at the local level.

Sex offenders have challenged residence restrictions in court and, like RCNL, this legislation has been deemed constitutional. The first case to be heard at the State Supreme Court level was in Iowa, which had enacted some of the strictest statewide residence restrictions in the nation. In 2005, the Eighth Circuit Court of Appeals upheld the Iowa statute that prohibited sex offenders from living within 2000 feet of designated places where children congregate (*Doe v. Miller*, 2005). Reversing the decision of the Court before it, the Court held that residence restrictions are not, on their face, unconstitutional. Once they were deemed constitutional, the number of states with residence restrictions doubled between 2005 and 2007. Some states enacted residence restrictions because of the fear that sex offenders would converge on their states if they did not enact such laws (Levenson, 2009).

The question then becomes, are the laws necessary and do they protect the public? Some studies have shown that sex offenders do live within close proximity of schools, day cares, and playgrounds. Walker, Golden, and VanHouten (2001) found that a higher percentage of child sex offenders (48 percent) lived within 1000-foot buffer zones around schools, day care centers, and parks than did nonchild sex offenders (26 percent). In New York City, approximately 85 percent of the highest risk offenders lived within five blocks of a school. This is in contrast to other studies; Tewksbury and Mustaine (2006) found that less than a quarter of sex offenders lived near a park or playground, and approximately one in seven lived near a school, community center, or library. The empirical research, however, does not indicate that this close proximity leads to higher levels of offending. The Colorado Department of Public Safety (2004) found that child sexual abusers who recidivated did not live any closer to schools, day care centers, or parks than the child sexual abusers who did not recidivate. These findings were replicated in Florida, as recidivism rates were not associated with the distance sex offenders lived from where children congregate (Zandbergen, Levenson, & Hart, 2010).

As with RCNL, residence restrictions lead to collateral consequences for sex offenders subject to them. Residence restrictions create barriers that make it difficult for sex offenders to reintegrate back into society (Zevitz & Farkas, 2000). Mercado, Alvarez, and Levenson (2008) showed that this legislation increases transience and homelessness, and may cause offenders to move further from supportive environments and employment opportunities. Offenders subject to residence restrictions are not only likely to lose their homes and be evicted from their residences but are also more likely to feel socially stigmatized, lose their jobs, have relationships end, and be subject to harassment from the public (Levenson, D'Amora, & Hern, 2007; Levenson & Hern, 2007; Tewksbury, 2005; Zevitz & Farkas, 2000). In a study addressing the impact on offenders subject to residence restrictions, Levenson and Cotter (2005) found that 57 percent of offenders had difficulty finding affordable housing, 48 percent suffered financially, and 60 percent suffered emotionally as a result of residence restrictions. Additionally, Mercado, Alvarez, and Levenson (2008) found that 35 percent of the offenders in their sample were not able to live with supportive family members.

One of the factors of concern with residence restrictions is the limit on available places for sex offenders to legally live. The Minnesota Department of Corrections (2003) reported that residence restrictions create a shortage of available housing alternatives for sex offenders, which they said may force them into isolated areas that lack services, employment opportunities, and/or adequate social support. This is similar in most jurisdictions, which only have a limited number of residential areas that are not within the restricted limit. For instance, Wartell (2007) found that only 27 percent of available living space within the city of San Diego was available to sex offenders. In Hamilton, Ohio, only 63 percent of the residential areas were available to sex offenders as a result of the 1000-foot residence restrictions. In New Jersey, Chajewski and Mercado (2008) found that 1000-foot residence restrictions would require 31 to 65 percent of offenders to move from their current locations.

Compounding the problem of a lack of legal areas in which sex offenders can reside, the areas in which sex offenders must relocate is often in socially undesirable neighborhoods (Tewksbury & Mustaine, 2008; Mustaine & Tewksbury, 2011). Mustaine and Tewksbury (2011) found that sex offenders live in high concentrations in areas with more concentrated economic disadvantage, more residential instability, and higher rates of robbery and child sexual abuse. These high concentration areas of sex offenders, deemed sex offender "colonies" (see When Laws Go Too Far: The Emergence of the Sex Offender "Colonies"), and may actually lead to an increase rather than a reduction of recidivism. In addition to all of these arguments against the legislation, there are practical shortcomings in it as well. For instance, sex offenders may live the regulated distance from where children congregate, but there are no restrictions on whether sex offenders can live next door to children, in the same apartment buildings as them, or even in the same homes as them (unless there are case-specific regulations). Plus, sex offenders are not restricted from spending time where children congregate, they are only restricted from residing there. Mercado, Alvarez, and Levenson (2008) found that 62 percent of the sample of sex offenders in their study said they would be able to reoffend if they wanted to, despite any residence restrictions. As such, residence restrictions should be reexamined to determine whether they are socially, economically, and ethically necessary.

GPS MONITORING

One way to monitor the whereabouts of sex offenders is to track them through electronic surveillance. This is most commonly done through the use of Global Positioning System (GPS) devices connected to electronic bracelets. Beginning in New Mexico in 1984, states began to monitor various types of criminal offenders with GPS devices as an alternative to incarceration (Levenson & D'Amora, 2007). The offenders wear an electronic bracelet while they are on probation, parole, or on house arrest, which allows the supervising agency to monitor the offenders' locations. There are three types of GPS supervision: active, passive, and hybrid systems. Active supervision tracks and monitors offenders' movements throughout the day and provides real-time information for law enforcement. Passive supervision, on the other hand, allows the offenders to upload information from their electronic bracelets at the end of the day. Hybrid systems are a combination of both the active and passive systems, transmitting information after longer periods of time than with the active systems but alerting the authorities instantly if the offenders are out of range (IACP, 2008).

The supervision of sex offenders through the use of GPS devices is unique to other types of offenders. Some sex offenders are monitored while on probation or parole, like other types of offenders. However, some states also require all registered sex offenders to be monitored whether or not they are under the care of correctional services. Florida was the first state to use GPS to track sex offenders under community supervision (Johnson, 2002). Since the implementation of the Jessica Lunsford Act in 2005, Florida requires all convicted child sexual abusers who are living in the community to wear a GPS device for the rest of their lives (Padgett, Bales, & Blomberg, 2006). More than half of the states now use GPS tracking of sex offenders, and six states currently require lifetime supervision

VIGNETTE

WHEN LAWS GO TOO FAR: The Emergence of the Sex Offender "Colonies"

Residence restrictions were enacted to protect the public, particularly children, from sex offenders by restricting the areas in which the offenders can reside. In doing so, they required that sex offenders could not live within a certain distance from places where children congregate. Some states and local jurisdictions enacted extreme measures, saying that offenders could not live within 2000 or more feet from any place where children may congregate. With few choices of where they could reside, sex offenders in some jurisdictions became transient and began "residing" in the only places available to them. Often they ended up living together in large numbers or "colonies" as they became known, in run-down motels, parking lots, or even under bridges. The most high profile case of a sex offender colony was the one formed under the Julia Tuttle Bridge in Miami-Dade County, Florida.

Following the death of Jessica Lunsford in Florida in 2005, Florida enacted Jessica's Law, which increased penalties for sex offenders and enhanced supervision of them in the community. Nine-year old Jessica was abducted from her home by John Couey, a previously convicted sex offender, who was staying in a trailer across the street from where she lived. The community was outraged that a known sex offender could rape and kill a neighbor, and Florida became one of many states to enact highly stringent sex offender legislation.

Several local jurisdictions in Florida passed residence restrictions limiting sex offenders from residing 2,500 feet from schools, parks, bus stops, and homeless shelters. There were no residential areas in some cities, including those in Miami-Dade County, where sex offenders could legally live. As a result, sex offenders in the Miami-Dade area moved to a camp under the Julia Tuttle Causeway, where more than 100 offenders lived between 2006 and 2010. The offenders lived in tents and shared generators. There was no running water and no protection from the elements. Reports likened the encampment to a "ghetto," "shantytown," and a "leper colony."

The sex offenders living under the Causeway had to register as sex offenders with the Causeway as their formal address. Representatives from the Department of Corrections would check on them every evening to ensure they were in their "residence" from 6 P.M. to 7 A.M. But the sex offender colony was highly controversial, and no single state or local agency wanted to be responsible for overseeing it. The Department of Corrections eventually absolved themselves of responsibility, the City of Miami filed a lawsuit against the state, and the ACLU filed a lawsuit against the city of Miami citing a "public health and safety crisis." The encampment was eventually shut down, and the offenders relocated. But the Julia Tuttle Causeway colony serves as an example of what can happen when legislation is taken too far, with politicians and lobbyists concerned with nothing other than NIMBY: not in my backyard.

Questions
1. Where should sex offenders be allowed to live? If there should be restrictions on where they live, explain why and how that would lead to better protection of children.
2. Under the Adam Walsh Act, adolescent sex offenders would be registered offenders subject to residence restriction guidelines. Should adolescent offenders have been allowed to live in the Causeway colony?

(Colorado, Florida, Missouri, Ohio, Oklahoma, and Wisconsin) (IACP, 2008). The number of states using GPS is likely to increase, as the AWA supports pilot programs for states to implement this legislation.

GPS tracking can be useful as one tool for the supervision of sexual offenders in the community. According to the International Association of Chiefs of Police (2008, p. 7), GPS tracking of sex offenders can assist agencies with court processes, violation hearings, case management planning, and investigating failure-to-register cases; serve as a tool to enhance other methods of supervision; monitor offenders' daily activities; and analyze data location points to identify specific patterns of movement and frequently visited locations, which may warrant further investigation. There are, however, disadvantages as well. GPS tracking is expensive; the tracking devices costs up to $15 per offender per day, not including the resources necessary for the supervising agents (Meloy & Coleman, 2009). GPS monitoring also requires an increase in other resources, such as the workload of the agents who must monitor the offenders, respond to GPS alerts, and maintain the tracking equipment. The most important limitation of the GPS tracking is that it cannot prevent crimes from occurring; it is useful instead as an informational tool and resource that agents can use to respond to offenders' actions (Meloy & Coleman, 2009). The tracking of offenders' movements is also not helpful with certain types of offenses. It cannot, for instance, detect whether the offenders are accessing inappropriate material on a computer or abusing someone within the home.

There is limited empirical support that GPS monitoring of sex offenders reduces recidivism or helps to protect the community (Brown et al., 2007; Meloy & Coleman, 2009). Studies in California and Tennessee showed that there were no significant differences in recidivism or technical violations between sex offenders who were monitored with GPS and those who were not (Tennessee Board of Probation and Parole, 2007; Turner et al., 2007). Despite the lack of empirical support, the Tennessee Board of Probation and Parole (2007, p. 4) stated that GPS monitoring "provides officers with a unique supervision tool and has potential in aiding officers greatly." Turner et al. (2007) found that although GPS tracking did not reduce offending, it did appear to reduce the level of absconding in sex offenders. More research needs to be done to determine for whom this is most effective, for how long, and in what circumstances.

THE CONTAINMENT APPROACH: COLLABORATING FOR EFFECTIVE MANAGEMENT

Some jurisdictions have implemented a "containment approach" to the supervision of sex offenders who are living in the community. The containment approach is not a policy, but rather a victim-centered collaborative strategy among the agencies involved in supervising sexual offenders. These agencies variously include probation, parole, law enforcement, treatment providers, and victim service agencies. These agencies work together to hold offenders accountable through internal and external controls (English, 2009). English (2009; English, Pullen, & Jones, 1997) explain that this strategy consists of five tenets that work together to secure the highest degree of management and care of sex offenders.

1. *Overall Philosophy and Goal: Community and Victim Safety* Protection and recovery of the victim and the well-being of the community are the main concerns that guide policy development. The sex offender is able to live in the community and receive appropriate care and treatment, while supervisors ensure that the offender has no contact with the victim and is blocked from high-risk situations where contact could be made with potential future victims. For example, the supervisors should ensure that the offender's employment is appropriate and does not establish conditions that could lead to relapse. Housing is also important, and supervisors must also ensure that the offender is not living within close range of potential victims or, if the victim is in the household, the offender should be removed from the household (rather than the victim being removed).

2. *Sex Offender-Specific Containment: Individualized Case Management System* Each case is different, and the supervision and management of each offender should be tailored to the specific case. Three elements must be present in order to effectively manage the sex offender. First, the offender must participate in treatment, and the treatment must be sex offender specific. Many sex offenders have behavioral problems that require additional treatment, such as substance abuse, though they must also participate in a treatment program designed to highlight their potential for relapse of sexually deviant behavior. Second, specially trained monitors who understand the individual high-risk needs of sex offenders must supervise them. If the offender does not comply with the supervisors (for example, probation or parole officers), the offender should be sanctioned accordingly. Third, the offender should be subjected to polygraph examinations periodically to ensure that he or she is complying with the supervision requirements that have been imposed.

3. *Collaboration: A Multidisciplinary Approach* Although each agency must employ its own procedures, the supervising teams must collaborate on management strategies. Collaboration must occur at both the case management and policy levels (CSOM, 2000). Without collaboration, the effort of each agency would be fragmented and lacking in necessary resources, knowledge, and skills.

4. *Consistent Public Policies* Public policies must be informed, clear, and consistent. For instance, prosecutors should develop consistent strategies about disallowing sex offenders to accept plea bargains (to either a lesser sexual offense or a nonsexual offense); treatment providers should make consistent use of external measures (for example, the polygraph and the PPG, discussed

in the next chapter); probation and parole should establish consistent policies on revocation if conditions are violated; and child and family services or social services should create consistent policy on family reunification.

5. *Quality Control* There must be an evaluation of the system that is in place to see if the policy implemented results in effective management. Because the primary purpose of a containment approach is community protection and restorative justice for the victim, any assessment process must acknowledge these facts.

The containment approach was developed by researchers at the Colorado Division of Criminal Justice. Colorado has been a leader in sex offender management strategies, developing policies based upon research (Ackerman & Terry, 2009). The Colorado General Assembly created the Sex Offender Management Board (SOMB), whose members represent the Department of Corrections, the Department of Public Safety, the Department of Human Services, the Public Defender's Office, district attorneys, treatment providers, and other relevant stakeholders. The SOMB was established to develop guidelines for the treatment and supervision of sex offenders (Colorado Department of Public Safety, 2008), and Colorado has consistently developed policies and guidelines based upon empirical research. The state and the SOMB are committed to maintaining research-based, best practices in an effort to manage offenders and promote public safety (Lowden, English, Hetz, & Harrison, 2003) with continuous evaluation and revisions of their guidelines.

Other states have implemented similar collaborative approaches to Colorado. For instance, the Minnesota Department of Corrections created a Sex Offender Supervision Study Group, tasked with making recommendations that would improve the management and supervision of sex offenders in the community (Minnesota Department of Corrections, 2000). In their report, the Study Group made recommendations about methods of supervision (both intensive supervised release and specialized caseloads), optimum caseload size, housing, risk assessment, supervision training, and probation and post-release programming funding. Minnesota is also responsible for supporting research studies on various issues related to sex offender management, and creating guidelines based upon the empirical findings of these studies (Minnesota Department of Corrections, 2007a, 2007b).

Another state that is a leader in data-driven sex offender policies is Washington (Ackerman & Terry, 2009). The state legislature created the Washington State Institute for Public Policy (WSIPP), whose researchers work together with state agencies and universities to ensure that sound research is conducted and that important policy questions are answered based on data. Research at WSIPP is conducted at the direction of the state legislature when significant state level issues arise (Ackerman & Terry, 2009). WISPP has published about 60 reports related to sex offenders since 1991 on topics focusing on civil commitment of sex offenders, female and juvenile offenders, RCNL, and various management policies.

All three of these states are leaders in sex offender practice and policy. The reason for this is their reliance on data-driven models of policy development and their support for extensive research to guide current and future policies. None of these states has yet implemented the AWA, largely because the RCNL procedures they currently have in place are considered best practices for sex offender management, based upon findings from empirical research. These states are also focused on the necessity to balance the rights and needs of sex offenders and the community, understanding the need for protection of the community through victim-centered approaches to sex offender management.

REENTRY AND REINTEGRATION

The aim of sex offender policies and management strategies is community protection, but at what expense? How limited should the rights be of sex offenders who are living in the community? Should sex offenders have the same civil liberties as nonsexual offenders, or should they be restricted in terms of employment, housing, education, and recreation? Limiting the rights of sex offenders could have a negative effect, actually leading to an increase rather than decrease in recidivism. For sex offenders who have been incapacitated and must reenter society, reintegration into the community can be difficult if not impossible because of the management and supervision policies in place. Yet successful reintegration is a critical component to reducing recidivism.

Reintegration into the community is difficult for many offenders, and even more so for sex offenders with the considerable restrictions of RCNL, residence restrictions, GPS monitoring, and other, individualized intensive supervision policies. Many sex offenders perceive this legislation as impeding their ability to find and maintain employment and housing, and restricting their ability to develop appropriate social relationships (Mercado, Alvarez, & Levenson, 2008). It can also lead to harassment and attacks. In fact, much of the research in this area has found that supervision and management policies have a negative affect on the reintegration of sex offenders in society (Levenson & D'Amora, 2007; Levenson & Cotter, 2005; Tewksbury & Mustaine, 2006; Tewksbury & Zgoba, 2010; Zevitz, 2006).

Housing

A basic necessity for sex offenders living in the community is affordable housing, but the ability of sex offenders to find affordable, appropriate housing has been complicated by two factors: RCNL and residence restrictions. Suresh et al. (2010) note that the ability to find housing is a result of both social processes (for example, the reaction of the community to notification of sex offenders in their neighborhoods) and restrictions on where offenders can legally live. Zevitz and Farkas (2000) found that sex offenders who were subject to high levels of notification in the community had great difficulty finding any housing. Many communities do not want sex offenders to move into their neighborhoods, and notification about sex offenders may lead to resident mobilization against the offenders, pushing them toward more disadvantaged neighborhoods (Hughes & Kadleck, 2008).

Residence restrictions have exacerbated the housing problems for sex offenders. Because they are barred from living within a certain distance from where children congregate, they are often unable to live in any socially desirable areas (Levenson & Cotter, 2005; Tewksbury & Mustaine, 2006). Additionally, these restrictions lead to frequent relocation, often to more socially disorganized areas (Mustaine et al., 2006). These socially disorganized neighborhoods are characterized by populations with high levels of unemployment, lower levels of educational achievement, high rates of poverty, low rates of home ownership, and lower median housing values (Mustaine et al., 2006; Mustaine & Tewksbury, 2008; Suresh et al., 2010). The neighborhoods themselves tend to have vacant lots, vacant houses and litter, and neighborhoods with high levels of poverty are predictors of where sex offenders live (Suresh et al., 2010).

It is not only the physical characteristics of the neighborhoods that are problematic. Sex offenders who live in socially disorganized neighborhoods tend to have higher levels of housing instability, have more difficulty finding and maintaining employment, and are located farther from services such as treatment programs (Levenson & Hern, 2007). Sex offenders also have difficulty finding housing with or close to family; Levenson and Cotter (2005) found that 44 percent of their sample was unable to find housing with family members because of residence restrictions. These restrictions on housing for sex offenders may lead to unintended consequences. In addition to creating problems of emotional distress (Levenson & Cotter, 2005), they lead to higher levels of absconding. The 2000-foot residence restrictions that were implemented in Iowa led to the displacement of thousands of sex offenders, and the number of sex offenders who absconded more than doubled within six months of the implementation of the law (Levenson, 2008).

Employment and School

Convicted felons often have difficulty securing jobs upon reentering the community. It is even more difficult for convicted sex offenders to gain employment, as they experience more barriers than the majority of offenders as a result of the conditions of RCNL and community supervision restrictions (Brown, Spencer, & Deakin, 2007). Yet employment is a critical component of reentry and reintegration for sex offenders. Studies indicate that employment is one dynamic factor correlated to recidivism rates, in that offenders who are employed are less likely to reoffend (Hanson & Harris, 1998).

Employment is one form of social tie to the community that has been linked to desistence from offending in adulthood. Kruttschnitt, Uggen, and Shelton (2000) studied all sex offenders released from prison and jail or sentenced to probation in the state of Minnesota in 1992 and followed them to determine whether employment and social ties to family impacted their recidivism. They found that the sex offenders who had stable employment at the time of sentencing were about 37 percent less likely to reoffend than sex offenders who did not have stable employment at that time.

Despite the importance of employment and job stability, sex offenders are prohibited from working in certain jobs. They are unable to work in educational environments or any other place where they would have access to children such as the medical field, homeless shelters, bus drivers, or in residential buildings (CSOM, 2002, p. 3). RCNL and other sex offender management policies make it difficult for offenders to be hired for jobs that are not strictly prohibited as well, including professional jobs. Even when sex offenders are employed, they may face difficulty integrating into the workplace environment.

According to the Center for Sex Offender Management (2002), four factors should be considered when approving employment for sex offenders: community needs, supervision program needs, employer needs, and offender needs. The number one concern should be community safety, and the only jobs offered should be those that do not expose the offender to high-risk situations. The jobs must also be flexible in allowing the offender to attend any meetings that are a necessary part of the supervision program, such as treatment groups. The offender and the employer must also have input into the job selection process; the employer must ensure that the offender is able to integrate into the workplace and perform the necessary duties of the job, whereas the offender should be satisfied with the job. If the employer and the supervising agency remain in contact regarding the offender's progress, there will almost certainly be a reduction in workplace risk.

Another obstacle of reintegration for sex offenders involves educational institutions. In most states, RCNL requires that school officials be notified about pupils who have committed a sexual offense, whether those are juvenile offenders attending school (public or private) or university-level students. Whether this information can be released to other students at the school is controversial, both legally (violating FERPA laws) and socially. The requirement under the AWA that juvenile sex offenders are subject to notification requirements means that this information will now be public. For the juvenile sex offender, notification may lead to social isolation and actually increase offending (Cochrane & Kennedy, 2010).

Because all jurisdictions have approached the registration and notification requirements for juveniles differently, there is little empirical evidence of the effect of the legislation on juvenile offenders. The AWA calls for a study to evaluate the effectiveness of supervision and monitoring of offenders in regard to where they live, work, and attend school.

Recreation and Social Relationships

The boundaries between community protection and individual rights become even less clear if the sex offender is not employed but is at an establishment, such as a church, recreationally. Social ties to the community and social networks can assist with reintegration and reduce the likelihood of reoffending. However, attending such events provides opportunities for offenders to be in close proximity to children. To ban church attendance would certainly pose constitutional challenges, yet it is a forum through which sex offenders can socially, and legally, spend time with children. In fact, sex offender treatment providers encourage offenders to join social groups in order to assist them in developing age-appropriate and socially appropriate relationships. Institutions such as churches create ideal opportunities for sex offenders to reintegrate into society and provide social opportunities for them.

There is little guidance or uniformity on the supervision of sex offenders' social and recreational activities. For instance, should a sex offender be allowed to attend any sporting events where children may participate or watch the event? This would include nearly every sport, both team (for example, baseball, basketball, football, soccer) and individual (for example, swimming, figure skating, tennis, gymnastics). Should the sex offender be able to participate in recreational activities such as shopping at a mall or going to a movie?

Sex offenders are likely to encounter potential victims nearly every time they are in public. It is not possible to completely remove them from society, short of incapacitation. To limit the social activities of sex offenders completely would lead to greater levels of social isolation for sex offenders, who are already stigmatized through the RCNL requirements (McAlinden, 1999). The stress, social isolation, and stigma from sex offender legislation could reinforce the low self-esteem that leads to reoffending. As such, it is important to strive for a balance of rights for both sex offenders and the communities they live in.

In sum, research indicates that the various sex offender laws that have been enacted to protect the public are not the panacea the community anticipated (Levenson & Hern, 2007). The growing body of research assessing the efficacy of these laws shows little empirical support for the community mandates. In fact, many studies have reported on the collateral consequences of the legislation, particularly the inability to find adequate housing, high levels of unemployment, social isolation, strain, and decreases in social support (Levenson & Cotter, 2005; Tewskbury, 2005; Zevitz, 2006).

CHAPTER SUMMARY

- Several sex offender laws have been enacted at the federal, state, and local level to enhance sanctions for sex offenders and improve the supervision and monitoring of sex offenders in the community.

- RCNL is the most extensive federal legislation for sex offenders. The aim of RCNL is to inform the public about known sex offenders who pose a high risk to the community with the aim of preventing recidivism.

- The AWA is federal legislation that imposes uniform requirements on states for RCNL. It is controversial for its requirements that states use a conviction-based assessment process, that all adolescent offenders over age 14 are subject to the RCNL requirements, and for the increase in economic burden on the states as a result of the enhanced supervision requirements. As a result, most states are not compliant yet with this legislation.

- The courts have addressed many constitutional issues related to RCNL, including ex post facto, due process, privacy, double jeopardy, cruel and unusual punishment, bill of attainder, and equal protection. Despite these claims, the U.S. Supreme Court decided in 2003 that both registration and community notification statutes are not punishment and do not violate the civil liberties of offenders.

- Studies of the efficacy of RCNL indicate that it provides little, if any, benefit at reducing recidivism or increasing the protective behaviors of the public.

- States and local jurisdictions have passed laws to further monitor the behavior of sex offenders in the community. The most common laws are residence restrictions and GPS monitoring. Like RCNL, studies do not show that residence restrictions reduce recidivism, protect the public, or increase the safety of children.

- The protection of the public is important and is the basis for the current sex offender laws. However, it is also important to balance the rights of sex offenders and the community. Some states, such as Colorado, Washington, and Minnesota, have made efforts to enact data-driven legislation, such as containment approach models, and should be reviewed for their best practices.

- Those who supervise sex offenders need to help them reintegrate into the community. Sex offenders need housing, employment, and the possibility of forming social and sexual relationships with agemates. With the internal controls learned during treatment, as well as effective external management by a collaborative supervisory team, most sex offenders should be able to reintegrate safely into the community.

DISCUSSION QUESTIONS

1. What are the primary benefits and drawbacks to RCNL? How does the Adam Walsh Act enhance those benefits and/or drawbacks?

2. There are now many ways to monitor sex offenders in community, including RCNL, residence restrictions, and GPS monitoring. Do these laws make the community safer? Explain why or why not.

3. Should all sex offenders be subject to RCNL, residence restrictions, and GPS monitoring? If not, who should be exempt?

4. Is it possible to balance the rights of sex offenders and the public?

5. The goal of sex offender legislation is to prevent sexual offending and recidivism. Do the current sex offender laws achieve this goal? What changes would you recommend to achieve this goal?

11

Assessment and Treatment of Sexual Offenders

The assessment and treatment of sexual offenders has developed substantially over the last 40 years. In an article summarizing the history of assessment, treatment, and theories of sexual offending, Marshall (1996) stated that there were few acceptable methods of assessing and treating sex offenders prior to the 1970s. Most early treatment strategies were based on the assumption that child sexual abusers were motivated by deep-seated psychological problems or pathologies. Early treatment models were medical (castration or chemical treatments) or psychoanalytic, with later treatments focusing on behavioral and then cognitive-behavioral techniques. Understanding what types of treatment work, for whom, and in what situations is particularly important today, since many states now mandate treatment for sex offenders living under correctional care in the community.

As treatment has developed, studies of treatment efficacy have proliferated. The findings of these studies have produced varied, and often conflicting, results. This is largely the result of methodologies with varying samples (such as the types of offenders and sample size), outcome variables (such as the definition of recidivism), control group design (for example, matching controls, nonequivalent controls), type of treatment (and, relatedly, when year or decade of treatment participation), length of follow-up, and evaluator (Losel & Schmucker, 2005). However, meta-analyses of studies on treatment efficacy show that, overall, treatment significantly lowers the rate of recidivism for sex offenders albeit with moderate effect (Hanson et al., 2002; Losel & Schmucker, 2005).

This chapter discusses the development of sex offender treatment and the types of treatment programs that are most commonly in use today. It also reviews studies on treatment efficacy, both in prison and in the community, and the factors associated with a reduction in recidivism. Though studies indicate that treatment can significantly reduce recidivism, questions remain about the ethics of treatment, for whom it is most effective, and whether unique populations (for example, deniers) should also participate in treatment.

HISTORY OF TREATMENT

Experts who evaluated and treated sex offenders originally thought sexual offending was the result of individual psychopathology. As such, many of the first treatments were either medical or psychoanalytic in nature. They were based on a medical model, which implied that offending was a disease that was out of the control of the individual. At the beginning of the 20th century, Freud claimed that deviant behavior was not likely to change; if treatment through psychoanalysis was to work, it would have to be lengthy, because the deviant behavior was a deep-rooted aspect of the person (Freud, 1953).

At this same time, many habitual sexual offenders were physically castrated, and this practice continued for many years for those sexual offenders who did not respond to psychotherapy (Sturup, 1971). Castration seemed to be the most effective way to reduce the hypersexuality of the sex offenders, though it only reduced the libido and did not affect the underlying "perversion" (Sturup, 1971). Tauber (1940) also noted that castration did not seem to affect the sexuality of the adult male on a purely biological basis. Others such as Hackfield (1935) found that castration was an immediate and effective "cure" for sexual offending, though with the limitation that the treatment was not fully effective for psychotic men and/or women.

Medical treatments for sex offenders surfaced in the 1940s, when researchers began linking hormonal reactions to sexual behavior. The first hormonal treatment used was an estrogen called *stilboestrol*, in an experiment by Dunn (1940) on one incarcerated sex offender. Estrogen proved to be fairly successful at reducing deviant sexual behavior when tested on a larger sample (Foote, 1944); however, it was not widely used because of its side effects, which included vomiting, nausea, and feminization (Bowden, 1991; Bradford, 1990).

The idea that sexual offending was a medical problem continued through the 1950s, when the Fauteaux Committee in Canada stated that research should be carried out on sex offenders once they are removed from the population. In the 1960s, a number of new pharmacological treatments were developed to control sexual behavior. Some of the first studies were conducted using the tranquillizers thioridazine (Sanderson, 1960) and fluphenazine (Bartholomew, 1968), both of which caused the reduction of sexual interest in some offenders. The two most common pharmacological treatments for deviant sexual behavior— cyproterone acetate (CPA) and medroxyprogesterone acetate (MPA)—were synthesized in 1961 and 1968 respectively, and are still used by some practitioners today for "chemical castration." Other agents such as benperidol and progestogens were also developed in the 1960s, but were not as widely circulated as CPA and MPA. Antiandrogen treatments have also helped many sex offenders regulate their behavior, though they are best used in a combination of treatments that also include some form of psychological therapy (Money et al., 1975).

In the 1950s, psychological methods of treatment for sexual offenders began to change. It was German-born psychologist Hans Eysenck's criticism of traditional psychotherapy that facilitated the move toward behavioral therapy as the preferred form of psychological treatment (Marshall, Anderson, & Fernandez, 1999). Many researchers at this time believed that sexual offending resulted from deviant sexual arousal; therapeutic practices were therefore developed to modify deviant fantasies. They took various forms, such as operant conditioning (Skinner, 1953), aversion therapy (McGuire & Vallance, 1964), orgasmic reconditioning (Marquis, 1970), and shaping (Bancroft, 1971). The focus was not only on modifying serious sexual fantasies, such as those about children, but also on eliminating homosexual desires.

Many clinicians continued to utilize these behavioral techniques through the 1970s, though the research that was conducted on the efficacy of these techniques was often on small samples of patients. For example, Wijesinghe (1977) studied four male patients who were each treated with six sessions of massed electrical aversion therapy in a single day. He found that with subsequent support, all four patients showed stable treatment effects at follow-up more than 18 months after treatment. Quinsey, Bergersen, and Steinman (1976) used classical conditioning aversion therapy on 10 child sexual abusers and noted that after these techniques were used the child sexual abusers showed a marked increase in sexual preferences for adults. Quinsey (1973), who is one of the leading researchers in the use of the penile plethysmograph (PPG), discussed how penile volume is not an infallible method of predicting a child abuser's dangerousness. He stated that just because an individual undergoes aversion therapy, does not necessarily mean decreased dangerousness. Quinsey suggested at that time that much more research is needed to determine the relationship between penile volume and recidivism/dangerousness.

Behavioral models of treatment were limited in their scope and concentrated on single elements of deviant behavior. Two groups of researchers in the early 1970s—Gene Abel and his colleagues and William Marshall and his colleagues—expanded on these and made the programs multimodal in nature by adding components such as social skills training. Abel, upon recognizing the prevalence of cognitive distortions (CDs) in sex offenders, modified behavioral treatment programs so that they were cognitive-behavioral in nature to address these distortions.

In the 1980s, Pithers and colleagues adapted the therapeutic technique of relapse prevention (RP) to help sex offenders; this was said to be the most important development for sex offender research of that decade, as offenders were finally trained to recognize and manage their fantasies and behavior that could not be cured (Marshall, 1996). Other developments in the 1980s involved cognitive restructuring, victim empathy training, the refinement of sexual arousal monitoring, and an increased validity of phallometric testing (Prentky, 1994).

A significant addition to treatment in the 1990s was the use of the polygraph. The polygraph results are used only for treatment purposes, and the results are not valid in a courtroom. The primary benefit of the polygraph is that offenders tend to be truthful to the treatment providers when they know they are going to be tested on a polygraph. One study showed a significant increase in truthful admissions for both inmates and parolees by the second administration of a polygraph, though the most important result from their study is the high level of deception practiced by sex offenders (Ahlmeyer, Heil, McKee, & English, 2000). The most recent developments in treatment over the last decade involve adaptations of the RP model: the Self-Regulation and Good Lives Models of self-management, both of which emphasize positive aspects of the offenders lives as well as risk management.

The current state of understanding about the treatment of sexual offenders is that sexual offending is the result of a complex matrix of social, psychological, and developmental problems. Additionally, recent research has focused on the role of opportunity in offending, particularly in situations where abusers have developed mentoring or nurturing relationships with those whom they abuse.

"Nothing Works"

Although treatment for sex offenders has continued to develop since the 1970s, it hit many philosophical and political roadblocks at that time. The 1960s were a decade that epitomized the "rehabilitative ideal," with correctional programs for various types of offenders expanding rapidly. Many of these programs were established quickly and without adequate planning and assessment, and as a result many were not as effective as it was originally hoped they would be (Ross & McKay, 1980). The 1970s brought about a decline in this "rehabilitative ideal" for all correctional treatment programs (Andrews, Zinger et al., 1990), and the declining faith in sex offender treatment programs was consistent with these beliefs. Politicians of all parties were turning against the notion of rehabilitation; liberals felt that offenders were being coerced into treatment, and conservatives wanted retribution rather than rehabilitation for hardened criminals (Andrews, Zinger et al., 1990). Some researchers at this time were proclaiming that correctional treatment does not work (Lipton, Martinson, & Wilks, 1975; Martinson, 1974; Wilks & Martinson, 1976). Other researchers (Chaneles, 1976; Hallack & White, 1977; Serrill, 1975; Smith & Berlin, 1977), led by Palmer (1975), analyzed the treatment regimes and rash judgments made by those dubbed as the "nothing works" theorists and claimed that treatment *does* work for some individuals. Many agreed that "the effectiveness of correctional rehabilitation is dependent upon what is delivered to whom in particular settings" (Andrews, Zinger et al., 1990, p. 372). Gendreau and Ross (1979) considered the biggest problem with the efficacy debate to be the lack of objectivity from the researchers who were arguing their points, describing those from the differing disciplines as "strangers trying to communicate in different languages by raising their voices." In defending the notion that rehabilitation can work, he said that "the 'nothing works' belief reduced to its most elementary level suggests that criminal offenders are incapable of relearning or acquiring new behavior. Why should this strange learning block be restricted to this population?" (Gendreau & Ross, 1979, p. 465).

In the 1980s, there was an increased acceptance of rehabilitative beliefs, yet criticism still existed. Several researchers (Furby, Weinrott, & Blackshaw, 1989; Walker, 1989; Whitehead & Lab, 1989) produced critical evaluations of treatment efficacy, concluding that no data existed to show that treatment could be effective. These researchers failed to take into consideration the methodological problems of the studies they were evaluating (Marques, Day, Nelson, & West, 1994). Other researchers who did take these problems into consideration proclaimed that positive results have been produced through multimodal cognitive-behavioral programs (Andrews, Zinger et al., 1990; Marques, Day et al., 1994; Marshall & Barbaree, 1990b).

Professionalization of Treatment

The 1980s also saw the rise in the professionalization of treatment for sex offenders. Not only was research increasing exponentially at this time, but researchers and practitioners also created the first professional association specific to this population. In 1984, the first version of the Association for the Treatment of Sexual Abusers (ATSA) was formed (formerly called ABTSA, Association for the Behavioral Treatment of Sexual Aggressives).

ATSA is a nonprofit organization, whose members include scholars and practitioners who work with and/or study sexual abusers. ATSA facilitates the exchange of information for scholars and practitioners through its annual conferences, Listserves, newsletters, and the academic journal *Sexual Abuse: A Journal of Research and Treatment*. ATSA also publishes standards and guidelines for practitioners who treat sexual offenders, which are evidence based and provide information about the best practices in evaluating and treating sexual offenders (Murphy, McGrath, & Christopher, 2008).

The ATSA website provides an overview of the history of the organization (see http://www.atsa.com/atsaHis.html). Jim Haaven, one of the founding members of ATSA, states that these founders were "a group of people with a common interest and need to learn more about sex offending issues, realizing we knew little to nothing, willing and able to be curious, collaborative, and inclusive of ideas and opinions." Roger Little, another founding member, is quoted as saying: "I might add, almost everything we thought we knew at that [first] meeting has proved to be not true." Similarly, Ron Langevin, the founding editor of *Sexual Abuse*, commented on the need for more information about the population of sexual offenders in his opening editorial in 1988. Langevin (1988, pp. 5–6) stated,

> Child sexual abuse is also a deep concern at present, in part, a response to the efforts of Women's Rights groups and changing social legislation requiring professionals to report abuse of children. On many important questions, we lack information.... Sex offenders against children and women have also received limited research attention. The bulk of treatments for the offenders have been tried out on homosexual men.

There is little convincing evidence that these methods are effective at rehabilitating sex offenders. New directions are being explored to help them to adjust to their sexual anomaly and to prevent relapse.

Although treatment programs were rapidly expanding and scholarly research on sexual offending and treatment had developed substantially by the mid-1980s, rigorous research had yet to be done with this population. Little was known at that time about the efficacy of different types of treatment programs, or the best ways in which to assess the risks and needs of the offenders who participated.

ASSESSMENT FOR TREATMENT

In order for the treatment of sex offenders to be effective at reducing recidivism, treatment providers must be able to accurately assess the risks and needs of the offenders (Andrews, Zinger et al., 1990; Glaser, 1974; Gleuck & Gleuck, 1950; O'Connell, Leberg, & Donaldson, 1990; Perkins, 1991; Ross & Gendreau, 1980). Studies have shown that inappropriate matching of risks and needs can actually increase recidivism among offenders (Andrews, Bonta, & Hoge, 1990).

There are various components to a thorough evaluation of sex offenders prior to treatment. According to the ATSA (2005) guidelines, the evaluator should use multiple sources of information in the evaluation. A thorough evaluation of the sex offender before treatment would include, when appropriate: a completed investigation of the background of the offender, based on an interview with the offender; a review any available official documents (for example, police records, victim statements); and interviews with those who know the offender (for example, family members, employers); physiological testing; psychometric testing; and actuarial testing. ATSA (2005) also cautions that the evaluator should be trained for any of the evaluations that are given, or should rely on someone who is trained, and should be aware of the special needs of unique populations (for example, developmentally disabled, non-English speaking).

Background Information

Treatment can only be effective if the treatment providers know the full nature of sexual thoughts, feelings, and behaviors of the offenders. As such, they should conduct extensive background checks of the offenders' histories (ATSA, 2005; O'Connell et al., 1990). A client interview is important, particularly to note whether and how the offenders' accounts of their behavior differ from official documentation on the offenses. In checking records to validate the offender's history, the evaluator should ideally review criminal justice documents (particularly police reports and presentence investigation reports), victim statements, and any past treatment or medical records (ATSA, 2005; Longo, 1983).

An important variable in risk assessment is the offender's past criminal history, particularly if the crimes are of a violent or a sexual nature (Hanson &

Bussiere, 1996; Mair & Stevens, 1994; Marshall & Eccles, 1991; Nicholaichuk, 1996; Scully, 1990); and some researchers have found that offenders who have at least two past violent offenses are at the highest risk of reoffense. Also important is whether there are discrepancies between the offenders' accounts of their behavior and official records. Any denial or minimization of behavior should be addressed in the treatment process.

Physiological Testing

Physiological tests should be conducted, when appropriate, to measure the level of deviant sexual arousal in offenders. The primary way in which this is done is through a PPG, though it can be measured through a psychophysiological hand monitor or a volumetric phallometer. The offenders are shown various images of adults, children and objects, some sexual and some control, and their level of sexual arousal is measured. One common assessment system for such an evaluation is the Abel Screening Tool (Abel, Lawry, Karlstrom, Osborn, & Gillespie, 1994), where offenders must answer a questionnaire and rank slides on their level of erotic arousal while their responses are being physiologically measured.

Though the PPG is an important tool in measuring sexual arousal patterns, it alone is not sufficient as an evaluation instrument. When offenders are assessed with a PPG, they are exposed to erotic stimuli, and it is difficult to identify deviant sexual attraction through reaction to erotic images alone. Rapists often show equal arousal to consenting and nonconsenting sex, and many "normal" individuals show some level of arousal to inappropriate stimuli (for example, erotic pictures of children) (Marshall & Eccles, 1991). Unless the offender is sadistic or has a high level of fixation with children, it is often difficult to differentiate between "normal" and "deviant" arousal patterns. Second, not all sexual offenders are driven by sexual needs, and the arousal patterns will not explain much about why the offender sexually offends. As Marshall and Eccles (1991, p. 256) state, the most important element in a rape is not the deviant sexual arousal but rather the frame of mind of the offender at the time of the act. This is also true for regressed child sexual abusers, who are primarily attracted to agemates but have abused children; they rarely show arousal patterns that are different from the general population of males.

Psychometric and Actuarial Testing

A thorough pretreatment assessment of sex offenders should include a battery of psychometric tests to assess variables such as intelligence, psychopathology, personality, social attitudes, morality, respect for others, and the presence of negative emotional states (ATSA, 2005; West, 1987). Psychologists use a variety of personality inventories to assess sex offenders, as well as actuarial assessments to evaluate the risk of the offenders (discussed in detail in Chapter 10). The most common large-scale personality inventories used for this purpose are the Minnesota Multiphasic Personality Inventory (MMPI) and the Millon Clinical Multiaxial Inventor

(MCMI). Both assess the presence of personality traits and symptoms of psychopathology. The MMPI measures general personality and symptom domains, while the MCMI measures Axis I and Axis II disorders.

In addition to the general personality inventories, clinicians have developed numerous evaluative instruments that are devoted to measuring traits specific to sexual offending. An example of this type of assessment is the Multiphasic Sex Inventory (MSI), which measures sexual cognitions. Others assessments distinguish between different types of offenders. For example, Knight, Prentky, and Cerce (1994) constructed the Multidimensional Assessment of Sex and Aggression (MASA), which differentiates between rapist subtypes. Another example comes from Hillbrand and Waite (1994), who developed the Experience Sampling Method (ESM) to measure thoughts and their relations to mood states. They constructed the ESM because they claimed that most psychometric tests were inadequate at addressing psychological determinants (for example, fantasies, defenses, and mood states) and how they interact with environmental determinants (for example, precipitating stressors, victim availability, and disinhibitors).

Though these evaluation instruments can be useful, clinicians should also use actuarial assessments to evaluate offenders' risk levels. The most common risk assessment instruments are the Sex Offender Risk Appraisal Guide (SORAG), Rapid Risk Assessment of Sexual Offense Recidivism (RRASOR), Static-99 (and the revised Static-99R and Static-2002), the Minnesota Sex Offender Screening Tool-Revised (MnSOSTR), the Violence Risk Appraisal Guide (VRAG), and the Psychopathy Checklist-Revised (PCL-R). These instruments can be used to assess the risk of offenders based upon the stable characteristics (those that are stable over time) and dynamic characteristics (those factors that change) of the offenders. As with the assessment of risk in the community, the most common risk assessment tool for treatment is the Static-99.

TYPES OF TREATMENTS

There are various types of treatment available for sex offenders today. These can be delivered to offenders who are living in the community or incapacitated. The treatment format may be group therapy, individual therapy, or as a combination of the above. This section provides information about the most common types of treatments, how they are delivered, for whom, and in what settings.

Cognitive-Behavioral Treatment

Cognitive-behavioral programs are the most common form of treatment for sex offenders today. The goals of cognitive-behavioral programs are to have the offenders achieve the following:

> recognize their problems and behaviors;

> and the feelings that led to their deviant behavior;

> and eventually eliminate their CDs;

- Accept responsibility for their behavior;
- Reevaluate their attitudes and behaviors;
- Acquire prosocial expressions of sexuality;
- Gain a higher level of social competence;
- Be able to identify their high-risk situations; and
- Understand the repetitive nature of their behavior and be able to break the sequence of offending.

Many treatment programs in the community are ATSA certified, meaning that they follow a specific cognitive-behavioral regime developed by researchers in the field (see http://www.atsa.com for more details). According to ATSA guidelines, cognitive-behavioral treatment programs should address RP knowledge and skills, cognitive restructuring, empathy enhancement, interpersonal skill training, emotional management, and sexual arousal control (ATSA, 2005). Despite the general agreement that cognitive-behavioral treatment is the most effective way in which to treat sex offenders, researchers are continually assessing treatment components and addressing ways in which treatment can improve. For example, researchers have recommended that treatment providers should reassess the purposes of and ways in which they address CDs (Mann & Shingler, 2006), enhancing victim empathy (Wastell et al., 2009), and RP (Ward & Hudson, 2000). That said, the overall issues addressed in cognitive-behavioral programs are unlikely to change, even as we learn more about who can be successfully treated and through what processes.

Targeted Areas of Treatment Many sex offenders lack victim empathy, and as such this is a critical part of most treatment programs (Wastell, Cairns, & Haywood, 2009). Empathy is "the capacity to perceive another's perspective, to recognize affective arousal within oneself and to base compassionate behavioral responses on the motivation induced by these precepts" (Pithers, 1994, p. 565). The empathy deficits of sex offenders may result from the lack of intimate relationships (Ward, Hudson, Marshall, & Siegert, 1995) or the sexual offender's inability to attribute appropriate thoughts and feelings to others (Keenan & Ward, 2000). According to Keenan and Ward (2000), some sex offenders lack the awareness and understanding of others' beliefs, needs, and particular perspectives. These broad deficits lead to more specific deficits in intimacy, empathy, and cognition. In her study, Scully (1990) found that 54 percent of rapists felt nothing toward their victims at the time of the offense, and Langevin, Wright, and Handy (1988) found a positive correlation between denial and empathy scores. One goal of sex offender treatment programs is therefore to make offenders understand the consequences of sexual abuse for their victims (Abel & Rouleau, 1995; Marshall, 1996).

Some cognitive-behavioral programs utilize a system of role-playing to induce empathy in offenders, since some sex offenders respond better to concrete rather than abstract tactics (Groth, 1983). In this method of therapy, the offender acts out the role of his victim(s) while the treatment providers or other members of the group take the role of the offender. Through the physical act of playing the role of the victim, the offender is often able to understand for the first time the amount of fear that he instilled in the victim at the time of the attack and the subsequent harm that was caused.

Despite the prominent role that victim empathy training takes in cognitive-behavioral treatment, studies are mixed about the efficacy. Even when sex offenders show increased empathy as a result of the treatment, this does not necessarily lead to a reduction in recidivism (Wastell et al., 2009). Wastell et al. (2009) noted that while treatment may improve offenders' scores on measures of empathy, it does not necessarily improve the ability for offenders to recognize affective cues in other people.

Sex offender treatment should also help offenders to better understand appropriate, prosocial sexual behavior, from general sex education to arousal reconditioning. Some sex offenders are raised in sexually dysfunctional homes and thus lack an understanding of normal sexual behavior (Saunders-Wilson, 1992). They may also suffer from sexual dysfunctions (for example, premature ejaculation) that, when in conjunction with other predisposing and triggering factors, may lead them to commit a sexual offense (West, 1987). As such, general sexual education is an important part of many cognitive-behavioral treatment programs.

For those offenders who fantasize about inappropriate sexual stimuli—whether children, violence, or situations of power and control—treatment can help to recondition their arousal patterns. The treatment provider teaches the offenders how to retrain their sexual fantasies, usually through classical conditioning, with negative consequences occurring when the offender experiences deviant thoughts. The treatment provider may use smelling salts (Marshall, 1996) or other devices such as rubber bands (the offenders put the bands around their wrists and snap them when a deviant thought occurs). Arousal reconditioning requires the cooperation of the offender, because unless the offender is aroused by known stimuli and arousal rates are recorded on a PPG, the offender knows if he is having inappropriate fantasies.

Although it is necessary for sex offenders to redirect their inappropriate sexual interests toward appropriate adult channels, they are not able to maintain proper social relationships without also improving their social skills. Lack of social competence increases the likelihood of offending behavior by blocking legal sexual outlets. Until offenders acquire appropriate conversational skills, living skills, and use of leisure time, they are likely to experience anxiety in adult relationships (Marshall & Barbaree, 1990b). The three sets of social skills in which sex offenders are generally deficient include *decoding skills*, or the interpretation of situations and other people's behavior; *decision skills*, or considering possible responses to situations and choosing the best option; and *enactment skills*, where the decided response is carried out (Marshall & Eccles, 1991, p. 250). Without prosocial attitudes and expressions of sexuality, it is probable that offenders will experience negative emotional states such as stress, anger, and loneliness. Strategies for controlling negative emotional states are included in most group processes in addition to the social skills training, as these states may act as triggering factors for deviant sexual behavior and offenders must learn how to effectively deal with such emotions. Negative emotional states are also commonly experienced prior to relapse, and as such are targeted in the treatment process.

Arguably, one of the most critical stages of treatment is RP. RP is defined as a "maintenance-oriented self-control program that teaches sex offenders how to determine if they are entering into high-risk situations, self-destructive behavior, deviant cycle patterns, and potential reoffenses" (Alaska Department of Corrections Offender Programs, 1996, p. 5). This strategy for maintaining treatment-induced changes was originally developed as a model for controlling substance abuse, and was later adapted by Pithers, Marques, Gibat, and Marlatt (1983) to address deviant sexual behavior. RP teaches offenders how to interrupt the succession of events that lead to the commission of sexual offenses over time and across situations, and requires offenders to analyze the factors that have previously led them to commit offenses. Upon determining what constitutes a high-risk situation for the offenders, they are then taught coping strategies and given general instructions on problem-solving procedures so that they can devise their own avoidance strategies upon termination of treatment.

The role of the treatment provider is to help develop realistic expectations for the offenders regarding their fantasies and behaviors. Offenders are taught that if they experience a *lapse* (fantasy or initial occurrence of sexually deviant behavior), it will not necessarily lead to a *relapse* (performance of and complete return to pattern of sexually deviant behavior) (Pithers et al., 1983). Pithers explains that a relapse usually occurs after the offender makes a series of "seemingly irrelevant decisions" (SIDs). An SID is a minor decision that is relatively harmless on its own, but several SIDs can lead to an offense. For example, a child sexual abuser will not necessarily commit an offense if he drives past a school; however, this is an SID because it is the first in a series of decisions that may put the offender at risk of committing an offense.

There are a number of factors that can trigger a relapse, and these are similar to the factors that help cause the original instance of offending behavior. Most commonly, relapses are triggered by negative emotional states—in Pither's study, 75 percent of relapses were precipitated by negative moods and feelings such as anger and depression (Pithers et al., 1983). These emotional states can lead to fantasies or cause an offender to act upon fantasies that he has already been having. If RP strategies are successful, then the offender's perception of self-control should be maintained until a high-risk situation occurs. Upon reaching such a situation, the offender will increase his self-confidence if he copes successfully with the situation and will similarly feel a sense of failure and helplessness if he is unsuccessful. RP should help offenders to maintain the changes that have been induced by other components of the treatment programs, providing offenders with "cognitive and behavioral skills that will reduce the probability of another offense" (Pithers et al., 1983, p. 239).

Despite its proliferation in treatment programs throughout the 1980s and 1990s, some researchers have become critical of the traditional RP model and have proposed alternative strategies for understanding and managing sexual behavior. The two most notable alternative theoretical models are the Self-Regulation

Model and the Good Lives Model (Lindsay et al., 2007). The Self-Regulation Model takes into consideration both internal and external processes that allow offenders to achieve goal-oriented behaviors over time and in various contexts (Laws & Ward, 2006). This model consists of nine phases: (1) life event, (2) desire for offensive sex, (3) goals for sexual offending, (4) planning strategy, (5) high-risk situation, (6) lapse, (7) sexual offense, (8) evaluation, and (9) attitude to future offending (Laws & Ward, 2006, pp. 247–251). Ward and Stewart (2003) proposed the Good Lives Model (later updated to the Good Lives Model – Comprehensive; Ward & Gannon, 2006), which is based on the premise that sexual offenders seek to attain basic goals (for example, family, employment, community, personal well-being) as part of a "good lives" plan to achieving a well-balanced life. However, they often try to fulfill these goals through the commission of harmful behavior toward others. Treatment, then, is geared toward helping the offenders develop the skills to achieve these goals in prosocial ways. Both the Self-Regulation and Good Lives Models have shown positive outcomes in assessment studies, though more thorough evaluation should be conducted to fully understand their impact.

The Group Treatment Process   Most cognitive-behavioral programs are conducted through group processes, called by some the "cornerstone of therapy" (Hagan et al., 1994). There are two main reasons for this: namely, that peer confrontation tends to be the most effective way to overcome CDs (Marshall et al., 1999), and it is the most cost-effective form of treatment when resources are limited (Houston et al., 1995). Group therapeutic sessions generally address both *offense-specific targets* (for example, denial and minimization, victim harm and empathy, deviant sexual fantasies, distorted attitudes, beliefs, and perceptions, and RP) and *offense-related targets* (for example, anger management, social skills, assertiveness training, life management skills, marital therapy, and substance abuse therapy) (Marshall, 1996).

Group treatment processes are effective in many areas of psychotherapy, and sex offender treatment is no exception. Peer confrontation may be helpful in making sex offenders admit their offenses and acknowledge responsibility for their offenses—two main goals of treatment. According to Yalom's (1985) general psychotherapeutic framework for group processes, group therapy sessions develop in stages. Houston et al. (1995) have described the three stages of group treatment programs for sex offenders, utilizing Yalom's framework, as the initial stage, the stage of conflict, and the cohesive stage. In the initial stage, the offenders search for similarities—between themselves and their problems—and establish a hierarchy within the group. There is a struggle at this time to establish roles, and there is a search for approval with each other and with the treatment providers. The second stage consists of a competition for dominance among the group members, as well as feelings of hostility toward the treatment providers and attempts to sidetrack from the actual topic of treatment. The third stage is one of cohesion, the point at which the group will finally be able to achieve work without distraction. Although they have noted other issues involved with group processes, it is these stages that have appeared consistently in various types of group therapy.

In addition to the stages of treatment that take place in group processes, each individual offender also experiences distinct stages of change. Prochaska and DiClemente (1982) described five stages of change that the offender may encounter, although all stages are not necessarily experienced by all individuals. The first stage is *precontemplation*, where the offender can be classified as a "denier." He does not yet acknowledge that he has a problem, and he is defensive and unmotivated to change. The second stage is one of *contemplation*, where the offender acknowledges that a problem does exist yet minimizes the problem or the extent of damage that has resulted from the problem. The third stage is *preparation*, where the offender recognizes the significance of his problem and is finally motivated to change his behavior. The fourth stage is one of *action*, where he participates in the treatment program in an effort to change his behavior. The fifth stage is one of *maintenance*, where change is consistently sustained upon termination of the program. In applying these stages of change to the sex offender, Kear-Colwell and Pollock (1997) have also added a sixth stage to this process: *relapse*. When the offender is unable to sustain change and "slips" into deviant fantasies and subsequently deviant action, he relapses and returns to either the precontemplation or the contemplation stage of change.

Group processes are particularly important for offenders in these first two stages of change. Most sex offenders at first deny or minimize their offenses to some extent, and studies have shown that offenders do exhibit a gradual change throughout the treatment process in the amount of information that they are willing to reveal about themselves (Perkins, 1991). Marshall (1994) examined a treatment program for offenders who deny or minimize their offenses, showing how denial can be overcome in a group treatment context. In this study, the offenders had to disclose the nature and extent of their offenses in detail to the group, including thoughts, feelings, and emotional states. The role of the treatment provider was only to explain what the disclosures revealed, while it was the group's task to encourage and/or challenge the offender who was speaking. In addition, the treatment provider had to distinguish for the group the difference between the crime and the offender—the offender himself is not heinous even though he committed heinous crimes. It was found that when the offenders were encouraged and treated with respect, their self-confidence increased and they were more likely to admit their offenses.

There are two ways in which group treatment processes can be conducted: through confrontational or motivational approaches (Miller & Rollnick, 1991). The *confrontational approach* aggressively challenges offenders about their behavior in an effort to overcome denial, rationalizations, and deceit, and it does so by disempowering the offender and putting the responsibility of change with the treatment provider. It encourages self-labeling and attacks the self-image and self-esteem of the offenders, which can cause some to take up a position of "psychological reactance"—they argue for their position of not having a problem rather than taking the responsibility to change the problem (Brehm & Brehm, 1981; Kear-Colwell & Pollock, 1997; Miller & Rollnick, 1991). As a result, some researchers have argued strongly against taking a confrontational approach in treatment (Fernandez, 2006).

In opposition to the confrontational approach, the *motivational approach* leaves the responsibility to change with the offender. The treatment provider does so by creating "cognitive dissonance," or a psychological discomfort that acts as a motivator for the offender to change (Miller & Rollnick, 1991). Some researchers believe that the motivational approach is best when working with deniers, as it encourages them to consider changing their behavior rather than staying in the precontemplation stage of denial (Garland & Dougher, 1991; Kear-Colwell & Pollock, 1997). Fernandez (2006) also encourages the use of positive language in the treatment session and the focus on positive goals, with an understanding of the offenders' strengths.

MEDICAL TREATMENT

Some sex offenders are offered pharmacological treatment in lieu of, or in addition to, cognitive-behavioral treatment. The purpose of these pharmacological treatments, which are usually injections of antiandrogens, is to reduce the sexual drive of the offenders and, subsequently, their sexually offending behavior. As stated previously, the first hormonal treatment used to control deviant sexual behavior was estrogen. Although not in use for long, it was beneficial in showing researchers that hormonal treatments were capable of decreasing levels of sexual drive. It also became clear to the researchers who used estrogen that side effects may occur with some individuals using hormonal treatments. One hormonal treatment used today is CPA, which works as an antiandrogen and antigonadotrophin to reduce sexual drive (Bowden, 1991). Several studies have shown positive effects from the use of CPA, both in Europe and in North America (Marshall & Eccles, 1991), including reductions in ejaculate, erections, and sexual fantasies. Despite its apparent successes in these areas, CPA, as well as a similar hormonal treatment called ethinyl estradiol, does not seem to have any effect on sexual fantasy or erectile responses outside of experimental situations, and it does not necessarily reduce sexual aggression (Bowden, 1991; Bradford, 1990). As for side effects, CPA can cause depression, breast enlargement, increased weight, and osteoporosis; however, these effects are limited and usually occur after years of treatment. In a case study of the effects of MPA, one pedophile who had been treated over a period of four years was diagnosed with Cushing's Syndrome and adrenal insufficiency (Krueger, Hembree, & Hill, 2006). There are, however, alternatives to MPA that may have similar beneficial effects, such as gonadotropin-releasing hormone agonists.

The most common hormonal agent used to control sexual deviancy is MPA, which is administered in weekly doses to reduce serum testosterone levels. Also referred to as *Depo-Provera*, this hormonal agent causes a temporary "chemical" castration for the length of time it is used (Solicitor General of Canada, 1990). Although it causes reversible testicular atrophy, there are ethical considerations with its use as well as questions about the long-term benefits for those who cease taking the weekly doses. Studies have produced conflicting results as to the effects of Depo-Provera years after treatment ends. Two early studies reported that it has many beneficial effects, including decreased frequency of erections, reduced sexual drive, and reduced orgasm rates, which continued for several years upon cessation of treatment in some patients (Blumer & Migeon, 1975; Money, Wiedeking, Walker, & Gain, 1976). Another study, however, showed that almost all of those who terminated the doses of Depo-Provera against medical advice relapsed, as did a small number of patients who were still taking doses of the hormonal agent (Berlin & Meinecke, 1981). Research has shown that it does have positive effects for most offenders who comply with the treatment protocol, and because it is administered through weekly injections, its compliance can be documented (Berlin, 1989). Still, some offenders will prematurely end treatment, saying they are "cured," thus potentially bringing about adverse consequences. Though sexual drive can be measured during treatment through blood tests (measuring serum testosterone levels), self-ratings, or with penile plethysmographs, when treatment has ended, the benefits are often only measurable through reconviction rates (Bowden, 1991).

Pharmacological treatments are generally offered to paraphiliacs, particularly pedophiles, rather than rapists or child sexual abusers such as intrafamilial offenders who do not experience intense sexual urges. The function of pharmacological treatments is to reduce sexual drive, and as such they are generally helpful for sexual offenders who have difficulty resisting their strong sexual urges without such treatment. The use of these drugs, however, is limited without additional psychological treatments. For example, antiandrogens and antigonadotrophins can reduce sexual drive but not nonsexual violence, and they cannot change the types of sexual urges (Bowden, 1991). Additionally, there are difficulties to administering pharmacological treatments to incarcerated offenders. There is a requirement for the indefinite continuation of treatment, and it is unclear whether there will be any benefits for offenders who terminate usage prematurely. Also, informed consent is necessary for pharmacological treatments, and because they are likely to be offered only in exchange for parole or reduced sentences, it is assumed that consent will not always be entirely voluntary (Bradford, 1990).

Another medical treatment offered to sex offenders is physical castration, though it is now rare for this to be offered even when offenders request the procedure. Despite the fact that castration dramatically reduces the circulating testosterone (the hormonal effect that induces sexual drive), the effects of castration are not complete. Many offenders who have been castrated stayed sexually active for a while after the surgical procedure (Heim, 1981). Because of the numerous ethical problems associated with physical castration, it is more common for chemical castration to be offered through the use of Depo-Provera. Some researchers encourage the use of hormonal treatment, saying that it effectively reduces sexual drive and that compliance can be monitored (Bowden, 1991). There are, however, problems with hormonal treatments; it is suggested that even though testosterone is the main contributor to sexual arousability and functioning, it is not the only contributor (Bradford, 1990; Perkins, 1991). Therefore, chemical castration, which affects serum testosterone levels, may reduce but not eliminate the problem of sexual aggression.

Pharmacological treatment is controversial; sex offenders under the care of correctional authorities in some states are denied this treatment, whereas other states make it mandatory in order for offenders to be released. Inappropriate sexual behavior may be the result of a biological drive in some individuals, and as such medical treatment may help to suppress intense urges. Nonetheless, there are ethical considerations with its use as well as questions about the long-term benefits for those who cease taking the weekly doses. As such, the mandated use of this chemical is questionable except in serious cases driven by physiological needs.

California was the first state to require mandatory chemical castration for offenders convicted of two or more predatory sexual offenses. After one sexual offense, this is an optional treatment that will allow the offender to serve his sentence in the community rather than in prison. Several other states have since enacted laws that allow for the discretionary use of Depo-Provera for sex offenders living in the community. To date only one follow-up study has been published on the efficacy of pharmacological treatments based on this legislation, which was passed in Oregon in 1999. Maletzky, Tolan, and McFarlaned (2006) evaluated the recidivism rates of 275 men within three groups: those who were evaluated to need MPA who eventually went on to actually receive it; men recommended to receive MPA who, for a variety of reasons, did not receive the medication; and men deemed not to need MPA. They found that the men who received treatment were significantly less likely to recidivate, particularly in regard to sexual offenses. Thus, initial studies indicate a positive effect, but more studies would have to be done to discern for which types of offenders this is effective.

Community versus Prison Treatment

Once convicted, sex offenders are likely to serve part, if not all, of their sentence in the community. One condition of a community sentence is almost always that the offenders participate in a treatment program. As such, sex offender-specific treatment programs are available in many communities in the United States. Most correctional institutions will also offer some form of treatment to sex offenders, though these programs are less likely to be sex offender-specific and are more likely to focus on offense-related factors such as anger management or substance abuse. With the increase in sex offenders being incarcerated, however, some prisons have established sex offender-specific treatment programs.

Prison and community-based treatment programs establish the same goals for sex offenders. However, treatment providers face practical problems in prison that are not present in the community. Examples of such problems include difficulties in securing treatment rooms, getting prisoners unlocked at a particular time, continual interruption, and fitting the treatment program into the prison regime (Houston et al., 1995). Some researchers say that treatment works best in the community, for the reasons listed, and because offenders in prison are not subject to the environmental triggers that are present in the community (Kear-Colwell & Pollock, 1997; West, 1985). Others say that all treatment programs vary, whether they are outpatient or institutional (Marshall & Barbaree,

1990b), and that, overall, treatment programs in prison are as effective as those in the community (Marshall & Eccles, 1991). It is important to offer offenders the option of treatment in prison, as one researcher states that "if one enters prison because of an inability to cope successfully with a sexual orientation directed towards children, in most cases there is little reason to believe that prison alone will alter that situation" (Berlin, 1989, p. 234).

One problem with institutional treatment programs is that the offenders are rarely followed up with long-term supervision and maintenance upon release from prison. There tends to be little communication among the various organizations about what treatment has occurred, and what is still needed for each offender. The lack of communication extends to the prisons themselves, as the institutions rarely communicate with each other about what aspects of treatment are most effective and upon whom, and what programs are being run where. There are no uniform prison treatment programs run federally or on a statewide basis in the United States. In Canada, there are some excellent prison treatment programs offered in Ontario, and there is a multisite, uniform treatment program at a number of prisons across England and Wales called the *Sex Offender Treatment Programme*. See "The Sex Offender Treatment Programme", below, for more information about that program.

Some states, such as Minnesota, Colorado, and Washington, have established treatment programs in prison and they continue to provide resources for offenders after their release. Evaluating programs in Minnesota, Duwe, and Goldman (2009) found that prison-based treatment programs produced a significant, but modest, reduction in sexual recidivism rates. They also found that the programs were similarly effective for a variety of offenders, including adult rapists and child sexual abusers as well as for those who abused children they knew and strangers. This is similar to the findings of international studies of sex offender treatment programs in prison. O'Reilly et al. (2010) evaluated a treatment program in prison in Ireland and found that program participants showed statistically significant improvement on some but not all self-report measures of CDs, empathy, interpersonal skills, self-regulation, and RP.

VIGNETTE

The Sex Offender Treatment Programme

Most cognitive-behavioral treatment programs in the United States follow general guidelines, as set out by ATSA. However, each program is unique and designed as per the needs of the population. In England, however, there is a uniform treatment program in 25 prisons called the Sex Offender Treatment Programme (SOTP). This program is an example of how to establish and run a multisite treatment program for all types of sex offenders is a variety of prisons.

In 1990, one of the most serious riots in the history of British prisons occurred at HMP Strangeways, which houses numerous sex offenders. The riot provoked an inquiry into prison conditions, and as a result Lord Woolf, a prominent British judge, offered recommendations on the reevaluation of sex offenders' situations in prison.

At this time, sex offenders were segregated from the general prison population for their own protection and, though some incarcerated sex offenders were offered treatment, the treatment was erratic and there was no continuity or consistency in the programs (Programme Development Section, 1997a). Lord Woolf recognized sex offenders as constituting "a group with special needs," believing that it is the responsibility of the prison to provide regimes that are not damaging for the prisoners (Prison Reform Trust, 1990, p. 24). As a result of his report, the Criminal Justice Act, passed in 1991, increased the demands on the prison and the probation services to better provide for sex offenders, stating that "without treatment, they are likely to leave prison as dangerous, if not more dangerous, than when they entered and highly likely to reoffend" (Guy, 1992, p. 2). The number of sex offenders in British prisons increased nearly 300 percent from 1980 to 1990 (Grubin & Thornton, 1994), a rate similar to that of the United States. This increase led to heightened interventions and expectations that prisons should be capable of treating sex offenders before they are released into society (Guy, 1992).

The prison service developed its national initiative based on evidence of effective treatment programs in Canada. Dr. William Marshall, an expert on treatment for sex offenders, helped them to establish a cognitive-behavioral treatment program for sex offenders who were incarcerated. It was geared toward offenders who were assessed to be a high risk to the community upon release. High-risk offenders were those who exhibited three or more of the following characteristics: having four or more convictions of any kind, any previous conviction for a sex offense, a current conviction of a sex offense against three or more victims, a current or previous conviction for a nonsexual assault, and a current sentence of at least four years (Grubin & Thornton, 1994). The SOTP follows exclusionary guidelines similar to those used by Marques and her colleagues at the Atascadero State Hospital (Marques, Nelson et al., 1994), including that offenders who suffer from an acute mental illness, have an IQ below 80, risk self-injury, suffer from severe paranoia or personality disorder, have chronic brain damage, or are for some other reason unsuitable medically are not eligible to participate in SOTP (Clarke, 1997).

All prisons with the SOTP follow a strictly structured program. The main, or Core, program addresses offense-specific targets, or the primary issues common to most sex offenders, whereas an Extended Program addresses offense-related targets, such as intimacy, marital, and relationship problems. There is also a Booster Program, which acts as a refresher course for those offenders who are serving long sentences. Its main function is to reinforce the understanding of RP strategies for offenders who participated in treatment well before their release dates. A fourth supplementary program has been introduced for those who deny their offenses. A fifth supplementary program is an adapted version of the Core Program and has been established for those who are learning disabled and require different communication methods from the verbal and written communications utilized in the Core Program.

The treatment providers, or tutors, are drawn from all disciplines within the prison system. Though there is a general assumption that treatment providers are clinicians with years of psychological training, the SOTP employs multidisciplinary teams comprised mainly of lay treatment providers—often corrections officers in the prison. These multidisciplinary teams have shown to be as effective in group work as those with all professionals, as the importance lies in the personal qualities of the tutors rather than their education (Mann & Thornton, 1997). There are three tutors assigned to work with each treatment group, with at least one being male and one being female. Those who have recently completed the training course are teamed with more experienced tutors, and, when possible, there is at least one tutor with a professional background on each group.

As with all studies of treatment efficacy, program evaluations have been mixed but show encouraging results. Short-term evaluation studies have shown that treatment is effective for some individuals, yet change was greatest with high-risk offenders to whom treatment risks and needs were matched. In one study that measured change in rapists only, 11 of the 22 variables analyzed showed significant change; however, all but one of the variables changed at least slightly in a positive direction (Bowers, 1996). Beech, Fisher and Beckett (1998) found that sex offenders who participated in the SOTP showed improvements in nearly all dynamic risk factors. Many of the offenders showed change not only through the psychometric tests that were administered but also through their actions in the prison as observed by the prison officers (Beech et al., 1998; Clark, 1996). A two-year follow-up of 647 released offenders indicated that treated offenders had significantly lower recidivism rates than untreated offenders (Friendship, Mann, & Beech, 2003). To date, no long-term, methodologically rigorous studies have been conducted on the SOTP. It does, however, show promise in modeling a sex offender treatment program in prison.

Questions
1. Would it be possible to establish a multisite, uniform treatment program in the United States? What would be the obstacles to doing so?
2. What are the benefits and problems with having correctional officers as treatment providers?
3. What would be the best way to evaluate the efficacy of the SOTP?

VARIABLES AND CONTROVERSIES
WITH TREATMENT

Despite the positive outcomes of many sex offender treatment programs, which are discussed in the next section, there are several controversial issues in regard to who participates in programs, who serves as treatment providers, in what contexts the treatment takes place, and under what conditions the offenders agree to participate. Ethical questions arise, such as whether treatment is truly voluntary and whether certain offenders can and should be excluded from participation. Some researchers have even gone as far as to say treatment is in itself punishment. Not only are these issues philosophically important, but they can also affect the treatment outcome. In particular, outcome may vary depending on the risk level of the offenders (and whether treatment matches the risks and needs of the participants); individual characteristics, including personality traits, such as psychopathy levels, and motivation to participate; and the treatment itself, including the therapeutic climate of the group, the composition of the group, and treatment provider characteristics (Harkins & Beech, 2007b; Marshsall & Moulden, 2006).

Ethics of Sex Offender Treatment

Cognitive-behavioral treatment programs, sometimes in combination with medical treatment, may help reduce the recidivism of sex offenders. However, some researchers (Birgden & Cucolo, 2011; Glaser, 2009) have argued that treatment programs for sex offenders are unethical as offered today. Glaser (2009) states that sex offender treatment providers breach ethical principles by putting the interest of the community ahead of the well-being of the sex offenders, restricting confidentiality, and coercing offenders into treatment. He has concluded that treatment programs have in essence become punishment for the offenders, and calls treatment providers agents of social control (Glaser, 2010). Birgden and Cucolo (2011) have also concluded that the political mandate governing societal responses to sex offenders render many treatment programs unethical. Like Glaser, they state that the rights of the community take precedence over the rights of offenders, and that treatment-as-management is ineffective and therefore unethical.

Though it is challenging to balance the rights of the community and the rights of sex offenders, most treatment providers and researchers would not consider sex offender treatment to be inherently unethical. In a direct response to Glaser's (2010) assertions, Prescott and Levenson (2010) stated that treatment is not punishment and, even when mandated, can adhere to the professional codes of ethics and a human rights model of treatment. Ward (2010) also argues against the central tenets of Glaser's (2010) arguments. He points out that treatment does not necessarily have to support either the protection of the community or the rights of sex offenders, but instead can fulfill the well-being of the offenders while enhancing community protection.

One of the arguments for treatment being unethical is the question of whether treatment for offenders is truly voluntary. Even though treatment programs must be voluntary and offenders who participate must sign informed consent agreements (according to the ATSA guidelines), offenders often have to choose between treatment participation and increased sanctions. Alternatively, they may be offered more lenient sentences if they do agree to participate. Terry and Mitchell (2001) stated that approximately half of the offenders participating in a prison treatment program in England said they were doing so either for incentives within the prison or because they had to in order to be eligible for parole. This has been supported by other studies measuring motivation to participate in treatment programs in prison in England (Theodosi & McMurran, 2006). Similarly, Grubin and Gunn (1990) interviewed rapists and found that 73 percent of their sample said they either did not want or need treatment, though 41 percent of those said that they would participate if they were expected to do so while in prison.

Not all researchers believe that voluntariness is an absolute variable. Bowden (1991), for example, describes voluntariness as a matter of degree, saying that prisoners are not in a position to choose freely. He states, "We should be treating those accused of criminal acts, despite the commonly held view that the voluntariness of their consent is compromised by their position" (p. 133). Prescott and Levenson (2010) noted that many clients who participate in treatment do so without absolute voluntariness, as they may be encouraged to do so by family, friends, or the legal system. In this sense, sex offenders are no different from other clients in treatment.

A question then arises as to whether treatment can be effective for offenders who participate for reasons other than the motivation to change their behavior.

One study showed that there is no difference in the reduction of CDs for offenders with adult victims who were and were not motivated to participate in a treatment program (Terry & Mitchell, 2001). Alternatively, a study by Pelissier (2007) showed that treatment retention was significantly related to higher scores of motivation to change behavior. Pelissier (2007) also showed, however, that education and treatment participation within three months of incarceration were correlated to treatment retention, and she did not provide follow-up information on the link between retention rates and efficacy.

Yet another ethical dilemma is that full disclosure of thoughts, feelings, and behaviors during treatment—in other words, fulfilling the purpose of treatment—may result in further punishment for the offenders. Offenders in prison or who are civilly committed (discussed in Chapter 12) may not be released or gain early release without participating in treatment, but genuine disclosures of their offenses and/or sexual thoughts during treatment may reduce their chances of parole or release. Other offenders will agree to take hormonal treatments or participate in a psychological treatment program while serving a community sentence, therefore avoiding a prison sentence altogether. The result of this trade-off—a lesser sentence for treatment participation—may cause the sex offenders to be "involuntary clients" (Groth, 1983). The ethics of this retributive rehabilitation will likely be debated for many years to come.

Treatment Staff

Treatment will only be effective if delivered by adequately trained staff whose attitudes toward offenders are positive and supportive. A successful treatment provider will be one who carefully adheres to ethical codes of the treatment profession (ATSA, 2005) and has the ability to understand the challenges in working with this population (Perkins, 1991). Research has shown that positive staff attitudes are critical in facilitating change in offenders (Glaser, 1969), and as such it is important for sex offenders to perceive the treatment staff as having positive attitudes toward them and the treatment programs. Staff should be "direct, open, truthful, and consistent in their attitudes" (Groth, 1983, p. 168). They should not be uncomfortable around sex offenders or when dealing with sexual issues, and training should increase their confidence in working with these offenders (Hogue, 1995).

Even skilled clinicians and adequately trained staff can have difficulty in delivering treatment programs to sex offenders for a sustained period of time. The most common problems that tend to develop include countertransference, burnout, and negative psychological effects. *Countertransference* refers to the emotional responses that treatment providers experience in relation to the offenders (Houston, Wrench, & Hosking, 1995). This can include negative or positive emotional responses, both of which limit objectivity of the treatment. Empathy for the offenders could lead to the lack of objectivity in treatment delivery (Greer & Stuart, 1983), thereby reinforcing the excuses and justifications of the offenders. Alternatively, the treatment providers may experience negative emotional reactions to sex offenders upon hearing about the nature of their offenses and their attitudes toward their actions and their victims. Problems arise when this contempt becomes destructive to the rehabilitative efforts of the treatment programs. As Glaser states, people "view themselves on the basis of their perception and interpretations of how others view them" (Glaser, 1974, p. 146). If offenders perceive staff to have negative feelings toward them, they are likely to develop low self-esteem and self-confidence, even viewing themselves as victims.

Burnout is another significant problem facing treatment staff. Sex offender treatment programs tend to require a highly intensive and emotional workload (Longo, 1983; Marshall et al., 1999), as well as a commitment of several months if not years. This can lead to the third problem, a range of negative effects on the treatment providers that range from mild anxiety to severe psychological morbidity (Clarke, 2011). In their study of sex offender treatment providers in Australia, however, Hatcher and Noakes (2010) found low levels of vicarious trauma, compassion fatigue, and burnout in their sample. They did note that organizational factors were correlated to psychological well-being, including perceived levels of environmental safety. They found that the treatment providers in their sample were able to accommodate the traumatic material from the programs, suggesting that future research assess the resilience literature to better understand what qualities might protect treatment providers from negative psychological consequences.

Assessment for Treatment Participation: Exclusion Criteria

One debate concerning sex offender treatment programs involves which offenders should be excluded from participating in treatment. Most treatment programs exclude some offenders from participating, though who is excluded varies from program to program. An example of one study, conducted by Marques and her colleagues at the Atascadero State Hospital in California, used the following guidelines for their treatment program: subjects consisted of all child sexual abusers 18–30 months from their dates of release; they were 18–60 years of age; they had no more than two prior felony convictions; they admitted to committing their offenses; they had no pending warrants or arrests; their IQ was estimated to be at least 80; they spoke English; they had no psychotic or organic disorders; they did not require nursing care; and they had not exhibited any severe management problems in prison (Marques, Nelson et al., 1994, p. 579). Many of these factors are typical of program requirements, and offenders who do not fit the assessment criteria will not be able to participate in programs. Questions have been posed as to whether treatment is effective or whether lower recidivism rates actually reflect the self-selection into the treatment program by those who are most likely to succeed (Doren & Yates, 2008).

Though all programs vary in regard to who is excluded, the most common factors considered are denial of the offense, psychopathy (or other serious mental disorders), and low intelligence. Many treatment programs exclude "deniers" on the basis that they are not likely to make progress if they do not admit their offenses, and they may disrupt the treatment program for others in the group (Yates, 2009). However, some researchers have argued that deniers should not be categorically excluded from treatment (Levenson, 2011; Yates, 2009). Yates (2009) points out that denial in and of itself is not necessarily a risk factor for reoffending, but instead it should be considered a CD that can be addressed in the treatment program. Levenson (2011) recommends offering a reasonable time period for therapeutic engagement rather than excluding all those who do not admit their offenses at the assessment stage.

Sex offenders may also be excluded from treatment programs based on the level of their cognitive functioning. Those who are developmentally disabled or who have an IQ of below a certain level (usually 75–80) are often excluded from cognitive-behavioral treatment programs. The reason is that many of the concepts presented in the programs are abstract, and those who are developmentally disabled may not be able to understand these concepts and be able to adapt their behavior as a result of them. Some programs are adapted to offenders who are developmentally disabled, and these have shown promising results. Craig, Stringer, and Moss (2006) evaluated developmentally disabled offenders who participated in a treatment program and found that the group had significantly enhanced their socialization skills and also showed improvement in sex knowledge and honesty. However, they did not find any change in the offenders' attitudes and CDs about sexual offending.

Many treatment programs also exclude offenders who score high on the PCL-R. The argument for exclusion is that they have a high likelihood of dropping out of the treatment program prior to completion, or treatment may actually be harmful because it provides them with manipulative or interpersonal skills that will increase their likelihood of recidivism (Seto & Barbaree, 1999). Olver and Wong (2011) examined the predictors of dropout from sex offender treatment programs and found that two factors accounted for approximately 70 percent of cases: never being married and scoring high on the Emotional facet of Factor I of the PCL-R. Roche et al. (2011) examined levels of psychopathy and the effect on empathy, and found that higher levels of psychopathy corresponded to lower levels of empathy. This relationship held true even with longer times in treatment.

Though the literature has consistently shown that sex offenders who score high on the PCL-R have a higher risk of reoffense, this does not mean that treatment is ineffective or even harmful. When using actuarial methodology, Barbaree, Langton, and Peacock (2006) found that treatment does not increase recidivism in a sample of psychopaths. Abracen et al. (2008) have also noted that there is little empirical support for the notion that psychopaths cannot be effectively treated. They suggest that treatment efficacy should be studied more closely for all groups of high-risk offenders, including psychopaths as well as those with paraphilias, substance abuse problems, and other high-risk characteristics.

MEASURING TREATMENT EFFECTIVENESS

The biggest question about sex offender treatment is whether it is effective, and if so for whom, what types of treatment, and in what situations. The literature is rife with studies evaluating treatment efficacy, though many of these show conflicting results. The primary reason for this is the differing methodologies of the studies, which makes it difficult to generalize the findings from any single study to larger body of treatment literature. Despite these differences, various meta-analyses in the last decade indicate positive outcomes overall for sexual offenders who have completed treatment programs.

Methodological Considerations

When considering the study findings on treatment efficacy, it is important to understand the methodology used and any limitations based on the study design. It is also important to understand differences between various study designs, as differing methodologies will produce differing results. Key factors to consider are the dependent variables (what is being tested, and how those terms are defined), sample, type and location of treatment, follow-up period, design, and evaluator (Losel & Schmucker, 2005).

Dependent Variables   The first issue to understand in an evaluation study is what is being measured. The majority of program evaluations try to determine whether a program is "effective," but effective is defined differently in nearly every study. Many use official data to gauge whether sex offenders have recidivated, but there is no single definition of recidivism (Marshall & Barbaree, 1990b). A *recidivist* is variously defined as an individual who commits another sexual offense (only), an individual who commits another violent offense and/or sexual offense, or an individual who commits any other offense (including a violent or sexual offense). Depending on which definition is used, studies produce distinctly different rates of efficacy.

Some researchers also claim that measuring recidivism through official statistics is not sufficient for program evaluations, as the recorded levels underestimate the true rate of reoffense (Marques, Day et al., 1994). Self-report surveys can supplement official statistics to help better understand rates of unreported behaviors or to understand levels of variables related to offending (for example, posttreatment levels of CDs, victim empathy) (Marshall, 1994). Self-reports also have considerable limitations; however, and there is no single way in which the dependent measure can be accurately measured.

Sample   Sex offenders constitute a heterogeneous group of individuals, and treatment programs can vary greatly in terms of their participants. The treatment participants may differ in regard to the age of their victims (for example, adult or child victims); their relationship to the victims (for example, intrafamilial or extrafamilial child abuser); and by type of offense (for example, contact or non-contact (exhibitionism, viewing child pornography) offenses). Some treatment groups include only a specific type of offender, such as child sexual abusers. Others combine multiple types of offenders together, with the understanding that all sexual offenders exhibit certain characteristics such as CDs. Treatment groups may also differ based upon inclusion/exclusion criteria. Some will include high-risk offenders, such as those who score high on the PCL-R, while others exclude all offenders deemed high risk. The composition of the treatment group will affect the outcome of the program.

Follow-Up Period   The rate of recidivism for sex offenders, however defined, will vary depending on the length of the follow-up period in which the offenders are being assessed. Follow-up periods vary drastically, from a year, to five years, to ten years, or longer. Some studies provide recidivism data for multiple years, to show the differences in recidivism over time. Soothill et al. (1976, p. 169) claimed that recidivism is most apt to occur soon after the offender is released from prison; however, one-quarter of the recidivists in their study were reconvicted after 10 years. As such, little can be gained from evaluation studies with only short periods of follow-up.

Type and Location of Treatment   Treatment outcome will also vary depending upon the type of treatment, location, and time period when the treatment took place. The outcome of cognitive-behavioral treatment is likely to differ from pharmacological treatment, behavioral, or other psychological treatments, and treatments with a combination of approaches. Additionally, even programs that use the same approach have changed over time to include additional components. For instance, cognitive-behavioral programs in the 1970s did not incorporate RP, some programs in the 1980s began to incorporate RP, and nearly all cognitive-behavioral programs in 1990s incorporated it. As a result, evaluations of cognitive-behavioral treatment may vary by decade.

Location of treatment may also affect the outcome. Treatment in prison may differ from treatment in the community, and even treatment programs in prison may vary depending on the timing of the treatment. Studies do not provide definitive answers as to when treatment should be offered to offenders who are incarcerated. Some say that treatment should be administered at the end of the offender's sentence, just before their release into the community (Longo, 1983). Others say that treatment is most effective at the beginning of the sentence with a "refresher" course at the end.

Type of Design   All treatment studies should use comprehensive designs, have a sufficient base rate, account for attrition, use proper assessment procedures, use statistical methods that account for a cumulative survival or failure rate of the offenders, and treatment providers must adhere to treatment protocol (Marques, Day et al., 1994; Marshall, 1994). Most importantly, treatment efficacy cannot be accurately measured without an appropriate control or comparison group. Ideally, offenders who want to participate in a treatment program would be randomly allocated to either a treatment or a control group; however, this is rarely possible or ethical (Marshall, 1994). Studies can still have a high level of rigor even without an uncompromised random design, as long as there is a control group with an equivalent matching sample. Additionally, Harkins and Beech (2007a) recommend examining more proximate outcomes, such as change within treatment, in addition to recidivism outcomes.

Evaluator   Program evaluations must be objective, and it is best for those evaluating the offenders not to be directly involved with the program. If treatment providers do the evaluations, the offenders may manipulate and con them so that they can be assessed positively; if program directors do the evaluations, they will likely be biased in their results in order to make the treatment appear effective. As such, it is best, when possible, for evaluations to be done through those in contact with the offenders but who do not have a stake in the outcome of the treatment program.

Study Findings

Despite the substantial methodological considerations for assessing sex offender treatment programs, several studies provide robust analyses of data on treatment efficacy. In their meta-analysis of 43 studies comparing sex offenders who participated in cognitive-behavioral treatment to controls, Hanson et al. (2002) found lower recidivism rates in treated sex offenders for both sexual and general recidivism. The offenders who were treated showed a sexual recidivism rate of 10 percent, while those who were not treated had a sexual recidivism rate of 17 percent. These findings are similar to Losel and Schmucker (2005), who conducted a meta-analysis containing 80 comparisons between treatment and control groups with more than 22,000 individuals. Unlike most studies, which focus on U.S. and/or Canadian and British populations, Losel and Schmucker (2005) evaluated studies worldwide that had been published in English, German, French, Dutch, and Swedish. They found a sexual recidivism rate of 11.1 percent for treated sexual offenders and a sexual recidivism rate of 17.5 percent for non-treated offenders, a reduction of 37 percent. They also found a reduction in the general recidivism rate of treated offenders of 31 percent. Unlike Hanson et al. (2002), they included pharmacological and psychological programs in their analyses.

Many of the treatment efficacy studies have examined outcomes based upon type or characteristics of the offenders. To summarize these findings, the offenders least likely to recidivate are intrafamilial child sexual abusers, offenders who are older (for example, over age 40), and those with no past offenses. The offenders most likely to recidivate are those who are younger, have used violence, and have committed one or more previous sexual offenses (Hanson & Bussiere, 1996; 1998; Williams, 1996). Some researchers have also found that offenders who are unemployed, had older or multiple victims, and who did not admit their offenses are at a high risk to reoffend (Berliner, Schram, Miller, & Milloy, 1995). While offenders with high PCL-R scores are considered high risk to reoffend, some studies have shown low rates of sexual recidivism for that treated group of offenders (Abracen et al., 2011). Abracen et al. (2011) found that the high PCL-R group showed substantially lower than predicted rates of sexual offending over a nine-year follow-up period. Similarly, Beech and Ford (2006) found that child sexual abusers who scored high or very high on the Risk Matrix 2000 responded well to treatment. Though they were more likely to sexually recidivate than child sexual abusers who scored lower on this assessment, the high-risk offenders who responded to treatment and did not leave the program did not reoffend within two years.

Study findings vary in regard to whether treatment is equally effective for different groups of offenders. Hanson and Bussiere (1996) found that offenders who have sexually abused young boys or both boys and girls are at a greater risk to commit another sex offense, and those who raped adult females are at a greater risk to commit a nonsexual violent offense. Zgoba and Levenson (2008) also found that rapists were significantly more likely than other sexual offenders to commit further nonsexual offenses, and tended toward committing more sexual offenses as well. Harkin and Beech (2008), however, found no differences in recidivism rates by type of offender.

Additionally, some studies find that offenders who drop out of treatment, regardless of offender type, are actually at an equal or higher risk to reoffend than those who do not participate at all. In their study of 195 sex offenders who were referred to a prison-based, cognitive-behavioral treatment program, McGrath, Cumming, and Livingston (2003) found that the sexual recidivism rate for treated offenders was 5.4 percent, compared to 30.6 percent for those who did not complete treatment, and 30.0 percent for the no-treatment groups. Browne et al., (1998) stated that treatment drop out was best predicted by time spent in prison, commission of a violence-related index offense, commission of noncontact offenses, unemployment, substance abuse, and delinquent/disruptive behavior during treatment. Thus, it is not surprising that this group of offenders would be at a higher risk of recidivating, since these variables are also associated with risk of reoffense.

Based on these meta-analyses and other treatment studies, certain factors appear to positively influence treatment outcomes. Multicomponent cognitive-behavioral treatment programs have shown the most promising results (Losel & Schmucker, 2005; Marques, Day et al., 1994; Marshall, 1994; Marshall et al., 1999). For certain high-risk offenders where high sexual arousal plays a role in the offending behavior, pharmacological treatments should be considered in addition to cognitive-behavioral programs (Losel & Schmucker, 2005; Solicitor General of Canada, 1990). The use of polygraphs in the treatment process also appears to have some effect on recidivism. McGrath et al. (2007) showed that treated offenders who had received polygraph examinations in treatment had significantly lower recidivism rates for nonsexual violent offenses, though this effect was not significant for sexual offenses or nonviolent offenses. Interestingly, the meta-analysis by Losel and Schmucker (2005) showed that cognitive-behavioral treatment programs in the 1990s and 2000s were no more effective at reducing recidivism than those in the 1980s.

Not all studies have shown positive outcomes, and some researchers continue to argue that there is no evidence treatment works (Rice & Harris, 2003). In a methodologically rigorous evaluation of the Sex Offender Treatment and Evaluation Program (SOTEP), Marques et al. (2005) found no significant effects between treated and untreated offenders. Zgoba and Levenson (2008) also found no differences between treated and untreated sex offenders in levels of sexual recidivism, based on a seven-year follow-up study of sex offenders in

New Jersey. However, they did find that untreated sex offenders reoffended more quickly than treated sex offenders. Even Losel and Schmucker (2005, p. 135), whose meta-analysis found significant reductions in recidivism, stated that "Bearing the methodological problems in mind, one should draw very cautious conclusions from our meta-analysis." They recommend that future research should include high-quality evaluations to determine what works for whom and under which circumstances.

CHAPTER SUMMARY

- There are a number of treatment regimes available to sex offenders in prison and in the community. Researchers have found that multimodal cognitive-behavioral treatment programs have the greatest potential of all treatment regimes to reduce recidivism.

- Most cognitive-behavioral treatment programs consist of group therapy, where the offenders are encouraged to take responsibility for their offenses, modify their CDs, acquire an understanding of prosocial sexual fantasies and behavior, learn social skills to help them achieve normal adult relationships, gain an understanding of the harm they have caused to their victims, and control their negative emotional states.

- Cognitive-behavioral programs are relatively short term, and many offenders need lifelong supervision and maintenance to control their behavior. Nonetheless, studies show that these programs, particularly when employed with RP strategies, can reduce the rate of reoffense for some offenders.

- For offenders who have high levels of deviant sexual arousal, hormonal treatments can be used concurrently with cognitive-behavioral treatment programs to reduce the likelihood of recidivism.

- For any treatment program to be effective, the offenders' risks and needs must be matched. Though most thorough cognitive-behavioral programs follow an ATSA-approved regime, these programs must still be tailored to the specific individuals in order to adequately treat them.

- Studies of the efficacy of sex offender treatment programs are mixed. However, the majority of studies find that sex offender treatment programs significantly reduce recidivism rates.

DISCUSSION QUESTIONS

1. Is treatment for sex offenders ethical? Why or why not?

2. Why is it important to offer sex offenders, who are receiving hormonal treatments (for example, Depo-Provera), cognitive-behavioral treatment as

well? What problems might arise if the cognitive-behavioral treatment is not offered?

3. How can you determine whether or not treatment is effective? What are some common methodological problems with studies on treatment efficacy?

4. What are the primary challenges of sex offender treatment programs? Can these challenges be overcome, and if so how?

5. Should any sex offenders be excluded from treatment? If so, what types of offenders and why? What should be done with those offenders who are excluded from group treatment programs?

DID YOU KNOW...?

There are many myths about sex offenders, treatment, and recidivism. Here is a brief myth/fact sheet:

MYTH: Treatment for sex offenders does not work.

FACT: Most studies indicate that treatment is effective at reducing recidivism for sex offenders. Treatment outcome is often based upon the appropriate matching of the risks and needs of the offenders.

MYTH: Sex offenders can be "cured" in treatment.

FACT: Even though treatment can significantly reduce recidivism for sex offenders, they are not "cured." Sex offenders must understand their high-risk factors and manage their behavior, much like individuals with substance abuse problems.

MYTH: Most sex offenders recidivate.

FACT: Though sexual offenses are greatly underreported, studies consistently show that sex offenders have low levels of recidivism. Most sexual offenders are not convicted of multiple sexual offenses.

MYTH: Sex offenders commit only sexual offenses.

FACT: Most sex offenders do not "specialize" in committing sex crimes. Sex offenders who do recidivate are more likely to commit nonsexual offenses than sexual ones.

© Cengage Learning

12

Incapacitating Sex Offenders

Modern-day sex offender legislation that has been enacted since the 1990s primarily focuses on the management and supervision of sex offenders in the community. However, states have also enacted legislation that allows for sex offenders to be incapacitated in secure facilities after the completion of their criminal sentences if they are assessed as having a mental abnormality or personality disorder and are dangerous. Labeling such an offender a "sexually dangerous person" or a "sexually violent predator" (SVP), the purpose of this legislation is to incapacitate recidivist sexual offenders who are "more likely than not to reoffend" until they are rehabilitated (Seling, 2000). This legislation assumes a relationship among mental disorder, risk, and sexual violence, yet the medicalization of sexually deviant behavior is not grounded in "empirically demonstrated empiricism or articulated legal standard" (Janus, 1997, p. 350).

SVP legislation is controversial in terms of its aim, effectiveness, and constitutionality, and has been criticized on both legal and scientific grounds (Elwood, 2009). This legislation is largely based on the ability of clinicians to accurately predict whether a convicted sex offender will commit another offense in the future. Though the risk assessment process for civil commitment is similar to that used for Registration and Community Notification Laws (RCNL) and treatment, civil commitment leads to a much greater restriction of civil liberties. The Supreme Court has declared SVP legislation constitutional, though legal challenges against it are continuing. Alternative methods of controlling dangerous sexual predators, such as mandatory chemical castration of recidivist offenders who live in the community, are also being implemented in some states. All of these reactions—particularly the incapacitation of a sexual offender for treatment—serve to medicalize the problem of sexual offending. The presence in a hospital-type setting allows moral problems (such as sexual offending) to be recast (by the offenders themselves as well as society) as medical problems, and thus may make offenders less inclined to take responsibility for their actions. This chapter provides an overview of the SVP legislation and commitment process, as well as the medical and legal implications of the legislation.

SVP LEGISLATION

SVP legislation is, essentially, recycled Mentally Disordered Sex Offender (MDSO) laws from the 1930s. As discussed in Chapter 2, during the 1930s states began implementing sexual psychopathy legislation for recidivist sexual offenders. Psychopathy statutes were passed on the principle that sexually deviant behavior results from a diagnosable disorder and is treatable. If an individual was diagnosed as a sexual psychopath, he or she would be civilly committed to a mental institution until rehabilitated (Alexander, 1993). Sexual psychopathy laws, like many of the modern laws concerning sex offenders, were constructed through reactive decision-making and passed after emotionally charged sex crimes occurred. The MDSO legislation was problematic for several reasons, most obviously the subjective process for commitment and the difficulty of assessing whether offenders should be released. All states differed in their definitions of "sexual psychopathy," though most states required that the individuals suffered from a mental illness and were dangerous. Dangerousness predictions at this time were subjective and could not be predicted with much accuracy, and as such commitment standards were disputed (Sutherland, 1950). Several psychiatric and mental health organizations suggested that these laws should be repealed, and by 1990, sexual psychopathy laws existed in only 13 states (American Psychiatric Association, 1999). At this time, however, there was another wave of highly publicized cases of sexual assaults on children, which led to the modern day commitment laws that exist today.

In the 1990s politicians, with much public pressure, began to assert that the sex offender legislation in place at that time was insufficient at protecting the public from serious sexual predators like Earl Shriner (discussed in Chapter 10). As a result, Washington enacted the Community Protection Act (CPA) in 1990, allowing for the civil commitment of such individuals. Since that time, 20 states have implemented civil commitment statutes and several others are likely to do so with the passage of the Adam Walsh Act (AWA).

Definition of an SVP

To be designated an SVP, an offender must: (1) have been convicted of or charged with a sexually violent offense, (2) suffer from a mental abnormality or personality disorder, and (3) be likely to engage in future acts of sexual violence as a result of the mental abnormality or personality disorder if not confined to a secure facility. SVP legislation was implemented by states specifically to target "a small but extremely dangerous group of SVPs who do not have a mental disease or defect that renders them appropriate for involuntary treatment" (Kansas SVPA

§59–29a). The statute requires more proof than a "mere predisposition" to violence; rather, it requires proof of past sexually violent behavior and a present mental condition that is likely to cause similar violent behavior in the future.

The type of mental disorder that may predispose an offender to commit future acts has been debated since the inception of SVP legislation (Elwood, 2009). The most common mental disorders for SVPs are paraphilias and personality disorders (Ellwood, 2009; Elwood, Doren, & Thornton, 2008). Levenson and Morin (2006) found that the statistically significant predictors of an SVP designation in Florida include diagnoses of pedophilia and paraphilia not otherwise specified (NOS), psychopathy, actuarial risk assessment scores, younger age of victim, and nonminority race. This is similar to the population of SVPs in Washington, who are most commonly diagnosed with pedophilia, alcohol or substance abuse, paraphilia NOS, personality disorder NOS, and an antisocial personality disorder (Jackson & Richards, 2007).

To date, SVP legislation has been administered on a state level. However, section 301 of the AWA brings this to a federal level by establishing grants for the development of civil commitment programs for SVPs. Called the Jimmy Ryce State Civil Commitment Program for Sexually Dangerous Persons, this section is named after the Florida statute of the same name. Jimmy Ryce was a nine-year-old boy who was kidnapped, raped, murdered, and dismembered by Juan Carlos Chavez in 1995. Although Chavez did not have a history of incarceration in the state of Florida, the premise of the Jimmy Ryce Act is to indefinitely commit sexual predators to an appropriate "secure facility" for treatment upon completion of their criminal sentences.

States are eligible for support under the AWA if they establish a civil commitment program or submit a plan for such a program within a two-year compliance period. The AWA also creates guidelines for the civil commitment process, including the definition of an SVP, the institution of proceeding, the psychiatric examination, the hearing, the determination and disposition, and discharge procedures. Under the AWA, the criteria for commitment is broader than in states previously; an offender may be civilly committed if he has been convicted of a sexually violent offense or merely "has been deemed by the State to be at high risk for recommitting any sexual offense against a minor" (AWA, Sec. 301(c)(3)(A)(ii)).

The Commitment Process

Thus far, the U.S. Supreme Court has heard SVP cases from the states of Kansas and Washington and also on the federal level, and has rendered this legislation constitutional. As a result, the SVP statutes in these states have served as a template for other states that have since enacted similar legislation. The commitment process in Washington, the first state to enact SV legislation, is as follows (Washington State Department of Corrections, 2012).

First, the sex offender is referred to the court within three months of his or her release from prison. The prosecuting attorney files the petition, which is followed by a hearing to determine whether there is probable cause to believe that the sex offender is, in fact, an SVP. At this hearing, the sex offender has due process rights similar to those in a criminal trial, including the right to notice of the hearing, an opportunity to be heard, right to counsel, right to present evidence, right to cross-examine witnesses, and the right to view and copy all petitions and documents in his or her file. If the court establishes that probable cause does exist, the sex offender is then transferred to a facility for evaluation.

Once the offender is in a facility, a psychiatrist does a risk assessment of the offender. If a sex offender is assessed as dangerous, the next step in the commitment process is a trial. The trial must be held within 45 days, and the offender has a right to counsel, a jury trial, and an examination by an expert of his or her choice. Again, this is similar to a criminal trial. In Washington, the prosecuting attorney must prove the case beyond a reasonable doubt; however, because it is a civil trial, some states use a standard of only clear and convincing evidence. Because this is a jury trial, the verdict must be unanimous. If the jury does not meet a unanimous verdict, the court must declare a mistrial and set a retrial date within 45 days. If the jury does return a unanimous verdict that the offender is an SVP, he or she is transferred to a Special Commitment Center (SCC) for "control, care, and treatment" until rehabilitated. In order to be rehabilitated, the SVP's condition must change so that he or she is no longer a danger to others and can be safely released into the community or to a less restrictive alternative (LRA) than the SCC (to a facility with conditions similar to those of a minimum-security prison or a halfway house, for example). As a result of an injunction in 1994, Washington State was required to construct an LRA that would be available to offenders nearing discharge.

A petition for conditional release to an LRA may be made once the offender's condition has changed so that he or she no longer fits the definition of an SVP. Once the offender has petitioned the court, a hearing is set. The offender is not present at this hearing, though he or she has a right to counsel at this time. In order to release the offender to an LRA, the offender must agree to abide by conditions stated in the judgment. This includes, among other conditions, participation in a treatment program with a qualified provider in the facility. The treatment provider must take responsibility for treating the offender and must report to the court regularly on the patient's progress. The LRA must also agree to accept the offender, and the facility must be secure enough to ensure community protection. Once the offender is situated in the LRA, he or she is not allowed to leave the facility without authorization. It is the authority of the facility to ensure the protection of the community by strict supervision of the offender, with a report to the court if the offender disobeys the regulations of the facility. The offender who is in the LRA facility will be reviewed annually until he or she is "rehabilitated" and there is an unconditional discharge. Once an offender is completely discharged from the facility, he or she is subject to the RCNL of the county to which he or she moves.

State Variation in SVP Statutes

Most states follow a commitment procedure similar to the one in Washington. Due to its many legal precedents, all states must abide by certain standards, such as due process rights during the commitment process, availability of treatment, and LRA facilities. Nonetheless, there are variations in each state.

- **Thresholds for Commitment** States use different standards of dangerousness in order to commit an offender. Sex offenders in Minnesota must be "highly likely" to recidivate in order to be committed, while in Washington they must have an "extremely high" rating of dangerousness for confinement. In Wisconsin, however, they are incapacitated if they are "most likely to reoffend" and "are distinctively dangerous." This is similar to the difference in standards with psychopathy commitment statutes, and the result is a differential in numbers of those committed.

- **Standards of Proof for Commitment** Standards of proof vary from state to state. Most states require the same standard for commitment as with a criminal trial: proof beyond a reasonable doubt. Other states, such as Florida and New Jersey, require the lesser standard of "clear and convincing evidence" that is generally required in civil trials. Though the commitment process is civil in nature, it resembles a criminal trial in several regards (for example, due process rights allotted, removal of civil liberties). As such, most states require a standard equal to that of criminal trials.

- **Length of Commitment** In most states, a sex offender, once committed, will remain incapacitated indefinitely until rehabilitated. These states have a process whereby the offenders can apply for release. However, in some states, such as California, the standard is that an offender must be reevaluated every two years in order to determine if he or she should remain committed. The offender goes through a similar (though less involved) trial process as with the original commitment process.

- **Facility** The facilities in which offenders are incapacitated vary greatly and include special wings of prisons, state hospitals, and special commitment facilities built specifically for the SVP population. As more SVPs are committed, however, more states are developing expansion projects or building facilities specifically for this population. This has happened in Iowa, California, Minnesota, Wisconsin, Florida, Kansas, and Washington, with a reevaluation of the needs of the state every five to seven years (Harris, 2009). Other states, such as Texas, have an outpatient-only program of commitment.

- **Cost** The cost of the facilities differs greatly. Taking into consideration housing and treatment cost as well as legal fees, the average cost of commitment is $97,000 per offender per year (Gookin, 2007). All facilities are required to staff treatment providers, who must be available to all offenders who desire to participate in a treatment program. Additionally, the cost of legal fees is high in every state because of the many appeals, but a state such as California, which repetitions the court for commitment every two years, has higher legal fees than other states. As a result, California has the highest cost of commitment among all states.

- **Psychopathy Statutes** Some states, such as Minnesota and New Jersey, use more that one commitment statute. Minnesota still applies the sexual psychopathy statutes as well as an SVP statute. For its psychopathy statute, called the *Psychiatric Personality Act*, Minnesota follows the "utter inability test"; to be committed, the offender must exhibit an "utter lack of power to control [his or her] sexual impulses" (*State ex rel. Pearson v. Probate Court of Ramsey County*, 1939). The Sexually Dangerous Persons (SDP) Act was implemented in 1994 as a result of Dennis Linehan, who could not be committed under the Psychiatric Personality Act upon completion of his criminal sentence because there was no "clear and convincing evidence that appellant has an utter lack of power to control his sexual impulses" (*In re Linehan*, 1994). After his release, the Minnesota legislature passed the SDP Act, allowing for the civil commitment of persons who suffer from "certain disorders and dysfunctions and are dangerous to the public."

The most thorough comparison of SVP statutes by states was published in 2007, comparing states on numbers of offenders committed and released, and the cost of commitment broken down by type of cost (Gookin, 2007). The report showed that the total number of SVPs committed by 2007 was 4534, with 494 discharged and 85 who died while in custody. Florida had the highest number of SVPs committed, at 942, while California had the most discharged at 96. The majority of SVPs who were discharged were released as a result of a court decision, not on the basis of treatment staff recommendations.

The total cost of commitment in all states was $454 million, ranging from $1.2 million (in Texas, the outpatient program) to $147.3 million (in California, with a new facility specifically built for SVPs). The average cost per resident per year ranged from $17,391 in Texas to $166,000 in California, and the cost of commitment is more than $100,000 per resident per year in seven states. In California, this is four times the cost of incarcerating an offender in prison, while in Texas the cost of the commitment program is nearly equal to the cost of incarceration.

THE ROLE OF MENTAL HEALTH
IN SVP LEGISLATION

The legal process of civil commitment for sex offenders necessarily involves the mental health profession. By definition, an *SVP* is an offender assessed as "dangerous," and mental health professionals must determine whether offenders meet that standard. Additionally, mental health professionals must treat offenders who are incapacitated and determine whether and when the offenders are "rehabilitated." Despite the centrality of mental health processes to SVP legislation, they raise many ethical issues. With this system of therapeutic jurisprudence, mental health professionals are ultimately responsible for the well-being of offenders and the public.

Assessing "Dangerousness"

An important step of the commitment process is the risk assessment. As described in Chapters 10 and 11, the assessment of risk is critical in order to determine the level of risk an offender poses to the community (for RCNL) and to match the risks and needs of the offenders (in treatment). However, the assessment process for civil commitment requires that clinicians determine, to the greatest extent possible, whether an offender is likely to commit another sexual offense in the future. Clinicians use the same type of actuarial assessment described previously, such as the Static-99, in conjunction with a clinical assessment (Jackson & Hess, 2007). These actuarial assessment tools are used to predict the likelihood of future offending behavior based on past offenses or personal (static) characteristics. If the offender displays characteristics similar to a class of offenders who have shown a high degree of recidivism, it is postulated that the offender will follow the same pattern of reoffense.

There are both scientific and ethical problems inherent in this type of dangerousness assessment. Most importantly, it is not possible to predict with certainty whether an offender will commit an offense in the future. Actuarial instruments can predict the risk of offending better than chance (Hanson & Morton-Bourgon, 2004), but the accuracy is generally low to moderate. Though several scholars have estimated the predictive accuracy of such instruments (Hanson & Morton-Bourgon, 2004), other scholars have argued that actuarial assessments do not predict risk, but rather compare an offender's risk level to that of similar groups of offenders (Doren, 2002).

However narrowly the prediction of dangerousness is defined, the question remains whether it is ethical to incapacitate an individual who shows some level of risk of future violence, and what is the appropriate threshold of risk determined to be high enough to incapacitate an offender. In some states, such as Washington, an estimated sexual recidivism risk of 50 percent or greater is required for civil commitment (Sreenivasan et al., 2007). In other words, sex offenders can be committed if they have an equal likelihood of committing another offense or not. Other states use vague terms, such as "highly likely" to recidivate, which allows for a vague interpretation of the threshold for commitment.

In addition to the ethical question about risk predictions generally, it is not clear how accurate the predictions actually are. According to Gottfredson and Moriarty (2006, p. 183), predictive accuracy of actuarial risk assessment instruments depend upon "the reliabilities of the items of information used, the method(s) used to combine items of information, the reliability of the criterion variable chosen, the kinds of measurements used, the base rate, the selection ratio used, and the representativeness of samples employed." Yet sexual offenders have a low base rate of reoffending, making it difficult to predict future risk of offenders in this group. Studies have also shown conflicting levels of reliability for some instruments used in civil commitment. Boccaccini et al. (2012) examined the field reliability of the Static-99 for civil commitment purposes, and found that in nearly half of the cases, evaluators assigned different total scores to the same offenders. Based on these findings, the authors suggest that evaluators and systems should consider procedures for accounting for measurement error.

Treatment

The treatment of SVPs also presents several quandaries for mental health care professionals. There are three problems in particular with the treatment of SVPs who are civilly committed: the treatment may not be appropriate for them, they may decide not to participate in treatment, and, if they do participate, genuine disclosures in treatment may prohibit them from being released. Approximately two-thirds of the sex offenders who are civilly committed actually participate in treatment, and it is unclear whether cognitive-behavioral treatment is effective for those SVPs who do participate in a program. Numerous legal cases in Washington in 1994 sparked the modification of treatment procedures, though despite the improved efforts at treating SVPs, very few offenders are deemed "rehabilitated" and released.

The majority of treatment programs for civilly committed sex offenders are cognitive behavioral, just as in the community. As was discussed in Chapter 11, treatment is only likely to be effective if the risks and needs of the offenders are accurately assessed and the treatment program can address those needs. Most cognitive-behavioral treatment programs in prison and in the community have exclusionary criteria, prohibiting offenders from participating if they have certain characteristics such as certain mental disorders, high levels of psychopathy, are violent, and so forth. But the sexual offenders who are civilly committed tend to have many of those characteristics, and are in fact the offenders who would be excluded from participating in most standard cognitive-behavioral treatment programs. Additionally, many of the SVPs have "special needs"—meaning, in addition to being dangerous sex offenders with mental abnormalities, they have developmental disabilities, neurological impairments, or mental illnesses (Seling, 2000). SVP legislation then requires that offenders participate in treatment programs that they would have likely not qualified to participate in another environment.

Treatment for SVPs, as with offenders in the community, is voluntary. However, SVPs will not be released until they are rehabilitated, and so there is some incentive, or coercion, to participate in treatment. Yet, many SVPs do not participate in treatment once incapacitated. Some choose not to participate, but for others there is no program that can address their risks and needs. Leroy Hendricks claimed that although he was civilly committed on the basis of rehabilitation, no treatment was offered to him in the hospital. SVPs remain committed indefinitely until rehabilitated and, thus, must participate in treatment; yet, there may be no treatment available for the offenders. It is difficult to understand how such a situation can be regarded as anything other than punitive in nature.

Another problem with treating sex offenders who have been civilly committed is the paradox presented by their treatment disclosures. In order to be rehabilitated, they must fully address their offending behavior, including CDs, fantasies, and (lack of) victim empathy. However, most are aware that genuine disclosures of their deviant acts and fantasies during treatment may reduce their chances of release. SVPs who have inappropriate sexual thoughts and fantasies are not likely to be designated as "rehabilitated," even if they learn in treatment to manage their behavior through relapse prevention techniques.

Release

Once treated, mental health professionals must then determine whether the SVPS are sufficiently "rehabilitated." It is a challenge for clinicians to make this assessment, however, for several reasons. Risk level is determined largely upon the risk assessment instruments, yet these instruments are largely based upon the static characteristics of the offenders, or those factors that do not change. SVPs who are assessed as high risk offenders prior to commitment are likely to always be high risk according to these instruments because the factors associated with their offenses, criminal history, and family history will not change. There is also little opportunity for offenders to modify their behaviors while confined in order to sufficiently alter the assessment of their risk based upon dynamic characteristics. Thus, the determination of risk and level of rehabilitation is dependent largely upon the clinical assessment of the offenders.

The clinical assessment of the SVPs while incapacitated in necessarily subjective, as each case is unique and there is no designated definition of "rehabilitated." SVPs will always present some level of risk to the community, so the clinicians must identify what level of risk is acceptable for release. Because future violence is difficult to predict, most clinicians admit that if they are going to err in their judgments, they will do so on the side of society (Alexander, 1993). If a psychologist approves an offender's release, he or she is deemed responsible for any actions the offender takes once in the community. One example of this is the release of Raymond Alves, a rapist, from a New Jersey prison in March 2000. Psychologists Judith Frankel and Jack Gibbons assessed him and approved his release into the community, though he was discharged before anyone could impose registration requirements upon him. When the Commissioner of Corrections realized the mistake, Alves was declared a fugitive. For the next 11 days he traveled by bus through 17 cities and eventually came back to New Jersey (Hanley, March 23, 2000). In order to point blame at an individual rather than the system for this lapse in communication, the commissioner fired the two psychologists (Hanley, March 17, 2000).

LEGAL ARGUMENTS ABOUT SVP LEGISLATION

SVP legislation involves involuntary civil commitment, a concept that is not new and exists in every state for the mentally ill. Involuntary civil commitment originated as a last resort, whereby the state had the power to assist people with mental disorders or illnesses who were unable to recognize their problems or help themselves. These statutes require proof of a mental disability that gives rise to a substantial threat of serious harm to oneself or others. Involuntary civil commitment statutes have continuously withstood constitutional challenges, despite the infraction on civil liberties to those confined.

Almost immediately after its inception, claimants challenged the SVP laws in the courts on several grounds, including ex post facto application, double jeopardy, due process, equal application, vagueness of the statute, and definition of an

SVP. The statute itself has been challenged, as well as its application to individuals. In addition to being the first state to enact legislation, Washington was also the first state to test the constitutionality of the law in a state court in *In re Young* (1993) and several other cases followed suit. However, it was the Kansas statute, implemented in 1994, that first reached the U.S. Supreme Court in 1997.

The first two cases that set a precedent for the constitutionality of civil commitment statutes did not even concern sexual offenders, though both cases are cited often in SVP decisions. The case of *O'Connor v. Donaldson* (1975) is the first to analyze the constitutionality of civil commitment generally and the limitations of indefinite commitment. Kenneth Donaldson, who suffered from paranoid schizophrenia, remained civilly committed in Florida for approximately 15 years despite several petitions for release. Though the Court found that he was mentally ill, they stated that this finding alone does not justify confinement. He was not deemed to be a danger to himself or others, and the Court therefore ordered that he be released.

The second case looked at the other tenet of commitment statutes, that of dangerousness. Until 1992, civil commitment was tolerated without firmly establishing the presence of a serious mental disorder. At this time, however, the Court passed down a decision in *Foucha v. Louisiana* (1992) that offenders can only be detained involuntarily if they have a "mental illness" or "mental abnormality," even if they remain a danger to themselves or others. Terry Foucha was an armed burglar who was found insane and committed to hospital. When he sought to be released, two psychiatrists diagnosed him as having an untreatable antisocial personality and declared that he was dangerous and should therefore be detained. The Court ruled that as long as he could not be treated, his confinement was no longer justifiable. To confine someone in hospital who is dangerous but does not have a mental disability would merely be substituting hospital for prison. The importance of this case lies in its emphasis on the necessity of treatment in order for a commitment order to be upheld, and has been cited in many SVP cases that followed.

The first critical case regarding an SVP in Washington was that of Terry Young (*In re Young*, 1993). When the court heard his case in 1993, it declared that the SVP clause of the CPA is, indeed, civil rather than criminal in nature. As such, it is not unconstitutional on grounds of double jeopardy and ex post facto application of the statute, and it does not violate any substantive due process rights. It did, however, affirm that an individual who is not incarcerated at the time of referral must have committed a recent, overt act to indicate that he or she may require incapacitation. Though the court stated that less restrictive alternatives must be considered for the individual referred for commitment, it also said that the statute is not "void for vagueness." The court in *Young* followed the *Foucha* decision, claiming that dangerousness alone is not enough to warrant confinement; there must be evidence of a mental disability as well, whether it is mental illness or abnormality.

Similarly to Washington, the Minnesota court declared civil commitment of sexual offenders constitutional in the case of *In re Linehan* (1994). Dennis Linehan, like most sexual offenders whose cases have come before the appellate courts, had an extensive history of sexual offending. He not only had several convictions for abusing children, but his offenses escalated in intensity over time and ranged from window peeping to murder. In *Linehan*, the state court declared Minnesota's SDP Act a civil rather than criminal law, confirming the decision in *Young*. Linehan petitioned for a *writ of certiorari* (a request for review of a case) from the U.S. Supreme Court, though shortly before granting the writ the Court decided *Kansas v. Hendricks* (1997).

In 1997, the first real test of SVP legislation occurred in the case of *Kansas v. Hendricks*. Leroy Hendricks had a long history of sexual deviancy, and he was convicted of molesting several young boys and girls, beginning in 1955. He was diagnosed as a pedophile, and although he attempted several treatment programs, he was never able to complete them. He explained to psychologists that he harbored strong sexual desires for young children, and he says that when he is "stressed out" he cannot control his urges to molest. As a result, he was registered as a SVP and incapacitated. This is the first time the court stated that pedophilia could be considered a mental abnormality, and that the purpose of the commitment was to hold Hendricks until his mental abnormality no longer caused a threat to others. Prior to this, the court did not consider a paraphilia, an antisocial personality or personality disorder, to be a mental illness, and individuals diagnosed with these were therefore not confined.

Hendricks challenged his civil commitment under the Kansas SVP Act on substantive due process grounds, and claimed that the act established criminal proceedings in violation of the ban on double jeopardy and ex post facto laws. Though it rendered its decision in a 5–4 split, the Supreme Court upheld Hendricks's civil commitment and declared the Kansas SVPA constitutional on all grounds. The Court supported the former state court decisions in *Young* (1993) and *Linehan* (1994), stating that the SVP Act is a civil rather than a criminal statute. As such, it does not violate double jeopardy clauses by adding additional punishment, because the purpose of civil commitment is neither retribution nor deterrence. The Court held that

> a state statute providing for the involuntary civil commitment of sexually
> violent predators ... does not violate the double jeopardy clause of the
> Federal Constitution's Fifth Amendment where, because the state did not
> enact the statute with punitive intent, the statute does not establish crim-
> inal proceedings, and involuntary commitment pursuant to the statute is
> not punitive; thus, for purposes of analysis under the double jeopardy
> clause, (1) initiation of commitment proceedings under the statute against
> a person upon his imminent release from prison after serving a sentence
> for the offenses which led to his being declared a violent sexual predator
> does not constitute a second prosecution, and (2) the person's involuntary
> detention under the statute does not violate the double jeopardy clause,
> even though that confinement follows a prison term.

Similarly, the Court stated in regard to ex post facto application of the law,

> A state's provision for the civil commitment of sexually violent preda-
> tors does not violate the Federal Constitution's prohibition of ex post

facto laws ... where the provision does not (1) impose punishment, in that because the state did not enact the statute with punitive intent, the statute does not establish criminal proceedings, and involuntary commitment pursuant to the statute is not punitive, (2) criminalize conduct which was legal before the provision's enactment, nor (3) deprive a person subject to the provision of any defense that was available to him at the time of his crimes.

The Court dismissed the notion that the term "mental abnormality" was vague or too lax a standard for commitment, thereby violating due process rights. The Court claimed that "legal definitions which must take into account such issues as individual responsibility and competency need not mirror those advanced by the medical profession." It further stated that "this Court has never required States to adopt any particular nomenclature in drafting civil commitment statutes and leaves to the States the task of defining terms of a medical nature that have legal significance." To illustrate varying psychiatric definitions from previous cases, the Court used as examples the cases of *Addington v. Texas* (1979) (interchanging the terms "emotionally disturbed" and "mentally ill") and *Jackson v. Indiana* (1972) (interchanging the terms "incompetency" and "insanity"). In regard to the wording of the Kansas SVP Act, the Court said,

> A state's definition of "mental abnormality," in a statute providing for the involuntary civil commitment of sexually violent predators—which statute requires as a prerequisite to commitment a finding that a person has been convicted of or charged with a sexually violent offense and suffers from a mental abnormality or personality disorder which makes the person likely to engage in the predatory acts of sexual violence—as a congenital or acquired condition affecting the emotional or volitional capacity which predisposes the person to commit sexually violent offenses in a degree constituting such person a menace to the health and safety of others satisfies substantive due process under the Federal Constitution's Fourteenth Amendment, in that such definition requires a finding of both dangerousness and an inability to control that dangerousness; while a finding that a person is dangerous, standing alone, is ordinarily not a sufficient ground upon which to justify indefinite involuntary commitment of that person, a civil commitment statute may be upheld where it couples proof of dangerousness with proof of some additional factor, such as mental illness or mental abnormality, which serves to limit involuntary civil confinement to those who suffer from a volitional impairment rendering them dangerous beyond their control; and the diagnosis of a person as a pedophile, which qualifies as a mental abnormality under the statute, suffices for due process purposes.

Though the Court here attempts to distance itself from the field of psychiatry, the two are inextricably linked in cases of civil commitment. Without the use of psychiatry, there would be no risk predictions of dangerousness. The Court depends on these predictions to incapacitate offenders under the SVP

Act, stating that "the Act unambiguously requires a precommitment finding of dangerousness either to one's self or to others, and links that finding to a determination that the person suffers from a 'mental abnormality' or 'personality disorder.'" Additionally, it is the psychiatric professional who eventually determines if an offender is "rehabilitated" and therefore eligible for release.

Perhaps the most startling point made in the Hendricks case was the acceptance of lack of treatment once incapacitated. Hendricks argued that treatment was not offered to him once he was detained, and the Court ruled that the SVP Act is not punitive even if it fails to offer treatment for the mental abnormality. Quoting *Jacobson v. Massachusetts* (1905), the Court stated,

> The liberty secured by the Constitution of the United States to every person within its jurisdiction does not import an absolute right in each person to be, at all times and in all circumstances, wholly free from restraint. There are manifold restraints to which every person is necessarily subject for the common good. On any other basis organized society could not exist with safety to its members.

Basing his opinion on this, Justice Clarence Thomas claimed that preventive detention was an acceptable means of incapacitation for dangerous sexual offenders. This is true despite the fact that the Court called treatment "at best" an "incidental" objective. Even the program director at the hospital testified that Hendricks had not participated in any "meaningful treatment," nor had many other SVPs. The doctor further testified that the hospital does not have adequate staffing for this population and that the SVPs were receiving "essentially no treatment." Prior to this case, the Court had allowed preventive detention in the *United States v. Salerno* (1987) but only that which was "strictly limited in duration." Civil commitment statutes are not limited, but are rather indefinite in most states. Despite this constriction on civil liberties, the conservative milieu of the Court prevailed.

The case of *Kansas v. Hendricks* (1997) set a precedent for civil legislation, and politicians in other states immediately began proposing legislation allowing civil commitment. Preventive detention for sexual predators became the politically popular mandate once it was deemed constitutional. Although some researchers and civil libertarians thought that the legislation would eventually be ruled unconstitutional, it has not been yet.

Since the Hendricks decisions, the courts have heard several other cases addressing more specific issues within the law. Several cases in Washington State addressed the issue of whether confinement is punitive at the SCC, including *Young v. Weston* (1999) (holding that the statute is not punitive), *In re Turay* (1999) (holding that commitment is constitutional), *In re Campbell* (1999) (holding that the statute is constitutional in its application), and *Seling v. Young* (2001). The primary issue addressed in *Seling v. Young* (2001) was not whether the statute itself was constitutional on its face but rather as applied to Young. Young argued that it is unconstitutional because there is an absence of adequate treatment. Because his confinement is indefinite, the Washington statute imposed a punitive measure because there was a lack of quality treatment to help him get better.

The Court disagreed with this "as applied" analysis, and in an 8–1 decision affirmed the constitutionality of the SVP Act.

Two other cases have reached the U.S. Supreme Court since Hendricks: *Kansas v. Crane* (2002) and *U.S. v. Comstock* (2010). In *Kansas v. Crane*, the Court confirmed that an SVP could be civilly committed on the basis that he suffers from an emotional or personality disorder, rather than a complete volitional impairment. Michael Crane was diagnosed with exhibitionism and an antisocial personality disorder, but he did not suffer from a complete lack of volitional control. The Court stated that although there must be some lack of control determination, it only had to prove serious difficulty in controlling behavior in order for an SVP to be civilly committed. In *U.S. v. Comstock*, the Court decided that the federal government held the authority to civilly commit sex offenders under the Necessary and Proper Clause.

UNDERSTANDING THE GOALS AND EFFICACY OF SVP LEGISLATION

The goal of SVP legislation is protection of the public from sexual offenders who have a high likelihood of committing another offense in the future. SVP legislation approaches this goal through two tactics: incapacitation and rehabilitation. SVPs are incapacitated, to protect society, and rehabilitated, to help the offenders. Though incapacitation will effectively eliminate the chance of re-offense while the SVP is confined, there is little evidence that SVP legislation is effective at protecting the community in the long term. It is also necessary to weigh the costs of the civil commitment legislation with the potential benefits; does the outcome justify the selective incapacitation for this group of offenders, and if so what should the threshold for commitment be?

Opponents of SVP legislation have criticized the ethics of the legislation, the shortcomings in treatment for SVPs who are incapacitated, the financial costs, and the difficulty in measuring the efficacy of the legislation. Though a key purpose of civil commitment is ostensibly rehabilitation, some scholars, justices and mental health professionals have suggested that incapacitation is only a pretext to punishment with the proportionality of punishment replaced by a public safety model (Erickson, 2008). The preconceived notion of sex offenders is that they are a unique class of individuals who should be incapacitated for the good of society. SVP legislation allows sex offenders to be incapacitated for offenses they may commit, after completing their criminal sentences. Pretextual decisions often lack support in empirical evidence, which may prove contrary to the preconceived biases.

The efficacy of treatment for SVPs is also not clear. Studies have shown that treatment reduces recidivism in offenders living in the community, but offenders designated as SVPs are often excluded from those treatment programs. Thus, it is not clear whether treatment would be effective for these offenders in any environment. However, treatment in a hospital environment may have even greater obstacles. Commitment of sex offenders into a secure facility may actually serve to retard treatment efforts by removing responsibility for criminal conduct from the offenders. This medicalization of behavior forestalls any personal attributions of agency or responsibility for that condition, and implies that the offender lacks the ability to respond to criminal justice sanctions (Erickson, 2008). Problems put down to a putative disease process (an attribution that can only be facilitated by a hospital setting) may actually increase recidivism through implanting the idea that it is not the offender but rather his or her putative medical problems that control the offender's response to a situation, in which, for example, he or she is faced with the opportunity to reoffend. As such, SVP legislation may actually impede the treatment effort, making worse the problem that we ostensibly seek to "cure" (yet covertly seek to punish).

The effectiveness of treatment for SVPs is also difficult to assess because so few offenders are released once committed. As of August 2007, approximately 10 percent of SVPs who had been civilly committed since 1990 had been released (Gookin, 2007). In some states, such as, Minnesota, which has the highest rate of commitment per capita of states with SVP legislation, no offenders had been discharged as of 2011 (Office of the Legislative Auditor, 2011). With a low base rate of reoffending for sex offenders generally, and so few SVPs being released from commitment, it is not possible to accurately assess the efficacy of treatment for SVPs.

The cost of SVP legislation is extraordinary, at nearly $100,000 per resident per year. This cost covers the confinement, clinical treatment, and legal assistance of the offenders, as well as the increasing cost of medical coverage for those who are older or in need of special medical services. This is approximately three-times the cost of incarceration, and the question arises as to whether SVP legislation uses state resources that may be better spent on other tactics for monitoring, supervising, and treating sex offenders. Considering that the size of the SVP population is growing, and few offenders are released once incapacitated, this cost may become impossibly burdensome on some states.

The question is, what is good sex offender legislation? As noted by Vess (2009), there is substantial misunderstanding about the risks posed by sex offenders and our ability to accurately assess those risks. Community protection laws exist and are unlikely to be rescinded, but to be effective and ethical they must protect both the community and the rights of offenders. SVP legislation restricts the civil liberties of offenders to a greater extent than nearly any other laws within the criminal justice system; as such, it should be reserved for only those offenders who are assessed as the highest possible risk to the community. But there is inconsistency in how risk is assessed, the accuracy of those assessments, and the threshold for which offenders are deemed as having a high enough level of risk that they need to be indefinitely incapacitated. Risk is a dynamic concept that is subject to environmental and personal factors (Vess, 2009), and as such assessments should be interpreted with caution both for commitment and release from an institution.

The goal of any community protection laws for sex offenders should be to help them take responsibility for their actions. The SVP, by definition, is dangerous as a result of a mental abnormality or personality disorder that must be treated. Yet, the best policy for management and supervision of sex offenders is one that does not remove responsibility of behavior from the offenders through the medicalization of their condition. Offenders must take responsibility for their actions and combine internal and external forms of control in order to adequately manage their offending behavior.

CHAPTER SUMMARY

- SVP legislation is similar to the sexual psychopathy legislation enacted in the 1930s. Both allow for the indefinite civil commitment of sexual offenders into a secure facility instead of (psychopathy) or after (SVP) a criminal sentence, with the possibility of release once the person is no longer a danger as a result of a mental illness (psychopathy) or mental or personality disorder (SVP).

- SVP legislation follows a utilitarian principle: The protection of society from sex offenders who may reoffend is the most important goal. Civil commitment is based on the prediction of clinical experts that an individual is at risk to reoffend. The courts established a medical justification for commitment in *Foucha v. Louisiana* (1992) and supported this justification in *Kansas v. Hendricks* (1997) and *Kansas v. Crane* (2002).

- Risk assessments to determine whether sex offenders should be civilly committed raise ethical concerns. There is no standard threshold of risk for which offenders should be committed, and are there no satisfactory methods for determining who should be released once committed. Though actuarial instruments are increasingly accurate at predicting levels of risk (low, moderate, high), they cannot say whether an individual will in fact commit an offense in the future.

- Civil commitment is expensive, at approximately three times the cost of prison. Costs of civil commitment will only increase, as offenders continue to be incapacitated and few offenders are released.

DISCUSSION QUESTIONS

1. What is the aim of SVP legislation? Does it fulfill this purpose?
2. How is SVP legislation similar to a criminal sentence? How does it differ?
3. Explain why incarceration in prison is punishment, but civil commitment in a secure facility is not.
4. Should the criminal justice process include a system of therapeutic jurisprudence? Why or why not?
5. At what point is a civilly committed sex offender "rehabilitated"? How can this be measured?

VIGNETTE

IDENTIFYING AN APPROPRIATE RESPONSE TO THE SERIOUS SEX OFFENDER: The Jessica Lunsford case

In February 2005, nine-year old Jessica Lunsford was abducted from her home in Homosassa, Florida, raped, and killed. The perpetrator, John Couey, was a career criminal who confessed to walking into her unlocked house at night and going into her room, where he put his hand over her mouth to keep her from screaming and kidnapped her. The coroner found that she had been sexually assaulted and asphyxiated, though the exact sequence of events is unknown because Couey was high on drugs and could not produce a timeline of actions he took against her. Three weeks after she disappeared, the police found her body in a shallow grave at the home where Couey was living—only 150 yards from her home. As a result of her death, her father pleaded for renewed, harsher penalties for known sex offenders. Jessica's tragic case drew the sympathies of the public and politicians alike. Shortly after her murder, the legislature moved quickly to enact new legislation, which became known as the Jessica Lunsford Act.

The case of John Couey is an interesting one, raising questions about what type of legislation might have prevented Jessica's murder, and whether it would have been possible to accurately assess the risk he posed. Couey had a substance abuse problem and a history of previous arrests and convictions, primarily for property offenses such as burglary. He also had one conviction for indecent exposure, resulting from exposing himself to a five-year-old girl. Though he was registered as a sex offender, he was not assessed as high risk to commit another sexual offense in the future. The question is, should mental health professionals have been able to discern that he was in fact at risk of committing a serious sexual offense? What should have been the supervision and management strategy for a "generalist" offender like John Couey?

This case presents an example of a serious offender who did not fit the assessment criteria for being a SVP. Even though he committed one of the most horrific acts of sexual abuse and murder of a child in recent memory, his past sexual offenses did not lead to a prediction of future dangerousness. He is not alone, however. Other offenders who committed notoriously heinous acts also would have escaped detection. For instance, in February 2002, seven-year-old Danielle van Dam disappeared from her bedroom in San Diego, California. David Westerfield, who lived two houses away from the van Dams, was arrested nearly three weeks later and charged with murder, kidnapping, and possession of child pornography. Westerfield had no previous convictions; he was well-educated, successful in business, had previously been married, and had two college-age children. This case is an important reminder that some of the most serious sexual offenses have been perpetrated by offenders who would not have been subject to any of the community protection laws now in place.

The Jessica Lunsford Act, passed to better monitor offenders like John Couey, did enhance regulatory measures of sex offenders living in the community, which may have helped to identify Jessica before she was killed. Among other things, it requires lifetime GPS tracking of offenders released from prison, increases the sanctions for failure to register, and enhances the sanctions for any sexual offenses against children under the age of 12 (Florida Department of Law Enforcement, 2005).

Questions
1. Should John Couey have been assessed as a high-risk offender after his first conviction? Why or why not?
2. Is there any legislation that could have prevented Jessica from getting kidnapped? What about Danielle van Dam?
3. Is it possible to predict who will commit serious sexual offenses like the murders of Jessica and Danielle?

Bibliography

PRINT AND ONLINE SOURCES

Abel, G. G., Becker, J. V., & Cunningham-Rathner, J. (1984). Complications, consent, and cognitions in sex between children and adults. *International Journal of Law and Psychiatry.* 7: 89–103.

Abel, G. G., Becker, J. V., Cunningham-Rathner, J., Mittelmen, M., & Rouleau, J. L. (1988). Multiple paraphiliac diagnoses among sex offenders. *Bulletin of the American Academy of Psychiatry and the Law.* 16: 153–168.

Abel, G. G., Becker, J. V., Mittelmen, M. S., Cunningham-Rathner, J., Rouleau, J. L., & Murphy, W. D. (1987). Self-reported sex crimes of nonincarcerated paraphiliacs. *Journal of Interpersonal Violence.* 2: 3–25.

Abel, G. G., Becker, J. V., & Skinner, L. (1980). Aggressive behavior and sex. *Psychiatric Clinics of North America.* 3: 133–151.

Abel, G. G., & Blanchard, E. B. (1974). The role of fantasy in the treatment of sexual deviation. *Archives of General Psychiatry.* 30: 467–475.

Abel, G. G., Blanchard, E. B., & Becker, J. V. (1978). An integrated treatment program for rapists. In R. T. Rada (ed.), *Clinical Aspects of the Rapist.* New York: Grune & Stratton.

Abel, G. G., Lawry, S. S., Karlstrom, E., Osborn, C. A., & Gillespie, C. F. (1994). Screening tests for pedophilia. *Criminal Justice and Behavior.* 21: 115–131.

Abel, G. G., Mittelmen, M. S., & Becker, J. V. (1985). Sexual offenders: Results of assessment and recommendations for treatment. In M. H. Ben-Avon, S. J. Hucker, & C. D. Webster (eds.), *Clinical Criminology: The Assessment and Treatment of Criminal Behavior.* Toronto, ON: M and M Graphics.

Abel, G. G., & Osborn, C. (1995). Pedophilia. In L. Diamant & R. D. McAnulty (eds.), *The Psychology of Sexual Orientation, Behavior, and Identity: A Handbook.* Westport, CT: Greenwood Press.

Abel, G. G., Osborn, C. A., & Twigg, D. A. (1993). Sexual assault through the lifespan: Adult offenders with juvenile histories. In H. E. Barbaree, W. L. Marshall, & S. M. Hudson (eds.), *The Juvenile Sex Offender.* New York: Guilford.

Abel, G. G., & Rouleau, J. L. (1990). The nature and extent of sexual assault. In W. L. Marshall, D. R. Laws, & H. E. Barbaree (eds.), *Handbook of Sexual Assault: Issues, Theories and Treatment of the Offender*. New York: Plenum.

Abel, G. G., & Rouleau, J. L. (1995). Sexual abuses. *Clinical Sexuality*. 18: 139–153.

Abel, G. G., Rouleau, J. L, & Cunningham-Rathner, J. (1986). Sexually aggressive behavior. In W. Curran, A. McGarry, & S. Shah (eds.), *Psychiatry and Psychology: Perspectives and Standards for Interdisciplinary Practice*. Philadelphia: FA Davis.

Abracen, J., Looman, J., Ferguson, M., Harkins, L., & Mailloux, D. (2011). Recidivism among treated sexual offenders and comparison subjects: Recent outcome data from the Regional Treatment Centre (Ontario) high-intensity Sex Offender Treatment Programme. *Journal of Sexual Aggression*, 17(2): 142–152.

Abracen, J., Looman, J., & Langton, C. M. (2008). Treatment of sexual offenders with psychopathic traits: Recent research developments and clinical implications. *Trauma, Violence, & Abuse*. 9: 144–166.

Abraham, K. (1927). *The Experiencing of Sexual Traumas as a Form of Sexual Activity*. Selected Papers of Karl Abraham, M. D. London: Hogarth Press.

Abrahamsen, D. (1950). Study of 102 sex offenders at sing sing. *Federal Probation*. 26: 26–31.

Ackerman, A., & Terry, K. J. (2009). Leaders in sex offender research and policy. In R. Wright (ed.), *Sex Offender Laws: Failed Policies, New Directions*. New York: Springer.

Ahlmeyer, S., Heil, P., McKee, B., & English, K. (2000). The impact of polygraph on admissions of victims and offenses in adult sexual offenders.

Sexual Abuse: A Journal of Research and Treatment. 12: 123–138.

Aiken, M., Moran, M., & Berry, M. J. (2011). *Child Abuse Material and the Internet Cyberpsychology of Online Child-Related Sex Offending*. Paper presented at the 29th Meeting of the INTERPOL Specialist Group on Crimes against Children Lyons, France, 5–7 September, 2011.

Akerstrom, M. (1986). Outcasts in prison: The cases of informers and sex offenders. *Deviant Behaviour*. 7: 1–12.

Alaska Department of Corrections Offender Programs. (1996, August). *Sex Offender Treatment Program: Initial Recidivism Study*. Available at: http://www.uaa.alaska.edu/just/reports/9602

Alexander, R. (1993). The civil commitment of sex offenders in light of Foucha v. Louisiana. *Criminal Justice and Behavior*. 20: 371–387.

Allard-Dansereau, C., Haley, N., Hamane, M., & Bernard-Bonnin, A. C. (1997). Pattern of child sexual abuse by young aggressors. *Child Abuse and Neglect*. 21: 965–974.

Allard-Dansereau, C., Hebert, M., Tremblay, C., & Bernard-Bonnin, A. C. (2001). Children's response to the medical visit for allegations of sexual abuse: Maternal perceptions and predicting variables. *Child Abuse Review*. 10: 210–222.

Allison, J. A., & Wrightsman, L. S. (1993). *Rape: The Misunderstood Crime*. Newbury Park, CA: Sage.

American Academy of Pediatrics, Committee on Child Abuse and Neglect. (1991). Guidelines for the evaluation of sexual abuse of children. *Pediatrics*. 87: 254–260.

American Association of University Women. (2001). *Hostile Hallways: Bullying, Teasing and Sexual Harassment in School*. Washington, DC: AAUW.

American Civil Liberties Union. (1998). *Lifestyle Discrimination in the Workplace: Your Right to Privacy under Attack.* New York: ACLU.

American Psychiatric Association. (1968). *Diagnostic and Statistical Manual of Mental Disorders: DSM-II* (2nd ed.). Washington, DC: APA.

American Psychiatric Association. (2000). *Diagnostic and Statistical Manual of Mental Disorders: DSM-IV-TR* (4th ed.). Washington, DC: APA.

American Psychiatric Association. (1999). *Dangerous Sex Offenders: A Task Force Report of the American Psychiatric Association.* Washington, DC: APA.

American Psychiatric Association. (2010). *DSM 5 Development: Paraphilias.* Available at: http://www.dsm5.org/pro posedrevision/pages/paraphilias.aspx

Amir, M. (1971). *Patterns in Forcible Rape.* New York: Columbia University Press.

Anderson, A. L., & Sample, L. L. (2008). Public awareness and action resulting from sex offender community notification laws. *Criminal Justice Policy Review.* 19: 371–396.

Anderson, D. (2011, December 24). Plenty of Disgrace and Distress in a Year of Sports Headlines. *New York Times.* Retrieved from http://www .nytimes.com/2011/12/25/sports/ plenty-of-disgrace-and-distress-in- year-ofsportsheadlines.html?_ r=1&scp=1&sq=sandusky% 20syracuse&st=cse

Andrews, D. A., Bonta, J., & Hoge, R. D. (1990). Classification for effective rehabilitation: Rediscovering psychology. *Criminal Justice and Behavior.* 17: 19–52.

Andrews, D. A., & Kiessling, J. J. (1980). Program structure and effective correctional practices: A summary of the CaVIC research. In R. R. Ross & P. Gendreau (eds.), *Effective Correctional Treatment.* Toronto: Butterworth.

Andrews, D. A., Zinger, I., Hoge, R. D., Bonta, J., Gendreau, P., & Cullen, F. T. (1990). Does correctional treatment work? A clinically relevant and psychologically informed meta-analysis. *Criminology.* 28: 369–397.

Andrews, D. J. (1999). *Healing in Congregations in the Aftermath of Sexual Abuse by a Pastor.* Dissertation from Hartford Seminary; available through University Microfilms International, Ann Arbor, MI.

Apfelberg, B., Sugar, C., & Pfeffer, A. Z. (1944). A psychiatric study of 250 sex offenders. *American Journal of Psychiatry.* 100: 762–770.

Araji, S. (1997). *Sexually Aggressive Children: Coming to Understand Them.* Thousand Oaks, CA: Sage.

Arata, C. M. (1998). To tell or not to tell: Current functioning of child sexual abuse survivors who disclosed their victimization. *Child Maltreatment.* 3: 63–71.

Associated Press. (2010, April 5). Boys Scouts Sued in a Sex-Abuse Case. *The Washington Time.* Retrieved from http://www.washingtontimes.com/ news/2010/apr/5/boy-scouts-sued- in-a-sex-abuse-case/

Association for the Treatment of Sexual Abusers. (2005). *ATSA Practice Standards and Guidelines for the Evaluation, Treatment and Management of Adult Male Sexual Abusers (2004).* Beaverton, Oregon: Association for the Treatment of Sexual Abusers.

Awad, G. A., & Sanders, E. B. (1989). Adolescent child molesters: Clinical observations. *Child Psychiatry and Human Development.* 19: 195–206.

Awad, G. A., & Sanders, E. B. (1991). Male adolescent sexual assaulters: Clinical observations. *Journal of Interpersonal Violence.* 6: 446–460.

Babchishin, K. M., Hanson, K. R., & Chantal, A. (2011). The characteristics of online sex offenders: A meta-analysis.

Sexual Abuse: A Journal of Research & Treatment. 23: 92–123.

Bagley, C., Wood, M., & Young, L. (1994). Victim to abuser: Mental health and behavioral sequels of child sexual abuse in a community survey of young adult males. Child Abuse and Neglect. 18: 683–697.

Baker, A. J. L., Tabacoff, R., Tornusciolo, G., & Eisenstadt, M. (2001). Calculating number of offenses and victims of juvenile sexual offending: the role of posttreatment disclosures. Sexual Abuse: Journal of Research and Treatment. 13: 79–90.

Baker, T., Skolnik, L., Davis, R., & Brickman, E. (1991). The social support of survivors of rape: The difference between rape survivors and survivors of other violent crimes and between husbands, boyfriends, and women friends. In A. W. Burgess (ed.), Rape and Sexual Assault III: A Research Handbook. New York: Garland.

Bales, K. (2007). Ending Slavery: How We Free Today's Slaves. Berkeley; University of California Press.

Banbury, A. (2004). Coercive sexual behavior in British prisons as reported by adult ex-prisoners. The Howard Journal of Criminal Justice. 42(2): 113–130.

Bancroft, J. (1971). The application of psycho physiological measures to the assessment and modification of sexual behaviour. Behaviour Research and Therapy. 9: 119–130.

Bancroft, J. (1978). The relationship between hormones and sexual behavior in humans. In J. Hutchison (ed.), The Biological Determinants of Sexual Behavior. West Sussex, UK: Wiley.

Bandy, R. (2011). Measuring the impact of sex offender notification on community adoption of protective behaviors. Criminology & Public Policy. 10(2): 237–263.

Banks, D., & Kyckelhahn, T. (2011). Characteristics of Suspected Human Trafficking Incidents, 2008-2010. Washington, DC: U.S. Department of Justice.

Barbaree, H. E., Hudson, S. M., & Seto, M. C. (1993). Sexual assault in society: The role of the juvenile offender. In H. E. Barbaree, W. L. Marshall, & S. M. Hudson (eds.), The Juvenile Sex Offender. New York: Guilford.

Barbaree, H. E., Langton, C., & Peacock, E. (2006). Sexual offender treatment for psychopaths: is it harmful? In W. L. Marshall, Y. M. Fernandez, L. E. Marshall, & G. A. Serran (eds.), Sexual offender treatment: Controversial issues (pp. 225–239). John Wiley and Sons.

Barbaree, H. E., Seto, M. C., & Peacock, E. J. (2001). Evaluating the predictive accuracy of six risk assessment instruments for adult sex offenders. Criminal Justice and Behavior. 28: 490–521.

Barbaree, H. E., Seto, M. C., Serin, R. C., Amos, N. L., & Preston, D. L. (1994). Comparisons between sexual and non-sexual rapist subtypes: Sexual arousal to rape, offense precursors and offense characteristics. Criminal Justice and Behavior. 21: 95–114.

Baron-Evans, A. (2008). Still time to rethink the misguided approach of the sex offender registration and notification act. Federal Sentencing Reporter. 20(5): 357–361.

Bartholomew, A. (1968). A long-acting phenothiazine as a possible agent to control deviant sexual behavior. American Journal of Psychiatry. 124: 917–923.

Bartholomew, K. (1990). Avoidance of intimacy: An attachment perspective. Journal of Social and Personal Relationships. 7: 147–178.

Bass, E., & Davis, L. (1988). The Courage to Heal. New York: Harper & Row.

Bates, A., & Metcalf, C. (2007). A psychometric comparison of internet and non-internet sex offenders from a community treatment sample. *Journal of Sexual Aggression.* 13(1): 11–20.

Baxter, D. J., Marshall, W. L., Barbaree, H. E., Davidson, P. R., & Malcolm, P. B. (1984). Deviant sexual behavior: Differentiating sex offenders by criminal and personal history, psychometric measures, and sexual response. *Criminal Justice and Behavior.* 11: 477–501.

Beauregard, E., & Mieczkowski, T. (2009). Testing the predictive utility of the Static-99: A Bayes analysis. *Legal and Criminological Psychology.* 14: 187–200.

Beck, V. S., Clingermayer, J., Ramsey, R. J., & Travis, L. F. (2004). Community response to sex offenders. *Journal of Psychiatry and Law.* 32(2): 141–168.

Beck, V. S., & Travis, L. F. (2006). Sex offender notification: An exploratory assessment of state variation in notification processes. *Journal of Criminal Justice.* 34(1): 51–55.

Becker, J. V. (1990). Treating adolescent sex offenders. *Professional Research Psychology and Practice.* 21: 362–365.

Becker, J. V. (1998). What we know about the characteristics and treatment of adolescents who have committed sexual offenses. *Child Maltreatment.* 3: 317–330.

Becker, J. V., Cunningham-Rathner, J., & Kaplan, M. S. (1986). The adolescent sexual perpetrator: Demographics, criminal history victims, sexual behaviors and recommendations for reducing future offenses. *Journal of Interpersonal Violence.* 1: 421–445.

Becker, J. V., & Hunter, J. A. (1997). Understanding and treating child and adolescent sexual offenders. In T. H. Ollendick & R. J. Prinz (eds.), *Advances in Clinical Child Psychology.* New York: Plenum.

Becker, J. V., Hunter, J. A., Stein, R. M., & Kaplan, M. S. (1989). Factors

associated with erection in adolescent sex offenders. *Journal of Psychopathology and Behavioral Assessment.* 2: 355–363.

Becker, J. V., & Kaplan, M. S. (1998). The assessment of adolescent sexual offenders. *Advances in Behavioral Assessment of Children and Families.* 4: 97–118.

Becker, J. V., Kaplan, M. S., Tenke, C. E., & Tartaglini, A. (1991). The incidence of depressive symptomatology in juvenile sex offenders with a history of abuse. *Child Abuse and Neglect.* 15: 531–536.

Becker, J. V., & Stein, R. M. (1991). Is sexual erotica associated with sexual deviance in adolescent males? *International Journal of Law and Psychiatry.* 14: 85–95.

Beech, A. R., Elliott, I. A., Birgden, A., & Findlater, D. (2008). The Internet and child sexual abuse: A criminological review. *Aggression and Violent Behavior.* 13: 216–228.

Beech, A., Fisher, D., & Beckett, R. (1998). *An Evaluation of the Prison Sex Offender Treatment Programme: A Report for the Home Office by the STEP Team.* London: Home Office Information Publications Group.

Beech, A., & Ford, H. (2006). The relationship between risk, deviance, treatment outcome and sexual reconviction in a sample of child sexual abusers completing residential treatment for their offending. *Psychology, Crime & Law.* 12(6): 685–701.

Bender, L., & Blaue, A. (1937). The reaction of children to sexual relations with adults. *American Journal of Orthopsychiatry.* 7: 500–518.

Beneke, T. (1995). Jack and Ken. In P. S. Searles & R. J. Berger (eds.), *Rape and Society.* Boulder, CO: Westview.

Bennett, S. (2002, August 24). Big Brothers + Big Sisters = Big Disaster? *World Daily Net.* Retrieved from http://www.wnd.com/news/article.asp?ARTICLE_ID=28723

Benoit, J. L., & Kennedy, W. A. (1992). The abuse history of male adolescent sex offenders. *Journal of Interpersonal Violence*. 7: 543–548.

Bensley, L. S., Van Eenwyk, J., & Simmons, K. W. (2000). Self-reported childhood sexual and physical abuse and adult HIV-risk behaviors and heavy drinking. *American Journal of Preventative Medicine*. 18(2): 151–158.

Berger, R. J., Searles, P., & Neuman, W. L. (1995). Rape-law reform: Its nature, reform and impact. In P.S. Searles & R. J. Berger (eds.), *Rape and Society*. Boulder, CO: Westview.

Berlin, F. S. (1989). The paraphilias and Depo-Provera: Some medical, ethical and legal considerations. *Bulletin of the American Academy of Psychiatry and the Law*. 17: 233–239.

Berlin, F.S., Galbreath, N.W., Geary, B., & McGlon, G. (2003). The use of actuarials at civil commitment hearings to predict the likelihood of future sexual violence. *Sexual Abuse: A Journal of Research and Treatment*. 15: 377–382.

Berlin, F. S., & Meinecke, C. F. (1981). Treatment of sex offenders with antiandrogen medication: Conceptualization, review of treatment modalities, and preliminary findings. *American Journal of Psychiatry*. 74: 596–601.

Berliner, L., & Conte, J. R. (1995). The effects of disclosure and intervention on sexually abused children. *Child Abuse and Neglect*. 19: 371–384.

Berliner, L., Schram, D., Miller, L. L., & Milloy, C. D. (1995). A sentencing alternative: a study of decision making and recidivism. *Journal of Interpersonal Violence*. 10: 487–502.

Berry, J. (1992). *Lead Us Not into Temptation: Catholic Priests and Sexual Abuse of Children*. New York: Image Books.

Berry, J. (2006). Sexual exploitation of children over the internet: What parents, kids and congress need to know about child predators. *U.S. House of Representatives Committee on Energy and Commerce Hearing* (pp. 1–12). Washington, DC.

Berson, N. L., Herman-Giddens, M. E., & Frothingham, T. E. (1993). Children's perceptions of genital examinations during sexual abuse evaluations. *Child Welfare*. 72: 41–49.Birgden, A., & Cucolo, H. (2011). The treatment of sex offenders: Evidence, ethics, and human rights. *Sexual Abuse: A Journal of Research and Treatment*. 23(3): 295–313.

Blackburn, A. G., Mullings, J. L., & Marquart, J. W. (2008). Sexual assault in prison and beyond: Toward an understanding of lifetime sexual assault among incarcerated women. *The Prison Journal*. 88(3): 351–377.

Blasko, B. L., Jeglic, E. L., & Mercado, C. C. (2011). Are actuarial risk data used to make determinations of sex offender risk classification? An examination of sex offenders selected for enhanced registration and notification. *International Journal of Offender Therapy and Comparative Criminology*. 55(5): 676–692.

Blume, E. S. (1990). *Secret Survivors: Uncovering Incest and Its Aftereffects in Women*. New York: Ballantine.

Blumer, D., & Migeon, C. (1975). Hormone and hormonal agents in the treatment of aggression. *Journal of Nervous and Mental Disorders*. 160: 127–137.

Blumstein, A., Cohen, J., Roth, J., & Visher, C. A. (1986). *Criminal Careers and "Career Criminals."* Washington, DC: National Academy Press.

Blundell, B., Sherry, M, Burke, A., & Sowerbutts, S. (2002). Child pornography and the internet: Accessibility and policing. *Australian Police Journal*, 56(1): 59–65.

Boccaccini, M. T., Murrie, D. C., Mercado, C., Quesada, S., Hawes, S., Rice, A. K. et al. (2012). Implications of Static-99 field reliability findings for score use and reporting. *Criminal Justice and Behavior.* 39(1): 42–58.

Bolen, R., & Scannapieco, M. (1999). Prevalence of child sexual abuse: A corrective meta-analysis. *Social Service Review.* 73: 281–313.

Boney-McCoy, S., & Finkelhor, D. (1995). Psychosocial sequelae of violent victimization in a national youth sample. *Journal of Consulting and Clinical Psychology.* 63: 726–736.

Bono, A. (2004, February 13). Picture of Child Sex Abuse in U.S. Society Clouded by Lack of Data. *Catholic News Service.* Retrieved from http://www.catholicnews.com/data/abuse/abuse19.htm

Boston Globe. (2004). *The Boston Globe Spotlight Investigation: Abuse in the Catholic Church.* Retrieved from http://www.boston.com/globe/spotlight/abuse/

Bourke, M., & Hernandez, A. (2009). The "Butner study" redux: A report of the incidence of hands-on child victimization by child pornography offenders. *Journal of Family Violence.* 24(3): 183–191.

Bowater, B. (2008). Adam Walsh child protection and safety act of 2006: Is there a better way to tailor the sentences of juvenile offenders? *Catholic University Law Review.* 57: 817.

Bowden, P. (1991). Treatment: Use, abuse and consent. *Criminal Behaviour and Mental Health.* 1: 130–141.

Bowers, L. (1996). *An Evaluation of the Effectiveness of the First Version of the Core Programme for Rapists.* Prepared for the SOTP Accreditation Panel, London.

Boyle, P. (1994). *Scout's Honor: Sexual Abuse in America's Most Trusted Institution.* Rocklin, CA: Prima Publishing.

Brackenridge, C. H. (1994). Fair play or fair game? Child sexual abuse in sports organizations. *International Review for the Sociology of Sport.* 29(3): 287–298.

Brackenridge, C. H. (1997). "He owned me basically." Women's experiences of sexual abuse in sport. *International Review for the Sociology of Sport.* 32: 115–130.

Bradford, J. (1990). The antiandrogen and hormonal treatment of sex offenders. In W. L. Marshall, D. R. Laws, & H. E. Barbaree (eds.), *Handbook of Sexual Assault: Issues, Theories and Treatment of the Offender.* New York: Plenum.

Bradford, J., & MacLean, D. (1984). Sexual offenders, violence and testosterone: A chemical study. *Canadian Journal of Psychiatry.* 29: 335–343.

Bradley, A. R., & Wood, J. M. (1996). How do children tell? The disclosure process in child sexual abuse. *Child Abuse and Neglect.* 20: 881–891.

Brannigan, A., & Gibbs Van Brunschot, E. (1997). Youthful prostitution and child sexual trauma. *International Journal of Law and Psychiatry,* 20(3): 337–354.

Brannon, J. M., & Troyer, R. (1995). Adolescent sex offenders: Investigating adult commitment-rates four years later. *International Journal of Offender Therapy and Comparative Criminology.* 39: 317–326.

Brehm, S. S., & Brehm, J. W. (1981). *Psychological Reactance: A Theory of Freedom and Control.* New York: Academic.

Breiner, S. J. (1990). *Slaughter of the Innocents: Child Abuse through the Ages and Today.* New York: Plenum.

Briere, J., & Runtz, M. (1989). The trauma symptom checklist (TSC-33). *Journal of Interpersonal Violence.* 4: 151–163.

Briggs, F. (1995). *From Victim to Offender: How Child Sexual Abuse Victims Become Offenders.* St Leonards, Australia: Allen & Unwin.

Briggs, P., Simon, W. T., & Simonsen, S. (2011). An exploratory study of internet-initiated sexual offenses and the chat room sex offender: Has the internet enabled a new typology of sex offender? *Sexual Abuse: A Journal of Research & Treatment.* 23(1): 71–91.

Bringer, J. D., Brackenridge, C. H., & Johnston, L. H. (2001). The name of the game: A review of sexual exploitation of females in sports. *Current Women's Health Reports.* 1(3): 225–231.

Brochman, S. (1991). Silent victims: Bringing male rape out of the closet. *The Advocate.* 582: 38–43.

Brody, S., & Tarling, R. (1980). *Taking Offenders Out of Circulation.* Home Office Research Study 64. London: HMSO.

Brown, K., Spencer, J., & Deakin, J. (2007). The reintegration of sex offenders: Barriers and opportunities for employment. *Howard Journal of Criminal Justice.* 46(1): 32–42.

Brown, M. E., Hull, L. A., & Panesis, L. K. (1984). *Women Who Rape.* Boston: Massachusetts Trial Court.

Brown, T., McCabe, S., & Welford, C. (2007). *Global positioning system (GPS) technology for community supervision: Lessons learned.* Washington, DC: National Institute of Justice, Office of Justice Programs, Department of Justice.

Browne, K. D., Foreman, L., & Middleton, D. (1998). Predicting treatment drop-out in sex offenders. *Child Abuse Review.* 7(6): 402–419.

Browning, C. R., & Laumann, E. O. (1997). Sexual contact between children and adults: A life-course perspective. *American Sociological Review.* 62: 540–560.

Brownmiller, S. (1975). *Against Our Will: Men, Women and Rape.* New York: Bantam.

Bumby, K. M., & Bumby, N. H. (1997). Adolescent female sexual offenders.

In B.K. Schwartz & H. R. Celini (eds.), *The Sex Offender, Vol. II: New Insights, Treatment Innovations and Legal Developments.* Kingston, NJ: Civic Research Institute.

Bumby, K. M., & Hanson, D. J. (1997). Intimacy deficits, fear of intimacy, and loneliness among sex offenders. *Criminal Justice and Behavior.* 24: 315–331.

Bund, J. M. (1997). Did you say chemical castration? *University of Pittsburgh Law Review.* 59: 157.

Buntin, S. (2011). The high price of misguided legislation: Nevada's need for practical sex offender laws. *Nevada Law Journal.* 11: 770.

Bureau of Justice Statistics. (1998). *Child Victimizers: Violent Offenders and Their Victims.* Washington, DC: U.S. Department of Justice.

Bureau of Justice Statistics. (1999). *Felony Sentences in State Courts, 1996.* Washington, DC: U.S. Department of Justice.

Bureau of Justice Statistics. (2004). *Data Collection for the Prison Rape Elimination Act of 2003. BJS Status Report.* Washington, DC: U.S. Department of Justice.

Burgess, A. W. (ed.). (1991). *Rape and Sexual Assault III: A Research Handbook.* New York: Garland.

Burgess, A. W. (1995). Rape trauma syndrome. In P.S. Searles & R. J. Berger (eds.), *Rape and Society.* Boulder, CO: Westview.

Burgess, A. W., Hartman, C., Ressler, R. K., Douglas, J. E., & MacCormack, A. (1986). Sexual homicide: A motivational model. *Journal of Interpersonal Violence.* 1: 251–272.

Burgess, A. W., & Holstrom, L. L. (1974). Rape trauma syndrome. *American Journal of Psychiatry.* 131: 981–986.

Burkhardt, S. A., & Rotatori, A. F. (1995). *Treatment and Prevention of Child*

Sexual Abuse: A Child-Generated Model. Washington, DC: Taylor & Francis.

Burt, M. (1980). Cultural myths and supports for rape. *Journal of Personality and Social Psychology.* 38: 217–230.

Burton, D. L. (2000). Were adolescent sexual offenders children with sexual behavior problems? *Sexual Abuse: Journal of Research and Treatment.* 12: 37–48.

Burton, D. L., & Meezan, W. (2004). Revisiting recent research on social learning theory as an etiological proposition for sexually abusive male adolescents. *Journal of Evidenced-Based Social Work.* 1: 41–80.

Burton, D. L., Miller, D. L., & Shill, C. T. (2002). A social learning theory comparison of the sexual victimization of adolescent sexual offenders and nonsexual offending male delinquents. *Child Abuse and Neglect.* 26: 893–907.

Busby, K., Downe, P., Gorkoff, K., Nixon, K., Tutty, L., & Ursel, E. J. (2000). *Examination of innovative programming for children and youth involved in prostitution.* Winnipeg, Manitoba: RESERVE. http://www.harbour.sfu.ca/freda/reports/gc204.htm

Butler S. M., & Seto M. C. (2002). Distinguishing two types of adolescent sex offenders. *Journal of the American Academy of Child & Adolescent Psychiatry.* 41: 83–90.

Bunzeluk, K. (2009). *Child sexual abuse images: Analysis of websites by Cybertip.ca.* Winnipeg: Canadian Centre for Child Protection.

Cafardi, N. (2008). *Before Dallas: The U.S. Bishops' Response to Clergy Sexual Abuse of Children* New York: Paulist.

Cairns, K. (1999). *Surviving Paedophilia: Traumatic Stress after Organised and Network Child Sexual Abuse.* Staffordshire, UK: Trentham Books.

Calder, M. (2004). *Child sexual abuse and the internet: Tackling the new frontier.* Dorset, UK: Russell House Publishing.

Calder, M. C., Hanks, H., Epps, K. J., Print, B., Morrison, T., & Henniker, J. (2001). *Juveniles and Children Who Sexually Abuse: Frameworks for Assessment.* Dorset, UK: Russell House.

Caldwell, M. F. (2007). Sexual offense adjudication and sexual recidivism among juvenile offenders. *Sexual Abuse.* 19: 107–113.

Caldwell, M. F., Ziemke, M. H., & Vitacco, M. J. (2008). An examination of the sex offender registration and notification act as applied to juveniles: Evaluating the ability to predict recidivism. *Psychology, Public Policy & Law.* 14: 89–114.

Calhoun, K. S., & Atkeson, B. M. (1991). *Treatment of Rape Victims: Facilitating Psychosocial Adjustment.* Elmsford, NY: Pergamon.

Calley, N. G., & Gerber, S. (2008). Empathy-promoting counseling strategies for juvenile sex offenders: A developmental approach. *Journal of Addictions and Offender Counseling.* 28: 68–85.

Campbell, R. (1998). The community response to rape: Victim's experiences with the legal, medical and mental health systems. *American Journal of Community Psychology.* 26: 355–379.

Campbell, R. (2005). What really happened? A validation study of rape survivors' help seeking experiences with the legal and medical systems. *Violence and Victims.* 20: 55–68.

Campbell, R., Wasco, S. M., Ahrens, C. E., Sefl, T., & Barnes, H. E. (2001). Preventing the "second rape": Rape survivors' experiences with community service providers. *Journal of Interpersonal Violence.* 16: 1239–1259.

Campis, L. B., Hebden-Curtis, J., & DeMaso, D. R. (1993). Developmental differences in detection and disclosure of sexual abuse. *Journal of* the *American Academy of Child and Adolescent Psychiatry.* 32: 920–924.

Canada. (1984). *Sexual Offenses against Children.* Ottawa: Canadian Government Publishing Centre.

Canestrini, K. (1999). *The Method of Risk Assessment Used for the New York State Sex Offender Registration Act.* National Conference on Sex Offender Registries. Proceedings of a BJS/SEARCH conference.

Caputo, A. A., Frick, P. J., & Brodsky, S. L. (1999). Family violence and juvenile sex offending: The potential mediating role of psychopathic traits and negative attitudes toward women. *Criminal Justice and Behavior.* 26: 338–356.

Carpenter, D. R., Peed, S. F., & Eastman, B. (1995). Personality characteristics of adolescent offenders: A pilot study. *Sexual Abuse: A Journal of Research and Treatment.* 7: 195–203.

Carpentier, J., Leclerc, B., & Proulx, J. (2011). Juvenile sexual offenders: Correlates of onset, variety, and desistance of criminal behavior. *Criminal Justice and Behavior.* 38(8): 854–873.

Carr, J. (2001). *Theme paper on child pornography for the 2nd world congress on commercial sexual exploitation of children.* Available at: http://www.csecworldcongress.org/PDF/en/Yokohama/Background_reading/Theme_papers/Theme%20paper%20Child%20Pornogrpahy.pdf

Catholic League for Religious and Civil Rights. (2004). *Sexual Abuse in Social Context: Catholic Clergy and Other Professionals.* Available at: http://www.bishop-accountability.org/reports/2004_02_CatholicLeague_SexualAbuse.htm

Center for Sex Offender Management. (2000, January). *Community Supervision of the Sex Offender: An Overview of Current and Promising Practices.* Available at: http://www.csom.org/pubs/supervision2.html

Center for Sex Offender Management. (2000, October). *The Collaborative Approach to Sex Offender Management.* Available at: http://www.csom.org/pubs/collaboration.html

Center for Sex Offender Management. (2002, January). *Time to Work: Managing the Employment of Sex Offenders under Community Supervision.* Washington, DC: U.S. Department of Justice, Office of Justice Programs.

Chajewski, M., & Mercado, C. C. (2008). An analysis of sex offender residency restrictions in Newark, New Jersey. *Sex Offender Law Report.* 9: 1–6.

Champion, D. J. (1994). *Measuring Offender Risk: A Criminal Justice Sourcebook.* Westport, CT: Greenwood.

Chaneles, S. (1976). Prisoners can be rehabilitated—Now. *Psychology Today.* 10: 129–133.

Charles, G., & McDonald, M. (1996). Adolescent sex offenders. *Journal of Youth and Child Care.* 11: 15–25.

Child Maltreatment Report. (2001). Washington, DC: Children's Bureau, Administration on Children, Youth and Families.

Christiensen, K., Elers-Neilson, M., LeMaire, L., & Sturup, G. K. (1965). Recidivism among sexual offenders. *Scandinavian Studies in Criminology.* 1: 55–85.

Chuchmach, M., & Patel, A. (2010, April 9). ABC news investigation: USA swimming coaches molested, secretly taped dozens of teen swimmers. *ABC New.* Retrieved from http://abcnews.go.com/Blotter/abc-news-investigation-usa-swimming-coaches-raped-molested/story?id=10322469

Cipolat, U. (1996). *Rape before the International Criminal Tribunal for the Former Yugoslavia: The Tadic/"F" Case.* LLM dissertation, Yale Law School.

Claiborne, R. (2002, January). *Protected Priest: Archdiocese Admits Priest Should Have Been Reported for Molesting Children.* Available at: http://abcnews.go .com/sections/wnt/DailyNews/ pedophile_priest020125.html

Clancy, S. A. (2009). *The Trauma Myth: The Truth About the Sexual Abuse of Children—and Its Aftermath.* New York: Basic Books.

Clark, D. (1996). *Behavioural Changes Following Completion of the Core Programme.* Prepared for the SOTP Accreditation Panel, London.

Clarke, J. (1997). *HM Prison Service's Sex Offender Treatment Programme: An Overview.* Treating Sex Offenders in a Custodial Setting, HMP Brixton.

Clarke, J. (2011). Working with sex offenders: Best practices in enhancing practitioner resilience. *Journal of Sexual Aggression.* 17(3): 335–355.

Clarke, N. K. (1993). Sex offenders: An overview. In N.K. Clarke & G. M. Stephenson (eds.), *Sexual Offenders: Context, Assessment and Treatment.* Division of Criminological and Legal Psychology Paper No. 19. London: Home Office.

Cochrane, D. L., & Kennedy, M. A. (2010). Attitudes towards Megan's law and juvenile sex offenders. *Justice Policy Journal.* 7(1): 1–35.

Cohen, L. E., & Felson, M. (1979). Social change and crime rate trends: A routine activities approach. *American Sociological Review.* 44: 588–608.

Cohen, M. L., Garofolo, R., Boucher, R., & Seghorn, T. (1971). The psychology of rapists. *Seminars in Psychiatry.* 3: 307–327.

Colorado Department of Public Safety, Sex Offender Management Board. (2004). *Report on safety issues raised by living arrangements for and location of sex offenders in the community.* Denver: Colorado Department of Public Safety.

Colorado Department of Public Safety. (2008). *Sex Offender Management Board.* Available at: http://dcj.state. co.us/odvsom/sex_offender/

Colton, M., Roberts, S., & Vanstone, M. (2010). Sexual abuse by men who work with children. *Journal of Child Sexual Abuse.* 19: 345–364.

Connell, R. (1990). The state, gender, and sexual politics: Theory and appraisal. *Theory and Society.* 19: 507–544.

Conte, J. R. (1991). The nature of sexual offences against children. In C. R. Hollin & K. Howells (eds.), *Clinical Approaches to Sex Offenders and Their Victims.* West Sussex, UK: Wiley.

Conte, J. R., Wolf, S., & Smith, T. (1989). What sexual offenders tell us about prevention strategies. *Child Abuse and Neglect.* 13: 293–301.

Coolidge, F. L., & Segal, D. L. (1998). Evolution of personality disorder diagnosis in the diagnostic and statistical manual of mental disorders. *Clinical Psychology Review.* 18: 585–599.

Cooper, A., McLaughlin, I. P., & Campbell, K. M. (2000). Sexuality in cyberspace: Update for the 21st century. *Sexual Addiction & Compulsivity.* 3(4): 521–536.

Cooper, C. L., Murphy, W. D., & Haynes, M. R. (1996). Characteristics of abused and non-abused adolescent sexual offenders. *Sexual Abuse: Journal of Research and Treatment.* 8: 105–119.

Corlew, K. R. (2006). Congress attempts to shine a light on a dark problem: An in-depth look at the prison rape elimination act 2003. *American Journal of Criminal Law.* 33(2): 157–190.

Correctional Service of Canada. (1996). *Case Studies of Female Sex Offenders.* Ottawa: Correctional Service of Canada.

Coxe, R., & Holmes, W. (2001). A study of the cycle of abuse among child molesters. *Journal of Child Sexual Abuse*. 10: 111–118.

Coyne, J., & Berry, A. (2000). *Rape as an Adaptation?* Retrieved September 27, 2003, from http://www.eurowrc.org/06.contributions/1.contrib_en/11.contrib.en.htm

Craig, L. A., Stringer, I., & Moss, T. (2006). Treating sex offender with learning disabilities in the community. *International Journal of Offender Therapy and Comparative Criminology*. 50(4): 369–390.

Criminal Law Revision Committee. (1984). *Sexual Offences: Fifteenth Report*. London: HMSO.

Cuklanz, L. M. (1996). *Rape on Trial: How the Mass Media Construct Legal Reform and Social Change*. Philadelphia: University of Pennsylvania Press.

Cullen, F. T., & Gendreau, P. (1989). The effectiveness of correctional rehabilitation. In L. Goodstein & D. L. MacKenzie (eds.), *The American Prison: Issues in Research Policy*. New York: Plenum.

Cumming, G., & Buell, M. (1997). *Supervision of the Sex Offender*. Orwell, VT: Safer Society Press.

Curtis, R., Terry, K., Dank, M., Dombrowski, K., & Khan, B. (2008). *Commercial sexual exploitation of children in New York City, volume one: The CSEC population in New York City: Size, characteristics, and needs*. Washington, DC: National Institute of Justice (Award 2005-LX-FX-0001).

Dank, M. (2008). The Safe Harbor for Exploited Youth Act: Recognizing that sexually exploited children are not "offenders." *Sex Offender Law Report*. 9(6): 81–96.

Danni, K. A., & Hampe, G. D. (2000). An analysis of predictors of child sex offender types using pre-sentence investigation reports. *International*

Journal of Offender Therapy and Comparative Criminology. 44: 490–504.

Darke, J. L. (1990). Sexual aggression: Achieving power through humiliation. In W. L. Marshall, D. R. Laws, & H. E. Barbaree (eds.), *Handbook of Sexual Assault: Issues, Theories and Treatment of the Offender*. New York: Plenum.

Davis, G., & Leitenberg, H. (1987). Adolescent sex offenders. *Psychological Bulletin*. 101: 417–427.

Davis, M. H. (1983). Measuring individual differences in empathy: Evidence for a multidimensional approach. *Journal of Personality and Social Psychology*. 44: 113–125.

Davis, R. C. (1987). *Crime Victims: Learning How to Help Them, Research in Action*. Washington, DC: U.S. Department of Justice, National Institute of Justice.

De Francis, V. (1971). Protecting the child victim of sex crimes committed by adults. *Federal Probation*. 35: 15–20.

De River, J. P. (1949). *The Sexual Criminal: A Psychoanalytic Study*. Springfield, IL: Charles C. Thomas.

Debra Lafave: Crossing the Line. (2006). *Dateline*. NBC Broadcasting.

Demichele, M., Payne, B. K., & Button, D. M. (2008). Electronic monitoring of sex offenders: Identifying unanticipated consequences and implications. *Probation and Parole*. 46: 119–135.

Dennison, S. M., Stough, C., & Birgden, A. (2001). The big 5 dimensional personality approach to understanding sex offenders. *Psychology, Crime & Law*. 2: 243–261.

Devoe, E. R., & Coulborn-Faller, K. (1999). The characteristics of disclosure among children who may have been sexually abused. *Child Maltreatment: Journal of the American Professional Society on the Abuse of Children*. 4: 217–227.

Dewan, S. (2006, December 19). Georgia man fights conviction as molester. *New York Times.* Retrieved from http://query.nytimes.com/gst/full page.html?res=9A01E0D9133 1F93AA25751C1A9609C8B63

Dewan, S. (2007, April 16). Dropped duke charges renew hope in georgia. *New York Times.* Retrieved from http://www.nytimes.com/2007/04/16/us/16rape.html

Dickens, B. (1985). Prediction, professionalism, and public policy. In C. D. Webster, M. H. Ben-Aron, & S. J. Hucker (eds.), *Dangerousness: Probability and Prediction, Psychiatry and Public Policy.* New York: Cambridge University Press.

Dietz, P., Hazelwood, R., & Warren, J. (1990). The sexually sadistic criminal and his offenses. *Bulletin of the American Academy of Psychiatry and the Law.* 18: 163–178.

DiGiorgio-Miller, J. (1994). Clinical techniques in the treatment of juvenile sex offenders. *Journal of Offender Rehabilitation.* 21: 117–126.

DiGiorgio-Miller, J. (1998). Sibling incest: Treatment of the family and the offender. *Child Welfare League of America.* 78: 335–346.

Dipietro, E. K., Runyan, D. K., & Fredrickson, D. D. (1997). Predictors of disclosure during medical evaluation for suspected sexual abuse. *Journal of Child Sexual Abuse.* 6: 133–142.

Donohue, W. A. (1996). *A Review Essay of Philip Jenkins's Pedophiles and Priests. Catalyst Online.* Retrieved from http://www.catholicleague.org/catalyst.php?year=1996&month=May&read=61

Doren, D. M. (2002). *Evaluating Sex Offenders: A Manual for Civil Commitments and beyond.* Thousand Oaks, CA: Sage.

Doren, D. M., & Yates, P. M. (2008). Effectiveness of sex offender treatment for psychopathic sexual offenders. *International Journal of Offender Therapy & Comparative Criminology.* 52(2): 234–245.

Dorsett, K. (1998). Kansas v. Hendricks: Marking the beginning of a dangerous new era in civil commitment. *DePaul Law Review.* 48: 113–159.

Dover, K. J. (1978). *Greek Homosexuality.* Cambridge, MA: Harvard University Press.

Downey, M. (2008, January 16). Our opinion: Learn from Genarlow; House bill 908 fails to distinguish between dangerous offenders and those who pose little risk. *The Atlanta Journal-Constitution.* 14A.

Dube, S. R., Anda, R. F., Whitfield, C. L., Brown, D. W., Felitti, V. J., Dong, M., & Giles, W. H. (2005). Long-term consequences of childhood sexual abuse by gender of victim. *American Journal of Preventative Medicine.* 28(5): 430–438.

Dumond, R. W. (2000). Inmate sexual assault: The plague that persists. *The Prison Journal.* 80(4): 407–414.

Dunn, C. (1940). Stiloestral induced gynacomastatia in the male. *Journal of the American Medical Association.* 115: 2263–2264.

Duwe, G., & Goldman, R. A. (2009). The impact of prison-based treatment on sex offender recidivism: Evidence from Minnesota. *Sexual Abuse: A Journal of Research and Treatment.* 21(3): 279–307.

Eby, K. K., Campbell, J. C., Sullivan, C. M., & Davidson, W. S. (1995). Health effects of experiences of sexual violence for women with abusive partners. *Health Care for Women International.* 16: 563–576.

ECPAT International Online. (2005). Retrieved from http://www.ecpat.net/eng/Ecpat_inter/projects/monitoring/online_database/countries.asp.

Ehrenkranz, J., Bliss, E., & Sheard, M. (1974). Plasma testosterone: Correlation with aggressive behavior and social dominance in man. *Psychosomatic Medicine.* 36: 469–475.

Eigenberg, H. M. (2000). Correctional officers and their perceptions of homosexuality, rape, and prostitution in male prisoners. *The Prison Journal.* 80(4): 415–433.

Elliot, D., & Briere, J. (1994). Forensic sexual abuse evaluations of older children: Disclosures and symptomatology. *Behavioral Sciences and the Law.* 12: 261–277.

Elliot, M., Browne, K., & Kilcoyne, J. (1995). Child sexual abuse prevention: What offenders tell us. *Child Abuse and Neglect.* 19: 579–594.

Elliott, I. A., Beech, A. R., Mandeville-Nordon, R., & Hayes, E. (2009). Psychological profiles of internet sexual offenders: Comparisons with contact sexual offenders. *Sexual Abuse: A Journal of Research and Treatment.* 21(1): 76–92.

Ellis, E. M., Atkeson, B. M., & Calhoun, K. S. (1981). Sexual dysfunction in victims of rape. *Women and Health.* 5: 39–47.

Ellis, H. (1899/1942). *Studies in the Psychology of Sex* (2 vols.). New York: Random House.

Ellis, L. (1989). *Theories of Rape: Inquiries into the Causes of Sexual Aggression.* New Yo rk: Hemisphere.

Elwood, R. W. (2009). Mental disorder, predisposition, prediction, and ability to control: Evaluating sex offenders for civil commitment. *Sexual Abuse: A Journal of Research & Treatment.* 21(4): 395–411.

Elwood, R. W., Doren, D. M., & Thornton, D. (2008). Diagnostic and risk profiles of men detained under Wisconsin's sexually violent person law. *International Journal of Offender Therapy and Comparative Criminology.* 54(2): 187–196.

English, K. (2009). The containment approach to managing sex offenders. In R. G. Wright (ed.) *Sex Offender Laws: Failed Policies, New Beginnings.* New York; Springer

English, K., Pullen, S., & Jones, L. (1997). *Managing Adult Sex Offenders in the Community: A Containment Approach.* NIJ Research in Brief. Washington, DC: Department of Justice, National Institute of Justice.

Enniss, B. (2008). Quickly assuaging public fear: How the well-intended Adam Walsh Act led to unintended consequences. *Utah Law Review.* 697–717.

Epps, K. (1993). A survey of experience, training, and working practices among staff working with adolescent sex offenders in secure units. In N. K. Clarke & G. M. Stephenson (eds.), *Sexual Offenders: Context, Assessment and Treatment.* Division of Criminological and Legal Psychology Paper No. 19. London: Home Office.

Epps, K. J. (1999). Causal explanations: Filling the theoretical reservoir. In M. C. Calder (ed.), *Working with Young People Who Sexually Abuse: New Pieces of the Jigsaw Puzzle.* Dorset, UK: Russell House.

Erickson, S. K. (2008). The myth of mental disorder: Transsubstantive behavior and taxometric psychiatry. *Akron Law Review.* 42: 67.

Erickson, W. D. (1987). Frequency of MMPI two-point code types among sex offenders. *Journal of Consulting and Clinical Psychology.* 55: 566–570.

Erickson, W. D., Walbek, N. H., & Seely, R. K. (1987). The life histories and psychological profiles of 59 incestuous stepfathers. *Bulletin of the American Academy of Psychiatry and the Law.* 15: 349–357.

Erooga, M., & Masson, H. C. (eds.). (1999). *Children and Young People*

Who Sexually Abuse Others: Challenges and Responses. London: Routledge.

Estes, A. (1999). "A pure predator"— Sources: Defrocked priest faces rape charges. *The Boston Herald* [online]. Available at: http://www.lexisnexis. com /us/lnacademic/

Estes, R. J., & Weiner, N. A. (2001). *Commercial sexual exploitation of children in the U.S, Canada, and Mexico*. University of Pennsylvania.

Estrich, S. (1987). *Real Rape*. Cambridge, MA: Harvard University Press.

European Sourcebook of Crime and Criminal Justice Statistics—2006 (3rd ed.). (2006). The Hague: Ministry of Justice. Available at: http://www.euro peansourcebook.org/esb3_Full.pdf

Evans, D. R. (1968). Masturbatory fantasy and sexual deviation. *Behaviour Research and Therapy*. 6: 17–19.

Ewing, C. (1985). Preventive detention and execution: The constitutionality of punishing future crimes. *Law and Human Behavior*. 15: 139–163.

Fagan, J., & Wexler, S. (1988). Explanations of sexual abuse assault among violent delinquents. *Journal of Adolescent Research*. 3: 363–385.

Farr, C., Brown, J., & Beckett, R. (2004). Ability to empathize and masculinity level: Comparing male adolescent sex of offenders with a normative sample of non-offending adolescents. *Psychology, Crime and Law*. 10: 155–167.

Farrell, D. P., & Taylor, M. (2000). Silenced by God: An examination of unique characteristics within sexual abuse by the clergy. *Counselling Psychology Review*. 15: 22–31.

Farrell, G. (1995). Preventing repeat victimization. In M. Tonry & D. P. Farrington (eds.), *Crime and Justice: A Review of Research. Vol. 19: Building a Safer Society: Strategic Approaches to Crime Prevention*. Chicago, IL: University of Chicago Press.

Farrington, D. P. (2003). Developmental and life-course criminology: Key theoretical and empirical issues: The 2002 Sutherland award address. *Criminology*. 41: 221–256.

Federal Bureau of Investigation. (1992). *Ted Bundy Multiagency Investigative Team Report*. Washington, DC: U.S. Department of Justice.

Federal Bureau of Investigation. (2000). *Crime in the United States, 2002*. Washington, DC: U.S. Department of Justice.

Federal Bureau of Investigation. (2003). *Crime in the United States, 2002*. Washington, DC: U.S. Department of Justice.

Fehrenbach, P. A., & Monastersky, C. (1988). Characteristics of female adolescent sexual offenders. *American Journal of Orthopsychiatry*. 58: 148–151.

Fehrenbach, P. A., Smith, W., Monastersky, C., & Deisher, R. W. (1986). Adolescent sex offenders: Offender and offense characteristics. *American Journal of Orthopsychiatry*. 56: 225–233.

Felson, M., & Clarke, R. V. (1998). *Opportunity Makes the Thief: Practical Theory for Crime Prevention*. Police Research Series, Paper 98. London: Policing and Reducing Crime Unit: Research, Development and Statistics Directorate.

Fenichel, O. (1945). *The Psychoanalytic Theory of Neurosis*. New York: Norton.

Fernandez, Y. M. (2006). Focusing on the positive and avoiding negativity in sexual offender treatment. In W. L. Marshall, Y. M. Fernandez, L. E. Marshall, & G. A. Serran (eds.), *Sexual offender treatment: Controversial issues* (pp. 225–239). New York: John Wiley and Sons.

Ferrara, M. L., & McDonald, S. (1996). *Treatment of the Juvenile Sex Offender: Neurological and Psychiatric Impairments*. Northvale, NJ: Jason Aronson.

Ferraro, M., Casey, E., & McGrath, M. (2004). *Investigating child exploitation and pornography: The internet, the law and forensic science.* Boston: Elsevier.

Feyerick, D., & Steffen, S. (2009, April 7). "Sexting" lands teen on sex offender list. *CNN's American Morning.* Retrieved from http://articles.cnn.com/2009-04-07/justice/sexting.busts_1_phillip-alpert-offender-list-offender-registry?_s=PM:CRIME

Finkelhor, D. (1980). Sex among siblings: A survey report on its prevalence, its variety, and its effect. *Archives of Sexual Behavior.* 9: 171–194.

Finkelhor, D. (1984). *Child Sexual Abuse: New Theory and Research.* New York: Free Press.

Finkelhor, D. (1986). *A Sourcebook of Child Sexual Abuse.* London: Sage.

Finkelhor, D. (2008). *Childhood Victimization: Violence, Crime, and Abuse in the Lives of Young People.* New York: Oxford University Press.

Finkelhor, D., Hotaling, G., Lewis, I. A., & Smith, C. (1990). Sexual abuse in a national survey of adult men and women: Prevalence, characteristics, and risk factors. *Child Abuse and Neglect.* 14: 19–28.

Finkelhor, D., & Jones, L. M. (2004). *Sexual Abuse Decline in the 1990s: Evidence for Possible Causes.* Washington, DC: U.S. Department of Justice, Office of Juvenile Justice Programs.

Finkelhor, D., & Ormrod, R. (2001, September). *Crimes Against Children by Babysitters.* Washington, DC: Juvenile Justice Bulletin.

Finkelhor, D., & Ormrod, R. (2004). "Prostitution of juveniles: Patterns from NIMBRS." *Juvenile Justice Bulletin.* U.S. Department of Justice, Office of Justice Programs, Office of Juvenile Justice and Delinquency Prevention

Finkelhor, D., Ormrod, R. K., Turner, H. K., & Hamby, S. L. (2005). The victimization of children and youth: A comprehensive, national survey. *Child Maltreatment.* 10(1): 5–25.

Finkelchor, D., & Williams, L. (1988). *Nursery Crimes: A Study of Sexual Abuse in Daycare.* Newbury Park, CA: Sage.

Finn, P., & Lee, B. (1987). *Serving Crime Victims and Witnesses.* Washington, DC: U.S. Department of Justice, National Institute of Justice.

Firestone, P., Bradford, J. M., Greenberg, D. M., & Serran, G. A. (2000). The relationship of deviant sexual arousal and psychopathy in incest offenders: Extra familial child molesters and rapists. *Journal of the American Academy of Psychiatry and the Law.* 28: 303–308.

Fitch, J. H. (1962). Men convicted of sexual offences against children: A descriptive follow-up study. *British Journal of Criminology.* 3: 18–37.

Fitzpatrick, L. (2008). Top Ten Underreported Stories of 2008. *Time* [serial online]. Retrieved from http://www.time.com/time/specials/2008/top10/article/0,30583,1855948_1861760_1862212,00.html

Fletcher-Stack, P. (1999). Pressure to Forgive Challenges Mormon families, Divides Wards. *The Salt Lake Tribune* [online]. Retrieved from Lexis-Nexis.

Florida Department of Law Enforcement. (2005). *Technical Assistance Paper: The Jessica Lundsford Act.* Available at: http://info.fldoe.org/docushare/dsweb/Get/Document-3151/k12_05-107a.pdf

Floud, J., & Young, W. (1981). *Dangerousness and Criminal Justice.* S. L. Radzinowicz, series ed. London: Heinemann.

Flynn, K. A. (2000). *Clergy Sexual Abuse of Women: A Specialized Form of Trauma.* Dissertation from Claremont Graduate University; available from University Microfilms International, Ann Arbor, MI.

Fones, C. S. L., Levine, S. B., Althof, S. E., & Risen, C. B. (1999). The sexual struggles of 23 clergymen: A follow-up study. *Journal of Sex & Marital Therapy.* 25: 183–195.

Foote, R. (1944). Hormone treatment of sex offenders. *Journal of Nervous and Mental Diseases.* 99: 928–929.

Forbes, S. G. (2011). Sex, cells, and SORNA: Applying sex offender registration laws to sexting cases. *William and Mary Law Review.* 52(5): 1717–1746.

Ford, M. E., & Linney, J. A. (1995). Comparative analysis of juvenile sexual offenders, violent nonsexual offenders, and status offenders. *Journal of Interpersonal Violence.* 10: 56–71.

Fowler, S. K., Blackburn, A. G., Marquart, J. W., & Mullings, J. L. (2010). Would they officially report an in-prison sexual assault? An examination of inmate perceptions. *The Prison Journal.* 90(2): 220–243.

Francis, P. C., & Turner, N. R. (1995). Sexual misconduct within the Christian Church: Who are the perpetrators and those they victimize? *Counseling and Values.* 39: 218–227.

Franket al. (1985). Induced abortion operations and their early sequelae. *Journal of the Royal College of General Practitioners.* 35: 175–180.

Fredrickson, R. (1992). *Repressed Memories: A Journal to Recovery from Sexual Abuse.* New York: Simon & Schuster.

Freeman, N. J., & Sandler, J. C. (2008). Female and male sex offenders: A comparison of recidivism patterns and factors [electronic version]. *Journal of Interpersonal Violence.* 23(10): 1394–1413.

Freeman-Longo, R. E. (1996). Feel good legislation: Prevention or calamity. *Child Abuse and Neglect.* 20: 95–101.

Freeman-Longo, R. E., & McFadin, B. (1981). Sexually inappropriate behavior: Development of the sexual offender. *Law and Order.* 29: 21–23.

French, R. (June 14, 2007). Three Insurers Shed Light on Protestant Church Sex Abuse. *The Houston Chronicle* [online]. Retrieved from http://stopbaptist-predators.org/article07/three_insurers_shed_light.html

Freud, S. (1905). My views on the part played by sexuality in the aetiology of the neuroses. In S. Freud (ed.), *Collected Papers, Vol. II* (1959). New York: Basic Books.

Freud, S. (1905/1953). *Three Essays of the Theory of Sexuality: The Complete Psychological Works of Sigmund Freud* (Standard ed., Vol. 7). London: Hogarth.

Freud, S. (1907). Sexual enlightenment of children. In S. Freud (ed.), *Collected Papers, Vol. II* (1959). New York: Basic Books.

Freud, S. (1959). *Collected Papers, Vol. II.* New York: Basic Books.

Freund, K. (1963). A laboratory method of diagnosing predominance of homo- and hetero-erotic interest in the male. *Behavior Research and Therapy.* 1: 85–93.

Freund, K. (1990). Courtship disorder. In W. L. Marshall, D. R. Laws, & H. E. Barbaree (eds.), *Handbook of Sexual Assault: Issues, Theories and Treatment of the Offender.* New York: Plenum.

Freund, K., & Kuban, M. (1994). The basis of the abused abuser theory of pedophilia: A further elaboration on an earlier study. *Archives of Sexual Behavior.* 23: 553–563.

Freund, K., McKnight, C. K., Langevin, R., & Cibiri, S. (1972). The female child as a surrogate object. *Archives of Sexual Behavior.* 2: 119–133.

Frick, P. J. (1998). *Conduct Disorders and Severe Antisocial Behaviour.* New York: Plenum.

Friendship, C., Mann, R. E., & Beech, A. R. (2003). Evaluation of a national prison-based treatment program for sexual offenders in England and

Wales. *Journal of Interpersonal Violence.* 18: 744–759.

Frohmann, L. (1995). Discrediting victims' allegations of sexual assault: Prosecutorial accounts of case rejections. In P.S. Searles & R. J. Berger (eds.), *Rape and Society.* Boulder, CO: Westview.

Frosch, J., & Bromber, W. (1939). The sex offender: A psychiatric study. *American Journal of Orthopsychiatry.* 9: 761–777.

Frumkin, J. (2008). Perennial punishment? Why the sex offender registration and notification act needs reconsideration. *Journal of Law and Policy.* 17: 313–358.

Fry, L. J. (2008). The use of hotspots in the identification of the factors that predict human trafficking. *International Journal of Criminal Justice Sciences.* 3(2): 71–83.

Furby, L., Weinrott, M., & Blackshaw, L. (1989). Sex offenders recidivism: A review. *Psychological Bulletin.* 105: 3–30.

Gabor, T. (1990). Looking back or moving forward: Retributivism and the Canadian Sentencing Commission's proposals. *Canadian Journal of Criminology.* 32: 537–546.

Gallagher, B. (2000). The extent and nature of known cases of institutional child sexual abuse. *British Journal of Social Work.* 30: 795–817.

Gannon, T. A., Rose, M. R., & Ward, T. (2008). A descriptive model of the offense process for female sexual offenders [electronic version]. *Sexual Abuse: A Journal of Research and Treatment.* 20(3): 352–374.

Ganzar, V. J., & Sarason, I. G. (1973). Variables associated with recidivism among juvenile delinquents. *Journal of Consulting and Clinical Psychology.* 40: 1–5.

Garland, R., & Dougher, M. J. (1990). The abused/abuser hypothesis of

child abuse: A critical review of theory and research. In J. R. Feierman (ed.), *Pedophilia: Biosocial Dimensions.* New York: Springer.

Garland, R., & Dougher, M. J. (1991). Motivational intervention in the treatment of sex offenders. In W. R. Miller & S. Rollnick (eds.), *Motivational Interviewing: Preparing People to Change Addictive Behaviour.* New York: Guilford.

Garlick, Y. (1989). *Intimacy Failure, Loneliness and the Attribution of Blame in Sexual Offending.* Master's thesis, University of London.

Geberth, V. J. (1996). *Practical Homicide Investigation: Tactics, Procedures, and Forensic Techniques.* Boca Raton, FL: CRC.

Gebhard, P. H., & Gagnon, J. H. (1964). Male sex offenders against very young children. *American Journal of Psychiatry.* 6: 576–579.

Gebhard, P. H, Gagnon, J. H, Pomeroy, W., & Christenson, C. (1965). *Sex Offenders: An Analysis of Types.* London: Heinemann.

Gendreau, P., Goggin, C., & Paparozzi, M. (1996). Principles of effective assessment for community corrections. In R.P. Corbett & M. K. Harris (eds.), A review of research for practitioners. *Federal Probation.* 60: 64–70.

Gendreau, P., & Ross, R. R. (1979). Effective correctional treatment: Bibliotherapy for cynics. *Crime and Delinquency.* 25: 463–489.

Gendreau, P., & Ross, R. R. (1987). Revivification of rehabilitation: Evidence from the 1980s. *Justice Quarterly.* 4: 349–408.

Gerdes, K. E., Beck, M. A., Cowan-Hancock, S., & Wilkinson-Sparks, T. (1996). Adult survivors of childhood sexual abuse: The case of Mormon women. *Affilia.* 11(1): 39–60.

Gigeroff, A. K., Mohr, J. W., & Turner, R. E. (1968). Sex offenders on probation: Heterosexual pedophiles. *Federal Probation.* 32: 17–19.

Glaser, B. (2009). Treaters or punishers? The ethical role of mental health clinicians in sex offender programs. *Aggression & Violent Behavior.* 14(4): 248–255.

Glaser, B. (2010). Sex offender programmes: New technology coping with old ethics. *Journal of Sexual Aggression.* 16(3): 261–274.

Glaser, D. (1969). *The Effectiveness of a Prison and Parole System.* Indianapolis, IN: Bobbs-Merrill.

Glaser, D. (1974). Remedies for the key deficiency in criminal justice evaluation research. *Journal of Research in Crime and Delinquency.* 11: 144–154.

Gleuck, S., & Gleuck, E. T. (1950). *Unraveling Juvenile Delinquency.* Cambridge, MA: Harvard University Press.

The Globe Spotlight Team. (2006). Church allowed abuse by priest for years. *The Boston Globe* [online]. January 6, 2002. Available at: http://www.boston.com/globe/spotlight/abuse/chronological.htm.

Goetz, D. (1992). Is the pastor's family safe at home? *Leadership.* 13: 38–44.

Golding, J. M. (1996). Sexual assault history and women's reproductive and sexual health. *Psychology of Women Quarterly.* 20: 101–121.

Good, O. S. (2001, July 24). Public hears pitch for group home: Advocate says facility for young sex offenders would be safest in state. *Rocky Mountain News,* p. 20A.

Goodman-Brown, T. B., Edelstein, R. S., Goodman, G. S., Jones, D. P, & Gordon, D. (2003). Why children tell: A model of children's disclosure of sexual abuse. *Child Abuse and Neglect.* 27: 525–540.

Goodstein, L. (2003). Decades of damage; trail of pain in Church crisis leads to nearly every diocese. *New York Times,* p. 1.

Goodstein, L. (2003, August 11). Ousted members say Jehovah's Witnesses' policy on abuse hides offenses. *New York Times* [online]. Retrieved from http://www.nytimes.com/2002/08/11/us/ousted-members-say-jehovah-s-witnesses-policy-on-abuse-hides-offenses.html

Gookin, K. (2007). *Comparison of State Laws Authorizing Involuntary Commitment of Sexually Violent Predators: 2006 Updated, Revised* (Washington State Institute for Public Policy, document number 07-08-1101). Retrieved March 5, 2009, from http://www.wsipp.wa.gov.

Gordon, A., & Porporino, F. J. (1990). Managing the treatment of sex offenders: A Canadian perspective (Resesarch Report No. B-05). Ottawa: Correctional Service of Canada.

Gottfredson, M. R., & Hindelang, M. J. (1977). A consideration of telescoping and memory decay biases in victimization surveys. *Journal of Criminal Justice.* 5: 205–216.

Gottfredson, S. D., & Moriarty, L. J. (2006). Statistical risk assessment: Old problems and new applications. *Crime and Delinquency.* 52(1): 178–200.

Gould, M. A. (1994). *Differences Between Male Intrafamilial and Extrafamilial Child Sexual Abusers in Situational Disinhibition Factors of Alcohol Use (MAST) and Stress (SRE).* PhD dissertation, The Fielding Institute.

Gozdziak, E. M., & Collett, E. A. (2005). Research on human trafficking in North America: A review of literature. *International Migration.* 43(1/2): 99–128.

Grace, S., Lloyd, C., & Smith, L. J. F. (1992). *Rape: From Recording to Conviction.* Home Office, Research and Planning Unit Paper No. 71. London: HMSO.

Gragg, F., Petta, I., Bernstein, H., Eisen, K., & Quinn, L. (2007). *New York Prevalence Study of Commercially Sexually Exploited Children*. New York: WESTAT for the New York State Office of Children and Family Services.

Graham, J. R. (2005). *MMPI-2: Assessing Personality and Psychopathology* (4th ed.). New York: Oxford University Press.

Grant, C., & McDonald, M. (1996). Adolescent sexual offenders. *Journal of Child and Youth Care*. 11: 15–25.

Grant, H., & Terry, K. J. (2001). *Report on the Management and Care of Sex Offenders in New York City*. Presentation to the Sex Offender Management Team.

Grant, H., & Terry, K. J. (2011). *Law Enforcement in the 21st Century* (3rd ed.). Boston, MA: Allyn & Bacon.

Graves, R. B., Openshaw, D. K., Ascione, F. R., & Ericksen, S. L. (1996). Demographic and parental characteristics of youthful sexual offenders. *International Journal of Offender Therapy and Comparative Criminology*. 40: 300–317.

Gray, A. S., & Pithers, W. D. (1993). Relapse preventions with sexually aggressive adolescents and children: Expanding treatment and supervision. In H. E. Barbaree, W. L. Marshall, & S. M. Hudson (eds.), *The Juvenile Sex Offender*. New York: Guilford.

Gray, S. H. (1982). Exposure to pornography and aggression towards women: The case of the angry male. *Social Problems*. 29: 387–398.

Green, R. (1994). Recovered memories of sexual abuse: The unconscious strikes back or therapist induced madness? *Annual Review of Sex Research*. Mt. Vernon, IA: Society for the Scientific Study of Sex.

Greenfeld, L. A. (1997). *Sex Offenses and Offenders: An Analysis of Data on Rape and Sexual Assault*. Washington, DC: U.S. Department of Justice, Bureau of Justice Statistics.

Greenland, C. (1984). Dangerous sex offender registration in Canada, 1948-1977: An experiment that failed. *Canadian Journal of Criminology*. 26: 1–12.

Greer, J. G., & Stuart, I. R. (eds.). (1983). *The Sexual Aggressor: Current Perspectives on Treatment*. New York: Van Nostrand Reinhold.

Gries, L. T., Goh, D. S., & Cavanaugh, J. (1996). Factors associated with disclosure during child sexual abuse assessment. *Journal of Child Sexual Abuse*. 5: 1–20.

Griffin, S. (1979). *Rape: The Power of Consciousness*. New York: Plenum.

Grisso, T., & Appelbaum, P. S. (1992). Is it unethical to offer predictions of future violence? *Law and Human Behavior*. 16: 621–633.

Grisso, T., & Appelbaum, P. S. (1993). Structuring the debate about ethical predictions of future violence. *Law and Human Behavior*. 17: 482–485.

Groth, A. N. (1979). *Men Who Rape: The Psychology of the Offender*. New York: Plenum.

Groth, A. N. (1983). Treatment of the sexual offender in a correctional institution. In J.G. Greer & I. R. Stuart (eds.), *The Sexual Aggressor: Current Perspectives on Treatment*. New York: Van Nostrand Reinhold.

Groth, A. N., & Burgess, A. W. (1977). Motivational intent in the sexual assault on children. *Criminal Justice and Behavior*. 4: 253–264.

Groth, A. N., & Burgess, A. W. (1980). Male rape: Offenders and victims. *American Journal of Psychiatry*. 137: 806–810.

Groth, A. N., Hobson, W. F., & Gary, T. S. (1982). The child molester: Clinical observations. In J. Conte &

D. A. Shore (eds.), *Social Work and Child Sexual Abuse*. New York: Haworth.

Groth, A. N., Longo, R. E., & McFadin, J. D. (1982). Undetected recidivism among rapists and child molesters. *Crime and Delinquency*. 28: 102–106.

Groth, A. N., & Loredo, C. M. (1981). Juvenile sex offenders: Guidelines for assessment. *International Journal of Offender Therapy and Comparative Criminology*. 25: 31–39.

Grubesic, T. H., Murray, A. T., & Mack, E. A. (2007). *Geographic Exclusion: Spatial Analysis for Evaluating the Implications of Megan's Law*. National Institute of Justice's 9th Annual Crime Mapping Conference, Pittsburgh, PA.

Grubin, D., & Gunn, J. (1990). *The Imprisoned Rapist and Rape*. London: Home Office.

Grubin, D., & Prentky, R. (1993). Sexual psychopathy laws. *Criminal Behaviour and Mental Health*. 3: 381–392.

Grubin, D., & Thornton, D. (1994). A national program for the assessment and treatment of sex offenders in the English prison system. *Criminal Justice and Behavior*. 21: 55–71.

Grubin, D., & Wingate, S. (1996). Sexual offence recidivism: Prediction versus understanding. *Criminal Behaviour and Mental Health*. 6: 349–359.

Gurley, G. (2001, March). Pleasures to the fur. *Vanity Fair*. 174–196.

Gutheil, T. G. (2000). Preventing "critogenic" harms: Minimizing emotional injury from civil litigation. *Journal of Psychiatry and the Law*. 28: 5–18.

Guy, E. (1992). The prison service's strategy. In Prison Reform Trust (ed.), *Beyond Containment: The Penal Response to Sex Offending*. London: Prison Reform Trust.

Hackfield, A. W. (1935). The ameliorative effects of therapeutic castration in habitual sex offenders. *Journal of Nervous and Mental Disease*. 82: 169–181.

Hagan, M. P., Gust-Brey, K. L., Cho, M. E., & Dow, E. (2001). Eight year comparative analyses of adolescent rapists, adolescent child molesters, other adolescent delinquents, and the general population. *International Journal of Offender Therapy and Comparative Criminology*. 45: 314–324.

Hagan, M. P., King, R. P., & Patros, R. L. (1994). The efficacy of a serious sex offenders treatment program for adolescent rapists. *International Journal of Offender Therapy and Comparative Criminology*. 38: 141–150.

Hall, G. C. N., & Hirschman, R. (1992). Sexual aggression against children: A conceptual perspective of etiology. *Criminal Justice and Behavior*. 19: 8–23.

Hallack, S. L., & White, A. D. (1977). Is rehabilitation dead? *Crime and Delinquency*. 23: 372–382.

Hamilton, M. A. (2010, April 15). *How Other Religious Organizations Echo the Roman Catholic Church's Rule against Scandal—A Precept That Entrenches and Perpetuates Cycles of Child Sex Abuse: Church of Jesus Christ of Latter-Day Saints*. Available at: http://writ.news.findlaw.com/hamilton/20100415.html

Hammer, E. F. (1957). A psychoanalytic hypothesis concerning sex offenders. *Journal of Clinical and Experimental Psychology*. 18: 341–360.

Hammer, E. F., & Glueck, B. C. Jr. (1957). Psychodynamic patterns in sex offenders: A four-factor theory. *Psychiatric Quarterly*. 31: 325–345.

Hammett, T. M., Harmon, P., & Maruschak, L. M. (1999). *1996-1997 Update: HIV/AIDS, STDs and TB in Correctional Facilities: Issues and Practices*. Washington, DC: US Department of Justice. Retrieved December 7, 2004, from http://www.ncjrs.org/txtfiles1/176344.txt

Hanley, R. (2000, March 17). Psychologists fired after disputed release of rapist. *New York Times*, p. B:1.

Hanley, R. (2000, March 23). Freed rapist traveled openly by bus across east and south during nationwide manhunt. *New York Times*, p. B:5.

Hanser, R. D., & Mire, S. M. (2008). Juvenile sex offenders in the United States and Australia: A comparison. *International Journal of Law, Computers and Technology*. 22: 101–114.

Hanson, R. F., Saunders, H. S., Saunders, B. E., Kilpatrick, D. G., & Best, C. (1999). Factors related to the reporting of childhood rape. *Child Abuse and Neglect*. 23: 559–569.

Hanson, R.K. (1998). What do we know about sex offender risk assessment? *Psychology, Public Policy, and Law*. 4: 50–72.

Hanson, R. K. (2000). *Risk Assessment*. Association for the Treatment of Sexual Abusers. Available at: http://www.atsa.com/pdfs/InfoPack-Risk.pdf

Hanson, R. K. (2006a). Does Static-99 predict recidivism among older sexual offenders? *Sexual Abuse: A Journal of Research & Treatment*. 18(4): 343–355.

Hanson, R. K. (2006b). Screening for positions of trust with children. *Research Summary Public Safety and Emergency Preparedness Canada*. 11: 1–3.

Hanson, R. K. (2006c). Stability and change: Dynamic risk factors for sexual offenders. In W. L. Marshall, Y. M. Fernandez, Marshall, & G. Serran (eds.), *Sexual Offender Treatment*. New York: John Wiley & Sons.

Hanson, R. K., & Bussiere, M. T. (1996). *Sex Offender Risk Predictors: A Summary of Research Results*. Available at: http://www.csc-scc.gc.ca/crd/forum/e082/e

Hanson, R. K., & Bussiere, M. T. (1998). Predicting relapse: A recta-analysis of sexual offender recidivism studies. *Journal of Consulting and Clinical Psychology*. 66: 348–362.

Hanson, R. K., Gizzarelli, R., & Scott, H. (1994). The attitudes of incest offenders: Sexual entitlement and acceptance of sex with children. *Criminal Justice and Behavior*. 21: 187–202.

Hanson, R. K., Gordon, A., Harris, A. J. R., Marques, J. K., Murphy, W., Quinsey, V. L., & Seto, M. C. (2002). First report of the collaborative outcome data project on the effectiveness of psychological treatment for sex offenders. *Sexual Abuse: A Journal of Research and Treatment*. 14: 169–194.

Hanson, R. K., & Harris, A. (1998). *Dynamic Predictors of Sexual Recidivism*. Ottawa: Office of the Solicitor General of Canada.

Hanson, R. K., & Harris, A. (2000). *The Sex Offender Need Assessment Rating (SONAR): A method for measuring change in risk levels*. Available at: http://www.sgc.gc.ca/epub/Corr/e200001b/e200001b.htm

Hanson, R. K., & Morton-Bourgon, K. (2004). *Predictors of Sexual Recidivism: An Updated Meta-Analysis* (Research Rep. No 2004-02). Ottawa: Public Safety and Emergency Preparedness Canada.

Hanson, R. K., & Slater, S. (1988). Sexual victimization in the history of child sexual abusers: A review. *Annals of Sex Research*. 1: 485–499.

Hanson, R. K., Stefly, R. A., & Gauthier, R. (1993). Long-term recidivism of child molesters. *Journal of Consulting and Clinical Psychology*. 61: 646–652.

Hanson, R. K., & Thornton, D. M. (1999). *Static 99: Improving Actuarial Risk Assessments for Sex Offenders*. Ottawa: Public Works and Government Services.

Hanson, R. K., & Thornton, D. M. (2000). Improving risk assessments for sex offenders: A comparison of three actuarial scales. *Law & Human Behavior.* 24(1): 119–136.

Hare, R. D., & Jutai, J. W. (1983). Criminal history of the male psychopath: Some preliminary data. In K. T. Van Dusen & S. A. Mednick (eds.), *Prospective Studies of Crime and Delinquency.* Boston: Kluwer-Nijhoff.

Hare, R. D., & MacPherson, L. M. (1984). Violent and aggressive behavior by criminal psychopaths. *International Journal of Law and Psychiatry.* 7: 35–50.

Harkins, L., & Beech, A. R. (2007a). Measurement of the effectiveness of sex offender treatment. *Aggression & Violent Behavior.* 12(1): 36–44.

Harkins, L., & Beech, A. R. (2007b). A review of the factors that can influence the effectiveness of sexual offender treatment: Risk, need, responsivity, and process issues. *Aggression & Violent Behavior.* 12(6): 615–627.

Harkins, L., & Beech, A. R. (2008). Examining the impact of mixing child molesters and rapists in group-based cognitive-behavioral treatment for sexual offenders. *International Journal of Offender Therapy & Comparative Criminology.* 52(1): 31–45.

Harlow, C. W. (1999). *Prior Abuse Reported by Inmates and Probationers* (NCJ 172879). Washington, DC: U.S. Department of Justice.

Harris, A. J. (2005). *Civil Commitment of Sexual Predators: A Study in Policy Implementation.* New York: LFB Scholarly Publishing.

Harris, A. J. (2009). The civil commitment of sexual predators: A policy review. In R. Wright (ed.), *Sex Offender Laws: Failed Policies, New Directions.* New York: Springer.

Harris, A. J., & Lobanov-Rostovsky, C. (2010). Implementing the Adam Walsh Act's sex offender registration and notification provisions: A survey of the states. *Sexual Abuse: A Journal of Research and Treatment.* 21(2): 202–222.

Harris, G. T., Rice, M. E., & Quinsey, V. L. (2003). A multisite comparison of actuarial risk instruments for sex offenders. *Psychological Assessment.* 15(3): 413–425.

Harris, J., & Grace, S. (1999). *A Question of Evidence? Investigating and Prosecuting Rape in the 1990s.* Home Office Research Study 196. London: Home Office.

Harris, V. (2000). The antecedents of young male sex offenders. In G. Boswell (ed.), *Violent Children and Adolescents: Asking the Question Why* (pp. 138–150). London: Routledge.

Hart, T. C., & Rennison, C. (2003). *Reporting Crime to the Police, 1992–2000.* Washington, DC: U.S. Department of Justice, Bureau of Justice Statistics.

Hartley, C. C. (1998). How incest offenders overcome internal inhibitions through the use of cognitions and cognitive distortions. *Journal of Interpersonal Violence.* 13: 25–39.

Hartley, C. C. (2001). Incest offenders' perceptions of their motives to sexually offend within their past and current life context. *Journal of Interpersonal Violence.* 16: 459–475.

Hastings, T., Anderson, S. J., & Hemphill, P. (1997). Comparisons of daily stress, coping, problem behavior, and cognitive distortions in adolescent sexual offenders and conduct-disordered youth. *Sexual Abuse: A Journal of Research and Treatment.* 9: 29–42.

Hatcher, R., & Noakes, S. (2010). Working with sex offenders: The impact on Australian treatment providers. *Psychology, Crime & Law.* 16(1/2): 145–167.

Hayashino, D. S., Wurtele, S. K., & Klebe, K. J. (1995). Child molesters: An examination of cognitive factors. *Journal of Interpersonal Violence*. 10: 106–116.

Haywood, T. W., Grossman, L. S., & Kravitz, H. M. (1994). Profiling psychological distortions in alleged child molesters. *Psychological Reports*. 75: 915–927.

Hays, S. E. (1981). The psychoendocrinology of puberty and adolescent aggression. In D.A. Hamburg & M. B. Trudeau (eds.), *Biobehavioral Aspects of Aggression*. New York: A. R. Liss.

Hazelwood, R. R. (1983, September). The behavior-oriented interview of rape victims: The key to profiling. *FBI Law Enforcement Bulletin*. 52: 8–15.

Hazelwood, R. R., Dietz, P. E., & Burgess, A. W. (1983). *Autoerotic Fatalities*. Lexington, MA: Lexington Books.

Heffernan, K., Cloitre, M., Tardiff, K., Marzuk, P. M., Portera, L., & Leon, A. C. (2000). Childhood trauma as a correlate of lifetime opiate use in psychiatric patients. *Addictive Behaviors*. 25(5): 797–803.

Heim, N. (1981). Sexual behavior of castrated sex offenders. *Archives of Sexual Behavior*. 10: 11–20.

Helmus, L., Thornton, D., Hanson, R. K., & Babchishin, K. M. (2011). Improving the predictive accuracy of Static-99 and Static-2002 with older sex offenders: Revised age weights. *Sexual Abuse: A Journal of Research and Treatment*. 39: 1–38.

Hemphill, J. F., Hare, R. D., & Wong, S. (1998). Psychopathy and recidivism: A review. *Legal and Criminological Psychology*. 3: 139–170.

Henry, O., Mandeville-Norden, R., Hayes, E., & Egan, V. (2010). Do internet-based sexual offenders reduce to normal, inadequate and deviant groups? *Journal of Sexual Aggression*. 16(1): 33–46.

Hershkowitz, I., Lanes, O., & Lamb, M. E. (2007). Exploring the disclosure of child sexual abuse with alleged victims and their parents. *Child Abuse and Neglect*. 31: 111–123.

Herman, J., & Hirschman, L. (1977). Father-daughter incest. *Signs*. 4: 735–756.

Herman, J. L. (1990). Sex offenders: A feminist perspective. In W. L. Marshall, D. R. Laws, & H. E. Barbaree (eds.), *Handbook of Sexual Assault: Issues, Theories and Treatment of the Offender*. New York: Plenum.

Heyman, B. (1997). *Risk, Health and Healthcare: A Qualitative Approach*. London: Edward Arnold.

Hickey, N., McCrory, E., Farmer, E., & Vizard, E. (2008). Comparing the developmental characteristics of female and male juvenile who present with sexually abusive behaviour. *Journal of Sexual Aggression*. 14(3): 241–252.

Hicks, R. D. (1991). *In Pursuit of Satan*. New York: Prometheus.

Hillbrand, M., & Waite, B. M. (1994). The everyday experience of an institutionalised sex offender: An idiographic application of the experience sampling method. *Archives of Sexual Behavior*. 23: 453–463.

Hiller, S. (1998). The problem with juvenile sex offender registration: The detrimental effects of public disclosure. *Boston University Public Interest Law Journal*. 7: 271–272.

Hilliker, D. R. (1997). *The Relationship between Childhood Sexual Abuse and Juvenile Sexual Offending: Victim to Victimizer*. Dissertation from Ohio State University; available through University Microfilms International, Ann Arbor, MI.

Hindelang, M., Gottfredson, M., & Garofalo, J. (1978). *Victims of Personal Crime: An Empirical Foundation for a Theory of Personal Victimization*. Cambridge, MA: Ballinger.

Hite, S. (1976). *The Hite Report: A Nationwide Study of Female Sexuality.* New York: Seven Stories Press.

Hite, S. (1982). *The Hite Report on Male Sexuality.* New York: Ballantine Books.

Hogue, T. E. (1995). Training multi-disciplinary teams to work with sex offenders: Effect on staff attitudes. *Psychology, Crime and Law.* 1: 227–235.

Holland, G. (2005). Identifying victims of child abuse images: An analysis of successful identifications. In E. Quayle & M. Taylor (eds.), *Viewing Child Pornography on the Internet: Understanding the Offense, Managing the Offender, Helping the Victims* (pp. 75–90). Lyme Regis, UK: Russell House.

Hollin, C. R., & Howells, K. (1991). *Clinical Approaches to Sex Offenders and Their Victims.* West Sussex, UK: Wiley.

Holmes, R. M. (1991). *Sex Crimes.* Newbury Park, CA: Sage.

Holmes, R. M., & Holmes, S. T. (2002). *Sex Crimes: Patterns and Behavior.* Newbury Park, CA: Sage.

Homes, M. M., Resnick, H. S., Kilpatrick, D. G., & Best, C. L. (1992). Rape-related pregnancy: Estimates and descriptive characteristics from a national sample of women. *American Journal of Obstetrics and Gynecology.* 175: 320–324.

Hood, R., & Shute, S. (1996). Protecting the public: Life sentences, parole, and high risk offenders. *Criminal Law Review.* 788–800.

Horwitz, A. V., Widom, C. S., McLaughlin, J., & White, H. R. (2001). The impact of child abuse and neglect on adult mental health. *Journal of Social Behavior.* 42: 184–201.

Houston, J., Wrench, M., & Hosking, N. (1995). Group processes in the treatment of child sex offenders. *Journal of Forensic Psychiatry.* 6: 359–368.

Howard League Working Party. (1985). *Unlawful Sex.* London: Waterlow.

Howells, K. (1981). Adult sexual interest in children: Consideration relevant to theories of aetiology. In M. Cook & K. Howells (eds.), *Adult Sexual Interest in Children.* London: Academic.

Hucker, S. J., & Bain, J. (1990). Androgenic hormones and sexual assault. In W. L. Marshall, D. R. Laws, & H. E. Barbaree (eds.), *Handbook of Sexual Assault: Issues, Theories and Treatment of the Offender.* New York: Plenum.

Hughes, L. A., & Kadleck, C. (2008). Sex offender community notification and community stratification. *Justice Quarterly.* 25(4): 647–671.

Hunter, J. A., Jr., & Becker, J. V. (1994). The role of deviant sexual arousal in juvenile offending: Etiology, evaluation and treatment. *Criminal Justice and Behavior.* 21: 132–149.

Hunter, J. A., Figueredo, A. J., Malamuth, N. M., & Becker, J. V. (2003). Juvenile sex offenders: Toward the development of a typology. *Sexual Abuse: A Journal of Research and Treatment.* 15: 27–48.

Hunter, J. A., Lexier, L. J., Goodwin, D. W., Browne, P. A., & Dennis, C. (1993). Psychosexual, attitudinal and development of an adolescent female sex offender. *Journal of Sex Research.* 29: 131–139.

Inciardi, J. A., Pottieger, A. E., Forney, M., Chitwood, D. D., & McBride, D. C. (1991). Prostitution, IV drug use, and sex-for-crack exchanges among serious delinquents: Risks for HIV infection. *Criminology.* 29(2): 221–235.

International Association of Chiefs of Police. (2008). *Tracking Sex Offenders with Electronic Technology: Implications and Practical Uses for Law Enforcement.* Washington, DC: U.S. Department of Justice.

Interpol. (2011). *Protecting Children from Actual and Virtual Abuse Focus of Interpol Expert Meeting.* Available at: http://www.interpol.int/News-and-media/News-media-releases/2011/PR071

Irons, R., & Laaser, M. (1994). The abduction of fidelity: Sexual exploitation by clergy—experience with inpatient assessment. *Sexual Addiction and Recovery.* 1: 119–129.

Isley, P. J. (1991). Adult male sexual assault in the community: A literature review and group treatment model. In A. W. Burgess (ed.), *Rape and sexual assault III: A research handbook.* New York: Garland.

Isley, P. J. (1997). Child sexual abuse and the Catholic Church: An historical and contemporary review. *Pastoral Psychology.* 45: 227–299.

Isley, P. J., & Isley, P. (1990, November). The sexual abuse of male children by church personnel: Intervention and prevention. *Pastoral Psychology.* 39: 85–99.

Jackson, R. L., & Hess, D. T. (2007). Evaluation for civil commitment of sex offenders: A survey of experts. *Sexual Abuse: A Journal of Research and Treatment.* 19: 425–448.

Jackson, R., & Richards, H. (2007). Diagnostic and risk profiles among civilly committed sex offenders in Washington State. *International Journal of Offender Therapy and Comparative Criminology.* 51(3): 313–323.

Jacob Wetterling Resource Center. (2008). Available at: http://www.jwrc.org/Home/tabid/36/Default.aspx

Jacobs, W. L. (1999). *The Utilization of Offense Characteristics in the Classification of Male Adolescent Sexual Offenders.* Dissertation from Florida State University; available through University Microfilms International, Ann Arbor, MI.

Jacobs, W. L., Kennedy, W. A., & Meyer, J. B. (1997). Juvenile delinquents: A between-group comparison study of sexual and nonsexual offenders. *Sexual Abuse: A Journal of Research and Treatment.* 9: 201–217.

Janicki, M. A. (2007). Better seen than herded: Residency restrictions and global positioning system tracking laws for sex offenders. *The Boston University Public Interest Law Journal.* 16: 285–311.

Janus, E. S. (1997). The use of social science and medicine in sex offender commitment. *New England Journal on Criminal and Civil Commitment.* 23: 347–386.

Janus, E. S., & Meehl, P. E. (1997). Assessing the legal standard for predictions of dangerousness in sex offender commitment proceedings. *Psychology, Public Policy, and Law.* 3: 33–64.

Janus, E. S., & Prentky, R. (2008). Sexual predator laws: A two-decade retrospective. *Federal Sentencing Report.* 21(2): 90–99.

Jehu, D. (1988). *Beyond Sexual Abuse: Therapy with Women Who Were Childhood Victims.* West Sussex, UK: Wiley.

Jenkins, P. (1998). *Moral Panic: Changing Concepts of the Child Molester in Modern America.* New Haven, CT: Yale University Press.

Jenkins, P. (2001). *Beyond Tolerance: Child Pornography on the Internet.* New York: University Press.

Jenkins, P. (1995). Clergy sexual abuse: The symbolic politics of a social problem. In J. Best (ed.), *Images of Issues* (2nd ed., pp. 105–130). New York: Aldine De Gruyter.

Jenkins, P., & Maier-Katkin, D. (1991). Occult survivors: The making of a myth. In J. Richardson, J. Best, & D. Bromley (eds.), *The Satanism Scare.* New York: Aldine & Gruyter.

Jennings, K. T. (2000). *Female Sexual Abuse of Children: An Exploratory Study.* Dissertation from the University of Toronto; available through University Microfilms International, Ann Arbor, MI.

John Jay College. (2004). *The Nature and Scope of Sexual Abuse of Minors by Catholic Priests and Deacons in the United States, 1950-2002.* Washington, DC: USCCB.

John Jay College. (2006). *The nature and scope of sexual abuse of minors by Catholic Priests and Deacons in the United States, 1950–2002: Supplementary report.* Washington, DC: United States Conference of Catholic Bishops.

Johnson, J. T. (1992). *Mothers of Incest Survivors: Another Side of the Story.* Bloomington: Indiana University Press.

Johnson, K. (2002). States' use GPS offender tracking systems. *Journal of Offender Monitoring.* 15(2): 21–26.

Jones, L. M., & Finkelhor, D. (2004). *Sexual abuse decline in the 1990s: Evidence for Possible causes* (Juvenile Justice Bulletin No. NCJ1999298). Washington, DC: Office of Juvenile Justice & Delinquency Prevention.

Jones, T. R., & Pratt, T. C. (2008). The prevalence of sexual assault violence in prison: The state of the knowledge base and implications for evidence-based correctional policy making. *International Journal of Offender Therapy and Comparative Criminology.* 52(3): 280–295.

Kafka, M. P. (2004). Sexual molesters of adolescents, ephebophilia, and catholic clergy: A review and synthesis. In R. K. Hanson, F. Pfäfflin, & M. Lütz (eds.), *Sexual Abuse in the Catholic Church: Scientific and Legal Perspectives.* Vatican: Libreria Editrico Vaticana.

Kahn, T. J., & Chambers, H. J. (1991). Assessing reoffense risk with juvenile sexual offenders. *Child Welfare.* 70: 333–344.

Karpman, B. (1954). *The Sexual Offender and His Offenses: Etiology, Pathology, Psychodynamics and Treatment.* New York: Julian.

Kasl, C. D. (1990). Female perpetrators of sexual abuse: A feminist perspective. In M. Hunter (ed.), *The Sexually Abused Male, Vol. 1: Prevalence, Impact and Treatment.* New York: Lexington Books.

Katz, N. (1997). "Homosexual" and "heterosexual": Questioning the terms. In M. Duberman (ed.), *A Queer World: The Center for Lesbian and Gay Studies Reader.* New York: New York University Press.

Kavoussi, R. J., Kaplan, M., & Becker, J. V. (1988). Psychiatric diagnoses in adolescent sex offenders. *Journal of the American Academy of Child and Adolescent Psychiatry.* 27: 241–243.

Kear-Colwell, J., & Pollock, P. (1997). Motivation or confrontation: Which approach to the child sex offender? *Criminal Justice and Behavior.* 24: 20–33.

Keary, K., & Fitzpatrick, C. (1994). Children's disclosure of sexual abuse during formal investigation. *Child Abuse and Neglect.* 18: 543–548.

Keenan, T., & Ward, T. (2000). A theory of mind perspective on cognition, affective, and intimacy deficits in child sex offenders. *Sexual Abuse: A Journal of Research and Treatment.* 12(1): 49–60.

Kelly, A. F. (1998). Clergy offenders. In W. L. Marshall & Y. M. Fernandez (eds.), *Sourcebook of Treatment Programs for Sexual Offenders.* New York: Plenum.

Kelty, R., Kleykamp, M., & Segal, D. R. (2010). The military and the transition to adulthood. *The Future of Children.* 20(1): 181–207.

Kempe, R. S., & Kempe, C. H. (1978). *Child Abuse.* London: Fontana/Open University.

Kemper, T. S., & Kistner, J. A. (2010). An evaluation of classification criteria of juvenile sex offenders. *Sexual Abuse: A Journal of Research and Treatment.* 22(2): 172–190.

Kemshall, H. (2001). *Risk Assessment and Management of Known Sexual and Violent Offenders: A Review of Current Issues.* Police Research Series, Paper 140. London: Home Office.

Kendall-Tackett, K. A., Williams, L. M., & Finkelhor, D. (1993). Impact of sexual abuse on children: A review and synthesis of recent empirical studies. *Psychological Bulletin.* 113: 164–180.

Kenny, D. T., Keogh, T., & Seidler, K. (2001). Predictors of recidivism in Australian juvenile sex offenders: Implications for treatment. *Sexual Abuse.* 13: 131–148.

Kernsmith, P. D., Comartin, E., Craun, S. W., & Kernsmith, R. M. (2009). The relationship between sex offender registry utilization and awareness. *Sexual Abuse: A Journal of Research and Treatment.* 21(2): 181–193.

Kidd, S. A., & Krall, M. J. (2002). Suicide and Prostitution among street youth: A qualitative analysis. *Adolescence.* 37: 411–430.

Kingston, D. A., Yates, P. M., Firestone, P., Babchishin, K., & Bradford, J. M. (2008). Long-term predictive validity of the Risk Matrix 2000. *Sexual Abuse: A Journal of Research & Treatment.* 20(4): 466–484.

Kinsey, A. (1948). *Sexual Behavior in the Human Male.* Philadelphia: Saunders.

Kinsey, A., Pomeroy, W., Martin, C., & Gebhard, P. (1953). *Sexual Behavior in the Human Female.* Philadelphia: Saunders.

Kinsey, A. C., Pomeroy, W. B., Martin, C. E., & Gebhard, P. H. (1990). *Sexual Behavior in the Human Female.* Philadelphia: Saunders.

Knight, R. A., & Prentky, R. A. (1990). Classifying sexual offenders. In W. L. Marshall, D. R. Laws, & H. E. Barbaree (eds.), *Handbook of Sexual Assault: Issues, Theories and Treatment of the Offender.* New York: Plenum.

Knight, R. A., & Prentky, R. A. (1993). Exploring characteristics for classifying juvenile sex offenders. In H. E. Barbaree, W. L. Marshall, & S. M. Hudson (eds.), *The Juvenile Sex Offender.* New York: Guilford.

Knight, R. A., Prentky, R. A., & Cerce, D. D. (1994). The development, reliability and validity of an inventory for the multidimensional assessment of sex and aggression. *Criminal Justice and Behavior.* 21: 72–94.

Knight, R. A., Prentky, R. A., Schneider, B., & Rosenberg, R. (1983). Linear causal modeling of adaptation and criminal history in sex offenders. In K. T. Van Dusen & S. A. Mednick (eds.), *Prospective Studies of Crime and Delinquency.* Boston: Kluwer-Nijhoff.

Knopp, F. H. (1984). *Retraining Adult Sex Offenders: Methods and Models.* Syracuse, NY: Safer Society Press.

Knopp, F. H. (1985). *The Youthful Sex Offender: The Rationale and Goals of Early Intervention and Treatment.* Syracuse, NY: Safer Society Press.

Knowles, G. J. (1999). Male prison rape: A search for causation and prevention. *The Howard Journal.* 38(3): 267–282.

Kobayashi, J., Sales, B., Becker, J. V., Figueredo, A. J., et al. (1995). Perceived parental deviance, parent/child bonding, child abuse and child sexual aggression. *Sexual Abuse: Journal of Research and Treatment.* 7: 25–44.

Kogan, S. M. (2005). The role of disclosing child sexual abuse on adolescent adjustment and revictimization. *Journal of Child Sexual Abuse.* 14: 25–47.

Kolker, R. (May 14, 2006). On the Rabbi's knee. *New York Magazine* [online]. Retrieved from http://nymag.com/news/features/17010/

Koss, M. P., Gidycz, C. A., & Wisniewski, N. (1987). The scope of rape: Incidence and prevalence of sexual aggression in a national sample of higher education students. *Journal of Consulting and Clinical Psychology.* 55: 162–170.

Koss, M. P., & Harvey, M. R. (1991). *The rape victim: Clinical and community interventions* (2nd ed.). Newbury Park, CA: Sage.

Kotrla, K. (2010). Domestic minor sex trafficking in the United States. *Social Work.* 55(2): 181–187.

Kraemer, B. D., Salisbury, S. B., & Spielman, C. R. (1998). Pretreatment variables associated with treatment failure in a residential juveniles sex offender program. *Criminal Justice and Behavior.* 25: 190–202.

Krafft-Ebing, R. V. (1886/1965). *Psychopathia Sexualis.* New York: Putnam.

Kreutz, L. E., & Rose, R. M. (1972). Assessment of aggressive behavior and plasma testosterone in a young criminal population. *Psychosomatic Medicine.* 34: 321–332.

Krone T. (2004). A typology of online child pornography offending. *Trends & Issues inCrime and Criminal Justice, 279.* Available at: http://www.aic.gov.au/publications/tandi/index.html

Krueger, R. B., Hembree, W., & Hill, M. (2006). Prescription of medroxyprogesterone acetate to a patient with pedophilia, resulting in cushing's syndrome and adrenal insufficiency. *Sexual Abuse: A Journal of Research & Treatment.* 18(2): 227–228.

Kruttschnitt, C., Uggen, C., & Shelton, K. (2000). Predictors of desistance among sex offenders: The interactions of formal and informal social controls. *Justice Quarterly.* 17: 61–87.

La Fond, J. Q. (1999). Can therapeutic jurisprudence be normatively neutral? Sexual predator laws: Their impact on participants and policy. *Arizona Law Review.* 41: 375.

La Fontaine, J. (1994). *The Extent and Nature of Organised and Ritual Abuse.* London: HMSO, Department of Health.

La Fontaine, J. S. (1990). *Child Sexual Abuse.* Cambridge, UK: Polity.

LaFave, O., & Simon, B. (2006). *Gorgeous Disaster: The Tragic Story of Debra Lafave.* Beverly Hills: Phoenix Books.

Lagon, M. P. (2008). Trafficking and human dignity. *Policy Review.* 152: 51–61.

Lakey, J. F. (1992). Myth information and bizarre beliefs of male juvenile sex offenders. *Journal of Addictions and Offender Counseling.* 13: 2–10.

Lamb, S., & Edgar-Smith, S. (1994). Aspects of disclosure: Mediators of outcome of childhood sexual abuse. *Journal of Interpersonal Violence.* 9: 307–326.

Landis, J. T. (1956). Experiences of 500 children with adult sexual deviation. *Psychiatric Quarterly.* 30: 91–109.

Lane, N. J. (1995). *The Abuse of Power by Church and Society toward Women with Disabilities: The Theological and Spiritual Implications of Sexual Abuse of the Vulnerable by the Powerful.* Dissertation from the Union Institute; available through University Microfilms International, Ann Arbor, MI.

Lane, S. L. (1997). Assessment of sexually abusive youth. In G. D. Ryan (ed.), *Juvenile Sexual Offending: Causes, Consequences, and Correction.* West Sussex, UK: Wiley.

Lang, R. A., Flor-Henry, P., & Frenzel, R. R. (1990). Sex hormone profiles in pedophilic and incestuous men. *Annals of Sex Research.* 3: 59–74.

Lang, R. A., Pugh, G. M., & Langevin, R. (1988). Treatment of incest and pedophilic offenders: A pilot study. *Behavioral Sciences and the Law.* 6(2): 239–255.

Langan, P. A., & Harlow, C. W. (1992). *Child Rape Victims, 1992*. Washington, DC: U.S. Department of Justice, Office of Justice Programs, Bureau of Justice Statistics.

Langan, P. A., & Harlow, C. W. (1994). *Child Rape Victims, 1992*. Crime Data Brief. Washington, DC: U.S. Department of Justice.

Langevin, R. (1983). *Sexual Strands: Understanding and Treating Sexual Abnormalities in Men*. Hillside, NJ: Erlbaum.

Langevin, R. (1988). Editorial: Sexual abuse. *A Journal of Research and Treatment*. 1: 5–6.

Langevin, R., Bain, J., Ben-Aron, M., Coulthard, R., Day, D., Handy, L., Heasman, G., Hucker, S. J., Purins, J. E., Roper, V., Russon, A. E., Webster, C. D., & Wortzman, G. (1985). Sexual aggression: Constructing a predictive equation. A controlled pilot study. In R. Langevin (ed.), *Erotic Preference, Gender Identity and Aggression in Men: New Research Studies*. Hillsdale, NJ: Erlbaum.

Langevin, R., & Curnoe, S. (2004). The use of pornography during the commission of sexual offenses. *International Journal of Offender Therapy and Comparative Criminology*. 48(3): 572–586.

Langevin, R., & Lang, R. A. (1985). Psychological treatment of paedophiles. *Behavioral Sciences and the Law*. 3: 403–419.

Langevin, R., Lang, R. A., & Curnoe, S. (1998). The prevalence of sex offenders with deviant fantasies. *Journal of Interpersonal Violence*. 13: 315–327.

Langevin, R., & Watson, R. (1991). A comparison of incestuous biological and stepfathers. *Annals of Sex Research*. 4(2): 141–150.

Langevin, R., Wortzman, G., Wright, P., & Handy, L. (1989). Studies of brain damage and dysfunction in sex offenders. *Annals of Sex Research*. 2: 163–179.

Langevin, R., Wright, P., & Handy, L. (1988). Empathy, assertiveness, aggressiveness, and defensiveness among sex offenders. *Annals of Sex Research*. 1: 533–547.

Langevin, R., Wright, P., & Handy, L. (2004). Use of the MMPI and its derived scales with sex offenders: Reality and validity studies. *Sexual Abuse: A Journal of Research & Treatment*. 3: 245–291.

Langstrom, N., & Grann, M. (2000). Risk for criminal recidivism among young sex offenders. *Journal of Interpersonal Violence*. 15: 855–873.

Lanning, K. (1986). *Child Molesters: A Behavioral Analysis for Law Enforcement Officers Investigating Cases of Sexual Exploitation*. Washington, DC: National Center for Missing and Exploited Children.

Lanyon, R. I. (1991). Theories of sex offending. In C. R. Hollin & K. Howells (eds.), *Clinical Approaches to Sex Offenders and Their Victims*. West Sussex, UK: Wiley.

Largen, M. A. (1991). Confidentiality in the sexual assault victim/counselor relationship. In A. W. Burgess (ed.), *Rape and Sexual Assault III: A Research Handbook*. New York: Garland.

Laumann, E. O., Gagnon, J. H., Michael, R. T., & Michaels, S. (1994). *The Social Organization of Sexuality: Sexual Practices in the United States*. Chicago, IL: University of Chicago Press.

Laws, D. R., Hanson, R. K., Osborn, C. A., & Greenbaum, P. E. (2000). Classification of child molesters by plethysmographic assessment of sexual arousal and a self-report measure of sexual preference. *Journal of Interpersonal Violence*. 15: 1297–1312.

Laws, D. R., & Ward, T. (2006). When one size doesn't fit all: the reformulation of relapse prevention. In W. L. Marshall, Y. M. Fernandez, L. E. Marshall, & G. A. Serran (eds.), *Sexual* offender treatment: *Controversial issues* (pp. 225–239). New York: John Wiley and Sons.

Lawson, L., & Chaffin, M. (1992). False negatives in sexual abuse disclosure interviews: Incidence and influence of caretaker's belief in abuse in cases of accidental abuse discovery by diagnosis of STD. *Journal of Interpersonal Violence.* 7: 532–542.

Lazebnik, R., Zimet, G. D., Ebert, J., Anglin, T. M., Williams, P., Bunch, D. L., & Krowchuk, D. P. (1994). How children perceive the medical evaluation for suspected sexual abuse. *Child Abuse and Neglect.* 18: 739–745.

Lees, S. (1996). *Carnal Knowledge: Rape on Trial.* London: Hamish Hamilton.

Leiter, R. A. (ed.). (1999). *National Survey of State Laws* (3rd ed.). Farmington Hills, MI: Gale.

Letourneau, E. J., Bandyopadhyay, D., Armstrong, K. S., & Sinha, D. (2010). Do sex offender registration and notification requirements deter juvenile sex crimes? *Criminal Justice and Behavior.* 37: 553–569.

Letourneau, E. J., Levenson, J., Bandyopadhyay, D., Armstrong, K. S., & Sinha, D. (2010). The effects of sex offender registration and notification on judicial decisions. *Criminal Justice Review.* 35: 295–317.

Letourneau, E. J., & Miner, M. H. (2005). Juvenile sex offenders: A case against the legal and clinical status quo. *Sexual Abuse: A Journal of Research & Treatment.* 17(3): 293–312.

Levenson, J. S. (2008). Collateral consequences of sex offender residence restrictions. *Criminal Justice Studies.* 21(2): 153–166.

Levenson, J. S. (2009). Sex offender residence restrictions. In R. Wright (ed.), *Sex offender laws: Failed polices, new directions.* New York: Springer Publishing Company.

Levenson, J. S. (2011). "But I didn't do it!": Ethical treatment of sex offenders in denial. *Sexual Abuse: A Journal of Research & Treatment.* 23(3): 343–364.

Levenson, J. S., & Cotter, L.P. (2005). The impact of sex offender residence restrictions: 1,000 feet from danger or one step from absurd? *International Journal of Offender Therapy and Comparative Criminology.* 49(2): 168–168.

Levenson, J. S., & D'Amora, D. A. (2007). Social policies designed to prevent sexual violence: The emperor's new clothes? *Criminal Justice Policy Review.* 18(2): 168–199.

Levenson, J. S., D'Amora, D., & Hern, A. (2007). Megan's law and its impact on community re-entry for sex offenders. *Behavioral Sciences and the Law.* (25): 587–602.

Levenson, J. S., & Hern, A. (2007). Sex offender residence restrictions: Unintended consequences and community re-entry. *Justice Research and Policy.* 9(2): 59–73.

Levenson, J. S., Letourneau, E., Armstrong, K., & Zgoba, K. M. (2010). Failure to register as a sex offender: Is it associated with recidivism? *Justice Quarterly.* 27(3): 305–331.

Levenson, J.S., & Morin, J. W. (2006). Factors predicting selection of sexually violent predators for civil commitment. *International Journal of Offender Therapy & Comparative Criminology.* 50(6): 609–629.

Leversee, T. (2010). Typology research: Refining our understanding of a diverse population. In G. Ryan, T. Leversee, & S. Lane (eds.), *Juvenile Sexual Offending: Causes, Consequences and Correction.* Hoboken, NJ: Wiley & Sons.

Levine, J. P. (1976). The potential for crime over reporting in criminal victimization surveys. *Criminology.* 14: 3.

Lewis, C. F., & Stanley, C. R. (2000). Women accused of sexual offenses.

Behavioral Sciences and the Law. 18: 73–81.

Lidz, C. W., & Mulvey, E. P. (1995). Dangerousness: From legal definition to theoretical research. *Law and Human Behavior.* 19: 41–48.

Lieb, R., & Matson, S. (1998). *Sexual Predator Commitment Laws in the United States: 1998 Update.* Olympia, WA: Washington State Institute for Public Policy.

Lightfoot, L. O., & Barbaree, H. E. (1993). The relationship between substance use and abuse and sexual offending in adolescents. In H. E. Barbaree, W. L. Marshall, & S. M. Hudson (eds.), *The Juvenile Sex Offender.* New York: Guilford.

Lindsay, W. R., Ward, T., Morgan, T., & Wilson, I. (2007). Self-regulation of sex offending, future pathways and the good lives model: Applications and problems. *Journal of Sexual Aggression.* 13(1): 37–50.

Lindsey, R. E., Carlozzi, A. F., & Eells, G. T. (2001). Differences in the dispositional empathy of juvenile sex offenders, non-sex offending delinquent juveniles and nondelinquent juveniles. *Journal of Interpersonal Violence.* 16: 510–523.

Lipton, D., Martinson, R., & Wilks, J. (1975). *The Effectiveness of Correctional Treatment.* New York: Praeger.

Lipton, D. N., McDonel, E. C., & McFall, R. M. (1987). Heterosocial perception in rapists. *Journal of Consulting and Clinical Psychology.* 55: 17–21.

Lisak, D., & Ivan, C. (1995). Deficits in intimacy and empathy in sexually aggressive men. . *Journal of Interpersonal Violence.* 10: 296–308.

Littel, K. (2000). *Engaging Advocates and Other Victim Service Providers in the Community Management of Sex Offenders.* Washington, DC: U.S. Department of Justice, Office of Justice Programs.

Littel, K. (2001). *Sexual Assault Nurse Examiner (SANE) Programs: Improving the Community Response to Sexual Assault Victims.* Washington, DC: U.S. Department of Justice, Office for Victims of Crime.

Litwack, T. R. (1993). On the ethics of dangerousness assessments. *Law and Human Behavior.* 17: 479–482.

Lloyd, C. (1991). The offense: Changes in the nature and pattern of sex offences. *Criminal Behavior and Mental Health.* 1: 115–122.

Loeber, R., & Farrington, D. (1998). Serious and violent juvenile offenders. *Juvenile Justice Bulletin.* U.S. Department of Justice, Office of Justice Programs, Office of Juvenile Justice and Delinquency Prevention.

Loftus, E. (1993). The reality of repressed memories. *American Psychologist.* 48: 518–537.

Loftus, E. (1994). Therapeutic recollection of childhood abuse. *The Champion— National Association of Criminal Defense Lawyers.* 18: 5–10.

Loftus, E. F., & Davies, G. M. (1984). Distortions in the memory of children. *Journal of Social Issues.* 40: 51–67.

Loftus, J. A., & Camargo, R. J. (1993). Treating the clergy. *Annuals of Sex Research.* 6: 287–303.

Logan, W. A. (2008). Sex offender law and policy: Criminal justice federalism and national sex offender policy. *Ohio State Journal of Criminal Justice.* 6: 51.

Longo, R. (1983). Administering a comprehensive sexual aggressive treatment program in a maximum-security setting. In J.G. Greer & I. R. Stuart (eds.), *The Sexual Aggressor: Current Perspectives on Treatment.* New York: Van Nostrand Reinhold.

Looman, J., Gauthier, C., & Boer, D. (2001). Replication of the Massachusetts Treatment Center child molester typology in a Canadian sample. *Journal of Interpersonal Violence.* 16: 753–767.

Losel, F., & Schmucker, M. (2005). The effectiveness of treatment for sexual offenders: A comprehensive meta-analysis. *Journal of Experimental Criminology.* 1(1): 117–146.

Lowden, K., English, K., Hetz, N., & Harrison, L. (2003). *Process Evaluation of the Colorado Sex Offender Management Board Standards and Guidelines.* Denver, CO: Sex Offender Management Board.

Lundberg-Love, P. K. (1999). The resilience of the human psyche: Recognition and treatment of the adult survivor of incest. In M. A. Paludi (ed.), *The Psychology of Sexual Victimization: A Handbook.* Westport, CT: Greenwood.

Lussier, P., Beauregard, E., Proulx, J., & Nicole, A. (2005). Developmental factors related to deviant sexual preferences in child molesters. *Journal of Interpersonal Violence.* 20: 999–1017.

Lussier, P., LeBlanc, M., & Proulx, J. (2005). The generality of criminal behavior: A confirmatory factor analysis of the criminal activity of sex offenders in adulthood. *Journal of Criminal Justice.* 33: 177–189.

MacLeod & Sarago. (1987). Family secrets: Child sexual abuse. *Feminist Review*, p. 7.

MacMillan, H. L., Fleming, J. E., Trocmé, N., Boyle, M. H., Wong, M., Racine, Y. A., et al. (1997). Prevalence of child physical and sexual abuse in the community: Results from the Ontario Health Supplement. *Journal of the American Medical Association.* 278: 131–135.

MacMillan, H. L., & Munn, C. (2001). The sequelae of child maltreatment. *Current Opinion in Psychiatry.* 14(4): 325–331.

Mair, J. S., Frattaroli, S., & Teret, S. P. (2003). New hope for victims of prison sexual assault. *Journal of Law, Medicine & Ethics.* 31: 602–606.

Mair, K. J., & Stevens, R. H. (1994). Offending histories and offending behaviour: A ten-year follow-up of sex offenders tried by sheriff and district courts in Grampian, Scotland. *Psychology, Crime and Law.* 1: 83–92.

Malamuth, N. (1981). Rape proclivity among males. *Journal of Social Issues.* 37: 138–157.

Malamuth, N. (1986). Predictors of naturalistic aggression. *Journal of Personality and Social Psychology.* 50: 953–962.

Maletzky, B. M., Tolan, A., & McFarland, B. (2006). The Oregon Depo-Provera program: A five-year follow-up. *Sexual Abuse: A Journal of Research & Treatment.* 18(3): 303–316.

Mallie, A., Viljoen, J., Mordell, S., Spice, A., & Roesch, R. (2011). Childhood abuse and adolescent sexual re-offending: A meta-analysis. *Child & Youth Care Forum.* 40(5): 401–417.

Mann, R. E., Hanson, R. K., & Thornton, D. (2010). Assessing risk for sexual recidivism: Some proposals on the nature of psychologically meaningful risk factors. *Sexual Abuse: A Journal of Research & Treatment.* 22(2): 191–217.

Mann, R. E., & Shingler, J. (2006). Collaboration in clinical work with sexual offenders: Treatment and risk assessment. In W. L. Marshall, Y. M. Fernandez, L. E. Marshall, & G. A. Serran (eds.), *Sexual offender treatment: Controversial issues* (pp. 225–239). New York: John Wiley and Sons.

Mann, R. E., & Thornton, D. (1997). *The Evolution of a Multi-Site Sex Offender Treatment Programme.* London: HM Prison Service, Programme Development Section.

Mapes, B. E. (1995). *Child Eyewitness Testimony in Sexual Abuse Investigations.* Brandon, VT: Clinical Psychology Publishing.

Margolin, L. (1991). Child sexual abuse by nonrelated caregivers. *Child Abuse & Neglect.* 15: 213–221.

Marques, J. K. (1999). How to answer the question "Does sex offender treatment work?" *Journal of Interpersonal Violence.* 14: 437–451.

Marques, J. K., Day, D. M., Nelson, C., & West, M. A. (1994). Effects of cognitive-behavioral treatment on sex offender recidivism: Preliminary results of a longitudinal study. *Criminal Justice and Behavior.* 21: 28–54.

Marques, J.K., Nelson, C., West, M. A., & Day, D. M. (1994). The relationship between treatment goals and recidivism among child molesters. *Behavior Research and Therapy.* 32: 577–588.

Marques, J. K., Wiederanders, M., Day, D. M., Nelson, C., & van Ommeren, A. (2005). Effects of a relapse prevention program on sexual recidivism: Final results from California's Sex Offender Treatment and Evaluation Project (SOTEP). *Sexual Abuse: A Journal of Research & Treatment.* 17(1): 79–107.

Marquis, J. N. (1970). Orgasmic reconditioning: Changing sexual object choice through controlling masturbation fantasies. *Journal of Behavior Therapy and Experimental Psychiatry.* 1: 263–271.

Marshall, L. E., & Marshall, W. L. (2002). The role of attachment in sexual offending: An examination of preoccupied-attachment-style offending behavior. In B. Schwartz (ed.), *The Sex Offender: Current Treatment Modalities and Systems Issues.* New York: Civic Research Institute.

Marshall, L. E., & Moulden, H. M. (2006). Preparatory programs for sexual offenders. In W. L. Marshall, Y. M. Fernandez, L. E. Marshall, & G. A. Serran (eds.), *Sexual Offender Treatment.* London: John Wiley & Sons.

Marshall, W. L. (1989). Intimacy, loneliness and sexual offenders. *Behavior Research and Therapy.* 27: 491–503.

Marshall, W. L. (1993). The role of attachment, intimacy, and loneliness in the etiology and maintenance of sexual offending. *Sexual and Marital Therapy.* 8: 109–121.

Marshall, W. L. (1994). Treatment effects on denial and minimization in incarcerated sex offenders. *Behavior Research and Therapy.* 32: 559–564.

Marshall, W. L. (1996). Assessment, treatment and theorizing about sex offenders: Development during the past twenty years. *Criminal Justice and Behavior.* 23: 162–199.

Marshall, W. L., Anderson, D., & Fernandez, Y. (1999). *Cognitive Behavioral Treatment of Sexual Offenders.* Toronto, ON: Wiley.

Marshall, W. L., & Barbaree, H. E. (1990a). An integrated theory of the etiology of sexual offending. In W. L. Marshall, D. R. Laws, & H. E. Barbaree (eds.), *Handbook of Sexual Assault: Issues, Theories and Treatment of the Offender.* New York: Plenum.

Marshall, W. L., & Barbaree, H. E. (1990b). Outcome of comprehensive cognitive-behavioral treatment programs. In W. L. Marshall, D. R. Laws, & H. E. Barbaree (eds.), *Handbook of Sexual Assault: Issues, Theories and Treatment of the Offender.* New York: Plenum.

Marshall, W. L., Barbaree, H. E., & Eccles, A. (1991). Early onset and deviant sexuality in child molesters. *Journal of Interpersonal Violence.* 6: 323–336.

Marshall, W. L., Barbaree, H. E., & Eccles, A. (1993). A three-tiered approach to the rehabilitation of incarcerated sex offenders. *Behavioral Sciences and the Law.* 11: 441–455.

Marshall, W. L., & Eccles, A. (1991). Issues in clinical practice with sex offenders. *Journal of Interpersonal Violence.* 6: 68–93.

Marshall, W. L., & Eccles, A. (1993). Pavlovian conditioning processes in adolescent sex offenders. In H. E. Barbaree, W. L. Marshall, & S. M. Hudson (eds.), *The Juvenile Sex Offender*. New York: Guilford.

Marshall, W. L., Eccles, A., & Barbaree, H. E. (1991). Treatment of exhibitionists: A focus on sexual deviance versus cognitive and relationship features. *Behavior Research and Therapy*. 29: 129–135.

Marshall, W. L., Hudson, S. M., Jones, R., & Fernandez, Y. M. (1995). Empathy in sex offenders. *Clinical Psychology Review*. 15: 99–113.

Marshall, W. L., Laws, D. R., & Barbaree, H. E. (1990a). Issues in sexual assault. In W. L. Marshall, D. R. Laws, & H. E. Barbaree (eds.), *Handbook of Sexual Assault: Issues, Theories and Treatment of the Offender*. New York: Plenum.

Marshall, W. L., Laws, D. R., & Barbaree, H. E. (1990b). Present status and future directions. In W. L. Marshall, D. R. Laws, & H. E. Barbaree (eds.), *Handbook of Sexual Assault: Issues, Theories and Treatment of the Offender*. New York: Plenum.

Marshall, W. L., & Pithers, W. D. (1994). A reconsideration of treatment outcome with sex offenders. *Criminal Justice and Behavior*. 21: 10–27.

Marshall, W. L., Serran, G. A., & Marshall, L. E. (2006). Situational and dispositional factors in child sexual molestation: A clinical perspective. In R. Wortley & S. SMallbone (eds.), *Situational Prevention of Child Sexual Abuse. Crime Prevention Studies, Volume 19*. Monsey, NY: Criminal Justice Press.

Martinson, R. (1974). What works? Questions and answers about prison reform. *Public Interest*. 35: 22–54.

Mashberg, T., & Convey, E. (2002). Secret file full on Geoghan—Archdiocese told he was "real danger." *The Boston Herald*. Available at: http://www.lex isnexis.com/us/lnacademic/

Masters, W. H., & Johnson, V. E. (1966). *The Human Sexual Response*. Oxford: Little Brown.

Masters, W. H., & Johnson, V. E. (1970). *Human Sexual Inadequacy*. New York: Bantam Books.

Matthews, J. K. (1998). An 11-year perspective of working with female sexual offenders. In W. L. Marshall, Y. M. Fernandez, S. M. Hudson, & T. Ward (eds.), *Sourcebook of Treatment Programs for Sexual Offenders*. New York: Plenum.

Matthews, J. K., Matthews, R., & Speltz, K. (1991). Female sexual offenders: A typology. In M. Q. Patton (ed.), *Family Sexual Abuse: Frontline Research and Evaluation* (pp. 199–219). Newbury Park, CA: Sage.

Matthews, N. A. (1994). *Confronting Rape: The Feminist Anti-Rape Movement and the State*. J. Urry, series ed. Routledge, London: International Library of Sociology.

Matthews, R., Hunter, J. A., & Vuz, J. (1997). Juvenile female sexual offenders: Clinical characteristics and treatment issues. *Sexual Abuse: Journal of Research and Treatment*. 9: 187–199.

Matthews, R., Matthews, J. K., & Speltz, K. (1989). *Female Sexual Offenders: An Empirical Study*. Orwell, VT: Safer Society Press.

McAlinden, A. M. (1999). Sex offender registration: Some observations on "Megan's Law" and the sex offenders act of 1997. *Crime Prevention & Community Safety*. 1(1): 41–53.

McAnulty, R. D. (1995). The paraphilias: Classification and theory. In L. Diamant & R. D. McAnulty (eds.), *The Psychology of Sexual Orientation, Behavior, and Identity: A Handbook*. Westport, CT: Greenwood Press.

McCall, W. (2010, April 23). Boy Scouts' Sex Abuse Penalty: $18.5 Million for Abused Scout. *Huffington Post*. Retrieved from http://www.huffing

tonpost.com/2010/04/23/boy-scouts-sex-abuse-pena_n_550369.html

McCann, S. R. (1999, October 17). Clergy Ignores Victims, Allege LDS Plaintiffs. *The Salt Lake Tribune* [online]. Retrieved from Lexis-Nexis.

McCartan, F. M., Law, H., Murphy, M., & Bailey, S. (2011). Child adolescent females who present with sexually abusive behaviours: A 10-year UK prevalence study. *The Journal of Sexual Aggression*. 17(1): 4–14.

McCarthy, J. (2009). *The relationship between possessing child pornography and child molestation.* Dissertation from the Graduate Center, CUNY; available through University Microfilms International, Ann Arbor, MI.

McCloskey, S. H., & Ramos-Grenier, J. (2006). Theoretical consideration of female sexual predator serial killers in the United States. *Journal of Criminal Justice*. 34(3): 251–259.

McDevitt, P. J. (1999). *Priests as Victims of Childhood Sexual Abuse: The Effects of Disclosing a History of Childhood Sexual Abuse on the Capacity for Empathy.* Dissertation from Loyola College, MD; available through University Microfilms International, Ann Arbor, MI.

McGrain, P. N., & Moore, J. L. (2010). Pursuing the panderer: An Analysis of United States v. Williams. *Journal of Child Sexual Abuse*. 19: 190–203.

McGrath, R. J., Cumming, G. F., Hoke, S. E., & Bonn-Miller, M. O. (2007). Outcomes in a community sex offender treatment program: A comparison between polygraphed and matched non-polygraphed offenders. *Sexual Abuse: A Journal of Research & Treatment*. 19(4): 381–393.

McGrath, R. J., Cumming, G. F., & Livingston, J. A. (2003). Outcome of a treatment program for adult sex offenders: From prison to

community. *Journal of Interpersonal Violence*. 18(1): 3–17.

McGrath, R.J. (1994). Sex offender risk assessment and disposition planning: A review of clinical and empirical findings. *International Journal of Offender Therapy and Comparative Criminology*. 35: 328–350.

McGreal, C. (2010, April 29). Sexual Abuse Scandal Rocks Boy Scouts of America after $18.5m Payout. *The Guardian*. Retrieved from http://www.guardian.co.uk/world/2010/apr/29/boy-scouts-sexual-abuse-dykes/print

McGuicken, G. K., & Brown, J. (2001). Managing risk from sex offenders living in communities: Comparing police, press, and public perceptions. *Risk Management: An International Journal*. 3: 331–343.

McGuire, R. J., Carlisle, J. M., & Young, B. G. (1965). Sexual deviations as conditioned behavior: A hypothesis. *Behavior Research and Therapy*. 3: 185–190.

McGuire, R. J., & Vallance, M. (1964). Aversion therapy by electric shock: A simple technique. *British Medical Journal*. 2: 594–597.

McLaughlin, B. R. (1994). Devastated spirituality: The impact of clergy sexual abuse on the survivor's relationship with God and the church. *Sexual Addiction and Compulsivity*. 1: 145–158.

McLaughlin, J. (1998). Technophilia: A modern day paraphilia. *Knight Stick: Publication of the New Hampshire Police Association*. 51: 47–51.

McKibben, A., Proulx, J., & Lusignan, R. (1994). Relationships between conflict, affect and deviant sexual behaviors in paedophiles and rapists. *Behavior Research and Therapy*. 32: 571–575.

McMullen, R. J. (1992). *Male Rape: Breaking the Silence on the Last Taboo.* London: GMP.

Medaris, M. (1995). *Child Sexual Exploitation: Improving Investigations and Protecting the Victims*. Washington, DC: U.S. Department of Justice, Office of Juvenile Justice and Delinquency Prevention.

Medea, A., & Thompson, K. (1974). *Against Rape: A Survival Manual for Women*. New York: Farrar, Straus & Giroux.

Megargee, E. I. (1981). Methodological problems in the prediction of violence. In J. R. Hays, T. K. Roberts, & K. S. Soloway (eds.), *Violence and the Violent Individual*. Lancaster, UK: Spectrum.

Melloy, K. (2009, October 14). Ultra-Orthodox Jews no longer ignoring child sexual abuse. *Edge* [online]. Retrieved from http://www.edge-boston.com/index.php?ch=news&sc=&sc3=&id=97689&pf=1

Meloy, M. L., & Coleman, S. (2009). GPS monitoring of sex offenders. In R. Wright (ed.), *Sex Offender Laws: Failed Policies, New Directions*. New York: Springer.

Mendola, M. J. (1998). *Characteristics of Priests and Religious Brothers for Evaluation of Sexual Issues*. Dissertation from Antioch University, the New England Graduate School; available through University Microfilms International, Ann Arbor, MI.

Mercado, C. C., Alvarez, S., & Levenson, J. S. (2008). The impact of specialized sex offender legislation on community re-entry. *Sexual Abuse: Journal of Research & Treatment*. 20(2): 180–205.

Meyer-Bahlberg, H. (1987). Commentary on Bain's "hormones and sexual aggression in the male." *Integrative Psychiatry*. 5: 89–91.

Meyers. L., & Greenberg, R. (2007, November 11). New evidence in Jehovah's witnesses allegations. *MSNBC* [online]. Retrieved from http://www.msnbc.msn.com/id/21917798/

Mezey, G. C., & King, M. B. (eds.). (2000). *Male Victims of Sexual Assault* (2nd ed.). Oxford: Oxford University Press.

Miccio-Fonseca, L. C. (1998). Adult and adolescent female sex offenders: Experiences compared to other female and male sex offenders. *Journal of Psychology and Human Sexuality*. 11: 75–88.

Michels, S. (2009, May 5). Orthodox Jewish community struggles with abuse allegations. *ABC News* [online]. Retrieved From http://abcnews.go.com/print?id=7376057

Miethe, T. D., Olson, J., & Mitchell, O. (2006). Specialization and persistence in the arrest histories of sex offenders: A comparative analysis of alternative measures and offense types. *Journal of Research in Crime and Delinquency*. 43: 204–229.

Miller, W. R., & Rollnick, S. (1991). *Motivational Interviewing: Preparing People to Change Addictive Behavior*. New York: Guilford.

Minden, P. B. (1991). Coping with interpersonal violence and sexual victimization: Perspectives for victims and care providers. In A. W. Burgess (ed.), *Rape and Sexual Assault III: A Research Handbook*. New York: Garland.

Miner, M. H. (2002). Factors associated with recidivism in juveniles: An analysis of serious juvenile sex offenders. *Journal of Research in Crime and Delinquency*. 39: 421–436.

Miner, M. H., & Dwyer, S. M. (1997). The psychosocial development of sex offenders: Differences between exhibitionists, child molesters and incest offenders. *International Journal of Offender Therapy and Comparative Criminology*. 41: 36–44.

Minnesota Derpartment of Corrections. (2000). *Sex offender supervision: 2000 Report to the legislature*. St. Paul: Minnesota Department of Corrections.

Minnesota Department of Corrections. (2003). *Level three sex offenders residential placement issues.* St. Paul: Minnesota Department of Corrections.

Minnesota Department of Corrections. (2007a). *Residential proximity & sex offense recidivism in Minnesota.* St. Paul, MN: Minnesota Department of Corrections.

Minnesota Department of Corrections. (2007b). *Sex Offender Recidivism in Minnesota.* St. Paul, MN: Minnesota Department of Corrections.

Mitchell, K. J., Finkelhor, D., & Wolak, J. (2003). The exposure of youth to unwanted sexual material on the internet: A national survey of risk, impact and prevention. *Youth & Society.* 34(3): 330–358.

Mitchell, K. J., Finkelhor, D., & Wolak, J. (2010). Conceptualizing juvenile prostitution as child maltreatment: Findings from the National Juvenile Prostitution Study. *Child Maltreatment.* 15(1): 18–36.

Mitchell, K. J., Jones, L. M., Finkelhor, D., & Wolak, J. (2011). Internet-facilitated commercial sexual exploitation of children: Findings from a nationally representative sample of law enforcement agencies in the United States. *Sexual Abuse: A Journal of Research & Treatment.* 23(1): 43–71.

Mitchell, K. J., Wolak, J., & Finkelhor, D. (2008). Are blogs putting youth at risk for online sexual solicitation or harassment? *Child Abuse and Neglect.* 32: 277–294.

Mitchell, K., Wolak, J., & Finkelhor, D. (2010). *The National Juvenile Online Victim Study: Methodology Report.* New Hampshire; Crimes against Children Research Center.

Moffitt, T. E. (1993). Adolescence-limited and life-course-persistent antisocial behavior: A developmental taxonomy. *Psychological Review.* 100(4): 674–701.

Mohr, J. W., Turner, R. E., & Jerry, N. B. (1964). *Pedophilia and Exhibitionism: A Handbook.* Toronto, ON: University of Toronto Press.

Monahan, J. (1981). *Predicting Violent Behavior: An Assessment of Clinical Techniques.* Beverly Hills, CA: Sage.

Mondimore, F. M. (1996). *A Natural History of Homosexuality.* Baltimore, MD: Johns Hopkins University Press.

Money, J. (1970). Use of androgen depleting hormone in the treatment of male sex offenders. *Journal of Sex Research.* 6: 165–172.

Money, J., & Ehrhardt, A.A. (1972). *Man & Woman, Boy & Girl.* Baltimore: Johns Hopkins University Press.

Money, J., Wiedeking, C., Walker, P., Migeon, C., Meyer, W., & Borgaonkar, D. (1975). 47, XYY and 46, XY males with antisocial and/or sex-offending behavior: Antiandrogen therapy plus counseling. *Psychoneuroendocrinology.* 1(2): 165–178.

Money, J., Wiedeking, C., Walker, P. A., & Gain, D. (1976). Combined anti-androgen and counselling program for treatment of 46, XY and 47, XYY sex offenders. In E. Sachar (ed.), *Hormones, Behavior and Psychopathology.* New York: Raven.

Moore, B. S. (1990). The origins and development of empathy. *Motivation and Emotion.* 14: 75–79.

Moore, K. A., Nord, C. W., & Peterson, J. L. (1989). Nonvoluntary sexual activity among adolescents. *Family Planning Perspectives.* 21: 110–114.

Morrison, T. (1999). Is there a strategy out there? Policy management perspectives on young people who sexually abuse others. In M. Erooga & H. C. Masson (eds.), *Children and Young People Who Sexually Abuse Others: Challenges and Responses.* London: Routledge.

Moster, A. N., & Jeglic, E. L. (2009). Prison warden attitudes towards prison rape and sexual assault: Findings since the prison rape elimination act (PREA). *The Prison Journal.* 89(1): 65–78.

Moulden, H. M., Firestone, P., & Wexler, A. F. (2007). Child care providers who commit sexual offences: A description of offender, offence, and victim characteristics. *International Journal of Offender Therapy and Comparative Criminology.* 51: 384–406.

Moyer, W. (2007, August 27). Child Sexual Abuse by Protestant Clergy Difficult to Document. *Binghamton Press & Sun-Bulletin* [online]. Retrieved from http://stopbaptist-predators.org/article07/child_sex_abuse_by_protestant_clergy.html

Mullvihill, M., Wisniewski, K., Meyers, J., & Wells, J. (2003). Losing track: Florida's sex offenders flock to Mass., then disappear. *Boston Herald.* Retrieved from http://www.boston-herald.com/news/local_regional/sex10312003.htm

Muraschak, L. M. (1999). *HIV in Prisons 1997* (NCJ Publication No. 178284). Washington, DC: National Institute of Justice.

Murphy, W. D. (1990). Assessment and modification of cognitive distortions in sex offenders. In W. L. Marshall, D. R. Laws, & H. E. Barbaree (eds.), *Handbook of Sexual Assault: Issues, Theories and Treatment of the Offender.* New York: Plenum.

Murphy, W. D., McGrath, R. J., & Christopher, M. G. (2008). Evidence for the development of the ATSA practice standards and guidelines for the treatment of adult male sexual abusers. *Journal of Forensic Psychology Practice.* 8(1): 77–88.

Mustaine, E. E., & Tewksbury, R. (2011). Residential relegation of registered sex offenders. *American Journal of Criminal Justice.* 36(1): 44–57.

Mustaine, E. E., Tewksbury, R., & Stengel, K. M. (2006). Social disorganization and residential locations of registered sex offenders: Is this a collateral consequence? *Deviant Behavior.* 27(3): 329–350.

Nash, C., & West, D. J. (1995). Sexual molestation of young girls: A retrospective survey. In D. J. West (ed.), *Sexual Victimization.* Brookfield, VT: Gower Publishing.

Nathan, P., & Ward, T. (2002). Female sex offenders: Clinical and demographic features. *Journal of Sexual Aggression.* 8: 5–21.

National Adolescent Perpetrator Network. (1993). The revised report from the National Task Force on Juvenile Sexual Offending. *Juvenile and Family Court Journal.* 44: 1–120.

National Campaign to Prevent Teen and Unplanned Pregnancy (NCPTUP). (2009). *The National Campaign to Prevent Teen and Unplanned Pregnancy Survey.* Retrieved January 08, 2011, from http://www.thenational campaign.org/sextech/PDF/Sex-Tech_Summary.pdf

National Center for Victims of Crime. (1997). *Male Rape Information Sheet.* Available at: http://www.rapecrisis-cen-ter.com/Male%20Rape%20Infor%20Sheet.html

National Coalition for the Protection of Children and Families. (2002a). *Current Statistics.* Available at: http://www.nationalcoalition.org/safety.phtml?ID=53

National Coalition for the Protection of Children and Families. (2002b). *Pornography and the Internet.* Available at: http://www.nationalcoalition.org/safety.phtml?ID=18

National Data Archive on Child Abuse and Neglect, Family Life Development Center, Cornell University. (2011). *National Child Abuse and Neglect Data System (NCANDS): Detailed Case Data Component (DCDC).* Available at:

http://www.ndacan.cornell.edu/
ndacan/Datasets/Abstracts/Dataset
Abstract_NCANDS_General.html

National Institute of Justice. (1992). *When the Victim Is a Child* (2nd ed.). Washington, DC: U.S. Department of Justice, Office of Justice Programs.

National Report Series. (2000). *Children as Victims. 1999 National Report Series, Juvenile Justice Bulletin.* Washington, DC: U.S. Department of Justice, Office of Juvenile Justice and Delinquency Prevention.

Negligent Hiring. (2006, January 1). *Goliath business news, security management.* Retrieved from http://goliath. ecnext.com/coms2/gi_0199-5159952/Negligent-hiring.html

Nelson, S. (2002). Physical symptoms in sexually abused women: Somatization or undetected injury? *Child Abuse Review.* 11: 51–64.

Neustein, A., & Lesher, M. (2008). A single-case study of rabbinic sexual abuse in the Orthodox Jewish community. *Journal of Child Sexual Abuse.* 17(3–4): 270–289.

New York City Alliance Against Sexual Assault. (2001). *Comprehensive Sexual Assault Treatment Programs: A Hospital-Based Model.* New York: NYC Alliance.

Nicholaichuk, T. P. (1996). *Sex Offender Treatment Priority: An Illustration of the Risk/Need Principle.* Available at: http://www.csc-scc.gc.ca/crd/forum/e082/e

Nieto, M., & Jung, D. (2006). *The Impact of Residency Restrictions on Sex Offenders and Correctional Management Practices: A Literature Review.* Sacramento, CA: California Research Bureau.

O'Brien, M., & Bera, W. H. (1986). Adolescent sexual offenders: A descriptive typology. *Preventing Sexual Abuse: A Newsletter of the National Family Life Education Network.* 1: 2–4.

O'Connell, M. A., Leberg, E., & Donaldson, C. R. (1990). *Working with Sex Offenders: Guidelines for Therapist Selection.* Newbury Park, CA: Sage.

Odem, M. E. (1995). *Delinquent Daughters: Protecting and Policing Adolescent Female Sexuality in the United States.* Chapel Hill, NC: University of North Carolina Press.

O'Donnell, I. (2004). Prison rape in context. *British Journal of Criminology.* 44: 241–255.

O'Donohue, W. T., & Geer, G. H. (1992a). *The Sexual Abuse of Children: Volume I: Theory & Research.* Hillsdale, NJ: Lawrence Erlbaum Associates.

O'Donohue, W. T., & Geer, G. H. (1992b). *The Sexual Abuse of Children: Volume II: Clinical Issues.* Hillsdale, NJ: Lawrence Erlbaum Associates.

Office of the Legislative Auditor. (1994). *Sex Offender Treatment Programs.* St. Paul, MN: Office of the Legislative Auditor.

Office of the Legislative Auditor. (2011). *Civil Commitment of Sex Offenders.* St Paul, MN: Office of the Legislative Auditor.

Office for Victims of Crime. (2001). *First Response to Victims of Crime 2001.* Washington, DC: U.S. Department of Justice, Office for Victims of Crime.

Oken, D. (2007). Evolution of psychosomatic diagnosis in DSM. *Psychosomatic Medicine.* 69: 830–831.

Olafson, E. (2004). Child sexual abuse. In B. J. Cling (ed.) *Sexualized violence against women and children* (pp. 151–187). New York: Guilford Press.

Oliver, J. M. (2004). *Psychopathy in Child Molesters: Affective Differences Between Incest and Extra-Familial Offenders.* PhD dissertation, University of Louisville.

Olver, M. E., & Wong, S. (2011). Predictors of sex offender treatment dropout: Psychopathy, sex offender risk, and responsivity implications. *Psychology, Crime & Law.* 17(5): 457–471.

Olweus, D., Matteson, A., Schalling, D., & Low, H. (1980). Testosterone, aggression, physical, and personality dimensions in normal adolescent males. *Psychosomatic Medicine.* 42: 253–269.

O'Reilly, G., Carr, A., Murphy, P., & Cotter, A. (2010). A controlled evaluation of a prison-based sex offender intervention program. *Sexual Abuse: A Journal of Research & Treatment.* 22(1): 95–111.

O'Reilly, G., Morrison, T., Sheerin, D., & Carr, A. (2001). A group-based module for adolescents to improve motivation to change sexually abusive behavior. *Child Abuse Review.* 10: 150–169.

Orlando, D. (1998). Sex offenders. *Special Needs Offenders Bulletin.* Washington, DC: Federal Judicial Center.

Otto, R. K. (2002). Use of the MMPI-2 in forensic settings. *Journal of Forensic Psychology Practice.* 2: 71–91.

Oxnam, P., & Vess, J. (2006). A personality-based typology of adolescent sex offenders using the Millon Adolescent Clinical Inventory. *New Zealand Journal of Psychology.* 35: 36–44.

Padgett, K. G., Bales, W. D., & Blomberg, T. G. (2006). Under surveillance: An empirical test of the effectiveness and consequences of electronic monitoring. *Criminology Public Policy.* 5(1): 61–91.

Paine, M. L., & Hansen, D. J. (2002). Factors: Influencing children to self-disclose sexual abuse. *Clinical Psychology Review.* 22: 271–295.

Pallone, N. J. (1990). *Rehabilitating Criminal Sexual Psychopaths: Legislative Mandates, Clinical Quandaries.* New Brunswick, NJ: Transaction.

Palmer, T. (1975). Martinson revisited. *Journal of Research in Crime and Delinquency.* 12: 133–152.

Paludi, M. A. (1999). *The Psychology of Sexual Victimization: A Handbook.* Westport, CT: Greenwood.

Parker, S. G. (2001). *Establishing Victim Services within a Law Enforcement Agency: The Austin Experience.* Washington, DC: U.S. Department of Justice, Office for Victims of Crime.

Parkinson, P. (2010). Breaking the long silence: Reports of child sexual abuse in the Anglican church of Australia. *Ecclesiology.* 6(2): 183–200.

Partners with Child Welfare League of America. (2010, June 21). *USA swimming.* Retrieved from http://www.usaswimming.org/ViewNews Article.aspx?TabId=0&itemid=2876&mid=8712

Pearson Assessments. (2009). *MMPI-2.* Available at: http://www.pearsonas sessments.com/mmpi2.aspx

Pearson, K. (2007). The trouble with Aileen Wuornos, Feminism's "first serial killer." *Communication and Critical/Cultural Studies.* 4(3): 256–272.

Pelissier, B. (2007). Treatment retention in a prison-based residential sex offender treatment program. *Sexual Abuse: A Journal of Research and Treatment.* 19(4): 333–346.

Pelka, F. (1995). Raped: A male survivor breaks his silence. In P.S. Searles & R. J. Berger (eds.), *Rape and Society.* Boulder, CO: Westview.

Perkins, D. (1991). Clinical work with sex offenders in secure settings. In C. R. Hollin & K. Howells (eds.), *Clinical Approaches to Sex Offenders and Their Victims.* West Sussex, UK: Wiley.

Perry A. E. (2012). Court decisions on child pornography and language use. *Sexual Assault Report.* 15(3): 38, 41, 43, 48.

Perry, N. W., & Wrightsman, L. S. (1991). *The Child Witness: Legal Issues and Dilemmas.* Newbury Park, CA: Sage.

Persky, H., Smith, K. D., & Basu, G. K. (1971). Relations of psychologic measures of aggression and hostility to testosterone in man. *Psychosomatic Medicine*. 33: 265–277.

Phan, D. L., & Kingree, J. B. (2001). Sexual abuse victimization and psychological distress among adolescent offenders. *Journal of Child Sexual Abuse*. 10: 81–90.

Piper, A. (1993). Truth serum and recovered memories of sexual abuse. *Journal of Psychiatry and Law*. 21: 447–471.

Piquero, A. R., Farrington, D. P., & Blumstein, A. (2003). The criminal career paradigm. In M. Tonry (ed.), *Crime and Justice: A Review of Research*. Chicago, IL: University of Chicago Press.

Pirke, K. M., Kockott, G., & Dittmar, F. (1974). Psychosexual stimulation and plasma testosterone in men. *Archives of Sexual Behavior*. 3: 577–584.

Pithers, W. D. (1994). Process evaluation of a group therapy component designed to enhance sex offenders' empathy for sexual abuse survivors. *Behavior Research and Therapy*. 32: 565–570.

Pithers, W. D., Kashima, K. M., Cumming, G. F., Beal, L. S., & Buell, M. M. (1988). Relapse prevention in sexual aggression. In R.A. Prentky & V. L. Quinsey (eds.), *Human Sexual Aggression: Current Perspectives*. New York: New York Academy of Science.

Pithers, W. D., Marques, J. K., Gibat, C. C., & Marlatt, G. A. (1983). Relapse prevention with sexual aggressives: A self-control model of treatment and maintenance of change. In J. G. Greer & I. R. Stuart (eds.), *The Sexual Aggressor: Current Perspectives on Treatment*. New York: Van Nostrand Reinhold.

Pithers, W. D., Beal, S., Armstrong, J., & Petty, J. (1989). Identification of risk factors through clinical interviews and analysis of records. In D. R. Laws (ed.), *Relapse Prevention with Sex Offenders*. New York: Guilford.

Plante, T. G. (2003). After the earthquake. *America*, p. 11.

Police Responses to Crimes of Sexual Assault. (2002). Available at: http://www.vaw,umn.edu/finaldocuments/consac3.html

Polizzi, D. M., MacKenzie, D. L., & Hickman, L. J. (1999). What works in adult sex offender treatment? A review of prison and non-prison based treatment programs. *International Journal of Offender Therapy and Comparative Criminology*. 43: 357–374.

Porter, R. (ed.). (1984). *Child Sexual Abuse Within the Family*. London: Tavistock.

Potas, I. (1982). *Just Deserts for the Mad*. Canberra: Australian Institute of Criminology.

Prendergast, W. E. (2004). *Treating sex offenders: A guide to clinical practice with adults, clerics, children, and adolescentsf.* New York: Haworth Press

Prentky, R. A. (1994). The assessment and treatment of sex offenders. *Criminal Justice and Behavior*. 21: 6–9.

Prentky, R. A., & Burgess, A. W. (1990). Rehabilitation of child molesters: A cost-benefit analysis. *American Journal of Orthopsychiatry*. 60: 108–117.

Prentky, R. A., Burgess, A. W., Rokous, F., Lee, A., Hartman, C., Ressler, R., & Douglas, J. (1989). The presumptive role of fantasy in serial sexual homicide. *American Journal of Psychiatry*. 146: 887–891.

Prentky, R., Harris, B., Frizzell, K., & Righthand, S. (2000). An actuarial procedure for assessing risk in juvenile sex offenders. *Sexual Abuse: A Journal of Research and Treatment*. 12: 71–93.

Prentky, R., Knight, R., & Lee, A. (1997). Risk factors associated with recidivism among extra-familial child molesters.

Journal of Consulting and Clinical Psychology. 65(1): 141–149.

Prescott, D., & Levenson, J. S. (2010). Sex offender treatment is not punishment. *Journal of Sexual Aggression.* 16(3): 275–285.

Prior, V. (2001). Invited comments to: Children's response to the medical visit for allegations of sexual abuse: Maternal perceptions and predicting variables. *Child Abuse Review.* 10: 223–225.

Prison Reform Trust. (1990). *Sex Offenders in Prison.* London: Prison Reform Trust.

Prison Reform Trust. (1991). *The Woolf Report: A Summary of the Main Findings and Recommendations of the Inquiry into Prison Disturbances.* London: Prison Reform Trust.

Pritt, A. F. (1998). Spiritual correlates of reported sexual abuse among Mormon women. *Journal for the Scientific Study of Religion.* 37: 273–285.

Prochaska, J. O., & DiClemente, C. C. (1982). Transtheoretical therapy: Toward a more integrative model of change. *Psychotherapy: Theory, Research and Practice.* 19: 276–288.

Programme Development Section. (1997a). *The Prison Service Sex Offender Treatment Programme.* Prepared for the SOTP Accreditation Panel, London.

Programme Development Section. (1997b). *Sex Offender Treatment Programme Accreditation Criteria 1997-8.* Prepared for the SOTP Accreditation Panel, London.

Pryor, D. (1996). *Unspeakable Acts: Why Men Sexually Abuse Children.* New York: New York University Press.

Quayle, E., & Jones, T. (2011). Sexualized images of children on the internet. *Sexual Abuse: A Journal of Research & Treatment.* 23(1): 7–21.

Quayle, E., Loof, L., & Palmer, T. (2008). *Child pornography and sexual exploitation of children online.* A contribution of ECPAT International to the World Congress III against sexual exploitation of children and adolescents.

Quayle, E., & Taylor, M. (eds.). (2005). *Viewing Child Pornography on the Internet: Understanding the Offense, Managing the Offender, Helping the Victims.* Dorset, UK: Russell House Publishing.

Quinsey, V. L. (1973). Methodological issues in evaluating the effectiveness of aversion therapies for institutionalized child molesters. *Canadian Psychologist.* 14: 350–361.

Quinsey, V. L., Bergersen, S. G., & Steinman, C. M. (1976). Changes in physiological and verbal responses of child molesters during aversion therapy. *Canadian Journal of Behavioral Science.* 8(2): 202–212.

Quinsey, V. L., Chaplin, T. C., & Varney, G. (1981). A comparison of rapists' and non-sex offenders' sexual preferences for mutually consenting sex, rape, and physical abuse of women. *Behavioral Assessment.* 3: 127–135.

Quinsey, V. L., Khanna, A., & Malcolm, P. B. (1998). A retrospective evaluation of the regional treatment centre sex offender treatment program. *Journal of Interpersonal Violence.* 13: 621–644.

Quinsey, V. L., Lalumiere, M. T., Rice, M. E., & Harris, G. T. (1995). Predicting sexual offences. In J. C. Campbell (ed.), *Assessing Dangerousness: Violence by Sexual Offenders, Batterers and Child Abusers.* Thousand Oaks, CA: Sage.

Quinsey, V. L., Rice, M. E., & Harris, G. T. (1990). *Psychopathy, Sexual Deviance and Recidivism Among Released Sex Offenders* (Research Report Vol. 7, No. 5). Pentanguishine, ON: Mental Health Centre.

Quinsey, V. L., Steinman, C. M., Bergerson, S. G., & Holmes, T. F. (1975). Penile circumference, skin conductance and ranking responses of child molesters and "normals" to sexual and nonsexual stimuli. *Behavior Therapy.* 6: 213–219.

Quinsey, V. L., Warneford, A., Pruesse, M., & Link, N. (1975). Released Oak Ridge patients: A follow-up study of review board discharges. *British Journal of Criminology.* 15: 264–270.

Rada, R. T. (1978). Classification of therapist. In R. T. Rada (ed.), *Clinical Aspects of the Rapist.* New York: Grune & Stratton.

Rada, R. T., Laws, D. R., & Kellner, R. (1976). Plasma testosterone levels in the rapist. *Psychosomatic Medicine.* 38: 257–268.

Rada, R. T., Laws, D. R., Kellner, R., Stiristava, L., & Peake, G. (1983). Plasma androgens in violent and non-violent sex offenders. *Bulletin of the American Academy of Psychiatry and the Law.* 11: 149–158.

Rape and Rape Prevention. (1999). Available at: http://www.estronaut.com/a/avoiding_rape.htm

Rape Crisis Federation. (2002, February 25). *Rape!* Notingham, UK: Rape Crisis Federation of Wales and England.

Ray, J. A., & English, D. J. (1995). Comparison of female and male children with sexual behavior problems. *Journal of Youth and Adolescence.* 24: 439–451.

Redding Police Department. (1996, July 29). *Parolees and Sex Offenders.* Available at: http://ci.redding.ca.us/rpd/rpdoff.htm

Redmon, J., & Joyner, T. (2007, October 27). Wilson rejoices: 4-3 decision frees Genarlow. *The Atlanta Journal-Constitution.* 1A.

Reiss, D., Grubin, D., & Meux, C. (1996). Young "psychopaths" in special hospital: Treatment and outcome. *British Journal of Psychiatry.* 168: 99–104.

Rennison, C. M. (2001). *Criminal Victimization 2000: Changes 1999–2000 with Trends 1993–2000.* National Crime Victimization Survey. Washington, DC: Bureau of Justice Statistics.

Rennison, C. M., & Rand, M. R. (2003). *Criminal Victimization, 2002.* Washington, DC: U.S. Department of Justice, Bureau of Justice Statistics.

Report: USA Swimming Coaches Abused "Dozens" of Teen Athletes. (2010, April 9). *The Raw Story.* Retrieved from http://rawstory.com/rs/2010/0409/report-usa-swimming-coaches-abused-dozens-teen-athletes/

Resnick, H. S., Acierno, R., & Kilpatrick, D. G. (1997). Health impact of interpersonal violence: Medicinal and mental health outcomes. *Behavioral Medicine.* 23: 65–78.

Ressler, R. K., Burgess, A. W., & Douglas, J. E. (1988). *Sexual Homicide: Patterns and Motives.* New York: Lexington Books.

Rhodes, A. (2002). *Fifth Grade Rapist Exposes Woeful Lapse in Bureaucratic Communication.* Available at: http://www.wgac.com/austin/01-16.html

Rice, M. E., & Harris, G. T. (2003). The size and sign of treatment effects in sex offender therapy. In R. A. Prentky, M. C. Seto, & A. Burgess (eds.), *Understanding and Managing Sexually Coercive Behavior.* New York: New York Academy of Sciences.

Rice, M. E., Quinsey, V. L., & Harris, G. T. (1991). Sexual recidivism among child molesters released from a maximum-security psychiatric institution. *Journal of Consulting and Clinical Psychology.* 59: 381–386.

Rich, L. L. (1995). *Right to Privacy in the Information Age.* Publishing Law Center. Available at: http://publaw.com/ privacy.html

Rich, P. (2011). *Understanding, Assessing, and Rehabilitating Juvenile Sexual Offending* (2nd. ed.). Hoboken, NJ: Wiley & Sons, Ltd.

Richardson, G., Kelley, T. P., Graham, F., & Bhate, S. R. (2004). A personality-based taxonomy of sexually abusive adolescents derived from the Millon Adolescent Clinical Inventory (MACI). *British Journal of Clinical Psychology*. 43: 285–298.

Righthand, S., & Welch, C. (2001). *Juveniles Who Have Sexually Offended: A Review of the Professional Literature*. Washington, DC: U.S. Department of Justice, Office of Juvenile Justice and Delinquency Prevention.

Rizzo, N. D. (1981). Can everyone be rehabilitated? *International Journal of Offender Therapy and Comparative Criminology*. 25: 41–46.

Robertiello, G., & Terry, K. J. (2007). Can we profile sex offenders? A review of sex offender typologies. *Aggression and Violent Behavior*. 12(5): 508–518.

Robson, B. (1999). *A Prison by Any Other Name*. Available at: http://www.citi-pages.com/databank/18/863/article3579.asp

Roche, M. J., Shoss, N. E., Pincus, A. L., & Menard, K. S. (2011). Psychopathy moderates the relationship between time in treatment and levels of empathy in incarcerated male sexual offenders. *Sexual Abuse: A Journal of Research & Treatment*. 23(2): 171–192.

Roesler, T. A., & Weissmann-Wind, T. A. (1994). Telling the secret: Adult women describe their disclosures of incest. *Journal of Interpersonal Violence*. 9: 327–338.

Rogers, C. M., & Terry, T. (1984). Clinical interventions with boy victims of sexual abuse. In I. Stewart & J. Greer (eds.), *Victims of Sexual Aggression*. New York: Van Nostrand Reinhold.

Romano, E., & DeLuca, R. V. (2001). Male sexual abuse: A review of effects, abuse characteristics, and links with later psychological functioning. *Aggression and Violent Behavior*. 6: 55–78.

Ronan, T. P. (1957). Report on Sex Problems Stirs British Debate. *New York Times*. Retrieved from http://query.nytimes.com/mem/archive/pdf?res=F20912F93F5D157A93C0AB1782D85F438585F9

Rondeaux, C. (2005, November 22). No jail time for Lafave. *St. Petersburg Times*. Retrieved from http://www.sptimes.com/2005/11/22/Tampabay/No_jail_time_for_Lafa.shtml

Ropelato, J. (2012). *Internet Pornography Statistics*. Available at: http://internet-filter-review.toptenreviews.com/internet-pornography-statistics.html

Rosetti, S. J. (1995). The impact of child sexual abuse on attitudes toward God and the Catholic Church. *Child Abuse and Neglect*. 19: 1469–1481.

Rosetti, S. J. (1997). The effects of priest-perpetration of child sexual abuse on the trust of Catholics in priesthood, church and God. *Journal of Psychology and Christianity*. 16: 197–209.

Rosman, J., & Resnick, P. (1989). Sexual attraction to corpses: A psychiatric review of necrophilia. *Bulletin of the American Academy of Psychiatry and the Law*. 17: 153–163.

Ross, D. F., Miller, B. S., & Moran, P. B. (1987). The child in the eyes of the jury: Assessing mock jurors' perceptions of the child witness. In S. J. Ceci, M. P. Toglia, & D. F. Ross (eds.), *Children's Eyewitness Testimony*. New York: Springer.

Ross, J. I., & Richard, S. C. (2002). *Behind Bars: Surviving Prison*. Indianapolis, IN: Marie Butler-Knight Publication.

Ross, R. R., & Gendreau, P. (eds.). (1980). *Effective Correctional Treatment*. Toronto, ON: Butterworth & Company.

Ross, R. R., & McKay, B. (1980). Behavioral approaches to treatment in corrections: Requiem for a panacea. In R. R. Ross & P. Gendreau (eds.), *Effective Correctional Treatment*. Toronto, ON: Butterworth & Company.

Rossow, I., & Lauritzen, G. (2001). Shattered childhood: A key in suicidal behavior among drug addicts? *Addiction*. 96(2): 227–240.

Rush, F. (1977). The great Freudian cover-up. *Trouble and Strife*. 4: 29–32.

Russell, D. E. H. (1975). *The Politics of Rape: The Victim's Perspective*. New York: Stein & Day.

Russell, D. E. H. (1984). *Sexual Exploitation: Rape, Child Sexual Abuse and Sexual Harassment*. Beverly Hills, CA: Sage.

Russell, D. E. H. (1986). *The Secret Trauma: Incest in the Lives of Girls and Women*. New York: Basic Books.

Ryan, G. (1999). Treatment of sexually abusive youth. *Journal of Interpersonal Violence*. 14: 422–437.

Ryan, G., Lane, S., Davis, J., & Issac, C. (1987). Juvenile sex offenders: Development and correction. *Child Abuse and Neglect*. 11: 385–395.

Ryan, G., Leversee, T., & Lane, S. (2010). *Juvenile Sexual Offending: Causes, Consequences and Correction*. Hoboken, NJ: Wiley & Sons.

Ryan, G., Miyoshi, T. J., Metzner, J. L., Krugman, R. D., & Fryer, G. E. (1996). Trends in a national sample of sexually abusive youth. *Journal of the American Academy of Child and Adolescent Psychiatry*. 35: 17–25.

Ryan, G. D. (1991). Historical responses to juvenile sexual offences. In G.D. Ryan & S. L. Lane (eds.), *Juvenile Sexual Offending: Causes, Consequences and Correction*. Lexington, MA: Lexington Books.

Salt Lake Tribune. (1999, October, 17). Bringing Abuse to Light. *Salt Lake Tribune* [online]. Retrieved from Lexis-Nexis.

Sample L. L., & Bray T. M. (2003). Are sex offenders dangerous? *Criminology & Public Policy*. 3: 59–82.

Sampson, A. (1992). Treatment programs: From theory to practice. In Prison Reform Trust (ed.), *Beyond Containment: The Penal Response to Sex Offending*. London: Prison Reform Trust.

Sanday, P. R. (1981). *Female Power and Male Domination*. New York: Cambridge University Press.

Sanderson, R. (1960). Clinical trial with millenil in the treatment of schizophrenia. *Journal of Mental Science*. 106: 732–741.

Saunders-Wilson, D. (1992). The need for sexual glasnost. In Prison Reform Trust (ed.), *Beyond Containment: The Penal Response to Sex Offending*. London: Prison Reform Trust.

Scaramella, J. J., & Brown, W. A. (1978). Serum testosterone and aggressiveness in hockey players. *Psychosomatic Medicine*. 40: 262–265.

Scarce, M. (1997). *Male on Male Rape: The Hidden Toll of Stigma and Shame*. New York: Insight Books.

Schissel, B., & Fedec, K. (1999). The selling of innocence: The gestalt of danger in the lives of youth prostitutes. *Canadian Journal of Criminology*. 41(1): 33–56.

Schlank, A. M., & Shaw, T. (1996). Treating sexual offenders who deny their guilt: A pilot study. *Sexual Abuse*. 3: 371–380.

Schmidt, N. B., Kotov, R., & Joiner, T. E., Jr. (2004). Evolution of classification in the diagnostic and statistical manual of mental disorders: Current problems and proposed alternatives. In N. B. Schmidt, R. Kotov, & T. E. Joiner, Jr. (eds.), *Taxometrics: Toward a New Diagnostic Scheme for Psychopathology*. Washington, DC: American Psychological Association.

Schneider, A. L., & Sumi, D. (1981). Patterns of forgetting and telescoping. *Criminology.* 19: 3.

Schwartz, B., & Cellini, H. (eds.). (1997). *The sex offender.* Kingston, NJ: Civic Research Institute.

Schwartz, B. K. (1995). Characteristics and typologies of sex offenders. In B. Schwartz (ed.), *The Sex Offender: Corrections, Treatment and Legal Practice* (Vol. 3). Kingston, NJ: Civic Research Institute.

Schwartz, B. K. (1999). The case against involuntary commitment. In A. Schlank & F. Cohen (eds.), *The Sexual Predator: Law, Policy, Evaluation and Treatment* (Vol. 2). Kingston, NJ: Civic Research Institute.

Scott, L. K. (1997). Community management of sex offenders. In B. Schwartz & H. Cellini (eds.), *The Sex Offender.* Kingston, NJ: Civic Research Institute.

Scott, M. B., & Lyman, S. M. (1968). Paranoia, homosexuality, and game theory. *Journal of Health and Social Behavior.* 9: 179–187.

Scully, D. (1990). *Understanding Sexual Violence: A Study of Convicted Rapists.* Cambridge, MA: Unwin, Hyman.

Scully, D., & Marolla, J. (1984). Convicted rapists' vocabulary of motive: Excuses and justifications. *Social Problems.* 31: 530–544.

Scully, D., & Marolla, J. (1985). "Riding the bull at Gilleys": Convicted rapists describe the rewards of rape. *Social Problems.* 32: 251–263.

Sealy, G. (2002, February). *The Talk in Church: Some Experts Say Abuse Cases Could Open Up Religious Sexual Discussions.* Available at: https://www.abcnews.go.com/sections/us/Daily-News/churchsex020222.html

Sebba, L. (2001). On the relationship between criminological research and policy: The case of crime victims. *Criminal Justice.* 1: 27–58.

Sebba, L. (1996). *Third Parties, Victims and the Criminal Justice System.* Columbus: Ohio State University Press.

Seghorn, T. K., & Cohen, M. (1980). The psychology of the rape assailant. In W. Cerran, A. L. McGarry, & C. Petty (eds.), *Modern Legal Medicine, Psychiatry and Forensic Science.* Philadelphia: FA Davis.

Seghorn, T. K., Prentky, R. A., & Boucher, R. J. (1987). Childhood sexual abuse in the lives of aggressive sexual offenders. *Journal of the American Academy of Child and Adolescent Psychiatry.* 26: 262–267.

Segraves, R., Balon, R., & Clayton, A. (2007). Proposal for changes in diagnostic criteria for sexual dysfunctions. *Journal of Sexual Medicine.* 4: 567–580.

Seidman, B. T., Marshall, W. L., Hudson, S. M., & Robertson, P. J. (1994). An examination of intimacy and loneliness in sex offenders. *Journal of Interpersonal Violence.* 9: 518–534.

Seifert, R. (1993). War and rape: A preliminary analysis. In A. Stiglmayer (ed.), *Mass Rape: The War against Women in Bosnia-Herzegovina.* Lincoln: University of Nebraska Press.

Seling, M. (2000). *A Treatment Program Overview.* Steilacoom, WA: Special Commitment Center.

Serin, R. C. (1991). Psychopathy and violence in criminals. *Journal of Interpersonal Violence.* 6: 423–431.

Serin, R. C., Malcolm, P. B., Khanna, A., & Barbaree, H. E. (1994). Psychopathy and deviant sexual arousal in incarcerated sexual offenders. *Journal of Interpersonal Violence.* 9: 3–11.

Serrill, M. S. (1975). Is rehabilitation dead? *Corrections.* 3: 21–26.

Seto, M. C., & Barbaree, H. E. (1999). Psychopathy, treatment behavior and sexual offender recidivism. *Journal of Interpersonal Violence.* 14: 1235–1248.

Seto, M. C., Cantor, J. M., & Blanchard, R. (2006). Child pornography offenses are a valid diagnostic indicator of pedophilia. *Journal of Abnormal Psychology*. 115(3): 610–615.

Seto, M. C., Karl Hanson, R., & Babchishin, K. M. (2011). Contact sexual offending by men with online sexual offenses. *Sexual Abuse: A Journal of Research & Treatment*. 23(1): 124–145.

Shakeshaft, C. (2004). *Educator Sexual Misconduct with Students: A Synthesis of Existing Literature on Prevalence*. Washington, DC: Planning and Evaluation Service, Office of the Undersecretary, US Department of Education.

Shaw, J. A., Lewis, J. E., Loeb, A., Rosado, J., & Rodriguez, R. A. (2000). Child on child sexual abuse: Psychological perspectives. *Child Abuse and Neglect*. 24: 1591–1600.

Shipley, S. L., & Arrigo, B. A. (2004). The female homicide offender: Serial murder and the case of Aileen Wuornos. *Women & Criminal Justice*. 15(3/4): 172–177.

Simkins, L. (1993). Characteristics of sexually repressed child molesters. *Journal of Interpersonal Violence*. 8: 3–17.

Simkins, L., Ward, W., Bowman, S., & Rinck, C. M. (1989). The Multiphasic Sex Inventory: Diagnosis and prediction of treatment response in child sexual abusers. *Annals of Sex Research*. 2: 205–226.

Simon, L. M. J. (2000). An examination of the assumptions of specialization, mental disorder, and dangerousness in sex offenders. *Behavioral Sciences and the Law*. 18: 175–308.

Simon, L. M. J., Sales, B., Kaskniak, A., & Kahn, M. (1992). Characteristics of child molesters: Implications for the fixated-regressed dichotomy. *Journal of Interpersonal Violence*. 7: 211–225.

Simon, T., Mercy, J., & Perkins, C. (2001, June). *Injuries from Violent Crime,*

1992–98. Washington, DC: U.S. Department of Justice, Bureau of Justice Statistics.

Simpson, T. L., & Miller, W. R. (2002). Concomitance between childhood sexual and physical abuse and substance use problems: A review. *Clinical Psychology Review*. 22: 27–77.

Sipe, A. R. (1995). *Sex, Priests and Power: Anatomy of a Crisis*. New York: Brunner/Mazel.

Sipe, A. R. (1999). The problem of prevention in clergy sexual abuse. In T. G. Plante (ed.), *Bless Me Father for I Have Sinned: Perspectives of Sexual Abuse Committed by Roman Catholic Priests*. Westport, CT: Praeger.

Sipe, A. W. R. (1990). *A secret world: Sexuality and the search for celibacy*. New York: Brunner/Mazel, Inc.

Sipe, R., Jensen, E. L., & Everett, R. S. (1998). Adolescent sexual offenders grown up: Recidivism in young adulthood. *Criminal Justice and Behavior*. 25: 109–124.

Skinner, B. F. (1953). *Science and Human Behavior*. New York: Macmillan.

Skogan, W. G. (1975). Measurement problems in official and survey crime rates. *Journal of Criminal Justice*. 3: 1.

Smallbone, S. W., & McCabe, B. (2003). Childhood attachment, childhood sexual abuse, and onset of masturbation among adult sex offenders. *Sexual Abuse: A Journal of Research and Treatment*. 15: 1–9.

Smallbone, S. W., & Wortley, R. K. (2004). Criminal diversity and paraphilic interests among adult males convicted of sexual offenses against children. *International Journal of Offender Therapy and Comparative Criminology*. 48: 175–188.

Smith, A. B., & Berlin, L. (1977). Can criminals be treated? *New England Journal on Prison Law*. 3: 487–502.

Smith, D. W., Letourneau, E. J., & Saunders, B. E. (2000). Delay in disclosure of childhood rape: Results from a national survey. *Child Abuse and Neglect*. 24: 273–287.

Smith, H., & Israel, E. (1987). Sibling incest: A study of dynamics of 25 cases. *Child Abuse and Neglect*. 11: 101–108.

Smith, L. M. (1994). Lifting the veil of secrecy: Mandatory child abuse reporting statutes may encourage the Catholic Church to report priests who molest children. *Law and Psychology Review*. 18: 409–421.

Smith, M., & Pazder, L. (1980). *Michelle Remembers*. New York: Congdon & Lattes.

Smith, W., & Monastersky, C. (1986). Assessing juvenile sex offender's risk of reoffending. *Criminal Justice and Behavior*. 13: 115–140.

Smith, W. R. (1988). Delinquency and abuse among juvenile sexual offenders. *Journal of Interpersonal Violence*. 3: 400–413.

Smith, W. R., Monastersky, C., & Deishner, R. M. (1987). MMPI-based personality types among juvenile sexual offenders. *Journal of Clinical Psychology*. 43: 422–430.

Snaith, P. (1983). Exhibitionism: A clinical conundrum. *British Journal of Psychiatry*. 143: 703–710.

Snyder, H. N. (2000). *Sexual Assault of Young Children as Reported to Law Enforcement: Victim, Incident, and Offender Characteristics, NIBRS Statistical Report*. Washington, DC: U.S. Department of Justice, Office of Justice Programs Bureau of Justice Statistics.

Solicitor General of Canada. (1990). *Management and Treatment of Sex Offenders*. Ottawa: Minister of Supply Services.

Soothill, K., Francis, B., Sanderson, B., & Ackerley, E. (2000). Sex offenders:

Specialists, generalists–or both? *British Journal of Criminology*. 40: 56–67.

Soothill, K. L., Jack, A., & Gibbens, T. C. N. (1976). Rape: 22 year cohort study. *Medicine, Science and the Law*. 16: 26–39.

Sorenson, T., & Snow, B. (1991). How children tell: The process of disclosure in child sexual abuse. *Child Welfare*. 70: 3–15.

Spinazzola, J., Ford, J. D., & Zucker, M. (2005). Complex trauma exposure, outcome, and intervention among children and adolescents. *Psychiatric Annual Journal*. 35(5): 433–439.

Sreenivasan, S., Garrick, T., Norris, R., Cusworth-Walker, S., Weinberger, L. E., Essres, G. et al. (2007). Predicting the likelihood of future sexual recidivism: Pilot study findings from a California sex offender risk project and cross-validation of the Static-99. *The Journal of the American Academy of Psychiatry and the Law*. 35: 454–468.

State of New York. (1999). *Governor Pataki Announces Latest Criminal Justice Reform; Civil Commitment of Sexually Violent Predators Protects New York Families* [press release]. Albany, NY: Press Office.

Steadman, H. J. (1972). The psychiatrist as a conservative agent of social control. *Social Problems*. 20: 263–271.

Sternac, L. E., & Segal, Z. V. (1989). Adult sexual contact with children: An examination of cognitive factors. *Behavior Therapy*. 20: 573–584.

Sternac, L. E., Segal, Z. V., & Gillis, R. (1990). Social and cultural factors in sexual assault. In W. L. Marshall, D. R. Laws, & H. E. Barbaree (eds.), *Handbook of Sexual Assault: Issues, Theories and Treatment of the Offender*. New York: Plenum.

Stirling, A. E., & Kerr, G. A. (2009). Abused athletes' perceptions of the coach-athlete relationship. *Sports in Society*. 12(2): 227–239.

Stone, A. (1985). The new legal standards of dangerousness: Fair in theory, unfair in practice. In C. D. Webster, M. H. Ben-Aron, & S. J. Hucker (eds.), *Dangerousness: Probability and Prediction, Psychiatry and Public Policy*. New York: Cambridge University Press.

Stone, N. (2011). The "sexting" quagmire: Criminal justice responses to adolescent's electronic transmissions of indecent images in the UK and the USA. *Youth Justice*. 11(3): 266–281.

Strahan, T. (1991). Women increasingly receive public assistance as abortion is repeated. *Association for Interdisciplinary Research in Values and Social Change Newsletter*. 4: 3–7.

Studer, L. H., Clelland, S. R., Aylwin, A. S., Reddon, J. R., & Monro, A. (2002). Rethinking risk assessment for incest offenders. *International Journal of Law and Psychiatry*. 23: 15–22.

Sturman, P. (2000). *Drug Assisted Sexual Assault*. London: Home Office, Police Research Award Scheme.

Sturup, G. K. (1971). Castration: The total treatment. *International Psychiatry Clinics*. 8: 175–196.

Sullivan, J., & Beech, A. (2004). A comparative study of demographic data relating to intra- and extra-familial child sexual abusers and professional perpetrators. *Journal of Sexual Aggression*. 10: 39–50.

Summit, R. C. (1983). The child sexual abuse accommodation syndrome. *Child Abuse and Neglect*. 7: 177–193.

Suresh, G., Mustaine, E. E., Tewksbury, R., & Higgins, G. E. (2010). Social disorganization and registered sex offenders: An exploratory spatial analysis. *Southwest Journal of Criminal Justice*. 7(2): 180–213.

Sutherland, E. (1950). The diffusion of sexual psychopath laws. *American Journal of Sociology*. 50: 142–148.

Syed, F., & Williams, S. (1996). *Case Studies of Female Sex Offenders in the Correctional Service of Canada*. Ottawa, ON: Correctional Service Canada.

Sykes, G. M., & Matza, D. (1957). Techniques of neutralization: A theory of delinquency. *American Sociological Review*. 22: 664–670.

Tappan, P. W. (1950). *The Habitual Sex Offender: Report and Recommendation of the Commission on the Habitual Sex Offender*. Trenton, NJ: Commission on the Habitual Sex Offender.

Taslitz, A. E. (1999). *Rape and the Culture of the Courtroom*. New York: New York University Press.

Tauber, E. S. (1940). Effects of castration upon the sexuality of the adult male: A review of relevant literature. *Psychosomatic Medicine*. 2: 74–87.

Taylor, M., & Quayle, E. (2003). *Child Pornography: An Internet Crime*. East Sussex, UK: Brunner-Routledge.

Taylor, M., Quayle, E., & Holland, G. (2001). Child pornography, the Internet and offending. *The Canadian Journal of Policy Research*. 2(2): 94–100.

Tennessee Board of Probation and Parole. (2007). *Monitoring Tennessee's sex offenders using global positioning systems: A project evaluation*. State of Tennessee, Board of Probation and Parole.

Terman, L. (1938). *Psychological Factors in Marital Happiness*. New York: McGraw-Hill.

Terry, K. J. (1999). *Analysing the Effects of Motivation on Sex Offenders in a Cognitive-Behavioural Treatment Programme*. Unpublished doctoral dissertation, Cambridge University, Cambridge, UK.

Terry, K. J. (2000). *Sustaining Employment: Factors Associated with Job Retention Among Ex-Offenders*. New York: Report for the Center for Employment Opportunities.

Terry, K. J. (2008). Stained glass: The nature and scope of sexual abuse crisis in the Catholic Church. *Criminal Justice & Behavior.* 35(5): 549–569.

Terry, K. J. (2011). What is smart sex offender policy? *Criminology and Public Policy.* 10(2): 275–282.

Terry, K. J., & Ackerman, A. (2008). Child sexual abuse in the Catholic Church: How situational crime prevention strategies can help create safe environments. *Criminal Justice and Behavior.* 35(5): 643–657.

Terry, K. J., & Ackerman, A. (2009). A brief history of major sex offender laws. In R. G. Wright (ed.), *Sex Offender Laws: Failed Policies, New Beginnings.* New York: Springer.

Terry, K. J., & Furlong, J. (2008). *Sex offender registration and community notification: A "Megan's Law" Sourcebook* (2nd ed.). Kingston, NJ: Civic Research Institute.

Terry, K. J., & Litvinoff, L. (2012). Child maltreatment in the context of religious organizations. In D. L. Chadwick (ed.), *Child Maltreatment* (4th ed.). St Louis, MO: STM Learning, Inc.

Terry, K. J., & Mitchell, E. W. (1999). The impact of voluntariness on treatment efficacy: Is motivation necessary? *Forensic Update.* 59: 7–12.

Terry, K. J., & Mitchell, E. W. (2001). Motivation in sex offender treatment efficacy: Leading a horse to water and making it drink? *International Journal of Offender Therapy and Comparative Criminology.* 45: 663–672.

Terry, K. J., Smith, M. L., Schuth, K., Kelly, J., Vollman, B., & Massey, C. (2011). *Causes and context of the sexual abuse crisis in the Catholic Church.* Washington, DC: United States Conference of Catholic Bishops.

Terry, K. J., & Tallon, J. (2004). *Child Sexual Abuse: A Review of the Literature.* New York: John Jay College Research Team.

Tewksbury, R. (1989). Fear of sexual assault in prison inmates. *The Prison Journal.* 69: 62–71.

Tewksbury, R. (2005). Collateral consequences of sex offender registration. *Journal of Contemporary Criminal Justice.* 21: 67–81.

Tewksbury, R. (2007). Effects of sexual assaults on men: Physical, mental, and sexual consequences. *International Journal of Men's Health.* 6: 22–34.

Tewksbury, R., & Lees, M. (2006). Consequences of sex offender registration: Collateral consequences and community experiences. *Sociological Spectrum.* 26(3): 309–334.

Tewksbury, R., & Mustaine, E. E. (2006). Where to find sex offenders: An examination of residential locations and neighborhood conditions. *Criminal Justice Studies.* 19(1): 61–75.

Tewksbury, R., & Mustaine, E. E. (2008). Where registered sex offenders live: Community characteristics and proximity to possible victims. *Victims & Offenders.* 3: 86–98.

Tewksbury, R., & West, A. (2000). Research on sex in prison during the late 1980s and early 1990s. *The Prison Journal.* 90(4): 368–378.

Tewksbury, R., & Zgoba, K. (2010). Perceptions and coping with punishment: How registered sex offenders respond to stress, internet restrictions, and the collateral consequences of registration. *International Journal of Offender Therapy and Comparative Criminology.* 54(4): 537–551.

Theodosi, E., & McMurran, M. (2006). Motivating convicted sex offenders into treatment: A pilot study. *British Journal of Forensic Practice.* 8(3): 28–35.

Thomas, T. (2000). *Sex Crime: Sex Offending and Society.* Devon: Willan.

Thompson, K. M., Wonderlich, S. A., Crosby, R. D., & Mitchell, J. E. (2001). Sexual victimization and adolescent weight regulation practices: A test across three community based samples. *Child Abuse and Neglect.* 25: 291–305.

Thornhill, R., & Palmer, C. (2000). *A Natural History of Rape: Biological Bases of Sexual Coercion.* Cambridge, MA: MIT Press.

Tjaden, P., & Thoennes, N. (2006). *Extent, Nature, and Consequences of Violence against Women: Findings from the National Violence against Women Survey* (NCJ 210346). Washington, DC: U.S Department of Justice and U.S. Department for Health and Human Services, Centers for Disease Control Prevention, National Institute of Justice.

Tomak, S., Weschler, F. S., Ghahramanlou-Holloway, M., Virden, T., & Nademin, M. E. (2009). An empirical study of the personality characteristics of internet sex offenders. *Journal of Sexual Aggression.* 15(2): 139–148.

Toobert, S., Bartelme, K. F., & Jones, E. F. (1959). Some factors related to pedophilia. *International Journal of Social Psychology.* 4: 272–279.

Tracy, F., Donnelly, H., Morgenbesser, L., & MacDonald, D. (1983). Program evaluation: Recidivism research involving sex offenders. In J.G. Greer & I. R. Stuart (eds.), *The Sexual Aggressor: Current Perspectives on Treatment.* New York: Van Nostrand Reinhold.

Transcript of Interview with LDS Church Officials. (1999, October 17). *The Salt Lake Tribune* [online]. Retrieved from Lexis-Nexis.

Travin, S., Cullen, K., & Protter, B. (1990). Female sexual offenders: Severe victims and victimizers. *Journal of Forensic Sciences.* 35: 140–150.

Turner, S. (2000). Surviving sexual assault and sexual torture. In G.C. Mezey & M. B. King (eds.), *Male Victims of*

Sexual Assault. Oxford: Oxford University Press.

Turner, S., Hess, J., Myers, R., Shah, R., Werth, R., & Whitby, A. (2007). *Implementation and Early Outcomes for the San Diego High Risk Sex Offender GPS Pilot Program.* Irvine, CA: Center for Evidenced-Based Correction.

Ukeritis, M. D. (2005, November). *Clergy Who Violate Boundaries: Sexual Abuse and Misconduct in a Sample of Canadian Men.* Annual Meeting of the Religious Research Association, Rochester, NY.

Ullman, S. E. (2007). Relationship to perpetrator, disclosure, social reactions, and PTSD symptoms in child sexual abuse survivors. *Journal of Child Sexual Abuse.* 16: 19–36.

Uniform Crime Report. (2009). *Crime in the United States.* Available at: http://www.fbi.gov/ucr/cius_02/html/web/appendices/07-append02.html

U.S. Department of Health & Human Services. (2010). *Fourth National Incidence Study of Child Abuse and Neglect (NIS-4), 2004-2009.* Available at: https://www.nis4.org/nishome.asp

U.S. General Accounting Office. (2003). *File-sharing programs: Peer-to-peer networks provide ready access to child pornography.* Washington, DC: U.S. G.A.O.

Uy, R. (2011). Blinded by red lights: Why trafficking discourse should shift away from sex and the "perfect victim" paradigm. *Berkeley Journal of Gender, Law & Justice.* 26(11): 204–219.

Valcour, F. (1990). The treatment of child sex abusers in the church. In S. J. Rosetti (ed.), *Slayer of the Soul: Child Sexual Abuse and the Catholic Church.* Mystic, CT: Twenty-third Publications.

Valente, S., & Wight, C. (2007). Military sexual trauma: Violence and sexual abuse. *Military Medicine.* 172: 259–265.

Vallerie, V. (1997). Relationships between alcohol, expectancies and sexual offenses in convicted offenders. In B. Schwartz & H. Cellini (eds.), *The Sex Offender.* Kingston, NJ: Civic Research Institute.

Van Dijk, J. J. M., Van Kesteren, J. N., & Smit, P. (2008). *Criminal Victimisation in International Perspective, Key Findings from the 2004-2005 ICVS and EU ICS.* The Hague: Boom Legal Publishers. Available at: http://rechten.uvt.nl/icvs/pdffiles/ICVS2004_05.pdf

Vandiver, D. M. (2006). Female sex offenders: A comparison of solo offenders and co-offenders. *Violence and Victims.* 21(3): 339–354.

Vandiver, D. M., Cheeseman Dial, K., & Worley, R. M. (2008). A qualitative assessment of registered female sex offenders: Judicial processing experiences and perceived effects of a public registry [electronic version]. *Criminal Justice Review.* 33(2): 177–198.

Vandiver, D. M., & Kercher, G. (2004). Offender and victim characteristics of registered female sexual offenders in Texas: A proposed typology of female sexual offenders [electronic version]. *Sexual Abuse: A Journal of Research and Treatment.* 16(2): 121–137.

Vandiver, D. M., & Teske, R., Jr. (2006). Juvenile female and male sex offenders: A comparison of offender, victim, and judicial processing characteristics [electronic version]. *International Journal of Offender Therapy and Comparative Criminology.* 50(2): 148–165.

Vandiver, D. M., & Walker, J. T. (2002). Female sex offenders: An overview and analysis of 40 cases [electronic version]. *Criminal Justice Review.* 27(2): 284–300.

Vasquez, B. E., Maddan, S., & Walker, J. T. (2008). The influence of sex offender registration and notification laws in the United States: A time-series analysis. *Crime and Delinquency.* 54(2): 175–192.

Veneziano, C., & Veneziano, L. (2002). Adolescent sex offenders: A review of the literature. *Trauma, Violence and Abuse.* 3: 247–260.

Vess, J. (2009). Fear and loathing in public policy: Ethical issues in laws for sex offenders. *Aggression and Violent Behavior.* 14(4): 264–272.

Viljoen, J. L., Elkovitch, N., Scalora, M. J., & Ullman, D. (2009). Assessment of reoffense risk in adolescents who have committed sexual offenses: Predictive validity of the ERASOR, PCL:YV, YLS/CMI, and Static-99. *Criminal Justice and Behavior.* 36(10): 981–1000.

Villmoare, E., & Neto, V. V. (1987). *Victim Appearances at Sentencing Hearings under California's Victims' Bill of Rights, Executive Summary.* Washington, DC: U.S. Department of Justice, National Institute of Justice.

Visgaitis, R. L. (2011). Retroactive application of the sex offender registration and notification act: A modern encroachment on judicial power. *Columbia Journal of Law and Social Problems.* 45: 273.

Vitello, P. (2009, October 14). Orthodox Jews rely more on sex abuse prosecution. *The New York Times* [online]. Retrieved from http://www.nytimes.com/2009/10/14/nyregion/14abuse.html

Vitiello, M. (2008). Punishing sex offenders: When good intentions go bad. *Arizona State Law Journal.* 40: 651–690.

Vogeltanz, N. D., Wilsnack, S. C., Harris, T. R., Wilsnack, R. W., Wonderlich, S. A., & Kristjanson, A. F. (1999). Prevalence and risk factors for childhood sexual abuse in women: National survey findings. *Child Abuse & Neglect.* 23: 579–592.

Von Hirsch, A., & Ashworth, A. (1996). Protective sentencing under section 2(2)(b): The criteria for dangerousness. *Criminal Law Review.* 175–183.

Walker, E. A., Katon, W. J., Hansom, J., Harrop-Griffiths, J., Holm, L., Jones, M. L., Hickok, L., & Jemelka, R. P. (1992). Medical and psychiatric symptoms in women with childhood sexual abuse. *Psychosomatic Medicine.* 54: 658–664.

Walker, J. T., Golden, J.W., & VanHouten, A. C. (2001). The geographic link between sex offenders and potential victims: A routine activities approach. *Justice Research and Policy.* 3(2): 15–33.

Walker, S. (1989). *Sense and Nonsense about Crime: A Policy Guide.* Pacific Grove, CA: Brooks/Cole.

Walrath, C., Ybarra, M., & Holden, E. W. (2003). Children with reported histories of sexual abuse: Utilizing multiple perspectives to understand clinical and psychosocial profiles. *Child Abuse and Neglect.* 27: 509–524.

Ward, C. (1995). Attitudes towards rape: Feminist and social psychological perspectives. In S. Wilkenson, series ed. *Gender and Psychology: Feminist and Critical Perspectives.* London: Sage.

Ward, C., & Inserto, F. (1990). *Victims of Sexual Violence: A Handbook for Helpers.* Kent Ridge: Singapore University Press.

Ward, T. (2010). Punishment or therapy? The ethics of sex offender treatment. *Journal of Sexual Aggression.* 16(3): 286–295.

Ward, T., & Gannon, T. (2006). Rehabilitation, etiology, and self-regulation: The Good Lives Model of rehabilitation for sexual offenders. *Aggression and Violent Behavior.* 11: 77–94.

Ward, T., & Hudson, S. M. (2000). A self-regulation model of relapse prevention. In D. R. Laws, S. M. Hudson, &

T. Ward (eds.), *Remaking Relapse Prevention with Sex Offenders: A Sourcebook.* Thousand Oaks, CA: Sage.

Ward, T., Hudson, S. M., Marshall, W. L., & Seigert, R. (1995). Attachment style and intimacy deficits in sexual offenders: A theoretical framework. *Sex Abuse.* 7(4): 317–335.

Ward, T., Hudson, S. M., & McCormack, J. (1997). Attachment style, intimacy deficiencies and sexual offending. In B. Schwartz & H. Cellini (eds.), *The Sex Offender.* Kingston, NJ: Civic Research Institute.

Ward, T., & Keenan, T. (1999). Child molesters' implicit theories. *Journal of Interpersonal Violence.* 14: 821–838.

Ward, T., Polaschek, D. L., & Beech, A. (2006). *Theories of Sexual Offending.* West Sussex, UK: Wiley.

Ward, T., & Siegert, R. J. (2002). Toward a comprehensive theory of child sexual abuse: A theory knitting perspective. *Psychology, Crime, and Law.* 9: 197–248.

Ward, T., & Stewart, C. A. (2003). The treatment of sex offenders: Risk management and good lives. *Professional Psychology: Research and Practice.* 34: 353–360.

Wartell, J. (2007). *Sex offender laws: Planning for an election.* San Diego: San Diego District Attorney's Office.

Washington State Department of Corrections. (2012). *Civil Commitment.* Available at: http://www.doc.wa.gov/community/sexoffenders/civil-commitment.asp

Wastell, C. A., Cairns, D., & Haywood, H. (2009). Empathy training, sex offenders and re-offending. *Journal of Sexual Aggression.* 15(2): 149–159.

Watanabe, T. (2002, March 25). Sex abuse by clerics: A crisis of many faiths. *Los Angeles Times* [online]. Retrieved from Lexis-Nexis.

Watkins, B., & Bentovim, A. (2000). Male children and adolescents as victims: A review of current knowledge. In G. C. Mezey & M. B. King (eds.), *Male Victims of Sexual Assault*. Oxford: Oxford University Press.

Watkins, J. G. (1993). Dealing with the problem of false memory in clinic and court. *Journal of Psychiatry and Law*. 21: 297–317.

Webb, L., Craissati, J., & Keen, S. (2007). Characteristics of internet child pornography offenders: A comparison with child molesters. *Sexual Abuse: A Journal of Research & Treatment*. 19(4): 449–465.

Weber, E. (1977). Incest: Sexual abuse begins at home. *Ms*. 5: 64–67.

Weeks, R., & Widom, C. S. (1998). Self-reports of early childhood victimization among incarcerated adult male felons. *Journal of Interpersonal Violence*. 13: 346–361.

Weinrott, M. R. (1996). *Juvenile Sexual Aggression: A Critical Review*. Portland, OR: Center for the Study and Prevention of Violence.

Weiss, K. (2002). Authority as coercion: When authority figures abuse their positions to perpetrate child sexual abuse. *Journal of Child Sexual Abuse*. 11: 27–51.

Welchans, S. (2005). Megan's law: Evaluations of sexual offender registries. *Criminal Justice Policy Review*. 16: 123–140.

West, D. J. (1985). Helping imprisoned sex offenders: Discussion paper. *Journal of the Royal Society of Medicine*. 78: 928–932.

West, D. J. (1987). Sexual crimes and confrontations: A study of victims and offenders. In A. E. Bottoms, series ed. *Cambridge Studies in Criminology*. Aldershot, UK: Gower.

Wexler, D. B. (1999). Introduction to the therapeutic jurisprudence symposium. *Arizona Law Review*. 41: 263.

Whitehead, J. T., & Lab, S. P. (1989). A meta-analysis of juvenile correctional treatment. *Journal of Research in Crime and Delinquency*. 26: 276–295.

Widom, C. S., Czaja, S. J., & Dutton, M. A. (2008). Childhood victimization and lifetime revictimization. *Child Abuse & Neglect*. 32(8): 785–796.

Widom, C. S., Schuck, A. M., & White, H. R. (2006). An examination of pathways from childhood victimization to violence: The role of early aggression and problematic alcohol use. *Violence and Victims*. 21: 675–690.

Wigamore, J. H. (2004). Child sexual abuse. In B. J. Cling (ed.), *Sexualized Violence Against Women and Children*. New York: Guilford Press.

Wijesinghe, B. (1977). Massed aversion treatment of sexual deviance. *Journal of Behavior Therapy and Experimental Psychiatry*. 8(2): 135–137.

Wilks, J., & Martinson, R. (1976). Is treatment of criminal offenders really necessary? *Federal Probation*. 40: 3–8.

Williams, L. M., & Finkelhor, D. (1990). The characteristics of incestuous fathers: A review of recent studies. In W. L. Marshall, D. R. Laws, & H. E. Barbaree (eds.), *Handbook of Sexual Assault: Issues, Theories and Treatment of the Offender*. New York: Plenum.

Williams, S. M. (1996). *A National Strategy for Managing Sex Offenders*. Available at: http://www.csc-scc.gc.ca/crd/forum/e082/e

Wilson, R. J., Abracen, J., Looman, J., Pichea, J. E., & Ferguson, M. (2011). Pedophilia: An evaluation of diagnostic and risk prediction methods. *Sexual Abuse: A Journal of Research & Treatment*. 23(2): 260–274.

Winick, B. J., & LaFond, J. Q. (eds.). (2003). *Protecting Society from Sexually Dangerous Offenders: Law, Justice and Therapy*. Washington, DC: American Psychological Association.

Wolak, J., Finkelhor, D., & Mitchell, K. (2011). Child pornography possessors: Trends in offender and case characteristics. *Sexual Abuse: A Journal of Research & Treatment.* 23(1): 22–42.

Wolak, J., Finkelhor, D., & Mitchell, K. J. (2005). *Child Pornography Possessors Arrested in Internet-Related Crimes: Findings from the National Juvenile Online Victimization Study.* Washington, DC: National Center for Missing & Exploited Children.

Wolak, J., Finkelhor, D., & Mitchell, K. J. (2011). How often are teens arrested for sexting? Data from a national sample of police cases. *Pediatrics.* 129(1): 1–10.

Wolak, J., Mitchell, K., & Finkelhor, D. (2004). *National Juvenile Online Victimization Study (N-JOV): Methodology Report.* Crimes against Children Research Center, University of New Hampshire.

Wolf, S. C. (1985). A multi-factor model of deviant sexuality. *Victimology: An International Journal.* 10: 359–374.

Wolfgang, M. E., Figlio, R. M., & Sellin, T. (1972). *Delinquency in a Birth Cohort.* Chicago, IL: University of Chicago Press.

Worling, J. R. (2001). Personality-based typology of adolescent male sexual offenders: Differences in recidivism rates, victim-selection characteristics, and personal victimization histories. *Sexual Abuse: A Journal of Research and Treatment.* 13: 149–166.

Worling, J. R., & Curwen, T. (2000). Adolescent sexual offender recidivism: Success of specialized treatment and implications for risk prediction. *Child Abuse and Neglect.* 24(7): 965–982.

Wormith, J. S., & Ruhl, M. (1986). Preventive detention in Canada. *Journal of Interpersonal Violence.* 1: 399–430.

Wortley, R. K., & Smallbone, S. (2006a). Applying situational principles to sexual offenses against children. In R. Wortley & S. Smallbone (eds.), *Situational prevention of child sexual abuse. Crime prevention studies, Volume 19.* Monsey, NY: Criminal Justice Press.

Wortley, R. K., & Smallbone, S. (2006b). *Child pornography on the internet.* Washington, DC: US Department of Justice, Center for Problem-Oriented Policing, Problem-Oriented Guides for Police No.41.

Wortley, R. K., & Smallbone, S. (eds.). (2006c). *Situational Prevention of Child Sexual Abuse. Crime Prevention Studies, Volume 19.* Monsey, NY: Criminal Justice Press.

Wright, R. (2009). Introduction: The failure of sex offender policies. In R. Wright (ed.), *Sex Offender Laws: Failed Policies, New Directions.* New York: Springer.

Wyatt, G. E., & Newcomb, M. D. (1990). Internal and external mediators of women's sexual abuse in childhood. *Journal of Consulting & Clinical Psychology.* 58: 758–767.

Wyatt, R. (2006). Male rape in U.S. prisons: Are conjugal visits the answer? *Case Western Reserve Journal of International Law.* 37(2&3): 579–614.

Yalom, I. D. (1985). *The Theory and Practice of Group Psychotherapy* (3rd ed.). New York: Basic Books.

Yates, P. M. (2009). Is sexual offender denial related to sex offender risk and recidivism? A review and treatment implications. *Psychology, Crime & Law.* 15(2/3): 183–199.

Yehuda, R., Friedman, M., Rosenbaum, T. Y., Labinsky, E., & Schmeidler, J. (2007). History of past sexual abuse in married observant Jewish women. *American Journal of Psychiatry.* 164: 1700–1706.

Yung, C. R. (2009). One of these laws is not like the others: Why the federal sex offender registration and notification act raises new constitutional questions. *Harvard Journal on Legislation.* 46: 369.

Zahn-Waxler, C., & Radke-Yarrow, M. (1990). The origins of empathic concern. *Motivation and Emotion.* 14: 107–130.

Zaitz, L., & Dungca, N. (2010, May 23). Boy Scouts Lagged in Efforts to Protect Children From Molesters. *The Oregonian.* Retrieved from http://blog.oregonlive.com/news_impact/print.html?entry=/2010/05/post_106.html

Zandbergen, P. A., Levenson, J. S., & Hart, T. C. (2010). Residential proximity to schools and daycares: An empirical analysis of sex offense recidivism. *Criminal Justice & Behavior.* 37: 482–502.

Zevitz, R. G. (2006). Sex offender community notification: Its role in recidivism and offender reintegration. *Criminal Justice Studies.* 19(2): 193–208.

Zevitz, R. G., & Farkas, M. A. (2000). The impact of sex offender community notification on probation/parole in Wisconsin. *International Journal of Offender Therapy & Comparative Criminology.* 44(1): 8–21.

Zgoba, K., & Levenson, J. S. (2008). Variations in the recidivism of treated and non-treated sexual offenders in New Jersey: An examination of three time frames. *Victims and Offenders.* 3(1): 10–30.

Zgoba, K., Veysey, B. M., & Dalessandra, M. (2010). An analysis of the effectiveness of community notification and registration: Do the best intentions predict the best practices? *Justice Quarterly.* 27(5): 667–691.

Zgoba, K., Witt, P., Dalessandro, M., & Veysey, B. (2008). *Megan's Law: Assessing the Practical and Monetary Efficacy* (Award no. 2006-IJ-CX-0018). National Institute of Justice, Office of Justice Programs: US Department of Justice.

Zgourides, G., Monto, M., & Harris, R. (1997). Correlates of adolescent male sexual offense: Prior adult sexual contact, sexual attitudes and use of sexually explicit materials. *International Journal of Offender Therapy and Comparative Criminology.* 41: 272–283.

Zimring, F. E. (2004). *An American travesty: Legal responses to adolescent sexual offending.* Chicago: University of Chicago Press.

Zimring, F. E., Jennings, W. G., Piquero, A. R., & Hays, S. (2009). Investigating the continuity of sex offending: Evidence from the second Philadelphia cohort. *Justice Quarterly.* 26: 58–76.

Zimring, F. E., Piquero, A. R., & Jennings, W. G. (2007). Sexual delinquency in Racine: Does early sex offending predict later sex offending in youth and young adulthood? *Criminology & Public Policy.* 6: 507–534.

LEGAL CASES

Addington v. Texas, 441 U.S. 418 (1979).

Artway v. Attorney General of New Jersey, 81 F.3d 1235, 1267 (3rd Cir. 1996).

Ashcroft v. Free Speech Coalition, 122 S. Ct. 1389 (2002).

Brown and others, 94 Cr.App R 302 CA, [1994] IAC 212 HL (1992).

Commonwealth of Pennsylvania v. Copenhefer, 587 Atl.2d 1353 (Pa. 1991).

Connecticut Department of Public Safety v. Doe, 123 S. Ct. 1160 (2003).

Doe v. Goff 306 Ill. App. 3d 1131 (1999).

Doe v. Miller, 405 F.3d 700 (8th Cir. 2005).

Doe v. Pataki, 940 F. Supp. 603, 620 (S.D.N.Y 1996).

Doe v. Poritz, 283 N.J. Super. 372, 661 A.2d 1335 (1995).

E. B. and W.P. v. Verniero, 119 F.3d 1077 (3rd Cir. 1997).

Foucha v. Louisiana, 504 U.S. 71 (1992).

Hammer v. Hammer, 418 N.W2d 23, 27 (Wis. Ct. App. 1987).

In re Campbell, 986 P.2d 771 (Wash. 1999).

In re Linehan, 518 N.W2d 609, 614 (Minn. 1994).

In re Turay, 986 P.2d 790 (Wash. 1999).

In re Young, 857 P.2d 989 (Wash. 1993).

Jackson v. Indiana 406 U.S. 715 (1972).

Jacobson v. Massachusetts, 197 U.S. 11, 26, 49 L. Ed. 643, 25 S. Ct. 358 (1905).

Kansas v. Crane, 534 U.S. 407 (2002).

Kansas v. Hendricks, 521 U.S. 346 (1997).

Lawrence v. Texas, 539 U.S. 558 (2003).

New York v. Ferber, 458 U.S. 747 (1982)

O'Connor v. Donaldson, 422 U.S. 563 (1975).

Opinion of the Justices to the Senate, 423 Mass. 1201, 698 N.E.2d 738 (1996).

Paul v. Davis, 424 U.S. 693 (1976).

People v. McClellan, 6 Cal.4th 367, 24 Cal Rptr.2d 739 (1994).

Ramona v. Isabella, Cal. Sup. Ct. C61898 (1994).

Rise v. Oregon, 59 F.3d 1556 (9th Cir. 1995).

Roe v. Wade, 410 U.S. 113 (1973).

Rowe v. Burton, 884 F. Supp. 1372 (D. Alaska 1994).

Russell and Stearns v. Gregoire, 124 F.3d 1079 (9th Cir. 1997).

Seling v.Young, 121 S. Ct. 727 (2001).

Skinner v. Oklahoma, 316 U.S. 535 (1942).

Smith v. Doe, 123 S. Ct. 1140 (2003).

Snyder v. State, 912 P.2d 1127 (Wyo. 1996).

State ex rel. Pearson v. Probate Court of Ramsey County, 205 Minn. 545, 555, 287 N.W. 297, 302 (1939).

State v. Cameron, 185 Ariz. 467, 916 P.2d 1183 (Ct. App/Div. 1 1996).

State v. Skroch, 883 P.2d 1256 (Mont. 1994).

State v. Ward, 123 Wash.2d 212, 737 P.2d 250 (1987).

Tyson v. Tyson, 727 P.2d 226, 229 (Wash. 1986).

United States v. Carey, 172 F.3d 1268 (1999).

United States v. Comstock, 560 U.S. ___ (2010).

United States v. Dost, 636 F. Supp. 828, 832 (S.D. Cal. 1986).

United States v. Hotaling, 599 F.Supp.2d 306, 322 (N.D.N.Y.2008).

United States v. Salerno, 481 U.S. 739, 95 L. Ed.2d 697, 107 S. Ct. 2095 (1987).

United States v. Williams, 553 U.S. 285 (2008).

Young v. Weston, 192 F.3d 870 (9th Cir. 1999).

LEGISLATION

PROTECT Act of 2003 (Pub.L. 108-21, 117 Stat. 650, S. 151).

Sexual Offences Act 1967, Chapter 60. Available at: http://www.legislation. gov.uk/ukpga/1967/60/pdfs/ukp-ga_19670060_en.pdf

Index

A

Abel, Gene, 60
abuse. *See* child sexual abuse; cycle of abuse theory; rape
academics. *See* schools
acceptance and healing, 195–196, 209–210
acquaintances. *See* victim-offender relationship
actuarial risk assessments, 227–230, 253–254
Adam Walsh Child Protection and Safety Act (2006), 219–220, 230–231
Addington v. Texas (1979), 287
adjudication process. *See* courts and adjudication process
adolescent offenders. *See* juvenile offenders
adolescent-oriented institutions, child sexual abuse, 162
 Big Brothers Big Sisters organization, 164–165
 Boy Scouts of America (BSA), 163–164
 child care settings, 162–163
 educator sexual misconduct, 162
 professional and legal remedies, 167
 schools, 162
 sporting organizations, 165–166
age, offense victims, 12
age of consent. *See* consent

aggression
 power and control-focused rapists, 99
 sadistic rapists, 98
 testosterone effects, 55
aggressive homosexual offenders, 114*t*, 115
alcohol and drug abuse
 juvenile offenders, 125
 triggering factors, 87–89
Alves, Raymond, 284
Amytal, 39
androgens, 55
antisocial personality disorder, 98
apparently irrelevant decisions (AIDs), 72
arousal reconditioning, 256
arrests and prosecutions
 civil commitment, 278
 New York City, 32
 political motivation, 33
art, drama, and literature, 24–25
Artway v. Attorney General of New Jersey (1996), 225
Ashcroft v. Free Speech Coalition (2002), 149–150
assessment and investigation
 criminal justice system, 197–198
 planning for treatment, 247
 police, 200–201
 sexually violent predators, 276, 279
Association for the Behavioral Treatment of Sexual Aggressives (ABTSA), 251

Association for the Treatment of Sexual
   Abusers (ATSA), 251
   guidelines, 252
Atascadero State Hospital (CA), 268
attachment theories of sexual deviancy,
   58–60
autoerotic asphyxia, 50

B

background information
   cycle of abuse, 62, 65, 83
   juvenile offenders, 122
   men and women offenders, 194
   rapists, 111
behavioral models, of treatment, 249
behavioral theory, 60–61
   historical perspectives, 27
   juvenile offenders, 128
   offense cycle, 71–73
   treatment of offenders, 248
benperidol, 248
Big Brothers Big Sisters, 164–165
bill of attainder clause, 224
biological theories of sexual deviancy, 55–57
Black Americans, 12
blame and culpability
   child abuse victims, 211
   medicalization of offenses, 284
   rape victims, 201
   secondary victims, 197
blockage in relationships, 66
bounded and unbounded surveys, 22
Boy Scouts of America (BSA), 163–164
Brownmiller, Susan, 57
Bureau of Justice Statistics, 12
burnout, in offender management staff, 268

C

California
   civil commitment, 280
   medical treatment of offenders, 262
   sexual psychopathy laws, 33
Campus Sex Crimes Prevention Act
   (2000), 218–219
castration and sterilization
   castration anxiety, 54
   historical perspectives, 31
   surgical castration, 248, 261

Catholic Church, child sexual abuse in,
   167–168, 172–177
Center for Sex Offender Management, 244
Child Maltreatment Reports, 14
child pornography, 5
   accessing, 140–143
   and child sexual abuse, 147–148
   COPINE scale, sexual images, 140, 141*t*
   definition of, 140
   distributing and accessing methods,
      internet, 141, 142*t*
   federal legislation prohibiting, 148, 149*t*
   regulating and policing, 148–152
   scope of, 143–144
   victims of, 145–147
Child protective services, 13
Child Protector and Sexual Predator
   Punishment Act (1998), 151–152
children
   men and boys sexual behavior, 25, 26–27
   Minnesota Student Survey, 12
   post-abuse investigation, 198–199, 200
   witnesses in court, 204–205
children, sexual development of
   Freud's theories, 54
   historical perspectives, 25, 26–27
   justification of sexual offenses, 81
   masturbation, 4
   sexual offenders, 65, 126, 127
children, sexual exploitation of
   human trafficking, 157–159
   juvenile prostitution, 154–157
   self-produced pornography, 152–154
   sexting, 152–154
   sexual offenders and internet, 140–152
children, social development of
   attachment theories of sexual
      deviancy, 58
   sexual offenders, 83–84
child sexual abuse, 15–16*t*, 62–63, 251
   adolescent-oriented institutions, 162–167
   biological theories, 56
   in Catholic Church, 167–168, 172–177
   classical conditioning aversion
      therapy, 249
   crime statistics, 15–16, 17
   disclosure, 19–21
   in Episcopalian churches, 169
   fantasies of sexual offenders, 86
   feminist theories of sexual deviancy, 57

historical perspectives, 25, 30
integrated theories of sexual deviancy, 67
in Jehovah Witnesses, 169–170
in Jewish Community, 171–172
juvenile offenders, 121
in Mormon churches, 170–171
non-catholic religious organizations,
    168–172
offense cycle, 79–80, 81–82
planning and grooming victims, 73–76
post-abuse investigation, 198–199
in Protestant churches, 168–169
psychosocial theories of sexual deviancy,
    61–63
repressed memories cases, 41
routine activities of sexual deviancy,
    63–64
in Southern Baptist churches, 169
types of molesters, 108, 109
victim empathy, 83–85
victims, 211
See also pedophilia
Child Sexual Abuse Accommodation
    Syndrome reporting model, 19
civil commitment. *See* commitment of
    offenders
classical conditioning aversion therapy
    on child sexual abuse, 249
classifications
    child molesters, 109, 109*t*, 110, 110*t*
    juvenile offenders, 129–131
    rapists, 97, 97*t*
    types of sexual offenders, 93
cognitive-behavioral theories, 60–61
    juvenile offenders, 134
    offense cycle, 77–78, 83
    treatment for offenders, 247–248, 249
cognitive-behavioral treatment, 254–260
    for disabled offenders, 269
    sex education, 256
cognitive dissonance, 260
cognitive distortions (CDs), 60, 77–78,
    249, 258
cognitive factors, rapists, 96
Colorado
    sexual offense definitions, 5
Colorado Department of Public Safety
    (2004), 236
Combating Paedophile Information Net-
    works in Europe (COPINE), 140, 141*t*

commitment of offenders
    historical perspectives, 32–34
    sexually violent predators, 276
Community Protection Act (1990),
    216, 277
community *vs.* prison treatment, 262–263
competency, child witnesses, 204
conditioning (behavioral theory), 61, 85
confrontational approaches, 259
conjugal visits, 182–183
*Connecticut Department of Public Safety v.
    Doe* (2003), 226
consent
    definition of sexual offenses, 4–7
    juvenile offenders and victims, 126
    laws, 30
    minimization of sexual offenses, 79–80
    pharmacological treatments, 261
constitutional issues, 278, 284–287
containment approach, supervision of sex
    offenders, 239–242
    collaboration, management strategies, 240
    community and victim safety, goal, 240
    consistent public policies, 240–241
    individualized case management
        system, 240
    quality control, 241
contemplation stage, 259
control and domination
    feminist theories of sexual deviancy, 57
    mass rape during war time, 100
    power and control-focused rapists,
        99–100
coping skills, 66–67, 195–196
costs, civil commitment, 280, 290
countertransference, 267
court cases
    Addington v. Texas (1979), 287
    Artway v. Attorney General of New Jersey
        (1996), 225
    Ashcroft v. Free Speech Coalition (2002),
        149–150
    *Connecticut Department of Public Safety v.
        Doe* (2003), 226
    *Doe v. Big Brothers Big Sisters of
        America,* 164
    Doe v. Goff (1999), 163
    Doe v. Pataki (1996), 226
    Doe v. Poritz (1995), 224, 225, 226
    Farmer v. Brennan, 179

court cases *(continued)*
 Foucha v. Louisiana (1992), 285
 Jackson v. Indiana (1972), 287
 Jacobson v. Massachusetts (1905), 288
 Kansas v. Crane (2002), 289
 Kansas v. Hendricks (1997), 286, 288–289
 Lamarche v. Big Brothers Big Sisters of America, 164
 Lawrence v. Texas (2003), 42
 New York v. Ferber (1982), 149
 O'Connor v. Donaldson (1975), 285
 Paul v. Davis (1976), 225, 226
 In re Campbell (1999), 288
 In re Linehan (1994), 285, 286
 In re Turay (1999), 288
 In re Young (1993), 285, 286
 Roe v. Wade (1973), 37
 Russell and Sterns v. Gregoire (1997), 225
 Seling v. Young (2001), 288
 Skinner v. Oklahoma (1942), 31
 Smith v. Doe (2003), 226
 State ex rel. Pearson v. Probate Court of Ramsey County (1939), 281
 United States v. Carey (1999), 152
 United States v. Dost (1986), 149
 United States v. Hotaling (2011), 151
 United States v. Salerno (1987), 288
 United States v. Williams (2008), 151
 U.S. v. Comstock (2010), 289
 Young v. Weston (1999), 288
courts and adjudication process, 202–205, 211
 child witnesses, 211
 civil commitment, 279, 280, 284–287
courtship disorder, 98
crime rate
 National Child Abuse and Neglect Data System, 13
 sexual offenses, 17
 Uniform Crime Reports, 11
criminal justice system
 child victims, 211
 crime reporting, 10–11
 investigating abuse, 197–198
criminal records, juvenile offenders, 133
criminals
 Alves, Raymond, 284
 Dodd, Wesley Alan, 41
 Fish, Albert, 32
 Foucha, Terry, 285
 Hendricks, Leroy, 286–288
 Linehan, Dennis, 285, 286
 Shriner, Earl, 41
critogenesis, 198, 212
cruel and unusual punishment clause, 224
cultural factors
 feminist theories of sexual deviancy, 57–58
 historical perspectives of sexual behavior, 24–27
cyber sex offenders, 144–145, 146*t*
 See also Internet and websites
cycle of abuse theory, 62
cyproterone acetate (CPA), 248, 249
 hormonal treatments, 260

D

date rape, 99
decision, social skills, 256
decoding, social skills, 256
denial
 by offenders, 78–80
 by victims, 195
Department of Health and Human Services, 13
Depo-Provera, 260
depression
 in abuse victims, 192
 triggering factors, 88
deviant sexual behavior, triggering factors for, 256
Diagnostic and Statistical Manual of Mental Disorders (DSM), 38
 paraphilias of, 45–46
disclosure of child sexual abuse, 19–21
Dodd, Wesley Alan, 41, 216
Doe v. Big Brothers Big Sisters of America, 164
Doe v. Goff (1999), 163
Doe v. Pataki (1996), 226
Doe v. Poritz (1995), 224, 225, 226
dolls (interviewing tool), 200–201
domestic violence. *See* home environment
Donaldson, Kenneth, 285
double jeopardy, 223
drama (literature), 25
drug abuse. *See* alcohol and drug abuse
due process rights
 civil commitment, 280, 287
 report on sexual psychopathy, 35

E

eating disorders, 192, 210
effectiveness
of offender treatment, 270–274
Egypt, ancient, 25
Ellis, Havelock, 29
emotional congruence, 66
emotional relationships
attachment theories of deviancy, 58
child molesters' lack of, 101
integrated theories of deviancy, 65
routine activities of sexual deviancy,
63–64
empathy
juvenile offenders, 127–128, 134
for victims, 83–85, 267
employment for sex offenders, 243–244
enactment, social skills, 256
End Child Prostitution, Child
Pornography, & Trafficking of
Children for Sexual Purposes
(ECPAT), 155
England
ethnicity and rape, 12
prison treatment program in, 266
Victims' Charter, 203
entitlement, sexual, 84–85
ephebophiles, 104
Episcopalian Church, child sexual abuse
in, 169
escalation of sexual offenses
report on sexual psychopathy, 34
estrogen, 248
ethics
medical treatment of offenders, 265–267
risk predictions, 279
ethinyl estradiol, 260
eugenics, 31
Europe
historical perspectives of sexual behavior,
25–26
evidence, medical examinations, 199
evolutionary biology theory of rape,
56–57
Experience Sampling Method
(ESM), 254
experimentation, juvenile offenders,
127, 129

ex post facto application, 223–224, 286
extrafamilial sexual abusers, 102–105

F

families
juvenile offenders and victims, 127
regressed child molesters, 106
response to child sexual abuse, 197
theories of sexual deviancy, 54–55
victim disclosure of abuse, 20
fantasies
offense cycle, 71–73, 77, 85–87
of sexual offenders, 86
fantasy necrophile, 51
Farmer v. Brennan, 179
fear
disclosure of abuse, 20
victims, after abuse, 196
Federal Bureau of Investigation (FBI)
historical perspectives, 33
National Incident-Based Reporting
System, 11
Uniform Crime Reports, 10
female juvenile sex offenders, 123–124
female sex offenders, 20, 111–116, 113*t,*
114*t*
female sexual predators, 114, 114*t*
feminist theories
rape reform laws, 205–206
of sexual deviancy, 44, 57–58
fetishism, 47
Finkelhor, David, 65
Finkelhor model, 65
Fish, Albert, 32
fixated child molesters, 105, 108*t,* 109*t*
Florida
civil commitment, 280
fluphenazine, 248
follow-up to offender treatment
measuring recidivism, 247, 271
fondling
juvenile offenders, 130
Foucha, Terry, 285
Foucha v. Louisiana (1992), 285
Fourth Amendment, 151, 152
Frankel, Judith, 284
Freud, Sigmund, 29, 54
frotteurism, 48

G

Gauthe, Reverend Gilbert, 167
gender issues
    disclosure of abuse, 20
    feminist theories of sexual deviancy, 58
    historical social roles, 27, 30
Geoghan, John, 167
Gibbons, Jack, 284
global positioning system (GPS)
    monitoring, 235, 237, 239
Good Lives Model, 258
government agencies
    child protective services, 13
Greece, ancient, 24–25
grief, 195, 196
grooming victims, 73–77
group-based treatment
    juvenile offenders, 134
    rape victims, 210
group treatment process, 258–260
guilt and shame
    family reaction to child abuse, 196–197
    juvenile offenders and victims, 127
    offense cycle, 80–81
    victims, 211

H

healing and resolution, 195, 210
Health and Human Services
    Department, 13
Hebrew culture, 26
Hendricks, Leroy, 286–288
Heterosexuality, 38
heterosexual nurturers, 114, 114t
Higher Education Act (1965), 219
Hispanic Americans, 12
history
    mass rape during war time, 100
    prosecution of rape cases, 205
    sexual psychopathy legislation, 277
    social perception of sexual offenders,
        3–4, 24–42
    theories of sexual deviancy, 44–45
    treatment of offenders, 247, 248–250
home environment
    after child sexual abuse, 197
    female offenders, 113
    juvenile offenders, 125

homicidal necrophile, 51
homosexual criminals, 114t, 115
homosexuality, 24–25, 34, 38
Hoover, J. Edgar, 33
hormones
    imbalance or deficiencies, 27, 56
    treatment for offenders, 248, 261
hospitals, post-abuse procedure, 198–199
human trafficking, 157–159
    defined, 158
Human Trafficking Reporting System, 158
humiliation, 99
hypnosis, 39
hypochondria, 191

I

incarceration and prisoners
    background of offenders, 194
    civil commitment in prisons, 278
incest
    juvenile offenders, 127
    offense cycle, 73–75, 83
    regressed child molesters, 107
index offenses (Uniform Crime Reports), 10
injuries, physical
    types of abuse, 191
In re Campbell (1999), 288
In re Linehan (1994), 285–286
In re Turay (1999), 288
In re Young (1993), 285, 286
integrated theories of sexual deviancy,
    64–69
international issues (war rapes), 100
Internet and websites, 51, 128, 140–152
    sex trafficking, 158
    See also child pornography
interviews and questioning
    bounded *vs.* unbounded surveys, 22
    post-abuse investigations, 200–201
intimate relationships
    attachment theories of sexual
        deviancy, 59
    rapists' lack of, 98
intrafamilial sexual abusers, 102–105
Iowa
    sexually violent predators, 280
    sexual psychopathy laws, 33
IQ (intelligence quotient)
    testing juvenile offenders, 124

J

Jackson v. Indiana (1972), 287
Jacobson v. Massachusetts (1905), 288
Jacob Wetterling Crimes against
  Children and Sexually Violent
  Offender Registration Act (1994),
  216–217
Jehovah Witnesses, child sexual abuse in,
  169–170
Jewish Community, child sexual abuse
  in, 171–172
juvenile offenders, 118–138
  alcohol and drug abuse, 125
  background information, 122
  behavioral theory, 128
  child sexual abuse, 121
  classifications, 129–131
  cognitive-behavioral theories, 134
  consent, 126
  criminal records, 133
  empathy, 127–128, 134
  experimentation, 127, 129
  families, 127
  female, 123–124
  fondling, 130
  group-based treatment, 134
  guilt and shame, 127
  home environment, 125
  incest, 127
  IQ (intelligence quotient) testing, 124
  long-term risk and treatment, 135
  mental illness and abnormalities, 124
  motivation, 134
  non-sex offenses, 124–126
  paraphilias, 130
  pedophilia, 128
  pornography, 128
  psychopathology, 124–125
  registration of sex offenders, 135
  research and reports, 120–123,
    126, 131
  schizophrenia, 125
  self-esteem, 129
  sexual arousal, 128, 133, 134
  sexual knowledge, 126–127, 129, 133
  social skills and socialization, 128
  statistics, 121
  taboos, 127
  treatment programs, 131–132, 133, 134

Uniform Crime Reports (UCRs), 121
  victim-offender relationship, 121, 126
juvenile prostitution, 154–157

K

Kanka, Megan, 42, 217
Kansas
  sexually violent predators, 277–278,
    280, 285
Kansas v. Crane (2002), 289
Kansas v. Hendricks (1997), 286, 288–289
Kinsey, Alfred, 36
Krafft-Ebing, Richard von, 4, 28–29

L

*Lamarche v. Big Brothers Big Sisters of
  America,* 164
Lawrence v. Texas (2003), 42
lawyers, rape cases, 206
legislation
  rape reform laws, 205–206
  reaction to public panic, 31, 32
  sexually violent predators, 35, 42, 277–291
  victims' rights, 202–203
lesbians, 25
less restrictive alternative (LRA)
  facilities, 279
Liberal Era, 37
Linehan, Dennis, 285, 286
literature and art, 24–25
long-term risk and treatment
  juvenile offenders, 135
Lychner, Pam, 218

M

male victims of abuse, 194–195, 210
market facilitators, 154
masculine aggressiveness, wartime rape, 183
Massachusetts Treatment Center: Child
  Molester Typology, 109, 110*t*
mass rape during war time, 100, 183
  See also military, sexual abuse
masturbation
  in Hebrew culture, 26
  social norms, 4
media portrayal, sex trafficking, 158
medical examinations and treatment, 199

medications and drugs
  Amytal, 39
  "morning after" pills, 198–199
  Rohypnol, 99
  treatment of offenders, 248
medroxyprogesterone acetate (MPA),
    248, 260
Megan's Law, 217–218
  origin, 42
memory
  repressed, 39–40
  telescoping, 21
mental illness and abnormalities
  juvenile offenders, 124
  sexually violent predators, 41, 285
  sexual psychopathy, 33
mental institutions, 32
Mentally Disordered Sex Offenders
    (MDSO) laws, 277
Michigan
  psychopathy laws, 32
Middle Ages, 25–26
military, sexual abuse, 183–184
Military Sexual Trauma (MST). *See*
    Post-Traumatic Stress Disorder
Millon Clinical Multiaxial Inventory
    (MCMI), 253
minimization of sexual offenses, 78–80
Minnesota
  registration of offenders, 284
  sexually violent predators, 285–286
  sexual psychopathy laws, 33,
    280–281
Minnesota Multiphasic Personality
    Inventory (MMPI), 253
Minnesota Student Survey, 12
Mormon churches, child sexual abuse in,
    170–171
motivation
  child molesters, 105, 108*t*
  juvenile offenders, 134
  rapists, 97*t*
motivational approaches, 260
MTC:CM3 child molester typology,
    109–110, 110*t*
Multidimensional Assessment of Sex and
    Aggression (MASA), 254
Multiphasic Sex Inventory (MSI), 254
murder and fatalities
  children, 31

N

narcissism, 58, 84
National Adolescent Perpetrator Network
    (NAPN), 120–121, 124, 131
National Campaign to Prevent Teen
    and Unplanned Pregnancy
    (NCPTUP), 153
National Child Abuse and Neglect Data
    System (NCANDS), 10*t*, 13, 14
National Crime Victimization Survey
    (NCVS)
  criminal justice statistics, 9
  juvenile offender statistics, 121
  reporting crimes, 12
National Incident-Based Reporting
    System (NIBRS), 9*t*, 11
  reporting crimes, 11
National Juvenile Online Victimization
    (NJOV) study, 142–143
National Youth Survey, 121
Native American culture, 26–27
necrophilia, 51
negative emotional states
  triggering factors, 87–89
negative emotions, 256, 257
New Jersey
  civil commitment, 280
New York City
  history of sexual crimes, 32
  New York v. Ferber (1982), 149
noncriminal homosexual offenders,
    114, 114*t*
non-sex offenses
  juvenile offenders, 124–126
  property offenses, 10
nonsexually motivated offenses, 99–101
normalcy and deviancy
  historical perspectives, 27–42
  Kinsey reports, 36
North Dakota
  sexual offense definitions, 5
notorious sex crimes
  historical perspectives, 28, 28*f*
  Washington state, 41

O

obscene phone calls, 48
O'Connor v. Donaldson (1975), 285

oedipal conflicts, 54
offense cycle, 71–77, 129
offense-related targets, 258
offense-specific targets, 258
The Office of Sex Offender Sentencing,
   Monitoring, Apprehending,
   Registering, and Tracking (SMART
   Office), 220
opportunistic rapists, 97*t*, 100–101
opportunities to abuse
   Finkelhor model, 66

P

pain and torture
   sadistic rapists, 98–99
Pam Lychner Sex Offender Tracking and
   Identification Act (1996), 218
paraphilias
   Diagnostic and Statistical Manual of
      Mental Disorders, 46
   high-contact, 48–52
   juvenile offenders, 130
   necrophilia, 51
   noncontact and minimal contact, 46–48
   and sexual disorders, 45–46
   sexual sadism, 50
parent-child relationship
   factors in becoming rapist, 101
   integrated theories of sexual deviancy, 65
   mothers and child abuse, 196
   parents of juvenile offenders, 125
   regressed child sexual abusers, 106
   theories of sexual deviancy, 54
parole
   historical perspectives, 33
Paul v. Davis (1976), 225, 226
pedophilia, 48
   juvenile offenders, 128
   Kansas v. Hendricks (1997), 286
   types of child sexual abusers, 104
penile plethysmograph (PPG), 86, 107,
   111, 249
penis envy, 54
persistence of offending behavior, 77–89
pharmacological treatments, 261
physiological testing, 253
planning and grooming victims, 73–77
Plato, 24
plea bargains, 203–205

police
   history of sexual crimes, 32
   investigating offenses, 197, 200–202
   reporting offenses, 10, 11
pornography
   juvenile offenders, 128
   See also child pornography
Porter, Reverend James, 167
positive reinforcement, 72–73
positivism, 31
posttraumatic stress disorder (PTSD),
   183–184, 189, 192
precontemplation stage, 259
pregnancy, 191, 199
preparation stage, 259
prepubescent, 49
pretextuality, 289
prison, and community-based treatment
   programs, 262–263
Prison Rape Elimination Act (PREA),
   181–182
prisons, sexual abuse in, 177–178
   prevalence and reporting of, 178–179
   Prison Rape Elimination Act (PREA),
      181–182
   sexual assaulters and victims, character-
      istics of, 180–181
   sexual assault prevention, 182–183
   victimization, effects of, 179–180
progestogens, 248
Progressive Era, 27
promiscuity, 30
property offenses, 10
Prosecutorial Remedies and Other Tools
   to End the Exploitation of Children
   Today (PROTECT) Act (2003), 219
prostitution, 31
PROTECT Act (2003), 151
Protection of Children from Sexual
   Predators Act (1998), 218
Protestant churches, child sexual abuse in,
   168–169
pseudo necrophile, 51
Psychiatric Personality Act (MN), 281
psychodynamic theories of sexual
   deviancy, 54–55
psychological effects of abuse
   children, 211
   critogenesis, 198
   rape victims, 191–195, 210–211

psychological reactance, 259
psychologists and researchers
  Abel, Gene, 60
  Brownmiller, Susan, 57
  Ellis, Havelock, 29
  Finkelhor, David, 65
  Frankel, Judith, 284
  Freud, Sigmund, 29, 54
  Gibbons, Jack, 284
  Kinsey, Alfred, 36
  Krafft-Ebing, Richard von, 4,
    28–29
psychometrical testing, 253–254
psychopathia sexualis, 51
Psychopathia Sexuality (Krafft-Ebing), 28
psychopathology
  historical perspectives, 27, 28–29,
    32–35, 248
  juvenile offenders, 124–125
  laws, 277, 280–281
  psychoanalysts' theories, 54–55
Psychopathy Checklist-Revised
  (PCL-R), 269
psychosocial theories of sexual deviancy,
  61–63
psychotherapy
  group treatment processes in, 258

Q

questioning. *See* interviews and
  questioning

R

race and ethnicity, 12
rape
  additional physical injuries during, 191
  evolutionary biology theory, 56–57
  feminist theories, 57
  forcible *vs.* statutory, 11
  integrated theories of sexual deviancy, 67
  offense cycle, 76–77, 79–80, 80–81
  police and victims, 201
  post-abuse medical exam, 198
  psychosocial theories of sexual devi-
    ancy, 62
  rape myths, 206, 208–209
  rape shield laws, 206
  rape trauma syndrome (RTS), 195–196

secondary victims, 196–197
social ideologies, 4
testosterone effects, 55
triggering factors, 87–89
types of rapists, 96–101, 97*t*
victim empathy, 83–85
victim support, 209–211
rationalization of sexual deviancy
  child sexual abuse, 65
  cognitive distortions, 60
  offense cycle, 71, 77–82
  triggering factors, 87
recanting testimony, 20
recidivism, 119–124, 233, 234,
  237, 239, 242, 243
  child molesters, 108*t*
  definition of, 247
  dependent variables, 270
  offense cycle, 79
  research, 4
  sexually violent predators, 282
  treatment of offenders, 271
registration and community notification
  laws (RCNL), 215
  collateral consequences of,
    234–235
  conviction/type of offense, 222
  efficacy of, 232–235
  goal of, 220, 233
  juveniles, registration of, 223
  legal challenges, 223–227
  length of registration/registration
    period, 222
  name removal from registry, 222
  notification method, registration
    agency, 223
  regulations and guidelines,
    220–223
  retroactive application of law, 222
  risk assessment, 222–223
  sanction, failing to register, 223
  time period, register/reregister, 222
registration of sex offenders
  juvenile offenders, 135
  Megan's Laws, 42
regressed child molesters, 106,
  108*t*, 109*t*
regular necrophile, 51
rehabilitation, 250
reinforcement of behaviors, 73

reintegration into community
  employment environments, prohibition, 243–244
  housing, 242–243
  recreation and social relationships, 244–245
relapse prevention (RP)
  definition, 257
  therapeutic technique of, 249
relapses and lapses, 259
religion
  history of sexual offenses, 26
religious institutions, sexual abuse, 167–177
  Catholic Church, 167–168, 172–177
  non-catholic organizations, 168–172
reporting sexual offenses, 18–21
  National Incident-Based Reporting System, 11
  telescoping, 21–22
  Uniform Crime Reports, 10–11
repressed memories, 39–40
reproduction, sex for, 56
research and reports
  acquaintance offenses, 16
  biological theories of sexual deviancy, 55–57
  integrated theories of sexual deviancy, 69
  juvenile offenders, 120–123, 126, 131
  Kinsey reports, 36
  Minnesota Student Survey, 12
  motivational approaches, 260
  National Youth Survey, 121
  prevalence of sexual offenses, 7–9, 17
  psychosocial theories of sexual deviancy, 62
  routine activities of sexual deviancy, 63
  sexual offenses, 18
  sexual psychopathy, 34–35
  social perception of sexual offenders, 4
  telescoping, 21–22
  telescoping surveys, 22
residence restrictions, 235–237
  goal of, 235
resistance to abuse, 75
resolution and healing, 195, 210
Respondent-Driven Sampling (RDS), 155
revictimization, 57, 197, 202, 203, 212

rights of offenders
  sexually violent predators, 278–279, 290
risk (community safety)
  sexually violent predators, 276, 279
risk assessment
  actuarial assessments, 227–230
  conviction-based approach, 230
  sex offender-specific tools, 227–230
Roe v. Wade (1973), 37
Rohypnol, 99
Rome, ancient, 25
routine activities theory (RAT), 63–64
  situational crime prevention strategies, 63–64
Russell and Sterns v. Gregoire (1997), 225

S

sadistic rapists, 97, 97t, 98–99
Sandusky, Jerry, 166
satanic abuse, 40, 41
scatologia. See obscene phone calls
schizophrenia
  civil commitment, 285
  juvenile offenders, 125
schools
  child sexual abuse, 162
  juvenile offenders, 124, 244
  reintegration for offenders, 244
secondary victims, 187, 196–197
seemingly irrelevant decisions (SID), 257
seemingly unimportant decisions (SUDs), 72
self-abusive behavior, 132
self-esteem
  child sexual abusers, 101
  juvenile offenders, 129
  offense cycle, 72, 88
self-produced pornography, 152–154
Self-Regulation Model, 258
Seling v. Young (2001), 288
sentencing and punishment
  crime statistics, 16
sex education
  to arousal reconditioning, 256
sex-force offenses, 107
Sex Offender Management Board (SOMB), 241
Sex Offender Registration and Notification Act (SORNA), 220, 230–231

sex offender-specific tools, 227–230
Sex Offender Treatment Programme
    (SOTP)., 263, 273
sex-pressure offenses, 107
sexting, 152–154
sex trafficking. *See* human trafficking
sexual arousal
    biological theories of sexual deviancy,
        55–57
    child sexual abusers, 107, 111
    juvenile offenders, 128, 133, 134
sexual assault nurse examiners (SANEs), 199
sexual behavior, 38
The Sexual Criminal (De River), 35
sexual disorders
    paraphilias, 45–46
sexual drive, 55
sexual dysfunction
    rapists, 97
    victims, after abuse, 193
sexual entitlement, 85
sexual knowledge, juvenile offenders,
    126–127, 129, 133
sexual liberation (1960s), 37
Sexually Dangerous Persons (SDP) Act
    (MN, 1994), 281
sexually violent predators (SVP), 276–291
    Washington state cases, 41
sexual masochism, 49
Sexual Offences Act, 38
sexual sadism, 49, 50
sexual victimization, 161
    in prison, 179–180
Shriner, Earl, 41, 216
situational crime prevention (SCP), 63
Skinner v. Oklahoma (1942), 31
Smith, Michelle, 40
Smith v. Doe (2003), 226
social learning theory, 128
social skills and socialization
    child sexual abusers, 101–102
    juvenile offenders, 128
    misreading social cues, 82
    theories of sexual deviancy, 59,
        62–63, 65
social views
    perception of sexual offenders, 3,
        27–41, 31–32
    of sexual behavior, 4–5, 24–27
sodomy, 6, 26

soldiers, mass rape, 100
Southern Baptist Church, child sexual
    abuse in, 169
Special Commitment Center (SCC), 279,
    288
sporting organizations, child sexual abuse,
    165–166
spouses
    historical perspectives, 25
    secondary victims, 197
    theories of sexual deviancy, 54–55
staff, offender treatment programs
    management of offenders, 267–268
*State ex rel. Pearson v. Probate Court of
    Ramsey County* (1939), 281
states
    child sexual abuse, 15–16t
    definition of mental abnormalities, 287
    sexually violent predators, 41, 279–281
    sexual offense terminology, 5
    sexual psychopathy laws, 33, 36
Static-99, 254
    assessment tool, 282
    risk assessment, 228–230
statistics
    child sexual abuse, 15–16t
    effect of telescoping, 21
    juvenile offenders, 121
    National Child Abuse and Neglect Data
        System, 14
    sexual offenses, 18
    Uniform Crime Reports, 11
statutory rape, 11
stilboestrol, 248
stress and stressors
    regressed child sexual abusers, 106
    triggering factors, 87–89
support services, abuse victims, 201,
    209–211
Symposium (Plato), 24

T

taboos
    juvenile offenders and victims, 127
telephone scatologia. *See* obscene phone
    calls
telescoping, 21–22
testosterone, 55
therapeutic jurisprudence (TJ), 281

therapy and counseling
  Freud, psychoanalysis, 54
  repressed memories, 41
  treatment of offenders, 248–249
thioridazine, 248
third-party exploiters, 154
Thomas, Clarence, 288
Timmendequas, Jesse, 217
To Catch a Predator, 150
touching and fondling
  offense cycle, 73–74
Trafficking Victims Protection Act (2000),
  158, 159
tranquillizers, 248
transvestic fetishism, 47
treatment programs
  assessment for, 252–254
  behavioral models of, 249
  child sexual abusers, 111
  commitment of offenders, 279
  juvenile offenders, 131–132, 133, 134
  polygraph used for, 250
  professionalization of, 251
  rehabilitative ideal for, 250
  sexually violent predators, 283,
    289–291
  sexual psychopathy report, 35
  social perception of sexual offenders, 4
  triggering factors, 87–89
  types of, 254–260
  victims of abuse, 209–211
triggering factors, 77
"T" visa, 159

U

underreporting sexual offenses, 18
  crime statistics, 17
  National Crime Victimization
    Surveys, 12
  Uniform Crime Reports, 11
Uniform Crime Reports (UCRs)
  criminal justice statistics, 9*t,* 10–11
  juvenile offender statistics, 121
United States v. Carey (1999), 152
United States v. Dost (1986), 149
United States v. Hotaling (2011), 151
United States v. Salerno (1987), 288
United States v. Williams (2008), 151
U.S. v. Comstock (2010), 289

V

victim-offender relationship
  child sexual abusers, 106
  crime statistics, 11–12, 16
  juvenile offenders, 121, 126
  rapist types, 101
  registration laws, 42
  victim disclosure of abuse, 20
victim protection measures,
  trafficking, 159
victims, 186–212
  crime statistics, 18
  disclosure, 19–21
  empathy for victims, 83–85, 134
  historical perspectives, 37
  minimization of sexual offenses, 80
  National Crime Victimization
    Surveys, 12
  resistance to abuse, 107
  support services, 201, 209–211
video recordings
  child victim interviews, 201
Violent Crime Control and Law
  Enforcement Act (1994), 217,
  218–219
virtual child pornography,
  150–151, 219
voyeurism, 45, 46*t,* 48
vulnerability, victims, 188

W

Walsh, Adam, 219
war rapes. *See* mass rape during war
  time
Washington
  registration laws, 216
  sexually violent predators, 41, 278–280,
    282, 283, 285–286
Washington State Institute for Public
  Policy (WSIPP), 241
websites. *See* Internet and websites
Wetterling, Jacob, 216
White Americans, 12
Wisconsin
  sexually violent predators, 280
witnesses, child, 200, 204–205
wives and husbands. *See* spouses
Wolff, Donald, 164

women
church abuse, 170–171, 172
female sex offenders, 20, 111–116,
113*t*, 114*t*
feminist theories of sexual deviancy, 57
historical roles, 27, 30
rapists' desire to humiliate, 99
sex offenders against, 251
status in society, 100
See also gender issues
Women's Christian Temperance Union
(WCTU), 30
women's rights movement (1970s), 37

workplace. *See* employment for sex
offenders

Y

young adult child exploiters, 114–115,
114*t*
Young v. Weston (1999), 288
youth offenders. *See* juvenile offenders

Z

zoophilia, 51

CPSIA information can be obtained
at www.ICGtesting.com
Printed in the USA
FFOW01n0532181215
19708FF